nternational Law

The International Library of Essays in Law and Legal Theory
Series Editor: Tom D. Campbell

Schools

Natural Law, Vols I & II *John Finnis*
Justice *Thomas Morawetz*
Law and Economics, Vols I & II *Jules Coleman and Jeffrey Lange*
Critical Legal Studies *James Boyle*
Marxian Legal Theory *Csaba Varga*
Legal Reasoning, Vols I & II *Aulis Aarnio and Neil MacCormick*
Legal Positivism *Mario Jori*
American Legal Theory *Robert Summers*
Law and Language *Fred Schauer*
Sociological Theories of Law *Kahei Rokumoto*
Rights *Carlos Nino*
Law and Psychology *Martin Levine*
Feminist Legal Theory *Frances Olsen*

Areas

Criminal Law *Thomas Morawetz*
Tort Law *Ernest Weinrib*
Contract Law, Vols I & II *Larry Alexander*
Anti-Discrimination Law *Christopher McCrudden*
Consumer Law *Iain Ramsay*
International Law *Martti Koskenniemi*
Property Law *Elizabeth Mensch and Alan Freeman*
Constitutional Law *Mark Tushnet*
Procedure *Denis Galligan*
Evidence and Proof *William Twining and Alex Stein*
Administrative Law *Denis Galligan*
Child Law *Harry Krause*
Family Law, Vols I & II *Harry Krause*
Welfare Law *Peter Robson*
Medicine and the Law *Bernard Dickens*
Commercial Law *Ross Cranston*
Communications Law *David Goldberg*
Environmental Law *Michael Blumm*
Conflict of Laws *Richard Fentiman*
Law and Religion *Wojciech Sadurski*
Human Rights Law *Philip Alston*
European Community Law *Francis Snyder*

Legal Cultures

Comparative Legal Cultures *Csaba Varga*
Law and Anthropology *Peter Sack*
Hindu Law and Legal Theory *Ved Nanda*
Islamic Law and Legal Theory *Ian Edge*
Chinese Law and Legal Theory *Michael Palmer*
Socialist Law and Legal Theory *W. Butler*
Japanese Law and Legal Theory *Kiochiro Fujikura*
Law and Development *Anthony Carty*
Jewish Law and Legal Theory *Martin Golding*
Legal Education *Martin Levine*

Future Volumes

Labour Law, Common Law and Legal Theory, Civil Law and Legal Theory, Law and Society, African Law and Legal Theory, Legal Ethics and Cumulative index.

International Law

Edited by

Martti Koskenniemi

Counsellor, Legal Affairs
Ministry for Foreign Affairs of Finland

NEW YORK UNIVERSITY PRESS
REFERENCE COLLECTION

Manufactured in Great Britain

First published in the U.S.A. in 1992 by
NEW YORK UNIVERSITY PRESS
Washington Square
New York NY 10003

Library of Congress Cataloging-in-Publication Data
International law / edited [by] Martti Koskenniemi.
p. cm. — (The International library of essays in law and legal theory)
Essays originally published in various journals from 1971 to 1990.
"New York University Press reference collection."
Includes bibliographical references and index.
ISBN 0-8147-4619-5
1. International law. I. Koskenniemi, Martti. II. Series.
JX1391.I634 1992
341—dc20 91-25106
CIP

Contents

Acknowledgements

The editor and publishers wish to thank the following for permission to use copyright material.

American Society of International Law for the essay: Thomas M. Franck (1988), 'Legitimacy in the International System', *The American Journal of International Law*, **82**, pp. 705–59.

The American University Journal of International Law and Policy for the essay: David Kennedy (1987), 'The Sources of International Law', *American University Journal of International Law and Policy*, **2**, pp. 1–96.

James Boyle (1985), 'Ideals and Things: International Legal Scholarship and the Prison-House of Language', *Harvard International Law Journal*, **26**, pp. 337–59. Copyright © James Boyle.

Anthony D'Amato (1984–5), 'Is International Law Really "Law"?', *Northwestern University Law Review*, **79**, pp. 1293–314. Copyright © Anthony D'Amato.

Denver Journal of International Law for the essay: Daniel W. Skubik (1986), 'Two Models for a Rawlsian Theory of International Law and Justice', *Denver Journal of International Law and Policy*, **14**, pp. 231–74. Copyright © by the Denver Journal of International Law.

Finnish Yearbook of International Law for the essay: Martti Koskenniemi (1990), 'The Normative Force of Habit: International Custom and Social Theory', *Finnish Yearbook of International Law*, **1**, pp. 77–153.

Harvard International Law Journal for the essay: Surakiart Sathirathai (1984), 'An Understanding of the Relationship Between International Legal Discourse and Third World Countries', *Harvard International Law Journal*, **25**, pp. 395–419. Permission granted by the Harvard International Law Journal. Copyright © 1984 by the President and Fellows of Harvard University.

Journal of International Affairs for the essay: Friedrich Kratochwil (1984), 'Thrasymmachos Revisited: On the Relevance of Norms and the Study of Law for International Affairs', *Journal of International Affairs*, **37**, pp. 343–56. Published by permission of the Journal of International Affairs and the Trustees of Columbia University in the City of New York.

The Royal Institute of International Affairs for the essay: Philip Allott (1971), 'Language, Method and the Nature of International Law', *British Year Book of International Law*, **XLV**, pp. 79–135. Published by Oxford University Press for the Royal Institute of International Affairs, London.

Sweet & Maxwell Limited for the essay: J.S. Watson (1980), 'A Realistic Jurisprudence of International Law', *The Year Book of World Affairs*, **30**, pp. 265–85.

Wisconsin International Law Journal for the essay: Nathaniel Berman (1988), 'Sovereignty in Abeyance: Self-Determination and International Law', *Wisconsin International Law Journal*, **7**, pp. 51–105. Copyright © by the Wisconsin International Law Journal.

Every effort has been made to trace all the copyright holders, but if any have been inadvertently overlooked the publishers will be pleased to make the necessary arrangement at the first opportunity.

Series Preface

The International Library of Law and Legal Theory is designed to provide important research materials in an accessible form. Each volume contains essays of central theoretical importance in its subject area. The series as a whole makes available an extensive range of valuable material which will be of considerable interest to those involved in the research, teaching and study of law.

The series has been divided into three sections. The Schools section is intended to represent the main distinctive approaches and topics of special concern to groups of scholars. The Areas section takes in the main branches of law with an emphasis on essays which present analytical and theoretical insights of broad application. The section on Legal Cultures makes available the distinctive legal theories of different level traditions and takes up topics of general comparative and developmental concern.

I have been delighted and impressed by the way in which the editors of the individual volumes have set about the difficult task of selecting, ordering and presenting essays from the immense quantity of academic legal writing published in journals throughout the world. Editors were asked to pick out those essays from law, philosophy and social science journals which they consider to be fundamental for the understanding of law, as seen from the perspective of a particular approach or sphere of legal interest. This is not an easy task and many difficult decisions have had to be made in order to ensure that a representative sample of the best journal essays available takes account of the scope of each topic or school.

I should like to express my thanks to all the volume editors for their willing participation and scholarly judgement. The interest and enthusiasm which the project has generated is well illustrated by the fact that an original projection of 12 volumes drawn up in 1989 has now become a list of some 60 volumes. I must also acknowledge the vision, persistence and constant cheerfulness of John Irwin and the marvellous work done by Mrs Margaret O'Reilly and Mrs Sonia Bridgman.

TOM D. CAMPBELL
Series Editor
The Faculty of Law
The Australian National University

Introduction

If, as some say, the era of modernity is drawing to a close, one may wonder what consequence this might have on the quintessentially modern idea of a universal Rule of Law. Though international lawyers have received much of their professional vocabulary from ancient sources – Roman law and Christian ethics – in a relevant sense their profession is based on distinctly modernist ideas about social organization and political legitimacy. Central to these ideas is the belief that human society is an artificial creation and that its only legitimate organizing principle is the Rule of Law – the principle that 'the health of the political realm is only maintained by conscientious objection to the political'.[1]

Much of our European-origined modernity – its historical optimism, its economic rationalism and even its ideal of the liberal *Rechtsstaat* – now appears increasingly problematic. Not surprisingly therefore, many feel that the international law of sovereign equality, based as it is on the same structure of ideas as that which has governed liberal politics for the past two centuries, cannot be expected to grapple successfully with some of modernity's most pressing global issues: war, political oppression, over-use of natural resources and massive human suffering caused by widespread poverty and over-population. International law, these critics have noted, has failed because it has been unable to deter politics: it has either capitulated to or been overrun by it.

That international law participates in the political struggle for economic and spiritual values has not been – and cannot be logically held as – sufficient reason for simply abandoning legal rhetoric in the communication between states. In fact, contemporary international lawyers point out that their law has come to cover an increasing array of subjects, such as human rights, economic development, uses of natural resources and the environment. New legal-bureaucratic international institutions have been erected and the work-load (and number) of jurists in foreign offices and international organizations continues to increase. The roster of cases at the International Court of Justice has never been as full as during the latter part of the 1980s and the volume of academic writing in the field shows no sign of decline. So it may seem only appropriate that the General Assembly of the United Nations declared, on 17 October 1989, the period 1990–99 as the 'Decade of International Law'.[2]

On the other hand, the recurrent disappointments experienced by jurists and diplomats trying to develop a full system of binding and effective standards for international conduct have had their effect. Many have accepted the realist point that classical internationalists failed because theirs had been a 'metaphysical... attempt to exorcise social events by the infatigable repetition of magic formulae'.[3] The academic doctrine of the past 30 years has been shaped by restatements of this position and a consequent turn away from such philosophically loaded subjects as the character of international law or state sovereignty, explanation for the law's binding force, or the ultimate reason for its validity. These have been replaced by a more sociological style with an empiricist or analytical programme. Instead of discussing binding force or international justice, lawyers have turned to describing diplomatic developments or interpreting and systematizing the rules inherited from the textbook tradition.

Yet, there is a tension between this confident pragmatism and the recognized threats to the system's overall viability. This tension has been inadequately dealt with by legal doctrine itself – though signs of a change in this respect are visible. The present volume of essays intends to make a contribution towards rehabilitating 'theory' – a post-realist theory which would articulate for international lawyers the experience of what some have (perhaps somewhat too hastily) called post-modernism. This introduction hopes to set that task in focus and indicate some of the accepted truths and consequent problems which today's theorists need to deal with in order to move beyond an impoverished pragmatism without engaging in uncritical Utopias.

This task cannot be undertaken without paying attention to intellectual developments in neighbouring disciplines and national societies. From linguists and social theorists, international lawyers might learn that norms, whether extracted from texts or social behaviour, are of necessity *indeterminate* and that the most down-to-earth pragmatic analyses of diplomatic behaviour or treaty text are conditioned by conceptual matrices which are the arena of political struggle. From historians and political philosophers they might receive understanding of the character of that struggle and their place in it. International lawyers would profit from the discussions concerning the legitimation crisis of the liberal *Rechtsstaat* – a crisis engendered by the realization that the neutrality of laws is even at best a half-truth concealing the many ways in which political power is channelled through the legal system. Yet, they should realize that the perceived alternatives – socialism in particular – have collapsed because of the absence of a credible system of laws as the reference-point for the distribution of social values.

To be sure, the realists always stressed the need for an interdisciplinary orientation. For many of them, however, coming back to international law once they had heard the sirene's song of sociology and politics, proved impossible. If they did return, their analyses often failed to appear relevant to practicing lawyers. It seems clear now that international lawyers cannot expect that their problems can be solved simply by flirtation with other areas of thought. Having located the problems of international law in the general framework of late modern social and political thought, international lawyers could do worse than look back at their historical continuities and inherited conceptual structures. The rest of this Introduction aims to set down some of those continuities and structures in a spirit of *reculer pour mieux sauter*; to enable the reader to appreciate the tradition to which the following essays pay the subtle compliment of criticism.

Beginnings: The Social Conception of International Law

With some simplification, it may be said that international law, as we know it, is a child of the Enlightenment. It is not mere coincidence that Emer de Vattel's *Droit des Gens ou Principes de la Loi naturelle appliqués aux affaires des Nations et des Souverains* (1758) – by far the most influential book on international law in the 19th century – came out only a decade after Montesquieu's *De l'esprit des lois* and four years before Rousseau's *Du contrat social*. Though the argument in these works is by no means identical, they share a new, modern outlook on the problem of the legitimacy of power. The authors do not look upon social life from the perspective of first principles or by way of commentary to higher authority. Each attempts to explain the conditions of a just society – in Vattel's case a society of states –

in the absence of pre-ordained social hierarchy. Each assumes that society is an artificial creation; that the justness of a society is measured not by some principles external to that order but by how well it fulfils the goals which are set to it by its members. As a distinctly *modern* utopia, post-Enlightenment international law constitutes itself through its consistent hostility towards what seems to it subjective, political, passionate, indemonstrable.

Two hundred years earlier, Francisco de Vitoria (1486–1546) – a Spanish theologist with a penchant for contemplating princely politics in Spain's newly-acquired colonies – delivered his *Relectiones De Indis* in 1532 as a gloss on a passage in St. Matthew. For him, legal argument had to be grounded in Christian faith – moreover, reasoning from something else than faith would be a sin even if the result were correct.[4] Such a position builds upon an unquestioned faith – a faith which is the measure of everything else and cannot therefore be itself meaningfully questioned. By mid-18th century, however, faith no longer seemed secure. The wars of the preceding century and a half had neither succeeded in preventing the spread of Protestantism nor ensured its final victory. Traditional religious institutions had become outdated and corrupt. Theological doctrine started to seem as a facade for secular politics.

The secularism of international lawyers is nicely present in their habit of dating, from Vattel onwards, the beginning of the modern states-system from the treaties of peace at Münster and Osnabrück (1648). *Cuius regio, eius religio* was a liberating slogan. Faith became now a state's 'private' matter – useful for sovereigns to the extent that it provided a pacifying cult for the unenlightened majority.[5] It was, however, useless as a legitimator of sovereign conduct and unnecessary for a full understanding of international politics. The Vattelian revolution was from a theological (passionate) into a secular (rational) conception, a *social conception of international law*.

A conception which denies the existence of a natural global *telos* (or at least man's capacity to know it) and which assumes international norms to be historical, social phenomena seems compelled to come to terms with at least two conundrums: first, the precise relationship between international law and international society and second, the possibility of binding law between sovereign entities. The first may be described as a problem of *applied social theory* dealing with what legal theorists have sometimes discussed under the title of 'relative autonomy'. It has to do with how to isolate what counts as 'international law' from the mass of social behaviour in which we see nations and their representatives engage themselves. The second may be understood as a problem of *political theory* seeking to explain when international constraint may be legitimately applied against formally equal and independent entities. The Vattelian conception of international law appealed to post-Enlightenment lawyers because it seemed to provide credible answers to these conundrums.

First, it provided a method which produced normative consequences out of observing social life itself, not from religious abstractions or rationalist fictions (such as Christian Wolff's timid hypothesis of the *Civitas Maxima*[6]). Where previous jurists had held a normative system constant to explore social behaviour, Vattelian moderns reversed this order. For them, the facts of international social life were given and the law something that had to be constructed from them. That the juristic *a priori* shifted from faith to 'facts', made possible methodological self-examination and engagement in a 'scientific' dispute about the validity of one's conclusions. In contrast to Grotius's indiscriminate use of whatever authority seemed available to support his preferred positions – criticized by Vattel as much as Rousseau – it now became possible (and frequent) for international jurists to reflect on the way they carried out their work.[7]

Second, and perhaps more importantly, the Vattelian revolution solved the problem of binding force by a wholesale appropriation of liberal politics from the national into the international sphere.[8] Order among sovereigns was possible if it relied upon value-neutral and (thus) verifiable rules of law whose content was determined by the states themselves, in a procedure to which they all took part. The social conception enjoyed a unique legitimacy because it directed the state's duties to the state itself and because of its apparent transparency; the way it seemed to reflect everyone's interests. As Vattel observed: 'La nature oblige tout homme à travailler à sa propre perfection & par là déjà il travaille à celle de la Société Civile'.[9] We recognize Vattel as a modern because his voice is ours: a voice of egalitarian individualism, transposed at the level of international life.

Principles of Coherence: The Classical Law

These moves did not, however, fully dispose of the problems of social and political theory. In the first place, it remained difficult to explain why conscientious scholars constantly drew differing normative conclusions from the same diplomatic facts. In the second place, the social conception was in danger of buying the legitimacy of its law at the cost of its binding force: by stressing the law's basis in sovereign policy, it easily collapsed into an apology to whatever states willed. Something was needed with which one could justify one's interpretation and choice of the relevant facts as well as argue that a state was legally prohibited from acting in any way it desired. In the absence of divine intervention, finding this 'something' became an urgent preoccupation.

A first solution was provided by naturalism. In fact, natural law was invoked by Grotius and Vattel precisely in order to defend the social conception against abstract ruminations about theological principle. Unlike faith, natural law seemed to provide universally valid directives which were within the grasp of every human being endowed with reason. Natural law and its derivatives (such as Vattel's 'voluntary law' – a law which was both distinct from simple consent but related to state behaviour in a way which ensured the system's realistic basis while allowing its binding force) provided convenient conceptual starting-points for endowing diplomatic intercourse with legal meaning and a foothold for overruling a sovereign's momentary political will.

But natural law's contextual flexibility has been reinterpreted as its political manipulability. Natural law, noted Professor Mendelson recently, 'inevitably results in prescriptions which, when they are not merely trite and over-general, are too subjective to command widespread agreement'.[10] Natural norms do have a place in modern international legal practice where they appear in arguments about 'basic human needs', 'minimum requirements of humanity' and the like. But the fact that arguments which smack of naturalism are resorted to only at the last instance and are then either accepted or rejected without further discourse gives expression to our *skepsis* about the capacity of natural reason. For the social conception of law, an articulation of the importance of 'nature' or 'reason' as a source of legitimate constraint is not only difficult but in apparent contradiction with the conception's democratic premises. To derive international human rights from international custom (habitual state behaviour plus the *opinio juris*) may be the only way for a modern liberal to explain them – however counter-intuitive and historically implausible a strategy it might be and whatever further problems it might cause.[11]

Post-naturalist international jurists work under a twofold pressure: on the one hand, there is the modern criticism of natural law as superstition; on the other hand, there is the conservative criticism of enlightenment thought leading into anarchy. A credible doctrine of international law has to present itself as concrete-scientific to avoid the former criticism and as autonomously constraining to avoid the latter. The solution to this problem, as it was crystallized in late-19th century textbooks (and continues to be defended today), built upon a combination of nationalism and an optimistic historicism with the liberal assumption of an essential harmony of interests.

By late 19th century, Utopian thought had given up federalism: international lawyers were among the 'realists' stressing that a credible world order could not discount the persistence of the states-system. As the law could not be deduced from divine imagination, it could only be 'scientifically' deduced from statehood. This had the additional advantage of being in conformity with political nationalism. A law which could be traced back to the nation itself – its will, its 'nature', its character, the *Volksgeist* – seemed not only more concretely social but also more legitimate in application than a law claiming superiority over nationhood. The idea of international law as *Koordinationsrecht*[12] is an internationalization of Rousseau's idealized Geneva: a community of equals voluntarily submitting to the Rule of Law.

From the beginning, nationalism merged with a distinctly European brand of historical optimism in a way which seemed concretely based on social facts and allowed lawyers to deal with the threat of anarchy posed by law based on the state's momentary, political will. This is the core of the much-misunderstood *Selbstverpflichtungslehre*, for example. On the one hand, as Jellinek famously argued, international law is to be based like any other law: on the will of the state. On the other hand, state will is not free (*Willkür*). The law exists to give expression to natural state purpose (*Staatszwecke*) as it enfolds in the nation's history. If the elite 'willed' something that would not be in accordance with such purpose – if it wished to break a treaty, for example – such will would not be given legal sanction. This is so because it is in the nation's historical self-interest that treaties be kept.[13]

This argument which both respects sovereignty and departs from voluntarism is a liberal strategy similar to the utilitarian justification of promise-keeping and the *Rousseausque* point about 'forcing men to be free'. It avoids extreme voluntarism and thus grounds a *de facto* coercive order. And it does this without violating the democratic premise that order should be created out of the interests of the members of society and not from an externally introduced *telos*. But it does this at the significant cost of having to rely on a largely unargued view that 'natural state purpose' coincides with the communal interest.

The harmony of interests – 'duty and true self-love point to the same path', as Phillimore argued[14] – was, as we have seen, assumed already by Vattel. Now, even for a Hegelian *Leugner des Völkerrechts* such as Adolf Lasson it was evident that though international law was not law in the same sense as municipal law (because a coercive normative order among sovereigns was an absurdity), all states had an interest in abiding by it. The reciprocal expectations created by and expressed through it were useful for all states – the enlightened egotism of nations was the basis if not of the legal character of *Völkerrecht*, at least of its political reality.[15] Or, as a more mainstream jurist observed: 'Eine sittlich correcte Politik kan niemals thun und billigen, was Völkerrecht verwirft'. The interest of the single nation is equivalent to that of the community and vice versa.[16]

The arguments from reciprocal and enlightened self-interest have been voiced throughout the 20th century as a response to the criticism concerning the absence of centrally-organized legislation, judicature and enforcement in international law. Lawyers have attempted to solve the problem of order among sovereigns by replacing providence with a sociological assumption concerning the ultimate harmony of interests between states and the international order – an argument greatly buttressed by the perspective of nuclear or environmental catastrophy. Conflict is a 'mistake' about one's own interests, a false consciousness which can be corrected by right reasoning – right reasoning being the sort of chain of arguments which leads to an arrangement in which no one's (rationally calculable) interests are thwarted.[17]

This rationalistic optimism was expressed, for example, in the Bryan Treaties of 1913–14 and thereafter in the Covenant of the League of Nations which provided for a 'cooling-off period' before states could resort to force and a procedure for peaceful settlement. The assumption was that war can be avoided if only statesmen are forced to talk about their differences as reasonable men. Here they would be aided by the force of an enlightened public opinion (an opinion *a priori* assumed to go against war) and the publicity accorded to the negotiations.[18]

The harmony of interests entails a law which is *procedural* in character, a law providing channels through which enlightened statesmen can agree – at least to defer their dispute to a third party. In a similar vein, modern international law moved away from just war doctrines – *jus ad bellum* – into regulating the conduct of war – *jus in bello*. Where the Christian doctrine about the just causes of war seemed either useless because so abstract, or, if taken seriously, put national causes in an unequal position, thinking of war as legally regulated procedure seemed doubly beneficial. It did not rank national policies substantively *vis-à-vis* each other and allowed integrating humanitarian considerations into the conduct of war.

The point has been made more recently by Terry Nardin that the legitimacy of international law is based on the way it expresses a procedural instead of a 'purposive' conception of international order.[19] Because the political goals of states differ, imposing one goal, one conception of the good life on all states by international law would not be acceptable – it would make international law look like imperialism in disguise. Instead, international law shall provide procedural channels through which disagreeing states can settle their differences and live peacefully without having to renounce their political goals. Whatever one may think of this (liberal) conception, it clearly provides the best mainstream rationalization for present international law – a law primarily, if not exclusively, setting up mechanisms for peaceful settlement, allocating competences (jurisdiction), and organizing co-operation through diplomatic contacts and multilateral organizations. Substantive norms have been so few or open-ended that following the law has not seriously prejudiced national policy.

The classical law, then, is a combination of several elements which together transfer liberal principles of legitimacy into international society. Statehood remains the legal expression of political nationalism. The destructiveness of nationalism is checked by reference to a historically-determined *Staatszwecke* or some conception of basic needs or interests of all peoples. The tension between the egoistic and communal strands of this structure is mediated by a political optimism relying on something not unlike the Mandevillian fable of the bees. The system is held together by jurists' descriptive style and their concentration on procedural instead of substantive norms.

The Structure of Modern Doctrines

Between Idealism and Realism

The confident structure of classical international law came under attack after the frustration of World War I. But though academic jurists were explicit and sometimes furious in their criticism, this criticism took two separate and apparently contradicting strands.

On the one hand, 19th century international law was accused of excessive *étatisme* and voluntarism which had corrupted its Grotian ideals. Its failure to prevent the Great War or even to regulate its conduct was understood through its excessive reliance on 'sovereignty' – the order it implied was too weak. Lauterpacht's important reconstructive work, for example, concentrated on showing how 19th century doctrines of 'political questions', *rebus sic stantibus*, and the view of international law as *äusseres Staatsrecht* did away with a truly binding international law altogether.[20] The argument was that pre-war doctrines had failed because they had been too close to state policy, in a sense, not Utopian enough.

Other post-war jurists, however, argued that the preceding generation had failed because it had engaged in speculative abstraction with insufficient regard for the changed conditions of power and political fact. A notorious example was the collapse of the impressive legal-conceptual framework on neutrality. The law had failed because it carried outdated ideas about legitimacy and order, because it was based on speculative hypotheses with no grasp of the reality of power. It was, in a word, too Utopian.

The reconstructive theories of these two groups of lawyers differed in a similar fashion. The former group tried to strengthen the autonomy of international law by re-emphasizing its connection with naturalistic principles[21] or the system's logical[22] or material[23] coherence. The latter group attempted to close the gap between the law and the conditions of international society by mediating constructions such as a sentiment of 'social solidarity'[24], the objective causality of biological laws[25] or the 'effectiveness of community prescriptions'[26].

The two interpretations of the failure of classical doctrine and the consequent reformisms created a sparkling theoretical debate among international lawyers from the 1920s until the early 1950s. The works by Lauterpacht, Kelsen, Verdross, Le Fur, Brierly, Bruns, Scelle, Politis, Krabbe and a host of others are interesting because they emanate from a belief in theory as a means to re-establish a credible international law. The inconclusiveness of that debate provides the immediate background for the pragmatic humility of modern academic writing.

So much has been said about the contrast between 'idealism' and 'realism' in international theory that one may wonder whether that contrast really has much explanatory force. The fact that the battle lines between modern international lawyers have been drawn along that contrast may indeed be less a definite statement of doctrinal possibilities than an obstacle for creative thought. In a relevant if not strictly logical sense the debate is circular and the opposition illusory.

Much of contemporary mainstream insists on a conception of international law as 'rules' whose legal character lies in their being verifiable regardless of differing political opinions or situations. This approach remains, however, vulnerable to the realist criticism concerning the indeterminacy of rules. Most fields of international law are covered by widely formulated directives such as 'self-determination', 'territorial integrity', 'non-use of force', 'self-defence' etc. which in legal argument can be opposed to each other and interpreted to support the most varied and often conflicting positions. International practice, including the pronouncements of the International Court of Justice, enables professional jurists to pick any number of precedents to support their particular rule and their preferred interpretation thereof.

To that extent, relying solely on rules seems not only a methodological mistake but an outright 'wasteful deception'[27] as it suggests that rules bind in a way in which they clearly do not. Yet, realist reconstructions remain just as vulnerable as those of their opponents. A law which does not tell states what to do but merely describes what they wish or have been doing is not really law at all. As norms cannot be deduced from (mere) factual descriptions, most realists have invested their descriptions already with normative sense, be it some 'goal values of human dignity', or a conception of the needs or interests of peoples.[28] The problem is, of course, that such hidden normativities remain vulnerable to the realists' own criticisms. Inasmuch as realism does not wish to appear merely resurgent naturalism (and this would be difficult to defend on its empiricist assumptions), its goal values or other such norms remain at least as (and probably more) abstract, indeterminate and controversial as rules.

The cul-de-sac created by looking at problems of international legality from the perspective of the idealism/realism debate was put in a nutshell by J.K. Stephen in a delightful little book over a century ago. He noted that:

> the adoption of the juridical method must lead to a confusion of international habits with international duties, or the mixture of the science of international relations as they are with that of international relations as they ought to be.[29]

To avoid becoming sociologists, lawyers adopt a moralist tone; to escape moralism, they shift back to sociology. Arguing for the relevance of international law by stressing its closeness with state practice, jurists may attain reliable descriptions of state conduct. But they lose the critical character (binding force) of their law – unless, like McDougal, they draw a constraining morality from a hat. Building the law's relevance on its distance from state practice, jurists may maintain its binding force but only at the expense of its verifiability and applicability – unless, like Alvarez, they derive their 'ought' from the 'is' of the character of international society, a theory of 'basic needs',[30] or the like. Stephen's point was that none of these avenues succeeds in attaining anything distinctly *legal*. Trapped between description and prescription the lawyer transforms either into an amateur sociologist or an abstract moralist.

This dilemma is not only about how academic lawyers should go about their doctrinal work – whether they should adopt a sociological or a normativist orientation. It suggests that international law may not carry any autonomous, impartial normative project for a world order at all. It either collapses into endless descriptions of existing political power – justifying the status quo as it goes along – or it remains just another harmless *chateau en Espagne*. In both cases, its neutrality turns out a deceptive myth.

Of course, some modern lawyers have taken an openly political approach. There have been conservatives, such as Professor H.A. Smith, who have felt that the world has changed in a totalitarian direction and argued that 'men must be persuaded, if not the truth of the Christian order, a natural law, a common standard above the human level by reference to which all human conduct can be judged'.[31] And there have been progressive liberals such as Richard

Falk or Third-World lawyers such as Mohammed Bedjaoui who have argued for an international law independent from prevailing (oppressive) economic and political structures and thus as a critical vehicle for global change.[32] Yet, these writings have carried a somewhat desperate tone. This is so because under the assumptions of the social conception of law calls for more openly political, moral, critical doctrines do not lend themselves to serious discussion. Inasmuch as we accept the liberal premise that politics is 'subjective' in some such sense that one person's (state's) political opinions cannot be legitimately opposed to that of another's – that is, if we think that the Rule of Law is the sole legitimate organizing principle of (international) society – then such calls can only be accepted or rejected *a priori*; but they seem unable to ground a rational, even less a recognizably legal argument at all.

Pragmatism and Beyond

The inconclusiveness of an international legal theory oscillating between idealism and realism and the minimal consequences for doctrinal work that such choice seems to have may explain something of the non-theoretical, pragmatic style of contemporary legal writing. Not that lawyers would have given up the social conception of law; on the contrary, doctrinal modernism is so thoroughly social, so confident in the transparency of its law that it has given up all attempt to argue its foundation. All that is left of what in the 19th century appeared as an elaborately theoretical discourse are scattered pieces of historical and sociological rhetoric which serve as introductions to the doctrinal topics but which bear little effect on normative outcomes.

Standard contemporary textbooks open up with a description of the 'international society', some short narrative about its development to its present 'stage' and a plea for taking the political context seriously. Why engage in abstractions if '[t]he significant question to ask about international law is whether the use of that term is in accordance with an accurate observation and study of the conduct of States'.[33] Even the most sophisticated among late modern lawyers argue from a pragmatic functionalism: 'C'est à une conception fonctionnelle du pouvoir, à une conception sociale du droit que s'attache notre enseignement'.[34] For the majority, it is enough to make brief reference to the political or 'process' aspect of their law – and then to continue with interpreting, systematizing and finally evaluating the materials inherited from the academic tradition itself.

To be sure, general treatments of international law appear every now and then. If they do not follow the textbook pattern, they are at their best perceptive commentaries on the interactions between normative rhetoric and international politics[35] or close but principled readings of limited legal materials,[36] and at worst either enthusiastic apologies for 'world order' or sophistic wrangles with conceptual apparatuses – often heavily burdened with neologisms. Most generalizing material is devoted to discussing the sources of international law or using sociological rhetoric in the treatment of a particular problem. These remain, however, isolated from the great debates concerning the character of and proper approach to the *Geisteswissenschaften*. Even developments in legal theory (in striking contrast to the situation half a century ago) fail, as a rule, to be reflected in writing about international law.

The turn to modern pragmatism is nicely illustrated in the stylistic and thematic development of the general courses given at the Hague Academy of International Law. During the interwar era, the courses were predominantly in the spirit of reconstructive doctrine. Many were dedicated to completely theoretical topics, such as the basis of obligation, the place and development of natural law or the fundamental rights of states. Some were really at least as much works of legal theory or political philosophy as (and some even much more so than) expositions of valid norms.[37]

In the more recent post-war era, however, purely theoretical lectures have disappeared (with the significant exceptions of two Italian lectures in the fifties).[38] Nobody has bothered to discuss 'foundations' in a separate course. The first post-war course expressly argues against theoretical work as it will inevitably fail to have a bearing on state practice.[39] A general course in 1965 stresses that what is now needed is a 'user's' point of view and keeping one's 'feet on the ground'. A search for principles might only distort the correct understanding of the legal process.[40] The general course has transformed from Utopian architecture into technical narrative, perpetuating the textbook style and structure.

Late modern doctrine struggles with what seems like the inter-war theorists' failure to provide a convincing explanation of the mistakes of classical doctrines and, consequently, a reliable mainstream of their own. Le Fur's moderate naturalism or Kelsen's logical normativism did provide critical outlooks but did this at the cost of their applicability in practice. Sociological approaches by lawyers such as Scelle or McDougal either ended up in behavioural description or were forced to rely on an implicitly political interpretation of state practice to seem normatively relevant. Contemporary pragmatism emerges from a silent rejection of *both* such strategies. It stresses the need to avoid the doctrinal extremes of pure conceptualism and sociologism and to provide:

> an intermediate position, one that maintains the distinctiveness of the legal order while managing to be responsive to the extralegal setting of politics, history and morality.[41]

This creates an eclectic mainstream which lives on styles borrowed from the most varied kinds of approach: naturalism, empiricism, consensualism and non-consensualism; teleological, linguistic, political, etc. justifications. This mainstream is curiously *ad hoc*. It stresses the contextuality of each outcome – thus undermining its claim for universality and impartiality. Reflection on theory is barred by the frustration theory creates and the apparent inability to do anything about it. At its worst, it degenerates into 'a specifically bureaucratic spirit which seeks to get the job done with the minimum of spiritual commitment and the maximum of personal security'.[42]

The theory of such a mainstream is a rhetoric of a *double association – dissociation*. It emphasizes the need for law to be a close reflection of society as well as the necessity of maintaining critical distance between the two. To counter the accusation that a doctrinal substance is too Utopian, lawyers have developed a sociological, functionalistic rhetoric – a rhetoric of context, interest and state behaviour – to defend it. To counter the accusation that such substance is just another political apology, lawyers defend it by showing its distance from context, interests and actual behaviour.

But of course doctrine cannot show that it simultaneously reflects society and is critical of it. The two strands provide a full criticism of each other. In a standard realist fashion, Francis Boyle recently attacked contemporary doctrine as 'obsessed with' rules and the legal/illegal distinction. For him, law and politics were not 'essentially independent of each other'.[43] Here, law is understood from the perspective of politics. But when Boyle wants to criticize recent United States' diplomatic action, he does this by appealing to binding international rules.[44] Now politics is judged from the perspective of rules. The method is in direct conflict with normative outcomes. This is a familiar dilemma for leftist writing. On the one hand, social facts are used to endow one's preferred norms with privileged legitimacy: the law I possess is correct because it is a faithful reflection of the (recent) changes in international society. On the other hand, the law thus defended is used to criticize the (oppressive) structures of present society. The tension between realism and idealism is *internal* to modern reformism. The norms embedded in the initial fact-description cannot be discussed because that would, to avoid circularity, have to be done *independently of facts*. And this would look like discussing abstract principles of (natural) justice.

Modern reconstructive works seem hampered by their uncertain oscillation between idealism and realism; conceptualism and empiricism. The answers the social conception provides to its questions of social and political theory do not match: its empiricist sociology cannot legitimize order among sovereigns.

To say that international law is a 'social' phenomenon – that it arises from or 'reflects' social events – does not by itself go far enough. The international 'society' is not as transparent as modern lawyers tend to think. It is an appropriate object of empirical analyses to the extent it consists of behavioural patterns and effective power. But these are not the only things it consists of. The meaning of behaviour and power – whether they give rise to 'law', for instance – is also determined by the normative concepts through which the participants – statesmen, diplomats, lawyers – look at what they are doing. Expressions such as 'state', 'treaty', 'asylum', 'self-determination', etc. do not simply reflect external events but *constitute what can be seen in them*. Conceptual analysis is just as necessary as it is, on the other hand, to realize that such concepts do not possess an autonomous meaning but can be construed usefully only in relation to particular constellations of (political) power.

Neither conceptualism nor empiricism provides a sustainable doctrine alone. A legal theory which hopes to avoid reductionism needs to explore the embeddedness of state power and international ideas in each other, the way in which international behaviour is induced by normative conceptions which, again, are constructed by reference to particular political environments. There are signs of such developments.[45] Anthony Carty's *The Decay of International Law?* makes a persuasive case for the relevance of history of ideas to an understanding of present international law and for attempts at the discursive validation of international norms.[46] David Kennedy's *International Legal Structures* analyses the internal structuring principles of the conceptual apparatus of international law.[47] Both of these strands are explored in the present writer's *From Apology to Utopia*,[48] while Thomas M. Franck looks at the question of rule-legitimacy and its relationship to notions of justice in his recent *The Power of Legitimacy among Nations*.[49]

A post-realist theory suggested by these and other[50] works aims to answer questions regarding the relationship of law and society and the legitimacy of constraint in a world of sovereigns as aspects of one single problem: the problem of power in concepts. On the one hand, it focuses attention on how lawyers' conceptual structures work so as to create patterns of preference for one type of substantive outcome to alternative ones. On the other hand, by disclosing the substantive values whose conflict is expressed in legal rhetoric, it suggests outcomes whose justice would be based on a more direct confrontation and choice between the values expressed by participants in the particular context.

Some Particular Controversies

It was noted above that every generalization about international law needs to give an account of the relationship between international law and international society as well as of the legitimacy of coercing a sovereign against its will. I shall now briefly illustrate how the tension between idealism and realism works so as to structure international legal doctrines with a close relationship to these two conundrums.

World Order

There is a vast literature on the conditions and legal character of 'world order'. Though this literature insists on realism, it remains divided both in its assessment of the present as well as its projection of the future. On the one hand, the present international economic and political structures are interpreted as oppressive collectivism. From this perspective, any legal project should strengthen sovereign autonomy. On the other hand, the present is routinely characterized in terms of excessive national egoism in a way to support the argument that international law is needed to increase communal solidarity. While this contrast is sometimes portrayed as another transformation of the idealist (more community)/realist (more autonomy) debate, this is not quite correct. For such perceptions and the resulting programmes hinge not on one's abstract view about whether it is better to live alone or in company but on inherently *political views about how one should live*. An Arab state might wish to stress its independence *vis-à-vis* the world at large or the developed West. Among other Arabs, however, emphasis might be more on co-operation and/or accommodation.

International law cannot take a stand on how states should live without losing its neutrality. The Rule of Law can seem legitimate only by being able to explain itself from the perspective of enhancing community (because it would otherwise support egoism) and safeguarding sovereignty (as its implications would otherwise remain collectivist). This is possible as long a legal concepts are formal, that is, stay at a sufficiently general and abstract level. But as soon as their interpretation or application seems to support some particular type of communal existence or some determined limit for sovereign authority, they become vulnerable from some opposing substantive perspective. From such perspective, formalism merely hides the law's preference for an objectionable substantive policy.[51]

A typical example of such argumentative deadlock is provided by the case of transboundary pollution. Here the affected state usually presents its case as a communitarian one while the polluting state refers to its sovereign right to engage in industrial activities.[52] Because both claims are legitimate *per se* and threaten each other, disputants usually supplement their initial positions by reversing them. The affected state may support its view by referring to its sovereign integrity while the polluting state might argue on the basis of the communal ideal of good neighbourliness which obligates states to tolerate minor inconveniences resulting from their physical proximity. As both states' positions are now communitarian as well as individualistic, neither strand (nor idealism/realism) alone may justify a resolution. A resolution is possible only by ascertaining the relevant environmental and economic values and establishing some kind of a 'balance' between them – that is, by actually setting up one substantive ideal of communal life and constructing the relationship between the disputing states on that ideal.[53]

The idealism/realism debate is only a (manipulable) surface for an essentially political debate about the right manner of living in the world of states. The debate seems interminable and inconsequential because it seldom reaches the relevant principles of political substance. Legal formalism – the way the concepts of international law sustain (and *must sustain*) communal as well as nationalistic ideas – does provide a language and a procedure through which statesmen and jurists can enter into a discussion. But it remains insufficient for reaching an outcome. Any specific outcome results from an ultimately political choice of interpreting the relevant facts and law in one way rather than another.

Legitimate Authority (Sovereignty)

There is a large doctrinal body dealing with the extent and delimitation of jurisdiction which is consequential on how states' legal authority is understood. There are two competing understandings. According to one, such authority follows from some determinate concentration of factual – effective – power within the state. According to another, such authority cannot be assumed to exist *ex hypothesi* but must in each case be established by reference to individual power-conferring norms.

The former approach seems defensible because it is so realistic: much of international case-law regarding territorial title, for example, seems to be about the search for effective possession in one or the other of the disputants. Authority involves also duties in respect of third states and local populations. Without manifestations of effective control, such duties could not seem adequately protected.[54] Still, mere effectiveness cannot be the sole basis for title. As H.L.A. Hart observed, there is a difference between gunman's orders and the law.[55] Thus, to achieve critical bite, the law must assume also that illegal occupation, however effective, cannot establish valid title.[56]

Most disputes about territorial title oppose empirical arguments about effectiveness with conceptual ones regarding anterior law. That these disputes seem so difficult to solve on *these terms* relates to the opposition being a false one: one cannot argue about the presence of 'effectiveness' without *a priori* (conceptual) criteria. And one cannot plausibly defend one's preferred *criteria* without linking them in some way to what is effectively supported by state practice. Again, the matter is not 'choosing' between facts or concepts but giving facts and concepts a defensible meaning. But because it is this act of projecting meaning which determines the sense of law (whether as facts or rules), that act cannot be justified by further reference to law: it is a political choice.

This is well-evidenced by recent practice concerning delimitation of sovereign authority. Far from being a matter of simply ascertaining the consequences of legal rules or effective power, the extent of sovereign authority has become the function of a balancing act by the legal body involved – a matter of finding an overall 'equitable result'.[57]

Binding Force (sources)

How can constraint among sovereigns be justified? Most international lawyers agree that a state can be bound at least if it so wills. Others have observed, however, that a pure voluntarism which allows *no* other ground apart from the state's own will as a justification for coercion does not really create binding law at all. The statement that international law is consensually based may reflect the mainstream understanding of the character of sources of international law. But it certainly does not convince critics of international law's constraining relevance as it stops where problems begin; at the point in which we want to overrule a state's present, politically-determined will.[58]

Pure non-consensualism – a view which sees consent as wholly irrelevant for the emergence of international norms – on the other hand, has little plausibility for modern lawyers. Will, at least, can be somewhat reliably known and there is little political difficulty in convincing states that they should be bound by what they will. Non-consensual principles of justice, of humanitarian ethics, of world order, reasonableness, good faith or whatever, render themselves to interminable interpretative controversies and, if applied, look like imperialism in the guise of moralist rhetoric.

Much international argument turns consensualism and non-consensualism against each other. Utopia argues that Apologia is bound by the norm N because that is what they had consented to. Apologia argues that applying N in these circumstances is unjust (because of changed circumstances, for example). At this point, it seems that the matter should be solved by preferring pure consensualism or pure non-consensualism. Apologia is bound if consent is what counts, released if justice is what is important. But the matter is not so simple. How do we *really* know if N was what had been agreed to? Or what basis is there to rely on the changed circumstances rule as the relevant consideration of justice – might not the *pacta sunt servanda* be equally just, though it renders the opposite result?

In legal practice, both states would develop their argument by taking their adversary's first position but challenging the adversary's interpretation of what it is that consent/justice requires. To respond to Utopia's initial claim about there having been an agreement, Apologia might deny that N was what had been consented to in the first place. To answer Apologia's claim about changed circumstances, Utopia might rely on the *pacta* rule or its derivatives (for example, it might say that it had relied on Apologia's apparent acceptance). Both states rely now on consent as well as principles beyond consent.

The case cannot be solved by taking either of the apparent alternatives of consensualism/non-consensualism. Solving it would seem to require looking into what Utopia and Apologia *really* had consented to or what it is that justice in this case *really* says. But neither question is amenable to an easy answer.

In the first place, under the democratic assumptions of Enlightenment political theory, 'will' (unlike 'reason') is a purely subjective thing. Even though I might (as an expert, for example) actually know better than you what you should will, I cannot invoke this argument to justify constraint against you, against what it is you now say you will (even though I think it is not your 'real' will). Arguing from knowing better ('objective interests') is a receipt for totalitarianism. That Rousseau used it in *Du contrat social* may have been due to pressures internal to his (liberal) theory – but it did come in handy to explain to Parisian intellectuals the necessity of Jacobin terror.

In the second place, how does one establish the validity of one principle of (non-consensual) justice against another? The Rule of Law was established precisely because 'justice' seemed so subjective, so manipulable – a matter of 'emotions', or 'evaluations', items which could not be rationally validated. Even if I, by some process which I have established, succeed in showing that the *pacta sunt servanda* is better, more just than the *rebus sic stantibus*, what justification have I to impose this outcome on you if you accept neither the outcome nor the process which I used (not to speak anything of imposing my deviating interpretation of that norm against you!)?

Doctrinal discussion on binding force swings between consensualism and non-consensualism without being able to fully accept either. The much-used strategies of justifying constraint by tacit consent seem helpful because they partake the character of both. Inasmuch as stress is on 'consent', principles of democratic legitimacy seem safeguarded. If emphasis lies on 'tacit', focus can be shifted away from real will on to legitimate expectations, actual behaviour and the overall context. The problem is that pursuing either of these avenues will very rapidly lead into full consensualism or full non-consensualism – and the consequent problems of binding force and democratic legitimacy.[59]

Beyond diplomatic necessity, binding force and legitimacy will remain matters of right action in a relevant context – a context which may or may not require paying at least lip service to the antropomorphic metaphor of a sovereign *voluntas*.

The Future of Utopia

In 1948 Kelsen wrote that '[f]rom a realistic point of view, the solution of the problem of peace can be sought only within the frame of international law'.[60] His distinctly modern Utopianism rejects the vision of a world federation, based on common religious or moral experience, and builds on the existing system of free and equal states. There is no such common experience: ideas about the good society are partial, subjective, socially conditioned. By contrast, the formalized states-system and the law supporting it constitute a value-free and uniquely rational, universal organization principle: 'the first and essential general principle of public international law is its quality of universality; that is to say, that it be recognized as a valid and applicable law in *all* countries, whatever their economic, socio-political or religious histories or traditions'.[61]

Such an outlook follows from liberal, Kantian ethics which stresses the neutrality and universal character of normative principles as a key to their uniquely rational legitimacy. But our late modern experience is that international law's universality is eroding. This may not be a surprise. For international law 'has suddenly to cope with a community of states and peoples in which there is no longer a shared cultural tradition'.[62] In fact, one of the most vocal concerns among international lawyers has been the fragmentation which seems to have hit international law. At least three developments come to mind.[63]

First, by far most of the *corpus* of international legal rules are regional in a wide sense; applicable and in fact applied only between governments with close historical, political or economic ties. There is even a strong analytical tendency to think of *all* international legal rules in terms of bilateral 'opposabilities', established by a continuous process whereby states present claims and counter-claims against each other and acquiesce in them.[64] Second, international law has tended to disintegrate into intellectual boxes of far-reaching functional specialization: human rights lawyers may feel as alien to integration lawyers as classical Grotians might feel estranged from both groups. Natural resources law, air and space law, law of the sea, humanitarian law, etc. have become so distinct that efforts towards connecting theory may seem like abstract academic exercises. Thirdly, and most remarkably, it has become a dominant practice to read the most varied contextual criteria into an assessment of states' international obligations. The recourse to equity whenever hard-and-fast rules seem absent or require interpretation is one such practice, particularly useful to deal with conflicts of jurisdiction. The granting of special privileges to developing states in treaty practice and the wide applicability of the *rebus sic stantibus* rule, or the good faith principle, achieve a tailoring of the law confronting each state so as to take account of its particular circumstance.

What should the theory of international law learn from this move from universality to context? Does it have more than a superficial connection with the debate about the end of modernity's legitimizing 'meta-narratives'?

Modern lawyers' realistic concentration on power and the states-system has an uneasy relationship with their assumption that even in the absence of sanctions states generally have good, selfish reasons to obey the law. For this commits them (as their 19th century predecessors) to the assumption of a transcendental, pre-existing harmony of interests between states. Such an assumption is not only implausible in that it ignores problems of scarcity and the experience of equally valid but incompatible goods.[65] It also represents an untenable conception of law as a transparent medium through which this pre-existing harmony is communicated to states.

But late modern experience itself – realism – tells us that social conflicts have not been solved in some transcendental code *ex ante*, a code combining the different *raisons d'état* into a consistent whole. Far from giving expression to such ideal harmony, international law has remained open for interpretative conflict. The attempts by modern lawyers to close recurrent 'gaps' in this system by appeal to deep-structural purposes or principles, economic or historical laws, human needs or interests, the logic of the balance of power or that of interdependence have not worked out too well. These connecting explanations were unable to sew the legal fabric together because they were themselves subject to political controversy. If they seemed unobjectionable in their conventional formulation, they remained so abstract as to accommodate any factual position; the more concrete they were made, the less they seemed to represent a universal law and the more politically biased they appeared.

To be sure, the law's rhetorical consistency provides a constraint for interpretative imagination – the concepts do privilege certain outcomes. But this is a far cry from it expressing any pre-existing harmony, even less a privileged project for a rational society. Interpretative conflicts are not misunderstandings about states' objective (even if unrecognized) interests. They are logical corollaries of the fact that the law is simply a set of concepts which can be arranged and rearranged to accommodate any conceivable substantive positions. Our ability to make distinctions – to separate the national–socialist *Grossraum* doctrine from unilateral extensions of maritime territory, for example – is prior to and determining of what we can see in law, not vice-versa. Likewise, there is no intrinsic meaning of 'self-defence' which we could apply to know the difference of meaning of United States military action in Panama in December 1989 and in Saudi Arabia in August 1990. Rather, our concept of self-defence is crucially dependent on the largely shared intuitions about this distinction. When such intuitions are not present, however, merely an insistence on the transparency of the legal concepts will prove a fruitless exercise.

The connection between the erosion of international law's universality and the debate about the end of modernity lies in the experience that social transformation cannot be achieved by appeal to pre-existing principles or great Utopias. There is no lawlike movement, no 'context of contexts' which could be abstracted in normative principles and enjoy a privileged legitimacy. State behaviour, diplomatic practices and economic constraints may be useful to know. But they provide no final, impartial and neutral law. 'History', writes Anthony Giddens, 'is not on our side, has no teleology, and supplies us with no guarantees'.[66] Though it is always possible to devise conceptual structures, such structures can never attain a true, primordial experience of social life. More often than not such structures provide legitimacy and a sense of fixity to social arrangements which are in truth both contingent and revisable. The move in legal practice to context and equity can be understood as a breaking down of this sense of fixity; a silent realization that legal concepts and categories might provide a context and a vocabulary for addressing social conflict – but that the substantive solution of conflict cannot be found from those concepts. It remains a matter of agreeing on how to live together accepting both difference and the tragedy of incompatible goods.

In this vein, international lawyers might do worse than set aside their search for the universal principles of world law. They could look at their own practice of constructing the law contextually, hesitantly and without the pretence of derivations from a unified 'system'. In such construction, notions, feelings, passions and the sense of justice play an uneradicable part. That is the part – 'politics' – which modernism has continuously attempted to suppress but which has re-emerged always as lawyers have had to look beyond routine. Looking at that 'other' side, trying to work out its substance and the ways in which it might match the aspirations whose incompatibility lies at the heart of social conflict provides a challenging enough programme for a reinvigorated international legal theory.

International law is a projection of what international lawyers think and do. This, again, is largely shaped by our socially-conditioned image of the 'international lawyer'. During the 20th century this image – and consequently the law – has undergone a metamorphosis from the academically-oriented Grotian 'adviser' to the technologically-oriented governmental bureaucrat. No wonder so little space seems available for theory! What needs articulation now is this new image of the lawyer as the conciliator, the all-around conflict-solver with a highly-trained sensibility for what is just in particular contexts and for particular participants. The breakdown of a universal law into contextual justice may indeed mark the end of the modern legal theory which attempted to establish the foundations for a context-less, uniquely rational legal doctrine and practice. May it be succeeded by a theory of law as conversation about the conditions of acceptable social arrangements and as criticism of the arbitrariness embedded in existing arrangements. If this sounds a bit high-pitched, then let me just borrow the following lines from an international lawyer with a sharp eye for theory but not known for engaging in eccentrics, James Brierly:

> We must not look for much help from the prolific growth of rules of general application such as is aimed at by projects of developing the law by codification, for that would assume a uniformity among states and their interests which often does not exist. It is more likely that the line of progress will be found to lie in the finding of particular solutions to particular problems; in the constitution, for example, of special regimes for special regions...or in the setting up of special functional organs with powers appropriate to their subject-matter. The legal purist may object that such an outlook means the continued presence of a strong political element in the international legal system, but the admixture is made inevitable by the nature of the entities with which the system has to deal.[67]

The Essays

The essays which follow have been chosen and arranged so as to illustrate the strength and weakness of realist thought in international law and what might lie 'beyond' realism. The fact that they are all by contemporary writers and link into a kind of a narrative (admittedly without a definite ending) has meant, together with the obvious constraint of space and exclusion of materials already widely reprinted, that they may not be strictly 'representative'. But they do make the best available case for taking seriously the insight that all doctrine is theory-dependent and that if one wishes to tackle seriously with doctrine or its outcomes, one had better be prepared to answer questions such as are raised in them.

The first three essays move within what I have called the realist debate. Professor Watson's is, in fact, a realist battle-cry. It is empiricist *sans peur et sans reproche* and also bedazzled by power: its empirical reality is the Hobbesian reality of egoistic sovereigns taking the posture of gladiators against each other. The essay is directed against an academic mainstream irrelevant and marginalized because too concerned with 'values' and too reliant on international organizations and courts to fulfil them. Such arguments are not new but they are powerful. They are in fact so powerful that most lawyers accept their premise – that law is determined by power – and try only to show erroneous the conclusion that this makes law relatively marginal.

The second and third essays move within the social conception but develop another understanding of the place and character of international legal norms in it. For D'Amato, the mainstream defence that 'most States obey most of the rules most of the time' is not really a credible one. That law is constantly 'used' and made reference to by states may only be evidence of its uncritical character, its capacity to accommodate any behaviour. The relevant question is: Do rules constrain? To show that they do, he interprets state behaviour as silent enforcement – as a play whereby states continuously allocate entitlements to each other and deprive each other of them. Professor Kratochwil's defence is of similar kind. He agrees that international law is indeed a social phenomenon and must be studied by studying international society. But its conceptualization solely in terms of power is a mistake. It forms rather a constantly on-going discourse through which decision-contexts are formulated and reciprocal expectations are created. As discourse, it 'functions to orchestrate and thereby facilitate societal interaction'.

The following two essays explore international lawyers' methodological options in a critical light. Dr Allott discusses the contrast between the traditional textbook style and the late modern technologico-sociological style of international legal writing. He makes no secret of having a clear preference for the controlled confusion of the traditional style – mixing the most various types of doctrinal argument with a confident reliance in a common framework of recognition in the reader. While the openly evaluative, technical style of McDougal and others may score highly on intellectual honesty and perhaps analytical clarity, its very openness and reliance on a rather unsophisticated utilitarianism renders it both amenable to cynical misuse and unsuitable for answering questions about the right legal decision to make. Professor Boyle examines doctrinal debate as a series of definitional exercises which introduce politics in legal outcomes under the pretext of disclosing the 'essence' of international law. While the attempt to fix law into objective essences (behaviour, rules, purposes) reflects the Utopian-rationalistic urge to constrain politics by something that is external to it, it may easily fall into dogmatic polemics which, Professor Boyle argues, 'are the antithesis of the Enlightenment vision of reason'. His own Utopia is a non-reifying legal argument and practice which involves the international lawyer in exploring the law's internal contradictions and, more physically, in 'international clinical programs'.

The third section expands upon attempts to think beyond realism by redefining the relationship between international law and international society. Professor Franck's essay does this by a theory of international legitimacy for which power is mixed with normative ideas and expectations. Though Professor Franck assumes that legal rules do exist in behaviour and have a 'function' to fulfil, he looks at how conforming behaviour is induced by the legitimacy, or justness, attached to the rules. The conception is social, yet departs from empiricism by concentrating on 'indicators of rule legitimacy' (determinacy, symbolic validation, coherence and adherence to hierarchy). The present writer's essay seeks a clearer break with the social conception. It uses the doctrine of international custom to show that neither of the mainstream alternatives – materialism and psychologism – provides a fully convincing account of the relationship of law and society in international affairs. Both are supplemented by unexplicated (though largely shared) ideals of the right conduct and only thereby attain plausible explanations for why some behavioural patterns might count as international custom.

The section on rethinking the substance of international law moves already quite far away from the realist debate. Professor Kennedy's long essay demonstrates how lawyers use arguments from consent and binding force so as to construct a legal architecture which guarantees a coercive order without derogating from sovereign authority. The discussion of three topics: unilateral declarations, *rebus sic stantibus*, and custom renders a description of a doctrinal argument which creates constantly new positions so as to be able to overcome the tension between order and sovereignty. Nathaniel Berman uses a similar type of method to look into the age-old quandary about the relationship of law and sovereignty through an examination of modern arguments about self-determination. He focuses on how self-determination bypasses the state system in situations in which the normal equilibrium between law and statehood has become disrupted. He shows how the difficult issue of the definition of the 'self' endowed with the 'right to become a full-fledged right-holder' is not determined by the application of pre-existing criteria but constructed with a view to restore that balance. Surakiart Sathirathai's essay looks into how even the legal rhetoric of those outside the law's privileged centre – Third World lawyers – is structured by the search for mediating strategies to deal with the tensions of liberal thought internal to that rhetoric. The power of conceptual structures is vividly illustrated in the taming of radical Third World policy by its entry into the modern international world of sovereign equals.

After these explorations of argumentative structure, Daniel Skubik's essay stands alone to direct attention to doctrine's normative aspects. His attempt to 'derive' universally applicable and neutral principles of international law from a Rawlsian 'original position' represents a late modern version of the Enlightenment project to harness politics by uniquely rational principles. Whatever one may think of such an approach or any other attempt to resuscitate the role of reason in politics (such as Habermas's theory of discursive validation as used by Anthony Carty, for example), something like it is clearly the most plausible normative strand *internal* to the social conception. It is this strand that lawyers need to pursue if they wish to remain within the modern project, or challenge if they want to abandon it.

Notes

1 Wight, Martin (1966), 'Western Values in International Relations', in Butterfield-Wight, *Diplomatic Investigations; Essays in the Theory of International Politics*, London: Harvard University Press, p 122.
2 UNGA Res. 44/23.
3 Morgenthau, Hans (1940), 'Positivism, Functionalism and International Law', *AJIL*, **34**, p. 260.
4 Vitoria, Francisco de (1917), 'De Indis et de Jure belli Relectiones', 1696 ed., Carnegie Endowment for International Peace *The Classics of International Law*, Washington, Sct. I, pp. 116–17.
5 Vattel, Emer de (1916), *Droit des gens ou Principes de la Loi naturelle appliqués aux affaires des Nations et des Souverains*, Carnegie Endowment for International Peace, Washington (Reprint of ed. of 1758) Vol. **I**, Bk.I, Ch.XII, paras 129–130 (pp. 118–120); Rousseau, Jean-Jacques (1987), *The Social Contract*, Bk. IV, Ch. 8 (*in fine*) Penguin, Harmondsworth, pp. 186–7.
6 Wolff, Christian (1933), 'Jus Gentium Methodo Scientifica Pertractatum', Carnegie Endowment for International Peace, *The Classics of International Law*, Oxford.
7 See, for example, Ompteda, D.H.L. (1785), *Litteratur des gesammten sowohl natürlichen als positiven Völkerrechts*, Regensburg: J.L. Montags; F. Kaltenborn von Stachau (1847), and Bulmerincq, A. von (1858), *Die Systematik des Völkerrechts von Hugo Grotius bis auf die Gegenwart*, Dorpat: Karow.
8 Much has been written about the domestic analogy. For a recent work, see Suganami, Hidemi (1989), *The Domestic Analogy and World Order Proposals*, Cambridge: Cambridge University Press.
9 Vattel, note 5 above, Book I, ch. II, para. 21, p. 27.
10 Mendelson, Maurice (1990), 'Practice, Propaganda and Principle in International Law', *Current Legal problems*, p. 3.
11 Cf. Koskenniemi, Martti (1990), 'The Pull of The Mainstream', review article; Meron: Human Rights and Humanitarian Norms as Customary Law, Oxford 1989, *Michigan Law Review*, **88**, pp. 1046–62.
12 See, for example, Kaufmann, Erich (1911), *Das Wesen des Völkerrechts und die Clausula Rebus sic Stantibus*, Tübingen.
13 Jellinek, Georg (1880), *Die rechtliche Natur der Staatenvertrage*, Berlin-Wien: A. Hölder, pp. 16, 38–9, 42–3.
14 Phillimore, Sir Robert (1879), *Commentaries upon International Law*, 3rd ed., Vol. **I**, London: Butterworths, p. 9.
15 Lasson, Adolf (1871), *Princip und Zukunft des Völkerrechts*, Berlin: Hertz, pp. 43–54 and *passim*.
16 Heffter, August Wilhelm (1888), *Das Europäische Völkerrecht der Gegenwart*, 8, Ausgabe, Bearb. von Heinrich Geffcken, Berlin: Müller, p. 9.
17 For the best account and criticism of international Utopianism and the 'harmony of interests', see Carr, E.H. (1951), *The Twenty-Years' Crisis 1919–1939*, 2nd ed., London: Macmillan, pp. 41–62. For analysis of contemporary Utopianism, see, for example, Taylor, Trevor (1985), 'Utopianism', in: Smith (ed.), *International Relations; British & American Perspectives*, Oxford: Blackwell, pp. 100–7.
18 See, for example, Bentham, Jeremy (1843), 'Principles of International Law', in Bentham, Works, vol. II (ed. by John Bowring) Edinburgh-London, p. 535 at 554–60. A sympathetic recent account of this Wilsonian optimism is provided in Moynihan, D.D. (1990), *On the Law of Nations*, Cambridge, Mass: Harvard University Press, pp. 33–54.
19 Nardin, Terry (1983), *Law, Morality and the Relations of States*, Princeton: Princeton University Press.
20 Lauterpacht, Hersch (1933), *The Function of Law in the International Community*, Oxford: Clarendon Press.
21 See, for example, Verdross, Alfred (1926), *Die Verfassung der Völkerrechtsgemeinschaft*, Wien-Berlin: Springer; (1923), *Die Einheit des rechtlichen Weltbildes auf Grundlage der Völkerrechtsverfassung*, Tübingen: Mohr.
22 Kelsen, Hans (1953), 'Théorie du droit international public', *RCADI*, **III**, 84, pp. 1–203.

23 Note 20 above. See also Lauterpacht, Hersch (1958), *Some Observations on the Prohibition of 'non Liquet' and the Completeness of Law*, Symbolae Verzijl, The Hague, pp. 196–221.
24 Duguit, Leon (1927), *Traité de droit constitutionnel*, Paris.
25 Scelle, Georges (1932, 1936), *Précis de droit des gens*, Vols **I–II**, Paris: Sirey.
26 McDougal, Myres S. (1953), 'International Law, Power and Policy; a Contemporary Conception', *RCADI*, **82**, pp. 133–259. See also Quadri, Rolando (1952), 'Le fondement du caractère obligatoire du droit international public', *RCADI*, **I**, 80, pp. 579–633.
27 Corbett, Percy (1951), *Law and Society in the Relations of States*, New York: Harcourt, Brace, p. 11.
28 See McDougal, note 26 above, and further, McDougal, Myres S. and Reisman, W. Michael (1983), 'International Law in Policy-Oriented Perspective', in Macdonald-Johnston (eds), *The Structure and Process of International Law*, The Hague: Nijhoff, pp. 103–29. For critical analyses, see, for example, Rosenthal, Bent (1970), *Etude de l'oeuvre de Myres S. McDougal en matière du droit international public*, Paris: L.G.D.J., especially pp. 127–44; Krakau, Knud (1976), *Missionsbewusstsein und Völkerrechtsdoktrin in den Vereinigten Staaten von Amerika*, Frankfurt am Main: Metzner especially pp. 474–504.
29 Stephen, J.K. (1884), *International Law and International Relations; An Attempt to Ascertain the Best Method for Discussing the Topics of International Law*, London: Macmillan, p. 45.
30 Alvarez, Alejandro (1959), *Le droit international nouveau dans ses rapports avec la vie actuelle des peuples*, Paris: Pédone.
31 Smith, H.A. (1947), *The Crisis in the Law of Nations*, London: Stevens, p. 102.
32 See Falk, Richard (1970), *The Status of Law in International Society*, Princeton: Princeton University Press; Bedjaoui, Mohammed (1979), *Towards a New International Economic Order*, Paris-London-New York: UNESCO.
33 Jessup, Philip C. (1958), *A Modern Law of Nations*, New York: Macmillan, p. 6.
34 Visscher, Charles de (1954), 'Cours général de principes de droit international public', *RCADI*, **II**, 86, p. 451.
35 See, for example, Corbett, note 27 above; Henkin, Louis (1979), *How Nations Behave. Law and Foreign Policy*, 2nd ed., New York: Columbia University Press; Cassese, Antonio (1986), *International Law in a Divided World*, Oxford: Clarendon Press.
36 For example, Fitzmaurice, Gerald (1987), *The Law and Procedure of the International Court of Justice*, (reprinted from articles in the *British Year Book of International Law*) Cambridge: Grotius Publication.
37 For a few examples, see, Kelsen, Hans (1926), 'Les rapports de systeme entre le droit interne et le droit international public, *RCADI*, **IV**, 14, pp. 231–331; Brierly, James L. (1928), 'Le fondement du caractère obligatoire du droit international', *RCADI*, **III**, 23, pp. 467–549;. Fur, Louis Le (1935), 'Règles générales du droit de la paix', *RCADI*, **IV**, 54, pp. 5–307; Kaufmann, Erich (1935), 'Règles générales du droit de la paix', *RCADI*, **IV**, 54, pp. 313–615; Djuvara, (1938), 'Le fondement de l'ordre juridique positif en droit international', *RCADI*, **II**, 64, pp. 485–616.
38 Ago, Roberto (1956), 'Science juridique et droit international', *RCADI*, **II**, 90, pp. 849–95; Ziccardi, Piero (1958), 'Le caractère de l'ordre juridique international', *RCADI*, **III**, 95, pp. 267–405.
39 Rolin, Henri (1950), 'Les principes de droit international public', *RCADI*, **II**, 77, p. 309.
40 Bishop, W.W. (1965), 'General Course on Public International Law', *RCADI*, **II**, 115, pp. 151, 170.
41 Falk, Richard (1969), 'The Interplay of Westphalia and Charter Conceptions of the International Legal Order', in Falk-Black (eds), *The Future of the International Legal Order*, Vol. I, Trends and Patterns, Princeton: Princeton University Press, pp. 34–5.
42 Allott, Philip (1988), 'State Responsibility and the Unmaking of International Law', *Harvard International Law Journal*, **29**, p. 10.
43 Boyle, Francis (1985), *World Politics and International Law*, Durham: Duke University Press, pp. 59–60, 81.
44 *Idem*, pp. 171–200.
45 For a brief analysis, see Kennedy, David (1988), 'A New Stream of International Law Scholarship', *Wisconsin International Law Journal*, 7, pp. 1–49.

46 Carty, Anthony (1986), *The Decay of International Law?*, Manchester: Manchester University Press.
47 Kennedy, David (1988), *International Legal Structures*, Baden-Baden: Nomos.
48 Koskenniemi, Martti (1989), *From Apology to Utopia; The Structure of International Legal Argument*, Helsinki: Finnish Lawyers' Publishing Company.
49 Franck, Thomas M. (1990), *The Power of Legitimacy among Nations*, New York: Oxford University Press.
50 See, in particular, Binder, Guyora (1988), *Treaty Conflict and Political Contradiction; The Dialectic of Duplicity*, New York: Praeger; Kratochwil, Friedrich (1989), *Rules, Norms and Decisions: On the Conditions of Practical and Legal Reasoning in International Relations and Domestic Affairs*, Cambridge: Cambridge University Press; Allott, Philip (1990), *Eunomia: A New Order for a New World*, Oxford: Oxford University Press; Fastenrath, Ulrich (1990), *Lücken im Völkerrecht. Zu Rechtscharakter, Quellen, Systemzusammenhang, Methodenlehre und Funktionen des Völkerrechts*, Berlin: Duncker & Humblot.
51 On the tension between international law's communal and individualistic strands, see Kennedy, David (1980), 'Theses on International Law Discourse', *German Yearbook of International Law*, 23, pp. 353–91. See also Koskenniemi, note 48 above, pp. 422–57.
52 For both of these claims, see Principle 21 of the Stockholm Declaration; Report of the UN Conference on the Human Environment, Stockholm 5–16 June 1972, UN Doc. A/Conf.48/14.
53 See, for example, Lammers, J.G. (1984), 'Balancing the Equities in International Environmental Law', *RCADI* Coll., pp. 153–64.
54 See, for example, *Island of Palmas* case, II United Nations Reports of International Arbitral Awards, pp. 839, 843–6.
55 Hart, H.L.A. (1961), *The Concept of Law*, Oxford: Clarendon Press, pp. 91 *et seq*.
56 See, for example, the UN Security Council Resolution condemning the Iraqi annexation of Kuwait, 662/1990 (9.8.1990).
57 Compare, in this respect, ICJ: *North Sea Continental Shelf* cases, Reports 1969, pp. 22–3 (paras 19–20) and *Tunisia-Libya Continental Shelf* case, Reports 1982, p. 59 (para. 70).
58 See also Charney, Jonathan (1985), *The Persistent Objection Rule and the Development of Customary International Law*, LVI BYIL, pp. 1–24.
59 See further Koskenniemi, note 48 above, pp. 270–341.
60 *Law and Peace* (1948), Cambridge: Harvard University Press, p. 28.
61 Jennings, Sir Robert (1986), 'Universal International Law in a Multicultural World', in *Liber Amicorum Lord Wilberforce*, Oxford: Clarendon Press, pp. 40–1.
62 *Idem*, p. 40.
63 For general discussions, see, for example, Fitzmaurice, Gerald (1973), 'The Future of Public International Law and that of the International Legal System in the Circumstances of Today', Institut de Droit International, *Livre de Centenaire 1873–1973*, pp. 196–328; Green, L.C. (1985), 'Is There a Universal International Law Today?', *Can YIL*, 1985, pp. 3–32; Weil, Prosper (1983), 'Towards Relative Normativity in International Law', *AJIL*, **77**, pp. 413–42.
64 See Koskenniemi, note 48 above, pp. 410–15 and notes therein.
65 Modern agnosticism has always had difficulty to face up with the tragedy of incompatible goods – hence its constant slide towards nostalgia and totalitarianism. See Berlin, Isaiah (1969), 'Two Concepts of Liberty', in *Four Essays on Liberty*, Oxford: Clarendon Press, pp. 118–72.
66 Giddens, Anthony (1990), *The Consequences of Modernity*, Stanford: Stanford University Press, p. 154.
67 Brierly, J.L. (1944), *The Outlook for International Law*, Oxford: Clarendon Press, p. 45.

Part I
The Realist Debate

[1]

A REALISTIC JURISPRUDENCE OF INTERNATIONAL LAW

By

J. S. WATSON

"*What you cannot enforce, do not command*"—Sophocles, *Oedipus at Colunnus.*

THAT international law lacks a competent body endowed with the power compulsorily to settle disputes, is a truism in the theory of international law. Likewise, the lack of a central source of authoritative rules, a legislature, is also routinely acknowledged by writers of all persuasions. To the layman, what this means is immediately apparent: international law cannot and does not behave in the same prescriptive manner that one has become accustomed to in dealing with domestic legal systems. There are, however, few theorists in international law who fully appreciate the extent of the problem so created. Rather than seek to discover the technique whereby the system operates, the tendency is clearly towards the suppression of this knowledge, while creating or advocating rules that require, for their successful implementation, the same degree of competence enjoyed by a domestic legislature or appellate judiciary. That international law requires, as a result of its decentralised nature, significantly greater attention to the questions of compliance and efficacy than one is accustomed to in the orderly environment of internal State law, is something that is quickly forgotten in the rush towards more attractive topics.

The result of this is that the norms generated by theorists are frequently not observed even by a majority of States. Consequently these rules do not have a normative function, nor are they descriptive of reality. But this does not seem to concern these writers for, as is so often the case in the social sciences, rather than question the utility or the validity of their theoretical framework, they adopt a posture reminiscent of Canute, to the effect that there is a considerable amount of behaviour that does not conform to their rules, and the sooner it stops the better. But the central question, how this "illegal" behaviour is to be made to stop, is seldom dealt with, beyond the proposal of schemes in treaty form that would work extremely well if only States would sign such treaties, and comply with them.[1] The underlying problem is that enforcement is seen as a

[1] See, *e.g.*, G. Clark and L. B. Sohn, *World Peace Through World Law*, 2nd ed. (1960).

separate topic, one that is to be considered only after the content of the substantive rules has been settled. In international law, however, enforcement and the feasibility of rules is part of the process whereby they are created.

The vain insistence that international reality must conform to carefully-deduced norms is due in large part to the extension into international law of the coercive habit of thought acquired by lawyers in domestic legal systems. As a result of this there is a widespread tendency to assume that international law may maintain a prescriptive function to the same degree that a domestic legal system can, despite its acknowledged lack of centralised authority or overall political stability. As a result of this one tends to find that many writers are quite comfortable with, for example, the reiteration of Lauterpacht's argument that Article 55 of the United Nations Charter contains a specific legal obligation for States to observe the human rights of their citizens, despite substantial evidence of contrary State practice. Widespread reports in the world Press and by non-governmental agencies,[2] such as the Red Cross and Amnesty International, of torture and unlawful incarceration of political prisoners in dozens of countries, and the killing of native populations, are, if they are acknowledged at all, regarded as reports of deviant or "illegal" conduct. Despite the clear lack of implementation, Lauterpacht's conclusion remains unaffected in the legal literature. Similarly the impotence of international law in the face of genocide in Burundi,[3] murder by the thousand in Uganda,[4] and by the million in Cambodia,[5] is only emphasised by reference to the verbal history of the General Assembly, or reasoning by analogy from the opinions of the International Court of Justice. The current failure of international law theorists to come to terms with the reality of the system's limitations is likewise clear in regard to the control of the use of force. Under prevailing theory, which has a strong tendency to isolate law from reality, the Kellogg-Briand Pact is still valid law, as are Articles 45 and 46 of the United Nations Charter. But whether it means anything to talk of such provisions as being valid is an elusive, and largely neglected, topic.

---

[2] On the increase in such organisations, see D. Weissbrodt, "The Role of International Nongovernmental Organisations in the Implementation of Human Rights," 12 *Texas International Law Journal* (1977), p. 293.

[3] "Massacre in the Heart of Africa," *The New York Times*, June 4, 1972, p. 2, col. 1; quoted in N. E. Leech, C. T. Oliver and J. M. Sweeney, *The International Legal System* (1973), p. 653.

[4] "Genocide in Uganda," *The Manchester Guardian* (Airmail Edition), Vol. 119, Nr. 18, October 29, 1978, p. 8, col. 3. The death role is put at 300,000.

[5] A United States Senate Report recently put the number of executions and deaths in Cambodia at 2·5 million, *Senate Report*, Nr. 95–1166, 95th Cong., 2nd Sess. (1978).

If law and legal theory are to have any useful function in international law beyond the making of value-judgments on the activities of individual States, it is imperative that more attention be given to the testing of conclusions and propositions of law against the prevailing international social reality. This is particularly true in view of the clear tendency in the literature towards reliance on verbal legal sources, such as General Assembly resolutions and World Court opinions, rather than on actual State practice. Since international law has no centralised institutional structure, validity can only be tested in relation to reality.

I—The Coercive, Centralised Model of Law

In a passage which ultimately formed the theoretical underpinning of his seminal work on human rights, Sir Hersch Lauterpacht stated that international law is superior to State law and has the ability to enforce its norms. He wrote: "The rights of man cannot, in the long run, be effectively secured except by the twin operation of the law of nature and the law of nations—both conceived as a power superior to the supreme power of the State."[6] While many would agree that international law, like natural law, is morally or conceptually superior to State law, that does not mean that it is politically superior. Likewise, the lack of enforcement mechanisms of the hierarchical type cannot be compensated for simply by "conceiving" of the one system as being superior to the other. If all that Lauterpacht was saying was that international law is morally superior, then that would be unobjectionable, but that is obviously not his position for he talks of "effectively" securing the rights of man, and subsequently added that "[i]t is only within the scheme of an overriding international order that we can give reality to the otherwise contradictory notion that the supreme authority of the State is limited and that the rights of man must be based on that limitation."[7] But he gives no evidence to support the contention of a supranational authority. Nor is there any discussion of how such a system might be brought about, or whether, as many believe, the creation of such a system might entail a greater violation of the rights of individuals than might be protected by its eventual implementation. Instead, in this and in his subsequent work on human rights in international law, he assumes the fully prescriptive model of international law, and proceeds to generate a normative structure which, when set against the reality of State behaviour, can only be characterised as

---

[6] H. Lauterpacht, "The Law of Nations, The Law of Nature and The Rights of Man," 29 *Grotius Society Transactions* (1943), p. 1.

[7] *Ibid*. p. 29.

totally inefficacious. Despite this, in the 30 years since Lauterpacht wrote the above passages, a vast literature on the role of general international law in protecting the rights of individuals has appeared. This literature depends, if one examines it closely, on a naturalistic view of international law as a superior force, and hardly ever does one encounter an attempt to demonstrate this superiority in any practical sense.

There clearly continues to be a bias in favour of Lauterpacht's position. A centralised, hierarchical, coercive legal system is seen as the only feasible solution to virtually every international problem, and little or no attention is given to the fact that the creation and implementation of such a system is a meta-legal issue, one which cannot be controlled by academic or judicial effort, no matter how well-intentioned or sincere. In addition, a supranational legal system cannot be built on the foundation of the current system of international law because the latter is an entirely different system. It does not rely on sanctions but on consent, mutual accommodation and reciprocity.

An example of this current bias can be found in the writings of Professor Falk who is representative in many respects of the "new" international lawyers. He does not present a test for legal validity, but rather seems to rely for support on the self-evident improvement to mankind that would result from a centralised system of enforcement. He is of the opinion that what is needed is "some form of central guidance"[8] and that this may be achieved by means of a populist transitional process which will, on the one hand, centralise control and planning and, on the other hand, decentralise political structures.[9] Quite apart from the intriguing question of the extent to which these two processes may be carried on simultaneously, he fails to provide any information not only on the advantages of such a world system, but also on its feasibility. He seems to be of the opinion that no one can seriously doubt that such a system would be better than the current horizontal structure and that there is really no need to explain how it will be brought about. He does, however, indicate that he sees a parallel between the shift, during the Middle Ages, from centralised Papal control to the State system, and a shift at the present time away from the State system to "some form of central guidance." While he uses the concept of central guidance throughout the article he at no time defines it even to the extent of whether it is primarily political, legal or spiritual in nature. We are once more presumed to believe that central guidance is better than

[8] R. Falk, "A New Paradigm for International Legal Studies: Prospects and Proposals," 84 *Yale Law Review* (1975), p. 969.

[9] *Ibid.* p. 1014.

horizontal reciprocity and mutual accommodation. Falk is not unaware of the vast difference between horizontal and vertical legal systems, between unilateral and reciprocal norms,[10] so this presumption in favour of the former cannot be attributed to oversight. As is so often the case with the "new" international lawyers a coercive model of international law is chosen without any assessment of the relative merits of international and supranational law. What is most interesting is that, although the more specific aspects of Falk's programme are attacked, this assumption of a prescriptive model as a goal meets little resistance. There is little need to defend it because it is so widely accepted amongst international lawyers as the only type of legal system. If international law is to be law "properly so called" then it must be modelled on its coercive domestic counterpart. That international law might be law "improperly so called" is one of the taboos of the discipline.

While one might be safe in assuming that Falk is not predicting or advocating the return of Papal rule, he gives no help to the curious in his elusive descriptions of what he envisions. Little help is given by his statement, "I believe that a paradigm shift is both necessary and possible in the years ahead, and that such a shift would help to influence the transitional process in the direction of preferred world order options,"[11] but the remark typifies the nature of Falk's overall argument. First, it hinges on his own personal belief that there is a holistic trend afoot. He gives no evidence of this, though evidence to the contrary immediately springs to mind: the widening gap between developed and undeveloped nations; the politicisation of voting in the United Nations resulting in such partisan behaviour as to render worthless much of its product; the paucity of cases before the International Court of Justice; the spread of nuclear and strategic arms throughout the world; the failure to reach agreement at the Law of the Sea conferences; and the lack of effective action taken in response to the massive violations of human rights in many countries. Falk does not show how such facts fit into his scheme. We are left to agree or disagree with his statement. Those who agree with him will feel that their position has been reinforced. Those who disagree will enjoy a similar experience.

A second problem of the "new" international lawyers' philosophy that is brought into focus by the above quotation, is that it is not at all clear whose preferences will be the basis of the "preferred world options." Falk seems to be of the opinion that world populism will produce a homogeneous value structure despite the widening

[10] R. Falk, "International Jurisdiction: Horizontal and Vertical Conceptions of Legal Order," 32 *Temple Law Quarterly* (1959), p. 295.

[11] *Op. cit.* in note 8, above, at p. 998.

gaps between rich and poor, developed and undeveloped, nations. While he shows from his perspective that there are weaknesses in the Clark-Sohn approach, the diplomacy of Henry Kissinger, and the Trilateral Commission, he makes no attempt to present the value preferences of his own world populist system. This lack of information is particularly unfortunate in view of the fact that he commences his article by saying that international lawyers have a key role to play in the creation of a central guidance system, "if they give self-conscious support to a set of *explicit* world order goals that structure both the means and the ends of transition."[12]

A final problem in Falk's position that is attributable to the prescriptive habit of thought is that he is clearly of the opinion that theory can affect reality to such an extent that academic advocacy alone may create world order. Again, this is a position that is shared by the "new" international lawyers, either openly, as in Falk's case, or more discreetly, as in those writers, discussed subsequently, who advocate modification of the concept of customary law formation. The idea that a few academic commentators can have a controlling effect on the flow of world events to the extent of substituting one universal *Grundnorm* for another is shown in a passage in which the transition to the State system is attributed to Hugo Grotius[13] as though Grotius' writing was the sole cause of the nation-State's evolution. Bringing this misconception up to date, Falk advocates the active participation of academics and international lawyers in a "paradigm shift" to his proposed system. This is perhaps the most unrealistic aspect of any world order project. While it is true that academics and international lawyers occasionally have access to those in power, their contribution to global policy is a small one indeed. The fact of the matter is that the functions of the academic and the lawyer are such as to preclude the success of their effective involvement. A lawyer canot be expected to put the advocacy of an unrevealed world order before the interests of his client. If he does, he is likely to be replaced by a lawyer with more predictable loyalties, and his brief foray into the realms of monism will have been in vain. As for academic involvement in such a scheme, the academic function is entirely incompatible with the unremitting advocacy of any idealistic order. Since the academic function is a very subjective activity at the best of times, being primarily concerned with the selection and sifting of material in order to present a coherent whole, any academic who is committed to one particular cause, and openly advocates such a cause without empirical data to support his position, immediately calls his or her professional judgment into

[12] *Ibid.* at p. 969 (italics added).
[13] *Ibid.* at p. 976.

question. While it is perfectly acceptable for an academic to adopt the role of advocate in private life, it must not, as Max Weber convincingly demonstrated,[14] be allowed to intrude on his professional activities.

For any academic activity to be of value to others, a clear distinction between the descriptive and the prescriptive aspects of one's work must be maintained. Before any normative activity can succeed, a firm descriptive base must first be built. This is particularly applicable to the study of international law where there is increased reliance on the descriptive aspect of the science of law due to the lack of norm-validating institutions. Curiously, it was the continual objective testing of theories against facts that was the theme running through the work on paradigms which Falk used as the basis for his argument. The major point that Kuhn was making was that when a scientific paradigm fails to account for available data then there is a need for a new paradigm. This new paradigm must then be tested by what Kuhn calls "normal science" and the eventual acceptance of the paradigm is dependent on its being "more successful than [its] competitors in solving a few problems that the group of practitioners has come to recognise as acute."[15] Thus, not only is Falk adopting Kuhn's view of scientific thinking and incorporating it into a normative science, against Kuhn's own advice,[16] but he is failing to use the approach properly by insisting on advocating a position where there is little or no empirical evidence to support it and indeed most would agree the vast weight of evidence is against it. The function of a paradigm is not normative, as Falk uses it, but descriptive, subject to subsequent empirical verification. In any event, just as a scientific rule cannot alter reality, a legal system cannot displace the political system on which it is based.

The idea that emerges from this loose mixture of *lex lata* and *lex ferenda*, of the advocate and the scholar, and of normative and scientific rules that is so typical of the "new" international law is that one is justified in reaching a conclusion concerning the existence of an international norm not so much on the basis of valid legal reasoning within the confines of the system's limited capacity, but rather on the basis of the overall desirability of the conclusion, and the goodness of the proponent's intentions. This naturalistic reasoning presupposes a legal system within which such conclusions may be enforced, regardless of their relationship to reality. It is thus, to a large extent, completely circular in that it assumes what it sets out to

[14] M. Weber. "On Science as a Vocation," in M. Truzzi (ed.), *Sociology: The Classic Statements* (1971), p. 22.

[15] T. S. Kuhn, *The Structure of Scientific Revolutions* (1964), p. 42.

[16] *Op. cit.* in note 8, above, at pp. 976–977.

prove. Before one can have a supranational legal order, one must have a pre-existing international political stability, for a viable coercive order is completely impossible in an unstable political environment. Historically law always follows, rather than precedes, the attainment of political stability. Its function is to dispense, in an orderly manner, the monopoly of political power and to ensure that this monopoly is not challenged by alternative systems, such as self help, that would be detrimental to the structure as a whole.

The preoccupation with the prescriptive model of international law is often evident in attempts to show that such a system is already in existence. One argument that is often made is that the United Nations is similar to a government in many respects. The multiple citation of resolutions,[17] or the alleged consistency of resolutions[18] are seen as being tantamount to an international common law. In a recent article by Brownlie[19] an attempt was made to show the parallel between the United Nations and a domestic government by means of emphasising the fact that the United Nations shared many flaws with governments. Among the shortcomings listed as being common to both were: budgets being less than is required for effective action; political weakness in the face of special interests; the use of discretion to avoid confrontation; inefficacious norms; and reliance on consensus rather than formal institutional mechanisms. That such similarities exist is undeniable, but the fact that an entity shares some of the commoner symptoms of governmental weakness could just as easily be applied to a tramway preservation society. What is lacking, and what Brownlie apparently would like to see, or would like to convince us exists, is the possession by that organisation of the degree of political power necessary for it to behave like a government, to enforce its directives and decisions. The argument that international law, or in this instance the United Nations, is as inefficient as a domestic legal system can be, ignores the fact that in a domestic legal system enforcement is always possible by a third party as a last resort. The fact that this heavy reliance on force is not clearly visible at all times is the result of other mechanisms such as the "habit of obedience"[20] which appear after

---

[17] An example of this argument may be found in S. A. Bleicher, "The Legal Signficance of Re-citation of General Assembly Resolutions," 63 *American Journal of International Law* (1969), p. 444.

[18] See, *e.g.*, R. Higgins, "The United Nations and Lawmaking: The Political Organs," *Proceedings of the American Society of International Law* (1970), p. 37.

[19] I. Brownlie, "The United Nations as a Form of Government," 13 *Harvard International Law Journal* (1972), p. 421; For a similar argument see J. H. E. Fried, "How Efficient is International Law?" in K. W. Deutsch and S. Hoffman (eds.), *The Relevance of International Law: Essays in Honour of Leo Gross* (1968), p. 63.

[20] H. L. A. Hart, *The Concept of Law* (1961), pp. 49–64.

the passage of time. This does not mean, however, that force is not the ultimate basis of law. No matter how inept a government might be, such power is always latent within the system. This power cannot be created by wishful thinking, or projected into reality by a comparison of symptoms of its absence. It is either there or it is not, and it is on this fact that all efficacious, prescriptive legal systems are built.

Support for this position, which has frequently been put forward by Schwarzenberger,[21] comes, rather surprisingly, from the writings of Hans Kelsen. Kelsen, in trying to remove the non-legal elements from legal theory, rested the validity of individual norms within a legal system on the validity of superior norms in the same hierarchy. Ultimately, the validity of this hierarchy depends on the validity of the *Grundnorm*. As long as one confines one's inquiry to the lower levels of Kelsen's system this theory is indeed potentially pure of meta-legal factors. But, if one addresses the question of the *Grundnorm's* validity, it quickly becomes apparent that the validity of his system depends on social and political facts, on power. The key to this lies in what Kelsen terms "the principle of effectiveness." In discussing this principle Kelsen states: "Every single norm loses its validity when the total legal order to which it belongs loses its efficacy as a whole. The efficacy of the entire legal order is a necessary condition for the validity of every single norm of the order. A *conditio sine qua non* but not a *conditio per quam.*"[22] Thus even Kelsen's pure theory ultimately depends on metapositive factors, the efficacy of the system or the power behind the law. According to him a system which is not efficacious is not legally valid, and efficacy is simply a social fact, not unlike the habit of obedience, for "[t]he content of the basic norm is determined by the facts through which an order is created and applied, to which the behaviour of the individuals regulated by this order by and large conforms ... the validity of a legal order is thus dependent upon its agreement with reality, upon its 'efficacy.'"[23]

II—Custom and Majority Rule

(a) *The Traditional Approach*

The preceding examples of writers dealing directly with the need for, or the desirability of, a supranational system is only the tip of the iceberg. The major areas in which supranational aspirations are

[21] G. Schwarzenberger, *International Law and Order* (1971), p. 1; "International *Jus Cogens*?" 43 *Texas Law Review* (1965), pp. 456–457.

[22] H. Kelsen, *General Theory of Law and State* (1945), p. 118.

[23] *Ibid.* at pp. 119–120.

evident are the developing areas of international law, such as the protection of human rights, the calls for a new international economic order, and international environmental law. While the goals are admirable and possibly beyond reproach from a humanistic viewpoint, it is very doubtful whether the approach that is being taken has any significant chance of success. Unlike Lauterpacht, Falk, Brownlie and the many other writers who confront directly the issue of supranational enforcement, the advocates of the "new" international law usually take a more indirect approach. What they do is to make what appear, at first sight, to be innocuous changes in the definition of custom. But on closer examination it becomes readily apparent that they have moved the theoretical basis of obligation from consent to majority rule. The approach is a little more subtle, but the efficacy, and hence the utility, of the result is no greater.

Consent is a crucial element in the overall functioning of effective international law, and any theory that disregards it is certain to experience severe problems in compliance, when looked at from the normative viewpoint, and in accuracy, when looked at from the descriptive viewpoint. This is so because, without organs of magisterial competence, international law must avoid unilateral commands and gain compliance by eliciting the support of States. This is the reason for the heavy reliance on consent in the traditional theory. It springs, not from a desire to maintain or further the prestige of the nation-State, as is so often charged, but rather from a realisation that since nation-States as a matter of fact are the primary wielders of power in the world, their co-operation is essential for the success of the limited normative role of international law. By requiring consent, express or tacit, on the part of States, the effectiveness of international norms is made possible.

The traditional concept of custom requires that two elements be present, the actual practice of States and *opinio juris*, the sense of obligation. When both of these are present then the rule in question is law. But it is not law in the unilaterally-sanctioned sense that one is familiar with in domestic legal systems. International custom receives a limited prescriptive effect in the following manner. The practice of States is the result of a complex, fluid process of mutual accommodation, trade-offs and reciprocity. It is, for each State, the end result of an evaluation of what it considers to be behaviour rightly expected of it by other States and also an indication of how it wishes to be treated in return by those States. Because of the reciprocal element that is inherent in the process, the practice of States tends towards uniformity in space and time. It is this uniformity that is its primary attraction since States, wishing to make the conduct of their international affairs easier, see the benefit to their own individual decision-making in maintaining this practice. This is the *opinio juris* element; States simply feel obligated, in a reciprocal sense based ultimately on self-interest, to behave as they have been behaving in the past. The prescriptive element at the core of international law is thus the norm that, in the main, the current practices ought to continue. Since there is considerable self-interest in this general maintenance of practice, since the system involves a reciprocal element, and especially since States are already behaving in the indicated manner, the system is virtually self-enforcing. Custom, the basis of all international law is thus primarily descriptive. The normative element is dependent on a community perception of the need for stability and the maintenance of expectations based on prior activity.

(b) *The "New" Approach*

The central theme of the new theory of custom is dependent on the view that the political organs of the United Nations must be endowed with legislative competence. Since this position is clearly untenable on the basis of the treaty obligations involved, another basis has to be found. The alternative method is custom, misconstrued. In an address to the American Society of International Law, Rosalyn Higgins, one of the leading advocates of this position, presented her argument.[24] It is that the resolutions of the General Assembly and Security Council can be used to fulfil the practice element of custom. There is, she says, no longer any need for an analysis of individual State practice, one need only refer to the practice of these organs. While she admits that there is a problem with regard to *opinio juris*, since the motivation for voting in a particular way on any resolution is often unconnected with a legal evaluation of its substance, she considers that problem insufficient to prevent the creation of law.

The problem with her approach is that it fails to provide rules that are self-enforcing, a problem that is absent if one limits oneself to the traditional definition. Higgins' approach fails to appreciate the horizontal enforcement mechanism of international custom outlined above. By using the practice of an organ rather than the practice of States, majority rule is obviously being introduced. Furthermore, even if an organ is perfectly consistent over a substantial period of time, the positions taken by its constituent members may have been anything but consistent. In almost every instance of voting in the political organs of the United Nations there is a sizeable minority which votes negatively. Since the factors that go into

[24] *Op. cit.* in note 18, above.

determining the vote are primarily political and ad hoc, this minority will not contain the same States in each instance of voting. Thus it is possible for a majority of States to have voted against a proposition at some time during the history of a perfectly cosistent practice by an organ. If a State is required to conform with this "practice" it should be able to point to negative votes cast by it, and characterise those as an objection to the evolving custom. If Higgins wishes to view positive votes as legally significant for custom, then negative votes must be accorded equal treatment. In addition, if a State has consistently voted against a position, has never acted in accordance with the proposed rule and has no intention of ever acting in accordance with it, then one has a very difficult enforcement problem indeed. Under the traditional theory such a State would not be bound, indeed it is unlikely that there would be a binding customary rule at all. Yet under the "democratic" approach currently in vogue such an objecting State would be bound. But bound by what? Since there is no way of requiring compliance, the best that can be said is that the objecting State is morally bound. While a certain amount of leverage can be gained from establishing moral obligation, Higgins' argument is based ostensibly on legal techniques and is thus not a proof of moral obligation. Nor can it be said to be proof of legal obligation since, while she may be correct in asserting that "[t]he interest of the vast majority is a real and legally relevant one,"[25] that does not by itself require the conclusion that valid international law has been created.

Not only is the practice of States dispensed with as a constituent element of custom under the new approach, but *opinio juris* also receives short shrift. Even if States were voting on the basis of purely legal assessments of the general propositions on which the resolutions were based, there would still remain a serious problem. As already indicated, custom is essentially descriptive, the prescriptive, *opinio juris*, element being dependent on the accuracy of the description of State practice. Under the new approach *opinio juris* cannot mean the same as it does in the traditional definition since the element of practice is missing. *Opinio juris* thus becomes oriented towards what the law ought to be rather than what the current practice is. It is *opinio juris de lege ferenda* rather than *opinio juris de lege lata*. This change, which is easy to overlook, makes the question of the efficacy of the rules produced a major problem, even an insoluble one. Since the *opinio juris* element does not relate to a current state of affairs, which would requie virtually no enforcement, but relates instead to a future situation in which reality must

[25] *Ibid.* at p. 42.

be made to conform to the law, it would require a supranational authority for this to be successful. But hypothetical legal systems cannot achieve concrete results. The conclusions presented are thus invariably attractive, but cannot be implemented.

Despite such problems, a considerable number of writers have endorsed this position. Akehurst, for example, has rejected the "restrictive" definition[26] of traditional international law in favour of a broader, more dynamic view. The fact that the traditional definition is "restrictive" for very sound reasons received little or no attention. Akehurst does, however, avoid the problems faced by Higgins' acceptance of *opinio juris de lege ferenda* and instead limits the material that may form the basis of custom to the "practice" of the General Assembly where the assertions made concern *lex lata*.[27] This removes part of the problem, but by no means all of it for, by including statements about law within "State practice" rather than insisting on the traditional requirement of actual State activity, the enforcement problem still remains. This is so because there is considerably less commitment to a position that is taken by mere vote at an Assembly meeting than is the case when a State is faced with the decision of whether or not to behave in a particular manner. This inconsistency is not due entirely to a lack of good faith on the part of States. More often than not States fail to live up to such announced standards for a variety of reasons that were not considered or foreseen at the time of the vote. For example, internal political pressure may have built up unpredictably, opposing the position taken. Economic pressures likewise can have a decisive effect on the relationship between verbal and actual behaviour, as has been shown most clearly in the history of the economic sanctions imposed on Rhodesia. That there was a gap between announced standards and subsequent practice on the part of many States is all the more relevant here in view of the mandatory nature of the Security Council's actions. To sum up, a State that is actually involved in an international activity has a higher commitment to that activity than it does in a mere vote because the activity involves the entire filtering process of reciprocity and mutual accommodation that is the very core of international law. A State must assess whether the position it takes is not only one which it is willing to advocate for itself but is also one which it is willing to tolerate when adversely applied to it by other States. This is a far cry from voting for or against a non-binding resolution in New York City.

---

[26] M. Akehurst, "Custom as a Source of International Law," XLVII *British Year Book of International Law* (1974–75), p. 1.

[27] *Ibid.* at p. 6.

III—The Role of the International Court of Justice

(a) *Academic Commentary*

Another symptom of the presumption in favour of too great a prescriptive role for international law is to be found in the use of the opinions of the International Court of Justice as sources of law. Brownlie, for example, in discussing the General Assembly's tendency to act *ultra vires* stated that this had been "legitimated by the advisory opinion of the International Court in the Namibia case."[28] This statement is indicative of the extent to which the juridical positivism of a common law system tends to be transferred into the international arena. The Court is treated as though it were a fully competent domestic court, the opinions of which may be analysed in order to find generally-binding law. But the use of this technique assumes yet again the existence of a supranational authority where none exists. *Stare decisis* does not, and cannot, apply in the present international system. The International Court of Justice, consistent with the traditional theory of international law, bases its jurisdiction firmly on State consent.[29] This acknowledgment of the importance of State consent has the effect of substantially increasing the compliance rate of the Court's judgments since, in deciding whether to appear before the Court, a State can assess its own willingness to comply with an adverse decision. A State that is not willing to comply with such a decision will simply not appear before the Court. This system is clearly unsatisfactory to those who think in terms of coercive legal orders, but it is the prevailing system nonetheless. The Court, on the basis of the terms of its Statute and as a matter of political reality, cannot create a legal rule adverse to a State that is not a party to the proceedings, which is the essence of the *stare decisis* philosophy. To assume that it can is to lose oneself in a world of unenforceable norms.

Indeed, even when State consent is taken into account, there is no guarantee that compliance will result. The continuing lack of implementation of the Corfu Channel Judgment, to mention only one example, is indicative of this. If there are problems under the traditional system then, it is submitted, there will be a significant increase in non-compliance if the theoretical base of international law is allowed to shift towards any presumption of magisterial competence on the part of the Court.

The juridical positivism of the "new" international lawyers is categorically dismissed by Article 59 of the Court's Statute which

[28] Brownlie, *op. cit.* in note 19, above, pp. 422–423.

[29] Art. 36, Statute of the International Court of Justice.

quite clearly states that the opinions of the Court are not law-creating in any general sense, but only affect the specific case submitted to the Court.[30] While it may be true that the opinions of the Court are of great persuasive value they are not sources of law and thus, along with the writings of academic commentators, are relegated to the position of "subsidiary means for the determination of rules of law" in Article 38 of the Statute.[31] Thus, in order to reach the conclusion that the Court has "legitimated" any historical activity of the General Assembly, one must ignore completely three valid treaty provisions of the Statue of the International Court of Justice. If the aim is to establish a system of supranational law by such dexterity, one might consider that in doing so the prevailing legal norms of the present system are being ignored. It is curious to disregard law, however "restrictive" it may be, in order to attempt to create a higher order which, it is safe to assume, is worthy of our attention because it is based on the rule of law. *Ex injuria jus non oritur.*

Another question that merits attention is the relationship between custom and the Court as sources of law. Akehurst, for example, relies very heavily on the Court's opinions in putting forward his broader theory of custom, citing in the process passages from about a dozen cases. But he does not discuss the legal significance of these cases as they relate to the creation of law. In view of Article 38 of the Court's Statute, there is reason to doubt that the Court's opinions can ever have any effect on the definition of what constitutes custom. It would appear that, as a primary source of law, custom is of a much higher priority than the "subsidiary means" of judicial decisions. Clearly, since custom is a source of law and the Court is not, the Court does not have the power, as it is presently constituted, to alter the definition of custom in any significant way. Akehurst, Higgins *et al.* must demonstrate on what basis the Court is empowered authoritatively to alter a primary source of law to the extent they advocate. Perhaps there is a convincing argument. If so, it needs clearly to be made.

A final point merits attention on the question of the academic treatment of the Court's role as lawmaker. If the Court cannot, under Article 59, create generally binding norms in contentious cases, precisely what is the legal significance of an advisory opinion? Brownlie's statement, quoted above, clearly envisions an advisory

[30] *Ibid.* Art. 59 which states, "The decision of the Court has no binding force except between the parties and in respect of that particular case."

[31] *Ibid.* Art. 38 which states, "The Court ... shall apply ... subject to the provisions of Article 59, judicial decisions and the teachings of the most highly qualified publicists of the various nations, as subsidiary means for the determination of rules of law."

opinion "legitimating" *ultra vires* United Nations activity. Yet an advisory opinion is not even binding on the organisation that requested it. This extremely liberal use of juridical positivism is increasingly common in articles purporting to generate rules in the developing areas of international law. The 1971 opinion on South-West Africa is a particular favourite since there are many passages in it which indicate, as one writer put it, "an extended role for the Court and for international law and organisation."[32] The quoted writer is thus not only assuming that the Court has law-making power and the power to modify the basic principles of international law, but also that it may do so on the basis of an advisory opinion. Unfortunately, no indication is given of the extent to which this position is accepted in the practice of States. Schwelb, long an advocate of the protection of human rights in international law, and a writer to whom the discipline owes a great deal, also fell prey to the temptation. He cited the 1971 Opinion[33] and concluded therefrom that there was an obligation on South Africa flowing from it. He was reinforced somewhat in his conclusion by being able to point to the fact that the decision was in agreement with the writings of Hersch Lauterpacht, but with respect to all concerned, the fact that two "subsidiary means" agree, especially when one of those means is only an advisory opinion, is not a particularly strong indication of valid law. Schwelb's perception of the court in common law terms is further evidenced by his use of the distinction between *ratio decidendi* and *obiter dictum* in his analysis,[34] a technique also used by Akehurst.[35]

(b) *Judicial Activism*

For some time, the view that the International Court of Justice could adopt a law-creating role was confined largely to academic circles. While there were writers whose theories assumed, explicitly or implicitly, the superiority of international law in terms of power, this philosophy did not appear significantly in the Court's opinions. There was always a minority on the Court that felt that it should take a more dynamic role, but it was only recently that this position came to the fore. Attention became focused on Judge Tanaka's Dissenting Opinion in the 1966 decision on South-West Africa[36] which,

---

[32] N. K. Hevener, "The 1971 South-West African Opinion, A New International Juridical Philosophy," 24 *International and Comparative Law Quarterly* (1975), p. 807.

[33] E. Schwelb, "The International Court of Justice and The Human Rights Clauses of the Charter," 66 *American Journal of International Law* (1972), p. 346.

[34] *Ibid.* at p. 350.

[35] *Op. cit.* in note 26, above, at p. 33.

[36] *South-West Africa, Second Phase*, I.C.J. Reports 1966, p. 248.

despite its being a dissent,[37] was cited and discussed frequently as support for the evolution of a dynamic theory. His statements concerning the development of international law by consensus rather than by consent were obviously welcome to the "new" international lawyers. For example, without explaining the source of authority or competence of the political organs, he stated, "the accumulation of *authoritative* pronouncements such as resolutions, declarations, decisions, etc., concerning the interpretation of the Charter by the *competent* organs of the international community can be characterised as evidence of the international custom referred to in Article 38 (1) (*b*)."[38] What Judge Tanaka did, as Lauterpacht had suggested, was to place international law on a par with natural law and attempt to create, particularly in the context of human rights, an area of *jus cogens*. The attempt fails to take account of the fact that State practice has not yet achieved the standards of behaviour that are advanced, nor does it suggest any means of implementation. Central to this dynamic view of international law is a disregard for State sovereignty, evidenced by unsuccessful attempts to show that Article 2 (7) of the Charter is now invalid, either on a legal or on a practical basis.[39] That this disregard should produce little in the way of concrete results should serve as a warning to the Court that it is reaching the limits of its usefulness to international law, and the limits of tolerance of nation-States.

By 1971, the dynamic philosophy of the Court's function had spread, and it was on this basis that the Court could conclude that South Africa was under an obligation to terminate its administration and occupation of the territory of Namibia. The efficacy problem of the new philosophy is indicated by the fact that, seven years after the decision, South Africa still occupies and administers the territory. The issue is thus much more crucial to the future of a viable international law than whether some academic theories are more valid than others. The issue now involves the Court's own credibility. Since the Court has to rely on an amalgam of non-coercive techniques for its effectiveness, its credibility is perhaps its greatest asset. Further, even if one were willing to discard the role of third-party adjudication as being irrelevant to a horizontal legal order, the fact

[37] In line with the cavalier treatment of legal materials it is not unusual to see a dissenting opinion analysed in much the same way as the Court's majority opinion. In view of Art. 59 of the Court's statute, this practice is, however, probably defensible. For other examples see, *op. cit.* in note 17, above, at p. 448; and in note 18, above, at pp. 39 and 47.

[38] *Op. cit.* in note 36, above, at p. 292 (italics added).

[39] For an assessment of the various arguments that have been presented in an attempt to undermine the authority of Art. 2 (7) see J. S. Watson, "Autointerpretation, Competence and the Continuing Validity of Article 2 (7) of the United Nations Charter," 71 *American Journal of International Law* (1977), p. 60.

remains that there is a symbiotic relationship between the Court's credibility and that of the entire legal order.

Those who are concerned with the viability of the international legal order, as well as those who are concerned with the role of the Court, should assess whether the modest gains that accrue from the attempt at a dynamic role is really worth the risk. A cavalier treatment of the realities of the international legal system by the Court can very quickly call into question the efficacy and the validity of the entire system. If this is done without any concrete results being achieved to compensate for it, then one has paid very dearly indeed for the luxury of adding the phrase "international law" to what might otherwise be a perfectly defensible position.

The gap of seven years since the Court's decision indicates that even if South Africa were to withdraw from Namibia in the near future, it will be more the result of political pressure from African and Western countries than the result of a supranational legal order. Even those who insist on a very loose definition of law must see the need for a reasonably close causal connection between the announcement of a norm and its subsequent implementation. The *ad hoc* and relatively unpredictable processes of international politics must be kept separate from international law if the latter is to have any meaning of its own.

What the Court must bear in mind is that, relying as it does on consent, the adoption of a dynamic, teleological reasoning process is likely to be counterproductive. Rather than causing States to behave in conformity with its "common law" directives, the effect will be to discourage States from ever appearing before the court. If States cannot be sure of the rules which will be applied by the Court, and cannot predict the approach that will be taken, there is little likelihood that even the historically sparse use of the Court will continue. This would seem to be supported by the slimness of the last three volumes of the reports, following two further instances of dynamic legal reasoning. In both the Fisheries Jurisdiction Case[40] and the Nuclear Tests Case[41] interim measures of protection were ignored by Iceland and France respectively. One author, in a detailed and sympathetic analysis of these two cases noted the liberalisation of the circumstances in which such relief may be granted, and stated: "The expansionist tendency inevitably conflicts with the fundamental rule that the jurisdiction of an international tribunal depends upon consent ... the Court cannot afford to reach decisions ...

[40] *Fisheries Jurisdiction (United Kingdom* v. *Iceland), Interim Protection,* I.C.J. Reports 1972, p. 12.

[41] *Nuclear Tests (Australia* v. *France), Interim Protection.* I.C.L. Reports 1073, p. 99.

which suggest support for rules which are too far advanced for community acceptance."[42]

IV—The Legality of a Coercive System

In the previous discussion of the process whereby custom, the effective basis of international law, creates a limited prescriptive effect due to the shared self-interest of States in the maintenance of predictable behaviour patterns, the emphasis was placed on the internal aspect of reciprocity and no mention was made of the external (coercive) methods of inducing compliance. The external methods comprise the varying degrees of force that can be used by other interested States either to force the deviant State into immediate compliance, or else to intimidate that and other States to such an extent that they will be deterred from future noncompliance. This technique, self-help, is often seen as forming an integral part of the international legal system[43] and it obviously has great attraction for those who insist on a coercive element in the definition of law.

There are however, two problems with this attempt at indirect enforceability in international law. The first is that the use of even a modicum of force is an unlikely and an inappropriate response to a violation of the typical international norm. It is highly unlikely, for example, that it would follow the violation of treaty provisions on topics such as import quotas, the exchange of technical information or maritime safety. In these and the vast majority of cases the motivation for compliance is still the internal one of keeping one's word for the general benefit, *pacta sunt servanda*. The typical response to a violation of an international norm falls well short of coercion in even the loosest sense of the word, and usually takes the form of protest, or the withdrawal of benefits of approximately the same level in a related or unrelated area. This process of trading one minor violation for another is well within the reciprocal, self-adjusting model of international law. In all but the most highly-charged issues coercion is an unlikely and an inefficient response to norm violation, and thus may be discounted as a viable enforcement mechanism.

The second reason for rejecting the use of force in this connection is that it is illegal.[44] Articles 2 (3) and 2 (4) of the Charter prohibit

[42] P. J. Goldsworthy, "Interim Measures of Protection in the International Court of Justice," 68 *American Journal of International Law* (1974), pp. 262–263.

[43] See, *e.g.*, H. Kelsen, *Principles of International Law* (1952), p. 14.

[44] This point is more fully developed by Fitzmaurice in "The Foundations of the Authority of International Law and the Problem of Enforcement," 19 *Modern Law Review* (1956), p. 1.

self-help in very specific terms. The philosophy behind this was to put a monopoly of the legitimate use of force into the hands of the Security Council. In attempting to reach that goal, by oversight or by intention, these articles, and Article 2 (4) in particular, imposed a general ban on the use of force. Even more important for our purposes is that Article 2 (4) also bans the threat of force, for it is the deterrent effect of the threat of force that is at the core of any coercive system.

The instances in which the use of force is permitted the organisation are of little help to those who see this ban as an unwelcome predicament. The Security Council is permitted to use force in obtaining compliance with an individual judgment of the International Court of Justice,[45] but not its "common law." It may also use forceful means to cope with breaches of the peace under Chapter VII[46] but the latter is obviously not addressed to matters of routine enforcement of legal rules. Even if it were, it is not likely that disinterested or unaffected States would be sufficiently motivated to involve themselves in the enforcement of rules affecting only a few States. The history of the collective security system is sufficient proof of that. Finally, Article 51, which permits the use of force to individual States in self-defence, is no less helpful to the advocates of self-help since it only permits the use of force "if an armed attack occurs."

International law has thus outlawed coercion by other States as a means of compliance with its norms. While this might dismay those with a coercive concept of law, it is entirely consistent with the perception of international law as a decentralised, reciprocal system based ultimately on State consent.

V—Conclusions

Most legal theories presuppose the existence of developed legal institutions and their test of legal validity is invariably tied to some such source, be it the sovereign, the legislature or the courts. In international law there are no such institutions and thus the validity of its rules must be founded on some other basis. This other basis, this other "institution," is the practice of sovereign States. This is acknowledged in the traditional concept of custom which has long formed the ultimate basis for legal validity.

International law cannot, by its own terms and as a matter of political reality, prescribe rules of conduct except in a very limited

[45] Art. 94 (2) of the UN Charter.

[46] *Ibid*. Art. 39.

sense. Its prescriptive effect is entirely dependent on the accuracy of the codification of State practice. Any attempt at altering or studiously ignoring this basic fact by superimposing a simplistic model of coercive law derived from domestic law is destined to result in inefficacious rules and sterile theory. To do so is to ignore the unique nature of international law, and to emphasise its weaknesses rather than its strengths.

[2]

Northwestern University Law Review
Printed in U.S.A.
Vol. 79, Nos. 5 & 6

IS INTERNATIONAL LAW REALLY "LAW"?*

*Anthony D'Amato***

Many serious students of the law react with a sort of indulgence when they encounter the term "international law," as if to say, "well, we know it isn't *really* law, but we know that international lawyers and scholars have a vested professional interest in calling it 'law.'" Or they may agree to talk about international law *as if* it were law, a sort of quasi-law or near-law. But it cannot be true law, they maintain, because it cannot be enforced: how do you enforce a rule of law against an entire nation, especially a superpower such as the United States or the Soviet Union?

I. The "Enforcement" Argument

One intriguing answer to these serious students of the law is to attempt to persuade them that enforcement is not, after all, the hallmark of what is meant, or what should be meant, by the term "law." As Roger Fisher observed, much of what we call "law" in the domestic context is also unenforceable.[1] For example, where the defendant is the United States, such as in a case involving constitutional law, how would the winning private party enforce his or her judgment against the United States? Upon reflection, we see that the United States, whenever it loses a case (and these cases are very frequent—the myriad cases involving income taxes, social security benefits, welfare, and the like), only complies with the court's judgment because it wants to. The winning private party cannot hold a gun to the head of the United States to enforce compliance, even if there were a natural meaning to the term "head of the United States." We can go even further than Professor Fisher did: every criminal law prosecution is a case of an individual pitted against the state (or the "people" of the state). What is to stop the state from saying, "you were acquitted by the jury, but that was a travesty of justice, so we're

** Professor of Law, Northwestern University. A.B., Cornell University (1958); J.D., Harvard University (1961); Ph.D., Columbia University (1968).

[1] *See* Fisher, *Bringing Law to Bear on Governments*, 74 HARV. L. REV. 1130 (1961), excerpted in B. WESTON, R. FALK & A. D'AMATO, INTERNATIONAL LAW AND WORLD ORDER 125-30 (1980). Professor Fisher has greatly elaborated on ways of improving governmental compliance with international law, and in the process, by implication, indicated how various enforcement mechanisms work against governments. *See* R. FISHER, IMPROVING COMPLIANCE WITH INTERNATIONAL LAW 39-72, 236-300 (1981).

going to imprison you anyway"? How does the defendant, in handcuffs, stop the state from going ahead? In some countries, at some times, we have heard of dictators or military regimes proceeding with the imprisonment and execution of defendants who were acquitted by their own courts. In terms of power, there is nothing to stop the United States from disregarding adverse judgments of its own courts. In this sense, therefore, a great deal of what we normally call "law" in the United States is unenforceable by private parties arrayed against the state.

It is no objection to this line of reasoning, by the way, to dismiss it as far-fetched. If one objects that the United States, in any event, routinely complies with adverse judgments of its own courts, then the international lawyer can answer that the same is true of rules of international law. As Louis Henkin put it, "almost all nations observe almost all principles of international law and almost all of their obligations almost all of the time."[2]

But a more substantial critique of Professor Fisher's analogy between cases involving the government as a party and international-law cases is that *most* domestic litigation, after all, does *not* involve the government as a party. Most cases involve one citizen against another ("citizen" including artificial persons such as corporations), and as to *those* cases the law is enforced by the full sovereign powers of the state against the losing litigant. This majority of cases, then, tends to define what we mean by "law"; it constitutes the paradigmatic instance of law. Therefore, the argument goes, the minority of cases that do involve the state or the United States as a party are, in a sense, parasitic upon the paradigmatic instance. We tend to regard this latter minority of cases as "law" only because they share certain attributes with the generality of cases. But if we look hard at this minority of cases where the government is a party, we must concede that they are not really "law" because, at bottom, they are unenforceable. They only appear to be law when looked at uncritically. In short, this line of argument *concedes* Professor Fisher's major premiss—that international-law cases are similar to domestic cases where the government is a party—but denies his minor premiss, that such cases are instances of "law." Hence, international law is no more "law" than is constitutional law or even criminal law. As John Austin stated, both constitutional and international law are merely "positive morality."[3]

[2] L. HENKIN, HOW NATIONS BEHAVE 47 (2d ed. 1979). This statement in a sense follows tautologically from the fact that there is an international system of legal rules. Clearly, the rules that have evolved over time are the ones that nations have found to be in their collective self-interest; this is simply a Darwinian process applied to customary international law. Professor Henkin's statement, however, while tautological, is not vacuous; after all, nations might have instead evolved into a non-rule anarchical system.

[3] J. AUSTIN, THE PROVINCE OF JURISPRUDENCE DETERMINED 127 (Hart ed. 1954). Austin, however, did not know much about classic international law; he was somewhat taken in by writers who included only treaties as international law. The term "international law" itself was after all

One might object and say that it is frivolous to exclude the vast body of constitutional law and criminal law cases from what we mean by "law." If you say that, then you see the force of Professor Fisher's argument. You are well on your way to accepting the "reality" of international law. But I have presented the skeptical argument against Professor Fisher's view because I want to be rigorous and not have to rely on an argument by analogy, which is ultimately the kind of argument that Professor Fisher has used.

Let us then consider a second line of reasoning against the proposition that enforcement is the hallmark of law. This argument is not associated with any particular writer, because it relies on early conceptions of law and also on the philosophy of law itself. If we consider what law is *not*, we soon realize that it is *not* a rationale for the application of force. It is not a system of "might makes right" in the sense that the state constantly has to compel people, at gunpoint, to behave in a certain way. If you look through a volume of cases, or even a volume of statutes or annotations, you will find that most of the matters therein concern the working-out of private arrangements in a complex society. Most of "law"concerns itself with the interpretation and enforcement of private contracts, the redress of intentional and negligent harms, rules regarding sales of goods and sales of securities, rules relating to the family and the rights of members thereof, and other such rules, norms, and cases. The rules are obeyed not out of fear of the state's power, but because the rules by and large are perceived to be right, just, or appropriate. No state could possibly compel people to obey all these rules at gunpoint; there would not be enough soldiers and policemen to hold the guns (a sort of extreme Orwellian vision of society), they would have to sleep sooner or later, and then anarchy might break out.

Even more fatal to this view of extreme enforcement is that the state would need many rules to channel the behavior of the enforcers themselves. For instance, how would all these police officials and soldiers know what rules they must enforce, and who would make sure that they enforced the rules as written? We would need another phalanx of soldiers to police the enforcers.[4] And on top of that, another layer of officials pointing the guns at the heads of the gun-pointers. The whole process would break down of its own weight. Indeed, Orwell in his novel, *1984*, avoided the question of how to coordinate and control the activities of the officials of the state he described. He simply referred to the state in the abstract as exercising monolithic power over the citi-

---

invented by Austin's contemporary, Jeremy Bentham, and Bentham was philosophically inimical to unwritten law. *See* J. BENTHAM, AN INTRODUCTION TO THE PRINCIPLES OF MORALS AND LEGISLATION 326 n.1 (2d ed. Oxford 1948) (1st ed. Oxford 1789).

[4] The argument is elaborated and extended in A. D'AMATO, JURISPRUDENCE: A DESCRIPTIVE AND NORMATIVE ANALYSIS OF LAW 7-8, 151-53 (1984) [hereinafter cited as A. D'AMATO, JURISPRUDENCE], and in D'Amato, *Legal Uncertainty*, 71 CALIF. L. REV. 1, 39 n.78 (1983).

zenry, finessing the real problem of how to organize such a state so as to control the controllers.

If law is not, by and large, a body of rules that are enforced at gunpoint, what is an individual rule of law? Is it, as the nineteenth century positivists maintained, a command of the state that is backed by the state's enforcement power?[5] To be sure, some "laws" might be just that: a dictator issues a command for his personal indulgence or whim, and if he has sufficiently satisfied his close advisers and the military in other areas, they will probably enforce his command. But most laws will not have this characteristic. Indeed, looking at the matter more microscopically, what is it that *forces* a judge to decide the case before her on the basis of precedent and statutes? Is another judge holding a gun to her head? Does she examine whether the law will be enforced to see whether it is law? How does she know, in advance of her own decision, what will be enforced?

This point came up in the famous case of *Marbury v. Madison*,[6] familiar to generations of American law students but often misinterpreted. In that case, Chief Justice Marshall's "bottom line" was that the Supreme Court had no original jurisdiction to issue writs of mandamus. In short, there was no power to enforce that which the plaintiff demanded. If "law" were coincident with enforceability, then, since under Marshall's reasoning there was not power of enforcement in the Supreme Court because it lacked *jurisdiction*, nothing Marshall said in his opinion would have had any legal significance. To put it another way, lacking a "remedy," the plaintiff would have no "right," not even a right to get a decision from the Court on the question of "right."

But Marshall took an entirely different tack. He *began* with the question: does the plaintiff have a right? He then asked the second question: if the plaintiff has a right, does he have a remedy? And his third question was, if the plaintiff has a remedy, can the relief issue from this Court? By putting the questions in this order, Marshall did the opposite of what the positivists would require. By dealing first with the question of "right," Marshall was able to address that question wholly apart from whether there was a remedy or whether the remedy was available from the Supreme Court. As all law students know, Marshall answered his own question that there was indeed a right, and secondly, there being a right meant that the plaintiff had a remedy. By going through this reasoning, Marshall was able to establish the groundwork for his path-breaking assertion of judicial review of questions of constitutionality. He held that, in the face of a right and remedy, the congressional statute purporting to grant that remedy to the Supreme Court as a matter of original jurisdiction violated the Constitution. Marshall would

[5] *See* A. D'AMATO, JURISPRUDENCE, *supra* note 4, at 118-22 (tracing the command theory of law from Hobbes through Bentham and Austin).

[6] 5 U.S. (1 Cranch) 137 (1803).

not have been able to make his assertion of judicial review if he had begun and ended his opinion with the simple sentence, "we have no jurisdiction; case dismissed." Hence, we see that in a case where by the Court's own admission it lacked jurisdiction and the power of enforcement, nevertheless the Court was able to establish a point of fundamental substantive significance.

Marshall's persuasiveness was dependent upon a consensus at the time he wrote his opinion that there could be such a thing as a "right" without a real remedy. This was part of a larger conviction in those days that the "law" itself was not something that only works when a policeman is standing by ready to enforce it physically. Law indeed is something that is opposed to force. Right is not the same thing as might. In Continental countries, the word for "law" is, as translated, the word "right." In law, there is a fundamental element of right, of justice, dating back to Cicero's and St. Thomas' equation of "right reason" with the natural law (the latter being those reasonable rules that accommodate the peaceful affairs of persons in a society).[7]

Under this argument that we are developing, the relation of force to law, of might to right, is a contingent and not a necessary relation. We can imagine a society under law where there is no force. People obey the laws, and no one disobeys. There is no need, in this idyllic utopia, for enforcement, because there is universal willing compliance. Surely we cannot claim that such a society does not have "law." It is clear that the society is one that is under law, and that the contingent use of force is simply not necessary. To take an example closer to home, suppose that in some state of the Union there has not been a kidnaping since that state entered the Union. Would we say that the law against kidnaping in that state is not a law? Certainly no one would argue that if a law is so successful that it never needs enforcement, it is not a law. Thus, we can conclude from this hypothetical that enforcement is not intrinsic to, is not necessary to, the idea of law.

But you might object that enforcement must potentially be present, even if it is not invoked. In other words, in the state that has no kidnaping, it is nevertheless true that if someone commits this crime—or even contemplates committing it—the potential for enforcement is ever-present. It is this potential for enforcement, after all, that the positivists insist upon when they draw our attention to the necessary connection between a rule of law and its enforcement.

To take care of this objection, we may simply modify our previous

---

[7] "Natural law" is not something handed down from on high, nor is it the a priori speculations of "right reason." Rather, it may best be described in modern terms as those systemic rules that have survived through evolution over time as best fitting the mutual needs of a society. An example of this approach, though not in those terms, is found in J. FINNIS, NATURAL LAW AND NATURAL RIGHTS (1980). For a categorical historical perspective, see D'Amato, *Lon Fuller and Substantive Natural Law*, 26 AM. J. JURIS. 202 (1981).

hypothetical of the idyllic utopia. Assume not only that they have never had a need to enforce their laws, but also that they have no enforcement machinery—no police, no jails, no sheriffs, no marshals. They can still have a system of laws, as complex as you please, even without the potential for enforcement.

Yet you might now object that we cannot prove something about the nature of law, an all-too-human institution, by postulating the existence of a utopia where the inhabitants never break the law. Can we modify our utopia to make it seem more realistic? Suppose occasionally someone breaks the law, but is ostracized from society. Suppose one who breaches a contract is considered a moral renegade who should not be entrusted with any further business dealings. These expressions of sharp social disapproval, and occasionally of ostracism, may work to discourage the few people who would disobey the law. They may not always work, but they may be potent enough to deter most of the people (a minority to begin with) who might consider breaking the law. Thus, our not-perfect utopia now consists of a regime where almost all of the laws are obeyed almost all of the time, where occasional disobedience is met with sharp social disapproval, and where occasionally, despite the "mechanism" of social disapproval, occasional violations of the law occur.[8] Is this not, nevertheless, a legal system?

A positivist might happen to object to this concept as follows: the idea of social disapproval, and sometimes social ostracism, is the same thing as a sanction. It constitutes a way of enforcing the law. Hence, by introducing this social-disapproval factor into the utopia, we have simply underscored the original point—that law (except in idyllic utopias which do not exist) depends upon potential enforcement.

But if that is the positivist's position, then the international lawyer should gladly concede the point. For international law recognizes that the social-disapproval factor operates as a sanction. A nation among the community of nations which violates the law, for example, by disregarding a treaty obligation, would certainly be subject to social disapproval by the other nations. In this sense, international law is really "law."

Now it is perhaps the positivist's turn to beat a hasty retreat. The positivist may now want to retract the equation of social disapproval with "sanction," for fear of including international law under the term "law." Instead, the positivist will retreat to the original position that physical or even violent enforcement is necessary to make law "law," and hence international law is not "law." We may, however, suspect that the positivist is reshaping definitions in order to *exclude* the international-law case, rather than to arrive at a general definition of law.[9] Consistent

---

[8] *See* M. BARKUN, LAW WITHOUT SANCTION (1968); *cf.* Reisman, *Sanctions and Enforcement*, in INTERNATIONAL LAW ESSAYS 381, 383-89 (1981) (group and community norms provide a "civic" sanction, distinguishable from a state-imposed public sanction).

[9] This is analogous to H.L.A. Hart's exclusion of international law from "mature" legal sys-

with this position, the positivist will have to argue that any legal system in which social disapproval functions as the sole sanction (for example, in a peaceful tribal society) does not have "law." "Law" is present only when, in addition to social disapproval, there is physical coercion stemming from the sovereign power of the state. But what if there is no *need* for this physical coercion? The positivist must then conclude that there is no law.

Such a position would be difficult to defend, for if there is a society where people are so law-abiding that they get along only with the social-disapproval sanction, that society manifests a rather good case of "law." It is strange to insist that, for there to be law, physical coercion must also be used even if there is no need for it.

Yet the serious student of law may not be satisfied with the preceding argument in its entirety. We want to ask what happens if the need for physical coercion should arise. In the international system, at least, we have states which occasionally break the rules of international law and which seem not to be deterred by expressions of social disapproval from the other states. This is a reality of international life. Therefore, unlike the tribal society where social disapproval may constitute an effective sanction, international society needs a physical sanction to underscore its legal rules. Otherwise, the rules will occasionally be flouted. Perhaps they will be ignored most often when the "chips are down," which is exactly when they most need to be enforced. How can we call such a system, dependent for its support on so feeble a mechanism as social approval, a "legal" system?

It is hard to discern the logic behind the preceding objection, even while it is easy to understand it. We all recognize, and regret, that rules of international law are flouted on occasion, and we are all too aware of the fact that an outraged world public opinion simply is incapable of discouraging the violation. Should our conclusion then be that the rules of international law are not "law" as we know the term, because as we know the term the "law" involves the concept of physical enforcement? Yet, even in asking this, we acknowledge that physical enforcement is not a *necessary* characteristic of law (our "utopian" examples). And we also acknowledge that, even in domestic cases, where the state is one of the parties, we cannot meaningfully speak of physical enforcement (Professor Fisher's argument). These two arguments destroy most of the logical force of our position that international law is not really law, and yet, we may cling to that position.

Some early writers on the law of nations attempted to meet the enforcement objection head-on, by asserting that rules of international law

tems, because it lacks a "rule of recognition" (Hart's equivalent of the positivist's command-backed-by-sanction). *See* H.L.A. HART, THE CONCEPT OF LAW 208-31 (1961); D'Amato, *The Neo-Positivist Concept of International Law*, 59 AM. J. INT'L L. 321 (1965) (natural-law critique of Hart).

are indeed enforced by the mechanism of war. A nation that violates the rules will be the object of a "just war" initiated precisely to punish the transgressing nation and to enforce the validity of the rules.[10] This argument today sounds like an archaic ploy, for we know enough about wars to have learned that the "transgressing" state may occasionally win if it has the physical power to do so. Physical might bears no necessary connection to international right. Interestingly, the concept of a "just war" has become, if possible, even more archaic under the collective security mechanisms of the League of Nations and its successor the United Nations. These bodies, in principle at least, are designed to stamp out acts of aggression wherever they occur. In other words, they are not set up for the purpose of enforcing international law, but simply for the purpose of enforcing international peace. It follows that if the peace is unjust, it will be enforced anyway. The United Nations seems to call for a "cease fire" in disregard of the merits of the local conflict, and it appears to be less concerned with enforcing international law than with enforcing a prohibition against the use of force no matter what the justification.

Yet there is something in the notion of a "just war" that may help us to fashion a more compelling case for the proposition that international law is really "law" than the other arguments we have examined. I will try to show in Part Three that what I will label as reciprocal-entitlement violation is a mechanism akin to the old "just war" notion that underlies a realistic enforcement mechanism for international law.

At present, we may conclude tentatively as follows:

(1) The fact that some states disobey periodically some rules of international law does not itself mean that those rules are not rules of "law," because even in domestic society some people (e.g., criminals) break the law from time to time.

(2) On the other hand, the fact that most states obey most rules of international law most of the time is not enough to call those rules "legal" because we are especially concerned with "important" cases where states may get away with violating rules of international law. If states can violate rules with impunity when it is in their national interest to do so, how can we call those rules "law"?

(3) We recognize, even though it makes us somewhat uncomfortable, that international law is more properly analogized to domestic cases where the state is a party than to domestic cases where one citizen sues another. Under this conception, we concede that our usual notions of "enforcement" are not appropriately applied to the state. But because we recognize as "law" those domestic cases involving the state as a party, we should also recognize as "law" those international controversies involving states as parties.

---

10 *See* 2 L. Oppenheim, International Law 177-79 (H. Lauterpacht 7th ed. 1952); M. Walzer, Just and Unjust Wars (1977).

(4) We further concede that physical coercion is not a necessary component of "law." However, we are reluctant to conclude that it is totally unnecessary, because we have seen too many cases where a nation violates international law and gets away with it because of the lack of an effective enforcement mechanism.

(5) Hence, we are somewhat, though not totally, persuaded that international law can properly be labelled "law" for most purposes. But we may remain unconvinced, at this point, that it is *really* "law."

II. THE "VERBAL" ARGUMENT

Let us for the moment look at the question whether international law is really law from an entirely different angle. Suppose we were to read all the communications that governments officially make to one another: letters, speeches, proclamations, treaties, agreements, diplomatic initiatives, and so on. Suppose we read these with an eye toward whether the language contained in these communications refers to "law" and is "legal" language. In brief, we would be engaging in a "content analysis" of these communications to see whether what is being asserted and claimed therein can properly be called "legal."[11] We will find that, indeed, much of the content of intergovernmental communications is self-consciously grounded in legal terminology. There should be nothing surprising about this, considering the fact that lawyers typically help draft these documents and speeches. We will find, indeed, that the more important the communication the more likely it is cast in legal terms, and the more likely it is that lawyers have played a role in drafting it.

We might then want to argue that, given the reality of this legal language, it would be rather absurd to maintain that "law" is *not* involved in these intergovernmental communications. If the relevant actors call it "law," who are we to say that they are all wrong? Rather, is it not our job, as observers or scholars, to employ the terms the way the relevant actors intend those terms to be employed? Thus, the very utilization of legal language in intergovernmental communications is an argument for the proposition at least that governments resort to "law" in their attempts to influence each other; or refer to "law" in an attempt to appear to be legal and thus ward off disapproval of other states.

We might want to add to this argument the position taken by the "policy-oriented jurisprudence" of Myres McDougal and his colleagues, including Harold Lasswell, Michael Reisman, Lung-chu Chen, and others.[12] We might collect on a library shelf their voluminous works and

---

[11] *See* P. STONE, D. DUNPHY, M. SMITH & D. OGILVIE, THE GENERAL INQUIRER (1966); *cf.* D'Amato, *Psychological Constructs in Foreign Policy Prediction*, 11 J. CONFLICT RES. 294 (1967) (content analysis of writings of foreign policy actors to derive predictive "general constructs" of such behavior).

[12] For a good summary statement, with bibliographic references, see McDougal & Reisman,

ask, "what have they written about?" If our answer is not "law," what is it? To be sure, when we take their books down from the shelf and look into them, we begin to get an extraordinarily broad definition of "law." The concept is so broad, indeed, that we wonder if there is anything which they can properly call "non-law." They cite works from the social sciences, from the humanities, as well as works on international law and international politics. Their idea of international law is that it is a process of authoritative decision-making, but then they seem to view "authoritative" so broadly as to encompass just about any decision made by any international decisionmaker.[13] Finally, they disassociate law from enforcement. Legal rules, according to Professor McDougal, "exhaust their effective power when they guide a decision-maker to relevant factors and indicate presumptive weightings."[14]

According to the policy-oriented jurisprudence school, therefore, international law is nothing other than international communication. Under the first argument I made in this Part, the prevalence of legal language in international communication indicates that nations are talking about, and believe they are talking about, "law" in the positions they take vis-a-vis each other. Under the second McDougal-type argument, international communication itself is "law" irrespective of its being couched in legal terms. Taken together, both of these positions may convince the reader that international law is really law.

In the past, I was intrigued by the law-as-communication approach.[15] Recently, I have become uneasy with it, in part because it proves too much. *Any* international contention couched in legal language (or even, following McDougal, not couched in legal language) becomes "law." Yet surely the "law" is not everything. It does not include contradictory positions, although McDougal comes perilously close to this in his notion of the complementarity of customary prescriptions.[16] If international "law" says that nations may or may not attack one another, that the high seas are free to all and closed to all, that genocide is both permissible and prohibited, then I would conclude that there is no international "law" worth talking about on these points. (Someone who disagreed with me would probably say that the "verbal" argument I have

---

International Law in Policy-Oriented Perspective, in THE STRUCTURE AND PROCESS OF INTERNATIONAL LAW: ESSAYS IN LEGAL PHILOSOPHY DOCTRINE AND THEORY 103 (1983).

13 *See, e.g.*, M. MCDOUGAL, H. LASSWELL & L. CHEN, HUMAN RIGHTS AND WORLD PUBLIC ORDER 161-363 (1980).

14 M. MCDOUGAL, STUDIES IN WORLD PUBLIC ORDER 887 n.109 (1960).

15 *See, e.g.*, D'Amato, *The Relation of Theories of Jurisprudence to International Politics and Law*, 27 WASH. & LEE L. REV. 257 (1970); *cf.* D'Amato, *What "Counts" as Law?*, in LAW-MAKING IN THE GLOBAL COMMUNITY 83 (N. Onuf ed. 1982) (attempting to put the law-as-words approach in perspective).

16 For a critique, with references to Professor McDougal's writings, see A. D'AMATO, THE CONCEPT OF CUSTOM IN INTERNATIONAL LAW 220-26 (1971).

outlined in this Part compels the conclusion that there *is* international law, but that its content is incoherent.)

The other misgiving I have about the verbal argument is that scholars are, after all, not precluded from criticizing the propriety of the use of language by other persons. Even though international communications are couched in legal terms, an observer does not have to conclude that the use of those legal terms is proper. In the insurance business, contracts between insurance companies are called "treaties," even though this is not the use of the term that international lawyers recognize. An international lawyer is not precluded from criticizing the terminology of "treaties" if that criticism throws some light on what insurance companies are really doing. For example, does the use of the term "treaty" imply that rules of international law relating to treaty interpretation should be followed in disputes among insurance companies, instead of domestic contract rules? The answer is no, and thus the term "treaty" can be criticized as misleading. Similarly, we might properly criticize the resort to legal terminology in international communications if we can show that it is not really "law" that is being invoked.

We may therefore conclude this Part by saying, simply, that the prevalance of legal language in international communications *adds* to our previous conclusions that international law is properly called "law" for most purposes and in most contexts. We still, however, reserve final judgment on the question whether it is really "law."

III. The "Reciprocal Entitlements" Argument

I believe that a conclusive argument can be fashioned that international law is really law, by showing that international law is enforceable in the same way that domestic law is enforceable. Of course, I cannot make the claim that international law is always enforced. Rather, what I shall proceed to do is to take a closer look at what we mean by enforcement, and then show that it is applicable equally to the domestic and to the international legal systems.

When we examine the concept of enforcement of law, we find that law can be enforced in many ways. For example, a parent might frown upon a child who does not brush his teeth, or might express stern disapproval. This tends to "enforce" the law, although as we saw in Part I it is not a satisfactory concept when we think of enforcement.[17] For it is too easy for the child, or the nation, to decide to violate the law and pay the mild price of incurring social displeasure.

Thus, we want to narrow the concept of enforcement. Perhaps a good way to begin to narrow it is to exclude all modes of "enforcement" that are extrinsic to the legal system itself. Social disapproval, for instance, is extrinsic to the legal system as is social approval. These are

[17] *See supra* text accompanying notes 3-5.

external mechanisms for enforcing, or more accurately reinforcing, the law, but we know intuitively that they are not provided by or required by the law itself. (If the law *required* them, then you would have the regressive problem of how to force people to socially disapprove of a miscreant's behavior.)

When we look at the legal system itself, we find that it typically provides for deprivations, for disabilities. When a person disobeys the law, the law "punishes" him in some way. The possibility of punishment, in turn, is supposed to deter a rational person from violating the law in the first place.

Enforcement thus consists of some form of legally imposed sanction. A monetary fine is an example of a punishment that is not physical. Physical punishments include being deprived of your freedom, for example by being incarcerated or being forced to perform some kind of community service as part of your "sentence." In the extreme, you may be deprived of your life if convicted of a capital crime.

In this entire spectrum of legally imposed sanctions for violation of the law, we find that the law has removed one or more of your entitlements. I could use the word "rights" here—for example, your rights to life, to liberty, and to property. But the word "entitlements" is more precise, because it denotes legally recognized rights. If you claim a right that the law does not recognize (for example, a woman's claim to the right to vote before the Constitutional amendment of 1920 providing for universal suffrage), you do not have an "entitlement." Since we are talking about enforcement mechanisms intrinsic to the legal system, it is more precise to speak of entitlements than to speak of rights.

In all cases of law violation, the law responds by depriving you of one or more of your entitlements. You have a legal entitlement to liberty; you lose it if you commit a crime punishable by incarceration. You have a legal entitlement to your bank account; you lose it if you have failed to pay your taxes or if someone obtains a judgment against you and attaches it. You have an entitlement to performance under a private contract that you make with someone else; if you fail to perform your part of the bargain, a court may decide that you have forfeited your entitlement under the contract. Some of these entitlement deprivations that you suffer because you have violated the law can be effectuated against you without any need for physical enforcement. Your bank account can be taken away from you by a bookkeeping entry made in the bank pursuant to a court order. Your marriage can be legally dissolved by a court decree without your willing compliance or participation. Thus, when we think of legal enforcement, we need not imagine the use of physical force against the person of the law-violator, although, of course, in some cases physical force is appropriate. The deprivation of either your entitlement to liberty, or your entitlement to life, may result from your conviction of a major crime.

Furthermore, there would be no possibility of enforcement by entitlement deprivation if people were not assigned some entitlements in the first place. If you had no entitlements, you would obviously suffer no loss if the law deprived you of some of them. (There is no "law" in the "jungle.") However, we find in all legal systems without exception the legal recognition of certain rights of the people, which we call entitlements. At a minimum, there is recognition of life and liberty. With a set of entitlements, therefore, each person is vulnerable to removal of some of them by the law. Legal systems typically enforce their own rules by removing one or more entitlements of persons who violate the rules.

If the account I have just given of the function of entitlements in the enforcement of law is persuasive, and if it fully captures the more diffuse notion of enforcement, then we next can turn to the international legal system to see how the process of entitlements and entitlement-deprivations works to provide for the enforcement of legal rules.

Let us imagine a primitive international situation. Two nations are at war with each other, but are weary of it and are interested in the possibility of peace. The problem now is how to send a peace ambassador from one nation to the other. The war between them is so total and brutal that no one wants to be an emissary for fear of being killed by the other side. We assume that this is the first "case" of resolving the conflict between the two nations so there are no prescribed methods of establishing peace.

Perhaps nation *A* could dispatch a particularly brave person who would carry a letter saying, "don't kill the bearer of this letter, as we are attempting to set up communications with you, and we promise to give safe conduct to any person you choose to send to us who has a letter from you. Moreover, as evidence of our good faith, you can hold the bearer of this letter hostage while your emissary is en route to us." Such a letter, of course, would not guarantee that its bearer would be safe. All we know is that, in some instances, letters such as this one actually worked.[18] We don't know much about those instances where the letter was ineffective and its bearer was killed. But in those cases where the letter worked, a primitive entitlement—a limited ambassadorial immunity—between the two nations was set up.

This single entitlement, however, is precarious, for the only remedy for entitlement violation by one nation is that of a reciprocal violation by the other nation of the same entitlement. Thus, suppose nation *A* is furious with the peace terms brought by nation *B*'s emissary, and responds by killing the emissary. In effect, nation *A* has opted to resume total war. Nation *B*, it is true, can retaliate by killing the emissary it is holding, but nation *A* presumably had already taken this possibility into account and

[18] *Cf.* G. Schwarzenberger, The Inductive Approach to International Law 75-78 (1965).

decided to "sacrifice" its own emissary. The two nations have thus destroyed the only entitlement that existed between them. They revert to a lawless state of war, from which extrication will now be harder given the unfortunate experience with the emissaries. Clearly the entitlement of diplomatic immunity would have had a better chance to survive had there been a second and different entitlement between the two nations. Then a threat by one nation to destroy the diplomatic immunity could be countered by a threat to destroy the other unrelated entitlement.

Thus, stability has a better chance the more entitlements there are. It is not the purpose of this essay to discuss historically how entitlements arose among nations, or how they became more complex and differentiated. Yet we might briefly consider the perspective of a new nation (perhaps a nation that has just received its independence from a colonial power).

Our new nation receives at its birth a host of entitlements. It has not chosen nor selected any of these entitlements; instead they are, so to speak, thrust upon the new nation. The first entitlement is of fundamental importance: the entitlement of statehood, which means, in the international system, that our new nation is a geographic entity entitled to exert its own legal jurisdiction in the area within its boundaries and to claim the inviolability of those boundaries against all other states. The legal sanctity of its borders signifies that our new state is a state in a community of states, and not merely a gang of thieves subject to the untrammelled degradations of other neighboring gangs. Indeed, it appears that the very definition of a state, or nation, involves an entitlement to the sanctity of its borders. Without such boundaries, the entity is hardly a "state." Yet, the boundaries are boundaries only by virtue of their recognition by all the other states in the system.

In sum, still considering this first entitlement, our new nation depends for its very identity upon the recognition of other similar states in the community of states. I am not talking about de jure recognition; rather, all that is necessary is a sense in the international community that the new state is enclosed by international boundaries, and those boundaries, like all boundaries, are lines that differentiate the internal affairs of the state from the external affairs and cannot be crossed at will by military forces in either direction. This notion of a boundary is so fundamental that the Vienna Convention on the Law of Treaties specifically excepts boundary-establishing treaties from the normal rules of *rebus sic stantibus*,[19] and the World Court in its leading decision in the *Continental Shelf Cases* made it clear that the normal generation of customary international law cannot affect ownership of territory (in those cases, the submerged land areas) absent a showing of consent from the owner.[20]

[19] Vienna Convention on the Law of Treaties, art. 62, *adopted* May 12, 1969, 8 I.L.M. 679, 702 (1969).

[20] North Sea Continental Shelf (W. Ger. v. Den., W. Ger. v. Neth.), 1969 I.C.J. 3. This case has

Our new state might, therefore, look upon the international law of the sanctity of its boundaries as a gift of a valuable entitlement. But the entitlement carries with it reciprocal duties, so that it is not necessarily a gift. The entitlement provides that our new nation must respect the borders of all the other states. Suppose our new nation is very powerful militarily, and expansionist-minded; it might want to extend its boundaries at the expense of its neighboring states. In that case, the entitlement of sanctity of boundaries is, in the first instance, more of a curse than a gift. (Later on, if the new state has succeeded militarily in extending its dominion, it might then want to establish the principle of sanctity of international boundaries, so as to secure its own gains.) Obviously, we cannot know, a priori, whether a new state likes or dislikes any particular entitlement. And that is indeed the point: the new entitlements that accrue to the new state at its birth are those that the international system has imposed upon the new state. If pressed to make a judgment whether the host of entitlements as a whole are a blessing or a curse to the new nation, we would conclude that, on the whole, the system of entitlements is beneficial to the new nation. This conclusion follows from the simple observation that international entitlements did not descend from God, but rather they evolved slowly over time to serve the collective self-interest of all the states. It is unlikely, therefore, that a system of rules that serves the collective self-interest would be inimical to the individual interests of any given state. Nevertheless, it is possible that *some* of the entitlements would be contrary to the interest of our new nation. If so, there is nothing our new nation can do about it. The list of entitlements is a given; they are thrust upon our new nation without its initial consent.

At least, there is no provable manifestation of initial consent by the new nation's. But there is an inferred consent which stems from our new nation taking its position among the community of nations. By asserting the inviolability of its borders from external attack, our new nation defines itself as a state that has internationally recognized boundaries. Indeed, it is hard to think of what our new nation would be if it did not have those boundaries, and therefore the inference of its consent to statehood is very powerful. Our new nation also has the entitlement to send ambassadors to other states who want to receive them; and even before the first treaty is concluded giving those ambassadors diplomatic protection, there is an international entitlement that they have initial diplomatic immunity to proceed to other countries to negotiate such treaties. Moreover, our new nation is the beneficiary of the whole set of entitlements regarding its capacity to enter into binding treaties with other nations, and to have those treaties construed and applied according to the customary international law regarding the interpretation of treaties. Ad-

been widely misinterpreted, and thus the statement in the text has been supported by an extensive argument given elsewhere. *See* D'Amato, *The Concept of Human Rights in International Law*, 82 COLUM. L. REV. 1110, 1142-44 (1982).

ditionally, our new nation, at birth, benefits from the entitlement that all nations are free to use the high seas, to send satellites into outer space, to claim for themselves a territorial sea, an underlying continental shelf, and an exclusive economic zone. It may be that our new nation does not border upon any ocean, or if it does so border, that there is no underlying continental shelf. All the international entitlements say is that if a nation does border on an ocean it is entitled to claim an exclusive territorial sea, and if it has a continental shelf it is entitled to claim certain exclusivities with regard thereto. The full list of entitlements embraces areas such as the entitlement to protect nationals abroad, the protection of the laws of war and rules regulating the conduct of hostilities, rules regarding the exertion of extraterritorial jurisdiction, and among other topics the following: international servitudes, succession of states, international rivers, lakes, canals and straits, polar regions, rights and duties of states in outer space, nationality and status of ships, piracy, slavery, international traffic in narcotics, nationality and statelessness, rights of aliens, asylum, extradition, international communications including satellites and "jamming" of broadcasts, immunities of states and their agencies and subdivisions, protection of human rights, diplomatic and consular privileges and immunities, status and privileges of international organizations, status of armed forces on foreign territory, limits of criminal jurisdiction, enforcement of foreign judgments and commercial arbitrations, treaties (entry into force, modification, termination), pacific blockade, reprisals, arms shipments, relations between belligerants and neutrals, etc. The point of making such a list is that for our new nation, all the specific entitlements in these subject-matter categories work two ways: first, to benefit our new nation to the extent that it has any interest in claiming any specific entitlement; and second, to impose upon our new nation the duty to respect those same entitlements when they are asserted against it by other nations.

Taken as a whole, these entitlements define what it is to be a "nation" or "state" in the modern world.[21] To be sure, these are the legal definitional parameters of a nation, but a nation is admittedly a legal fiction. As a construct of international law, a nation is nothing more nor less than a bundle of entitlements, of which the most important ones define and secure its boundaries on a map, while others define its jurisdictional competency and the rights of its citizens when they travel outside its borders.

Some writers have tried to base all these competences on the "consent" of the nation.[22] They are thus compelled by their own logic to

[21] *See* D'Amato, *supra* note 20, at 1113-15.

[22] *See, e.g.*, G. TUNKIN, THEORY OF INTERNATIONAL LAW 123-33 (1974); G. VAN HOOF, RETHINKING THE SOURCES OF INTERNATIONAL LAW 76-82 (1983). For a critique of "consent" theories, see A. D'AMATO, *supra* note 16, at 187-99. Even the writers who insist upon consent will accept *tacit* consent; yet it is a short move from tacit consent to inferred consent to legally inferred

assert that a new nation is not bound by any particular rule of international law until it has consented to that rule.[23] The new nation is then in a preferred position; it can pick and choose among the rules those that it likes. This pick-and-choose position is clearly wrong as a matter of historical fact as well as logic. Historically, existing nations have never allowed new nations to pick and choose, nor have new nations asserted a *tabula rasa* position.[24] Logically, if a new nation tried to assert such a position, the reaction of the other nations might well be that the new nation's *rights* as well as its duties are up for grabs, thus placing the new nation in a perilous position vis-a-vis its boundaries and other basic legal entitlements. Perhaps some such calculus has operated to dissuade any new nation from making the claim that these writers assert.

"Consent" is an elusive notion for yet another reason. If international law is truly grounded in each nation's consent, then what is to stop a nation from withdrawing its consent at any time? Specifically, when a nation finds a particular rule of international law disadvantageous to it, it could simply withdraw consent—even up to the very moment of application of the unwanted rule. The result would be to wipe out the notion of "law." Of course, some writers, focusing on consent, claim that international law is illusory anyway.[25] That claim begs the question, for if international law is real, as I have been arguing, then "consent" does not explain its application to states. What the writers are trying to say is that consent is such a powerful explanatory mechanism that international law as a result is not real. This puts a theoretically false cart before the horse.

If one wants to insist upon finding a role for the concept of consent, it may be useful to view consent in the following way: A nation is a bundle of entitlements which define what the nation is. In choosing to exist as a nation, the nation has consented to the bundle of entitlements. However, this scholastic exercise in logic, the sort that Pascal liked to satirize, is only necessary if someone is actively worried about the concept of consent and its role in international law. The simple conclusion

consent, *i.e.*, that given all the other elements that constitute a norm of international law, consent ultimately is inferred. To the extent that writers espouse consent out of a notion of the sovereignty of national *will* (an insistence based on positivist theory), none of them has ever answered the following question: what happens if a state, having given its consent to a rule, wants to change its mind? Such a change of mind would appear logically to be precluded by consent theory (at least, if that theory purports to explain how nations become obligated), and yet would seem to be required by the predominance of the will.

23 *See, e.g.*, VAN HOOF, *supra* note 22, at 78. *Accord* E. ZOLLER, PEACETIME UNILATERAL REMEDIES: AN ANALYSIS OF COUNTERMEASURES 6 (1984).

24 A. D'AMATO, *supra* note 16, at 191-92.

25 *See, e.g.*, Watson, *Legal Theory, Efficacy and Validity in the Development of Human Rights Norms in International Law*, 1979 U. ILL. L.F. 609, 632-35; *cf.* Tieya, *The Third World and International Law*, in THE STRUCTURE AND PROCESS OF INTERNATIONAL LAW, *supra* note 12, at 955 (recognizing continued validity of international law, but noting chances due to emergence of Third World interests).

follows that a nation is coextensive with its international legal entitlements.

This conclusion in turn illustrates why, as a matter of its very identity, a state should act in such a manner as to preserve its entitlements. Yet, its identity as a state, its "bundle of entitlements," is dependent upon the acquiescence of all the other states in the system. Since every state has the same bundle of entitlements—otherwise there would be legal inequality among states, a proposition that has never seriously been advocated—the other states in the system have an obvious interest in acquiescing in the entitlements of any given state. In this manner, a new state starts out, as we have seen, with its full complement of entitlements.

But just as all the states in the international legal system have a collective interest in acquiescing to all the entitlements for any given state in the system, they also have an interest in preserving the entitlements per se. For ease of illustration, let us consider the previously mentioned entitlement of diplomatic immunity. All the states in the system have an interest in the preservation of this particular entitlement. The existence of this entitlement, like other entitlements, helps define what a state is and what the international legal system is. The system would be something different, perhaps diminished, if the entitlement of diplomatic immunity were undermined.

To preserve this entitlement, the states in the system collectively will allow certain actions to be taken against any given state which violates the entitlement of diplomatic immunity. Prior to 1979, it would have been difficult to come up with a single example of a state which directly violated that entitlement. In nearly every case up to 1979 in which a diplomat's life or liberty was threatened, the host state immediately took action against those persons who threatened the diplomat. If the host state itself wanted to expel the diplomat, it would arrange for the diplomat's return. But in 1979, after some radical students occupied the American Embassy in Tehran, the government of Iran took the unprecedented step of ratifying the action and holding the American diplomatic personnel hostage. This was a case of a deliberate violation of international law, the violation of the entitlement of diplomatic immunity. To allow it to go unremedied would constitute a threat to the existence of that entitlement in the international legal system.

What legal recourse did states have to prevent the erosion of such an entitlement? An obvious move would be to allow the United States to violate Iran's similar entitlement by arresting diplomatic and consular officials of Iran who were physically present in the United States at the time of the takeover of the American embassy in Iran. While this tit-for-tat strategy is generally regarded as legal under international law, it is not always a particularly effective strategy.[26] As we saw previously in

[26] For a recent, provocative explication of the tit-for-tat strategy, see R. AXELROD, THE EVOLU-

the idealized example of two states at total war, the tit-for-tat strategy would simply eliminate the incipient ambassadorial-immunity entitlement and plunge the states back into the chaos of total war. Today, under a more developed international legal system, the tit-for-tat strategy might not have as negative an outcome, but it nevertheless could operate to erode rather than to preserve the entitlement in question. For instance, if the United States had jailed all Iranian diplomatic and consular officials, such an action at least in theory could be interpreted not as an attempt to punish Iran for its initial act but rather as a recognition that Iran's act was correct and that in fact diplomats are not entitled to immunity—I say "in theory" because this example may appear to be far-fetched. But since the content of international law depends upon the recognition of what the entitlements are by all the states in the system, the action I have just hypothesized by the United States and Iran might well be interepreted as a new understanding of the entitlement of diplomatic immunity, i.e., that such immunity exists no longer. Consider the following more realistic example of the same theoretical process: nation *A* announces a territorial sea of 300 miles from its coastline; nation *B* argues that *A* has illegally infringed upon the high seas by attempting to expropriate part of it, and in retaliation, nation *B* proclaims its own 300-mile territorial sea. Despite what nation *B* said, the action it took tends to reinforce *A*'s claim. Thus, rather than challenging *A*'s claim to a 300-mile territorial sea, *B* has reinforced it. A new rule, giving coastal states a much larger area of jurisdiction over the high seas will evolve. And the old entitlement—that the high seas were open to all nations—will partly be eroded by these new claims for an extensive territorial sea. Thus, the tit-for-tat strategy, in this example, not only fails to deter the original entitlement violation but in fact reinforces it.

The United States, in fact, did not retaliate by jailing Iranian consular and diplomatic officials, although that action was considered and reported in the press.[27] Instead, the United States took steps that were also justified under international law and which constitute a more sophisti-

---

TION OF COOPERATION (1984). *See also* A. RAPOPORT, STRATEGY AND CONSCIENCE 48-57 (1964); A. RAPOPORT, FIGHTS, GAMES, AND DEBATES 166-79 (1960). The most complete analysis of the legality of countermeasures under international law is E. ZOLLER, *supra* note 23. However, it is not clear whether Professor Zoller confines her conclusions to countermeasures which do not violate an independent norm of international law (i.e., those which may simply violate a state's treaty commitments or other such obligations owing to a particular state). In the *Case Concerning the Air Service Agreement (U.S. v. France)*, appended to Professor Zoller's book, the Arbitral tribunal concludes:

> Under the rules of present-day international law, and unless the contrary results from special obligations arising under particular treaties, notably from mechanisms created within the framework of international organisations, each State establishes for itself its legal situation vis-a-vis other States. If a situation arises which, in one State's view, results in the violation of an international obligation by another State, the first State is entitled, within the limits set by the general rules of international law pertaining to the use of armed force, to affirm its rights through counter-measures.

Id. at 166-67.

[27] *See* N.Y. Times, Dec. 13, 1979, at § Al, col. 5.

cated (though, as we shall see, perhaps more dangerous) method of enforcement. The United States "froze" approximately thirteen billion dollars of Iranian deposits in American banks and in various European banks where the United States, through American corporations, had the power to act.[28] If it were not for the initial Iranian act of holding the American diplomats hostage, the United States would be unjustified under inter-national law in violating the Iranian entitlement to the use of its own bank deposits abroad. Indeed, by freezing the Iranian assets, the United States was effectively confiscating the interest those assets would have earned.[29] This was a direct deprivation of Iranian property by the United States. Yet there was no condemnation of the American action by the international community; instead, the American action in violating a different Iranian entitlement from the one that Iran violated in the first place (diplomatic immunity) was tolerated by general silence, whereas governments from all over the world expressly condemned Iran's seizure of the American embassy. The workings of international law are rarely as explicit as scholars might like them to be, but I believe we are entitled to infer from the reaction of the community of nations that they did not perceive a threat to the shared entitlement of keeping state-owned deposits in foreign banks as a result of the American action, but rather regarded the U.S. action as a temporary infringement of an Iranian entitlement for the limited purpose of enforcing the original entitlement of diplomatic immunity.[30] Thus, the international community implicitly accepted the legality of a strategy that violates an offending nation's entitlements in order to repudiate that nation's initial offence. In the Iran-United States case, the strategy worked well, for the American diplomatic personnel were all safely returned to the United States, and the United States lifted the freeze on Iranian assets.

Of course, I am not attempting here to support my theory of a reciprocal-violation-of-a-different-entitlement by the single case of the American hostages in Tehran. The pattern is a general one and can be substantiated by numerous examples.[31] Moreover, the tit-for-a-different-tat pattern "makes sense" in a legal system that does not have a central court of compulsory jurisdiction, a world legislature, and a world police

---

28 *See* Nickel, *Battling for Iran's Frozen Billions*, FORTUNE, Dec. 15, 1980, at 117.

29 At the time the $13 billion was blocked, interest rates were approximately 15%. The assets were blocked for slightly over one year. At compound interest, this amounts to interest earned, and unpaid, of over two billion dollars. When the hostages were returned to the United States, the United States agreed to pay, in partial settlement, interest of $800 million to Iran, as reported in the New York Times. *See* N.Y. Times, Jan. 21, 1981, at § A9, col. 1.

30 Two judges out of the fifteen on the World Court felt that the blocking of Iranian assets should be set off against any reparations owing to the United States, but all fifteen members of the Court agreed that Iran's initial detention of the American diplomatic and consular personnel was unlawful. *See* United States Diplomatic and Consular Staff in Tehran (U.S. v. Iran), 1980 I.C.J. 3, 51 (Morozov, J., dissenting); *id.* at 58 (Tarazi, J., dissenting).

31 *See generally* E. ZOLLER, *supra* note 23.

force.[32] The absence of these institutions does not mean that international law isn't really law; rather, it simply means that international law is enforced in a different way.

There is a danger in relying on the enforcement of international law by allowing a retaliatory deprivation of the offending nation's entitlement. The danger is the potential escalation of entitlement violations, ultimately leading to international anarchy. In the idealized case where there was only one entitlement, its destruction put the nations back into anarchy. The same result is possible if in the modern world there is runaway destruction of many entitlements. But the fact that law can become ineffective doesn't mean that it isn't law in the first place. Some people expressed fear when President Richard Nixon faced impeachment that he might order the military to seize Congress and the Supreme Court and proclaim himself immune from any attempt to dislodge him as President. While this may not have been a very realistic fear, if such a scenario had occurred, it would mean that constitutional law had deteriorated; but it would not mean that no constitutional law existed prior to Nixon's seizure of the reins of government. Similarly, while international law could destroy itself through a runaway series of violations of entitlements, until then it polices itself by the meta-rule I have described: That it is legal to deter the violation of an entitlement by threatening a counter-violation of the same or a different entitlement. This latter enforcement action is the "physical sanction" provided by the international legal system, just as the rules regulating police, prison officials, sheriffs, etc., are its domestic legal equivalents.

IV. Conclusion

International law is enforced by the process I have described as re-

32 The employment of a different countermeasure raises the question of proportionality of response. International law has not evolved a specific measure of proportionality, but it is at least clear that the countermeasure cannot be wholly disproportionate to the initial delict. The *Air Service Case*, in E. Zoller, *supra* note 23, at 167, calls attention to the possibility of a wholly different countermeasure, and states that it should be measured in terms of quality as well as quantity in order to judge proportionality. Interestingly, the social science literature bears out the effectiveness of quantitatively non-measurable responses so long as there is an ordinal ordering of preferences. As Axelrod demonstrates, *supra* note 26, at 17-18, the payoffs of the two players need not be comparable, nor symmetric, nor measurable on an absolute scale, and there is no need to assume rationality on the part of the players. The only ordering of preferences is that a nation prefers there to be no rule violation, and prefers taking a countermeasure in the event of a rule violation rather than letting the violator get away with a rule violation. In turn, taking countermeasures, in an iterated series (which for international purposes can extend over the centuries) is a stable and robust strategy for deterring the initial delict. Nations in their interactions seem to have evolved a tit-for-tat or a tit-for-a-different-tat strategy in their numerous interactions over the centuries, and this probably accounts for the stability of international legal rules. The tit-for-a-different-tat strategy is actually codified in the Vienna Convention on the Law of Treaties, art. 60, *supra* note 19, at 701, allowing a party to suspend *any* treaty obligation or obligations if the other party commits a material breach of any of its obligations.

ciprocal-entitlement violation. The violation may be of the same entitlement or, more likely now days, of a different entitlement. But it is on the whole an effective process—as effective for the international legal system as is the enforcement of most laws in domestic systems via the state-sanctioned deprivation of one or more entitlements held by individual citizens or corporations. Occasionally people or states will break laws despite the presence of enforcement machinery, but that does not mean that there were no laws to begin with. Nor, as I have tried to argue, should we swing to the opposite side of the spectrum and say that enforcement has nothing to do with whether laws exist. We don't need to take such an extreme position with respect to international law because there is, in fact, enforcement, resulting in a stable system of international entitlements. It is impossible to understand why nations do or refrain from doing the things they do without understanding what entitlements are included in the bundle and how nations act to preserve their full complement of existing entitlements. In this sense, international law is a very realistic component of the picture that political scientists try to draw of how nations behave. The "serious students of law" who claim that international law isn't really "law" make the same mistake that some political scientists make in ignoring norms in order to be "scientific" in their "descriptions." A state cannot be described without reference to its entitlements, nor can its actions be fully understood without reference to the steps it takes to preserve those entitlements.

[3]

Friedrich Kratochwil

THRASYMMACHOS REVISITED:

On the Relevance of Norms and the Study of Law for International Relations

Introduction

The place of norms in political life has always been controversial probably because of their counterfactual validity. The possibility of violating norms has made the explanation and prediction of human action in terms of norms particularly difficult.[1] Thus the search for causes of human behavior has been concerned mainly with the discovery of less problematic factors that could be imputed as constants in explaining particular decisions.

Such explanations, be they cast in terms of power, interest, drives, or race were thought to be more parsimonious than the complicated description of circumstances and applicable norms in a given situation. Thereby a more objective or in any case scientific explanation of human action, it was hoped, would become possible.[2] Consequently, norms have been understood solely as ideological reflections, deceptions, subterfuges or simply as an impediment to the achievement of one's goals in a "rational" way.

One of the most principled discussions in which the relevance of a normative order for man and society is defended is Plato's *Republic*. Significantly, it is also entitled a dialogue "on justice." There the debate about the relevance of norms in individual and social life takes a "theological" turn when Thrasymmachos, the sophist, maintains that the gods, as symbols and guarantors of the normative order either do not exist or do not care and are therefore irrelevant. If indeed they do care, Thrasymmachos contends they can be bribed, thus calling into question the whole prospect of a normative order.[3]

Many students of international relations voice similar objections concerning the status of legal prescriptions in the international arena. In a realm governed by great insecurity, marginally rather than widely shared values, and great competitiveness, a modified version of the three "Thrasymmachian objections" appears relevant. Thus modern sophists argue plausibly that: 1) international law does not exist, i.e., any norm which might exist in the international arena is not legal; 2) if legal norms exist they are ineffective, and; 3) even if legal norms exist and are relevant to decisions they are con-

I wrote this Article while I was a Post Doctoral fellow of the Alexander Humboldt Foundation, whose generous support is hereby gratefully acknowledged. I also want to thank Nicholas Onuf for his valuable criticism.

1. Carl Hempel, *Aspects of Scientific Explanation* (New York: Free Press, 1965), chap. 4.
2. The argument that a "political", i.e., structural explanation of international relations is required is made in Kenneth Waltz, *Theory of International Politics* (Reading, Mass.: Addison Wesley Co., 1979).
3. Plato, *Republic*, Book II, 365d-366b. For an interpretation of the sophistic argument and Plato's response see Eric Voegelin, *Order and History*, vol. 3, *Plato and Aristotle* (Baton Rouge: University of Louisiana Press, 1957), chap. 3.

0022-197x/83/1314-0343$01.50/0

stantly abused in the interest of the powerful. For these reasons the idea of an impartial regulatory system is fanciful indeed.

These assertions speak to three different aspects of the legal *problematique* in any society. The first and most radical objection, but also perhaps the easiest to refute, is based on a particular definition of law. A conceptual clarification can quickly show the inadequacies of a preconceived idea of law derived exclusively from a particular subset of legal prescriptions.[4] For example, using criminal law as the model means to mistake a part of law for law in its entirety. This shows two things. First, the question of the existence or non-existence of international law cannot be answered by nominal definitions as e.g. in Austin's theory: law is the command of the sovereign; since there is no sovereign in international relations therefore there is no law. As a corollary, it is only against the background of a broader definition of law that the question of the status of international law can be discussed intelligently.

The second aspect of the legal *problematique* deals with the influence of norms upon decision-making and, in particular, the constraining force of prescriptions. To focus exclusively on the constraining aspect of prescriptions—as opposed to a fuller account which includes the justificatory, enabling and communicative aspects of norms—leads to serious distortions concerning the efficacy of law in social life.

The final objection focuses on the jurisprudential issue of the link between a set of legal prescriptions and the requirements of a formal or substantive conception of justice. This in turn not only includes the specification of such criteria as fairness, impartiality or equity, but entails a critical appraisal of the actual strategies by which a more principled and just order can emerge from the interactions between states.

Those familiar with the legal literature will recognize that these three theses can serve as convenient categories in classifying a variety of scholarly efforts. The first question deals mainly with the problem of Austinian positivism and its reformulation by legal theorists such as H.L.A. Hart.[5] The third issue is most explicitly treated by writers who share a world order perspective.[6] The second issue, the influence of norms on policy-makers, has not received sufficient attention. In this context it is important to note that the work on regimes is characterized by an egregious lack of familiarity with legal theory.[7]

It is through the prism of this second objection that the other two sophistic theses, and their problematic character will be examined. This will not only help develop a broader understanding of the functions and limitations of law in general, but will highlight the distinctive features of the international legal order. Furthermore, a more appropriate appraisal of the weaknesses of international law becomes possible. This appraisal avoids mistaking the "cops and robber" model of law for an adequate formulation of the role of norms in social life.

4. For a more extensive treatment of differing concepts of law and its implications for international law, see Friedrich Kratochwil, "Is International Law Proper Law?" *Archives for Philosophy of Law and Social Philosophy* 69, no. 1 (1983), 13-46.

5. H.L.A. Hart, *The Concept of Law* (Oxford: Clarendon, 1961).

6. For a short description of the world order approach, see Saul H. Mendlovitz, ed., *On the Creation of a Just World Order* (New York: The Free Press, 1975).

7. Stephen Krasner, ed., *International Organization* 36, no. 2 (Spring 1982).

Such an approach is indebted to linguistic conceptual analysis and jurisprudence rather than to the positivist understanding of science. It is useful in clarifying some of the epistemological problems of the present "regime" discussion in international relations and it has important repercussions for the building of international relations theory.

The next section begins with an argument about the "ineffectiveness" of international legal prescriptions. In this context the conceptualization of rules and norms as constraints is shown to be faulty and to lead to a mistaken view of the role of norms in social life. After determining the function of norms, the following section will examine the question of their legal character. The final section is devoted to a short summary and some concluding considerations concerning the status of theory building in international relations.

The Efficacy of International Legal Prescriptions

Law can be defined "as a set of prescriptions (rules and principles) that impartial judges apply to a case at hand in order to render an authoritative decision."[8] This conception of law avoids the excesses of Austinian positivism (command of a sovereign) and is specific enough to serve as a useful point of departure. Unless appropriately modified, however, this preliminary definition, which focuses upon important differences between political and legal decision-making as subcategories of "authoritative" decisions, is problematic at best. The problem is brought out by reflecting briefly on the meaning of the term "rule of law." A government of laws does not refer to the government of judges, but, as Morton Kaplan and Nicholas de B. Katzenbach have aptly put it, it refers to:

> ... the larger formal process through which the members of the society pursue and realize values in an orderly way. It scarcely requires argument that law viewed as a body of authoritative rules pervades all the institutions of modern democratic government and is no monopoly of judges. ...
>
> Legislators, administrators and judges are all parts of a related process; all are subject to legal rules, and all invoke legal rules in the performance of their official tasks. They play different roles and the role of each is related in important ways to the existence of and the role played by the others.[9]

Three points are worth pondering in this context. There is the implicit argument that law is best understood as a special type of rules guiding conduct, rather than as a set of commands. Secondly, there is the distinction between the narrow conception of law as applied by impartial third parties and the wider context in which rules are used, invoked and utilized. The third point concerns the importance of legal rules for the performance of duties. Law, therefore, is not simply a "constraint," but it also functions to orchestrate and thereby facilitate, societal interaction.[10] These two functions emphasize the performative and pragmatic dimensions of law, and as such are usually neglected in the normal definition of the functions of law.[11]

From this preliminary analysis it becomes obvious that the conception of law as a coercive order needs

8. Morton Kaplan and Nicholas de B. Katzenbach, *The Political Foundations of International Law* (New York: Wiley, 1961), 4.

9. Kaplan and Katzenbach, 4.

10. For a discussion of the function of law as a means of communication, see William Coplin, "International Law and Assumptions about the State System," *World Politics* 17, 615-35.

11. J.L. Austin, *How to Do Things with Words* (Cambridge: Harvard University Press, 1962).

revision.[12] The efficacy of law cannot be assessed simply in terms of the compliance or noncompliance with prohibitions. Such a procedure would be inaccurate, because it mistakes laws for commands, and because complying with prescriptions is an intensely dynamic process as opposed to passively following rules.

Mistaking legal prescriptions for commands has a long and distinguished ancestry shared by such unlikely companions as positivists, voluntarist philosophers and theologians.[13] But even in the last case, when the obligatory character of prescriptions is derived from an absolute sovereign—God—the language distinguishes between a command and a commandment. While commands are always situation-specific, commandments (which show rule-like characteristics) are always thought to be applicable to broad classes of events.[14] Rules, as Hart points out, are standing orders.[15] This is elucidated when rules are stated in the "if-then" form.[16] Rules are also valid *erga omnes* (applicable to all) and are different from commands. After all, the famous gunman asking for your wallet is not claiming to have established a norm also applicable to him or herself.[17] This surely is not part of the language game of asking for "your money or your life." Even when rules empower someone to issue commands in specific situations, the command and the rule are clearly distinguishable.[18] As Kaplan and Katzenbach state, rules that empower in this sense are always part of a larger normative context.

Two corollaries follow from this. First, it appears not only that one cannot equate rules with commands, but that a variety of different rule types exist, each of which exhibits characteristic differences in the incentives for compliance. Although prohibitions are adequately represented as constraints, rules that empower or enable are not. Thus while enforcement according to the "cops and robber" model of criminal law may increase compliance with a certain type of prescription, and thus the effectiveness of a certain part of the legal order, it is clearly irrelevant to the compliance patterns of enabling rules. A serious effort in ascertaining the effectiveness of legal prescriptions in general would entail: first, the differentiation of several type of rules; second, an analysis of the social situation to which these rules correspond, and third, an empirical account of actual compliance patterns. It should be obvious that such an enterprise is at odds with the facile arguments about the ineffectiveness of the legal order mentioned above in the second sophistic objection. Actors, in the domestic as well as the international order, are not simply constrained by rules. Rules enable them to act, to pursue goals, to communicate, to share meanings, to criticize claims and justify actions. Indeed, the blueprint image of a society in which legal norms program individual action has been justly criticized by sociolo-

12. On the argument that law is a coercive order, see Hans Kelsen, *Principles of International Law*, 2nd ed. (New York: Holt, Rinehart and Winston, 1966).

13. For a good conceptual distinction, see Thomas Mayberry, "Laws, Moral Laws and God's Commands," *The Journal of Value Inquiry* 4, no. 4 (Winter 1970), 287-92.

14. Alf Ross, *Directives and Norms* (London: Routledge, Kegan and Paul, 1968).

15. Hart, chaps. 2, 3.

16. Gidon Gottlieb, *The Logic of Choice* (London: Allen and Unwin, 1968).

17. For a discussion of the "gun man example" see Hart, chap. 2.

18. For a further discussion of the situation specific form of commands in contrast to the standing order character of rules see Ross, *Directives and Norms*, 99.

gists.[19] The inappropriateness of viewing laws merely as a system of sanctions or constraints has also been noted in the jurisprudential literature.[20]

These theoretical considerations conform with an unprejudiced assessment of the empirical evidence. While it is true that the international legal order is not very successful in preventing international violence, the relevance of norms in international life is manifest in the thousands of transactions that take place every day. It is precisely because policy-making machinery has become bureaucratized that it increasingly needs standard operating procedures by which to function. These conditions can be best structured by the application and invocation of norms.[21]

The fact that legal prescriptions are not particularly effective in preventing violence in the international, as well as in the domestic context is not new. In both arenas the legal order is continuously violated. What distinguishes the failure of international law from that of the domestic legal order is less the frequency of violations than the catastrophic consequences these failures have for international relations. While the daily death toll from violent crimes in American cities alone might amount to 30 victims, it does not have the same saliency as a guerrilla attack or military expedition which claims ten or twenty lives and which is quickly adduced as proof for the failure of international law.

In addition, the scope of war distinguishes it from private acts of unauthorized violence. The destruction wrought, and the possibility of escalation, clearly sets international violations apart from even the worst failures of the domestic legal order, with the exception of internal strife and civil war. The issue, therefore, is not the weakness of the international prohibitions against violence but rather more effective prevention of violence. This in turn presents an array of new puzzles. Would a world in which no legal prescriptions exist against the resort to force be better off? Arguments could be made that this might lead to a less cynical attitude concerning violations. There might also be trade-offs between an increased observance of the rules of warfare *(jus in bello)* and the free resort to violence *(jus ad bellum)* as defined by the UN regime. As Louis Henkin has shown, however, the argument is not persuasive, conceptually or historically.[22]

Would it be more effective to rely on other mechanisms to the exclusion of legal considerations? Sometimes a *Realpolitik* policy depending on competing national interests and the balance of power is mentioned in this context. The balance of power model, however, can only be an effective and rational policy within a framework of conventions with normative status. Even the most hardened realists confess that the application of force is a very costly way to achieve one's objectives in international relations and that sensible powers have therefore followed a policy of "prestige."[23] Prestige itself, however, is an ambiguous

19. Judith Blake and Kingsley Davis, "Norms, Values and Sanctions," *Modern Sociology*, Robert Harris, ed., (Chicago: Rand MacNally, 1964).

20. David Miers and William Twining, *How to Do Things With Rules* (London: Weidenfeld and Nicholson, 1976).

21. Louis Henkin, *How Nations Behave*, 2nd ed. (New York: Columbia University Press, 1980).

22. On the controversy between Thomas Franck and Louis Henkin see Thomas Franck, "Who Killed Article 2.4?" *American Journal of International Law* 64 (1970), 809-37; Louis Henkin, "The Reports of the Death of Article 2.4 are Greatly Exaggerated," *American Journal of International Law*, 65 (1971), 545-48.

23. Robert Gilpin, *War and Change in World Politics* (Cambridge: Cambridge University Press, 1981).

concept. It might simply mean establishing a "bad reputation" similar to gangsters attempting to keep challenges to their position to a minimum. But even in that case prestige is tied to some type of rule-governed expectations about the likelihood, scope and domain of retaliatory action. The more explicit this framework becomes the more prestige becomes mediated by the normative order.[24] This means in turn that power and influence are derived from the role as a protector of certain rules and core values of the game as exemplified in the notion of a Great Power or of hegemonic leadership.[25] Whether it is useful to endow these "rules of the game" with the dignity of some type of legal prescriptive force as some scholars seem to suggest, is a difficult question.[26] Nevertheless it shows that the alleged antinomy between "power" "balancing" and "rule following" is a mistaken one.

The role of such hegemonic aspirations is perhaps best exemplified in Thucydides' record of the Periclean Funeral Oration.[27] All those who read or interpret this book as an example of the inevitability of hegemonic wars, caused by the law of uneven growth, miss an important part of the Thucydidean intention.[28] The shifts in key governing concepts of the political discourse that occurred during the war brought about the destruction of a common normative framework.[29] The ethos of the protagonists decays and finally destroys even the set of conventions which distinguished Hellenic from barbaric society. Both cities become oppressors of their allies and lose power and prestige as the war is finally decided by an outside power, Persia.

Another possible substitute for norms is deterrence.[30] But as Alexander George and Richard Smoke have shown, the numerous failures of deterrence demonstrate its limited effectiveness.[31] Not only is such a system dependent on common sense to function, but substantive norms also provide templates in case the normal interaction has broken down.

These remarks do not necessarily prove the importance of legal prescriptions, but they do show that realist and capability analyses, deriving everything from "structural givens," are seriously misleading.[32] Realist and capability analyses share a certain naiveté about the complexities of human life, a shortcoming often attributed to legal scholars. Only legalism of the worst kind could assume that through the proliferation of prescriptions and the criminalization of international law, the problem of war could be eliminated. However, it is an equally

24. Friedrich Kratochwil, "On the Notion of Interest in International Relations," *International Organization* 36, no. 1 (1982), 1-30.

25. On the importance of a common understanding of legitimacy see Henry Kissinger, *A World Restored* (New York: Gosset and Dunlop, 1964); on the notion of a "Great Power" see Martin Wright, *Systems of States*, Hedley Bull and Carsten Holbraad, eds., (Leicester: Leicester University Press, 1977).

26. Richard Falk, "The Interplay of Westphalia and Charter Conceptions of the International Legal Order," *The Future of the International Legal Order*, Cyril Black and Richard Falk, eds., 4 vols. (Princeton: Princeton University Press, 1969), vol. 1, chap. 2.

27. Thucydides, *The Peloponnesian War*, Book II, 34-36.

28. In this context, I object strongly to Gilpin's "leninist" interpretation of politics. See Gilpin, *War and Change*.

29. Thucydides, *Peloponnesian War*, Book III, 82-95.

30. See Robert Jervis for critical remarks about "security regimes" in which the role of norms is considered secondary to the utility calculations of each player. Robert Jervis, "Security Regimes," *International Regimes*, Krasner, ed., 357-78.

31. Alexander George and Richard Smoke, *Deterrence in American Foreign Policy* (New York: Columbia University Press, 1974).

32. See Klaus Knorr, *The Power of Nations* (New York: Basic Books, 1975); David Baldwin, "Money and Power," *Journal of Politics* 33 (1971), 578-614; see Joseph Nogee, "Polarity: An Ambiguous Concept," *Orbis* 18 (Winter 1978), 1193-1224.

naive conception that the only reality of international politics is power as gauged by national capabilities.

While the preceding paragraphs illustrate how difficult it is to maintain that norms are nonexistent in the international arena, there still remains the question of whether these norms can really be called "legal." The attribution of a legal character to norms requires more than simply demonstrating that norms exist in the international arena and that norms indeed mold decisions. Thus, Austinian jurisprudence did not deny the existence of norms but maintained that they are merely norms of comity or morality.

While it may be difficult to draw a clear line between legal prescriptions and moral principles—some moral precepts such as "promises have to be kept" are inherent to legal systems—a demarcation criterion between legal prescriptions and other norms serves as an important device in further clarifying the functions of law. The next section will consider this problem and then approach the last objection mentioned above, i.e. the "partial" character of norms.

The Character of International Legal Prescriptions

Having shown the rule-guided character of human action in the domestic as well as the international arena, the problem remains to distinguish legal rules from other rules guiding interactions. There seem to be two ways to approach the character of a rule. The rule can be traced back to its origin or it can be distinguished according to its influence on an actor's decision. While fundamentalist mullahs and positivists prefer the formal tests—law is what originates from God or a basic norm—the pressure test of legal obligation is usually preferred by sociologists and psychologists. Psychologists distinguish legal norms by the *severity* with which they pressure the individuals to act in accordance with the rule in question.

Both approaches create severe difficulties for the determination of the legal character of norms in the international arena. Although some norms can conveniently be traced back to a source, such as those created by a treaty, the establishment of a pedigree of a norm often depends upon the logical closure of the legal system. This can easily be seen when two norms, both traceable to a valid source, lead to contradictory implications or when one party argues that "x" is a legal norm while the other party questions its legal pedigree. In such cases a rule is formulated at a meta-level, which decides the circumstances under which one norm is to be given preference over another. Or an authoritative decision is made of what the "law is," a task performed by adjudication. Since adjudicative procedures in either contentious cases or in the "advisory opinion" variety are rarely utilized in international relations, much of what is claimed to be legally relevant is never authoritatively decided. This is obviously one reason why the international legal system can be called "primitive." Nevertheless, it would not be very useful to call all the activities in which legal norms are invoked "nonlegal" simply because of the lack of authoritative decision. After all, states usually *do* make distinctions between their rights, and their desires and preferences, even if the latter are backed by persuasive reasons. Furthermore, such a perspective makes too much of the "ratio decidendi" (the reason for the decisions) of a judge and is clearly inapplicable to international law where *stare decisis* (to stand by that which was decided) is not established.[33]

33. See Miers and Twining, 159.

Another attempt to define a criterion of demarcation focuses on the type of psychological pressure generated by legal norms as opposed to rules of comity. On the one hand, legal norms are said to be characterized by a certain gravity and seriousness; on the other hand, it is maintained that legal rules are not as compelling as moral prescriptions. Thus it is not clear which type or degree of "seriousness of pressure" qualifies a rule as legal. In addition, the most severe psychological pressures in the international arena might not be generated by legal norms but by unilateral policy commitments. But such commitments do not qualify as moral imperatives or as legal obligations. Besides, no legal order can make the private feelings of an actor the ultimate test of legal obligations quite aside from the fact that "feelings" of pressure are probably a mistaken metaphor in the case of corporate actors.[34]

If the psychological pressure model is seriously deficient, then the guidance provided by rules must be conceptualized differently. The concept should not emphasize the psychological impact, but the explicitness and the contextual variation allowed in decision-making. Legal rules "provide relatively firm guidance not only with respect to ends but to the means adopted."[35] This distinguishes legal rules from morals. Moral precepts are practically context-free and do not provide for specific ranges of application. This accounts for the open-ended nature of the moral discourse. The specificity of legal norms, on the other hand, is perhaps clearest in the rules of evidence in a legal order. The search for "truth" in a legal proceeding is subordinate to provisoes specifying what counts as a "proof" and what facts are inadmissible.

Such a definition of law focuses no longer on certain institutions such as courts, or on the states or beliefs of the actors, but rather on the reasoning process (deliberation) of an actor in making decisions. The legal nature of norms can now be determined in a "system free" way. Neither logical closure nor particular institutions of a legal order are prerequisites for its existence. A legal order exists if actors accept certain rules as obligatory by making principled use of them in defining choices, by making demands as well as proposals for the settlement of disputes in terms of these rules, and by justifying action through their invocation.

In this way a legal order can be conceived of as a particular system of communicative action.[36] It informs the participants about the nature of the game by determining the type of actors who can make claims; it sets the range of permissible goals the actors can pursue, specifies the steps necessary to insure the validity of their acts and assigns priority and weight to different claims.[37] The legal order represents one of the primary means of organizing social life because it makes more specific the shared general notions in practical matters

34. For a discussion of the problem of political and legal obligation see Richard Flathman, *Political Obligation* (London: Croom Helm, 1972).

35. Gidon Gottlieb, "The Nature of International Law: Towards a Second Concept of Law," *The Future of the International Legal Order*, Cyril Black and Richard Falk, eds., vol. 4 (Princeton: Princeton University Press, 1972), chap. 9, 370.

36. See Jürgen Habermas, *Theorie des Kommunikativen Handelns*, 2 vols. (Frankfurt: Suhrkamp, 1981).

37. The informal organization of social life is thus dependent upon the workings of norms that make an intersubjective understanding possible. On the emergence of such norms out of iterative bargaining situations see Edna Ullmann-Margalit, *The Emergence of Norms* (Oxford: Clarendon Press, 1977); Philip Heyman, "The Problem of Coordination: Bargaining and Rules," *Harvard Law Review* 86 (March 1973) 707-78.

which allow for interdependent decision-making. Finally, the legal order deals with the problems that arise due to scarcity and the non-identical preferences of a multiplicity of actors. These last remarks deserve further exploration and will be helpful in clarifying the concept of a "primitive" order.

The term "shared meaning" is conventionally used to designate culture, which is a comprehensive system of symbols used to explain all or particular aspects of reality. This includes practices, mythical lores and conceptual schemes. Although law as a cultural scheme has its roots in myth and magic, it emancipated itself early from the mythical origins. Ultimate meanings are increasingly relegated to theology or philosophy. The validity of legal prescriptions becomes a matter of argumentation, through quoting relevant norms as an explanation for the espoused position. This means that law undergoes thereby not only a process of rationalization, but that law is increasingly oriented towards the practical aspects of life.[38]

But even within this realm of practical reason law becomes a much more restricted form of discourse. This becomes evident when comparing the moral and legal discourse. While from a moral point of view all norms have to satisfy the generalization criterion to be valid, the legal discourse allows for self-interested and thereby non-universal claims if they are rights.[39] Furthermore, rights as particularly insistent claims cannot simply be defeated by showing that the pursuit of some ultimate value, even if agreed upon, is impeded.[40]

Unlike moral precepts, the legal system has a tendency to develop procedures of internal validation by which norms can be created, altered or abolished. In this context it is important to remember that specific legislative institutions are historically rather late phenomena within legal orders and that most of the development of law takes place through judicial activity (interpretation, precedents). In addition, scholars try to introduce some consistency into often contradictory practices. Long before legal orders attain their full reality status in practice they existed as ideas which gave meaning and coherence to otherwise only vaguely related activities.[41]

These considerations lead to a more appropriate assessment of the international legal order as a primitive one. As previously mentioned, primitive does not refer to the lack of differentiation between mythical and legal concepts. International law is a purely secular construct and thus is distinguishable from morality, religion or mythical elaborations that endow the interaction of states with some utlimate meaning. This meaning is defined in either a philosophy of history or in a mechanical interpretation such as the balance of power.[42] After all, it was no accident that the legal conceptualization of international relations attained importance when the

38. Max Weber, *Rechtssoziologie*, Johannes Winckelmann, ed., (Neuwied: Luchterhand, 1960).

39. See Marcus Singer, *Generalization in Ethics* (New York: Knopf, 1960).

40. See Dworkin, *Taking Rights Seriously* (Cambridge: Harvard University Press, 1978).

41. See Nicholas G. Onuf, "The International Legal Order as an Idea," *American Journal of International Law* 73 (1979), 244-266.

42. On the process of differentiation and the elaboration of philosophical "Weltbilder" see Habermas, vol. 2, chap. 5. Although it is fashionable to interpret the balance of power as a logical outcome of an anarchic state it can easily be shown that the European balance of power was a rather unique phenomenon. It seems rather questionable to assume that the idea of a "balance" could have been persuasive to anyone who did not share the mechanical metaphors that came into fashion after Descartes and attained prominence with Newton's physics, which demonstrated the heuristic power of equilibrium analysis.

"right way of life" as an organizing principle of political life had to be abandoned. The wars of religion demonstrated that neither the old orthodoxies nor the new forces espousing a different way of life could organize the body politic. On the contrary, each day of continued warfare led to new savageries without resolving any of the ultimate issues; the creation of a legal order appeared to be the only possibility to provide a normative framework necessary for social coexistence. An intellectual construct created by scholars ranging from Grotius to Vattel, proved useful and the idea of a "legal order" attained an increasingly concrete status.

An important problem with the primitive law analogy is that it suggests that the international legal order is largely a customary order. One of the peculiarities of the international legal order is, however, that it presupposes the distinction between a public and a private legal sphere, a division usually undeveloped or absent in primitive customary systems. This has important repercussions for the role of public officials as "agencies" of the international legal order (the famous dedoublement fonctionelle of Scelle).[43] Thus unlike a primitive order where law is the set of customary norms everybody follows, international law is applied to problems by a special class of public officials. In this sense international law exhibits some features of a developed legal system. International law also possesses features of a customary order characterized by horizontal patterns of authority.[44] Finally, there is the rather unique feature of the prescriptions of transnational law.[45] These regulate the conduct of private associations, such as multinational corporations by creating a special regime.

Having stated to what extent the term primitive is equivocal and problematic when applied to the international legal order, it is now easier to show in what sense the term primitive can be used justifiably. The international legal system is most obviously primitive in that it does not automatically subject its members to the compulsory settlement of disputes by legal means. This weakness is not specific to international law, because the settlement of disputes through court proceedings is always difficult once organized groups are involved and once issues cannot be separated from the wider social context. The lack of institutionalization of the world political process limits the more effective utilization of the legal process.[46] Although international law provides for a rudimentary informal organization of social life among independent actors, there are no effective formal organizations that can translate interest and issues into policy. Collective goods on the international level are thus not provided or achieved suboptimally through hegemonic leadership and, infrequently, through some type of voluntary contributions. The world political process remains, in spite of all communications, sporadic, and is often characterized by bargaining and coercive moves rather than by persuasion and by appeals to common standards, shared values and accepted solutions. Thus not only can the legal process not be separated from the political process, but the impartiality of

43. Georges Scelle, *Droit International Public* (Paris: Doneat Montchrestien, 1948).

44. Richard Falk, "International Jurisdiction: Horizontal and Vertical Conception of Legal Order," *Tempade Law Quarterly* 32 (1959), 295-320.

45. On a clarification of the concept of "transnational law" see Wolfgang Friedmann, *The Changing Structure of International Law* (New York: Columbia University Press, 1964).

46. For a fundamental discussion on the social and theoretical preconditions of a functioning legal process see Michael Barkun, *Law Without Sanction* (New Haven: Yale University Press, 1968), chaps. 6-8.

legal reasoning is crucially impaired by the lack of authoritative decisions concerning the applicability and scope of legal norms.

International adjudicative institutions are more often than not quite limited in their ability to determine what the law is. This is either due to general jurisdictional limitations incorporated into the statute that brings such a "court" into existence, or to the further limitations under which the parties to a dispute agree to ask for a judicial decision.[47] Thus, quite apart from the hoary institutional problem of how authoritative decisions of international tribunals can be enforced, the problem of determining the applicable legal principle is often impaired by the narrow limits to the jurisdictional domain of such tribunals.[48] This has two corollaries: first, if the relevant legal rule or principle cannot be authoritively established, many issues remain unclear. An unknown rule can neither be followed nor violated. In this way one of the major advantages of a legal settlement is diminished: i.e. that future quarrels can be avoided by taking the authoritatively established rule into account. The second corollary is that substitutes have to be found so that such impasses do not become totally disabling characteristics of the legal order. In this context advisory opinions, decisions by national institutions and scholarly expositions have to be mentioned.

In an arena that does not accept the principle of *stare decisis*, opinions defining the scope of legal principles are of decisive importance. Their weight, however, will largely depend upon their persuasive power rather than their institutional authority. Only in this sense does the importance of advisory opinions by the International Court of Justice become understandable. This also explains why legal scholars' writings are considered a "subsidiary source" of international law.[49]

National institutions often fail in establishing "the law" because of their partisan nature. The observer is then confronted with practices varying from state to state. The most obvious example of the partisan nature of decision-making is evident in the regulations of administrative agencies, whose rulings are bound by national policy. But even the independent courts have considerable difficulty acting in a detached fashion. They might have to defer to the executive agencies because of constitutional considerations or are bound by national legislative interpretations or precedents. Thus while a decision of a national court settles a particular dispute which has international legal ramifications, and while its decision might be authoritative as a precedent within a given domestic legal system, it will often fail to be considered an authoritative decision on the international law level.[50]

The lack of international credibility of domestic decisions has important implications for an assessment of international law as an instrument that impartially protects the interests of all claimants. It is clear that those parties which have the most developed domestic organi-

47. See Leo Gross, "The ICJ: Considerations of Requirements for Enhancing its Role in the International Legal Order," *The Future of the International Court of Justice*, Leo Gross, ed., 2 vols. (Dobbs Ferry, N.Y.: Oceana, 1976) vol. 1, 27; Daniel Partan, "Increasing the Effectiveness of the International Court," *Harvard International Law Journal* 18 (1977), 559-75.

48. Oscar Schachter, "The Enforcement of International Judicial and Arbitral Decisions," *American Journal of International Law* 54 (1960), 1-24.

49. See Art. 36 of the ICJ statute.

50. Thus decisions of national courts concerning the expropriation of foreign property are notorious for not having established clear rules in spite of a considerable amount of case law. Even worse is the situation in such gray areas as "creeping expropriations" by means of fiscal laws, health, or labor regulations.

zational structures as well as the most far reaching interests can adjudicate the largest number of disputes. Although no modern nation is currently in the same privileged position as England was with respect to maritime trade, differentials of development and power still matter. To that extent the third sophist objection mentioned above is not always beside the point. An even-handed assessment must admit, however, that national courts occasionally deviate from established national policies and try to come to terms with the changing structure of international society, thereby providing important new crystallization points for the development of international law.

Finally, the lack of effective channels for an authoritative determination of what the law is and how it can be modified, changed or rescinded, sheds new light on the problem of compliance and legal change. Non-compliance is usually conceived of in terms of transgressions in which an actor works for advantages in hopes of not being discovered. Even in the domestic arena, however, there are cases of non-compliance in defense of a valued position and with the explicit purpose of changing an objectionable rule. Although the latter strategy might open the door for all types of extralegal considerations and thus weaken the strength and autonomy of the legal order, significant distinctions exist between these two cases. Cynical acts of rascality, therefore, are treated differently than actions of civil disobedience. Nothing in the nature of the international legal order allows the neglect of such crucial differences. Precisely because the means of peaceful change in the international arena are few, and by and large ineffective, the violation of a legal norm is often not a pure act of lawlessness but rather part and parcel of a larger bargaining game for change. It would be a legalism of the worst kind to reduce the problem of compliance to the technical problem of ensuring norm conformity at the least cost through the elaboration of repressive techniques, while leaving the issue of justifying actions in terms of broader principles, demands for justice and pleas for peaceful change to history and philosophy.

The Status of Law in International Relations Theory

At this point it is useful to summarize some of the major arguments. Taking the sophistic objections as a point of departure, the argument about the nonexistence and ineffectiveness of an international legal order was shown to be flawed for two reasons. First, social interactions are in need of norms, because only then can the problem of coordination and interference be regulated. Second, it became clear that the conceptualization of rules and norms as constraints is erroneous since norms are also enabling and empowering instruments. The phenomenal growth of international—or better—transnational law is a response to the increasing interdependence of international life.

This in turn made the characterization of law in general and international law in particular as a "system of sanctioning prescriptions" inappropriate. A more fundamental clarification of the concept of law was required. This essay developed a concept of law that focuses less on the organizational features of law enforcement or the systemic character of the norms, but rather of the *contexts* in which norms are used and on the particular style of *reasoning* by which they provide decision-making guidance. In this sense norms in the international arena were shown not to be simple rules of comity or morals but to exhibit legal character.

These theoretical considerations provided the necessary criteria to judge the "primitiveness" of the international legal order. Primitiveness was seen to be a rather equivocal characterization of a legal order which showed some interesting complicating features that make it a type of system *sui generis*. A discussion of the weaknesses of international law followed. Aside from the lack of enforcement, several problems that usually are not treated adequately, were emphasized. One point concerned the weakness of any legal order that deals with organized groups rather than individuals, in particular, with the issue of group violence. In this case the limits of law as a means of conflict resolution could clearly be perceived, in both the international and domestic arena. This led to a more principled discussion of the role of adjudicative procedures and their function in international life. In accordance with the main thrust of the literature, this article stated that the primary contribution of such proceedings is to develop international law as an authoritative statement of what the law is rather than the settlement of a particular dispute. The frequent lack of authoritative determinations was then diagnosed as one of the major weaknesses. This weakness cannot easily be overcome by national institutions, administrative or judicial, because their determinations are not usually disinterested choices. The role of scholars as a more objective forum was emphasized in this context.

The third section ended with some short remarks concerning the problem of compliance with existing norms and the unresolved problem of peaceful change. The problematic nature of change via noncompliance with an objectionable norm was pointed out.

What remains to be sketched are the implications of a legal approach emphasizing a particular style of deliberative reasoning for theory building in international politics. Since the newest rage in theorizing about international relations is a concern with "regimes," such a clarification appears useful, especially because none of the insights from international law or jurisprudence have been taken into account in the pertinent literature.[51] The subject of custom seems highly relevant to the regime discussion, but one cannot help thinking that busy social scientists are about to rediscover the wheel. Worse still, there are justifiable suspicions that the wheel will not be discovered unless fundamental changes are made in the research program.

Since norms and rules do not directly determine the outcome of decisions, what role do they play as underlying factors? While one could argue that norms influence events in a probabilistic fashion, this does not solve the dilemma. The concept of probability is problematic, and subjectivist and objectivist interpretations of probability appear to remain irreconcilable. Finally, what serves and is accepted as an explanation in given situation cannot be derived from the logical structure of the explanation but rather from interests guiding the inquiry and from contextual factors. Explaining often means elaborating, putting events in context, or perhaps only justifying the action in terms of vaguely articulated but shared standards.[52]

If this is correct—and all indications seem to corroborate the evidence—then the chances for a grand theory of international relations are small if not nonexistent. A grand theory of international relations is missing exactly for the same reasons that there is no grand

51. See Krasner, ed., *International Organization* 36 (Spring 1982).
52. See Hannah Pitkin, *Wittgenstein on Justice* (Berkeley: University of California Press, 1972).

theory of life. True, there are models for regularities which might in certain circumstances develop the firmness of lawlike forces, but this type of explanation remains tied to rigorous abstractions as the *homo oeconomicus* so amply demonstrates. The problem is not so much that these models are unreliable, but that they create blind spots (i.e., everything that does not fit these models is declared irrelevant). It is, however, simply not true that nothing sensible can be said and that nothing worth knowing exists outside the standard positivist framework.

Since the present article is indebted more to jurisprudence and conceptual analysis than the "grand theory" tradition of international relations, perhaps it illustrates a type of analysis which, through conceptual clarifications, can lead to deeper and deeper levels of reflection. It is a discourse rather than a theory. Such an approach is definitely useful when the role of law in social life is investigated. Since norms are not "causes" for behavior but are part of the deliberation necessary to make a choice, a contextual and interpretative frame of reference had to be chosen in order to "understand" human action. Only in this way can a particular type of question sensibly be asked without being ruled out by the framework. Thus what is at issue in explaining an action is often not the cause, but whether the decision could have been made differently, whether a choice was possible, whether responsibility was incurred and can be assessed, and whether good reasons can be provided for acting in this and not in another fashion. Since such assessments include normative terms a descriptivist framework is insufficient, as shown by G.E. Moore's argument concerning the "naturalistic fallacy."[53]

International relations specialists would do well to remember the limitations of the positivist approaches and to reflect critically upon them. An international jurisprudence in which this critical and reflective attitude is preserved is essential for the education of future decision-makers. Only in this way can the human project in the domestic and international arena be examined as a continuous creative effort. It is not determined by the "objective forces" of history or fate, but is a project for which everyone bears responsibility. The problem is not simply that Thrasymmachos can be shown to be mostly wrong, but he must be persuaded to better his ways.

53. G.E. Moore, *Principia Ethica* (Cambridge: Cambridge University Press, 1959).

Part II
Beyond Realism: Methodological Conundrums

[4]

LANGUAGE, METHOD AND THE NATURE OF INTERNATIONAL LAW*

By PHILIP ALLOTT[1]

A LITERARY approach to the presentation of international law persists. The style of the Early Fathers of international law has been handed down, almost as a tradition, through the eminent writers of international law's Scholastic period, in the middle and late nineteenth century, to most modern writers. There have been marginal changes of tone and vocabulary, but there has been preserved an underlying structure of thought and argument which is more literary than scientific and more businesslike than concerned. International law formerly shared this style and structure of thought and argument with at least one tradition of philosophy and the social sciences. But, in those studies, widely accepted and far-reaching changes of language and method have occurred over recent years, tending to replace the tone of the inspired dilettante with that of the technician. In international law, too, there have in recent years been a number of writers, particularly in the United States, who have adopted what appear to be a new style and a new method—novelties which have dismayed and disorientated some international lawyers but which, on closer analysis, raise important questions about the method and even the nature and function of international law. The present study considers the language of international law, its relationship to method and the contribution which a new style and method can make to international law.

I. Hall on a State's Rights in the Territorial Sea

As an illustration of the classical style, the following is an extract from a discussion of the legal character of the territorial sea in W. E. Hall's *International Law*:[2]

> Of the marginal seas, straits and enclosed waters which were regarded at the beginning of the present century as being susceptible of appropriation, the case of the first is the simplest. In claiming its marginal seas as property a State is able to satisfy the condition of valid appropriation, because a narrow belt along a coast can be effectively commanded from the coast itself either by guns or by means of a coast-guard. In fact also such a belt is always appropriated, because States reserve to their own subjects the enjoyment of its fisheries, or, in other words, take from it the natural products which it is capable of yielding. It may be added that, unless the right to exercise control were

[1] Legal Counsellor in the Foreign and Commonwealth Office. The views expressed are the author's personal views.

[2] (1st edn., 1880), pp. 125–6.

admitted, no sufficient security would exist for lives and property of the subjects upon land. . . . Accordingly, on the assumption that any part of the sea is susceptible of appropriation, no serious question can arise as to the existence of property in marginal waters.

(The words omitted are six lines in which the author illustrates the consequences which would follow if the coastal State did not have a right of control.)

By the standards by which English prose style is normally judged, this is a piece of good average English prose. The ideas are simply expressed; the vocabulary is neither too commonplace nor over-refined; the sentences are well-constructed and confident. It is not entirely free from patent ambiguity, for example in the third sentence and in the last quoted sentence. Also, there is a diffused ambiguity about the whole passage. Closer examination makes its validity and value difficult to assess. It should be stressed that the quoted passage is taken out of context, the context having, in particular, already carefully reviewed the development of the law and practice relating to the appropriation of the territorial sea. But the quoted passage is the essence of the writer's own view on the matter. It is the point at which he asks us to join him in drawing a conclusion as to the 'present state of the question'.

Hall, in the passage quoted above, uses three different general forms of proposition to support, or to tend to, the conclusion that a State has property in its marginal waters. Put in a highly abbreviated form for the purpose of demonstration they are:

1. A State may only appropriate what it can effectively control and a belt of marginal sea can be effectively controlled by the coastal State.
2. A narrow belt of water along their coasts is always appropriated by States.
3. If a belt of marginal sea were not appropriated by the coastal State, lives and property on land could not be sufficiently protected.

These three forms of proposition are archetypal in classical international law method and, in the present study, it will be necessary to refer to them on various occasions in different connections. They may be termed the 'autological' or deductive form ('given an underlying rule of internal logical consistency in international law, rule B follows, deductively or analytically or, in a sense, tautologically, from rule A'); the empirical form ('this is the practice of States, the situation of fact, the history of the matter'); and the teleological or policy form ('this is what leads to the best results').

To consider further the nature of these forms of argument and, incidentally, to show that none of Hall's argumentation works in any logical or even rigorous way to justify his conclusion, the arguments may be set out more fully as follows. The premises of the autological form are:

1 (*a*) a State may only appropriate what it can effectively control;
1 (*b*) a belt of marginal sea can be effectively controlled by the coastal State.

At first reading, the extract from Hall might seem to be implying as a conclusion that—

1 (*c*) therefore, the coastal State may appropriate a belt of marginal sea.

Unconsciously or even consciously, such an implication runs through the reader's mind at the first reading and colours his impression of the whole passage. But such a conclusion would involve an obvious fallacy. It would be correct if the 'only' element were omitted from 1 (*a*) and if 1 (*a*) were rewritten as—

1 (*aa*) a State may appropriate anything which it can effectively control.

If that were the first premise, then the conclusion would be correct as in 1 (*c*). But, of course, such a proposition would be a surprising rule of international law, justifying much which international law prohibits, for example in relation to the illegal acquisition of territory. In passing, it may be remarked that this kind of fallacy is relevant to current controversies of great importance as to the extent of the territorial sea and the rights of States in the sea-bed. The tendency of States to do anything which they consider themselves capable of doing and likely to get away with, is the very tendency which international law must often resist. It is also apparent that the autological form of argument depends for its validity and value on agreement as to the premises. The first premise is in the form of a statement of a rule of international law and this cannot be proved by empirical evidence in any direct sense. It is 'proved' either by reference to authority (a treaty, an authoritative writing, a decided case), or as the conclusion of an argument in the teleological form, or it is itself a ruling, that is to say, it is stated by an authoritative source in a situation where the mere statement of the proposition validates it (for example, in the course of a judgment of a court or the decision of an arbitral tribunal). (The first premise may also be derived by deduction from another rule of international law, but then precisely the same verification problem arises in respect of the rule from which it is derived.) It is obvious that each of the methods of verification referred to is itself liable to challenge and subject to verification. It would have to be shown that the authority relied upon is authoritative, that the policy considerations acceptably support the conclusion, that the authority pronouncing the proposition has authority to do so. Each of these 'proofs' is in its turn liable to challenge and subject to verification. Much more will be said below of this question of verification. For the present, it is enough to underline that the first proposition of an argument, such as in 1 (*a*) above, self-contained and confident as it may seem, is no more effective than the argument on which it is itself based. As regards 1 (*a*) itself, for example, one may immediately wonder whether it can be literally correct, for instance in relation to airspace (even if the effective control and appropriation of airspace were admittedly not matters of which Hall could have taken adequate account). One such doubt is enough to leave the reader uneasy about the validity of such a proposition in the context in which it is used.

As to the second premise, 1 (*b*), this again is liable to challenge and subject to verification. There are many doubts and objections which could be raised in respect of such a proposition.

But it may charitably be assumed that Hall did not intend, in using proposition 1 above, to imply any such conclusion as in 1 (*c*). It may be that he was merely reassuring the reader, as it were, on a technical point. Perhaps he was, in effect, saying that the correct conclusion to draw from 1 (*a*) and 1 (*b*) is—

> 1 (*cc*) therefore, a belt of marginal sea is not one of those things which a State cannot in principle appropriate (leaving on one side the question of whether, as a matter of law, it *may* appropriate a belt of marginal sea).

If this is to be taken as the real intention of the first proposition, then it cannot be said to have taken matters very much further forward, and all rests on the remaining propositions to show that a State *may* appropriate a belt of marginal sea.

Proposition 2 implies a second proposition of the form—

> 2 (*b*) that which States always do is permitted by international law.

This would lead to a conclusion—

> 2 (*c*) therefore, the appropriation by States of a narrow belt of water along their coasts is permitted by international law.

Proposition 2 (*b*) obviously cannot be right as it stands. Sometimes that which States do is something which is not permitted by international law. It would be absurd to say that international law requires States to do what States always do. This is, incidentally, an absurdity involved in Marxism: how can one distinguish between the relative values of events if one asserts that events determine their own value, unless one finds, as Marxists ultimately and mysteriously find, a set of values which are in some way autonomous of events? Similarly in international law, States do not 'always' do the same thing, which means that either everything which States do is permitted, however contradictory, or that there is some way of extracting a general rule from the particular and contradictory cases. And this is no doubt the relevance of the second proposition in Hall's argument. Proposition 2 (*b*) is probably a crude statement of the traditional view of customary international law. The traditional view would want to rewrite it as—

2 (*bb*) international law requires States to do that which States have customarily done in circumstances in which it may be inferred that they regard themselves as obliged to do what they do.

Other modifications of the argument would be needed. A proposition would have to be introduced—which might itself be controversial—that a State is permitted by international law to do that which it is not required by international law to refrain from doing. If 2 (*a*) were then rephrased to match 2 (*bb*)—by saying that a narrow belt of water is customarily claimed by States in circumstances, etc.—the conclusion at 2 (*c*) would be adequately supported. But all this is to read a good deal into what Hall has written, and the fact is that he does not assert, let alone provide evidence to support, a proposition that States claim a territorial sea *opinio juris*.

As in the case of proposition 1, however, it may be objected that, of course, Hall was not intending to assert any dramatic proposition about the self-justifying character of State practice or suggesting that the right to appropriate the territorial sea is sufficiently proved by the fact that States always do it. Perhaps he was again merely reassuring the reader, in effect saying: 'Look, what I am saying cannot be shocking because States always do what I say international law permits them to do.' But, even on such a basis, one would be entitled to raise some objections to the bold assertion of what States always do, and as to whether it follows from the fact that they assert the right to exclusive fisheries that they should be entitled to regard the territorial sea as their property for all purposes. But, whatever the substantive merits of the proposition, if the second proposition is again essentially another reassurance to the reader, then, so far as the strict demonstration of the conclusion is concerned, all must depend on the third proposition.

Proposition 3 looks much more like a direct piece of argument, although, as used by Hall, it is given the appearance of a makeweight by the introductory words—'It may be added that . . .'. The proposition seems to imply a second premise of the form—

3 (*b*) international law permits States to do that which must be done to ensure that lives and property on land can be sufficiently protected.

This would lead to the conclusion—

3 (*c*) therefore, international law permits the coastal State to appropriate a belt of marginal sea.

Put in this form the argument would be essentially autological—saying what the internal consequences of a given rule of international law are as applied to a given situation. But proposition 3 (*b*) is an unlikely sounding rule of international law and it does not seem likely that it would entirely reflect what Hall was saying or what his readers would generally understand him to mean. More likely is it that proposition 3 depends on a more generalized, teleological version of 3 (*b*) of the form—

3 (*bb*) It is the purpose of international law to bring about results which, taking into account the conflict of the reasonable interests of States, allow each State to maximize the protection of its most basic concerns as a State.

Another proposition would then have to be introduced on the lines—

3 (*bc*) the protection of lives and property on its land is one of the most basic concerns of a State.

If these two propositions are then read with a slight reworking of the original proposition 3, on the lines—

3 (*bcc*) the appropriation of a belt of marginal sea by the coastal State is a means for it to maximize protection of lives and property on its land consistently with the reasonable interests of other States—

then it would be possible to conclude—

3 (*c*) therefore, international law permits a coastal State to appropriate a belt of marginal sea.

This rather un-legal sounding argument is, strangely enough, the one which emerges most unambiguously from the extract quoted from Hall. It seems to do less violence to his text than the implications drawn in respect of the other two arguments. It is clearly not a mere 'reassurance' argument. It is a 'policy' argument relying on agreement between the writer and the reader on fundamental matters concerning international law itself and as to the correct relative weights to be given to the conflicting interests of the States involved.

Hence the net effect of Hall's argument may be put in this form: 'It is not inconsistent with other rules of international law (autological argument) nor with the settled practice of States (empirical argument) to say that it is a rule of international law that a coastal State may appropriate a belt of marginal sea (conclusion—rule of international law) and the enjoyment of such a right enables the coastal State fairly to protect its interests (teleological or policy argument).'

For the moment it is enough to note that three arguments of varying levels of abstraction and with quite different verification principles are put together to support a rule of international law which is of a quite different logical order, containing the 'may' form of the verb (which is essentially the same as the 'ought' form, into which the rule could easily be transposed).

II. Gidel on the Legal Character of the Territorial Sea

In order to get the classical style into focus, it is worth looking at it from another angle—as seen in an extended discussion of a highly controversial question by a distinguished French writer. In *Le Droit international public de la mer*,[1] Gilbert Gidel deals with the question of the legal character of the territorial sea at considerable length. Extracts quoted below have been translated for the purpose of the present study.

Gidel begins with the resounding statement that the question of the legal character of the territorial sea, which had been a matter of debate for a long time, should now be regarded as settled as a result of the Hague Codification Conference of 1930 in which the unanimous opinion of States had been expressed: to the effect that the territorial sea is a part of the territory of the coastal State and is under its sovereignty. He nevertheless goes on to consider the controversy which had previously existed.

He first states the two fundamentally opposed views. The one regards the territorial sea as a part of the high seas subject to certain restrictions in favour of the coastal State to meet its legitimate interests. The other view regards the territorial sea as part of the territory of the coastal State subject to certain restrictions on the powers of the coastal State. Gidel says that it is quite wrong to say, as some authors had said, that the two alternatives lead to the same results and that the dispute is purely verbal. On the contrary, legal consequences follow if the sovereignty theory is accepted, for example in that the coastal State can extend its powers up to the point where it meets the restrictions imposed by law. And, in any case, 'a general principle, in all juridical matters which admit of a general principle, is necessary as a guide in case of difficulties'.[2]

Already two methodological comments should be made. In the first place, Gidel's basic view, many times repeated in the subsequent discussion, is that the unanimous opinion of States expressed in the Hague Conference had resolved the matter. What are the implications of such an

[1] (1934), vol. 3, chapter I of book II. [2] Ibid., p. 155.

assertion? The opinions of governments were expressed in the form of their replies to the questionnaire sent to them prior to the Conference, and in the unanimous adoption at the Conference on a provisional basis of thirteen draft articles, one of which contained the 'sovereignty' thesis. But these articles were not inserted in any treaty at the time, owing to disagreements on other matters, and hence did not acquire any further positive legal significance. Also, there were forty-seven States represented at the 1930 Conference. What significance is to be attached to the fact that there are now more than 130 States in the world, many of which did not exist as such in 1930? Again, what significance is to be attached to the fact that, had the Conference been held, say, thirty years earlier, it is most unlikely that there would have been unanimity? (Indeed, Gidel himself makes this very point, using the year 1914, at another stage in his discussion of the matter.) Twenty-eight years later the Geneva Conference adopted a text almost identical, in this matter, to that adopted in 1930. This is now to be found in Article 1 of the Convention on the Territorial Sea and Contiguous Zone; but the precise words used, with their qualification relating to the 'other rules of international law', have enabled some writers to argue that governments did not simply accept the 'sovereignty' theory, but something more complicated. Finally, what is the significance of the word 'unanimously'? Would it have been enough if it had been the opinion of the overwhelming majority of governments? This has become a highly substantive question in relation to the various statements by majorities in the United Nations General Assembly as to the content of international law on a given subject. Despite these objections, it is perhaps true to say that, as with Hall in the extract previously considered, Gidel is partly reassuring the reader that the view which he is about to defend is that accepted by so many governments, even if it is not accepted by all writers. He is perhaps also saying that, in terms of the traditional view of customary international law, it cannot be insignificant that so many governments have expressed this opinion and will probably act accordingly in practice in the future.

The other methodological point to note is that Gidel has dismissed in short order the argument that the whole dispute is in any case only about words. To do this, (*a*) he gives an illustration of the consequences of adopting one theory (although it must be remarked that the illustration could be faulted as an answer to the argument in question, which could easily have been to the effect that, *provided that* the two theories are fully and efficiently worked out, they lead to the same thing); and (*b*) he asserts the utility of having a single general principle to resolve difficult cases. Similar objection could be taken to this point, on the grounds that it may be that, if both theories are fully and efficiently worked out, no *lacunae* need remain such as would be resolved differently by the different theories.

Gidel's next step, oddly enough, is to provide, very briefly, some supporting material for the sovereignty view. Twenty-three lines of text are introduced by the assertion:[1] 'The trend [in favour of the sovereignty view] is no longer in doubt today either in theory or in the field of positive law.' To support this, he refers to resolutions recently adopted, in fact after difficult and controversial discussion, by various international law associations; he refers to the work of 'the eminent professor and Judge of the Permanent Court, Mr. Bustamente' and to recent works by Fedozzi and Jessup. As to positive law, he refers again to the preparatory work and the draft article adopted by the Hague Conference. It is difficult to resist the impression that Gidel is here in the business of predisposing the reader before getting to his very full exposition of the views of other writers.

Gidel next relies on the researches of Raested (1913) to show that the dispute is of remarkably recent origin (mid-nineteenth century and later). He quotes Niemeyer, who had acted as scorer in the contest and who had found that, in writings between 1850 and 1914, there were twenty-two writers in favour of the sovereignty theory and twelve against. A footnote lists the names *à titre de curiosité* and mentions a particularly curious case, that of Perels who changed sides between his first edition of 1881 and his second edition of 1905. Gidel adopts the view of Fedozzi:[2]

> One must indeed subscribe to the summing-up of Fedozzi: 'The legal character of the *territorial* sea is that which is indicated by that expression taken in its literal sense and the doctrinal discussions which have gone on and have continued up to the present day have only complicated and confused a problem which, originally, had been exposed in the most simple and the most exact terms.'

The fact that these are the words of Fedozzi and not Gidel allows one to withold comment on such a dismissive statement, except to note that it asserts Gidel's conclusion for a third time, this time at the end of a purely historical passage, in a fashion which will find an echo in the extracts from the work of Professor McDougal considered below.

Gidel's detailed examination of the two theories begins with a distinction which he draws between two versions of the *mare liberum* theory—the 'coastal servitudes' system of de la Pradelle and the 'right of preservation' system of Fauchille. He says of the first version that the talent of its author was not able to assure its success despite its ingenuity and despite the fact that it seems to deal with the two facts that not only do the limits of territorial waters vary as between States, but also one and the same State may operate different limits for different purposes. He quotes Fauchille's criticism of it at length and says that de la Pradelle's theory rests on two essential ideas 'about which the least one can say is that they are of an extreme fragility'. The sea is *not*, says Gidel, *res communis* and he quotes in

[1] (1934), vol. 3, chapter I of book II, p. 156. [2] Ibid., pp. 157–8.

his support the 'vigorous words' of Charles Rousseau. And, 'the notion of international servitudes is, at the present time, almost universally rejected'.[1] Even those who admit the existence of international servitudes do not admit the existence of 'natural servitudes':[2]

> All servitudes presuppose the existence of two territories, two domains belonging to two different States, one of which is the servient and the other the dominant. Is this really the situation here? The dominant power exists without doubt: it is the territory of the coastal State. The existence of the servient power is more doubtful. To affirm it, the author must admit that the sea is a *res communis* and that it belongs, as such, to the community of States. For many authors such an idea is incorrect and it is certainly very disputable and is one on which this system of coastal servitudes, tottering despite the elegance of its presentation, does not manage to find any solid basis. In the end, this system, which would wish to be a reflection of the facts, does not square with them in various respects: what reality can a theory claim which refuses to the coastal State the right of police and the right of exclusive fishery in the waters which adjoin its territory?

Quite apart from the occasionally emotive use of language in this passage, it raises some problems from a methodological point of view. Gidel's refutation may be analysed as follows:

(1) Servitudes require that there are two 'land-owners': one owning the land over which the servitude exists; the other owning the adjoining land and enjoying the servitude;
(2) the sea is not owned by anyone, therefore one of the requirements for a servitude is not satisfied;
(3) in any case, a servitude as postulated by de la Pradelle does not give the coastal State rights which it in fact has (or, perhaps, must obviously have or should have).

As to the first point, Gidel, having implied that there are no such things as international servitudes (the concept is, he says, 'almost universally rejected') must be saying either that, if they did exist, they would have a certain character, or else that, working by analogy from domestic law, they would have to have this character. As to the second point, Gidel relies on the view of 'many authors' and, for himself, says that the concept is certainly very disputable. Needless to say, the dispute as to the legal character of the high seas is complicated and all one can say for present purposes is that it is surprising that Gidel did not admit that the sea may be, *in some special sense*, *res communis*. Indeed, at another point he admits that the sea, although it does not belong to all, 'must serve for use by all'. Perhaps he could have gone on to admit that it could be also said that all States therefore have, to this extent, rights in respect of the high seas. Could not this be regarded as making it a kind of *res communis*, so that it would be possible to say that

[1] (1934), vol. 3, chapter I of book II, p. 160. [2] Ibid., p. 161.

some kind of servitude may exist in respect of the territorial sea? The third point is difficult to assess. Either it is a policy assertion ('we must find an answer which allows the coastal State to do things which it obviously should be able to do') or it is an objection on inductive grounds ('you, de la Pradelle, have failed to find a theory which fits the facts'). Implicit here is the difficulty in arguing on its own level with a hypothesis (de la Pradelle's theory) which was presumably derived by induction from positive law but which may have been used to demonstrate by deduction the existence of other rules of law. To deal with such a hypothesis a more careful and subtle form of argument is required than that offered by Gidel.

One further point to make at this stage is to note how incestuous the discussion of this matter is. Gidel makes very extensive reference to the work of other writers and bestows appropriate epithets on each of them. He is able to sort out the good from the bad, the right from the wrong. He treats them as if they were natural events occurring and observed in an external world of fact. The writing is also incestuous in relation to the law itself. There is an assumption of a closed system of an almost theological character within which there can be right and wrong deductions—there are things which can be done with the concept of servitudes and things which cannot be done. The implication is that, for right-thinking men, there can be no two ways about the rightness and wrongness of such deductions.

Gidel next deals with Fauchille. He praises him for having disposed of de la Pradelle with 'decisive arguments'. But he condemns Fauchille for having, in his turn, put forward 'a system which also leads to inadmissible results and which, starting from the notion of a right of preservation, leads back to the most *a priori* concepts of natural law'.[1] It is not known whether Fauchille would have resented this charge that his theory was in the end a natural-law theory. It is interesting to note the tone of Gidel's remark. Despite the fact that natural law has survived as such in Catholic France, it is possible that Gidel thought that he had almost said enough by way of condemnation in exposing the natural-law character of Fauchille's theory. Natural law is a perennial problem of international law—if not *the* perennial problem. It will be contended below that Professor McDougal is only a contemporary actor in this continuing drama. But Fauchille's right of preservation is as much a 'policy' concept as a natural-law concept and it is possible to see here, in Gidel's attitude, an embryo which was to grow into the fully fledged modern-dress debate of recent years on law/policy. In a way reminiscent of McDougal, Fauchille argues that the right of preservation is a fundamental right which can be exercised on the sea, since the sea belongs to no one, on the condition that the State exercising the right respects the equal right of preservation of other States. Gidel has

[1] Ibid., pp. 161–2.

something to say at a later stage about this technique of postulating competing claims of States.

He reviews at length nine consequences which Fauchille had drawn from his theory and which Fauchille himself had contrasted with the consequences of the 'servitudes' theory. Gidel says why he sets them out at length:[1]

> . . . it is interesting to go through them in order to establish the numerous points on which both systems diverge from positive law. After going through them, one will be led to the inevitable conclusion that the only theory which is logically satisfying and in conformity with international practice is the old theory, from which it would have been better never to have departed, that the territorial sea is a part of the territory of the coastal State, over which it possesses the same rights as over its land territory.

It is important to note the phrases 'logically satisfying' and 'in conformity with international practice'. They are implied to be the true criteria for correct international law. They correspond to the autological and empirical forms of argument referred to in part I of the present study. Where, it may be asked, is the teleological or policy form of argument? This remains to be seen.

Gidel does not mince his words in commenting on Fauchille's views:[2]

> Here again this conclusion is in complete contradiction with positive law.—
> Nothing could be less correct (see below, Chapter II, right of innocent passage).

After Fauchille, he deals in fifteen lines with various halfway-house systems, ending with the laconic sentence:

> No doubt such systems barely provide explanations of the solutions laid down by positive law; but at least they have the advantage of not surrendering to a disregard of the realities.

Gidel's oracular references to 'positive law' call for comment. He appears to mean by this the first-level rules of international law which flow directly from the practice of States. It would follow that the exercise on which he, Fauchille and de la Pradelle were engaged in this particular matter, is a higher level of law-finding. It is the inductive process of arranging facts (the first-level rules of law) into a theory, rather than the construction of the rules from the raw material of State practice. Two problems arise, however. Gidel himself firmly asserts that legal consequences flow from adopting one or other of the various theories. It is, he says, not merely a verbal dispute. This must mean that the second-level theory affects and alters in some way the first-level rules, although it is on first level rules that the second-level theory was largely supposed to have been based or, at least, was constantly to be tested. It was noted above that this particular confusion means that it is difficult to know how to argue against the

[1] (1934), vol. 3, chapter I of book II, p. 163. [2] Ibid., p. 168.

second-level theory. It should now also be noted that this confusion gives rise to a more general difficulty. It may be impossible in principle to operate the inductive and deductive processes entirely separately in any piece of reasoning which is at all complex. But the total interpenetration and confusion of the two processes in writing such as Gidel's does not allow the reader any opportunity, or any easy opportunity, to know where he stands at any point in the course of the argument. He can never be sure whether, at any particular moment, he is on the way down from a higher to a lower level of abstraction, by way of deduction, or whether he is on the way up, by induction, from a lower to a higher level.

The second problem is that, if a theory is in some way an explanation of, or is constantly to be checked against, first-level rules, there must be some way of knowing what the first-level rules are. Gidel tends to be categoric about such rules. In one of the sharp comments quoted above, for example, he tells the reader to look at another chapter of his book to see that Fauchille is wrong in saying that foreign vessels cannot as of right use the territorial sea to travel from one port to another in the coastal State. But, generally, he simply asserts what is or is not consistent with positive law, despite the fact that there are clearly some serious differences of view among the writers as to the first-level rules in question. Gidel's own treatment of a first-level problem will be considered briefly below.

Before moving into forward gear in his treatment of the matter, Gidel delivers a sharp rebuke to those proto-McDougals who tried to resolve the problem by postulating competing claims by the coastal and non-coastal States, and, in doing so, he almost lights on one of McDougal's own terminologies:[1]

> Systems which have sought to reject the pure and simple sovereignty of the coastal State over the territorial sea have in reality started from an artificial opposition between the idea of the freedom of passage of foreign ships in the territorial sea and the idea of the rights and needs of the coastal State. This is a facile method, frequently useful for giving a gloss to the presentation of international law problems by setting against each other—and one can do it in almost every question because of the very nature of the relations to which international law applies—the 'cosmopolitan' principle, here the freedom of the seas, and the 'particularist' principle, here the sovereignty of the coastal State. It is a superficial method of exposition rather than a solid and profound way of looking at things. The truth is, at least in this question of the legal regime of the territorial sea, that freedom of navigation in the proximity of the coast and the needs or the 'rights' of the coastal State are not conflicting ideas, but two complementary ideas. It is this artificial opposition between the interests of the coastal State and those of other States which has led to the search for a different regime for the territorial sea from that of the land territory of the State.

It is possible to feel that Gidel is here almost on the point of breaking new and more subtle ground in his consideration of the matter, but that

[1] Ibid., pp. 168–9.

he is held back by his intellectual background which led him to prefer static and logically satisfying explanations rather than dynamic, amorphous and experientially satisfying explanations.

Gidel next states for the fifth and sixth times what he considers to be the correct view of the situation, separating them by a very brief statement of a further consideration of a rather different order:[1]

> The territorial sea is merely submerged territory; it differs from ordinary territory only in that a certain volume of water is interposed at each point of the territory between the earth itself and the air which, normally, lies immediately above it. The difference is physical; it comports no essential legal difference.

The use of the verb 'is' in the first sentence repays study. It is a rhetorical or hypothetical 'is'. Gidel then shows once again, but in more detail, how the Hague Conference supported the 'sovereignty' theory, albeit with nuances between the attitudes of the various governments. The next section entitled 'Causes which give to the maritime territory a legal aspect different from the land territory' should not be regarded as conflicting with the extract last quoted, which merely denied an 'essential legal difference'. The physical reasons for the differences are mentioned and Gidel says that the legal regime must change in step with changes in means of navigation, etc.—which comes near to being a policy consideration. The geographical and political reasons turn on the fact that the territorial sea is a 'frontier area', an area of contact between different political domains, the place of meeting of contradictory forces. Gidel had been impressed by some recent socio-anthropological work on the significance of frontier areas (translated into legal terms by de la Pradelle, who was apparently to be regarded as being as right on this matter as he was wrong about coastal servitudes). Gidel uses this interesting analogy to explain why, although the territorial sea is essentially no different from the land territory, it is nevertheless subject to a series of special rules, and why, incidentally, territorial waters are automatically transferred when territory is transferred and why they cannot exist except as an adjunct of land territory. It is difficult to know whether Gidel means the analogy to be taken literally, as international anthropological fact, or metaphorically, as a convenient way of picturing the situation, or inductively, as a *post hoc* rationalization of the peculiar legal rules relating to the territorial sea. Surprisingly, he deals with the Bynkershoek/Pufendorf protection theory only in a footnote, suggesting that it is too narrow as compared with his 'frontier area' theory.

After a short discussion of the word 'sovereignty' and after insisting that the coastal State has sovereignty and not merely sovereign rights over the

[1] (1934), vol. 3, chapter I of book II, pp. 169–70.

territorial sea, he states again the correct view as revealed by the 1930 Conference, and ends by saying:[1]

> Once it has been said that the coastal State possesses in respect of the territorial sea, which is submerged territory, the same powers as over its land territory, there is no need to draw up a restrictive list of such powers. On the contrary, the drawing-up of such a list is required by those doctrines which attribute to the coastal State only strictly limited rights in the adjacent waters. . . . [In accordance with the 'sovereignty' principle] the only powers excluded are those which customary law has limited (innocent passage), and those which the coastal State, to a greater or lesser extent, has by agreement or unilaterally given up.

It seems most probable that Gidel's academic colleagues would have read this part of his book as polemical. His view—the 'sovereignty' view—had won at the 1930 Conference and now was the time to administer the *coup de grâce* to the other views. But the fact is that all writing on international law, at least on controversial matters, must be intrinsically polemical. The writer has seen a way of putting the matter, has worked out, in the quiet of his study, what the rules of law must be, and his job is to get his reader to agree with him. At the same time, it is also the case that Gidel's is a leading work on the subject, consulted as a work of authority by practitioners of international law. It might seriously affect the attitude of a Government in a given situation if it were told that the legal position is that it may treat the territorial sea as if it were land territory, so long as it does not interfere with innocent passage and the other specific rights of other States. And reliance on the opposite thesis could, likewise, seriously affect the conduct of a government. Thus, Gidel's consideration of this subject is a contribution to the finding of international law, albeit at a certain level of abstraction.

It is not possible to demonstrate the point adequately within the compass of the present study, but the fact is that Gidel's method is not essentially different when he is dealing with more obviously detailed, first-level law-finding problems. With regard to the question of the passage of warships through the territorial sea, for example, he begins once again by saying that there is a great division of opinion in the matter. He states the general views of a number of writers and then quotes the relevant passage from Oppenheim (4th edition), saying that it seems the most 'judicious' treatment of the matter. Oppenheim considered that it was only possible to say two things with certainty on the question: first, that a usage had been established to the effect that passage should not be refused in time of peace, provided that it is innocent and does not constitute a threat; secondly, that it is a rule of customary international law that passage cannot be refused in areas of the sea which form part of international traffic routes. Gidel quotes to

[1] Ibid., pp. 191–2.

similar effect various codification documents, including the work of the 1930 Conference. As to the formula adopted by the latter, he says:[1]

> The formula satisfies the tendency expressed by the American and British delegations. The passage of foreign warships through the territorial sea is not a right, but something which is tolerated. This is the opinion which seems preferable. It is better suited to protecting certain States against the abuses to which they could be exposed because of turbulent or indiscreet neighbours.

Gidel then describes the way in which the 1930 Conference treated the question of whether the coastal State can regulate the passage of warships (answer: yes); and, in particular, whether it could require advance notification or authorization (answer: no). Gidel points to the fact that it is rare for national legislation to require such notification or authorization and refers to the replies of governments to the Codification Conference questionnaire.

As compared with the extract from Hall which was considered in Part I, Gidel's style is certainly more assertorical, more authoritarian, and, in one way, still more difficult to assess from a methodological point of view. The deduction/induction problem has been referred to above, but that is a general problem. The particular problem is the degree to which value-considerations are hidden. Academic values are openly exposed: 'incorrect'; 'judicious'; 'logically satisfactory'; 'very pertinent'; 'decisive argument'. But social, moral and political values are less apparent. There is a feeling almost of inhibition, preventing Gidel from going even as far as Hall in making his value-preferences explicit. But it is interesting to see that in the very last quoted extract he refers to the protection of the coastal State in an explicitly teleological or policy way; and the rather uncharacteristic discussion of the anthropological significance of frontier areas in the main body of the discussion could be a garbled form of policy argument: in effect saying that anthropologists tell us that peoples are very sensitive about frontier areas, and we, as international lawyers, should bear that in mind. Also, of course, there are countless choices made in the course of the discussion between alternative points of view and any choice, which is not analytical or tautological, involves the application of a value, however unexpressed or even concealed that value may be.

It remains to determine, in relation to both Hall and Gidel, how writing of this kind works in a useful way, and whether the method involved is characteristic of, and essential to, international law or whether it is fortuitous and replaceable.

[1] (1934), vol. 3, chapter I of book II, p. 284.

III. The Classical Method and the Nature of International Law

Writing such as that quoted from Hall and Gidel is made possible, in the first place, by a number of assumptions made by the writer about his audience. It proceeds on a basic assumption that the audience would be that cohesive élite to which the writers themselves belonged, that is to say, an élite sharing certain moral, political and social values, and values relating to the conduct of academic discourse. In the case of Gidel, there is also the impression that, within the cohesive élite, he had two kinds of audience in mind—his academic colleagues and his pupils (in the broad sense, meaning those who will use the book as a work of reference). To both audiences he directs a display of authority, in contrast with the sweet reasonableness of Hall's style. Gidel exercises skill in combining the *de haut en bas* variety of authority with what may be called the 'interpersonal domination' variety. But, in the case of both writers, the essence of the discourse is precisely the same. An argument is to be presented in such a fashion, and to be continued for just so long, as is necessary to produce a movement of assent in the mind of a sensible reader, on the assumption that the reader is not a Martian or even a Marxist, but a person who shares sufficient of the values of the writer to ensure that a dialogue between them is not a meaningless waste of time.

So far as the procedural values, the values of academic discourse, are concerned the writer, like a participant in a conversation, would not expect his audience to interrupt at each sentence with fundamental objections about method, verification procedures or basic assumptions. Nor would he expect that everything which he asserts without supporting argument or evidence would be immediately challenged on that ground as well as on its merits. Why should not a State appropriate what it cannot control? What precisely is meant by 'effectively' control? What sense of the word 'control' is intended? 'Appropriate' in what sense—complete property rights or a bundle of special rights or what? Must there be an act of appropriation or is it a deeming process? Do States really 'always' appropriate a territorial sea? What does 'always' mean—at all times or in all cases? Is it really the case that a State could not protect itself without a territorial sea? If so, should it not have a further belt of sea for the protection of the territorial sea, and why do not land-locked states have 'territorial lands'? What is the standard of 'sufficient' protection? Who is to judge? Does the answer vary as a function of time and place? Objections such as these, and those mentioned in Part II in relation to Gidel's writing, only touch the surface of the possible objections, serious and trivial, which could be raised from a philosophical point of view and from a methodological point of view.

There is an endless series of receding challenges which could be made at every level of meaning. But such challenges would have been in bad form in polite conversation and they would have been in bad form in academic discourse. The rules required that you could make one or two pertinent objections to reopen the matter, as it were, as a prelude to, and an excuse for, an exposition of your own point of view, the form of that exposition being essentially the same as the original statement.

The rules of academic discourse were based on convenience—debate would be tedious and unproductive in the absence of such rules. They also rested on an assumption that certain substantive values were shared, that there was much that went without saying. It is not suggested that all members of the cohesive élite agreed about everything important or even that they shared all their moral, political and social values. Indeed, one could argue that the two traditions of conservatism and liberalism, in Britain and the United States, and corresponding basic left/right divisions in other countries, are fundamentally different approaches to some of the most basic moral, political and social questions, to the extent of implying a conflict of some basic values. This has given a dialectical strength to these societies, as well as giving rise to a good deal of fruitless debate and social conflict; it remains to be seen whether monolithic societies which lack this institutionalized dialectical and dynamic conflict will be able to reconcile change with stability. But it is probably right to say, and not merely a pious assumption, that a society must have a shared substratum of values broad enough to permit that society to continue to cohere. Sharp debates and conflicts on such matters as law and order, the role of dissent, the outer limits of state authority, should reflect conflicts of judgment as to the application of shared values, if they are not to be radically destructive of the society in which they occur. A writer addressing the cohesive élite makes assumptions about such values; to a greater or a lesser extent he relies on them; he judges that they do not require to be demonstrated or even mentioned. Indeed, more often than not, explicit reference to such values may be destructive of them (and hence of an argument relying on them). It is possible to feel sure of such values of Western society as the primacy of the individual and the sanctity of human life more easily than to dispose of the philosophical problems which arise as soon as the words are uttered.

It may be said, with some temerity, that there is a British tradition in the presentation of philosophy and the social sciences in which the assumption made by the writer is of a particularly high degree of co-operativeness on the part of the reader. Although British philosophers and social scientists are now to some extent involved in a newer tradition, it remains true to say that, particularly in the fields of philosophy and political science, there has been a steady tradition of calm reflective writing, extending from Bacon and More to the present day, the characteristic tone of which is that of the library or the study, of the learned society or the club. The British form of academic discourse, while undoubtedly stimulating them, has tended to irritate the thinkers of continental Europe, because of its academic élitism, its hypocritical modesty and its lack of scientific or even human guts. The continental European alternatives to this calm and piecemeal British tradition have tended in the direction of holistic system (in the German tradition—Leibniz, Kant, Hegel) or passion and commitment (in the Romantic and French traditions—Voltaire (despite his obsession with Locke), Rousseau, Bergson, Sartre). Needless to say, there are many who do not fit easily, or the whole of whose writing does not fit easily, into such categories (Hobbes, Descartes, Marx, Freud, Russell). And it may be said that there are other British traditions, such as the polemical tradition (Swift, Burke, Shaw). But for present purposes the point is that there are various radically different ways of presenting philosophy and the social sciences—all with the aim of convincing a reader, but each adopting its own tactics—and that one of those ways has been, and has been recognized by professional philosophers as being, characteristically British.

This British tradition has contributed much by its calm speculation—for example in the fields of epistemology, ethics, language, the theory of government—by inviting the reader to think slowly and quietly and to form a view, preferably in the same sense as the writer's view, but in any case after the application of common sense and good faith. The method involved is inductive in a very broad sense. It asks the reader to take into his mind the diverse materials which are present in the writer's mind and to see whether he does not agree that the writer's conclusion is the sensible conclusion. The writer has formed a view of the matter, on the basis of all the heterogeneous associations attaching to it in his mind. He tries to ensure that similar associations, similar data and ideas, are in the reader's mind, partly explicitly, by setting out propositions and arguments and referring to facts, and partly relying on a broad assumption to the effect that the reader will have such-and-such ideas and facts in his mind, which, through his own associative process, he will see to be relevant or which will unconsciously condition his conclusion. If the conclusion reached by the reader is the same as that reached by the writer, then, given that both are sensible and intellectually experienced, that is already a significant fact. If the reader's conclusion is different, then it does not follow that one or the other conclusion is wrong. The writer's presentation of the matter may have been bad; the reader's approach may have been prejudiced or inattentive. This broad inductive method is, therefore, designed, at the risk of a play on words, to induce in the reader's mind a certain conclusion, not syllogistically or even logically, but by any suitable means. In practice, it has three main elements: (1) the mixing in the same paragraph, or even in the same sentence, of fact, inference and opinion; (2) the rhetorical repetition of the same or similar ideas in significantly different formulations; (3) the mixing in one argument of propositions whose verification principles are fundamentally different. The method can be said to be one of controlled intellectual confusion—controlled by its aim but confused by comparison with more rigorous forms of, and particularly with scientific, induction. The confusion is of the essence of the system—all kinds of consideration are equally capable of being incorporated in an argument: considerations of fact, logic and policy. And, indeed, the merit of the conclusion may often be measured by the extent to which it reconciles such diverse considerations.

In international law there have been a number of holistic efforts in the German tradition, of which the leading example is the work of Kelsen. But the overwhelming majority of writers on international law, at least until the advent of the modern United States writers, have followed in the diffused inductive tradition described above and exemplified by the extracts from Hall and Gidel. Taking this as an assumption for the purposes of further argument, it must be asked why such a thing should be the case. In the first place, it is possible that the important British writers of the late nineteenth century may have had an influence on the form as well as on the content of international law writing. It is true that those writers can be placed in the scholastic tradition on account of their success in giving an unwarranted appearance of precision to what should have been presented as more or less vague; and it is true that they had a corresponding 'authoritative' impact. But it seems most unlikely that their influence could be regarded as a sufficient cause. A second possibility is that the method is, in this context, not in the British tradition at all, but is the style of Grotius and the other creators of modern international law; and that their style was that of the then-existing common European culture. A third possibility is that the method reflects the nature of international law itself.

Grotius, at the very beginning of modern international law, was conscious of the problem of style and method. He tells us that he was concerned to avoid intellectual confusion:[1]

> In the whole course of my work I have had in view these things especially: to make my definitions and reasons as clear as I could: to arrange in due order the matters I had to treat of: and to distinguish clearly things which were really different, though they seemed identical.

This Cartesian aim (in fact, Descartes's *Discours de la méthode* appeared in 1637) was to some extent realized by Grotius in his writing, particularly in that he was unusually meticulous in signalling the kind of authority or

[1] *De Jure Belli et Pacis* (1625; ed. and trs. by Whewell, 1853), p. lxxvii.

argument on which he was relying at any particular time. He would expressly indicate what was demanded by natural law or the philosophers or the Roman law of nations or morality or, very occasionally, utility. To this extent he was a more articulated writer than almost all his successors.

So far as the substance of his method is concerned, Grotius made remarkably explicit, at the very beginning of his splendid work, the process by which he had found international law. Although his explanation cannot be regarded as a complete excuse for the rather hotchpotch nature of what followed, it is of the greatest significance in explaining the method and the nature of classical international law. He said that he had 'indicated the sources from which we derive our judgments, so that it may be easy to determine any question that may happen to have been omitted by us'. And also, he might have added, to determine the validity of the judgments which he does not omit to make:[1]

> In the first place, it was my object to refer the truth of the things which belong to Natural Law to some notions, so certain, that no one can deny them, without doing violence to his own nature. For the principles of such Natural Law, if you attend to them rightly, are of themselves patent and evident, almost in the same way as things which are perceived by the external senses; which do not deceive us, if the organs are rightly disposed, and if other things necessary are not wanting.

This reliance on natural law is no longer easy to accept as it stands. At another point in the argument, Grotius places natural law between nature and civil laws in a family hierarchy, saying that nature is the 'Grandmother of Civil Laws'. Despite such metaphors, it is not right to regard natural law as a rhetorical device or as a figure of speech in Grotius's work. To his contemporaries, a reference to natural law would normally be an impressive thing. Grotius himself asked that 'if I have said anything which is at variance with piety, good morals, with holy scripture, with the unity of the Christian Church, with truth in any form: let that be as unsaid'. The religious connotation of natural law, as sanctified by St. Thomas Aquinas, meant that it was an absolute limiting factor, which it was virtually sinful to disregard. Since Bentham, natural law has had to lead a rather shame-faced existence, at least in international law. It was John Stuart Mill who said that 'the writers on international law . . . having no positive law to write about and yet being anxious to invest the most approved opinions respecting international morality with as much as they could of the authority of law . . . endeavoured to find such an authority in nature's imaginary code'.[2]

This does not do justice to the role of natural law in international law. It has been said (possibly by Simone de Beauvoir) that in the present age there is only one moral problem, what to do about Communism. It could

[1] Ibid., p. lxv.

[2] *On Nature, the Utility of Religion and Theism* (1874).

be said that, in international law, there is really only one problem, what to do about natural law. In this sense natural law should be understood, not in its religious sense which would explain its existence in terms of the divine origin of nature, but in a secular sense. The question raised by natural law is whether it can be said that a legal system, such as international law, should conform to some general underlying pattern or principle, or whether it must be said that the rules of international law must justify themselves in their own terms and in terms of their end-purpose as being useful to, and accepted by, States. Grotius, in the passage just quoted, sees the rules of natural law as things which are patent and evident and which one cannot deny without doing violence to one's nature. Ignoring the low-class intellectual small print in what he says ('if you attend to them rightly' and 'if other things necessary are not wanting'), this is a useful secular definition of natural law. At another stage Grotius explicitly rejects the idea that international law is derived from, or to be identified with, natural law in any literal way. He explains how he has found the rules of natural law and of international law:[1]

> In order to give proofs on questions respecting this Natural Law, I have made use of the testimonies of philosophers, historians, poets, and finally orators. Not that I regard these as judges from whose decision there is no appeal: for they are warped by their party, their argument, their cause: but I quote them as witnesses whose conspiring testimony, proceeding from innumerable different times and places, must be referred to some universal cause; which, in the questions with which we are here concerned, can be no other than a right deduction proceeding from the principles of reason, or some common consent. The former cause of agreement points to the Law of Nature; the latter, to the Law of Nations: though the difference of these two is not to be collected from the testimonies themselves, (for writers everywhere confound the Law of Nature and the Law of Nations), but from the quality of the matter. For what cannot be deduced from certain principles by solid reasoning, and yet is seen and observed everywhere, must have its origin from the will and consent of all.

This short passage is of the greatest possible significance with regard to the style, the method and the nature of classical international law.

Two separate processes are inherent in this method of 'finding' the law. The first relates to the use of language and argument. In this respect Grotius's method is an excellent example of the diffused inductive method already described. In an almost chemical way, he mixes together a seemingly random collection of ideas about events (the historical record of State practice), ideas about ideas-about-events (the opinions of writers, lawgivers and governments) and the ideas of the author himself (which may be of any logical kind, of any degree of abstraction, contain any degree of opinion and be more or less openly value-laden). The accumulation of material is open-ended. It is a rag-bag or patchwork.

[1] *De Jure Belli et Pacis* (above, p. 98 n. 1), p. lxvi.

The number of separate and heterogeneous sources referred to admittedly makes it difficult to know how to derive a resultant from them. In discussing the law of the sea (Chapter III of Boook II), for example, how can one weigh against each other the views of Paulus the Jurist, Siculus and Demosthenes; the relevant rules of the Roman civil law; the requirements of natural law; the rules of the Roman law of nations; the views of Theophilus, Ulpian, Celsus and Pomponius; the activities of Lucullus and Sergius Orata and of the Megareans in the Peloponnesian War and of the Massilians and the Sinopians; the precedents of the Roman Erythaean tax and of the taxes levied by the Athenians in respect of the Hellespont; and so on and on? From time to time Grotius feels able to make a calculation from his sources. Having shown that the law of nature and practice support the right to possess small areas of the sea: '. . . but many things which are permitted by nature, the Law of Nations, by a bond of common consent, has prohibited'. Having shown that some ancient States, in practice and by treaty, exercised jurisdiction over areas of sea: '. . . but these examples do not prove the possession of the sea, or of the right of navigating, by occupation'.

It is amusing to note, incidentally, that Whewell's edition is an abridgement with some of Grotius's examples and quotations omitted, without their omission seeming to have much effect on the course of the argument. (Whewell's notes indicate the omissions.) Hall and Gidel, it will be recalled, were no different, even if they lacked Grotius's dazzling display of classical and historical reference. At some point they all ask us to make the leap across space from a collection of data to a conclusion. This leap is inherent in all inductive method. It is interesting, and a hopeful sign, that the problem of the mechanics of induction as it was posed by a philosopher (Hume) has now been passed to the psychologists for elucidation. For the physical sciences, however, although the hypothesis will always be more than the sum of the data, the identification and control of the data are more important than in the social sciences, or, at least, than in international law. At this first level the problem is, however, essentially the same and equally mysterious. As in the physical sciences, the fact that the method is not understood need not in itself mean that, in international law, the method is to be scorned.

The second process relates to the fact that writing about international law is writing about law. Another, equally puzzling, leap across space has to be made—from 'is' to 'ought'. Much effort has been spent by classical philosophy and legal philosophy on the problem of how such a leap can be made consistently with logic or, at least, with comprehensible intellectual processes. Essentially, the problem is that, from a logical point of view, manipulation of 'is' propositions should not lead to an 'ought' proposition.

The proposition that 'Ruritania is a State' and the proposition that 'A State ought to respect international law' might, in terms of everyday logic, lead to the conclusion that 'Ruritania ought to respect international law'. But the proposition that 'Ruritania is a State' and the proposition that 'international law is concerned with the rights and duties of a State' can only lead to the conclusion that 'international law is concerned with the rights and duties of Ruritania as a State'. Legal philosophers have tended to two alternative solutions to the problem. One is to introduce positive facts and to say that the 'ought' is put in by a lawgiver as a matter of fact and is not to be extracted as a matter of logical inference. The other is to look at the reality and to say that the 'ought' is in the mind of the perceiver of the rule, and attaches to any idea which he perceives to be a constraint on his choices of action or which he predicts as being likely to be so perceived by some person in a position to constrain him accordingly. International law has adopted another solution, partly because there is no lawgiver who can arbitrarily introduce the 'ought', and partly because, in the absence of both a lawgiver and a law-enforcer, international law would evaporate into pure subjectivism if it were to depend on the perceptions of its subjects for its validity. It is a solution which is applicable also to municipal law and, as such, is intellectually more satisfying than the alternatives referred to above.

The solution followed by traditional international law is to use the diffused inductive method to derive 'oughts' from miscellaneous sources. The three main sources of 'oughts' are: (1) an 'ought' derived as a pattern from the historical record of the practice of States; (2) an 'ought' derived as a pattern from the attitudes of other persons who have carried out the process of finding international law in the matter; (3) an 'ought' perceived by the person seeking to find law in the given situation. The rule of law is then itself a more general 'ought-pattern' derived from these sources.

An 'ought' statement can be said to be a pattern, in the form of a generalization or related to a particular case, linking values and preferences with potential or actual events.[1] The person finding the law perceives such a pattern, at the appropriate level of generalization (in relation to the passage of submarines through the territorial sea; passage of warships through the territorial sea; passage of ships through the territorial sea; passage of ships and aircraft through and over the territorial sea; the rights of one State in another State's territorial sea; the legal nature of the territorial sea; and so on). It is a pattern which fits in with other relevant patterns in his mind and is not inconsistent with any of them; it accords with patterns of his moral, social and political values and his basic legal values; it accords with the patterns of what he regards as practicable and sensible; it is

[1] Further discussion of this point is to be found in the Annexe, below, p. 134.

consistent with the views of those whose views he respects; and so on. He must then seek to lead the reader to form the same satisfying pattern in his own mind.

The practice of States is examined to see whether there emerges a pattern such as would emerge if States had been acting under the constraint of law. (This is the best meaning to give to the classical concept of *opinio juris*, which otherwise tends to the supposition of a situation in which States were *mistakenly* believing that there was a legal requirement to do what they were doing.) What is involved is, on the one hand, a pattern of practice extracted from the general record of the practice of States, and, on the other hand, a pattern of practice which would be observable if States had been acting under the constraint of law in the matter. If the patterns match, a provisional 'ought' is attached to the pattern of conduct in question.

The second pattern is extracted from the views of writers, lawgivers, governments and others who have sought to find the law in the matter. Writers are notoriously discordant on controversial matters, but a person finding the law may, and often does, detect a pattern in the writing and in the other authorities, and, if he does, he may regard such a pattern as significant.

The third pattern is derived from the values and attitudes of the person finding the law in the given situation. His values and attitudes will be derived, in their turn, from his personality, cultural environment and personal experience. He will be accustomed to making judgments in his daily life and in his work, and he must make judgments in the process of finding the law. Even Gidel made numerous judgments ('incorrect', 'illogical', 'preferable', and '*a priori*' and 'natural law' used opprobriously). Judgments are, or imply, an 'ought' and necessarily involve the application of values.

Returning to the two extracts from Grotius last quoted, it will be seen that ought-pattern no. (1) corresponds to his '. . . what . . . is seen and observed everywhere' and is deemed to have its origin in 'the will and consent of all'. Ought-pattern no. (2) is the 'conspiring testimony' of his witnesses. Ought-pattern no. (3) goes without saying, but is indicated in the phrases—'notions so certain that no one can deny them, without doing violence to his own nature' and 'the right deduction proceeding from the principles of reason'—which imply a subjective input.

It is important to note that these processes of pattern-finding, although here separated out, may be carried on simultaneously and need not in practice be separately signalled by the writer. It will be considered, in Part V below, whether there are any rules which should guide the writer in carrying out the process in his writing.

The process of finding patterns in heterogeneous material is a distinctive faculty of the brain. The process has not yet been rationalized; but it cannot be dismissed on the ground that it is irrational. It is a directly observable fact of everyday experience that the brain is able, not exceptionally but in the ordinary course of its functioning and possibly as the essential characteristic of its functioning, to perceive patterns, not only in the data presented by the senses, but also in the ideas and other patterns already stored in it. A pattern implies three things: selection (i.e. conversely, the discarding of some data as irrelevant—the State which did something different; the writer who held the other point of view); arrangement (putting the data into a certain relationship with each other—bringing together the facts that ships travel freely in the territorial sea and the fact that the coastal State sometimes exercises some kinds of jurisdiction in the territorial sea); and integration (as a result of which the pattern may be more than the sum of the parts, as the mind fills in gaps and joins up separate points: the best example being the way in which the patches of paint on a canvas are seen, beyond a certain critical distance from the canvas, as a portrait or a landscape containing much more detail than is on the canvas). Knowledge consists of established patterns of information. Reflective thought consists of the finding and ordering of such patterns into new patterns. It may be that the process is inexplicable in principle and that electronic machines will not be able to perceive significant patterns other than those which they are, directly or indirectly, programmed to perceive. In the meantime, artists and consumers of art will continue to see patterns in art objects and will relate them to their stored patterns of what is ugly or vulgar or original. Historians will continue to find patterns in the raw material of history, including the patterns formed by other historians and which have become part of that raw material. Lawyers will continue to detect, by an entirely mysterious process, the *ratio decidendi*, the essential pattern, of a decided case (discarding the fact that the plaintiff had two Christian names or red hair and retaining the fact that he had had two large whiskies before entering the defendant's premises) and they will relate that pattern to the essential pattern of the case before them. Most important of all, it will probably remain impossible ever to state all the elements which led to the formation of any such pattern. And this, by an application of an uncertainty principle, is likely to be a case of ultimate impossibility, impossibility in principle.

Grotius, in one of the extracts quoted above, speaks of the 'conspiring testimony' of the witnesses whom he was to consult. This evocative phrase is admittedly better in English translation than in the Latin original (*quod ubi multi diversis temporibus ac locis idem pro certo affirmant*). Better still might be 'converging testimony', since the process involved is that of detecting a convergence in the evidence explored. It should be emphasized that reliance in the foregoing discussion on the concept of pattern-finding is not intended to be an attempt to import any particular philosophical or psychological theory (the coherence theory, *Gestalt* psychology, structuralism, the theories of computer technology, for example) into international law. It is intended as a simple, more or less metaphorical, description of what happens in practice, to be verified by introspection. Even if such a presentation is difficult to accept, it surely cannot be difficult to see the traditional method of international law as that of listening to the voice of the practice of States, the voice of other writers, lawgivers and governments, and the voice of the writer's own intellect and experience, and to regard their converging testimony as significant. But, whatever explanatory metaphor is used, it is essential to make the point that such processes are not simply subjective and hence potentially cynical. Those who seek to find international law in a given situation are subject to two controlling factors which, in a sense, constitute international law's own verification procedure. The first is that it is not possible easily to delude an attentive reader into seeing a pattern which is not there. The second is that the rules of international law are put to the test, each and every day, in relations between governments. An international lawyer who persists in finding rules of international law which governments, international tribunals and his lawyer-colleagues never or seldom thereafter treat as law, may be on the side of the angels but will not in the end serve the useful purpose of contributing to the improvement of the quality of relations between States.

IV. McDougal and Burke on the Passage of Warships through the Territorial Sea

Having considered in a preliminary way the classical style and the classical method of international law, it is right to turn to a writer who is sometimes thought to have adopted a new style and a new method. What follows is a consideration of lengthy extracts from *The Public Order of the Oceans—A Contemporary International Law of the Sea* (1962) by M. S. McDougal and W. T. Burke. This is one of a number of works which Professor McDougal of Yale University has written with various collaborators. It is necessary to quote from it at length in order to do justice to the complex nature of the discourse involved. But the text will be considered as it stands, from the point of view of the random consumer, and not in the light of explanations which may be available elsewhere of the method and terminology used.

The particular matter to be considered is the authors' treatment of the controversial question of the passage of warships through the territorial sea.

(The authors' treatment of the question discussed in the extracts from Hall and Gidel has not been chosen because that question is not very systematically treated and the impression is given that such an abstract question is not at all to the authors' taste. Their treatment of a specific first-level topic is a much better example of their method at its best.) The authors adopt an inverted-pyramid style, however, with considerations set out in a broadly descending order of generality, so that it is necessary to consider a good deal of general material as part of the discussion of the particular topic.

The main discussion of the territorial sea is in a chapter entitled 'Claims to Authority over the Territorial Sea'. This matches the titles to other chapters, such as 'Claims to Authority over Internal Waters' and 'Claims to Shared Use and Competence upon the High Seas'. The title at once introduces a novel element, since it suggests that the chapter will be concerned, not simply with listing what States may lawfully do, but rather with what States actually *seek to do*, presumably with an analysis of the legal position in the event of incompatibility between what two States seek to do. From the practitioner's point of view, this is likely to be a natural and welcome approach, since this is just how day-to-day problems arise. We, or they, want to do this or that; what should their, or our, reaction be?

The next striking feature is that the chapter has an explicit methodological structure indicated by section-headings: Factual Background; Claims and Counterclaims: the Pattern of Controversy; Basic Community Policies; Particular Policies: Clarification of Policy, Trends in Decision, Appraisal and Recommendation. The Particular Policies section deals with five kinds of claim: claims to control access to the territorial sea; claims to apply policy in the territorial sea; claims to prescribe for activities directly relating to the use of the territorial sea; claims to prescribe and apply policy to persons aboard vessels in the territorial sea; claims to exclusive access to resources. There are obvious idiosyncrasies in these titles. The random consumer would be puzzled by the frequent and ambiguous use of the word 'policy'—in at least two senses: activity by a State; and theory regulating or applying to that activity. But the practitioner would also, once again, see that the 'claims' referred to are evocative of the kind of problems which arise in practice.

The Factual Background begins as follows:[1]

> The factors in the process of interaction in the territorial sea of greatest significance for State claims and community policy embrace again, as with respect to internal waters, such items as the location of the waters in relation to land masses and other waters (as affecting their indispensability or importance to international navigation), the types of uses sought, the characteristics of participants and their purposes, and the impacts, or potential impacts, of different activities upon the value processes of varying

[1] *The Public Order of the Oceans* (above, p. 105), p. 174.

communities. Though the greater the distance activities are removed from the shore, the less intense in rough proportion the unique interests of the coastal State are likely to be, there remain in the nearer territorial sea the potentialities of intense conflict between the inclusive and exclusive interests of States. Whatever the width claimed, and eventually to be honored, for the territorial sea, all States are thus intensely concerned with the allocation of rights of access and resource exploitation within such waters.

It should be noted that this does not purport to be an exhaustive survey of the factual considerations ('the factors . . . embrace . . . such items as . . .'). The Factual Background goes on to deal briefly and in general terms with examples of the conflicting interests of States:[1]

> The factors of most importance for the general community interest in the territorial sea are those which relate to the usefulness of this area for international transport and communication. . . . The exclusive interest of particular States in the territorial sea arises principally from the fact that this sea, like internal waters, affords an important means of access to coastal land masses. In the recent past this factor of facilitating access to the State has had a very considerable weight for the coastal State, since the oceans have served as a most convenient, and sometimes necessary, highway over which attacks and threats of attack could be launched by rival States. . . . Other exclusive interests arise from the conventional interactions in the territorial sea involving more prosaic events than threats to security. . . . Foreign vessels may seek to intrude upon fishing grounds considered to be reserved for exclusive exploitation by coastal nationals. Persons may attempt to use the unprotected water approaches to a State for evading coastal restrictions upon the ingress and egress of goods. . . . Finally, but by no means of least importance, both inclusive and exclusive interests are affected by the fact that the ocean areas close to land masses are very widely considered to be highly consequential as a source of food supply for an ever-increasing world population. There is a most profound community interest, engaging a progressively wider and more highly organized community attention, in assuring adequate production and distribution of food resources, including especially those available from the marine environment. . . .

The above are admittedly only extracts from more than five pages of text, but it is thought that they correctly represent the form and content of the original. As a preliminary comment, it might be mentioned that 'exclusive' and 'inclusive' interests, in the terminology used by the authors, apparently mean, respectively, an interest of a particular State which implies the exclusion of other States from the benefit involved, and an interest shared by States in general (cf. Gidel's reference to the 'cosmopolitan' and 'particularist' principles). The implications of these categories go beyond the question of method, but it should be noted in passing that they give rise to conceptual difficulties.

The considerations included in the Factual Background have a familiar ring. They echo considerations referred to in the extracts quoted from Hall and Gidel and which are commonly mentioned *en passant* in international

[1] Ibid., pp. 174–8.

law writing. The great virtue of the treatment given to them by McDougal and Burke is that not only are they stated more fully and more realistically, but also they are stated in a generally objective manner, with the minimum of policy comments. However, from a methodological point of view, it is not quite clear what the purpose or the effect of the Factual Background section is. The considerations are not exhaustive but they are extensive and fairly detailed. The reader will carry them in his mind, but probably not in such a way as will have much impact in the handling of specific topics. He will certainly be inclined to say: 'Ah yes, I can understand that the territorial sea is obviously a difficult and contentious area.' This in itself would be useful to a student or to one who had not realized the kind of pressures which exist in such an area. But from the point of view of finding the law, the section will probably tend to be treated as an overture, rather than as a first movement, arousing interest and the proper frame of mind without as yet asking the reader to apply himself to the legal substance.

The section entitled 'Claims and Counterclaims: the Pattern of Controversy' inevitably duplicates to some extent the factual background. It begins as follows:[1]

> The principal claims made by States to authority over the territorial sea are often characterized, in terms as sweeping as those with respect to internal waters, as assertion of 'sovereignty' over a part of State territory. The more specific claims comprising this alleged sovereignty include. . . .

There are then listed the five claims already mentioned above in describing the structure of the chapter, although, oddly enough, each of the claims is on this occasion formulated in a slightly different way from that in the section-headings. For example, the second claim is now said to be 'to apply *authority* to vessels' and the last claim is now said to be 'to exclusive *appropriation* of resources':[2]

> The major opposing claim to all of the claims affecting access and navigation is customarily expressed in terms of a right of innocent passage, and most of the discussion of claims to authority over the territorial sea has focused on this concept of innocent passage. This unfortunately has led observers to overlook that talking about innocent passage is but another, semantically equivalent, way of talking about the scope of coastal authority over access to the territorial sea.

This is a rather unusual excursion by the authors into Gidel country. The use of the word 'unfortunately' neatly gives the impression that, at last, the truth is told; whereas it might be more accurate to say that there can be no end to the kind of argument involved, which is metaphysical or, at least, relates to questions of propriety in applying the principles of deduction.

[1] *The Public Order of the Oceans* (above, p. 105), p. 179.
[2] Ibid., pp. 179–80.

The general nature of the various claims and counterclaims is then considered, with illustrations from national legislation. For instance:[1]

> Certainly the most direct and far-reaching assertion of coastal competence is that of continuing authority to deny all passage through the territorial sea, irrespective of its character or purpose. This claim may take the form of attempted suspension of all passage through the territorial sea or of assertion that vessels of a particular type or function are not entitled to use the territorial sea for passage. The counterclaim pressed by the flag State is for a right of access for passage on the ground either that the coastal State is not authorized by international law to forbid all passage through its territorial sea or that all vessels are entitled to a right of access for passage (assuming it is innocent) irrespective of their specialized use or purpose.

It is not at all clear what the precise nature of the concept 'claim' is supposed to be. In the above extract there are claims: of continuing *authority* to deny passage; of attempted *suspension* of passage; that certain vessels are not *entitled* to passage; to a *right* of access. The last claim is given two grounds: that the other State is not *authorized by international law*, etc.; and that vessels are *entitled* to a right of access. It is not clear whether the assertion is that this is what States do and claim in practice, or that this is the legal implication of what they do and claim in practice. From the passages here considered, which may not be a fair sample of Professor McDougal's technique in this matter, it appears that there is a mixture of claims actually made by States (as evidenced by national legislation) and claims implicit in the actions, and from the interests, of States. The methodological procedures for testing the two kinds of assertion are, of course, different. Once again, however, it must be said that this section on claims and counter-claims is likely to have only a broad effect in the process of leading the reader to form a view. At the end of it, he is likely to say: 'it is evident that international law in the matter must be expected to be such as would resolve a series of claims by States which are clearly incompatible as they stand.' More generally still, particularly if he is a student, he will have been led to a fuller awareness of the nature of international relations in this particular field and, hence, in general (*pace* Gidel's opinion that this is a superficial way of approaching international law).

Now that the authors have shown that the territorial sea is an area where the interests of States conflict and that these conflicts of interest are reflected in competing claims (sc. legal claims) to act in a certain way in relation to the territorial sea, the next section, called 'Basic Community Policies', sets out the general principles which are used, or, perhaps rather, are to be used, to resolve these competing claims:[2]

> All claims by coastal States to exercise authority affecting access to the marginal belt, and the opposing counterclaims by other States to be free of such authority, bring into

[1] Ibid., p. 180. [2] Ibid., pp. 184–7.

conflict the two fundamental policies that have traditionally been of paramount importance about use of the oceans of the world. In protection of widely recognized common interest, it has long been general community policy . . . to maintain the oceans as a common resource available for the peaceful use by all for the purposes of transportation and communication . . . [C]ommunity policy has also long established an opposing or limiting policy—that of recognizing the competence of the coastal State to promote or protect its aggregate value position by exercising authority over access to and passage in the territorial sea. . . . The compromise between these competing policies—which on the one hand call for free access to the territorial sea and on the other for restrictions of varying severity on that access—is given doctrinal expression in the concept of freedom of innocent passage. The common inclusive interest in assuring full and efficient use of the oceans is stressed in terms of freedom of passage, and the concurrent common exclusive interest in permitting the protection of coastal value processes is recognized in the qualification that to be privileged passage must be innocent, i.e. not offensive to certain coastal interests.

The perennial problem for authorized decision-makers in appraising claims and counterclaims involving passage in the territorial sea, including demands that they give greater weight to one or the other goal, has been that of determining what is reasonable, taking into account all factors in the context. The factors relevant to a determination of reasonableness may be considered most conveniently as relating, in threefold modality, to the claim of the coastal State, the counterclaim of the affected State or States, and the degree and modality of the interference demanded and effected by the claimed authority.

. . . The claim of the coastal State may be characterized initially in terms of the extensiveness of the authority asserted. . . . The interests coastal States seek to protect and to promote include power . . . wealth . . . and well-being.

. . . Among the factors characteristic of the counter-claim, the activity subjected to coastal authority is of primary importance. The main use of the territorial sea which is affected in this context is movement by passing vessels. . . .

. . . The modality and degree of interference effected by coastal authority are factors of great significance for policy.

. . . Turning to claims about resources, the most important task for policy is that of achieving *peacefully* the fullest shared use of the resources of the ocean consistent with maintenance of continued or enhanced supply. . . . Like most contemporary observers, we concur in the traditional balance, and place the greatest weight upon the importance of relative economy in exploitation, in concluding that a limited exclusive competence is the most desirable policy. . . .

If the extracts from Hall and Gidel are recalled to mind, it is apparent that we are, with these extracts from McDougal and Burke, in very different country. The structure of the argument is as follows—

1. There are, traditionally, two fundamental policies about the use of the oceans—that of maintaining the oceans as a common resource, and that of allowing the coastal State to protect itself.
2. The competing claims of the coastal State and other States in respect of the territorial sea produce a conflict in the application of the two

fundamental policies—the first suggesting that there should be free access to the territorial sea; the second suggesting that there should be restrictions in favour of the coastal State.

3. The conflict is resolved by a compromise expressed as 'innocent passage'.
4. But problems remain as to the content of 'innocent passage'. Such problems are to be resolved by weighing up all the factors involved and determining what is reasonable in the context.

There seem to be at least three strands of material involved in this: the policy factors which, as it were by introspection, one can see to be necessarily involved in resolving competing claims in this field; the policy attitudes which have been adopted 'traditionally' or as 'community policy' in the past; and the policy views of the writers. Examples of these three strands will be readily seen in the above extracts. It is extremely difficult for the reader to know how he should approach such material in seeking to form his own view. Proposition 1 above is, in appearance at least, a statement of historical fact, albeit at a rather abstract level. But the passages from Gidel discussed in Part II, and the phrenetic swordplay between the writers to whom he refers, show that it is simply not possible to assert, as if it were a fact, that the correct abstraction or generalization from past law and practice is such-and-such. How can one say whether there were two fundamental policies or whether a third more subtle fundamental policy developed, a *mare liberum* policy for the far seas and a *mare clausum* policy for the near seas? Also, the reader will want to know what he is buying in accepting such a proposition as proposition 1 above. Or, to take another example, the proposition in one of the extracts, that it is right 'to maintain the oceans as a common resource available for the peaceful use by all for the purposes of transportation and communication' may sound like the kind of proposition with which it is difficult to take issue. But situations could readily be imagined in which it would not be politic for a government, for example, to use such a proposition (for fear that it would be used as a first premise by another government for an argument leading to a highly unwelcome conclusion). It might be more politic in some situations to restate it as—'It is right that the oceans should be available to all as freely as possible consistently with the interest of all States in their security and well-being.' It is very difficult indeed for governments to be asked to adhere to general propositions of a policy-orientated kind, related to no particular case and the application of which to particular situations in the future is completely unpredictable, and might be highly prejudicial to their interests. The work of the United Nations Committees on the Principles of Friendly Relations between States and on the Question of Defining Aggression illustrates this difficulty.

The other major difficulty is in proposition 4. It is surprising, to say the least, to see that the criterion for determining what States may or may not do in relation to 'innocent passage' is to be what is 'reasonable', unless it is understood, which it is clearly not so far as McDougal and Burke are concerned, that what is reasonable is to be equated with what is required by international law. Having regard to the listing of the factors involved in reaching the decision, it is quite clear that the decision is to be taken in the manner, and on the intellectual bases, normally used by a competent administrator or legislator in taking policy decisions.

The next section deals with 'Particular Controversies' and the question of warships is mainly dealt with under 'Claims to comprehensive, continuing authority to deny all passage through the territorial sea'. There is first a subsection entitled 'Clarification of Policy' which makes more specific some of the considerations of policy discussed under 'Basic Community Policies'. The text considers the 'factors most pertinent for determining the reasonableness' of the claim of a coastal State to deny all passage:[1]

> Systematic consideration of these factors suggests that there ought to be no general arbitrary competence to deny all passage through the territorial sea whether within or without a strait, and that adequate protection can be accorded the coastal State in either type of area by recognition of an occasional exclusive competence to be exercised for a specified cause.

This is obviously an important turning-point in the presentation of the matter. The authors have now stated a conclusion using the 'ought' form of the verb. It is not clear whether the systematic consideration to which they refer consists of the material immediately following the passage quoted or whether they are telling us the results of a systematic consideration carried out by themselves but not set out in their book. The material which follows the quotation is not obviously systematic. It does not deal in turn with the four factors put forward for determining reasonableness, but concentrates on one of them:[2]

> Focusing explicitly upon the importance for international transportation of the area affected, we first consider community policy relating to straits.

The material which follows is extremely general in its terms, although it occupies eight pages, and also extremely subjective. After eighteen lines of discussion, the following first conclusion is reached:[3]

> It would appear, accordingly, that for community policy purposes all straits, irrespective of their utility at any particular period in time, ought to be treated alike for purposes of rejecting coastal authority to deny all passage.

[1] *The Public Order of the Oceans* (above, p. 105), p. 188. [2] Ibid. [3] Ibid., p. 189.

In balance against the high importance of straits for international navigation, already amply emphasized, there appears to be no coastal interest of sufficient gravity to merit authorizing the coastal state to deny all passage through a strait, except in time of highest expectations of violence.

After another sixteen lines, the first conclusion is in effect repeated:[1]

Because of the very intense general interest in the use of these areas for international transport it seems reasonable to require that individual States forgo so broad an exclusive competence.

The next paragraph deals with the alternative ways in which the protection of the interests of the coastal State can be secured. The conclusion is restated again after twenty lines:[2]

Recognition of a broader authority such as that to suspend all passage, without specification of reasonable cause, is therefore unnecessary for the reasonable protection of common coastal interests in a context such as this.

The text then goes on to consider the position in relation to territorial waters other than those in international straits.

Thus, in reaching the conclusion that a certain rule is reasonable, the authors have relied on assertions of fact (importance of straits to international navigation); judgments of value (freedom of navigation in straits is more valuable than freedom of action therein for coastal States); and statements referring to international law and custom ('the well-known right of innocent passage'). Rhetorical and logical support for their arguments has been found in: empirical evidence (for example, they refer to the factual paper on straits prepared by Commander Kennedy for the Geneva Conference); reference to authority ('traditionally recognized by international decision-makers'; 'the coastal State has long been considered competent'; 'the well-known right'; 'an authority long established in community expectations'); and, above all, appeals to shared values ('ought obviously'; 'it seems reasonable'; 'unnecessary'; 'no interest of sufficient gravity').

Turning at last to the authors' consideration of the right of passage of warships, it must be borne in mind that all that has gone before—the factual background, the analysis of claims and counterclaims, the basic community policies, the clarification of policy—should be regarded as gathered-in, as it were, to the consideration of this specific subject. At the same time, it should be said again that this method puts a strain on the ability of the reader to profit fully from the work, since it is not at all easy to bear in mind in any coherent way the considerations, often of an amorphous and generalized kind, which have gone before, not least because of the constant reformulation of the authors' arguments and conclusions in different terms.

[1] Ibid. [2] Ibid., p. 190.

After referring in twelve lines to the 'factors particularly relevant for policy' in this particular matter, the discussion continues as follows:[1]

From the perspective of one seeking to take into account both the inclusive interests of the general community of States and the exclusive interests of particular States, desirable community policy would appear to be that of assuring to all vessels of all types the right to innocent passage through the territorial sea. Such policy would explicitly reject the notion that the function of a vessel, either as a warship or as a fishing vessel, ought alone to be sufficient to warrant the conclusion that its mere presence is so prejudicial to exclusive interests that in no instance ought the right of innocent passage be available to protect access.

In considering this extract and those that follow, it is useful to put oneself in the position of a hypothetical government, and its legal advisers, who maintain that the passage of warships is not simply a matter of a right of innocent passage and that it requires the authorization of the coastal State (and there are such governments).[2]

It may be agreed that warships do have a special character and that they may threaten coastal interests. It need not, however, be assumed that these facts warrant withholding any access at all. The experience of many, if not all, maritime States suggests that coastal States have not in the past regarded passage of warships as necessarily threatening. . . . Insofar as history provides a guide for desirable policy there is, therefore, little justification for concluding that warships ought to be absolutely deprived of a claim to a right of passage.

It should be noted in passing that this reference to the historical record of State practice, striking as it is, is included as a possible, though somewhat uncertainly possible, 'guide for desirable policy'. The significance of such an indication need not be emphasized.

In thirteen lines the authors then consider the future position, in particular the present trend to more extensive breadths of territorial sea—[3]

Denial of a right of innocent passage would, in these circumstances, constitute a greater burden on passage than in the past when lesser breadths were claimed, yet because of progress in weapons technology, would offer much less protection against actual harm to coastal interests. For these reasons it appears desirable from a community policy perspective that there should be no special, discriminatory rule established in regard to access of warships.

This completes the 'clarification of policy' on the matter and the next section considers 'Trends in Decision'. This sets out, in great detail, historical facts and decided cases and describes the work of the International Law Commission and the Geneva Conference on the Law of the Sea (1958). This is followed by a section entitled 'Appraisal and Recommendation'. In relation to warships, this begins by saying—[4]

The rejection [by the Geneva Conference] of any arbitrary competence to deny access to the territorial sea fully accords with recommended policy and requires little

[1] *The Public Order of the Oceans* (above, p. 105), p. 192.
[2] Ibid., p. 193.
[3] Ibid., p. 194.
[4] Ibid., pp. 223–4.

comment in addition to that already offered in connection with straits. Because of the likelihood of future controversy, some further attention may however be given to appraisal of decisions about competence in regard to the access of warships.

The writers then argue the case again for rejecting the giving to the coastal State of a general right to exclude warships from its territorial sea. The arguments are similar in form to those already contained in the 'Clarification of Policy' and can be summarized as:

1. Warships are not a great enough threat to justify a comprehensive and continuing authority to exclude them.
2. Such a competence would entail drastic restriction on harmless and beneficial use of the territorial sea and might heighten international tensions.
3. Even if the coastal State should have some greater competence to qualify passage as non-innocent, an alternative method would be sufficient, for example a right to prevent access during times of particular tensions.

The authors' conclusion is also similar to that already quoted:[1]

> The occasional exclusive coastal competence represented by authority to suspend passage in the territorial sea temporarily for security reasons and by authority to prohibit passage as non-innocent would appear to be wholly adequate to provide protection for coastal interests. Special authority to control access of warships therefore seems unnecessary.

Once again, it must be said that the concluding passage is surprisingly discursive and literary in style. In particular, the reader is left uncertain as to the precise content of the solution proposed by the authors. It is not clear how 'temporarily for security reasons' is related to 'during times of particular tensions' and 'during the temporary periods in which outside threats are realistically perceived'—phrases used variously in the body of the discussion. Such variations of wording could be extremely significant in practice. Also, it is not clear whether the idea is to allow the coastal State to 'regard passage as non-innocent and subject to exclusion' in the exceptional cases (as suggested at one point in the body of the discussion) or whether the coastal State may also 'suspend passage in the territorial sea temporarily' (as the conclusion proposes). Again, such a difference could be significant in practice.

V. McDougal—A New Way of Presenting International Law?

It was necessary to quote from the work by McDougal and Burke at some length in order to establish precisely what are the innovations involved.

[1] Ibid., p. 226.

Two questions arise: is it a new way of presenting international law? Is it a new way of finding international law?

At the level of style and use of language and argument, there are features which are fully in line with the traditional style and method, and there are features which are different. The structure is made more apparent by the division of the material into sections with methodologically significant titles: factual background, basic community policies and so on. Also, the basic separation of the factual background and trends in decision (the historical setting) from the discussion of the policy considerations gives a radically different 'feel' to the writing, even if, in practice, the separation of the material is somewhat less rigid than the titles imply. Finally, there is no doubt that, in some respects, there is a good deal more material offered to the reader than in comparable works. This is particularly true in respect of the analysis of the factual and 'real' situation underlying the problem and in the very full, if expressly not exhaustive, exposition of the policy considerations.

The rather more aggressive style seems to invite the reader to be honest with himself and to face reality and reach a rational decision. This can be compared with Gidel's authoritarian style which, to one reader at least, gives the impression of asking him to accept what he is told by an authority rather than inviting him to share in reaching a sensible decision. On the other hand, because of the more explicit and articulated character of the argument in the McDougal and Burke writing, the reader is likely to feel inclined to resist and raise objections, particularly on 'policy' matters where he may feel that his personal opinion may also be worth something. He is certainly not left apathetic, but the urgency of the style and the nature of the arguments deployed may leave him unwilling either to assent to the authors' propositions or to form an articulated view in another sense.

Such differences, however, can hardly be said to amount to any radically new style or, at the superficial level of the manipulation of language and argument, method (leaving on one side, for the moment, the much more important question of whether they reflect an innovation in the method of *finding* international law). The essence of the classical method of presenting international law has been considered in Part III above, and the elements of the 'controlled intellectual confusion', which characterizes it, were set out. They are equally applicable to the writing of McDougal and Burke, as exemplified in the passage considered. The reader's mind, in order to form a general view on the basis of all the material provided, must take account of fact, inference and opinion mixed freely together; it must systematize many propositions of varying logical character and with different verification procedures; it must accommodate the repetition, which is a particularly striking feature of this writing, of similar ideas in constantly changing formulations. In the end, the authors must, as in the case of Hall and Gidel, rely on very many assumptions about their audience, their shared values (including their values of academic discourse), the correspondence of their inductive and deductive processes, and their willingness to approach the problem, and its discussion by the authors, with conventional seriousness and good faith.

Nevertheless, the writing of McDougal and Burke does raise one question about the presentation of international law which it would not be fair to overlook. The facts that the authors have taken the trouble to develop a new structure for the presentation of the material, new concepts for analysing the problem ('claims', 'community policy', 'exclusive and inclusive interests') and have sought to involve the reader in a new way, these are facts which call for appraisal in their own right. It is not easy to distinguish such an appraisal from the analysis of the underlying method of finding the law which they may reflect. But something can usefully be said in answer to the question: given that the method will inevitably be one of controlled intellectual confusion, are there any principles or ethics to judge whether a writer has controlled the confusion in a better or a worse way, or does anything go?

There can be no problem about intellectual confusion, controlled or not, in writing, including non-imaginative writing, whose prime purpose is to entertain, in the broadest sense of the word. The essayist is expected to confirm the reader in his familiar thoughts and to stimulate him gently by means of some unfamiliar and contentious ideas. It is of no great importance in the end whether we agree in detail or in general with a preface by George Bernard Shaw to one of his plays. Our minds will in any case have been slightly expanded by following through its argument, but we will not be greatly concerned if we do not regard ourselves as having come into the possession of a new, unassailable truth. The same may be said for artistic and literary criticism, where the writer is essentially asking the reader to feel with him. If the writer succeeds, the reader will have the same sense of certainty as the writer, based on the same completely uncertain grounds. As already mentioned, the situation was traditionally much the same in philosophy and the social and political sciences, and even in the physical sciences in their medieval days. But in the political and social sciences there is an additional element, which makes it necessary to ask whether such an intellectually relaxed approach is defensible. The additional element is that people may act significantly in relation to other people on the basis of the 'findings' of such studies. Of course, it is true to some extent of all intellectual activity that it may alter the conduct of other people. Even literary and artistic criticism may condemn a writer or an artist to poverty in a garret or it may make him successful and rich. But in the fields of political science, sociology and economics in particular, far-reaching courses of action may derive from writing which is successful, in the sense of being admired and accepted by the majority or by the influential. Rousseau and the Marx of the Communist Manifesto have had an actual effect on the lives of large numbers of people despite, or even because of, the essentially rhetorical and unscientific, not to say in a strict sense nonsensical, character of their writing. This means that there is, in these fields, the possibility for the writer to be a thinker and an actor in equal measure, a scientist and a politician at the same time. In such cases the vicious circle may indeed be completed by the apparent vindication and even validation of the writer's views by their being applied in practice under such conditions that their reality becomes the reality (cf. Marx). It is also possible that practice may seem to demonstrate the lack of validity of the writer's views (cf., for those not inside that particular vicious circle, Marx).

In writing about the law, the problem is still more acute. This is because it seems to be inherent in the nature of legal systems that writing about the law may itself constitute law. It may be that it is intrinsically impossible to devise a legal system so complete that the description and discussion of its interpretation and application will not tend actually to supplement its content. The common law is the clearest case; but even the codified systems, from Roman law onwards, show the same characteristic to a remarkable degree. To the extent that a court applies, in cases before it, what it finds in writings about the law, those writings can be said themselves to be law. And, even if such a radical equation of writing and law is not accepted from a formal point of view, there can be no denying the everyday fact that writings can be a major evidence of law and may have a decisive effect in individual cases. A court may be unable to repeat the process of collation and evaluation which a successful writer has carried out. The writer may appear to have consulted all the right sources and to have weighed up all the relevant considerations (or may have the reputation for having done so on other occasions), so that, on this occasion, the court puts its trust in his conclusion and applies it.

In international law, writing about the law has an especially significant function. Article 38 of the Statute of the International Court of Justice directs the Court to 'apply' international conventions, international custom, the general principles of law and 'judicial decisions and the teachings of the most highly qualified publicists of the various nations, as subsidiary means for the determination of rules of law'. There is a conflict in the drafting here, as the Statute tells the Court to *apply* the teachings of publicists and also to *use* them *as a means* for determining rules of law. But, in any event, the teachings of publicists are given a high place, equal to that of judicial decisions. This is not at all surprising in a legal system which has been predominantly a customary law system, where the custom has to be established by oral or written tradition.

Thus, the writer about international law has a correspondingly responsible task. If he purports to give a comprehensive view of the subject about which he writes, he has the responsibility to ensure that it is indeed comprehensive and that, so far as possible, his generalizations do justice to the evidence which is known to him (if all the evidence is not set out in his writing). If he purports to write from authority, that is to say, justifying what he says not so much by the comprehensiveness of the evidence as by the power of insight and generalization which he claims to have, through experience or otherwise, then he has a particular responsibility to write honestly, which means that he should not abuse his authority by propagating a partisan point of view without revealing it as such, and that he should admit doubt and ignorance when he is aware of it in himself. According to the analysis of 'pattern-finding' offered in Part III above, the reader is not merely an audience: he is an active participant in the process of finding the law. An essential element in the process is that the necessary pattern, or, more simply, conclusion should emerge in his own mind as a result of the process of diffused induction. It should emerge naturally, as it were, and not as a result of improper pressure or deception on the part of the writer.

In terms of criteria such as these, it must be said, with respect, that the extracts from McDougal and Burke score highly. There is no sleight-of-hand in the method. The form of the argument is always clear enough. The views and sympathies of the authors are always apparent. The reader's mind is able to roam freely in the policy considerations, for example, knowing that he should at that time be using a particular, and particularly subjective, area of his mind; a different area from that to be applied to the factual background or the case-history. That there are countervailing and, it is thought, overwhelming objections of a different kind to the method involved will be the theme of Part VI below. Also, it is only fair to record that, despite the methodologically explicit style, the reader's mind, or at least one reader's mind, is left unaccountably confused as he follows through the argument. Partly this may be due to an idiosyncratic English language style and vocabulary which the authors use (and which is, as it happens, less evident in the extracts quoted than elsewhere in the writing of Professor McDougal). But the kind of confusion and disorientation which is experienced can hardly be merely a matter of style or even of unfamiliarity. It must be related in some way to the substantive objections discussed in Part VI.

Two further points remain to be made on the problem of presenting international law. The first is to draw attention to the work of the

International Law Commission in relation to the various sets of draft articles which it has prepared as a basis for codification conventions. Not only has the Commission adopted for this work a remarkably economical and precise style (following, perhaps, a tradition established by the Harvard Research work), but the formulation of the commentaries on the articles with several clear and distinct points stated very simply in separate paragraphs, shows that it is not impossible to be both scientific and consumer-orientated. It is true that codification work is different from the discussion of abstract, controversial problems, but not so very different. The combined Commission product—of the Rapporteur's background papers, often analysing past practice and past attempts at codification, the records of the Commission's debates and the draft articles and commentaries produced by the Commission—is in some cases as scientific a treatment of a subject as has yet been achieved.

No one can presume to speak on behalf of all general practitioners of international law, but it is tentatively suggested that what a practitioner would be most happy to find, when he consults a work of learning for assistance in a problem which has arisen in practice, is a very extensive and self-contained description of what happened in similar situations in the past (without comment from the author); a statement of the areas of doubt which exist in the field (including references to the competing interests of States); followed by clear and direct quotations from well-known writers giving their view of the law; followed by the author's own views where they differ from the general trend or where the well-known writers do not speak with one voice. With such material before him, the practitioner's task of forming a view would be facilitated—a view ultimately depending on his own experience and judgment, but slightly more likely to be the view reached by other practitioners if they are all working on the same clear and complete material. This consideration underlines the great value to be attached to the efficient collection and publication of material on State practice and the widest possible dissemination throughout the world of leading textbooks and works of learning in all languages, so that practitioners everywhere can be working on the same material. It seems for some time to have been the policy of the International Law Commission to produce draft articles on as many subjects as possible, for adoption by governments in international conventions. A great contribution which could be made by a private foundation or association would be to organize a small group of leading scholars from widely differing backgrounds with the task of preparing detailed, systematic and up-to-date studies and, if appropriate, restatements of the law (with all relevant background material), not for adoption by, or even presentation to, governments, and certainly not for consecration by declarations or resolutions, but merely to exist as comprehensive and authoritative sources (one among many) *à toutes fins utiles*.

VI. McDougal—A New Way of Finding International Law?

The extracts quoted from McDougal and Burke in Part IV are distinguished from what has been described as the traditional method of finding international law, in two respects: (1) the authors appear to regard their task as that of constructing rather than finding the law; (2) they seem to imply an equation of the form: Fact $\times$ Policy $=$ Law.

In the first place, there appears to be a rejection of the traditional method on the ground that it treated international law as a rabbit to be produced from the hat of any international lawyer who could win the acquiescence of his admiring audience; and that the traditional method thus saw a virtue in the mysterious and fortuitous origin of the law, given that it is harder to disprove a mystery and that the mysterious is often easier to believe than the rational. If, on the contrary, one looks at the reality (so the presumed argument would continue), it is evident that all that there is on the ground is conflict between States which wish to act in mutually incompatible ways, in situations which are constantly varying over time; and it is the job of international law to find means of making the conflicting ways of States mutually compatible by showing to States the rules of adjustment and forbearance which they should sensibly follow.

There is a therapeutic value in such an approach. In the first place, it fits in well with the increased self-consciousness of international relations. Psychology, cybernetics, game theory and the open and intense debates about foreign affairs in many Western States have led to a situation where many governments, and those who influence them, are not simply doing what comes naturally. They are to some extent playing both sides of the dialectic. The Cuban missile crisis of 1962 is now a classic example of this tendency. This self-consciousness is itself, ironically enough, a complicating factor, which in some ways makes the problems still more difficult to deal with, but which, in any event, calls for more articulated consideration of the international relations options. (It might be mentioned, entirely incidentally, that two classic writers on game theory, von Neumann and Morgenstern, took the view that, in game theory, 'a guiding principle cannot be formulated by the requirement of maximising two (or more) functions at once'. It was, for them, virtually self-contradictory to offer such a principle as a rule of a game. Professor McDougal might, however, deny either the relevance of game theory to his method or else the analogy with his rules of law which seek to maximize the interests of the conflicting

States.) Secondly, for a variety of reasons—including the bitter experience of two world wars and subsequent multi-national conflicts, the advent of the new nations born in a spirit of idealism, the relative rise in significance of non-European areas of the world, and the cliché-forms of propaganda—a distinctly moralizing tone has for some years been present in international society, first clearly heard in President Wilson, but not entirely due to him. Governments are exhorted not simply to maximize their short-term benefits, but to consider the needs and concerns of other governments and the longer-term interests of the world community as a whole. Thirdly, the apparent decline in the number of values shared by all peoples of the now numerous nations of the world means that it is less easy to make assumptions about the attitudes and expectations of other States; and, as has been argued, international law has traditionally relied heavily on such assumptions. But this element of the present situation can easily be exaggerated, and it is possible to argue that, on the contrary, the astonishing fact is the extent to which basic human values are shared by the world community, despite its troubled recent history. But considerations such as these make it hard to deny the relevance of the McDougal approach, with its apparent implications that governments should not be naïve about the realities of any situation in which they find themselves; that they should respect and even make allowance in advance for the interests and aspirations of other States and for the interests and aspirations of the world community in general; and that they should not assume the automatic and continuing validity of the rules of good behaviour which they and like-minded governments have sought to follow.

So far as the content of the law is concerned, here again there is an immediate attraction in a generally relativist approach. The present time is not unique in having a strong sense of its own uniqueness. An element of our uniqueness is felt to be the intensity, the complexity, the gravity and the latent anarchy of the life in nations and between nations. How, it is asked, can problems arising in such a situation be resolved by invoking simplistic rules of law which may or may not have been good enough for an earlier world, which was at once more power-cynical and more innocent of the realities? The exploitation of the resources of the deep ocean sea-bed, the expropriation of foreign investments, the use of force to support or to suppress liberation movements, mutual defence of the 'achievements of Socialism', apartheid, the use of weapons of indiscriminate destruction, activities in outer space, the powers of political organs of international organizations—how, it is asked, can such matters be approached on the basis of *a priori* principles and rules? How can illumination be found in terms of the categories of traditional international law, when not only are they phenomena which were largely unforeseen by traditional international law, but also they are different in kind from the matters with which traditional international law had to deal? To anyone starting from such a conviction of the novelty of the present time, an approach must seem welcome which starts from the facts of a given situation and an analysis of the real State interests involved, refers to past law and practice as an incidental aid to reaching a right answer, by analogy or contrast, and seeks the rule which would be best for the world community as a whole. Its aim would be to find an answer to which all can assent rationally, not because others have assented to it in the past, but because it seems right and sensible for the situation as it now is. Arguments such as these are grossly over-impressed with the uniqueness of our times—an error due to a general decline in interest in history and a general sense of shame about the past. It can be argued that it is the duty of the international lawyer, like the moral philosopher and the theologian, not to become so desperate about the state of the world as to feel inclined to move into related, seemingly more practical and everyday, fields. On the contrary, his duty is to insist on the essential, objective element of his craft (law, morality, religion) ever more calmly and firmly as the need of the world for such things, whether or not the world realizes it, increases. At the same time, there is no doubt that the most conservative mind must occasionally long for more relevance and concern in some writing about international law.

But it does no justice to the McDougal approach to regard it as merely relativist. Because it is relativist and realist in nature, it cannot be accused of being out of touch, academic or irrelevant. But it is much more than relativist. It is, ironically, also an absolutist, idealist approach.

Its absolutist aspect is first revealed by the extreme subjectivism of the writing, which is assertoric rather than didactic; concerned almost to the point of being passionate. It is unashamedly and intentionally value-laden. It makes constant use of words such as: *fair*, *reasonable*, *right*, *incorrect*, *misleading*, *unfortunate*, *important*, *profound*, *vital*, *fundamental*, *of great significance*, *most desirable*, *arbitrary*, *intense*, *unnecessary*, *little justification*, *recommended*, *wholly adequate*, and, above all, *ought*, *should* and *may*. This aggressively subjective style may perhaps be intended to serve the incidental purpose of making the point that the objective style of traditional international law was bogus and concealed the inescapably subjective character of the whole exercise. What we are doing, this presumed argument would run, is to state plainly our views and our values. Of course, it is for our readers to object if they do not agree, but at least we can conduct an open argument rather than a polite charade. But it seems unlikely that the authors are merely issuing a rebuke to traditional international law. Given the seriousness and concern which are evident in their writing, and in all Professor McDougal's work, it seems clear that they are, in addition, claiming that their answers are not merely one set of possible answers, but that they are the right answers. Now, such a claim can only rest on one or other, or perhaps both, of two grounds: either that the judgments expressed in the writing conform to some given and settled system of values (by reference to which the reader also can measure those judgments), or that the judgments are in some way necessarily implied in the considerations which they set out. This second alternative, although in traditional logical theory it could only cover propositions of the same logical order, which logically support the conclusion (cf. the problem of going from 'is' propositions to an 'ought' conclusion), can, for present purposes, be taken to include the pattern-finding which, it has been suggested above, is characteristic of the method of traditional international law, and which does not rely on complete concordance between the value systems of the various participants in the process (the States involved in the State practice, those who have found the law in the past, those who are finding the law in the given situation, those who will apply the law) but only a sufficient concordance to enable a shared pattern to be extracted. It seems apparent on the face of it that Professor McDougal's method is not designed to find patterns from so wide a field of data. His remark quoted above—'. . . insofar as history provides a guide for desirable policy . . .'—shows that he does not entirely exclude the assistance of the record of State practice. And examples from State practice and references to the views of other writers are a feature, but a subordinate feature, of his writing. Excluding the possibility that he is merely manipulating words and concepts in a holistic, deductive way, it seems clear that the characteristic of his method is that it uses a concept known as 'policy' as a multiplier, as it were, to be applied to any material which comes to hand. And 'policy', in this sense, is a more or less ordered system of values. Even if exclusion of the alternative leads to this conclusion about his method, the conclusion can be verified less formally by referring to the language which he uses. The mere use of words such as those listed above is evidence enough that the essence of the appeal is to values which the author believes that his reader shares. He is saying: 'Our job is to find the reasonable answer; I have set out the relevant factual considerations; you and I know what is reasonable when we see it; let us see what is reasonable in the light of the factual considerations; if we disagree, let us discuss the matter further.'

The problem in the way of such a method is obvious. It is difficult to reach agreed conclusions if there is no shared system of values (as between the proponent of the proposition and the persons evaluating and applying it) or if there is insufficient concordance between their value systems so that, when a conflict of values occurs, there is no higher agreed value capable of resolving the conflict necessarily and automatically. Moral philosophers and political scientists have sought and, to their respective satisfactions, found many ways of circumventing this problem, usually in terms of one unquestionable proposition or principle or value or set of values, of so certain a character that no one can deny it without denying his own nature. There is no reason to think that Professor McDougal has adopted a Kantian solution, although it is interesting that his concept of 'community policy' could possibly be rationalized along the lines of the Kantian principle that the moral individual should adopt as his maxims those which could be the maxims of mankind in general. Again, there would seem to be too much of the *a priori* in McDougal to place him in the American traditions of pragmatism and realism. There is a certain Hegelian element (strictly, Hegel as 'realized' by the Marxists) in the basic concept of McDougal's method, that of States with competing interests which must be resolved into something which satisfies both sides and also satisfies the policy of the world community (world-spirit). None of the other conceptual devices which have been proposed in the history of moral and political philosophy would seem to be relevant, with one exception. That is the tradition of utilitarianism. There is abundant evidence, even in the extracts which have been quoted, that McDougal accepts the possibility of a 'calculus of values', in the style of Bentham; that, as Leibniz wished, he is saying—'let us calculate'. It seems clear that he feels able to weigh one interest against another, one value against another, one value-statement against another. The words 'weigh' and 'outweigh' are used on more than one occasion in such a context. It is highly speculative to suggest what the equivalents of 'pleasure' and 'pain' would be in McDougal's system; possibly 'humanity' and 'inhumanity'. His 'greatest happiness' principle might perhaps be on the lines: 'that is for the best which conduces to the greatest degree of humanity in the world community'. But it would be for him to say what the principle would be.

The obvious and frequently repeated philosophical objections to utilitarianism may have consigned it to the outer darkness so far as professional philosophers are concerned, but they cannot remove its appeal and its relevance in an everyday, practical context. Indeed, it can be said to underlie liberalism, democratic socialism and even the whole business of governing a mixed economy. Government consists of the establishing of priorities between desirable objectives and, more or less consciously, a principle such as the 'greatest happiness' principle has to underlie such a process to justify the priorities which are chosen. With it, there must necessarily be an acceptance of the possibility of weighing alternatives in terms of such a principle. Such a concept was particularly relevant in a society such as British society in the nineteenth century when countless social decisions had to be taken, decisions for which the Parliamentary and governmental machine was unprepared—choices between freedom and order, freedom from and freedom to, liberty and licence. These social and political and, indeed, moral choices were of a new kind—new in their gravity, urgency, intensity and in the scope of their consequences. It is not fanciful to argue that international society has been in a similar state in recent years. British society in the nineteenth century, and all other countries which have since gone through the same kind of process, had to take fundamental decisions about the distribution of wealth, the rights and powers of the masses, the limits of State intervention and *laissez-faire*. There are analogous international problems in the modern world: the extent of the right of the international community to concern itself with human rights and other matters arising *within* domestic societies; the relationship between the rich and militarily powerful nations and the poorer and more numerous nations; the problem of corporate action in fields such as population control, food supply and disaster relief. There is some similarity between the nineteenth-century struggle to resolve the conflicts between the exclusive and inclusive interests within a society, to use McDougal's terminology, and the conflicts of interest between States which are now so numerous and extensive. Just as utilitarianism, whether or not philosophically respected, provided a tone and a method (and, until the advent of Marxist Socialism, *the* tone and method) for internal political debate in the nineteenth century and up until the present time, so there is no reason why Professor McDougal's international utilitarianism should not do the same, with some escalation of fervour in its style, if need be, for international society in the second half of the twentieth century.

But there are two serious reasons why it would be regrettable, to say the least, if it were to become the tone and method for international *law*. The first is that it is a tone and a method for political, administrative and legislative debate and is not suitable for use by practitioners and governments applying law to the day-to-day conflicts of international relations. The second is that, whatever the high ideals of those who believe in it and practise it, the danger is that it will be a more apt weapon for those whom they would least wish to assist—the dialectical materialist and the cynical practitioner of *Realpolitik*.

International law is involved in answering questions of various kinds. (1) Is what we want to do lawful? (2) Is what they want to do lawful? (3) Was what we or they did lawful? (4) Hypothetically, what is the law relating to such a situation, what would the rights and duties of the participants in such a situation be? (5) Regardless of what the law has been thought to be, what should be the law relating to such a situation in the future? In answering each of these separate questions, it will be necessary to apply international law techniques in different ways. Also, such questions present themselves to different persons or bodies: to governments and their legal advisers; to international law consultants (acting for persons, companies or governments); to international courts and tribunals (and, sometimes also, to national courts); to international organizations; to international conferences (particularly codification conferences); to writers on international law. The needs, the expectations and the approach of each such person or group may differ.

Governments and practitioners of international law most often need to have rules of law in a form which not only gives an answer to questions such as (1) and (2) above, but also gives an answer which has a chance of being acceptable to other governments, an organization, a tribunal and so on. It is of no use for a government or a practitioner, in answering such questions, to assert rules which that government or practitioner has simply created *ad hoc*. Of course, governments and practitioners may argue diplomatically, or in a pleading before a tribunal, about the general merits of the situation, and seek to show that what they intend to do, are doing or have done is only fair and reasonable. But such an argument, which would not be a plea to law, is open to precisely parallel argument to opposite effect from the other side. To take the case of passage of warships through the territorial sea: it would not advance the cause of a government seeking to assert such a right of passage in a particular case and using the form of argument followed by McDougal and Burke, if another government, seeking to deny such a right in that case, were able to argue with equal vehemence and equally convincingly in the same kind of terms ('fair', 'reasonable', 'vital' and so on) to demonstrate the opposite conclusion. If governments were limited to such a form of argument, then the specifically legal character of the law would have ceased to exist. All would have become politics.

Now it might seem that this would be a more honest state of affairs. The charade, as advocates of another system sometimes allege the traditional system to be, would have ceased. But the strange fact is that not only do governments habitually talk and argue in terms of law, but also government decision-makers positively want to be told that there is relevant law governing certain situations. In the fluid and complex situations with which they are faced, it is often very welcome to them if they can safely exclude at least one area of variables from the situation, if they are told that one set of options must be regarded as closed. Admittedly and naturally, they also sometimes find it difficult to accept such advice, and sometimes, also, their legal advisers must be resolute in saying that the law is not clear enough in the area in question and that they must not be asked to close options, on legal grounds, which must in the circumstances be evaluated in political terms. But it would be a retrograde step if legal advisers were never able to meet this demand from their clients and were always obliged to say that, on the one hand, this may be the case and, on the other hand, that may be the case, and that the fair and reasonable conclusion seems to be such-and-such, but of course others may hold different views. In the form of discussion used by McDougal and Burke, the conclusion depends on an explicit weighing-up of conflicting values, interests and considerations and, in imitating such a procedure, a legal adviser would have great difficulty in conveying any assurance that his answer would be the same as that which another government or a tribunal would find.

At the same time, it must be admitted that such a method would be perfectly acceptable and, indeed, of great utility, in dealing with questions of the kind numbered (3), (4) and (5) above, at least in some circumstances. Question (3) might have to be answered by the International Court, and the Court may, as we have seen, range widely in finding the law. One could easily imagine situations in which, even when it had not been called upon to decide *ex aequo et bono*, the Court could look at the underlying interests of the States involved and of the international community in general, although it would be destructive of its character as a court of law if it were to follow such a procedure, in preference to the finding and applying of law, when relevant rules of law exist and are applicable. In cases where, however, there is an element of legislation in the Court's task in a particular case, such considerations could be properly regarded as relevant. Similarly, a text-writer called upon to answer question (4) could well find that the evidences of the law were insufficient to draw a clear conclusion and that a policy analysis, clearly and expressly demarcated as such, was necessary before a solution could be proposed. Finally, the method would be particularly relevant to question (5). A body such as the International Law Commission or a codification conference of governments could perfectly properly include policy analysis among the instruments which it uses to reach its conclusions. Article 13 of the United Nations Charter speaks of the 'progressive development of international law'. An international legislature, like a national legislature, cannot pluck new law out of the empty air.

But, it should be noted, legislators are more politicians than they are lawyers. And it is here that the policy method faces its second and more serious objection. It is very vulnerable to abuse and could be destructive of the nature of international law.

It has been suggested above that all legal systems are more or less dependent on jurisprudence, on the spontaneous creation of law—not by a legislature specifically empowered to create law, but by a mysterious alchemy. It is clearly inherent in such a situation that it is liable at any time to be condemned as the living-out of myth, as bondage to an illusion. It is also a commonplace, however, that three things can usually be said about social myths: that they continue to exert a power over the mind even when they are more or less known to be myths; that they often serve a positive and creative social function despite their mythical character; and that, precisely because of their mysterious and autonomous character, they are inevitably expressive of something real and profound in the society in which they develop. In other words, it is not enough to condemn a process or a system by saying that it is a myth. It must also be shown that it is a bad myth, counter-productive, destructive.

International law is not more mythical than domestic law. Indeed, because of the relative simplicity of international society (in terms of the number of participants) and the relatively exposed machinery of international society and of international law itself, it is arguable that international law is less mythical. The reason why the finding of international law has traditionally proceeded from a more or less disorganized consideration of what States have done in the past *opinio juris*, and of the views of past writers, lawgivers, governments and so on, is not any desire to justify what States did in the past as always right, nor any principle of 'whatever was, is right'; nor is it an attempt to foist on new States, and on new generations in old States, the rules concocted by old States and by the obsolete ruling classes of old States. Nor is it mere laziness. The past is relevant because international society, in a more evident way than domestic society, is an intensive dialectical process, a multiple dialectical process. International society evolves in consciousness through the interaction of States, but it is, like all societies at all times, threatened by the forces of anarchy, solipsism and entropy. From time to time these forces overwhelm the daily contact between governments, and wars and other critical events occur. But the daily contact of governments, because it proceeds peacefully for much of the time, albeit in continual confrontation and low-level friction, evolves critical paths or conventional programmes which favour its continuation and its orderly development. These critical paths and programmes evolve as if by a process of natural selection—those which are successful are retained by international society. Those which are not successful, which lead to heightened tension or tend to ultimate chaos, are avoided. Some of those critical paths and programmes which are retained are perceived as rules of international law.

Such a process, of discovering and constantly adjusting personal rules for survival, is common to all organisms. It has been well said that an organism is not only an organized thing; it is a thing organizing itself. The same can be said of international society and, indeed, of an individual person, who finds, as he develops, laws of his own personality which are asserted by his own particular intelligence, personality, circumstances and personal history as well as by his cultural environment. Their validity is tested pragmatically by their results. Continually, like a sophisticated electronic machine, a feedback process ensures that these personal laws are adjusted in the light of experience and in order to achieve new goals and meet new challenges. In a given situation, faced with a new challenge, it is theoretically possible for the individual to devise a complete new personal strategy for the occasion. But normally in practice, the process of so doing would be so complicated as to be impossible. Instead, he follows the strategy more or less dictated by the established laws of his personality. As John Stuart Mill said in a related context, of course the navigator cannot be expected to work out the tables of the Nautical Almanack each time he sets sail. As with the individual so with international society, the fact is that international society is a fairly experienced organism. With over five thousand years of recorded history behind it, a remarkably consistent pattern of experience has developed, the uniformity of which probably reflects the perennial features of the nature of man. Wars, alliances, the rise and fall of empires, plagues, natural disasters, ideological conflict, international crimes, the oppression of the weak, the tyranny of the majority—these are part of the everlasting story of history and are not modern inventions. The basic problems of States seeking to maximize their security and prosperity remain remarkably constant over so long a period of time, and the incompatibilities between numbers of States seeking to achieve this aim on a planet of limited dimensions and resources vary in degree over time, but hardly in kind. The relevance of the past is that it provides evidence of countless test-tube experiments of conflict-resolution. It is not the *theory* of what would be reasonable and what this or that State might seek to achieve or how it would react. It is the *story* of how the continuing problems have been presented and resolved or circumvented over a long period of time. The policy-analysis is performed in action and continuously.

In this sense, therefore, international law can be regarded as the natural law of international society, not in any religious sense but in a purely secular sense. It is the law by which international society prolongs its existence, and to find that law it is first necessary to discover how international society has managed to prolong its existence in the past. It is no chance or random series of events which resulted in the legal doctrines relating to the rights of States in respect of the territorial sea. It was due to no conscious evaluation of the policy considerations involved nor was it due to any disregard by States of their grave concerns in respect of such an area. The doctrines in question were the resultant of numerous different forces: the dialectic of the interests of States; the reflective consciousness of politicians and lawyers; the changing pattern of fact. Such doctrines are not a fact but a process and there can be no justification for stopping the process, or attempting to do so, and saying that, hereafter, the resultant will be taken from only such-and-such verbalized considerations—no justification, that is to say, except as an express act of legislation by the international community, an act which is political and executive as much as the meeting of warships in an actual territorial sea.

Professor McDougal is in the classic tradition of the opponents of the autonomous theory of law, a direct descendant of Bentham and Mill. It is a debate which will never be concluded; to which there can never be a right answer. Grotius, already in 1625, had words addressed to Professor McDougal:[1]

> I have refrained from discussing points which belong to another subject; as the Utility of this or that course; for these belong to a special Art, namely, the Art Political; which Aristotle rightly treats as a separate subject, mixing it with nothing of any other kind; thus differing from Bodinus, in whom this Art is confounded with *Jus* in our sense. In some cases, however, I have made mention of the Utility of acts; but collaterally only, and in order to distinguish that question the more plainly from the question of Right.

In support of Grotius's point, it can be said that a method which reduces law to policy flies in the face of consistent, historical, human experience of autonomous law, flies in the face of contemporary human experience, and does violence to the products of everyday intuition. But there is no way of winning such an argument on its own terms, except, possibly, by reference to a contemporary policy consideration.

If the finding of law is laid open to an explicit battle of interests and values conducted in words, who is then to be master? Or is there to be no master, and is the finding of the law to become an endless, actual or simulated, process of negotiation? It would not be surprising to find that Professor McDougal attached a correspondingly high value to treaties as a source of law. The fact that a codification treaty, for example, can be the product of the most explicit kind of policy-analysis must make it a worthwhile achievement, so far as he is concerned, at least as an interim achievement, pending the coming of the day when unwritten international law can also be found and applied in the proper, policy-orientated way. And it is no doubt right, even from the standpoint of the traditional method, to give a cautious welcome to codification treaties as providing a new plateau of agreement, as it were, from which the finding of international law can take off again. For various reasons, however, it is as well to sound a note of caution.

It is natural that Soviet writers should believe that treaties are a primary source of international law, superior to custom to the extent that they more

[1] *De Jure Belli et Pacis* (1625; ed. and trs. by Whewell, 1853), pp. lxxvii–lxxviii.

clearly and directly derive from the sovereignty of the State which, for Soviet writers and materialists in general, seems to be not only a basic datum of international society but also its basic norm. They do not reject the concept of custom in relation to international law. Unfortunately it is almost impossible to form any clear and definite picture of the Soviet rationale of international law, despite (or perhaps because of) the amount of material now available outside the Soviet Union. But it seems that custom is still regarded, in a distinctly old-fashioned way, as a more or less disembodied form of agreement between States. It is earnestly to be hoped that they will come more and more to see it as an autonomous source and a primary source of law, perfectly compatible with Marxism—if not more compatible, as being an objective expression of the dialectic, rather than a conscious and explicit manipulation of situations, as is the conclusion of treaties. In the meantime, it is no coincidence that the Soviet Union has initiated or wholeheartedly supported the work on the Declaration on the Principles of Friendly Relations between States and the work of the Special Committee on the Question of Defining Aggression and the various declarations adopted by the United Nations General Assembly. And it is certainly true that treaty law has come to occupy a relatively more significant place in international law in recent years—both in substantive treaties and in codification treaties. But should these developments be wholeheartedly welcomed?

Treaties give rise to a dilemma, a paradox. On the one hand, they have a totem-sanctity which has been recognized throughout recorded history. On the other hand, they can be seen as inimical to the existence of autonomous law in international society. In the first place, they are a political act, the product of an explicit confrontation between the potential contracting parties. This means that the norms which they contain will be a reflection of the power-relationship of the parties, a relationship which is itself an adventitious product of the circumstances which happen to exist at the time when the treaty is concluded. One valuable characteristic of customary international law is thereby removed—its emergence over a period of time during which short-term circumstances may average out. Secondly, treaties almost always give rise to serious problems when the circumstances change. International law may then be in equal disrepute if it holds a reluctant party to the agreed norms or if it allows one party to go free regardless of the norms. It is too soon yet to say how this problem will be resolved, if and when it arises in relation to the codification treaties concluded since 1945. But it seems probable that, sooner or later, there will be a cause for scandal when such a treaty is, in whole or in part, treated as a scrap of paper. Thirdly, treaties are generally regarded as a 'source of law', and not only by Soviet writers. It is not merely a verbal objection to say that this is highly regrettable. Treaties are a *product* of law. They are the concretization of the intention of States in a form which attracts the application of certain rules of law; they take that form in order to attract the application of those rules. If anything, treaties are a source of policies not of law. The regrettable consequence of regarding treaties as a source of law is that the consensual character of the treaty thereby appears to be the origin of the obligation. But *ad hoc* consent is a political act. It is a short step from here to removing the legal character (its autonomy from the will and the interests of its immediate subjects) from law altogether, and to regarding it as the pursuit of a State's interests by another, taboo-supported, means. And, of course, this is precisely the direction in which Soviet writers, with their materialist habits of mind, have sought to move international law; it explains why the Soviet Union is so comfortably at home in the codification field and in the near-law/near-politics world of the General Assembly declarations. The international utilitarian says: come, let us calculate, applying our calculus of values and policies to the real facts of the situation. The international materialist will say: yes, let us negotiate. They may find they are speaking the same language. It is greatly to be hoped that the materialist lawyer will come to recognize the degree to which his approach is blind to the long-term interests of his country and of the world community. Hopefully, too, the non-materialist policy-lawyer may find that it is the grammar, and not the language, which he and the materialist have in common, and he may, before it is too late, choose to regard with suspicion those who come bearing treaties.

It is respectfully suggested, in conclusion, that Professor McDougal's approach, as discussed above and, it is hoped, not caricatured, would seem to be essential in the process of making international lawyers more sensitive to the realities of an exceptionally complex and confusing world; that it is important as a contribution to the form and substance of international political science and international politics (the latter, in the sense of value-based dialogue about international matters); that, because of its comprehensiveness in certain respects and its explicit treatment of policy, it is of great utility in any international law activity where there is an openly legislative element; and that it can provide a rich source from which the traditional method of finding international law can draw. But it would be regrettable, to say the least, if such an approach were to be put forward or to be generally accepted as a substitute for the traditional method of finding international law, with that method's relative and highly convenient certainty, its remarkable flexibility and sensitivity over time, and, above all, with the strength which it gains from being found by men but created by international society itself.

ANNEXE[1]

Ought-patterns

On closer analysis, it is possible that the ought-pattern would be found to include two kinds of pattern representing, respectively, actual or hypothetical situations and potential situations into which such actual or hypothetical situations could be transformed. The 'ought' of the perceiver is attached to a pattern representing the paths (or intermediate patterns) by which the first kind of situation could be transformed into the second kind. This is a form of pattern which, as it were, makes trial adjustments of the focus, to make the two images (of the situation-patterns) converge. The patterns of the perceiver's values (which store the general matrices of what is desirable, fruitful, useful, etc. and which are functional to the brain and derived from experience, from examination of external sources of ought-patterns (State practice, the views of other writers, etc.) or excogitated by the perceiver as an expression of his own psychology) then scan the situation patterns and the focus pattern and cause a preference (consisting of a feeling of actual or expected reduction of tension flowing from the implementation of the preferred course of action and derived in the same kind of ways as the value patterns) to be attached by the perceiver to the potential situations and to the paths by which they can be realized. The pattern or patterns of such paths may then be externalized by the labelling of them with a provisional 'ought'. Whether or not the perceiver will perceive this provisional 'ought' as a rule of law will depend on other scanning processes applied to the provisional ought-pattern and to the patterns flowing from the other sources of law. (Such scanning may precede, accompany or follow the forming of his own 'ought' by the perceiver.) Whether or not the provisional ought-pattern will be treated as a rule of law will depend on the pattern emerging from the perceptions of others who have considered the matter (writers, governments, tribunals). Each time that a writer, a Government or a tribunal carries out the process (forming a pattern from the subject's own internal patterns and from the patterns of all those who have carried out the process before and whose results are known to the subject), the resulting pattern becomes more dense, more autonomous of the will of the subjects and, in this sense, more objective. Changes of fact (for example, the invention of new weapons), changes of value (for example, human rights concepts) and any other changes can alter the patterns at any time, gradually or suddenly and not necessarily by conscious adjustment on the part of the perceiver. It is a continuous, dynamic and cumulative process, taking place over time (and

[1] Referred to above, p. 102.

over a period of time longer than the lifetimes of individuals and even of States) and over space (taking in as many cultural backgrounds and value systems as participate in the process, but, because of its co-operative and objective character, not necessarily dominated by any one such background or system).

[5]

VOLUME 26, NUMBER 2, SPRING 1985

Ideals and Things: International Legal Scholarship and the Prison-house of Language

James Boyle*

INTRODUCTION

The search for a "theory" of international law, no less than the oft-repeated claims about "new directions," seems to me to be the incarnation, within the formalized language of scholarship, of a number of complex and contradictory yearnings—yearnings which are a central feature of the lives of international lawyers, scholars and activists. The strange thing about these yearnings (and it may also be sad, inevitable, or merely comical, depending on your perspective) is that the very language in which they are expressed tends both to exacerbate them and to deny us the possibility of ever dealing with them. I want to discuss these yearnings and the kinds of thinking they might lead us to engage in.

I have recently been reading the work of Alain Robbe-Grillet, a French writer who belongs to a school known as the chosists.[1] The chosists pay an inordinate amount of attention to the description of apparently unimportant household objects. This surfeit of description is supposed to bring on a sort of bittersweet melancholy. The reader contemplates the obsessive concern with the personification of the physical environment and thus becomes all the more aware of the fateful and absurd contrast between the infinite quality of human aspiration and the unrelenting indifference of a world of brute objects. Something in this idea reminds me very much of international legal scholarship.

The resemblance comes from more than the mere coexistence of lofty ideals with mundane reality. It also comes from the fact that the

* Assistant Professor, Washington College of Law, American University. Gary Peller, Peter Gabel, Richard Parker, and Roberto Unger all had a profound influence on the ideas presented in this essay. Henry Steiner was kind enough to comment on earlier versions of individual sections as they were produced. The Washington College of Law Research Fund provided financial assistance. My deepest debt of gratitude is to David Kennedy; his structuralist analysis of international law provided the spur for this focus on reification, many of the arguments developed here were originally worked out in conversation with him, and it would be hard to find the parts of this essay that do not reflect our three years of arguments about things international.

1. *See* A. ROBBE-GRILLET, POUR UN NOUVEAU ROMAIN (1963); *see also* J. STURROCK, THE FRENCH NEW NOVEL (1969).

very discourse in which we describe our experiences and hopes as lawyers and scholars is incapable of evoking (let alone exorcising) the feelings of cognitive dissonance that seem to be an occupational hazard of our profession.

Whereas the chosists spent their time describing trivial objects, international lawyers express their theoretical angst by defining international law.[2] It should be obvious that under this layer of definitionalism several very different activities are going on. Some people are trying to give a convincing account of the normative source of international law. Some are describing a normative meta-system that is supposed to give determinacy and neutrality to the everyday acts of legal interpretation within the international legal process. Others are engaged in the creation of models which, by describing how international law operates, will make it a more attractive problem-solving system to states and other international actors. Finally, some are combining all of these activities in an attempt to redefine the boundaries of the discourse in order to give more weight to the views of some particular group. All of these activities have been described as "definitions" of international law, or as attempts to answer the question "Is international law, law?" It is still true, despite Wittgenstein, that when people feel unsure as to what they should be doing they try to define the *essential elements* of their activity and thus, like medieval philsophers, to find refuge from the world in a prolonged contemplation of the word. My thesis in this article is that this fascination with definitions is not simply a "mistake." Instead I will argue that it is the manifestation of something rather more important: a pervasive reification[3] that operates on the level of everyday politics as well as in the conceptual netherworld of international legal scholarship. Here is a summary of my argument.

(1) Reification is hard to describe for two reasons. First, it is omnipresent and thus invisible. Second, when people do recognise its

2. For an earlier criticism see Williams, *International Law and the Controversy Concerning the World "Law"* 12 BRIT. Y.B. INT'L L. 146 (1945). Although Williams explains the linguistic fallacy inherent in the search, he does not deal with the connection that this essay tries to sketch out—that between "essentialism" and *social* reification such as sexism or role-fetishism. *See infra* note 3.

3. "Reification," in the narrow sense, is the making of a concept into a thing. In this essay I am talking about something broader and less exclusively conceptual. In this sense reification refers to the phenomena that link sexist advertisements to formalistic legal argument and then connects both of them to the debates about "what is law?". All these things rely on the *power* that can be exercised by incorporating a contentious political choice into the act of "re-presentation"; it doesn't matter whether it is Coke commercials presenting women as "essentially" sex objects, or judicial opinions defining sovereignty as an "essential" attribute of a state, the mechanism is the same. *See*, Gabel, *Reification in Legal Reasoning*, 3 RESEARCH IN L. & SOC. 25 (1980); Peller, *The Metaphysics of American Law* (forthcoming CALIF. L. REV.); Boyle, *The Politics of Reason* (forthcoming U. PENN. L. REV.).

existence, they explain it in very different ways. Its basic form is "the conversion of an idea into a thing" but there is much more to it than that. Some people see it as being an attempt to "naturalize" the here-and-now through the claim that it is actually the universal and timeless state of affairs. Others describe it as an attempt to deny both "contingency" and choice by incorporating some political decision about a subject into the *description* of that subject. The latter form is particularly easy to recognize because it depends on claims about "essences." For example, a sexist or racist comment will habitually be couched in the form of mere description. "That's a woman for you" or "It's human nature to be acquisitive" are statements which make political decisions about the role of women and the value of social change while disguising those decisions by incorporating them into the description of "the way things are." Who can argue with "the essential nature of women" or "human nature"? But this phenomenon of "reification" is more than just an argumentative trick which happens to be used both in international legal scholarship and in defenses of the status quo. It is the key to a particular kind of social theory—one that combines the traditional scholarly concern about the theory of the state with a predilection for small-scale descriptions of the realities of social power, in the workplace and the classroom as well as in the prison and the courtroom.

(2) One way to tackle the project of creating such a social theory would be to focus on the way that reification operates to 'close' the social world, the way that it makes the most mundane workplace hierarchy seem divinely ordained. "But what does all this have to do with international legal scholarship?", one might ask. Actually, I think that it has a great deal to do with international legal scholarship, but in order to make that point I will tackle the problem from another direction.

(3) For a long time I saw the problems with international legal scholarship as being a set of separate issues: a little xenophobia here, a little formalism there, a hint of technocracy and the rule of "the best and the brightest" somewhere else. But the more that I looked at it, the more that all the problems started to seem the same. Part of this can be dismissed as "concept fatigue," but I think that there is a sense in which all of the problems can usefully be understood to be the same—they all represent the reification, the "thing-ifying," of the ideals and aspirations that drew scholars to the subject in the first place.[4] This reification happens on many different levels. I have chosen

4. The reification that I have mentioned is rarely a deliberate attempt by a scholar to obscure the political implications of her work. It is more like a general "oppression of ourselves by ourselves" in which concepts are made into things and then treated as though they *were* things

to feature its effects in two main areas; scholarship about the "nature of" international law and the source of its "binding quality" and scholarship about doctrinal interpretation, application and effectiveness. By understanding the way that reification has operated to frustrate the goals of scholars in each of these areas we will not only be able to salvage a set of scholarly projects, but also to link scholarship to our everyday attempts to act as moral beings, whether we are dealing with a workplace dispute or an anti-nuclear campaign.

I. THE "NATURE" OF INTERNATIONAL LAW: SOURCES AND OBLIGATION

It is in scholarship that deals with the "nature," or "definition," or "source" of international law, or with its "binding quality," that one finds the most obvious form of reification—the search for "essences." In our century the dominant debate in this area of scholarship has been between the purveyors of natural law and the purveyors of positivism.[5] Through the use of hypothetical examples and ingenious scholastic conceits, both have attempted to show that *they* rather than the other group have actually discovered the "essence" of law in general and international law in particular. Like all such definitionalist debates, the resulting discourse may seem to be full of sound and fury and yet to signify nothing, but there is more to it than that.

As I pointed out earlier, there are a number of very different projects being carried out under the rubric of an investigation of the "source," or the definition of international law. Some scholars are attempting to prove that treaties are more authoritative than custom,[6] or vice versa,[7] while others are attempting to argue that some new "source," such as General Assembly resolutions or the dictates of utilitarian philosophy, should be given greater prominence as a fountain-head of authoritative norms.[8] Still others are trying to retell the story of international law in order to make it appear that the things we had thought of as defeats

---

which existed prior to our invention of them. Thus my argument is closer to being a critique of idolatry than a conspiracy theory. However, one should still remember that each time we give our own creations the status of golden idols and then worship them, we are reinforcing the grip of the status quo. So there *is* a sense in which reification is paradoxically both "innocent" and profoundly supportive of the existing structures of social power.

5. *See generally* A. NUSSBAUM, A CONCISE HISTORY OF THE LAW OF NATIONS (1947).

6. *See, e.g.*, G. TUNKIN, THEORY OF INTERNATIONAL LAW (1974) (given objective differences of interest between states of differing socio-economic systems, most international law must be formed by the explicit concordance of wills made possible by treaties).

7. *See, e.g.*, H. KELSEN, PRINCIPLES OF INTERNATIONAL LAW (1952) (custom is fundamental law-creating fact that gives international law its status as law).

8. *See, e.g.*, R. HIGGINS, THE DEVELOPMENT OF INTERNATIONAL LAW THROUGH THE POLITICAL ORGANS OF THE UNITED NATIONS (1963); M. BEDJAOUI, TOWARDS A NEW INTERNATIONAL ECONOMIC ORDER: NEW CHALLENGES FOR INTERNATIONAL LAW (1979).

were actually victories. By doing so they hope to stop the so-called "realists" from burying international law before it is dead.[9] But all these projects share one attribute: they are all in one way or another engaged in showing how, and under what conditions, authority can be distinguished from power, right from might, within the international legal system. In short, they are trying to develop some conceptual way of differentiating between law and politics. Once the lawyer has such a system, she can go down her conceptual checklist and make the decision "Is this Law or Not-law?" At the same time these theorists are trying to explain (again, on a *conceptual* level) why law has normative force—what are the hidden ingredients, the analytical components that imbue law with its authoritative status?

It is not that the task of explaining or justifying the normative force of international law is *conceptually* any more difficult than the equivalent task with respect to domestic law. In fact, the problems that theorists encounter are exactly the same; the difference comes from the absence of the veil of normality, of "natural-ness," that covers the internal operations of the state, the veil that would lead us to say that "it goes without saying" that the mugger's demand for one's wallet is "essentially" different from the state's demand for income taxes.[10] Now, of all the multitude of things one might think about this quality of "authoritativeness," one of the strangest would be the belief that there was something about legal norms, some conceptual thread woven into them, that distinguished them from other phenomena and thus provided the source, or test, or surety of their authoritative nature. Nevertheless, that is the line that legal theorists have taken—and if some, like Henkin, or Tunkin, seem to have moved beyond this fascination with conceptualism, it is only because they have shifted the axis along which one asks the questions.[11]

I have already said that one would have to embrace a complicated and unlikely set of ideas in order to believe that there was some point to a search for the "essence" of law. However, in order to believe that this essence not only existed, but that it would somehow provide the key to the normative force of law—the explanation of its "authority"—one would have to jettison most of the ideas about philosophy developed since the Enlightenment.

For a start, one would have to ignore the central insight that "social constructs," such as law, do not have some pre-existing shape prior to

9. *See, e.g.*, L. Henkin, How Nations Behave (1979); P. Jessup, A Modern Law of Nations (1968).

10. *See, e.g.*, H.L.A. Hart, The Concept of Law 79–88 (1961). Hart claims that the legal demand is perceived as more than mere force. But since the initial impulse of the discussion was to find out *why*, this does not get us very far.

11. *See infra* text accompanying notes 30–46.

human intervention. The idea of finding the essence or the real source of law distracts us from the reality that, in a very important sense, it is being created by our categories and definitions rather than being described by them. If we accept the pragmatists' insight that all definitional activity must be guided by some chosen purpose, then we must surely come to the conclusion that definitions can never be true or false but only useful or useless.[12] And if we accept that proposition, then post-medieval jurisprudence comes to resemble its scholastic ancestors fairly closely.

But there is one difference. The scholastic philosophers believed that timeless essences existed which could be uncovered by the exercise of "right reason." As I will try to demonstrate below, both the positivists and the natural law theorists relied on this notion of essences. But attacks on the essentialist approach were so common that they penetrated even the wall of anti-intellectualism surrounding lawyers and legal scholars. Consequently, the current justification for the definitional activity at the heart of international legal scholarship is not that it seeks transcendental essences, but that, being based on timeless and uncontroversial *purposes*, it provides us with a correct view of the "nature" of law. Of course, neutral, universally valid purposes seem about as likely as transcendental essences—and so they should, being basically the same thing—but the interesting thing about this strategy of confession and avoidance is that it has brought the cognitive dissonance in legal thought to the surface. On the one hand, this seems like a bad thing; scholarship appears simultaneously more irrelevant from practice and more Balkanized as these metaphysical "purposes" diverge, each claiming that it possesses the *real* fragment of the true cross.[13] On the other hand, this seems like a good thing. It brings us closer to the utopian goals that actually inspire, yet are denied by, these multifarious scholarly projects. I am going to discuss the history of this process in international legal thought about sources

12. *See* Cohen, *Transcendental Nonsense and the Functional Approach*, 35 COLUM. L. REV. 809, 835 (1935); L. WITTGENSTEIN, PHILOSPOHICAL INVESTIGATIONS 30 (G. Anscombe trans. 1958).

13. I am thinking of, for example, the different political agendas that are served by the theoretical approaches of McDougal, Tunkin, and Henkin. But this confused oscillation from essence to purpose is a more general jurisprudential phenomenon than these examples would indicate. For example, H.L.A. Hart oscillates between the realization that there are no "essences" and a series of attempts to resurrect essentialism on the basis of (supposedly uncontentious) purposes. Thus the chapter in *The Concept of Law* that deals with international law is devoted to an analysis of whether international law is "law." If one reads closely, one finds that law has been implicitly defined according to a set of purposes that are mentioned but never fully articulated, that there is no explanation of how these purposes could acquire the fundamental character that Hart imputes to them, and that the defects of this argument are compounded when the analogy is made from domestic law to international. *See* H.L.A. HART, *supra* note 10, at 1–13, 208–231.

in the hope that the critique I have outlined will allow us to conduct an investigation of the conceptual and political repression it has engendered. I will follow the argument I have laid out in this paragraph, beginning with the positivist/natural law debate, explaining the reliance that both sides put on reified essences, linking this reliance to the question "what is law," and finally describing the shift to "purposive" scholarship about sources—a shift that resurrected the same practices under different names.

The debate between positivism and natural law has dominated legal thought about the sources of international law. This definitional debate is harder to penetrate than one might expect. The main reasons for this are, first, that each side means something different by the question, "What is international law?", and second, that even when one looks *within* either camp, one finds that the question has markedly different implications in different situations. All the preconditions for a futile and circular discussion are thus present. In order to give the maximum of information about this debate in the minimum of space, I will list some of the main inquiries that are subsumed under the positivist and naturalist theories about the source of law. I will then try to show how the reification involved in the way the question was posed has limited, warped and frustrated both sets of theoretical efforts. Throughout the rest of this essay I will try to demonstrate that, at a minimum, the fact that so many people were asking so many different questions and believing that they were all the same question—"What is law?"—has stultified and trivialized the scholarly debate.

A. *Positivist Arguments*

Positivism is, or was until recently, the dominant school of jurisprudential thought in international law.[14] Confronted with the question "What is law?", positivists tended to give answers that concentrated on the institutional procedures of the state and the coercion it wielded.[15] This positivist "line" could be repeated at a number of different levels of abstraction. At the most abstract level, positivists claimed that the essence of law was that it was a command backed by a threat, or a norm stipulating a sanction—this was its imprimatur, the way that you could distinguish it from morals, religion or mere

14. *See* A. NUSSBAUM, *supra* note 5.

15. *See generally* H.L.A. HART, *supra* note 10; H. KELSEN, THE PURE THEORY OF LAW (1967).

habit.[16] Having set up such a reified description, positivists could then argue among themselves as to whether "international law" was really "Law". At a more concrete level, positivists claimed that the "hidden ingredient" that infused international law with normative force was some state-centered attribute such as the consent of the sovereign, rather than some more general "intangible" standard such as the sense of justice held by a nascent world-community.[17] Finally, at the most concrete level, positivists would use their definitional ideas as the basis for doctrinal arguments. But in order to do any of these three things they needed to somehow bring in the implicit purposes to which, for all their universalistic claims, their "definitions" had to appeal if they were to be convincing. This point is one of the major contradictions at the heart of classical international legal theory.[18]

In other words, my argument is that the positivists, at every level of their project, rested their claims to legitimacy on the supposedly

16. Notice that the task has already been implicitly structured by the assumption that law is to be distinguished from those things which are conceptually similar (other normative systems, or "norms" of behavior) rather than from those things that are ideologically, physically, or professionally similar. For example, what would jurisprudential scholarship look like if scholars had thought that the "obvious" task was to distinguish between law and the ideological belief that the social world is divided into a public and a private sphere; or between law and the sexist or racist prejudices that tend to support and reinforce the status quo; or between law and the acts of class violence carried out by the "invisible" hands of the market; or even to juxtapose "law-stuff" and the procedures and customs of accountants?

17. The "evolving world community" seems to be the main modern natural law idea in international law. Just as in domestic legal theory Dworkin has resurrected the idea that there are clear political rights prior to legal interpretation, so the international natural law thinkers have relied on a quasi-teleological notion that the normative consequences of some hypothetical trend towards internationalism can be both accurately identified and clearly applied. *See* R. DWORKIN, TAKING RIGHTS SERIOUSLY 81–130, 266–90 (1977). *See generally* P. JESSUP, *supra* note 9; C. JENKS, THE COMMON LAW OF MANKIND (1958).

18. For example, Hans Kelsen begins his *Principles of International Law*, *supra* note 7, with the claim that "the social phenomena called law present a characteristic in common, distinguishing them from other social phenomena of a similar kind." This characteristic is the only element "by which we are able to differentiate definitely and successfully between a legal and a moral or religious order." *Id.* at 3. This "criterion of law" is that, as a "coercive order", "[i]t provides for socially organized sanctions." *Id.* at 5. The question than becomes, "[i]s international law "law" in the true sense of the term?" *Id.* at 18. Kelsen's answer is that it is, provided that, "the forcible interference of a state in the sphere of interests of another state, [is], in principle, permitted only as a reaction against a delict, and accordingly the employment of force to any other end is forbidden . . . ." *Id.* The imprimatur of law is the application of coercive sanctions under a regime that distinguishes them from wrongful acts. The state is the body that applies these coercive sanctions against other states. One can identify legal obligations by knowing when a state has the (legal) power "to bring about a certain legal effect . . . , especially the power to apply the sanction . . . in case another individual does not fulfill his obligation." *Id.* at 8. If this seems obviously circular as well as deeply essentialist, one should remember that Kelsen thought that he had avoided these problems by postulating a "basic norm," "the hypothesis that international custom is a law-creating fact." *Id.* at 314. Kelsen thus follows all of the stages that I described as typical of an essentialist argument but, most important, he relies on the particular purpose underlying his study (the construction of a secular theory of the legal hierarchy which also separates fact and value) to confer a misplaced "universal" or "scientific" status on his ideas. *Compare* H. KELSEN, *supra* note 7, *with* L. WITTGENSTEIN, *supra* note 12.

universal character of their analysis of the international legal system.[19] Their arguments were supposed to have a fundamental quality precisely because they told us not "what is Law here and there; but what is Law; as Plato, Aristotle, Cicero and divers others have done."[20] But if, as I am claiming, the positivist analysis could only be convincing if it was actually shaped by some concrete, particular, contingent purpose, then the claims to universality cannot be taken seriously. The positivist view becomes just another way to slice up the world; but by the positivists' own standards this is not enough.

The point that I have just made may sound confusing in the abstract, but it is easy to grasp if we look at concrete examples. One of the implicit purposes to which positivism actually caters is the lawyer's need for operational definitions. If one needed to predict which pieces of paper would actually produce a formal reaction from some state organ, then the "evolving world consensus" is not going to be of much use, while a positivist's explanation of the procedural hierarchy might be. Of course this does not mean that positivism is the true definition of law. For example, one might also need to know, as a matter of practice, how far inside the Icelandic fishing limits one could get without being chased by the Icelandic coastguard, or which compensation procedures are accepted as legitimate by Third World states. What is more, we can certainly say that the answers to these questions are "the law on the subject," provided that we make clear how we are defining law and, more importantly, why we are doing so. The positivist has the same freedom, but she does not have the right to say that her definition is the "real" one. But if this is true—if all definitions are founded, implicitly or explicitly, on purpose and convention—then how can the positivist (or anyone else for that matter) use their definition of law as the basis for a claim about the essence of law, or about the normative source of law, or even as the basis for a doctrinal argument? And why did so few people notice that the arguments supporting such claims were threadbare?

I think that the answer to the last question lies in the fact that a vast number of intellectual projects are subsumed under the heading of the positivist definition of law. Even if we leave aside the ones that I mentioned earlier, such as the attempts to give more weight to General Assembly resolutions, or to utilitarian philosophy, one is still left with a staggering number of implicit purposes. Now if these purposes were shared by the reader, they could give a false patina of

19. *See* H. KELSEN, *supra* note 7, at viii, 3, 18. He contrasts the "political ideologies" of other theorists to the "scientific theory of international law," and claims to deal with "the element suited in *all regards* to form the decisive criterion for an investigation into the nature of law." *Id.* at 3 (emphasis added).

20. T. HOBBES, LEVIATHAN 311–12 (C. McPherson ed. 1968).

"correctness" to the theorist's claims of having discovered the essence of international law. Some theorists were attempting to vindicate scientistic views of knowledge and to maintain the logical positivist's dichotomy between fact and value.[21] Others were trying to establish the primacy of the national sovereign over competing centers of authority both within and outside the state. Still others, coming to an intellectual field that had been constructed around a definitionalist question (and coming to it in a historical era in which the lawyer's main task was to predict the reaction of state institutions to pieces of paper produced by other state institutions) actually thought that the positivist definition was *true* in a sense that the natural law definition was not. They did not see this quality of truthfulness as related to their historical, political or professional position, however. It was not that the positivist way of carving up the world was more useful in terms of certain functions of lawyers. Instead, it was that only positivism could accurately describe the *essence* of law.

The conceptual dogmatism I have been describing may sound unconvincing even when positivism is being applied to the standard, formalized posers of twentieth century jurisprudence. But its monomaniacal qualities become truly obvious when extended to history. Do "primitive" people fail to distinguish among the norms that govern their lives on the basis of whether the "source" of those norms was in religion, morality or the power of the state? Then that simply serves to show that they are, indeed, primitive. Since their societies have not yet "developed" a differentiated system of profane power and authority, they are obviously at an "earlier" and "lesser" stage of social development.[22] In other words, the positivist view has actually been read back into history as an indicator of some deep teleological process. And once one has this mythical teleology established in national legal systems one can then use it to "prove by analogy" almost anything one wants to about international law. How strange that this should be done by the same sort of people who, given their professional attachment to one of the drier forms of analytic philosophy, tended to react against Marxist history because of its theoretical reliance on an economic teleology.[23]

B. *Natural Law: The Arguments Reversed*

The main "opposition" to positivist international legal scholarship has always come from the proponents of natural law.[24] Positivists

---

21. *See* H. KELSEN, THE PURE THEORY OF LAW 1-3, 70-76 (1967).
22. *See* H.L.A. HART, *supra* note 10, at 89-91 ("primitive" vs. "developed" legal systems).
23. *See, e.g.*, H. KELSEN, THE COMMUNIST THEORY OF LAW (1955).
24. *See* A. D'ENTREVES, NATURAL LAW (1970).

asserted that the normative force of international law came from the fact that the sovereign had consented to it. The natural law thinkers claimed that this answer was insufficient. How could the sovereign bind itself to bind itself in the future? Why was the initial consent to law given higher normative status than some subsequent decision to renounce the applicability of international law? The natural lawyers argued that this circularity involved the positivists in an endless set of boot-strapping exercises in which they sought some higher source which could, in turn, imbue the sovereign's consent with the kind of normative force they wanted.[25] These "higher" sources generally had some kind of Latin tag, the most famous one being "pacta sunt servanda." Alternatively they relied on language of sublime generality, such as "states should act in such a way so as not to disappoint legitimate expectations." But neither Latin nor vagueness is protection against the realization that the process is endless. "Consent" must rely on a higher source if it is to bind the state to do something against its will. This higher source must rely on a still higher source and so on until one reaches something that can be called the "grundnorm," the "rule of recognition," or the "authority constituting social-legal construct," but which sounds like a definitional stop by any other name.[26]

How did the natural law theorists themselves resolve this problem of the source of legal authority? Whereas the positivists relied on state consent (validated by some mysterious normative background), the natural lawyers relied on some putative normative deep-structure which emanated from the commands of the deity, or from the dictates of right reason, or from a discoverable teleology immanent in the natural state of affairs. And this is where we get to the strange mirror images produced by the reified question at the heart of international legal theory. I say this because the natural lawyer must walk a narrow line between saying that this normative deep-structure is already clearly evidenced by the actions of states (and thus implying that whatever states do is legal) and saying that the deep-structure is *not* evidenced by what states do (and thus implying that it is hopelessly irrelevant). In order to "privilege" the particular line that she chooses, the theorist must thus give some subordinate importance to the consent and the actions of states. Thus whereas the positivists started by positing consent as the source of international law and were driven to rely on some ever-receding normative background, the natural lawyers

---

25. *Id.*

26. *See* H.L.A. HART, *supra* note 10, at 97–114 (rule of recognition); H. KELSEN, *supra* note 21, at 193–220 (*grundnorm* as transcendental-logical proposition); M. McDOUGAL, STUDIES IN WORLD PUBLIC ORDER (1960) (constitutive processes of authoritative decision-making).

started by relying on a deep normative order and ended up depending on manifestations of consent in order to save their project from being branded as either hopeless idealism or craven apologetics.[27]

The mirror-image structure to the arguments I have just described is no accident. If you found a discipline on a question like "What is law?", your arguments are bound to be circular. They will be circular because you will have to alternate between giving precedence to your theory and giving precedence to "the facts," and you will be unable to make it seem as though your choices in this regard are necessary unless you appear to be describing something fairly close to an "essence." This sounds more complicated than it is. Suppose you have a theory about what Law *really* is. Sometimes you will have to give "precedence" to your theory by saying that it shows that something normally talked about as law (say, international law) is not *really* Law at all. At other times you will have to give precedence to the "facts" by saying that a certain feature of "legal reality" shows that your ideas are true. For example, you might say that the familiar internal division of the law into substantive and procedural rules corroborated your theory's emphasis on the difference between rules granting authority and those exercising it. But in order to defend your choice of when to give precedence to the theory and when to the "facts," you would need a meta-theory which would run into the same problem. And so on, *ad infinitum*.

Now look at the framework of the theories put forward by positivists and natural lawyers. The oscillation between state consent and normative deep-structure that I described as a set of mirror-image arguments is simply a local version of the larger problem in the structure of jurisprudential discourse. This oscillation also reappears at each of the levels of abstraction that I described within the positivist and natural law theories. In other words, when the positivists or the natural law theorists use their theory about the essence of law to make further claims about the binding nature of international law, or even to make doctrinal arguments, the same oscillation makes their claims terminally unconvincing unless the indeterminacy of the analysis is concealed by a little judicious reification.

For example, a positivist might claim that the essence of law is that it is a norm that stipulates a sanction. International law is thus dependent on the right of a state to use sanctions, including force, if its legal rights have been infringed. Since this right of self-help is

27. David Kennedy's work on the history of international legal scholarship demonstrates the structural contradictions that this led to in the work of the early natural lawyers. *See* D. Kennedy, International Legal Structures (1984) (unpublished manuscript available in Harvard Law School Library).

actually the basis of the binding quality of international law, it cannot be abridged by international law; the state may make a political choice to revoke it, but it can never be legally alienated. The natural law theorist might respond by saying that the essential purpose of international law is to provide a stepping-stone to a peaceful world community; that its binding force depends on the fact that it serves this trans-historically valid normative goal of "world peace through world law"; and thus, that states not only can, but should legally renounce their rights of self-help. It is not simply that positivists and natural lawyers disagree. Rather, their debates are entirely circular. One could argue from the same positivist premises with just as much logic that, *because* the sanction provided by the right of self-help is the foundation of international law, the state must *always* be able legally to renounce that right; otherwise it is not truly a state and international law is not binding on it. Or, to complete the symmetrical pattern, the natural law premises can be made to produce the argument that because the goal of international law is, in a sense, to annihilate itself by moving to a world community, the one peaceful act which a state cannot take under international law is to renounce its right to self-help. Such an act could only be "legally" accomplished in a binding way under a "higher" stage of law than international law—perhaps under "world law."

My point is not that international lawyers had bad arguments. In a sense it is the reverse: their arguments were too good. Theorists founded their discussion of sources on a definitional question. They claimed that the authoritativeness of their arguments depended on the "universal quality" of their definitions of law. Yet they could only be convincing when they covertly appealed to some "purpose," be it the operational perspective of practitioners, or the teleological perspective of internationalists. In order to maintain their arguments, they had to believe (or at least, seem to believe) that their purpose was woven into the essence of law. But once they had "reified" law in this manner (by incorporating their choice into the concept itself) they were left with arguments that were completely "flippable." As my example above may have shown, the arguments are so "essentialist" that they have been emptied of all content. In the end, both the natural law and the positivist arguments become blank assertions. One might just as well say, "Because." This fate is not particular to the theorists I have been discussing. It will always be the fate of any inquiry founded on the definition, the "essence," or the "nature" of law, or of any other phenomenon for that matter.[28]

28. In a work in progress, I am attempting to describe the way that this process affects not only traditional analytic jurisprudence, but also the philosophy of science, aesthetic theory, linguistic philosophy and "meta-mathematics."

There is another level on which reification has operated in international law—the way in which it has presented the (mainly Western) theories of natural law and positivism as being neutral perspectives on the structure of law, in contrast to the culturally and ideologically influenced theories of the Third World or the Soviet Union. Again it is the claim to be dealing with the essence of law that supports these assertions of neutrality. The positivist (or the natural law theorist) is analysing the definitional components, the *form* of international law, not propounding an ideological view of the *content* of international law. The study of such ideological views is shunted off to some poor neighbor called "the sociology of international law," or "comparative international law," and the positivist emerges with renewed authority. The self-imposed constraints on the "object" of her study reflect the fact that her "discipline" is just as chastening as its name suggests; by excluding the messy and value-laden details of these "ideological views" the theorist supposedly justifies our reliance on her analytical power. As I now move to a discussion of contemporary thought about sources, I will try to show how Western "analytic" or "formal" jurisprudes produced exactly the same kind of arguments as the contemporary "ideological" theorists they have excoriated for being partisan.

C. *Contemporary Thought About Sources*

If one looks at some of the more influential jurisprudential works at the present one might think that theorists have finally escaped from the positivist/natural law merry-go-round. In a sense that is true. The works of Henkin, McDougal, and Tunkin are not as redolent of scholasticism as those of their predecessors.[29] But I would claim that they are all dependent on the same reified form of argument, the difference simply being that they have switched the reification from essence to purpose. Instead of resting their arguments on a search for the essence of international law, they claim to be working from (or towards) some timeless purpose, a "purpose" somehow "privileged" over all other purposes. Once again this process is a lot easier to understand when one has some examples.

1. Contemporary Thought: The USSR

As always, when one has a purpose, certain things recede into the background while others become more prominent. This is particularly obvious in the writings of the Soviet Union's foremost international

29. *See supra* text accompanying notes 18–26.

legal theorist, G.I. Tunkin.[30] In Tunkin's picture, international law is founded on a socio-economic reality which changes according to the logic of the "Marxist-Leninist science of foreign relations."[31] Thus law has, incorporated within itself, a profoundly historicist element. History is not seen as some external supplement to law, a transformatory medium in which law develops. Instead, history is embedded within law; it would be meaningless to talk of "law" without specifying the historical period because "law" is simply the conceptual working out of the logic of some particular stage in world history. This historicist element provides the deep purpose of law which, in Tunkin's theory, is that it should act as a temporary method of peacekeeping and as a mode of communication between "states of differing socio-economic systems", while the world makes the inevitable transition from capitalism to socialism.[32] This deep purpose is not simply an academic conceit or a theoretical ornament. Like the essences that the positivists relied on, it actually dictates the more concrete aspects of the theory. That is to say, Tunkin uses the "historical logic of international law" as a basis for the claims he makes about the "source" of international law, for the precedence he gives to some sources rather than others, and for the doctrinal arguments he puts forward, whether general (trends within the doctrine) or specific (correct resolution of this case).

There is also a further resemblance between Tunkin and the Western jurisprudes. The positivists and natural law theorists found themselves dealing with a world which they had structured according to a tension between two concepts—state consent and some general normative background. This tension could not be resolved, but resolution was exactly what their theorizing demanded. This contradiction played itself out on each successive theoretical level, in discussions of the "nature" of law, discussions of the source of its normative authority, and in the doctrinal arguments which were based on the master theory. Compare this with Tunkin's work.

In terms of the *nature of law* Tunkin must uphold the theory that law is a reflection of the interests of the dominant class in each society. Since he describes international law as being the result of the explicit concordance of the wills of states (thus safeguarding the Soviet Union from having Western legal norms imposed on it by custom), Tunkin must explain how a capitalist ruling class and a socialist ruling class could ever have anything sufficiently in common to actually make

---

30. *See, e.g.*,G. TUNKIN, THEORY OF INTERNATIONAL LAW (1974) [hereinafter cited as THEORY]; Tunkin, *The Contemporary Soviet Theory of International Law*, 31 CURRENT LEGAL PROBS. 177 (1978) [hereinafter cited as *Soviet Theory*]; Tunkin, *International Law in the International System*, 147 RECUEIL DES COURS 1 (1975) [hereinafter cited as *International Law*].

31. G. TUNKIN, THEORY, *supra* note 30, at 22.

32. *See id.* at 251–52. *See also* Tunkin, *International Law*, *supra* note 30, at 20.

law.[33] When he deals with the *source of law's normative authority*, Tunkin is faced with the task of showing that international law reflects, and to some extent reinforces, the inevitable historical progression from capitalism to socialism. At the same time, however, he must argue that it also represents a set of general, external standards which can command the respect of states of differing socio-economic systems precisely because those standards are neither completely manipulable, nor tilted in favor of one side or another.[34] Finally, on the level of *doctrinal argumentation* he must distinguish between those situations to which "general international law" applies[35] (such as, the law of non-intervention: Dominican Republic 1965, Chile 1976, Grenada 1984) and those situations to which the "more specialized" rules of socialist international law apply[36] (such as, the mutual security rules of the socialist brotherhood: Hungary 1956, Czechoslovakia 1968, Afghanistan 1980).

It does not seem to be stretching a point too far to say that these contradictions, appearing at each of our three levels of concreteness, are actually the same and that, on another level of generality, they are even the same as those faced by the positivists and the natural lawyers.

2. Contemporary Thought: Behaviorism and International Law

In a number of different ways, some of the most important contemporary Western work in international legal thought seems to be based on some kind of behaviorism. By "behaviorism" I mean a theoretical approach that focuses on the behavior of states and which has a philosophical commitment to the idea that one can somehow strip behavior of the explanations given for it by the actors themselves and thus reach a more profound understanding of what is really going on. In its most extreme forms, for example in the work of B.F. Skinner,[37] behaviorism dismisses as fallacy the claim that there are actually any "internal" thought processes at all. Everything is explained as the product of stimulus and response. In international law the method has not been applied in such an extreme way. The most one could say is that scholars have been attracted by the allure of "rigor" to which the social "sciences" have long appealed. An early article by Dahl captures this perspective rather neatly. He characterizes behaviorism

33. *See* Tunkin, *International Law*, *supra* note 30, at 19; Tunkin, *Soviet Theory*, *supra* note 30, at 177; Note, *Socialist Principles of International Relations*, 65 AM. J. INT'L L. 796 (1971).

34. *See* G. TUNKIN, THEORY, *supra* note 30, at 251.

35. *See id.* at 21–24.

36. *See* Tunkin, *International Law*, *supra* note 30, at 23; THE SOVIET STATE AND LAW 264 (V. Chkhikvadze ed. 1969); *see* HAZARD, *Renewed Emphasis on Socialist International Law*, 65 AM. J. INT'L L. 142, 145 (1971) (quoting Tunkin concerning Czechoslovakia).

37. *E.g.*, B.F. SKINNER, BEYOND FREEDOM AND DIGNITY (1972).

as being based on the belief that "additional methods and approaches existed or could be developed that would help to provide political science with empirical propositions and theories of a systematic sort, tested by closer, more direct, and more rigorously controlled observation of political events."[38]

Once again international lawyers are searching for the "real" story about what is going on. Faced with an international system that we cannot even describe without taking a political position, it is tempting to "simply look at what happens" without attempting to construct a descriptive or prescriptive international theory about it. The resulting attempts to construct theory-free statements about behavior are remarkably similar to traditional scholarship about sources. Both projects rely for their "authority" on a claim to be describing an essence, which is supposed to be prior to ideological interpretation or factional polemic. Or, to put it another way, in their attempt to escape the circular arguments of positivists and natural lawyers, behaviorist legal scholars actually rely on the same reification, the same essentialism, that was the cause of the very circles they were trying to avoid.

A most interesting example of the invidious effects that the dilemma of formalism and scientism can have is that of the Yale Studies in World Public Order, the series of books and research projects produced under the aegis of Myres McDougal.[39] To reduce the study of international legal discourse to a technocratic means-end manipulation of strategically useful concepts seems unhelpful. The fact that this manipulation almost always ends up favoring the American national interest is disquieting. To claim that one can inject a universal value ("human dignity") into an avowedly means-end technique is a contradiction in terms. For this to become one of the dominant approaches to international law is a travesty.

It could be objected that I have deliberately chosen a dogmatic, scientistic example to make my point. In order to show that the contradictions I describe extend even to the non-scientistic forms of behaviorism, I will use Louis Henkin's influential work on national behavior and international law as a further example.

Henkin may seem a dubious example of a behaviorist. Admittedly, his book is called *How Nations Behave*,[40] but he explicitly points out that he sees governments as being capable of "thought," "awareness" and other "internal" qualities that seem ill-suited to a theory which, in its most extreme forms, denies the reality of "consciousness."[41] On

---

38. Dahl, *The Behavioral Approach in Political Science: Epitaph For a Monument to a Successful Protest*, 55 AM. POL. SCI. REV. 763, 766 (1961).

39. *See, e.g.*, M. McDOUGAL, STUDIES IN WORLD PUBLIC ORDER (1960).

40. L. HENKIN, *supra* note 9.

41. *Id.* at 5.

the other hand, his central goal is to focus on "the influence of law on how nations behave," a subject to which jurisprudential discussion is only "incidental."[42] This sounds as though he believes that behavior can be stripped of its conflicting ideological "meanings" and analyzed from some independent standpoint. Let me say immediately that it is not so much that Henkin believes that he can provide a neutral or objective picture of what is going on, but rather that, like the legal realists, he thinks he can cut through the Gordian knots of formalist debate by presenting law as it appears in behavior. This interpretation is strengthened when one looks at the motivation for his project.

As the horrors of war fade from the minds of national elites, Henkin sees the slow decline of the old dreams of world peace through world law. How can he maintain or even expand the role of international law at a time when most people see it as an infinitely manipulable sham? Henkin's answer is that international law is actually much more important, much more influential on the day-to-day actions of states, than the old conceptual model of "hard legal rules" would have us imagine. In trying to prove that this is the case Henkin provides us with an excellent example of a major intellectual shift in conceptions about law, a shift that will be much more familiar if we compare it to its counterpart in domestic law. Richard Parker describes the domestic version of this shift, as manifested in constitutional law, in the following terms.

> The constitution of our polity—the essence of its "good order"—may be depicted, first of all, as inhering in the constitutional document or in a system of abstract doctrine of constitutional law. In that case, constitutional order is seen as transcending—disembodied from—the clash of wills and movement of passions that characterize day-to-day political life. It may then be enforced *on* political life to discipline those wills and passions. Its enforcement is necessarily a process totally divorced from politics—detached, objective, a matter of abstract legal "reason."
>
> At the other extreme, our constitutional order may be depicted as inhering not in a document or a doctrine, but in our day-to-day politics. In that case, it is seen not as transcending the political process, but as embodied in it. The political process, in turn, is seen not as threatening, but as operating spontaneously in "good order." We can count on our political system, once set up, to work well enough. Hence constitutional order need not be enforced on politics. It need hardly be enforced at all.[43]

---

42. *Id.* at x.
43. Parker, *The Past of Constitutional Theory and Its Future*, 42 Ohio St. L.J. 223, 225 (1981).

It seems to me that Henkin's work is a striking example of the second picture of law. Like the legal realists who transformed our understanding of constitutional law, Henkin is convincing until he tries to reconcile his picture of law as enmeshed in behavior with the picture provided by the "rule of law." At that point he is faced with an impossible task. As David Kennedy has pointed out,[44] Henkin, in order to make his project succeed, must claim that law is implicated in the actions of states, so that law is what states do. But, at the same time, he must maintain some residual amount of the first picture of law—the picture that law is separate from, and critical of, state behavior. If he does not retain this residual picture of law as a set of a-political rules, then it appears that anything that states do is legal. Thus Henkin would be contradicting the body of thought that forms the implicit background to his project, the ideology of the "rule of law" with its insistence on a sharp separation between law and politics. But the second picture is in tension with the first—to explain when law is behavior and when law is imposed on behavior he would need a meta-theory . . . and so on, and so on.

My point is not simply that Henkin's argument is contradictory—David Kennedy has provided a "close reading" of Henkin's work that goes into the aporetic structure of his ideas in detail.[45] Rather, I mean to point out that, once again, the search for the "stripped-down" reality of law leads us into a morass of question-begging, circular arguments.

Henkin's work is undoubtedly more advanced than the theories it criticizes. He even disavows the intention of providing an account that is more than "impressionistic." But underneath his impressionistic project lie two contradictory pictures of what law is all about. Like Holmes in the *Lochner* opinion,[46] Henkin is trying to create a vision of dynamic law, embedded in international social life. But, also like Holmes, he carries with him another, opposite image—the image contained in the ideal of the "rule of law." In this, other, image the law is a set of external rules that must sometimes be imposed on social life so that everyday reality can be forced to live up to the utopian blueprint contained in the legal documents.

It may provide an interesting comparison to note that Holmes, unlike Henkin, confronts this problem explicitly. He tries to establish a residual category, a "supplement" to his picture of law as being enmeshed in social life. This "supplement" expresses the opposite view of law. It talks of statutes being unconstitutional if they contravene

---

44. Kennedy, Book Review, 21 HARV. INT'L L.J. 301 (1980).

45. *Id.*

46. Lochner v. New York, 198 U.S. 45, 74 (1905) (Holmes, J., dissenting).

"fundamental principles as they have been understood by our peoples and our law."[47] But the supplement is "dangerous" to the main project. It is the expression of a contradictory "essence"—an opposing reification. The title of the theory may be different and a focus on behavior may seem to be a far cry from the positivist obsession with hierarchies of procedural norms. Nevertheless, both theories share exactly the same underlying structure, and both must conceal their definitional groundlessness by recourse to reification.

II. DOCTRINE

I want to move straight from this discussion of the scholarship about the nature and the source of international law, to a discussion of scholarship about doctrine. I will not attempt the same kind of analysis as I gave in the last section. Instead I will give a brief impressionistic account, relying on the familiarity of the picture I paint to compensate for the absence of citations to particular examples.

What are doctrinal articles about international law like? "Mush," says the cynic. "Just as definite as a domestic law article," says the scholar. Are they both right? One standard type of doctrinal article springs out of some recent happening—for example, the invasion of Grenada. The scholar gives a useful little potted history of the conflict, discusses the applicability of various norms, and then pronounces a conclusion. Unfortunately the very next article does the same, but comes to the opposite conclusion. Another type of article starts from some norm and then proceeds to discuss the extent to which it is obeyed by states. Things often look grim. "Ah ha!," says the cynic, "this all goes to prove my point. Even scholars cannot agree on the meaning of the law, and states do not obey it anyway. International law is a sham." "Not at all," says the scholar, "people disobey domestic law all the time and lawyers would not exist if there were not differing interpretations of the law. Yet neither of these two facts causes anyone to say that domestic law is a sham. Why should they do so over international law?" Standard argument is followed by standard response. Is there life beyond this debate?

I think that there is. Just as the arguments about sources were warped and frustrated by the implicit framework within which they were conducted, so the arguments about the interpretation, and even the effect of doctrine are constructed around a set of hidden premises that create and then perpetuate the sterile debate I have just described. In other words, I am claiming that scholarship about doctrine has its own pervasive reification, a reification that is similar in form to the

47. *Id.* at 76.

one that I described in my discussion of scholarship about sources. Let me explain what I mean.

Doctrinal scholarship often appears to be an attempt to show that rules can achieve determinacy, to show that there are correct interpretations of international legal norms. My claim is that this attempt is only explicable as the objectified manifestation of a different, more contentious political project. International lawyers are not attempting to show that rules are definite, firm and predictable because they believe this exercise will be good for their health. Their aspiration is to show that international law is a legitimate system for constraining power and irrationality, and, *in their minds*, they carry the assumption that it could only be such a system if there are neutral, objective answers to legal questions. This assumption is occasionally referred to in passing, is rarely debated and is hardly ever seriously questioned. Nevertheless, it is this assumption that provides the hidden logic to the debates about international legal doctrine.

The scholars of the Western countries have modelled international law along the familiar lines of liberal state theory. Their utopian vision is that politics can somehow be constrained by (a-political) rules.[48] This vision leads them to attempt to show that language can somehow provide a neutral conduit for power. The state's consent is to something called "a rule." This rule is made up of words and the words can be interpreted in a non-political way. Thus, ideological conflict can be separated from legal argument and the nation state can logically give its obedience to the resulting "objective" structure. In doing so it is merely following the lead set by its conceptual role model, the atomistic citizen, who makes decisions according to arbitrary, subjective value-judgments. An external source of power like "the law" might seem to pose an ineradicable danger to such a citizen, or to a nation-state. It is this problem which made theorists believe that the law's normative force would depend on the possibility of objective legal interpretation, on a body of materials and a mode of reasoning which, together, could triumphantly pierce the murky subjectivity of the social world.

So far I have suggested that the debate on "whether or not international law is mush" is actually a reified place-holder for a more important aspiration, the aspiration that law can be separated from, and then enforced on, politics. If this is true and we are dealing not with a mere argument over the meaning of doctrine but with a utopian vision expressed in the arcane iconography of the law, then we can begin to understand two features of this debate that otherwise seem inexplicable. First, there is the passion with which the debate has

---

48. *See* R. UNGER, KNOWLEDGE AND POLITICS 80–93 (1975).

been carried on. Second, there is the marked reluctance of international lawyers to incorporate the most basic insights from legal realism, post-Wittgensteinian linguistic philosophy, or any other source of knowledge that tends to undermine the possibility of neutral legal interpretation. These phenomena seem bizarre in the extreme if taken in isolation. They become meaningful only if one sees them as a manifestation of the utopian urges that often bring people to the study of international law in the first place but which most international legal scholarship seem so incapable of expressing.

But even if scholars did want to chain power with reason (or at least with words), this is surely not an unfamiliar, let alone reprehensible, ideal. In both international affairs and in the everyday pattern of Op-Ed pieces, civics classes, and bus-stop conversations that make up "the public sphere of debate," this ideal goes under the name of the rule of law. The defense of the rule of law can be the expression of a profoundly utopian goal. It should not be confused with apologetics simply because they are so often neighbors. But the thesis of this essay is that the ideal of power constrained by reason is expressed through a discourse, the professional language of scholarship as well as the ideology of the public sphere, which actually in some cruel fashion negates it, transforms it, turns its utopia into a suburb of the place we were trying to escape.

To those not interested in the mythology of the liberal state, or in the search for world peace through world law, this matter might appear to be happily irrelevant. It is not. If there is something interesting about this critique it is that it gives us insight into the mundane actuality of power, oppression and suffering as well into the formal language in which we express our opposition to these things. My argument is that legal theorists had the same fixations on the international level as they did on the domestic level and that the method they employed to deal with those obsessions is used in almost every situation of social power. Let us start with the theoretical obsessions and work down to this mysterious method.

Most of contemporary doctrinal scholarship is founded on two basic and mutually contradictory premises. The first is that values are subjective; there can be no demonstrably correct answer to a question that involves a value judgment. The second is the claim that words have "essences," or "core meanings," that can be interpreted mechanically, or at least neutrally. The second belief is necessitated by the first, but also denied by it. This is how it happens.

There is a "legitimating story" that supports the manifestations of the liberal state which appear in legal scholarship. This story operates to justify the exercise of power. But how is power to be justified if there can be no rational defense of value judgments? There are three answers. First, the market place is defensible because it merely records the (arbitrary) choices made by millions of consumers. Second, the democratic system of government is defensible because it merely records the (arbitrary) choices made by millions of voters. Third, the legal system is justifiable because the judge only applies the words of the law to the case in hand. There is simply no value choice to justify. In order to be true to the fundamental tenet that there are no moral or political essences that would allow us to know what "the good" was, and to act upon it, liberal thinkers have had to postulate that there were essences to *words* and that these essences would allow judges to make "correct" decisions without interposing their subjectivity. When legal theorists turned their eyes to international law, in which the problems of legitimacy were more obvious, it was not surprising that they would play out their obsession with words and values all the more strongly.

I want to discuss this obsession, and the utopian goals that fueled it, at the same time as I deal with the aspirations that motivated the search for an essence of law. After describing these various utopian goals, I will make some suggestions about what "new directions" in scholarship this mode of analysis actually suggests. In the last section, I will try to describe the implications of my argument for the teaching of international law; the arena in which most of these issues have had the greatest impact.

III. UTOPIAN ASPIRATIONS IN INTERNATIONAL LEGAL SCHOLARSHIP

If we look back over the discussion of scholarship about the nature and source of international law, it seems as though all of the theorists had a single desire, a single method. Tunkin seems to share a methodology with McDougal, McDougal with Kelsen, Kelsen with Jessup, Henkin, and Hart. All of them seem to be "using" reification to establish that the thing they want us to recognise about international law is already there woven into every strand. All we have to do is to admit its presence in, and its essentiality to, international legal discourse. The same seems to be true of doctrinal scholarship. Admittedly there is less hubris involved in the claim to have identified the essential meaning of a word within a rule than there is to the claim to have identified the essence of law. Nevertheless, the substance of the claims appear remarkably similar.

Why does this "reification" seem to reappear in every new theoretical project? Are the projects really all the same? The answer to the second question is "No." The answer to the first question depends on finding out why the projects are *not* the same. To do that, we need to look to the things that I have been calling the "utopian aspirations"—the implicit political, moral, and epistemological goals that seem to motivate each project.

Reason and Enlightenment

What do international lawyers want? A car in every driveway? Tofu in every pot? For me, the goals of scholarship are easiest to understand if one sees their relationship to politics and rationality. Like all "disciplines," international law is a "rationalist" project. One feature shared by all the scholarship we have looked at, doctrinal or jurisprudential, is the belief that (if carried on according to the plan put forward by that particular author) scholarship can live up to the image of reason exemplified by the Enlightenment. Knowledge itself will be a force for progress, moral autonomy and "the good." As it happens, I hold this vision of enlightened, critical self-reflection very dear. Yet the experience on which this essay is based is that the dominant forms of discourse, the ways of conceiving of the possible and desirable that we call "reason," may be far from emancipatory. Precisely because they are the dominant forms of discourse—be "they" positivist legal theory, traditional psychoanalysis, dialectical materialism, or representational painting—they exclude, "delegitimate," or undermine other modes of thought, other ways of life.[49] We are all aware that knowledge is power, and if we are not, we have everyone from Marx to the late Michel Foucault[50] to remind us. What does this mean for the utopian goals of scholarship?

I think that the answer is something of a paradox. In attempting to pursue their own versions of the Enlightenment project, scholars incorporated the antithesis of self-critical reason into their theories. Take Kelsen as an example. Kelsen's *Pure Theory of Law*[51] and his writings on international law are based on a particular vision of reason, a utopian vision of scientific thought, free from the distortions, myths and half-truths that he saw in moral, political and religious thinking. By knowing the limits of rational thought (which basically consisted of the realm of facts) we will free ourselves from the grandiose normative mysticism of natural law thought. But if we look more closely at Kelsen's theory we see not a hyper-rational, scientific analysis of law, but a dogmatic and repetitive brand of logical positivism, long

49. I may seem to be presenting a rather heartless picture in which theorists of different schools institutionalized the Enlightenment view of truth and thus destroyed it completely, amidst utterances of self-congratulation. The self-doubt brought on by the caricatured similarity in the theorists I have described is matched only by my amazement at the reappearance of essences in each new project.

50. *See, e.g.*, M. FOUCAULT, POWER/KNOWLEDGE (C. Gordon ed. 1980).

51. H. KELSEN, *supra* note 15.

discredited. Kelsen presents himself as an enemy of dogma, myth and medieval thought, and yet he bases his whole theory on those paradigmatically medieval devices, definitions and essences.

Kelsen is not the only one to use methods that are the epistemological antithesis of the Enlightenment vision of reason in an attempt to support a purportedly "rationalist" project. The depressing merry-go-round of positivist and natural law theories which I described in the section on sources is the result of precisely this contradiction. The "authority" that a theorist supposedly gains by describing the "essence" of law is exactly the kind of armor against rational inquiry that the Enlightenment vision of reason takes as its stock villain.

Contemporary thought is not as obviously internally contradictory until one realises that the "uncontentious" purposes animating each theory are actually extremely contentious, whether we are dealing with Tunkin's attempt to plug international law into the inexorable cycle of history, or McDougal's attempt to "square the circle" by claiming that his theoretical perspective is both a neutral means-end technique and normatively loaded in the service of "human dignity." Once again, "rational" projects are mounted on the basis of the philosophical techniques which insulate political choices from criticism, whether those techniques claim the imprimatur of "nature" or of "science" (natural, social, or Marxist-Leninist—pick one).

When we move our focus to doctrinal scholarship the picture looks more or less the same. The utopian aspiration at the heart of doctrinal scholarship was the attempt to cage power (whether of the state or the citizen) with rules. But, as I pointed out in the last section, this aspiration was pursued with tools that seem incompatible to the beliefs that motivated the pursuit in the first place. Let us assume, as liberal theorists do, that values are subjective, that there are no moral essences and thus that we must depend on the "artificial reason" of the law if we wish to restrain power. Where then, do we get these miraculous powers of neutral interpretation? Ah, from the "essential" meanings of words. But wait a minute . . . .

I do not mean to argue that there is no "felt-difference" between the proceedings of the International Court of Justice and the brainstorming sessions in a political affinity-group. Nor am I forgetting the long history of lynch-mobs and pogroms (to say nothing of the bombings of abortion clinics). What I am arguing is that it was never the essential meanings of words that allowed us to do the good things we associate with the rule of law. Nor was it the essential meaning of words that caused the *Lochner* case,[52] the *Korematsu* case,[53] or any other

52. Lochner v. New York, 198 U.S. 45 (1905).
53. Korematsu v. United States, 323 U.S. 214 (1944).

decision. In all of these cases, inescapably political choices are made—some of them systemic, some substantive. The utopian aspect of these choices does not come from any a-political process of neutral reason, but from the struggles and ideals of courageous men and women.

If as a last resort you wish to argue that it is a good thing to maintain the myth of the neutral rule of law (while privately acknowledging its emptiness), I would remind you that those who rely for their defense on myths are always misdirected and often disappointed. Besides, does it not seem a trifle Kafka-esque to be promoting myths we acknowledge to be false, all in the name of "enlightened reason?"

IV. "WHAT IS TO BE DONE?"

It would be fairly ironic if, at the end of a long essay about the perils of reification and the dangers of "the real level of what is going on," I was to provide a description of the "essence of good international law teaching and scholarship." Nevertheless, it would be craven, as well as unsatisfying, to finish a critique and not offer something in the way of a utopian proposal of my own. The suggestions that follow have their roots in the criticism of reification, but of course they are not logically derived from it.

Throughout this essay I have talked about the "utopian aims" of scholarship and of the ways that those aims are distorted or frustrated by the "language" in which they are expressed. But I have also fudged the question of what those utopian aims are; I only deal with their "manifestation" in scholarship about sources, doctrine and so on. I want to now make some implausible and "personal" claims about utopian thinking in international law.

The thing that first attracted me to international law was the lure of internationalism. There was a hefty dose of an adolescent desire to be truly cosmopolitan, there was some connection to my membership in the Campaign for Nuclear Disarmament, and there was the burgeoning outrage against war, famine and pestilence that we condescendingly refer to as "youthful idealism." If you had asked me then whether these ideas were connected to my other political views I might have given a confused answer about monopoly capitalism, or the Judeo-Christian ethic, but in reality I would not have made a connection between, say, my opposition to the sexist Student Union at my university and my belief in world peace through world law.

Things at present look a bit different. As this essay no doubt demonstrates, I now spend a lot of time thinking about reification—the way we turn other people, or social systems, or institutional hierarchies into objects which we then confront as disempowered observers. And a sense of outrage at this "objectification"—this fateful separation from "the Other," who is seen as "a woman," or "a Professor" or "a foreigner," or "a famine victim"—seems to me to be the general purpose fuel for a commitment to internationalism as well as to the demonstrations outside an all-male pub. Which is all very nice, but so what?

This essay is part of a symposium on new directions in international legal scholarship—a fairly abstruse subject, and one that does not seem likely to be connected to the intimate realities of our lives as lawyers, let alone those of the rest of the world's population, people who appear in our texts as populations to convince, victims of war, subjects of human rights violations, or, at best, as part of a "growing world consensus." I alluded to this disjunction—between the intensity of our aspirations and their impact on everyday life—in my comparison of international legal scholarship to the works of the chosist novelists. Is this the end of the story?

I think not. It is precisely because the utopian aims of international lawyers do express a hostility to the division of the world into Self and Other, North and South, Commie and Plutocrat, that their writing is still compelling even when it is covered over with medieval preoccupations about the "nature" of law. It is for the same reason that the disjunction between the world of international law as it is taught and written about, and the political and moral dilemmas of everyday life, that this disjunction is neither irrevocable nor completely disabling. As I have just argued, there is a plausible way of connecting these two arenas—of seeing internationalism as being inextricably intertwined with an opposition to sexism, racism and the calcification of authority. If we tried to concentrate on this connection and the general opposition to *social* as well as to *conceptual* reification that it suggests, what would our "new directions" look like?

For one thing, it would be hard to maintain the same kind of separation between "big" politics and "small" politics. This is not just a matter of realizing every day that there are things wrong with having a classroom structure in which "a professor" stands on a dais at the front of room and tells the people who are sitting down that they must always question authority and take the underdog's position. It is not just a matter of understanding that the teacher who is "Mr. Human Rights" may be dictatorial in the extreme in the classroom, or that the workplace hierarchies of "good" non-governmental organisations may mirror in microcosm the authoritarian politics of governments they condemn.

It more than understanding these things because it depends on a grasp of *how* they happen—the way that (public) politics is roped off from (private) work-life and thus the way that the fatal political paralysis induced by law school is amplified when we come to international politics. If I conceive of state politics as the only real politics, then I am unlikely to be able to conceive of being an effective political actor and doubly unlikely to be able to imagine myself as an effective actor in international political issues. So the University will go on investing in South Africa, and when I don't do anything about *that* it will be all the easier to explain the advantages of Krugerrands to my clients ten years hence, and still think I am an internationalist. After all, it's international law, isn't it?

What follows is an attempt to describe some of the other implications of this focus on both conceptual and social reification. I have chosen to deal with some of the areas that I criticised earlier (scholarship about sources and doctrine), but also to deal with the question of how one might teach using the kind of approach I outlined.

A. *Scholarship and Teaching About Sources*

It may seem bizarre to resurrect this category of scholarship. Surely it was the worst offender when it came to essentialism? Actually, in my own teaching, I have found that it was extremely important to start with a history and critique of the jurisprudence of international law. Otherwise students had the feeling that we were either trying to trick them into accepting a mass of formalistic premises (the same kind of premises they were so used to dissecting in their other first-year classes), or trying to make them believe that people could get excited about a set of definitional formulations that were obviously meaningless. I think of all the case-books that start with the *Lotus* case. Students who have carefully worked their way through the court's reasoning as to how international law is compatible with sovereignty are apt to drop international law straight away. Since the court starts out by trying to explain conceptually how it is that states can be bound when they do not want to be bound, it can hardly solve the problem by claiming that, because of their prior consent, they actually *do* want to be bound. It's just like saying that the small print in the contract represents the will of the parties. It may be an argument that convinces a judge, but it is not an answer to the question "under a will theory, how can this person be obligated to perform terms she did not know about?" In fact it is simply a restatement of the question. How many international law courses never get beyond the stage of restating the questions?

Instead of doing it that way, I introduce the court's heroic attempts to "answer the unanswerable" in terms of the utopian aims that motivated their project and the structural contradictions that made it impossible for them to complete it successfully. It is my perception at least, that rather than getting confused and angry at the circularity of the court's reasoning, the students come to see it as their first exposure to the legal version of a laudable internationalist aim.

I carry on using this general method as we deal with the ideas behind positivist, natural law, and behaviorist thinking. At the same time I try to introduce the class to some of the approaches to international law developed by scholars from the Third World and the USSR. My main aim here is to avoid the uncritical view that I described earlier. If the student decides that, say, Tunkin's ideas are both deeply apologetic and politically objectionable, that is fine. What I want to avoid is the belief that these "outsider's" views are somehow qualitatively distinct from the "real, neutral legal theory" produced by Western scholars. A modest enough little piece of relativism, but one that is more honoured in throwaway introductory lectures than in practice, as far as I can see.

B. *Doctrinal Scholarship and Teaching*

In terms of doctrinal scholarship, I think that we should pursue two apparently contradictory strategies. First, there is the possibility of developing a structuralist account of legal doctrine. Second there is the possibility of using the highly contextualized, politicized knowledge produced by working in clinical programs with international agencies and non-governmental organizations.

1. Structuralism and Doctrine

David Kennedy seems to have provided the best model for the structuralist part of the project.[54] A structuralist account takes the approach, familiar to the legal realists, of dealing with "binary oppositions," pairs of contradictory principles or premises about social life. It differs from the legal realist method in that it tries to explain all of the doctrine, or the legal arguments in a particular area, as being a product of the most basic of these tensions.

Kennedy's own work has focused on the conflict between the co-operative, communal, socialized aspect of international sovereignty, and the atomistic, individualized, and independent aspect. By using this familiar opposition, he tries to show how *all* of the rules, sub-rules and even the arguments by which they are manipulated, can be developed if one simply postulates an unconscious desire to "mediate the contradiction." By "mediating the contradiction" he means the attempt to make it seem as though the two aspects are actually perfectly compatible and thus that the doctrinal edifice has a suffi-

54. *See* Kennedy, *supra* note 27.

ciently coherent and logical structure to maintain its qualitative distinction from all that messy political and ideological conflict.

My favorite example of mediation is a theological one. If I believe that given the existence of a benevolent deity, virtue should be rewarded, but have the experience that wickedness is actually rewarded, I must develop a mediating structure to cover up the conflict between these two beliefs. A common mediator of this particular opposition is "God moves in mysterious ways"—asserting that some deep divine plan is actually going on underneath the (apparently) successful venality all around me. But this raises new problems. If God moves in mysterious ways, how can I ever know Her will with sufficient certainty to act on it as a good person myself? A new mediator must be deployed—common examples include direct, or textual revelation, preselection, or a sense of "reason" tilted toward the divine plan. But each of these . . . . And so on and so on.

If we look at international law this way, what happens? The focus on the generation of mediators for a set of recurring contradictions seems to capture something about the experience of "making a good legal argument." At the same time it becomes obvious that there is a Sisyphean quality to all of this. Why are we trying so hard to cover up these contradictions? Why does it seem as though law has this inner dynamic towards determinacy, this compulsion to make it look as though we are dealing with a "closed system?" One possible answer is the argument raised by my discussion of scholarship about sources and doctrine. The dominant background conception of "reason," self-interest and politics—and the utopian vision of power constrained by rules that is generated within that conception—seem to *require* a set of a-political rules. Since the mark of a neutral set of rules is their ability to provide one logically correct answer to each case, both the compulsive denial of contradiction and the doctrinal structure that this denial "generates" can be seen as products of the initial reification—the attempt to define "what law is," in order to separate it conceptually from morals and political argument.

Theoretically speaking this is all very tidy, but what use is it to teachers, students or practitioners? One of the exciting things about this kind of scholarship is that it lays out both doctrine and the arguments used to manipulate doctrine in a way that is almost reminiscent of classical legal thought, and yet it does so without the same tendency to turn what is into "what should be." In other words, structuralist legal theory has the analytical power of the great formalistic doctrinal edifices without the same commitment to apologetic politics.

What this means, I think, is that we can teach a large amount of doctrine and a large number of analytical techniques quickly, but because this method lays out doctrine in structural terms, we will not be concentrating on the trees to the exclusion of the forest. More importantly, we can give the student a perspective on doctrine that is neither formalistic, nor apologetic. Because the rules and the arguments used to manipulate them are presented as attempts to cover up a set of contradictions, the student does not get the misleading sense that these are the "right answers." What is more, there is no reason why this method should be confined to the (now-decaying) doctrinal structure established by the Western colonial powers. It is quite capable of being turned on the theoretical constructions produced by the USSR and the Third World.

2. Clinical Internationalism

I argued earlier that it was important to see the connection between internationalism and a general opposition to reification in social and intellectual life. I also claimed that this was necessary if we did not wish to become politically disempowered by a constraining vision of politics—"the only good politics is 'big' politics and I can't do anything to influence 'big' politics." One of the implications that I draw from this argument is that it is extremely important to show students that political activity with very real consequences can go on far away from the world of Kondratieff cycles, or trans- versus inter- nationalism. International clinical programs seem to provide the ideal method to accomplish this and at the same time to escape from the constraining world of formalistic international doctrinal scholarship.

Here we have some models to copy from, and some mistakes to avoid. The revolt against formalism in domestic law was connected with the idea that there were other methods to teach students than by relying on the antiseptic words of appellate opinions. This is the obvious connection between theory and practice, clinic and jurisprudence. The mistakes are also obvious. Clinical programs started out as being both politically and pedagogically threatening to the ideology of law schools. Gradually they have been assimilated; the ideals of "justice for all" and legal services for poor people have been traded in for video recorders and simulation classes. This is a mistake that international clinical programs in economic development or human rights should not make.

CONCLUSION

At the beginning of this essay I mentioned the chosists—those who sought to throw the universal quality of human aspiration into sharp relief by counterposing it against lengthy descriptions of objects. I said that international legal thought was similar to chosism, and in the body of the essay I have tried to show both why and how this could be the case. Theorists got their "authority" by being essentialist—by claiming they were dealing with the essence of law, or the "true" source of international obligations, or the "real" meaning of a doctrinal rule. I am going to assert blankly that they often wanted this authority for profoundly utopian reasons—internationalism, world peace through world law, enlightened international dialogue. Yet the fetishism of essences, the belief that this is how one showed oneself to be correct, actually subverts the commitment to enlightened rationality and replaces it with reified ideas, thus ruling out the possibility of real discussion.

So as we read international legal scholarship we might think that it is very like chosist writing—an ironic contrast between high aspiration and mundane description. The crucial difference is that scholars don't seem to *intend* the irony. They think that they are merely describing something—whether that "something" is a rule, or an obligation, or the source of law—when in fact they are putting forward a profoundly political set of arguments. For me it is this, the political effect of reification, that makes the critique put forward in these pages more than an academic exercise. There is something demeaning, something evil, about blindly obeying the imagined "dictates" of some social construct, whether it is the portrayal of women as sex objects, the ethnocentric circularity of positivist legal arguments, or the restrictive set of roles for "partner and associate," "child and parent." And this evil is precisely the one addressed by the critique of reification, or idolatry, or objectification. So what is one to do?

Part of the answer consists of presenting the structure of doctrine and the interplay of the arguments without pretending that they are the "real" level of what is going on. Part of the answer consists in trying to explain why all of the international legal scholars did what they did. It turns out, for example, that the international legal arguments of the USSR are a lot easier to understand if you can discern the mirror-image pattern of arguments that we found in Tunkin and Henkin, as well as in positivism and natural law. Part of the answer consists of thinking up methods of getting ourselves away from the objectified fantasy world of state sovereignty, and towards the actual human beings whose lives our abstractions affect—this means more international clinical programs, but is also means teaching and learning our subject by using poems and pictures as well as treaties and *travaux preparatoires*. Finally, and this seems to be the most important point, part of the answer consists in realizing that one should not divide one's life into tiny, discrete worlds—the struggle against racism and sexism and class-violence in one box, relationships with one's co-workers in another, the production of scholarly utopias in still another.

If one does this, one is simply recreating, in the social world, the kind of mirror-image contradictions that we saw in the conceptual structure of international law.

While I was writing this essay, I was looking for the best examples of attacks on reification; I hate to say this, but it ended up that my two favorites involved Marx[55] and God.[56] If one thing links Marx with the God of the Old Testament it is that both of them seemed to get fairly angry when people not only gave up their ability to choose, but gave it up to the very objects—be they industrial goods or the golden calf—that they had just created. International lawyers are making the same mistake. And that is something that even the chosists could understand.

55. *See* Marx, *Estranged Labour* (from *The Economic and Philosophical Manuscripts of 1844*) and *The Fetishism of Commodities and the Secret Thereof* (from *Capital*), in THE MARX-ENGELS READER 53–67, 215–25 (R. Tucker ed. 1972).

56. *See Exodus* 32:1–35, 34:17.

Part III
The Relationship between International Law and International Society Reconsidered

[6]

LEGITIMACY IN THE INTERNATIONAL SYSTEM

*By Thomas M. Franck**

INTRODUCTION

The surprising thing about international law is that nations ever obey its strictures or carry out its mandates. This observation is made not to register optimism that the half-empty glass is also half full, but to draw attention to a pregnant phenomenon: that most states observe systemic rules much of the time in their relations with other states. That they should do so is much more interesting than, say, the fact that most citizens usually obey their nation's laws, because the international system is organized in a voluntarist fashion, supported by so little coercive authority. This unenforced rule system can obligate states to profess, if not always to manifest, a significant level of day-to-day compliance even, at times, when that is not in their short-term self-interest. The element or paradox attracts our attention and challenges us to investigate it, perhaps in the hope of discovering a theory that can illuminate more generally the occurrence of voluntary normative compliance and even yield a prescription for enhancing aspects of world order.

Before going further, however, it is necessary to enter a caveat. This essay attempts a study of why states obey laws in the absence of coercion. That is not the same quest as motivates the more familiar studies that investigate the sources of normative obligation.[1] The latter properly focus on the origins of rules—in treaties, custom, decisions of tribunals, *opinio juris*, state conduct, resolutions of international organizations, and so forth—to determine which sources, qua sources, are to be taken seriously, and how seriously to take them. Our object, on the other hand, is to determine why and under what circumstances a specific rule is obeyed. To be sure, the source of every rule—its *pedigree*, in the terminology of this essay—is *one* determinant of how strong its pull to compliance is likely to be. Pedigree, however, is far from being the only indicator of how seriously the rule will be taken, particularly if the rule conflicts with a state's perceived self-interest. Thus, other indicators are also a focus of this essay insofar as they determine the capacity of rules to affect state conduct.

* Editor in Chief. The author acknowledges the generous support of the Filomen D'Agostino and Max E. Greenberg Research Fund of New York University School of Law, the very helpful advice of his colleagues Paul Chevigny, Ronald Dworkin, David W. Kennedy, David Richards, Alfred Rubin, Michael Sharpston and Roberto Unger, and the unstinting research assistance of Steven Hawkins, Laurie Oberembt and William Richter. Particular thanks are due to several colleagues on the Board of Editors, and Ag. R.-J. Dupuy of the Collège de France, who have made profoundly useful suggestions.

[1] *See especially* Schachter, *Towards a Theory of International Obligation*, 8 VA. J. INT'L L. 300 (1968).

This essay posits that, in a community organized around rules, compliance is secured—to whatever degree it *is*—at least in part by perception of a rule as legitimate by those to whom it is addressed. Their perception of legitimacy will vary in degree from rule to rule and time to time. It becomes a crucial factor, however, in the capacity of any rule to secure compliance when, as in the international system, there are no other compliance-inducing mechanisms.

Legitimacy is used here to mean that quality of a rule *which derives from a perception on the part of those to whom it is addressed that it has come into being in accordance with right process*. Right process includes the notion of valid sources but also encompasses literary, socio-anthropological and philosophical insights. The elements of right process that will be discussed below are identified as affecting decisively the degree to which any rule is perceived as legitimate.

I. Why a Quest for Legitimacy?

Why study the teleology of law? What are laws *for*? What causes obedience? Such basic questions are the meat and potatoes of jurisprudential inquiry. Any legal system worth taking seriously must address such fundamentals. J. L. Brierly has speculated that jurisprudence, nowadays, regards international law as no more than "an attorney's mantle artfully displayed on the shoulders of arbitrary power" and "a decorous name for a convenience of the chancelleries."[2] That seductive epigram captures the still-dominant Austinian positivists' widespread cynicism towards the claim that the rules of the international system can be studied jurisprudentially.[3]

International lawyers have not taken this sort of marginalization lying down. However, their counterattack has been both feeble and misdirected, concentrating primarily on efforts to prove that international law is very similar to the positive law applicable within states.[4] This strategy has not been intellectually convincing, nor can it be empirically sustained once divine and naturalist sources of law are discarded in favor of positivism.

That international "law" is not law in the positivist sense may be irrefutable but is also irrelevant. Whatever label is attached to it, the normative structure of the international system is perfectly capable of being studied with a view to generating a teleological jurisprudence. Indeed, international law is the *best* place to study some of the fundamental teleological issues that

[2] J. Brierly, The Outlook for International Law 13 (1944) (quoting Sir Alfred Zimmern).

[3] Austin believed that law was the enforced command of a sovereign to a subject. J. Austin, The Province of Jurisprudence Determined (1832); *see also* Janis, *Jeremy Bentham and the Fashioning of "International Law,"* 78 AJIL 405, 410 (1984). This Austinian view has been widely shared by critics. See, however, H. L. A. Hart, The Concept of Law, ch. 10 (1961); and Williams, *International Law and the Controversy Concerning the Word 'Law,'* 22 Brit. Y.B. Int'l L. 146 (1945).

[4] For the best recent exposition of this view, see A. D'Amato, *Is International Law Really Law?*, in International Law: Process and Prospect 1 (1987).

arise not only in the international, but also in national legal systems. This makes it odd that it is not more frequently used as a field for investigation.

Up to a point, the Austinians are empirically right. The international system of states *is* fundamentally different from any national community of persons and of corporate entities. It is not helpful to ignore those differences or to cling to the reifying notion that states are "persons" analogous to the citizens of a nation. Some of the differences are of great potential interest. In a nation, Machiavelli noted, "there cannot be good laws where there are not good arms."[5] In the international community, however, there are ample signs that rules unenforced by good arms are yet capable of obligating states and quite often even achieve habitual compliance. The Austinians, beginning with a defensible empirical observation about the difference between national laws and international rules, deduce from the difference that rules governing conduct which are not "law" in the positivist sense cannot usefully be studied as a system of community-based obligations. It is *this* deduction—not the empirical observation—which is wrong.

Indeed, it is precisely the curious paradox of obligation in the international rule system that should whet our speculative appetite, provoking the opening, not the closing, of jurisprudential inquiry. *Why should rules, unsupported by an effective structure of coercion comparable to a national police force, nevertheless elicit so much compliance, even against perceived self-interest, on the part of sovereign states?* Perhaps finding an answer to this question can help us to find a key to a better, yet realistic, world order. The answer, if there is one, may also incidentally prove useful in designing more widely obeyed, less coerced, laws for ordering the lives of our cities and states.

A series of events connected with the role of the U.S. Navy in protecting U.S.-flagged vessels in the Persian Gulf serves to illustrate the paradoxical phenomenon of uncoerced compliance in a situation where the rule conflicts with perceived self-interest. Early in 1988, the Department of Defense became aware of a ship approaching the gulf with a load of Chinese-made Silkworm missiles en route to Iran. The Department believed the successful delivery of these potent weapons would increase materially the danger to both protected and protecting U.S. ships in the region. It therefore argued for permission to intercept the delivery. The Department of State countered that such a search and seizure on the high seas, under the universally recognized rules of war and neutrality, would constitute aggressive blockade, an act tantamount to a declaration of war against Iran. In the event, the delivery ship and its cargo of missiles were allowed to pass. Deference to systemic rules had won out over tactical advantage in the internal struggle for control of U.S. policy.

Why should this have been so? In the absence of a world government and a global coercive power to enforce its laws, why did the U.S. Government, with its evident power to do as it wished, choose to "play by the rules" despite the considerable short-term strategic advantage to be gained by seizing the Silkworms before they could be delivered? Why did preeminent

[5] N. MACHIAVELLI, THE PRINCE 71 (L. de Alvarez rev. ed. 1981).

American power defer to the rules of the sanctionless system? At least part of the answer to this question, quietly given by the State Department to the Department of Defense, is that the international rules of neutrality have attained a high degree of recognized legitimacy and must not be violated lightly. Specifically, they are well understood, enjoy a long pedigree and are part of a consistent framework of rules—the *jus in bello*—governing and restraining the use of force in conflicts. To violate a set of rules of such widely recognized legitimacy, the State Department argued, would transform the U.S. posture in the gulf from that of a neutral to one of belligerency. That could end Washington's role as an honest broker seeking to promote peace negotiations. It would also undermine the carefully crafted historic "rules of the game" applicable to wars, rules that are widely perceived to be in the interest of all states.

Such explanations for deferring to a rule in preference to taking a short-term advantage are the policymaker's equivalent of the philosopher's quest for a theory of legitimacy. Washington voluntarily chose to obey a rule in the Persian Gulf conflict. Yet it does not always obey all international rules. Some rules are harder to disobey—more persuasive in their pull to compliance—than others. This is known intuitively by the legions of Americans who deliberately underreport the dutiable price of goods purchased abroad, and by the aficionados who smuggle Cuban cigars into the country behind pocket handkerchiefs, but would not otherwise commit criminal fraud. That some rules *in themselves* seem to exert more pull to compliance than others is the starting point in the search for a theory of legitimacy.

The questions raised by such examples of obedience and disobedience, however, are more interesting when examined in the context of the international than of the national community. It is the voluntariness of international compliance that heightens the mystery and lures us with the possibility of discovery. Thus, while the Austinians are right in pointing to important differences between the place of law in national society and the place of rules in the society of nations, those differences do not justify the closing of the international rule system to jurisprudential inquiry.

Indeed, such inquiry into the international system ought to be aided by the insights developed by the study of national and subnational communities. Research into the teleology of national legal systems has led the way to a recognition of the role of legitimacy, as distinct from coercion, as the key to legal order and systematic obedience. While most students of national systems, except perhaps for a few utopians such as Foucault,[6] agree with Machiavelli that governance requires *some* exercise of power by an elite supported by coercive force, few any longer believe the Austinians' claim that this necessary condition is also a sufficient one. Having reached this

[6] Foucault rejects all notions of dominance, whether embodied in theories of sovereignty (divine rule, autocracy, "public rights" and so forth) or embraced in "mechanisms of discipline," including, for example, "power that is tied to scientific knowledge." He visualizes, instead, a new form of "right," which is antidisciplinarian and divorced from concepts of sovereignty. M. FOUCAULT, POWER/KNOWLEDGE: SELECTED INTERVIEWS AND OTHER WRITINGS 106–08 (C. Gordon ed. 1980).

conclusion, most students of law, power and structure in society have sought to identify other characteristics that conduce to the rule of law. Ronald Dworkin identifies three such characteristics: *fairness*, *justice* and *integrity* (the last being a principled, more sensitive variant of consistency).[7] Jürgen Habermas emphasizes the role of discursive validation, following the tradition of Aeschylus and Aristotle.[8] Important scholarship on contract theory has demonstrated that coercion need not be an essential element in ensuring the efficacy of a contract, which is more accurately seen as self-enforcing obligation.[9] In fact, much recent work focusing on the phenomenon of obedience and obligation in national societies concerns itself primarily with noncoercive factors conducing to consensual compliance.

While some such studies have emphasized the role of strategic concepts that gain voluntary compliance by mutualizing advantage, others, beginning with the seminal work of Max Weber,[10] have emphasized the role of *legitimacy* and *legitimation*. Weber's analysis stressed process legitimacy. He hypothesized that rules tend to achieve compliance when they, themselves, comply with secondary rules about how and by whom rules are to be made and interpreted. In his view, a sovereign's command is more likely to be obeyed if the subject perceives both the rule and the ruler as legitimate. Somewhat different concepts of legitimacy have been developed by Habermas[11] and by neo-Marxist philosophers.[12] Oscar Schachter, working in the field of international normativity, has elucidated and emphasized the

[7] R. DWORKIN, LAW'S EMPIRE 176–224 (1986).

[8] According to Habermas:

> Legitimacy means that there are good arguments for a political order's claim to be recognized as right and just; a legitimate order deserves recognition. *Legitimacy means a political order's worthiness to be recognized.* This definition highlights the fact that legitimacy is a contestable validity claim; the stability of the order of domination (also) depends on its (at least) de facto recognition. Thus, historically as well as analytically, the concept is used above all in situations in which the legitimacy of an order is disputed, in which, as we say, legitimation problems arise. One side denies, the other asserts legitimacy. This is a *process* . . . .

J. HABERMAS, COMMUNICATION AND THE EVOLUTION OF SOCIETY 178–79 (T. McCarthy trans. 1979).

[9] Kronman, *Contract Law and the State of Nature*, 1 J. L., ECON. & ORG. 5 (1985).

[10] Weber postulates the validity of an order in terms of its being regarded by the obeying public "as in some way obligatory or exemplary" for its members because, at least in part, it defines "a model" which is "binding" and to which the actions of others "will in fact conform." At least in part, this legitimacy is perceived as adhering to the authority issuing an order, as opposed to the qualities of legitimacy that inhere in an order itself. This distinction between *an* order (command) and *the* order (authority) is easily overlooked but fundamental. 1 M. WEBER, ECONOMY AND SOCIETY: AN OUTLINE OF INTERPRETIVE SOCIOLOGY 31 (G. Roth & C. Wittich eds. 1968). For a critique, see Hyde, *The Concept of Legitimacy in the Sociology of Law*, 1983 WIS. L. REV. 379.

[11] "What are accepted as reasons and have the power to produce consensus . . . depends on the *level of justification* required in a given situation." J. HABERMAS, *supra* note 8, at 183.

[12] Hyde, for example, believes that the concept of legitimacy should be abandoned and replaced by investigation of "rational grounds for action." Hyde, *supra* note 10, at 380. *See also* Bos, *Friede Durch Volkerrecht—Oder Durch Volkerlegitimitat?*, 17 NEDERLANDS TIJDSCHRIFT VOOR INTERNATIONAAL RECHT 113 (1970).

role of "competence and authority" in endowing a rule with capacity to obligate.[13] All have in common, however, their emphasis on noncoercive factors as conducing to rule-compliant behavior.

It thus appears that, despite its residual Austinian propensities, national jurisprudence has quite a bit to say to the international system precisely because there is empirical evidence that, in both systems, noncoercive factors play an important part in conducing to rule/law-compliant behavior. The special value to both national and international jurisprudential inquiry of studying the international system, however, lies in its unalloyed noncoercive state. While the dependence of the international system on voluntary compliance is often (and justly) perceived as a weakness, it happens to afford a singular opportunity. Critics of efforts to study legitimacy as a noncoercive factor conducing to compliance in national legal systems have been able to argue that this factor necessarily eludes researchers because it cannot be isolated from other, authoritarian, elements compelling obedience.[14] That critique loses its force, however, in the international context. Thus, the operation of the noncoercive element, or, specifically, *legitimacy*, becomes easier to isolate and study in the interstate system than in societies of persons, where the coercive sovereign always lurks in the background.

Yet there is a stronger motivation for studying legitimacy in the international system than the academic objective of creating a bridge from national to international speculative jurisprudence. A teleology that makes legitimacy its hypothetical center envisages—for purposes of speculative inquiry—the possibility of an orderly community functioning by consent and validated obligation, rather than by coercion. This is surely the realistic approach to an international jurisprudential teleology: one that examines the objective properties of the global rule system so as to study whether and how it may advance or perfect itself in accordance with the propensities of those observable properties. That inquiry begins with the unexplained, yet evident, paradox that autonomous actors systematically engage in rule-determined conduct, not infrequently in the face of a strong countervailing desire to pursue realizable short-term gratification in violation of the rules.

Admittedly, the rule system of the community of states is far from perfected: absence of rules and disobedience continue to be important dissonant features. But it is too readily assumed that these deficiencies are attributable primarily to the lack of an Austinian sovereign with police powers. The weakness of this explanation is its failure to account for significant deviance: that many rules are obeyed much of the time. What if, instead, rule disobedience, or a rule void, were attributable—in whole or in part—not to the absence of coercive power to enforce the rules but to the perceived lack of legitimacy of the actual or proposed rules themselves and of the rule-making and rule-applying institutions of the international system? Put another way, perhaps failure to obey the rules can best be studied through a better understanding of its opposite: voluntary deference to them.

[13] Schachter, *supra* note 1, at 309.

[14] Hyde, *supra* note 10, at 411–17, 422–25.

That might be rather good news. Since the world is not about to create a global supersovereign with overriding enforcement powers, it might be encouraging to know that these are not the prerequisites of a developed, functioning international community. It would be even more helpful to know that the global system of rules could be further refined and developed, even in the absence of the Austinian factors, by augmenting the legitimacy of rules and institutions. It would spur the social imagination to realize that the creation of a global regime with enforcement power might only be the final culmination of a process capable of gradually perfecting the community, not the sine qua non for system building.

If such a noncoercive, or voluntarist, community were a reasonable goal of the study of legitimation, the resulting society of states would still not resemble the modern nation. In place of coercion, there is only the claim to compliance, based on social entitlement, which a legitimate rule makes on, and on behalf of, all members of the community. In this sense, the international community more closely resembles a membership club with house rules. Membership confers a desirable status, which is manifested when the members have internalized socially functional and status-rooted privileges and duties. Membership is reinforced by valid governance, shared experience, reciprocal gestures of deference and recognition, common rituals, mature common expectations and the successful pursuit of shared goals. Obedience to law, in contrast, at least in part is a recognition of the coercive power of the organized state.

In both the state and the voluntarist international system, obedience to commands is evidence of the existence of an organized community. The international community, however, does not closely resemble the modern state, precisely because the activist state exists to issue and enforce sovereign commands, while the more passive international community exists to legitimize, or withhold legitimacy from, institutions, rules and its members and their conduct. The legitimacy of a rule, or of a rule-making or rule-applying institution, is a function of the perception of those in the community concerned that the rule, or the institution, has come into being endowed with legitimacy: that is, in accordance with right process.

What "right process" means in practice is the subject of the remainder of this essay. Pursuing this line of inquiry, we will focus most of our attention on the legitimacy of *rules*, although attention will also have to be paid to the legitimacy of those institutions and processes through which the rules come into being. In our inquiry we will begin with the rules themselves: their literary structure, origins, internal consistency, reasonableness, utility in achieving stated ends and connection to the overall rule system, and the extent to which their origins and application comport with the international community's "rules about rules." It is the underlying hypothesis of this essay that rules, to varying degrees, contain the determining elements of their own legitimacy.

If legitimacy can be studied, it can also be deliberately nourished. There lies the practical rationale of this inquiry. Someday, perhaps, the international system will come to have law and legal institutions that mirror their domestic counterparts. But that is not now, and it is not likely to be in the foreseeable future. H. L. A. Hart put it more gently: "though it is consistent with the usage of the last 150 years to use the expression 'law' here, the absence of an international legislature, courts with compulsory jurisdiction, and centrally organized sanctions ha[s] inspired misgivings, at any rate in the breasts of legal theorists."[15] Such misgivings, however, are not a cause for despair, nor should they be the end of the road of theoretical inquiry. On the contrary, the misgivings are valid but, for that very reason, are precisely the right starting point in the search for those elements which conduce to the growth of an orderly voluntarist international community and system of rules.

Four elements—the indicators of rule legitimacy in the community of states—are identified and studied in this essay. They are *determinacy, symbolic validation*, *coherence* and *adherence* (to a normative hierarchy). To the extent rules exhibit these properties, they appear to exert a strong pull on states to comply with their commands. To the extent these elements are not present, rules seem to be easier to avoid by a state tempted to pursue its short-term self-interest. This is not to say that the legitimacy of a rule can be deduced solely by counting how often it is obeyed or disobeyed. While its legitimacy may exert a powerful pull on state conduct, yet other pulls may be stronger in a particular circumstance. The chance to take a quick, decisive advantage may overcome the counterpull of even a highly legitimate rule. In such circumstances, legitimacy is indicated not by obedience, but by the discomfort disobedience induces in the violator. (Student demonstrations sometimes are a sensitive indicator of such discomfort.) The variable to watch is not compliance but the strength of the compliance pull, whether or not the rule achieves actual compliance in any one case.

Each rule has an inherent pull power that is independent of the circumstances in which it is exerted, and that varies from rule to rule. This pull power is its index of legitimacy. For example, the rule that makes it improper for one state to infiltrate spies into another state in the guise of diplomats is formally acknowledged by almost every state, yet it enjoys so low a degree of legitimacy as to exert virtually no pull towards compliance.[16] As Schachter observes, "some 'laws,' though enacted properly, have so low a degree of probable compliance that they are treated as 'dead letters' and . . . some treaties, while properly concluded, are considered 'scraps of paper.' "[17] By way of contrast, we have noted, the rules pertaining to belligerency and neutrality actually exerted a very high level of pull on Washington in connection with the Silkworm missile shipment in the Persian Gulf.

The study of legitimacy thus focuses on the inherent capacity of a rule to exert pressure on states to comply. This focus on the properties of rules, of course, is not a self-sufficient account of the socialization process. How rules

[15] H. L. A. HART, *supra* note 3, at 209.

[16] Permissible activities of diplomats are set out in Article 3 of the Vienna Convention on Diplomatic Relations, Apr. 18, 1961, 23 UST 3227, TIAS No. 7502, 500 UNTS 95. Obviously, these do not include espionage.

[17] Schachter, *supra* note 1, at 311.

are made, interpreted and applied is part of a dynamic, expansive and complex set of social phenomena. That complexity can be approached, however, by beginning with the rules themselves. Those seemingly inert constructs are shaped by other, more dynamic forces and, like tree trunks and seashells, tell their own story about the winds and tides that become an experiential part of their shape and texture.

II. DETERMINACY AND LEGITIMACY

What determines the degree of legitimacy of any particular rule text or rule-making process? Or, to ask the same question another way: what observable characteristics of a rule or of a rule-making institution raise or lower the probability that its commands will be perceived to obligate? It is to such questions that the remainder of this analysis is addressed. One could approach the social phenomenon of noncoerced obedience directly, through such various openings as are afforded by the study of myths, game theory or contractarian notions of social compact. Instead, these and other socializing forces will be approached indirectly, through a unifying notion of *rule legitimacy*; that is, by approaching dynamic social forces through those rules which the society chooses to obey or to regard as obligatory. It should be borne in mind, however, that the norm-centered question—what is it about the properties of a rule that conduces to voluntary compliance?—is merely the lawyer's approach to larger sociological, anthropological and political questions: what conduces to the formation of communities and what induces members of a community to live by its rules?

Let us begin by examining the literary properties of the text itself that conduce to voluntary compliance or induce a sense of obligation in those to whom the rule is addressed.

Perhaps the most self-evident of all characteristics making for legitimacy is textual *determinacy*. What is meant by this is the ability of the text to convey a clear message, to appear transparent in the sense that one can see through the language to the meaning. Obviously, rules with a readily ascertainable meaning have a better chance than those that do not to regulate the conduct of those to whom the rule is addressed or exert a compliance pull on their policymaking process. Those addressed will know precisely what is expected of them, which is a necessary first step towards compliance.

To illustrate the point, let us compare two textual formulations defining the boundary of the underwater continental shelf. The 1958 Convention places the shelf at "a depth of 200 metres or, beyond that limit, to where the depth of the superjacent waters admits of the exploitation of the natural resources of the said areas."[18] The 1982 Convention on the Law of the Sea, on the other hand, is far more detailed and specific. It defines the shelf as "the natural prolongation of . . . land territory to the outer edge of the continental margin, or to a distance of 200 nautical miles from the baselines from which the breadth of the territorial sea is measured," but takes into

[18] Convention on the Continental Shelf, Art. 1, Apr. 29, 1958, 15 UST 471, TIAS No. 5578, 499 UNTS 311.

account such specific factors as "the thickness of sedimentary rocks" and imposes an outermost limit that "shall not exceed 100 nautical miles from the 2,500 metre isobath," which, in turn, is a line connecting the points where the waters are 2,500 meters deep.[19] The 1982 standard, despite its complexity, is far more determinate than the elastic standard in the 1958 Convention, which, in a sense, established no rule at all. Back in 1958, the parties simply covered their differences and uncertainties with a formula, whose content was left in abeyance pending further work by negotiators, courts, and administrators and by the evolution of customary state practice.[20] The vagueness of the rule did permit a flexible response to further advances in technology, a benefit inherent in indeterminacy.

Indeterminacy, however, has costs. Indeterminate normative standards not only make it harder to know what conformity is expected, but also make it easier to justify noncompliance. Put conversely, the more determinate the standard, the more difficult it is to resist the pull of the rule to compliance and to justify noncompliance. Since few persons or states wish to be perceived as acting in obvious violation of a generally recognized rule of conduct, they may try to resolve the conflicts between the demands of a rule and their desire not to be fettered, by "interpreting" the rule permissively. A determinate rule is less elastic and thus less amenable to such evasive strategy than an indeterminate one.

A good example of this consequence of determinacy is afforded by the recent litigation between Nicaragua and the United States before the International Court of Justice. From the moment it became apparent that Nicaragua was preparing to sue the United States, State Department attorneys began to prepare the defense strategy. One option considered was invoking the "Connally reservation," which, as part of the U.S. acceptance of the jurisdiction of the International Court of Justice, specifically barred the Court from entertaining any case that pertains to "domestic" matters *as determined by the United States*.[21] Yet the American lawyers chose not to use this absolute defense.[22] Instead, they tried in various other ways to challenge the Court's authority. They argued that the dispute was already before the Organization of American States and the UN Security Council; that it was

[19] United Nations Convention on the Law of the Sea, Art. 76, *opened for signature* Dec. 10, 1982, UN Doc. A/CONF.62/122, *reprinted in* UNITED NATIONS, OFFICIAL TEXT OF THE UNITED NATIONS CONVENTION ON THE LAW OF THE SEA WITH ANNEXES AND INDEX, UN Sales No. E.83.V.5 (1983), 21 ILM 1261 (1982).

[20] For a legislative history and analysis of the provisions of the 1958 Convention, see Whiteman, *Conference on the Law of the Sea: Convention on the Continental Shelf*, 52 AJIL 629 (1958).

[21] 92 CONG. REC. 10,694 (1946).

[22] As I have written elsewhere:

> That the Connally Reservation did not license the United States to refuse to litigate *any* case for *any* reason whatsoever, that a "good faith" caveat was to be implied, is to be given some support by the fact that Connally was not invoked by U.S. lawyers to withdraw the Nicaraguan case from the I.C.J.'s jurisdiction.

Franck & Lehrman, *Messianism and Chauvinism in America's Commitment to Peace Through Law*, in THE INTERNATIONAL COURT OF JUSTICE AT A CROSSROADS 3, 17 (L. Damrosch ed. 1987).

not a legal dispute at all, but a political one;[23] that Nicaragua, having failed to perfect its acceptance of the Court's compulsory jurisdiction, had no right to implead the United States. The failure of the lawyers to use the Connally shield is all the more remarkable because, whereas the reservation gave the United States a self-judging escape from the Court's jurisdiction, all the other defenses left the key jurisdictional decision up to the Court, which rejected every one.[24] Had the U.S. Government simply faced the Court with a "finding" that the mining of Nicaragua's harbors was a "domestic" matter for the United States, that would have ended the litigation. Instead, the United States went on to lose, not only on the matter of jurisdiction, but also, eventually, on the merits.[25]

Why was the Connally shield rejected? The answer, surely, lies in its determinacy. Anyone reading its language would instantly understand that the reservation, while rather open-ended, nevertheless was not intended to cover such matters as the CIA's alleged mining of the harbors of a nation with which the United States was not at war. Although the term "domestic matter" is not so determinate as to bar all differences of interpretation—that, after all, is why its interpretation was reserved to the U.S. Government and not left to the Court—*no* reasonable interpretation of the concept could be stretched to cover the events in question. The U.S. legal strategists, anxious to do everything possible to stay out of court, nonetheless were unwilling to subject their client to the obloquy that would have ensued had the Connally shield been deployed. Interest gratification, convenience and advantage were sacrificed so as not to be seen as absurd.

Such foreboding of shame and ridicule is an excellent guide to determinacy. If a party seeking to justify its conduct interprets a rule in such a way as to evoke widespread derision, then the rule has determinacy. The violator's evidently tortured definition of the rule can be seen to exceed its range of plausible meanings.

Thus, while it may be true in theory, as Wittgenstein has charged, that no "course of action could be determined by a rule because every course of action can be made out to accord with the rule,"[26] some rules are less malleable, less open to manipulation, than others. Although Wittgenstein's point has merit—and has recently been wittily adumbrated by Professor Duncan Kennedy[27]—in practice, determinacy is not an illusion. No verbal formulas are entirely determinate, but some are more so than others.

[23] The United States announced that the case involved "an inherently political problem that is not appropriate for judicial resolution." Department Statement, Jan. 18, 1985, DEP'T ST. BULL., No. 2096, March 1985, at 64, 64, *reprinted in* 24 ILM 246, 246 (1985), 79 AJIL 438, 439.

[24] Military and Paramilitary Activities in and against Nicaragua (Nicar. v. U.S.), Jurisdiction and Admissibility, 1984 ICJ REP. 392 (Judgment of Nov. 26).

[25] Military and Paramilitary Activities in and against Nicaragua (Nicar. v. U.S.), Merits, 1986 ICJ REP. 14 (Judgment of June 27).

[26] L. WITTGENSTEIN, PHILOSOPHICAL INVESTIGATIONS 81, para. 201 (G. E. Anscombe trans. 1953).

[27] Kennedy, *Towards a Critical Phenomenology of Judging*, 36 J. LEGAL EDUC. 518 (1986).

The degree of determinacy of a rule directly affects the degree of its perceived legitimacy. A rule that prohibits the doing of "bad things" lacks legitimacy because it fails to communicate what is expected, except within a very small constituency in which "bad" has achieved a high degree of culturally induced specificity. To be legitimate, a rule must communicate what conduct is permitted and what conduct is out of bounds. These bookends should be close enough together to inhibit incipient violators from offering self-serving exculpatory definitions of the rule. When almost everyone scoffs at such an exculpation, the outer boundary of the rule's determinacy has been established.

There is another sense in which determinacy increases the legitimacy of a rule text. A rule of conduct that is highly transparent—its normative content exhibiting great clarity—actually *encourages* gratification deferral and rule compliance. States, in their relations with one another, frequently find themselves tempted to violate a rule of conduct in order to take advantage of a sudden opportunity. If they do not do so, but choose, instead, to obey the rule and forgo that gratification, it is likely to be because of their longer term interests in seeing a potentially useful rule reinforced. They can visualize future situations in which it will operate to their advantage. But they will only defer the attainable short-term gain if the rule is sufficiently specific to support reasonable expectations that benefit can be derived in a contingent future by strengthening the rule in the present instance.

Let us consider the case of a foreign ambassador's son who has murdered someone in Washington, D.C. He is about to be "booked" by the District police when a message arrives from the State Department demanding his release. The Secretary of State announces that the culprit is to be sent home. Hearing of this, the public understandably is outraged; members of Congress complain to the President. Patiently, the Secretary of State explains that "almost all" states "almost always" act in accordance with the universal rules of diplomatic immunity, which protect ambassadors and their immediate family from arrest and trial.[28] Although in this instance, the Secretary continues, the rule does seem to work an injustice, in general it operates to make diplomacy possible. By gratifying popular outrage and violating the rule this time, the United States would weaken the rule's future utility, its reliability in describing and predicting state behavior. Alternatively, by acting in compliance with the rule, even at some short-term cost to its self-interest, the United States will reinforce the rule text and thus its future utility in protecting U.S. diplomats and their families abroad.[29] Indeed, a study by a committee of the British House of Commons—conducted after a shot from

[28] Vienna Convention on Diplomatic Relations, *supra* note 16, Arts. 31, 37.

[29] The Department of State, on Aug. 5, 1987, submitted its views on a " 'bill to make certain members of foreign diplomatic missions and consular posts in the United States subject to the criminal jurisdiction of the United States with respect to crimes of violence.' " The Department (Ambassador Selwa Roosevelt) "could not support the proposed legislation because it would be detrimental to U.S. interests abroad." If enacted, the law "would place the United States in violation of its international obligations" and would invite more harmful reciprocal action. Contemporary Practice of the United States, 82 AJIL 106, 107 (1988). For the text of Ambassador Roosevelt's statement, see also DEP'T ST. BULL., No. 2127, October 1987, at 29.

the Libyan embassy ("People's Bureau") on April 17, 1984, killed an on-duty London policewoman—came to something very like this conclusion despite the inflamed state of public opinion.[30]

Note, however, that this thoughtful argument by the Secretary against interest gratification only makes sense if the son's immunity is seen as part of a clearly understood normative package, that other countries will refrain from arresting members of the families of U.S. ambassadors on real or trumped-up charges. Such expectations of reciprocity are important threads in the fabric of the international system; but before an expectation of reciprocity can arise, there must be some mutual understanding of what the rule covers, what events constitute "similar circumstances." If the contents of the rule are vaguely defined and fuzzy—if some countries in some instances have extended immunity to the ambassador's children while others have not, or have done so only if no capital crime is involved, or only if the child was actually working for the embassy, or have not extended immunity to second sons, or daughters or stepchildren—the impetus for gratification deferral in the instant case would diminish. The demand for the trial of the ambassador's son might then be both reasonable and irresistible. It could quite easily be defended as not violating a "real" rule. The argument could also be made that bringing the son to trial would create no more hazards for American diplomats abroad than were already posed by the vagueness of the rule. If a norm is full of loopholes, there is little incentive to impose on oneself obligations that others can evade easily.

An excellent example of this cost of indeterminacy is offered by the rules prohibiting and defining aggression that were approved in 1974 by the General Assembly after some 7 years of debate. Among the actions branded as aggression is the "sending by or on behalf of a State of armed bands, groups, irregulars or mercenaries, which carry out acts of armed force against another State." Almost in the same breath, however, the text states that nothing in the foregoing "could in any way prejudice the right to self-determination, freedom and independence . . . of peoples forcibly deprived of that right . . . ; nor the right of these peoples . . . to seek and receive support." To confuse matters further, another article declares that no "consideration of whatever nature, whether political, economic, military or otherwise, may serve as a justification for aggression"; and yet another adds that in "their interpretation and application the above provisions are interrelated and each provision should be construed in the context of the other provisions."[31] Interrelated they may be, but like a tangled skein. Do they prohibit or encourage aid by one country to an insurgent movement in

[30] H.C. Foreign Affairs Committee, First Report, The Abuse of Diplomatic Immunities and Privileges, Report with Annex; Together with the Proceedings of the Committee; Minutes of Evidence Taken on 20 June and 2 and 18 July in the Last Session of Parliament, and Appendices (1984). *See also* Higgins, *The Abuse of Diplomatic Privileges and Immunities: Recent United Kingdom Experience*, 79 AJIL 641 (1985).

[31] Definition of Aggression, GA Res. 3314, 29 UN GAOR Supp. (No. 31) at 142, UN Doc. A/9631 (1974).

another? It is not that the individual mandates and caveats are opaque, but that, seeking to reconcile irreconcilable positions, they contradict one another. Such a muddled obligation, one would expect, could have little effect on the real-world conduct of states; and one would be right.

It happens—by way of contrast—that, in international practice, the rules protecting diplomats, as codified by the Vienna Convention, have a very high degree of specificity,[32] and they are almost invariably obeyed. So, too, are the highly specific rules, in another Vienna Convention, on the making, interpreting and obligation of treaties.[33] Among other subjects covered by determinate rules that exert a strong pull to compliance and, in practice, elicit a high degree of conforming behavior by states are jurisdiction over vessels on the high seas, and in territorial waters and ports,[34] jurisdiction over aircraft,[35] copyright and trademarks,[36] and international usage of posts,[37] telegraphs, telephones[38] and radio waves.[39] There is also a high degree of determinacy in the rules governing embassy property,[40] rights of passage of naval vessels in peacetime,[41] treatment of war prisoners[42] and the duty of governments to pay compensation—even if not as to the *measure* of that compensation—for the expropriation of property belonging to aliens.[43]

[32] *See* Vienna Convention on Diplomatic Relations, *supra* note 16, Arts. 27, 28.

[33] *See* Vienna Convention on the Law of Treaties, Arts. 6, 55, *opened for signature* May 23, 1969, UNTS Regis. No. 18,232, UN Doc. A/CONF.39/27 (1969), *reprinted in* 8 ILM 679 (1969), 63 AJIL 875 (1969).

[34] United Nations Convention on the Law of the Sea, *supra* note 19.

[35] Convention on Offenses and Certain Other Acts Committed on Board Aircraft, Sept. 14, 1963, 20 UST 2941, TIAS No. 6768, 704 UNTS 219.

[36] Universal Copyright Convention, July 24, 1971, 25 UST 1341, TIAS No. 7868 (revised version of 216 UNTS 132).

[37] *See* UNIVERSAL POSTAL UNION CONST., July 10, 1964, 16 UST 1291, TIAS No. 5881, 611 UNTS 7.

[38] *See* Telegraph and Telephone Regulations, with appendices, annex, and final protocol, Apr. 11, 1973, 28 UST 3293, TIAS No. 8586.

[39] *See* International Telecommunication Convention, Oct. 25, 1973, 28 UST 2495, TIAS No. 8572.

[40] *See* Vienna Convention on Diplomatic Relations, *supra* note 16, Art. 22 (which provides for inviolability of diplomatic missions and imposes a special duty on states to protect premises of missions on their territory). *See also* Convention on the Prevention and Punishment of Crimes Against Internationally Protected Persons, Including Diplomatic Agents, Dec. 14, 1973, 28 UST 1975, TIAS No. 8532, 1035 UNTS 167 (which criminalizes violent attacks upon the official premises of internationally protected persons).

[41] The right of innocent passage was specifically provided for in Article 14 of the Geneva Convention on the Territorial Sea and Contiguous Zone, Apr. 29, 1958, 15 UST 1606, TIAS No. 5639, 516 UNTS 205, and by Article 17 of the UN Convention on the Law of the Sea of 1982, *supra* note 19.

[42] *See* Convention Relative to the Treatment of Prisoners of War, Aug. 12, 1949, 6 UST 3316, TIAS No. 3364, 75 UNTS 135. For a complete treatment of war prisoners, see N. RODLEY, THE TREATMENT OF PRISONERS UNDER INTERNATIONAL LAW (1987).

[43] As to compensation for expropriated property, there is agreement in principle, but disagreement as to the measure of compensation. *See, e.g.*, Charter of Economic Rights and Duties of States, Dec. 12, 1974, Art. 2(2)(c), GA Res. 3281, 29 UN GAOR Supp. (No. 31) at 50, UN

What is interesting about these examples is that the high degree of textual determinacy goes together with a high degree of rule-conforming state behavior. When determinacy is absent, it is unlikely that states will have compunctions about not complying with the rule. Indeed, some rules are probably written with low determinacy so that noncompliance will be easy.

A good example is the abortive effort by the United Nations to draft a code for the prevention and punishment of terrorism. In 1972, at the initiative of Secretary-General Kurt Waldheim, the General Assembly tried its hand at devising a set of rules requiring states to act in concert against what was perceived as a global problem.[44] Two years of negotiations demonstrated the difficulty of coming to a commonly acceptable definition of the activity to be prohibited.[45] The Government of Senegal, for example, proposed on behalf of the Non-Aligned Group that the prohibition should include "acts of violence and other repressive acts by colonial, racist and alien régimes against peoples struggling for liberation, for their legitimate right to self-determination, independence and other human rights and fundamental freedoms." The same group urged an exception in favor of those committing terrorist acts on behalf of "the inalienable right to self-determination and independence of all peoples under colonial and racist régimes and other forms of alien domination," in recognition of "the legitimacy of their struggle, in particular the struggle of national liberation movements."[46] The Soviet Union demanded exemption from the prohibition on terrorism for "acts committed in resisting an aggressor in territories occupied by the latter, and action by workers to secure their rights against the yoke of exploiters."[47]

Understandably, the United States and other Western countries took the position that these exculpatory caveats, if adopted, would shape a definition

---

Doc. A/9631 (1974). *See also* Resolution on Permanent Sovereignty over Natural Resources, GA Res. 1803, 17 UN GAOR Supp. (No. 17) at 15, UN Doc. A/5217 (1962). Article 4 of the latter states in part concerning expropriation: "In such cases the owner shall be paid appropriate compensation, in accordance with the rules in force in the State taking such measures in the exercise of its sovereignty and in accordance with international law." *But see* Resolution on Permanent Sovereignty over Natural Resources, GA Res. 3171, 28 UN GAOR Supp. (No. 30) at 52, UN Doc. A/9030 (1973). Article 3 "affirms" that "each State is entitled to determine the amount of possible compensation and the mode of payment, and that any disputes which might arise should be settled in accordance with the national legislation of each State carrying out such measures."

[44] UN Docs. A/8791 and A/8791/Add.1 (1972).

[45] *See, e.g., Ad Hoc* Committee on International Terrorism, Observations of States Submitted in Accordance with General Assembly Resolution 3034 (XXVII), UN Docs. A/AC.160/1 and Adds. 1–2 (1973).

[46] UN Doc. A/AC.160/3/Add.2, at 3 (1973).

[47] UN Doc. A/AC.160/2, at 7 (1973). However, Ambassador Oakley has reported a new Soviet "awareness that distinctions must be made between so-called liberation movements and groups whose objectives and operations are primarily directed toward producing terror, and whose targets are often unrelated to their putative 'liberation' goals." Oakley, *International Terrorism*, 65 FOREIGN AFF. 628 (1987).

of terrorism that would exacerbate, rather than ameliorate, the problem. The loopholes would be so large as to permit unimpeded passage for almost any act of violence claimed to be directed against a wicked regime. On the other hand, few governments would be willing to implement a prohibition on all politically motivated violence against every regime, no matter how repressive. Even the United States has put forward the "Reagan Doctrine,"[48] with its sophisticated distinctions that exculpate external support for "good" insurgents against "bad" regimes, while excoriating support for "bad" insurgents against "good" regimes.[49]

The Reagan Doctrine was merely the most recent restatement of the "just war" notion, evolved by Christian thinkers in the time of Emperor Constantine to reconcile their pacifist theology with imperial military needs,[50] and reinterpreted by Augustine,[51] Aquinas[52] and Grotius.[53] Each version has sought to define the circumstances in which war is permissible, against the background of a more general prohibition. These efforts appeal to common sense and human decency. As long as there is no Austinian world sovereign and centralized world police force, there will be good (defensive) wars and bad (aggressive) wars. Articles 2(4) and 51 of the United Nations Charter[54] likewise seem to bless this distinction. The problem is to distinguish good violence from bad without the benefit of a papal decision.

This problem—how to tell the sheep from the goats—operates whenever a rule tolerates exculpatory distinctions. While simple rules inherently suffer from lack of humanity, reason and texture, more complex ones tend to be hard to apply or to make exculpation too easy. Thus we have a literary conundrum. In consequence of making a simple, but irrational, rule more complex, sensible and humane, the text may become too elastic to secure compliance. For example, applying the proposed international norms known as the Reagan Doctrine, Ambassador Jeane Kirkpatrick has argued that U.S. support for the Nicaraguan contras is permissible, but Soviet and Cuban support for the Sandinistas is not, because the contras are democrats fighting a totalitarian regime while the Sandinistas are totalitarians used by

[48] See Address by Ambassador Kirkpatrick, National Press Club (May 30, 1985), which in effect gave new life to the "just war" doctrine.

[49] On this policy, see Franck, *Porfiry's Proposition: Legitimacy and Terrorism*, 20 VAND. J. TRANSNAT'L L. 195, 218 (1987). *See infra* text accompanying note 55.

[50] F. RUSSELL, THE JUST WAR IN THE MIDDLE AGES 12 (1975).

[51] *Id.* at 18–20.

[52] T. AQUINAS, SUMMA THEOLOGIAE, Question 40, Art. 1 (T. Heath trans. 1972).

[53] *See* H. GROTIUS, ON THE LAW OF WAR AND PEACE (L. Loomis trans. 1949); Edwards, *The Law of War in the Thought of Hugo Grotius*, 19 J. PUB. L. 371 (1970). Grotius expressly contemplated intervention by a third state to protect the natural law rights of the citizens of another state. *See* bk. II, ch. XXV of H. GROTIUS, *supra* (entitled "On the Causes of Undertaking War on Behalf of Others").

[54] UN CHARTER. Article 2(4) seeks to curb aggressive wars by imposing the obligation on states to refrain from the threat or use of force against the territorial integrity or political independence of any state, while Article 51 provides support for the inherent right of individual or collective self-defense in case of armed attack.

Russians and Cubans to colonize Nicaragua.[55] A rule that lends itself to that interpretation, however humane and rational its intent, is unlikely to inhibit any state from pursuing every opportunity for short-term interest gratification. It will be dismissed from serious consideration by states as they weigh their options.

Determinacy thus poses a dilemma. As defined, the term "determinacy" has been used to indicate the clarity of the message transmitted by a rule to those at whom it is directed as a command. We have argued that greater clarity conduces to compliance. Now, however, it has become apparent that "clarity" is far from identical with simplicity. For example, the UN Charter, in Articles 2(4) and 51, sets out a simple rule pertaining to the use of force. It says, in substance, that a state may not use force against another except to respond to an *actual armed attack*. This rule, on its face, seems to enjoy a high level of determinacy. And in most instances of conflict, the rule also makes sense. It is usually possible, in these days of outer space sensing devices, to provide persuasive proof of which state initiated hostilities. Even without such evidence, the answer can usually be determined by looking to see which party is winning after the first day of fighting. Nevertheless, despite its superficial clarity, the rule—under certain circumstances—does not satisfy the test of genuine determinacy: it does not send a clear message as to its meaning in such a way as to promote compliance. This is because a literal reading of the law will produce absurd obligations at the margins of its application. Thus, the rule would seem to compel a state threatened by a nuclear attack to wait until it had actually been hit ("armed attack") before being permitted to use force in self-defense.[56] The rule would also require a tiny state like Israel or Singapore to wait until after an armed attack before striking back, even though it might well have been overrun in that first offensive. In Mr. Bumble's words, "If the law supposes that, the law is a ass—a idiot." Such a rule lacks essential legitimacy, because it is easy to

[55] Address by Ambassador Kirkpatrick, *supra* note 48. The Reagan doctrine is not the only 20th-century attempt to revive the just war doctrine. The Soviet Union has long maintained that "[j]ust wars . . . are not wars of conquest but wars of liberation, waged to defend the people from foreign attack and from attempts to enslave them, or to liberate the people from capitalist slavery, or, lastly, to liberate colonies and dependent countries from the yoke of imperialism." COMMISSION OF THE CENTRAL COMMITTEE OF THE C.P.S.U., HISTORY OF THE COMMUNIST PARTY OF THE SOVIET UNION (BOLSHEVIKS) 167–68 (1939). The modern non-aligned movement has also upheld the just war doctrine, one result being the provisions of Protocol I to the Geneva Conventions. *See, e.g.*, Art. 1(4), Protocol Additional to the Geneva Conventions of 12 August 1949, and Relating to the Protection of Victims of International Armed Conflicts, *opened for signature* Dec. 12, 1977, INTERNATIONAL COMMITTEE OF THE RED CROSS, PROTOCOLS ADDITIONAL TO THE GENEVA CONVENTIONS OF 12 AUGUST 1949, at 3 (1977), *reprinted in* 16 ILM 1391 (1977). This position was dramatically put forth in a 1973 General Assembly resolution: "colonial peoples have the inherent right to struggle by all necessary means at their disposal against colonial Powers and alien domination in exercise of their right of self-determination." GA Res. 3103, 28 UN GAOR Supp. (No. 30) at 142, UN Doc. A/9030 (1973). *See also* GA Res. 2105, 20 UN GAOR Supp. (No. 14) at 3, UN Doc. A/6104 (1965). For a case study, see Dugard, *SWAPO: The Jus ad Bellum and the Jus in Bello*, 93 S. AFR. L.J. 144 (1976).

[56] *See* Franck, *Who Killed Article 2(4)?*, 64 AJIL 809, 820–22 (1970).

predict that in at least some situations no state would abide by its strictures. If a patently absurd result—a *reductio ad absurdum*—accrues from the only possible application of the evident meaning of a simple rule in circumstances requiring a more calibrated response, then it becomes evident that the rule will not be taken seriously in those circumstances, and perhaps also not in others.

If simplicity of text is an invitation to *reductio ad absurdum*, which undermines the determinacy of a rule, and if complexity imposes an elasticity that deprives it of determinate meaning, what can be said about determinacy that is not self-contradicting? There is an answer to this riddle, but it requires attention to detail and, in particular, to content. A simple, straightforward rule—"red light to port, green light to starboard"—will have a high level of determinacy if the problem to which it is addressed is widely recognized as essentially binary: that is, capable of being resolved by an objective test of compliance involving a choice between only two options. A true-false test is binary in this sense. Most traffic regulations also are of this kind. So are prohibitions on specific acts as to which there is general agreement that no exculpatory exceptions are ever admissible. One example is aerial hijacking.[57] The United States, however ruefully, has prosecuted a gunman who seized an aircraft to escape from Eastern bloc oppression,[58] because it felt obliged to discharge its obligation under the Hague Convention either to prosecute or to extradite hijackers.[59] The binary view of hijacking—it either *is* or *is not*, but no excuse will avail—is also manifest in the accord signed by the United States and Cuba in 1973,[60] and in the 1978

[57] [Tokyo] Convention on Offenses and Certain Other Acts Committed on Board Aircraft, Sept. 14, 1963, 20 UST 2941, TIAS No. 6768, 704 UNTS 219; [Hague] Convention for the Suppression of Unlawful Seizure of Aircraft, Dec. 16, 1970, 22 UST 1641, TIAS No. 7192 [hereinafter Hague Convention]; [Montreal] Convention for the Suppression of Unlawful Acts Against the Safety of Civil Aviation, Sept. 23, 1971, 24 UST 564, TIAS No. 7570.

[58] This scenario most notably occurred when an East German hijacked a Polish airliner to West Berlin. As an outgrowth of the historical and jurisdictional freak that is Berlin, the hijacker was charged with crimes under West German law but prosecuted by the United States and tried in an American court. The U.S. ambassador to West Germany appointed a New Jersey federal district judge, Herbert Stern, to preside over the trial. *See* H. STERN, JUDGMENT IN BERLIN (1984). Judge Stern, applying U.S. constitutional law, determined that the defendant was entitled to a jury trial (despite the anomaly that juries generally do not exist under German law). United States v. Tiede, 86 F.R.D. 227 (U.S. Ct. Berlin 1979). Impaneling a jury of West Berliners to judge an East German "refugee" raised the specter that the jury would refuse to convict the defendant in the American tradition of jury nullification. *See* Lowenfeld, *Hijacking, Freedom, and the "American Way,"* 83 MICH. L. REV. 1000, 1005 (1985). In other words, the jury would in effect graft a complex clause upon the linear law of the Hague Convention. In the end, the jury did acquit the defendant of hijacking but convicted him of hostage taking. H. STERN, *supra*, at 350. Judge Stern, affronted throughout the trial by the American prosecutor's stance that the Constitution was inapplicable to West Berlin and skeptical that parole (which he thought appropriate) would be granted, sentenced the hostage taker to time served (9 months) and released him from custody. *Id.* at 369–70.

[59] Hague Convention, *supra* note 57, Arts. 7, 8.

[60] Memorandum of Understanding on Hijacking of Aircraft and Vessels and Other Offenses, Feb. 15, 1973, United States–Cuba, 24 UST 737, TIAS No. 7579.

Bonn Declaration adhered to by Canada, France, Italy, Japan, the United Kingdom, the United States and the Federal Republic of Germany,[61] which imposes collective measures against states that refuse to extradite or prosecute hijackers.[62] Similarly, there appears to be near-universal belief that an objective binary test should apply to hostage taking[63] and violence against diplomats.[64] Even Islamic and Soviet authorities joined in the UN Security Council[65] to condemn the Iranian violations of U.S. diplomatic immunity in Tehran in 1979, a decision that was reaffirmed by a nearly unanimous International Court of Justice.[66] It is not difficult to visualize other narrow

[61] *International Terrorism*, DEP'T ST. BULL., No. 2018, September 1978, at 5 [hereinafter Bonn Declaration].

[62] *Id.* This language tracks Articles 7 and 9(2) of the Hague Convention, *supra* note 57. The Bonn Declaration in effect grafts an enforcement mechanism upon the norms embodied in the Hague Convention. However, imposition of sanctions under the Bonn Declaration is not premised on violation of the Hague Convention. Accordingly, sanctions might be taken against a state that had refused to sign the Hague Convention, not on the basis of the duty to prosecute or extradite (assuming, as is likely, that that is not a duty under customary international law), but on the basis that the support of international terrorism violates international law. *See* Levitt, *International Counterterrorism Cooperation: The Summit Seven and Air Terrorism*, 20 VAND. J. TRANSNAT'L L. 37 (1987). *See also* Chamberlain, *Collective Suspension of Air Services with States Which Harbour Hijackers*, 32 INT'L & COMP. L.Q. 616, 628–32 (1983); Busuttil, *The Bonn Declaration on International Terrorism: A Non-Binding International Agreement on Aircraft Hijacking*, 31 INT'L & COMP. L.Q. 474 (1982). Specifically, the Seven would (1) "take immediate action to cease all flights to that country," and (2) "initiate action to halt all incoming flights from that country or" (3) "from any country by the airlines of the country concerned." Bonn Declaration, *supra* note 61.

[63] International Convention Against the Taking of Hostages, Dec. 17, 1979, GA Res. 34/146, 34 UN GAOR Supp. (No. 46) at 245, UN Doc. A/34/46 (1979). The negotiations for the Hostages Convention reveal the opposition that a straightforward rule, even one for a compartmentalized activity, faces. Attempts at a reformulation of the Convention ranged in sophistication. Several delegations suggested the Convention should only protect "innocent" hostages. *See, e.g.*, UN Doc. A/32/39, at 38 (1977) (statement of Egypt); *id.* at 40 (statement of Guinea, using Ian Smith as an illustrative guilty hostage). The Tanzanian delegate proposed an exculpatory clause and provided an umpire: "For the purposes of the Convention, the term 'taking of hostages' shall not include any act or acts carried out in the process of national liberation against colonial rule, racist and foreign regimes, by liberation movements recognized by the United Nations or regional organizations." UN Doc. A/AC.188/L.5 (1977). The Pakistani delegate wished to condition invocation of the Hostages Convention against national liberation movements on the target state's acceptance of both the Geneva Conventions and the 1977 Protocols. UN Doc. A/C.6/34/SR.62, at 2 (1979).

[64] Convention on the Prevention and Punishment of Crimes Against Internationally Protected Persons, including Diplomatic Agents, *supra* note 40. *See also* Convention to Prevent and Punish the Acts of Terrorism Taking the Form of Crimes Against Persons and Related Extortion that Are of International Significance, Feb. 2, 1971, 27 UST 3949, TIAS No. 8413. The latter, an OAS version of the Internationally Protected Persons Convention, specifically condemns all physical attacks on diplomats, "regardless of motive" (Art. 2). This protection afforded diplomats can be analogized to the 11th-century Peace of God doctrine, which declared certain classes, especially the clergy, exempt from all violence. F. RUSSELL, *supra* note 50, at 34.

[65] SC Res. 461, 34 UN SCOR (Res. & Dec.) at 24, UN Doc. S/INF/35 (1979).

[66] United States Diplomatic and Consular Staff in Tehran (U.S. v. Iran), 1980 ICJ REP. 3 (Judgment of May 24).

categories of international offenses that could be defined without exculpatory caveats: offenses against children,[67] the use of biological[68] and chemical weapons,[69] and offenses against nonbelligerent civilians.[70]

Issues that cannot be reduced to simple binary categories invite regulation by more complex rule texts which, while avoiding the problem of *reductio ad absurdum*, suffer the costs of elasticity. A rule finely calibrated to reflect complex considerations, embodying a textured system of regulatory and exculpatory principles, may suffer legitimacy costs because it invites disputes as to its applicability in any particular case. These costs, however, can be reduced by introducing a forum in which ambiguity can be resolved case by case. Such a legitimate forum mitigates the textual elasticity of the rule by introducing process determinacy. One example is a provision in the 1982 Law of the Sea Convention that deals with the allocation of continental shelf shared by two or more riparian states. The shelf should be apportioned, the rule says, "on the basis of international law . . . in order to achieve an equitable solution."[71] The evidently nonbinary quality of this rule, the vagueness of the notion of an "equitable solution," has been redressed effectively in a series of interpretations by the International Court of Justice. The judges have noted that the treaty sets "a standard, and it is left to the States themselves, or to the courts, to endow this standard with specific content."[72] This the Court has set out to do. In a 1969 opinion, the judges had ruled that there should be some relation "between the extent of the continental shelf areas appertaining to the coastal State and the length of its coast measured in the general direction of the coastline."[73] In a 1982 case between Tunisia and Libya[74] and a 1985 dispute between Libya and Malta,[75] they gave quite specific content to an "equitable solution." In this

[67] The rights of children were recently codified in the Draft Convention on the Rights of the Child, UN Doc. E/CN.4/1986/39. In addition, these rights are treated in the Declaration of the Rights of the Child, GA Res. 1386, 14 UN GAOR Supp. (No. 16) at 19, UN Doc. A/4354 (1959); the Universal Declaration of Human Rights, GA Res. 217A (III), UN Doc. A/810, at 71 (1948), Arts. 25, 26; the International Covenant on Civil and Political Rights, GA Res. 2200, 21 UN GAOR Supp. (No. 16) at 52, UN Doc. A/6316 (1966), Arts. 6, 14, 23, 24; and the International Covenant on Economic, Social and Cultural Rights, GA Res. 2200, *id.* at 49, Arts. 10, 12. *See* Bennett, *A Critique of the Emerging Convention on the Rights of the Child*, 20 CORNELL INT'L L.J. 1 (1987).

[68] Convention on the Prohibition of the Development, Production and Stockpiling of Bacteriological (Biological) and Toxin Weapons and on Their Destruction, Apr. 12, 1972, 26 UST 583, TIAS No. 8062.

[69] Protocol for the Prohibition of the Use in War of Asphyxiating, Poisonous or Other Gases, and of Bacteriological Methods of Warfare, June 17, 1925, 26 UST 571, TIAS No. 8061, 94 LNTS 65.

[70] Convention Relative to the Protection of Civilian Persons in Time of War, Aug. 12, 1949, 6 UST 3516, TIAS No. 3365, 75 UNTS 287.

[71] United Nations Convention on the Law of the Sea, *supra* note 19, Art. 83(1).

[72] Continental Shelf (Libyan Arab Jamahiriya/Malta), 1985 ICJ REP. 13, 30–31 (Judgment of June 3).

[73] North Sea Continental Shelf (FRG/Den.; FRG/Neth.), 1969 ICJ REP. 3, 54 (Judgment of Feb. 20).

[74] *See* Continental Shelf (Tunisia/Libyan Arab Jamahiriya), 1982 ICJ REP. 18, 35 (Judgment of Feb. 24).

[75] 1985 ICJ REP. at 44.

way, the elastic rule text has gained determinacy, just as the papacy once gave content to the vague notion of "just" wars.

Process determinacy is not solely the prerogative of courts. Any institution that is seen to be acting legitimately may be used for the purpose. "Acting legitimately" means here that those it addresses perceive the forum itself as having come into being in accordance with right process. In practice, the legitimacy of a forum can be tested in the same way as that of a rule: by reference to the determinacy of its charter, its pedigree, the coherence of its mandate and its adherence to the normative institutional hierarchy of international organization. Nowadays, the UN General Assembly and Security Council, as well as organs of regional organizations, sometimes play this clarifying role. They will only succeed, however, if they are seen to be acting in accordance with their specific mandate and the general principles of fairness; that is, in a disinterested, principled fashion and not simply to gratify some short-term self-interest of a faction. Moreover, each rule-decision emanating from a legitimate forum is itself subject to the test of its perceived legitimacy: its determinacy, coherence, and so forth.

To summarize: the legitimacy of a rule is affected by its degree of determinacy. Its determinacy depends upon the clarity with which it is able to communicate its intent and to shape that intent into a specific situational command. This, in turn, can depend upon the literary structure of the rule, its ability to avoid *reductio ad absurdum* and the availability of a process for resolving ambiguities in its application.

III. Symbolic Validation and Legitimacy

As determinacy is the linguistic or literary-structural component of legitimacy, so *symbolic validation*, *ritual* and *pedigree* provide its cultural and anthropological dimension. As with determinacy, so here, the legitimacy of the rule—its ability to exert pull to compliance and to command voluntary obedience—is to be examined in the light of its ability to communicate. In this instance, however, what is to be communicated is not so much content as *authority*:[76] the authority of a rule, the authority of the originator of a validating communication and, at times, the authority bestowed on the recipient of the communication. The communication of authority, moreover, is symbolic rather than literal. We shall refer to these symbolically validating communications as cues.

These three concepts—symbolic validation, ritual and pedigree—are related, but not identical. The *symbolic validation* of a rule, or of a rule-making process or institution, occurs when a signal is used as a cue to elicit compliance with a command. The cue serves as a surrogate for enunciated reasons for such obedience. The singing of the national anthem, for example, is a vocal and (on public occasions) a visual signal symbolically reinforcing the citizen's relationship to the state, a relationship of rights and duties. This

[76] Schachter, *supra* note 1, at 309–11. Schachter uses the terms "competence and authority" to cover some of the same matters. In his formulation, "whether a designated requirement is to be regarded as obligatory will depend in part on whether those who have made that designation are regarded by those to whom the requirement is addressed (the target audience) as endowed with the requisite competence or authority for that role." *Id.* at 309.

compliance reinforcement need not be spelled out in the actual words of the anthem (as it is not in the commonly used stanza of the American one). The act of corporate singing itself is a sufficient cue to validate the fabric of regularized relationships that are implicated in good citizenship. We are not really singing about bombs bursting in the night air, but about free and secret elections, the marketplace of ideas, the rule of valid laws and impartial judges.

Ritual is a specialized form of symbolic validation marked by ceremonies, often—but not necessarily—mystical, that provide unenunciated reasons or cues for eliciting compliance with the commands of persons or institutions. The entry of the mace into the British House of Commons is intended to call to mind the Commons's long and successful struggle to capture control of lawmaking power from the Crown. It functions as a much more direct, literal kind of symbolic validation than the "Star-Spangled Banner." Ritual is often presented as drama, to communicate to a community its unity, its values, its uniqueness in both the exclusive and the inclusive sense.

All ritual is a form of symbolic validation, but the converse is not necessarily true. *Pedigree* is a different subset of cues that seek to enhance the compliance pull of rules or rule-making institutions by emphasizing their historical origins, their cultural or anthropological deep-rootedness. An example is the practice of "recognition." When a government recognizes a new regime, or when the United Nations admits a new state to membership, this partly symbolic act has broad significance. It endows the new entity with a range of entitlements and duties, the concomitants of sovereignty. The capacity of states, and, nowadays, perhaps also of the United Nations, to confer sovereignty and its incidents in this fashion derives not from some treaty or other specific agreement but from the ancient practice of states and groupings of states, which legitimizes the exercise of this power.[77] The time-honored recognition practices by which status is conferred symbolically include such subsets as recognition "de facto" and "de jure," recognition of states and governments, the opening of diplomatic relations, and, in the United Nations, admittance to membership and acceptance of delegates' credentials. Along similar lines, Professor Schachter has observed that a body of rules produced by the UN legislative drafting body, the International Law Commission, will be more readily accepted by the nations "after [the Commission] has devoted a long period in careful study and consideration of precedent and practice." Moreover, the authority will be greater if the product is labeled *codification*—that is, the interpolation of rules from deep-rooted evidence of state practice—"than if it were presented as a 'development' (that is, as new law),"[78] even though the Commission (as a subsidiary of the General Assembly) is equally empowered by the UN Charter to promote "the progressive development of international law and its codification."[79] The compliance pull of a rule is enhanced by a demonstrable lineage. A new rule will have greater difficulty finding compliance, and even evidence of its good sense may not fully compensate for its lack of

[77] For a discussion of the origins of recognition policy and procedure, see 1 L. OPPENHEIM, INTERNATIONAL LAW 124–52 (H. Lauterpacht 8th ed. 1955).

[78] Schachter, *supra* note 1, at 310.

[79] UN CHARTER art. 13(1)(a).

breeding. Nevertheless, a new rule may be taken more seriously if it arrives on the scene under the aegis of a particularly venerable sponsor such as a widely ratified multilateral convention, or a virtually unanimous decision of the International Court of Justice.

Symbolic validation, ritual and pedigree are part of the legitimation strategy of all communities, all compliance-inducing rule systems. A study of the legitimacy of imperial authority in ancient China observes that rituals and symbols, "by endowing authority with mystical values and legitimacy, serve not merely to reflect authority but also to recreate and reinforce it. By such means the extent to which people are persuaded to accept a given authority goes far beyond the obedience normally elicited by force."[80] Similar observations have derived from the study of Aztec legitimation strategy, which was found to employ a social tactic making extensive symbolic resources available to achieve "political socialization."[81] For example, the government made a point of distributing food to the citizenry at certain state ceremonies. Feeding as Christian sacrament is also a symbolic validation of status as members of the mystical body of Christ, of hierarchic authority structure within that community, and serves as a renewal of commitment and obligation.

"Political legitimacy," a study of ancient China notes, "can be said to adhere to a regime and its authorities when the governed are convinced that it is right and proper to obey them and to abide by their decisions."[82] This conviction was cued symbolically in Aztec society by priests who provided "supernatural sanction for legitimate state authority,"[83] rather as did the Roman Pontifex Maximus.[84] But, in many societies, ritual and pedigree will have their symbolic roots in the cultural and political, rather than the religious, experience. In a posttheistic society, ritual is not discarded; rather, politics and history are substituted for magic and myth as the compliance-inducing or status-securing cue.

For example, in Britain the rule that a parliamentary bill becomes law only after receiving the assent of the Crown[85] certainly no longer relates to the divine right of monarchs. Although the Queen's title still claims that she rules "by the grace of God," it is not widely believed either that the Queen rules or, for that matter, that there is a God, particularly one involved in

[80] H. WECHSLER, OFFERINGS OF JADE AND SILK 21 (1985).

[81] Kurtz, *Strategies of Legitimation and the Aztec State*, 23 ETHNOLOGY 301, 309 (1984).

[82] H. WECHSLER, *supra* note 80, at 10. [83] Kurtz, *supra* note 81, at 306.

[84] The Pontifex's task, originally, was to legitimate political authority by appeasing the river god Tiber over whose banks the civil authorities had built a useful, but undeniably intrusive, bridge.

[85] When presenting bills for royal assent, the Speaker of the House of Commons pays homage to the Crown with the formula: "Be it enacted by the Queen's most Excellent Majesty, by and with the advice and consent of the Lords Spiritual and Temporal, and Commons, in this present Parliament assembled, and by the authority of the same, as follows . . . ." O. PHILLIPS, A FIRST BOOK OF ENGLISH LAW 118–19 (7th ed. 1977). The Crown's right to refuse assent to bills that have properly passed through both Houses of Parliament is "practically obsolete." A. DICEY, INTRODUCTION TO THE STUDY OF THE LAW OF THE CONSTITUTION 114 (9th ed. 1939). In fact, when the Unionists posited in 1913 that the reference to assent restored a real right of veto, the theory was criticized as "obviously absurd" and was said to have troubled the king. E. RIDGES, CONSTITUTIONAL LAW 106 (8th ed. 1950).

British government. A utilitarian explanation for the survival of the historic ritual of royal assent would have to look elsewhere.

Oddly, the very obsolescence of the practice of royal assent helps keep it alive. The act of seeking the Queen's signature on legislation, even when it is clear that she has no choice but to grant it, is not meaningless. It signifies the Government's acceptance of all the accumulated encrustation of customs that define and restrict British governmental powers and practices. The Speaker of the House, for example, assures the Queen that the bill has had its customary three readings in Parliament and has passed both Houses.[86] While meaning little in itself, since the governing party usually can command the parliamentary majority necessary to do what it wants, the ritual of three readings[87] symbolizes the governing party's subordination to orderly, unhurried parliamentary procedure. In an era of relentless bureaucratic momentum, these quaint historical-political rituals provide a delay for reflection and debate between the drafting of a bill and its implementation. The result is that the rituals of three readings and monarchial assent symbolically validate, cuing public compliance and serving to certify the legitimacy of the new law.

Of course, a bad law does not become a good one for having been anointed by parliamentary ritual and having received the blessing of pedigreed authority. A citizen who believes a law to be evil probably will not be induced to think otherwise by symbolic cues. Nevertheless, when decisions to comply or defy are made by those to whom a command is addressed, such cues, with their symbolic validation of its legitimacy, may tip the scales on the side of obedience.

The three-readings ritual is the secular analogue of the church's practice of "publishing the banns" of a proposed marriage on three successive Sundays before the actual nuptials are consecrated.[88] Even in this rational era, the publication of banns also has its residual validating force, which derives not from belief in the divine, but from faith in the evolutionary history that the ritual symbolizes. Just as the House of Commons's three readings celebrate the continuity of parliamentary democracy, the publication of banns symbolizes commitment to the social status of matrimony conferred by both the church and the acquiescent congregation. Both rituals constitute a recommitment to the society's procedural rules of recognition, the "rules of

[86] When a bill is presented to the Crown for assent, it bears an endorsement signed by the Speaker of the House certifying that the provisions of the Parliament Act have been complied with. Parliament Act, 1911, 1 & 2 Geo. 5, ch. 13, §2(2), *reprinted in* SELECT STATUTES, CASES AND DOCUMENTS 350, 352 (C. Robertson ed. 1935).

[87] For a full discussion of this ritual as it applies to the enactment of both public and private bills by the House of Commons and the House of Lords, see S. A. DE SMITH, CONSTITUTIONAL AND ADMINISTRATIVE LAW 265–71 (3d ed. 1977).

[88] The calling of banns is the public and official announcement of persons who intend to marry and is meant to discover whether the parties are free to marry and whether any impediment to their lawful and valid marriage may exist. The tradition that no marriage was to be celebrated until after a triple publication of the church's banns originated in the 8th century and was extended over all Christendom by Pope Innocent III in 1215. ENCYCLOPEDIC DICTIONARY OF RELIGION 357 (1979).

the game," about which more will be said below. These *secondary* rules about rules are particularly important because they are the yardstick by which all *primary* or substantive rules and commands can be tested. The legitimacy of secondary rules is particularly dependent on the length of their pedigree. They must be difficult to change if they are to be perceived as valid and able to validate. Thus, the secondary rules, as well as the primary rules made in accordance with them, derive their legitimacy in part from the rootedness of the former deep in the history and culture of the community. For this reason, a bill that did not undergo three readings and was not presented for the assent of the Crown would undoubtedly be perceived by Britons as lacking legitimacy, not because those rituals are believed to be powerful in themselves, but because the Government's failure to perform them would be seen as a repudiation of the ancient democratic essence of the British parliamentary system, of which the rites and pedigree are still potent cues.

As we have noted, validating cues are not a modern, or a western, invention. Pedigree is a particularly universal form of symbolic validation. Most societies make some form of linguistic connection between the concepts "old" and "venerable." In the ancient Aztec state, the rulers' hereditary relation to the Toltec dynasty "was the sacred source of legitimate power and authority,"[89] supplemented by a host of "pedigree nobles."[90] So, too, in the China of 1000 B.C., where the Mandate of Heaven doctrine endowed an ancient imperial series of rulers with historically pedigreed and ritually validated power that rested on an orderly system, or line, of succession.[91]

Ritual, too, is a pandemic validator of authority. The fundamental purpose of ritual in ancient China was to create a form of procedural legitimacy that Max Weber would have understood.[92] The point is illustrated by the story of Kao-tsu (206–195 B.C.). When Kao-tsu founded the Han dynasty, he and his followers were "rough and ready fellows" and, to put them at ease, the emperor abolished the "elaborate and bothersome" *Ch'in* ritual code. Unfortunately, this made a "shambles of court audiences" as the members of his court went about "getting drunk, hurling insults at one another, and hacking up the wooden pillars of the palace with their swords. To introduce some decorum . . . , Kao-tsu was moved to appoint an erudite named Shu-sun T'ung to provide him with a court ritual consonant with his modest personal capacity for performing ceremonial." The experiment proved a great success. The ritual "served as a powerful tool for dignifying and strengthening the ruler's position and for controlling the behavior of subordinates. It emphasized the large gap between the position of emperor and that of mere bureaucrat, prevented former associates from presuming upon past friendships, and helped keep subordinates agreeably subservient."[93]

In the modern state system, ritual and other kinds of symbolic validation play much the same role as in ancient and medieval national societies, inte-

[89] Kurtz, *supra* note 81, at 306.

[90] *Id.* at 308.

[91] H. WECHSLER, *supra* note 80, at 12–15.

[92] *See supra* note 10 (for Weber's perception that legitimacy in part stems from the authority issuing an order, rather than from the order itself).

[93] H. WECHSLER, *supra* note 80, at 25.

grating by inclusion and exclusion, seducing subjects into obeying rules and rulers, validating the exercise of power and generally contributing to the legitimization of the institutions and rules of the society. As a less-developed system, international society is underendowed with such symbolic validation, but what there is serves approximately the same legitimizing function as in ancient China, in the Aztec nation[94] and in modern parliamentary democracies.[95]

Despite their paucity, there are significant examples of attempts by the international system to legitimize itself through ritual and pedigree. One of the oldest and most universal was by using marriage between children of heads of state as symbolic emphasis for a practical political and social compact between nations, sometimes merely reifying the concept of a "family" of allied nations, at other times leading to—legitimizing—actual political union or federation. The practice was common not only among medieval European royal houses, but also in Asia, Africa and the precolonial Americas. For example, in Aztec Mexico, the "head of state established alliances with neighboring states through marriage. . . . Acamapichtli is reputed to have married twenty daughters of the chiefs of the clans that comprised Aztec society."[96]

One of the newest examples of symbolic international system legitimation is the creation of supranational agencies such as the United Nations Development Programme,[97] the International Bank for Reconstruction and Development[98] (the "World Bank"), the World Health Organization,[99] the Food and Agriculture Organization[100] and the United Nations International Children's Emergency Fund.[101] Their role is to distribute benefits to the deserving and the needy, either in tandem, or in competition, with the unilateral donations still given by one country to another.

The purpose of these agencies is largely and usefully instrumental. Nevertheless, the form of the organization is heavily symbolic. The World Bank, for example, could as well have been set up with only the 12 to 16 chief industrial nations as members, since they contribute almost all its working capital. Instead, the symbolic mingling of donors and recipients in the bank's governing organs and bureaucracy is intended to purge the assistance given of the aura of direct dependence between recipient and donor, a relationship in which gratitude has often been superseded by bitterness. By symbolic multilateralization, gratitude is directed to the agency, all of whose

[94] *See supra* text accompanying note 81.

[95] *See supra* text accompanying notes 86–87.

[96] Kurtz, *supra* note 81, at 308.

[97] *See* GA Res. 2029, 20 UN GAOR Supp. (No. 14) at 20, UN Doc. A/6014 (1965).

[98] Articles of Agreement of the International Bank for Reconstruction and Development, *opened for signature* Dec. 27, 1945, 60 Stat. 1440, TIAS No. 1502, 2 UNTS 134.

[99] WORLD HEALTH ORGANIZATION CONST., July 22, 1946, 62 Stat. 2679, TIAS No. 1808, 14 UNTS 186.

[100] UN FOOD AND AGRICULTURE ORGANIZATION CONST., Oct. 16, 1945, 12 UST 980, TIAS No. 4803.

[101] The United Nations International Children's Emergency Fund was founded by GA Res. 57, 1 UN GAOR (Res. pt.2) at 90, UN Doc. A/64/Add.1 (1946).

members participate, in most cases, as theoretical equals. This equality of participation is itself the symbolic representation of a confluence between sovereignty and interdependence that holds together the "community" of states.

The distribution of benefits by a global agency, with its own officials and symbols, also helps to create a sense of social solidarity—a primitive version of loyalty—between recipients (both persons and governments) and the international system (the "United Nations Family") of which the donor agency is a part, rather in the same way as did the Aztec rulers' ritual distribution of foodstuffs to subjects. This symbolic, as well as utilitarian, function of multilateral, institutionalized benevolence is familiar to anthropologists and sociologists who study the formation of national societies. In Aztec society, the "[c]onstruction and maintenance of temples and other public buildings appeased the gods, organized people's labor according to state directives and supported priests and other state functionaries."[102] The Pharaohs similarly sought to serve both personal and socializing objectives in the construction of the pyramids.[103] This concept of legitimization through the symbolism of public works has not been unknown, either, to American politicians from "Boss" Curley of Boston[104] to Nelson D. Rockefeller of New York.[105] It is also understood by the fledgling bureaucracy of the international system.

There are many other examples of ritual and other symbolic reinforcement of legitimacy in the international system. Thus, the United Nations Organization is authorized to fly its own flag, not only at headquarters, but also over regional and local offices around the world.[106] The flag has been used at the instigation of the Secretary-General to immunize such UN battle-front operations as clearing sunken ships from the Suez Canal in 1956

[102] Kurtz, *supra* note 81, at 310.

[103] Although many consider the pyramids to be solely the product of slave labor, evidence has been advanced indicating that the labor was in fact compensated. Thus, it is "probably nearer the truth [to] regard these monuments as vast public works providing economic security for a good part of the population." H. JANSON, THE HISTORY OF ART 40 (rev. ed. 1969). Erected as part of vast funerary districts, the pyramids were the scene of great religious festivities, both during and after the Pharaoh's lifetime. *Id.* at 38. At least as far as Old Kingdom pyramids are concerned, Pharaohs equipped their tombs as a "kind of shadowy replica of [their] daily environment for [their] spirit[s] . . . . [T]he Egyptian tomb was a kind of life insurance, an investment in peace of mind." *Id.* at 35.

[104] *See* J. DINNEEN, THE PURPLE SHAMROCK (1949) (which details the life of James Michael Curley, four-time mayor of Boston). *See also* E. O'CONNOR, THE LAST HURRAH (1956) (which, although fictional, is said to be based on Curley's life and career).

[105] In formulating the project for the Albany Mall, Governor Nelson Rockefeller suggested modeling New York's capitol on the palace of the Dalai Lama at Lhasa, Tibet. The revised version of the mall's plan incorporated architectural and symbolic elements from Lhasa, Washington, D.C., Brasília, Versailles, Rockefeller Center and St. Petersburg, and was meant to be "the most spectacularly beautiful seat of government anywhere in the world." Krinsky, *St. Petersburg-on-the-Hudson: The Albany Mall* (citing FORTUNE, June 1971, at 92), in M. BARASCH & L. SANDLER, ART THE APE OF NATURE 771, 778 (1981).

[106] The General Assembly adopted and authorized the use of the United Nations flag on Oct. 20, 1947. *See* GA Res. 167, 2 UN GAOR (96th plen. mtg.) at 338–39, UN Doc. A/414 (1947).

and protecting members of the Palestine Liberation Organization being evacuated from Lebanon in 1983.[107] The United Nations also issues stamps,[108] which not only are accepted for mail delivery by member states, but also generate a tidy independent income—some $8.6 million in 1986–1987.[109] Peacekeeping forces and truce observers under UN command and wearing UN symbols are stationed between hostile forces in Kashmir,[110] the Golan Heights,[111] Cyprus,[112] Lebanon[113] and Iran-Iraq.[113a] They are lightly armed, if at all, and palpably unable to defend themselves in the event of renewed hostilities; but, with their distinctive emblems, they have come to symbolize the world's interest in the continuance of an agreed truce or armistice. The blue and white helmets and arm bands also symbolize a growing body of rules applicable to peacekeeping operations, manifesting and reinforcing the authority of forces that usually are neither as numerous, nor as well armed, as those they must keep pacified. Their role is purely, but effectively, symbolic of the desire of bitter enemies—and the international community—to have respite from combat. Yet their token presence has a far more inhibitory effect on the behavior of states than can be explained by their minimal coercive power.[114] It is their perceived legitimacy, symbolically validated, that serves as their shield and usually induces more powerful forces to defer to their intangible authority.

The United Nations and its agencies also maintain headquarters and regional facilities that are accorded limited extraterritoriality and immuni-

[107] For the Secretary-General's operation to remove ships sunk in the Suez Canal during the 1956 war, see 1956 UN Y.B. 53–55; and GA Res. 1121, 11 UN GAOR Supp. (No. 17) at 61, UN Doc. A/3386 (1956). The Secretary-General also authorized, with the "support" of the Security Council, the flying of the UN flag on ships that would evacuate armed elements of the PLO from Tripoli. *See* UN Docs. S/16194, S/16195, 38 UN SCOR (Res. & Dec.) at 5–6, UN Doc. S/INF/39 (1983).

[108] The United Nations Postal Administration was established on Jan. 1, 1951. *See* GA Res. 454, 5 UN GAOR Supp. (No. 20) at 57–58, UN Doc. A/1775 (1950).

[109] The estimated 1986–1987 net revenue from the sale of postage stamps was $8,667,700. *See* Advisory Committee on Administrative and Budgetary Questions, First Report on Proposed Programme Budget for the Biennium 1986–1987, 40 UN GAOR Supp. (No. 7) at 209, UN Doc. A/40/7 (1985).

[110] The origin of the United Nations Military Observer Group in India and Pakistan (UNMOGIP) is found in a resolution of the UN Commission for India and Pakistan. *See* 3 UN SCOR Supp. (Nov. 1948) at 32, UN Doc. S/1100, para. 75 (1948). The Security Council subsequently authorized its operation. *See* SC Res. 91, para. 7, 6 UN SCOR (Res. & Dec.) at 1, 3, UN Doc. S/INF/6/Rev.1 (1951).

[111] The Security Council established the UN Disengagement Observer Force (UNDOF) for the Golan Heights on May 31, 1974. *See* SC Res. 350, 29 UN SCOR (Res. & Dec.) at 4, UN Doc. S/INF/30 (1974).

[112] The United Nations Force in Cyprus (UNFICYP) was formed by the Security Council on Mar. 4, 1964. *See* SC Res. 186, 19 UN SCOR (Res. & Dec.) at 2–4, UN Doc. S/INF/19/Rev.1 (1964).

[113] The United Nations Interim Force in Lebanon (UNIFIL) was created by the Security Council on Mar. 19, 1978. *See* SC Res. 425, 33 UN SCOR (Res. & Dec.) at 5, UN Doc. S/INF/34 (1978).

[113a] *See* Report of the Secretary-General, UN Doc. S/20093 (Aug. 7, 1988); SC Res. 619 (Aug. 9, 1988) (creating the force); GA Res. 42/233 (Aug. 17, 1988) (funding the force).

[114] For a discussion of the noncoercive role of UN peacekeeping forces, see B. URQUHART, A LIFE IN PEACE AND WAR 287–88, 342–43 (1987).

ties.[115] These have symbolic as well as practical significance. The extension of diplomatic immunity to top UN officials, privileges usually reserved for representatives of states, symbolizes the emergence of the Organization as an autonomous international actor, pedigreed in its own right. The functions and privileges of the agencies' resident representatives in various countries do not differ greatly, in practice, from those of ambassadors. Although it is not widely known, the Organization also levies an income tax[116] (staff assessment) on its employees who, with the exception of Americans, are immune from national taxation in recognition of the fact (noted by the U.S. Supreme Court in the domestic federal context[117]) that the right of states to tax federal instrumentalities must be limited because it necessarily encompasses the right to destroy.

A few more examples. Symbols of pedigree and rituals are firmly imbedded in state diplomatic practice. The titles ("ambassador extraordinary and plenipotentiary"), prerogatives and immunities of ambassadors, consuls and others functioning in a representative capacity are among the oldest of symbols and rites associated with the conduct of international relations. The sending state, by the rituals of accreditation, endows its diplomats with pedigree. They become, in time-honored tradition, a symbolic reification of the nation ("full powers" or *plenipotentiary*), a role that is ritually endorsed by the receiving state's ceremony accepting the envoy's credentials. These ceremonies, incidentally, are as old as they are elaborate and are performed with as remarkably faithful uniformity in Communist citadels as in royal palaces.[118] Once accredited and received, an ambassador *is* the embodiment of the nation. The status of ambassador, once conferred, carries with it inherent rights and duties that do not depend on the qualities of the person, or on the condition of relations between the sending and receiving states, or on the relative might of the sending state. To insult or harm this envoy, no matter how grievous the provocation, is to attack the sending state. Moreover, when an envoy, acting officially, agrees to something, the envoy's state is bound, usually even if the envoy acted without proper authorization.[119] The host state normally is entitled to rely on the word of an ambassador as if his or her state were speaking.

[115] *See* Convention on the Privileges and Immunities of the United Nations, *adopted* by the General Assembly Feb. 13, 1946, 21 UST 1418, TIAS No. 6900, 1 UNTS 1 (entered into force for the United States Apr. 29, 1970). *See also* Agreement Regarding the Headquarters of the United Nations, June 26, 1947, United States–United Nations, 61 Stat. 3416, TIAS No. 1676, 11 UNTS 11 (entered into force Nov. 21, 1947). *See further* Convention on the Privileges and Immunities of the Specialized Agencies, *approved* by the General Assembly Nov. 21, 1947, 33 UNTS 261.

[116] To rectify the inequalities it perceived in its original system of compensation, the United Nations subjected UN salaries to a tax assessed at a rate comparable to the employee's national income tax liability. GA Res. 239 (III), UN Doc. A/703, at 3 (1948), *as amended* by GA Res. 359 (IV), UN Doc. A/1949, at 1 (1949).

[117] McCulloch v. Maryland, 17 U.S. (4 Wheat.) 316, 347 (1819).

[118] *See* M. McCaffree & P. Innis, Protocol, The Complete Book of Diplomatic, Official and Social Usage 87–104 (1985).

[119] Legal Status of Eastern Greenland (Den. v. Nor.), 1933 PCIJ (ser. A/B) No. 53 (Judgment of Apr. 5).

The venerable ritual practices of diplomacy are almost universally observed, and the rules that govern diplomacy are widely recognized as imbued with a high degree of legitimacy, being both descriptive and predictive of nearly invariable state conduct and reflecting a strong sense of historically endowed obligation. When the rules are violated—as they have been by Iran and Libya in recent years[120]—the international community tends to respond by rallying around the rule, as the Security Council[121] and the International Court of Justice[122] demonstrated when the Iranian regime encouraged the occupation of the U.S. Embassy in Tehran. Violations of the elaborate rules pertaining to embassies and immunities usually lead the victim state to terminate its diplomatic relations with the offender.[123] The offended state—as Britain demonstrated after the St. James Square shooting—usually takes care not to retaliate by means that the rules do not permit.[124]

Related to the pedigreeing process of diplomatic accreditation, with its symbolic status of privileges and immunities, is the prevalent idea of sovereign immunity. That set of rules and practices has its roots in the medieval notion that the "king can do no wrong" and the monarch's claim that "I am the state." Nowadays, most governments can be sued in their own courts. Until at least the 1920s, however, nations, among themselves, generally continued to treat as sacrosanct not only foreign governments, but also all property of recognized foreign states and those activities and enterprises carried on in the foreign government's name.[125] Only in the last three

[120] For a discussion of the Iranian hostages incident, see Gross, *The Case of United States Diplomatic and Consular Staff in Tehran: Phase of Provisional Measures*, 74 AJIL 395 (1980). For an analysis of the Libyan violations, see Higgins, *supra* note 30.

[121] SC Res. 457, 34 UN SCOR (Res. & Dec.) at 24, UN Doc. S/INF/35 (1979) (adopted unanimously).

[122] *See* United States Diplomatic and Consular Staff in Tehran (U.S. v. Iran), Provisional Measures, 1979 ICJ REP. 7 (Order of Dec. 15); United States Diplomatic and Consular Staff in Tehran (U.S. v. Iran), 1980 ICJ REP. 3 (Judgment of May 24); United States Diplomatic and Consular Staff in Tehran (U.S. v. Iran), 1981 ICJ REP. 45 (Order of May 12).

[123] See, e.g., *France Breaks Iran Ties and Isolates Embassy*, N.Y. Times, July 18, 1987, at 1, col. 3, which followed the grant of sanctuary by the Iranian Embassy in Paris to a nondiplomat wanted for questioning in connection with terrorist activities.

[124] The British limited their reaction to the shooting of a policewoman from the premises of the Libyan People's Bureau to expulsion of the perpetrators and closing of the Bureau. *See* Higgins, *UK Foreign Affairs Committee Report on the Abuse of Diplomatic Immunities and Privileges: Government Response and Report*, 80 AJIL 135 (1986).

[125] In the *Steamship Pesaro* case, the U.S. Supreme Court refused to recognize the difference between ships held and used by a government for a public purpose and ships used by a government in trade. The latter "are public ships in the same sense that war ships are. We know of no international usage which regards the maintenance and advancement of the economic welfare of a people in time of peace as any less a public purpose than the maintenance and training of a naval force." Berizzi Bros. Co. v. S.S. Pesaro, 271 U.S. 562, 574 (1926). The Court expounded upon this doctrine in *The Navemar*, holding that, "[a]dmittedly a vessel of a friendly government in its possession and service is a public vessel, even though engaged in the carriage of merchandise for hire . . . ." Compania Espanola de Navigacion Maritima, S.A. v. Navemar, 303 U.S. 68, 74–76 (1938). For similar holdings in British cases, see The Jassy, 1906 P. 270; and The Gagara, 1919 P. 95.

decades have most nations begun to limit the immunity from suit of foreign governments and state commercial entities. While many nations now have restricted this status-based right of immunity by withdrawing it from purely *commercial* property and activities of foreign governments,[126] immunity continues to be granted to all officials and property engaged in *governmental* (public, or noncommercial) undertakings.[127] In practice, this means that immunity protects such officials, state property and governmental activity from legal action or, at a minimum, from the execution of a judgment against them.

Symbolically validated rules like these, precisely because they are old, or have been encrusted with quaint forms and rituals, seem easy prey to functionalist critique. They sometimes work an injustice, and they often appear anachronistic. On the other hand, a new rule, even if agreed upon, might not have the same capacity to obligate. To the extent that the legitimacy of a rule is dependent on symbolic validation, there is reason—albeit not invariably a decisive one—to leave the rule alone.

Symbols, ritual and pedigree are factors that cannot be made to order and rules endowed with them need to be husbanded. "No one makes up ritual or symbol any more than anyone makes up language," a study of ancient Chinese ritual has shown.

> Ritual and symbol arise without intention or adaptation to conscious purpose; they seem to be collective products worked out . . . over long periods of time. . . . Ironically, it appears that rituals and symbols must in some way already be regarded as "legitimate" in order for them to confer legitimacy on those who employ them.[128]

IV. Coherence and Legitimacy

Symbolic validation, like determinacy, serves to legitimize rules. But like determinacy, symbolic validation is not quite as simple a notion as it may initially appear. For example, as traditional Chinese practice makes clear, ritual invoked to enhance the capacity of a rule to compel compliance will

[126] The United States officially promulgated this policy in 1952, when the Department of State, by means of the "Tate letter," declared its adherence to the "restrictive theory" of sovereign immunity. Under this theory, immunity would be recognized with regard to sovereign or public acts (*jure imperii*) but not with respect to private acts (*jure gestionis*). Letter from Jack B. Tate, Acting Legal Adviser, Department of State, to Philip B. Perlman, Acting Attorney General, May 19, 1952, *reprinted in* 26 Dept. St. Bull. 984 (1952). For current European treatment of immunity, see the European Convention on State Immunity and Additional Protocol, 1972 ETS 74, *reprinted in* 11 ILM 470 (1972).

[127] Foreign Sovereign Immunities Act of 1976, 28 U.S.C. §§1330, 1602–1611 (1982). *See also* Higgins, *Recent Developments in the Law of Sovereign Immunity in the United Kingdom*, 71 AJIL 423 (1977). For judicial discussion of current U.S. practice and its history, see Broadbent v. Organization of Am. States, 628 F.2d 27 (D.D.C. 1980). U.S. application of the "commercial" activity concept under the doctrine of restrictive immunity is discussed in *id.* at 33–35; and the immunity accorded international organizations under the rubrics of restrictive and absolute immunity is treated in *id.* at 30–33.

[128] H. Wechsler, *supra* note 80, at 35.

only succeed if the rituals are themselves legitimate and are strictly observed. Similarly, a pedigree only confers actual rights and duties when the standards for pedigreeing are applied *coherently*. When, on the contrary, symbols, ritual and pedigree are dispensed capriciously, the desired effect of legitimization may not accrue.

Both determinacy and symbolic validation are connected to a further variable: coherence. The effect of incoherence on symbolic validation can be illustrated by reference to diplomatic practices pertaining to the ritual validation of governments and states. The most important act of pedigreeing in the international system is the deep-rooted, traditional act that endows a new government, or a new state, with symbolic status. When the endowing is done by individual governments, it is known as *recognition*.[129] The symbolic conferral of status is also performed collectively through a global organization like the United Nations when the members vote to admit a new nation to membership,[130] or when the General Assembly votes to accept the credentials of the delegates representing a new government.[131]

These two forms of validation are important because they enhance the status of the validated entity; that is, the new state or government acquires legitimacy, which, in turn, carries entitlements and obligations equal to those of other such entities. Such symbolic validation cannot alter the empirically observable reality of power disparity among states and governments, nor, properly understood, does it give off that cue. It does, however, purport to restrict what powerful states legitimately may do with their advantage over the weak. It is a cue that prompts the Soviets, however reluctantly, to do a lot of explaining when they invade Afghanistan. The pedigreed statehood of Afghanistan, together with the determinacy of the rules against intervention by one state in the internal affairs of another, then combine to render those Soviet explanations essentially unacceptable, global scorn evidencing the inelastic determinacy of the applicable rules. The practices of symbolic equality conferred by recognition also stipulate that the leader of tiny Bhutan must receive exactly the same number of volleys fired in salute as does the head of state of its huge neighbor, China. Recognition, as validation, has the effect of cuing the equal capacity of rich and poor, strong and weak, for acquiring rights and duties. It creates a presumption against all purported interpretations of existing rules—and against proposed new rules—that would make arbitrary distinctions between the rights and duties of different states or governments. Symbolic equality thus both affirms and reinforces real equality. Weaker nations, in particular, believe that ritual incantation of their symbolically validated status, at a minimum, has reduced somewhat the option of the powerful to treat the weak as tributary or

[129] For U.S. practices, see L. GALLOWAY, RECOGNIZING FOREIGN GOVERNMENTS: THE PRACTICE OF THE UNITED STATES (1978). An excellent treatment of recognition in general can be found in H. LAUTERPACHT, RECOGNITION IN INTERNATIONAL LAW (1947).

[130] J. DUGARD, RECOGNITION AND THE UNITED NATIONS (1987).

[131] See *infra* note 140 for illustrations of the converse, attempts to deny or rescind recognition by opposing delegates' credentials.

vassal states in contravention of the rights inherent in their status as states.[132]

These important benefits only accrue if the validation is effective; and it is only effective if the forms and standards have been followed.

Each kind of pedigreeing has its own rules and standards. No cue, no amount of ritual behavior, can achieve symbolic validation if its prescribed procedures are not followed or its public standards are violated. Graham Greene's "whisky priest" may have lost his faith,[133] but as long as he follows the rites, he remains an effective validator. Prescribed standards are the essential element in symbolic validation. For example, in 1948, the International Court of Justice was asked by the General Assembly to designate the test for admitting candidate states to UN membership.[134] The Court replied, essentially, by reciting the rules established by Article 4 of the UN Charter: that an applicant must be a state, peace loving, willing to accept the obligations of the Charter, able to carry them out, and willing to do so. The Court further explained that these were "not merely . . . the necessary conditions, but also . . . the conditions which suffice."[135] In other words, nations that objectively satisfy that standard are entitled to have their status validated. The standard is itself pedigreed by its inclusion in the UN Charter, the world's most inclusive multilateral treaty, and by its deep historical rootedness in analogous national recognition practices.[136]

Similarly, the legal adviser to the Secretary-General prepared a memorandum explaining the rules applicable to accepting or rejecting the credentials of a delegation when there is doubt about their validity, for example, during a civil war when there may be two adversary claimants. In such situations, too, UN members should be guided by Charter Article 4, the legal adviser said. Moreover,

> [w]here a revolutionary government presents itself as representing a State, in rivalry to an existing government, the question at issue should be which of these two governments in fact is in a position to employ the resources and direct the people of the State in fulfilment of the obligations of membership. In essence, this means an inquiry as to whether the new government exercises effective authority within the territory of the State and is habitually obeyed by the bulk of the population.[137]

[132] For example, a pledged word commits powerful as well as weak governments. There is widespread recognition by states, antedating the UN Charter, that a commitment equally obligates powerful, as weaker nations. *See* Legal Status of Eastern Greenland (Den. v. Nor.), 1933 PCIJ (ser. A/B) No. 53, at 22 (Judgment of Apr. 5).

[133] Greene shows that even though a priest may fall into a secularized life style, he retains his spiritual powers. A "whisky priest" is "a damned man putting God into the mouths of men," owing to his authority to perform communion. *See* G. GREENE, THE POWER AND THE GLORY 83 (1940).

[134] Admission of a State to the United Nations (Charter, Art. 4), 1948 ICJ REP. 57 (Advisory Opinion of May 28).

[135] *Id.* at 62, 63.

[136] *See* 1 L. OPPENHEIM, *supra* note 77, at 124–52.

[137] Letter to Trygve Lie, Mar. 8, 1950, Legal Aspects of the Problems of Representation in the United Nations, 5 UN SCOR Supp. (Jan.–May 1950) at 18, 22–23, UN Doc. S/1466 (1950).

Governments that do are eligible; those that do not are not. These standards are also rooted in venerable national recognition practices.

These standards for symbolic validation at the United Nations, like any rules, leave room for differences of interpretation in borderline cases where "willingness to carry out obligations" and "control over territory and population" are not wholly self-evident. Nevertheless, the standards have a fairly high degree of formal determinacy and are not difficult to understand, making it possible to dismiss bogus, self-serving interpretations. For example, it is surely not permissible to vote to deny membership to a new state on the ground that its president is black or that its inhabitants are poor. The standards also explain why even ardent Palestinian and Sahrawian representatives have not yet sought membership in the United Nations.

When the symbolic validation proceeds legitimately in accordance with its own prescription—when these rules are followed—it succeeds in its purpose. If validation is withheld in conformity with the same standards, the rejected candidate will be denied the hallmark of effective statehood. The legitimate refusal of governments, individually, and collectively in the United Nations, to validate the Bantustan "homelands"—which clearly do not meet the standard—has undoubtedly contributed to those pseudonations' failure to achieve the status of membership and equality in the international community.[138] Problems arise, however, when the standards are not applied coherently; that is, when they are applied to some but not to others equally entitled, or when the standards cease to be connected to principles of general applicability. For example, the United States Government led the fight that, for years, allowed the Nationalist regime on Taiwan, and not the Communist regime in Beijing, to occupy the Chinese seat in UN organs, on the ground that this "is a privilege and not a right."[139] The United States meant that symbolic validation could be withheld from the Beijing Government, even though it obviously met the traditional criteria, because those could be overridden by political considerations. More recently, African and Arab members of the General Assembly have led efforts to reject the credentials of the delegations from South Africa and Israel[140]

[138] The General Assembly condemned the establishment by South Africa of Bantu homelands (Bantustans) as an attempt artificially to divide the African people into "nations" according to their tribal origins, with the aim of weakening the African front in its struggle for its inalienable and just rights. GA Res. 2775E, 26 UN GAOR Supp. (No. 29) at 42, UN Doc. A/8429 (1971). The resolution passed by the resounding vote of 110 in favor, 2 opposed, with 2 abstentions. *See also* Report of the Secretary-General, UN Doc. A/8388 (1971) (transmitting consensus adopted on Sept. 13, 1971, by joint meeting of the Special Committee on *Apartheid*, the Special Committee on the Situation with regard to the Implementation of the Declaration on the Granting of Independence to Colonial Countries and Peoples, and the United Nations Council for Namibia); Dugard, *South Africa's "Independent" Homelands: An Exercise in Denationalization*, 10 DEN. J. INT'L L. & POL'Y 11 (1980) (for the development of the Bantustan policy).

[139] State Department Memorandum, *U.S. Policy on Nonrecognition of Communist China*, 39 DEP'T ST. BULL. 385 (1958).

[140] GA Res. 3207, 29 UN GAOR Supp. (No. 31) at 2, UN Doc. A/9631 (1974) (resolution on South Africa). When, in 1982, the Arab bloc decided to challenge the credentials of the

even though there is no question that these do meet the criteria for representing their respective countries. The General Assembly, with the support of the United States and a majority of Western and Third World nations, has also continued to seat the delegation of the Kampuchean regime headed by Prince Sihanouk even though it fails to control any significant part of the territory of the country it claims to represent. At least those who are responsible for the Kampuchean result have sought to justify themselves by proposing a new general rule: that a regime, even if it is in effective control, should not be rewarded for having been installed by foreign aggression.[141] That new rule may eventually acquire pedigreed legitimacy, but it has not done so as yet.

When the process of symbolic validation is abused by failure to follow its own procedural rules and standards, a divergence is likely to occur between the real world and the symbolic world, to the detriment of the status-validating processes and symbols. They may cease to be taken seriously. For example, at a time when the Chinese Communist regime was still being excluded from the United Nations, Secretary-General Dag Hammarskjöld nevertheless engaged in numerous important negotiations with Chou En-lai, Beijing's foreign minister.[142] The head of the UN Secretariat, it seems, did not feel constrained by the members' decision denying validation to the Communist authorities. Similarly, Hammarskjöld's successor, U Thant, vigorously pressed his negotiations with Hanoi during the Vietnam War,[143]

Israeli delegation, the United States announced it would boycott any UN body that excluded the Israelis and would also withhold its contribution amounting to 25% of the UN budget. T. FRANCK, NATION AGAINST NATION 217 (1985). Most recently, Oman, acting on behalf of 20 Arab states, proposed an amendment to exclude the credentials of Israel from General Assembly approval. The General Assembly voted not to act on this amendment. *Credentials Committee Reports Adopted*, UN CHRON., No. 1, February 1987, at 16. *See also* Halberstam, *Excluding Israel from the General Assembly by a Rejection of its Credentials*, 78 AJIL 179 (1984).

[141] Credentials of Representatives to the Forty-first Session of the General Assembly: First Report of the Credentials Committee, UN Doc. A/41/727, para. 12 (prov. ed. 1986).

> The representative of the United States of America stated that the credentials of the representatives of Democratic Kampuchea were in order, fulfilled the requirements of rule 27 of the rules of procedure, had already been accepted by the General Assembly in the past and should be accepted at the current session. The suggested alternative was a regime brought to power by a foreign military invasion and that was clearly not representative in any way, shape or form of the Kampuchean people.

Id.

[142] The Secretary-General conducted a series of talks with Chou En-lai "in the name of the United Nations" (*see* GA Res. 906, 9 UN GAOR Supp. (No. 21) at 56, UN Doc. A/2890 (1954)) in order to discuss the release of four U.S. fighter pilots shot down near the Yalu River between October 1952 and January 1953, while they were flying missions for the UN Command during the Korean War. See 2 PUBLIC PAPERS OF THE SECRETARIES-GENERAL OF THE UNITED NATIONS: DAG HAMMARSKJÖLD (1953–1956), at 415–59 (1972), for details of the Secretary-General's mission. *See also* T. FRANCK, *supra* note 140, at 136–37.

[143] In 1964 U Thant secretly informed President Johnson that he could arrange a meeting between the United States and North Vietnam. Believing he had secured the President's blessing, he proceeded to use his good offices to arrange a meeting in Rangoon. But when the United States failed to respond once the meeting had been agreed to by the North Vietnamese,

even though the UN political organs had never validated the nation of North Vietnam, let alone its governmental representatives.[144] The refusal to seat the South African delegates to the General Assembly likewise has not prevented Secretary-General Pérez de Cuéllar from negotiating with Pretoria over such matters as the future of illegally occupied Namibia.[145] With whom else, after all, *could* he negotiate that question?

To recapitulate: an act of recognition, the symbolic validation of a state or regime, has the capacity to bestow, symbolically, rights and duties on the recognized entity when, *but only if*, it is done in accordance with the applicable principled rules and procedures. Such pedigreed recognition, and its corporate UN equivalent, is everywhere accorded great weight. On the other hand, when the rules and standards for validation are violated, or are themselves unprincipled and capricious, then symbolic validation fails in its objective of bestowing status. Moreover, when validation is seen to be capricious, a failure to validate will do more to undermine the legitimacy of the validating process than of the state or government thus deprived of symbolic validation.

The failure of mystical ritual to do what it is invoked for is usually explained metaphysically. The excommunicate priest who elevates the host before the altar in a fraudulent Eucharist is left holding only bread and wine because his invalid orders cannot effect the miracle of transubstantiation. But failed validation can often be explained rationally. For example, the Ukraine has not been transformed into a sovereign and equal state by its membership in the United Nations. Membership held at variance with the Organization's own standards does not validate the Ukraine's statehood.[146] Similarly, when the United Nations wishes to engage in relief activities in Kampuchea, its officials do not deal with the symbolically validated government of Prince Sihanouk but, rather, with the "unrecognized" regime actually in control. The perverse use of validation, in both instances, fails to give or withhold status for reasons that are practical, rational and not in the least

---

Thant felt humiliated by the U.S. Government and leaked his story to the world. T. FRANCK, *supra* note 140, at 154–58.

[144] The People's Republic of China was admitted to the United Nations on Oct. 25, 1971, and Vietnam acquired membership only in 1977.

[145] For an account of how the Security Council directed Secretary-General Waldheim " 'to initiate as soon as possible contacts with all parties concerned' " so that the people of Namibia might exercise their right to self-determination and independence, see D. SOGGOT, NAMIBIA: THE VIOLENT HERITAGE 53–54 (1986).

[146] Despite the fact that the Soviet Constitution guarantees individual republics the right to secede from the Soviet Union, it was widely known that the Ukraine, like each of its sister republics, was considerably less independent than any American state and thus was otherwise ineligible for UN membership. Nonetheless, the West ultimately acceded to the Soviet request to admit two republics as UN members because it was viewed as a reasonable price to pay for Soviet participation in the United Nations. T. FRANCK, *supra* note 140, at 21. For a detailed history of the negotiations leading to the West's disposition of Stalin's initial request for membership for all 16 Soviet republics, see R. RUSSELL, A HISTORY OF THE UNITED NATIONS CHARTER 435, 533, 536–37, 539 n.49, 584, 597–98, 636 (1958).

metaphysical. If the valid procedural rules or standards are not applied, it is to be expected that no legitimacy will be conferred.

The costs to its legitimacy of applying a rule incoherently arise in three related, but different, senses. First, incoherence nullifies the flawed act of validating or withholding validation. Second, it undermines the standards, rules and processes for bestowing status or validity. Third, it derogates from the legitimacy of the institution that is charged with validating. Thus, in the UN context, when the General Assembly fails to follow the Organization's own rules, standards or procedures for accrediting delegates, it damages the claim of the whole UN system to be taken seriously as the symbolic bestower of status.

Dworkin has pointed out that coherence (he uses the term "integrity")[147] is a key factor in explaining why rules compel.[148] He observes that a rule is coherent when like cases are treated alike in application of the rule and when the rule relates in a principled fashion to other rules of the same system. Consistency requires that a rule (or, as we have noted, a ritual or standard), whatever its content, be applied uniformly in every "similar" or "applicable" instance. The opposite is what Dworkin calls "checkerboarding."[149]

There is another aspect of coherence. It encompasses the further notion that a rule, standard or validating ritual gathers force if it is seen to be connected to a network of other rules by an underlying general principle. This latter aspect of coherence merits closer examination.

Let us imagine that it has been generally agreed that the $1,010 billion debt of Third World states[150] should be retired by the borrowers' paying the lenders half the total amount owed. Both sides regard this compromise as the best deal they can get in present circumstances. The problem is one of coverage. How is the 50 percent repayment formula going to be implemented in practice? Who will repay what? Suppose it were suggested that states whose names begin with the letters *A–M* should repay their entire debt, while those whose names start with *N–Z* pay nothing. Such a rule has determinacy. Although some will fare better than others, no borrower state will be worse off with the compromise than without it. The compromise is also better for the lenders than being repaid nothing, and better for the borrowers than having to repay everything. Yet any such "checkerboard" compromise is likely to be rejected by both borrowers and lenders because of its manifest incoherence. Its incoherence makes it facially illegitimate.

To be legitimate, Dworkin points out, such a compromise must "aim to settle on some coherent principle whose influence then extends to the natural limits of its authority."[151] That means the compromise must connect what it does with some *rational principle of broader application*. The alphabetic

[147] R. DWORKIN, *supra* note 7.

[148] *Id.* at 190–92.

[149] *Id.* at 179.

[150] INTERNATIONAL BANK FOR RECONSTRUCTION AND DEVELOPMENT, WORLD DEBT TABLES, EXTERNAL DEBT OF DEVELOPING COUNTRIES, 1985–86, at xi (1986).

[151] R. DWORKIN, *supra* note 7, at 179.

compromise asserts a principle that distinguishes between countries—those which must repay and those to be forgiven—by means of a general principle that cannot be defended on any rational basis. The alphabetic compromise, like the flipping of a coin, is an admission that no rational principle can be found that will produce the desired result. Thus, the decision is left to chance: the "draw" of the alphabet. This establishes no generalizable rule, no principle to justify the basis for making a decision. It lacks coherence because it lacks nexus: both in logic and, more important, in practice. It fails to connect to a rational principle in general use. It establishes no basis for a continuing pattern of systemic interaction; it connects the particular decision to no sense of ongoing community. Even if there were other debt crises in the future, the alphabetic approach would merely become more indefensible as it lost its one vestigial merit: its randomness. Nothing in international life is ever resolved, or likely to be solved, by recourse to the alphabetic principle except seating arrangements at multinational conferences.

A coherent half-loaf compromise could be achieved by applying any one of various coherent, principled approaches. For example, debt forgiveness could be distributed on a sliding scale based on national income or on per capita productivity, the inverse of the scale of assessment used to tax UN members. Or each debtor's indebtedness could be reduced by a fixed percentage, as in a bankruptcy reorganization. Or all repayments could be stretched out in accordance with a schedule based on rise in productivity. Any of these methods of implementing the half-loaf compromise connects with a principle of distribution that commends itself rationally and has been, and will be, applied elsewhere. Coherence requires that the rule applied to a dispute about the distribution of debt relief should employ distinctions that are acceptable (or, at least, not unacceptable) in solving not only future instances of the same problem but also quite different distributive problems.

Dworkin illustrates the potency of coherence as a factor in legitimacy by asserting that a half-loaf regulation is even less acceptable than no loaf at all when it produces a checkerboard result. "Even if I thought strict liability for accidents wrong in principle," he has written, "I would prefer that manufacturers of both washing machines and automobiles be held to that standard rather than that only one of them be. I would rank the checkerboard solution not intermediate between the other two [no strict liability and universal strict liability] but third, below both, and so would many other people." Such "compromises are wrong, not merely impractical."[152] They are lacking in legitimacy.

A rule taxing only property with even-numbered addresses would be incoherent and lack legitimacy. The same rule would be perfectly coherent if odd-numbered properties, all being on the same side of each street, had received a 20-year tax abatement in return for yielding several feet of their frontal property to the city for the widening of roadways. A "selective service" lottery for induction into the armed services employs a purely random military draft, which may be justified as the fairest way to allocate a

[152] *Id.* at 182.

social burden in some circumstances. In other words, before a rule that is facially inconsistent in its application can be adjudged incoherent, it is necessary to determine not only that it applies unequally but also that no reasonable principle of general application can justify the inequality. If a rule is unequally applied, its legitimacy is placed in question. If the inequality is also unprincipled, the legitimacy of the rule—its capacity to obligate—will be severely depleted.

The idea that coherence is a key indicator of legitimacy may be illustrated further by reference to three recent developments in the international community: the emergence of a "right" to *self-determination*; the development of a notion of *state equality*, as exemplified by the voting system of the United Nations; and the entrenchment of free and nondiscriminatory terms of trade—the *most-favored-nation* system—in the General Agreement on Tariffs and Trade. Each has undergone a crisis of legitimacy occasioned by challenges to its normative coherence. Let us examine how each has attempted to meet that challenge and thus to protect its legitimacy.

The notion that national or ethnic groups are entitled to "self-determination" had its origins in the settlements made at the end of World War I. The U.S. delegation to the Versailles Peace Conference was firmly instructed to apply ethnic criteria to resolve all European territorial disputes and, to that end, President Woodrow Wilson saw to it that his team included historians, geographers and ethnologists.[153] Throughout the negotiations, Wilson insisted that settlements be based on "facts,"[154] by which he meant "racial aspects, historic antecedents, and economic and commercial elements."[155] Note, however, in passing, that this general principle need not be accepted as *just*. The legitimacy of a rule is conditioned by its coherence, but a rule may be quite coherent (in our sense of the term), as well as highly determinate and symbolically validated, and yet be thought unjust. Wilsonian self-determination, for example, may be legitimate yet work an injustice by transferring territories and resources in accordance with a general principle of ethnicity while ignoring considerations of economic well-being and the distributive claims of poor people.[156]

The Wilsonian principle achieved considerable coherence in the immediate period following World War I. Insistence on its application led to a plebiscite in Schleswig, which had been annexed by Prussia in 1864.[157] In 1920, Northern Schleswig voted to revert to Denmark, a verdict accepted by the Peace Conference.[158] The same principle governed the creation of Czechoslovakia, in accordance with the wishes of Wilson's Secretary of State Lansing, "that all branches of the Slav race should be completely freed from German and Austrian rule."[159] Similarly, the principle was used by Wilson

[153] R. S. BAKER, WOODROW WILSON AND WORLD SETTLEMENT 109 (1922).

[154] *Id.* at 187.

[155] *Id.*

[156] Franck & Hawkins, *Rawls' Theory of Justice in International Context*, 10 MICH. J. INT'L L. (1988).

[157] S. WAMBAUGH, PLEBISCITES SINCE THE WORLD WAR 14 (1933).

[158] 2 A HISTORY OF THE PEACE CONFERENCE OF PARIS 205 (H. W. V. Temperley ed. 1920).

[159] 4 *id.* at 261 (1921).

to oppose efforts by France to create a buffer Rhenish Republic[160] between itself and Germany. Wilson's chief adviser, Colonel House, was scornful of the French, who "do not seem to know that to establish a Rhenish Republic against the will of the people would be contrary to the principle of self-determination."[161] The compromise accommodated some elements of both French geopolitics and American moralism. A Saar buffer was established. However, it was not to be independent but administered through the League of Nations. Although the inhabitants were not allowed to be represented in the German Reichstag, their schools, language, laws and German nationality were left untouched.[162]

The principle of self-determination was also used in drawing the boundaries of an independent Poland on incontrovertible historical and ethnic grounds.[163] Wilson succeeded in his demand that the new Polish state "should be erected" to "include the territories inhabited by indisputably Polish populations."[164] Finally, Upper Silesia was divided by the League Council in 1921 along strictly ethnic lines.[165]

The coverage, in practice, of the concept of self-determination after World War I should not be exaggerated by dwelling exclusively on these dramatic instances. The rule was extended only—and, at that, imperfectly—to the European territories of the vanquished powers. It was not applied, for example, to the dispute between Sweden and Finland over the Aaland Islands.[166] The commission of inquiry appointed to settle that problem instead declared that "the principle had not yet attained the status of a positive rule of international law."[167] On the other hand, Britain claimed to be motivated by self-determination in the partition of Ireland.[168]

After World War II, however, the self-determination principle came to be applied even more generally. The United Nations Charter for the first time expressed a general obligation of states to help enable inhabitants of all dependent non-self-governing territories to make a meaningful choice of national destiny. By joining the United Nations, its members accepted "a sacred trust" to "develop self-government, to take due account of the political aspirations of the peoples, and to assist them in the progressive development of their free political institutions."[169] Some colonial territories that previously belonged to Germany or Japan were placed under a formal

[160] THE INTIMATE PAPERS OF COLONEL HOUSE 334 (C. Seymour ed. 1928).

[161] *Id.* at 345.

[162] 2 Temperley (ed.), *supra* note 158, at 182.

[163] R. S. BAKER, *supra* note 153, at 110–11.

[164] *Id.*

[165] D. FLEMING, THE UNITED STATES AND WORLD ORGANIZATION 153 (1938).

[166] L. BUCHHEIT, SECESSION 71 (1978). [167] *Id.*

[168] Linking the issue of Ireland to self-determination, Balfour wrote: "No one can think that Ulster ought to join the South and West who thinks that the Jugo Slavs should be separated from Austria. No one can think that Ulster should be divorced from Britain who believes in self-determination." Balfour, The Irish Question, Nov. 25, 1919, PRO CAB 24/93, *quoted in* T. G. FRASER, PARTITION IN IRELAND, INDIA AND PALESTINE 27 (1984). For Lloyd George's comments, see T. G. FRASER, *id.* at 38.

[169] UN CHARTER art. 73.

trusteeship system supervised by the United Nations, which aimed "to promote . . . progressive development towards self-government or independence as may be appropriate," in accordance with "the freely expressed wishes of the peoples concerned."[170]

The principle now applied equally to all: to colonies and to Europe, to victors and to vanquished. The first article of the Charter, enumerating the Organization's "Purposes and Principles," specifies an all-embracing obligation of members to develop "friendly relations among nations based on respect for the principle of equal rights and self-determination of peoples."[171] This casts the principle in terms of universal coverage. The term "peoples," moreover, recognizes the importance of the ethnic dimension in determining *who* is entitled to invoke self-determination. No boundary separates "peoples" entitled from "peoples" not entitled. Coherence was achieved and the rule acquired powerful legitimacy.

This is not merely a matter of theory or words. Very few rules of the international system have had as dramatic an impact. Beginning with India, Burma and the Gold Coast, Britain conceded self-determination to nearly one billion persons, with France, the Netherlands, Belgium, Spain and Portugal, albeit at first reluctantly, following suit. With a host of new nations seeking validation, UN membership nearly doubled between 1960 and 1980.[172] This was achieved almost entirely by voluntary compliance in deference to a legitimate rule, rather than by coercion.

The coherence of the rule, however, did not last. Even as these dramatic events were occurring, the same principle of self-determination was being denied all of Eastern Europe. Territories largely inhabited by Latvians, Poles, Germans, Romanians, Hungarians and Slovaks were arbitrarily annexed by neighboring states, and their populations often put to flight. Somewhat later, some of the very nations of a Third World that had just benefited from the application of self-determination refused to join in censuring the Soviet Union and Warsaw Pact nations during the invasion of Hungary in 1956 and of Czechoslovakia in 1968.[173] Nor was the principle disregarded only in Europe. No sooner had India become independent than its armed forces denied self-determination to the princely state of Kashmir, which might well have been entitled to it on ethnic, religious and legal grounds.[174] So, too, neither independent Nigeria nor the Organization of African Unity felt any obligation to permit self-determination to the ethni-

[170] *Id.* art. 76(b).

[171] *Id.* art. 1, para. 2.

[172] UN membership rose from 82 members at the beginning of 1960, 1959 UN Y.B. 539, to 154 by the end of 1980, 1980 UN Y.B. 1347.

[173] Saudi Arabia, Syria, Yemen, Yugoslavia, Afghanistan, Burma, Ceylon, Egypt, India, Indonesia, Iraq, Jordan, Libya and Nepal abstained from voting on a resolution condemning the 1956 Soviet invasion of Hungary. GA Res. 1004, ES-2 UN GAOR (564th plen. mtg.) at 7, 20, UN Doc. A/PV.564 (1956). Algeria, India and Pakistan abstained from voting on a Security Council resolution condemning the 1968 Soviet invasion of Czechoslovakia. 23 UN SCOR (1443d mtg.) at 28–29, UN Doc. S/PV.1443 (1968).

[174] India Independence Act, 1947, 10 & 11 Geo. 6, ch. 30.

cally and religiously distinct Ibo "nation" when it sought statehood for Biafra.[175]

Thus, the principle of self-determination began its descent into incoherence—in the sense of inconsistency of application—almost from the moment of its greatest apparent ascendance. Increasing incoherence became textually evident in 1960 with the General Assembly's adoption of the Declaration on the Granting of Independence to Colonial Countries and Peoples.[176] Drafted by the newly independent former colonies of Africa and Asia, it reiterated, on the one hand, "that all peoples have an inalienable right to complete freedom"[177] and demanded immediate implementation of this right "without any conditions or reservations in accordance with their freely expressed will and desire"[178] and regardless of "political, economic, social or educational preparedness."[179] On the other hand, the right was now to be applicable only to "territories which have not yet attained independence." The right was also offset by a new rule against any "attempt aimed at the partial or total disruption of the national unity and the territorial integrity of a country."[180]

The declaration thus revived the notion of the sanctity of existing boundaries and resistance to secession that informed the U.S. Civil War[181] and the decision in the Aaland Island case, but had briefly been disestablished by the notion of self-determination after World War I. In place of a coherent rule, there was now checkerboarding, with self-determination doctrinally sanctioned for some cases and prohibited for others. Not only has the coverage of self-determination shrunk, but also its boundaries—where it is applicable and where not—have become indistinct and incoherent. The standards for granting or withholding the right seem to lack connection to any underlying rational general principles.

This incoherence can be demonstrated by searching for applicable general principles that would justify the inconsistencies in the actual state practice since 1960. For example, Algeria was granted self-determination at the insistence of the world community, while Biafra was not. Is Algeria different from Biafra because the former is separated from France by water, while the latter is a contiguous part of the Nigerian landmass? Surely, this is not a

[175] Biafra declared its independence on May 30, 1967, but only five nations recognized its claim to independence. Neither the United Nations nor the OAU supported Biafran independence and the United Nations never even considered the issue. Nanda, *Self-Determination in International Law*, 66 AJIL 321, 326–27 (1972). *See also* 66 ASIL PROC. 58, 175 (1972).

[176] GA Res. 1514, 15 UN GAOR Supp. (No. 16) at 66, UN Doc. A/4684 (1960).

[177] *Id.*, Preamble.

[178] *Id.*, Art. 5.

[179] *Id.*, Art. 3.

[180] *Id.*, Art. 5.

[181] See, e.g., comments by President Lincoln:

> My paramount object in this struggle *is* to save the Union . . . . If I could save the Union without freeing *any* slave I would do it, and if I could save it by freeing *all* the slaves I would do it; and if I could save it by freeing some and leaving others alone I would also do that.

Letter from Abraham Lincoln to Horace Greeley, Aug. 22, 1862, *reprinted in* 5 THE COLLECTED WORKS OF ABRAHAM LINCOLN 388 (R. Basler ed. 1953).

principled distinction capable of being generalized. Many nations—the United States, the Philippines, Canada, Indonesia, India, China and the Soviet Union—have provinces or regions separated from the rest of their territory by salt water. Thus, the distance from Hawaii to Los Angeles is five times greater than that from Marseilles to Algiers. Understandably, an ultramarine principle has never been accepted in practice to define the boundaries of self-determination. No government is likely to accept a distinction that would allow the Canadian province of Prince Edward Island to enjoy the right of self-determination but not Quebec.

Other principles for making distinctions between those entitled and those not, encounter equal difficulty. A differentiation between oppressed "peoples" (entitled) and others (not entitled) has a certain moral attraction. But it is not generalizable and certainly fails to account for the actual behavior of states during the past 25 years in supporting or ignoring demands for self-determination. For example, even before their independence, the populations of Nigeria, India, Senegal and the Ivory Coast had far more say in their government than is currently enjoyed by the people of Latvia, Eritrea and the southern Sudan. Yet the international community has championed self-determination for the former, but not for the latter.

Likewise, attempts to introduce an economic variable to rationalize the "checkerboard" application of self-determination tends to be unsuccessful. It has been argued that Biafrans and other Nigerians have fared better by remaining united than they would have done had they separated.[182] But a strong case can also be made that Algeria and France would have prospered more had they remained together. And Katanga has surely suffered economically as a result of its continued union with Zaire, a denial of self-determination that was actually enforced by the United Nations.[183] The economic factor not only does not rationalize actual state practice, it is also probably bad theory. That economic considerations should or ever *will* trump political, cultural and ethnic ones is a very questionable basis for any agreed general principle.

A more defensible distinction makes self-determination applicable only to "peoples" who are treated *unequally* by government. This principle would

[182] An independent and united Nigeria was perceived to be a "model for Africa," a "key" to that continent's future stability and prosperity, because of its material wealth and rich culture. The "progressive Balkanization" of Nigeria, with its concomitant vast waste of human and social resources, was viewed with great anxiety as a tragedy for all Africa. 283 PARL. DEB. (5th ser.) 1367–76 (1967).

[183] The United Nations completely rejected the claim that Katanga was a sovereign independent nation. *See, e.g.*, SC Res. S/5002, 16 UN SCOR (Res. & Dec.) at 3, UN Doc. S/INF/16/Rev.1 (1961). The United Nations found itself at odds with Katanga. On Apr. 3, 1961, Katanga adopted a Decree on the State of Enmity with the United Nations, *reproduced in* J. GERARD-LIBOIS, KATANGA SECESSION 335–37 (R. Young trans. 1966), which, inter alia, forbade Katangans to enter into relations of any nature whatsoever with the United Nations or its agents. See also C. C. O'BRIEN, TO KATANGA AND BACK (1962), in which the author, a former representative of the United Nations in Katanga and former member of the Secretary-General's executive staff, offers a case history of UN experiences with Katanga.

explain why the inhabitants of a colony ruled by Britain or France might be entitled to self-determination, while Latvians or Biafrans were not. Even though preindependence Algeria did elect members to the French Assembly and Senate, the system of communal "colleges" then in operation gave a European vote ten times more weight than an Arab one.[184] Biafrans, by contrast, enjoyed the same rights as other Nigerians. Paradoxically, this basis for distinction may deny the right of self-determination to groups that are more oppressed than some to whom the right would accrue. Latvians, deprived of many basic freedoms, would have no right because they are treated no differently than other disempowered Soviet citizens. Thus, "peoples" of nations that treat everyone equally badly would have no right, while "peoples" treated quite well would be entitled to secede if they were not accorded quite as many rights as the most privileged of that populace.

Moreover, this theoretical basis for determining entitlement to self-determination, while coherent, and also rather congruent with prevailing state conduct, is hard to apply in practice. Once a secessionist movement is in full operation, its ethnic group is almost certain to encounter discriminatory treatment, as is demonstrated by the rise of anti-Tamil sentiment in Sri Lanka in tandem with the spread of Tamil insurrection. Secessionism and discrimination mutually reinforce one another, and it is difficult in particular instances to determine whether secessionism *caused* or *was caused by* unequal treatment.

Difficult or not, the search for a coherent general principle of coverage, or boundary, is important. If it fails, the once-dynamic right of self-determination will fall into incoherence and desuetude. As a rule of state conduct, it began to lose its power to obligate when it became a checkerboard of incoherent practice.

Coherence, in this sense, is fundamental to understanding why a rule text has sufficient legitimacy to affect the conduct of states. The power of coherence to validate derives from the phenomenon we have already identified: that the status of states is symbolically validated by admission into the community of states. It is by symbolic recognition of their membership in that community that states are confirmed in their equal capacity for rights and obligations. Coherence derives from—is the operational manifestation of —that community of rules. Dworkin, although focusing on a community of persons rather than of nations, explains *why* legitimacy is "grounded in" coherence.[185] Coherence demonstrates that states relate through more than random interactions; that they consciously accept responsibilities derived "from a more general responsibility" that is based on membership in a community. Thus, in the community of nations, each state must "treat discrete obligations that arise only under special circumstances, like the obligation to help a friend who is in great financial need, as derivative from and expressing a more general responsibility active throughout the association in different ways."[186] This concern, in principle, must be "an *equal*

[184] E. BEHR, THE ALGERIAN PROBLEM 38 (1961).
[185] R. DWORKIN, *supra* note 7, at 194. [186] *Id.* at 200.

concern for all members."[187] However, the concern is not incompatible with distinctions, so long as each distinction "fits a plausible conception of equal concern."[188] A plausible conception of equal concern is another way of describing a generalizable principle for determining the coverage of a rule-based obligation.

To take another example of such a search: the UN Charter, in Article 2, sets forth "the principle of the sovereign equality of all . . . Members." Article 27, however, provides that the five permanent members of the Security Council—Britain, China, France, the United States and the USSR—shall have a veto over substantive decisions. If states did not regard the United Nations as an aspect of a global community, this seeming contradiction would not matter. Life is full of contradiction. It only matters when a contradiction rises to the level of an incoherence that invalidates and illegitimatizes an aspect of the system of rules of a community to which the state belongs and by reference to which the state defines *its own legitimacy*. Does the contradiction between the voting procedure of the Charter and its rule of state equality invalidate the rules, the UN-based community and, thus, even the individual legitimacy of the members? To ask the question is to understand why states are reluctant to let the Charter fall into incoherence. Instead, they strive to find a reconciling "neutral principle,"[189] a rational distinction that could restore coherence and validate the "checkerboarding." The best one available is this: while all states are equal, some states, because of their special wealth and power, have greater obligations and responsibilities. Consequently, they may also be entitled to an enhanced vote in certain matters.

Unfortunately, this coherent conceptual justification for the privileges granted the "Big Five" in 1945 is not rationally defensible in 1988. In 1945, they really were the world's major powers, having vanquished the Axis and inherited the postwar leadership. Their special status had a certain plausibility, since the success of any important Security Council action would depend on their cooperation. Today, however, Britain, France and China are middle powers, and their role in the world and in the Organization has become no more important than that of some important states without the veto such as the Federal Republic of Germany, Brazil, Nigeria, India and Japan. The privilege bestowed by the rules has thus lost its rational persuasiveness as a boundary, a standard for making distinctions that connects with a rational general principle.

Apparently, this problem of incoherence, with its concomitant dangers, is recognized. While it has not been possible to amend the Charter, Britain, France and China, although casting occasional negative votes in the Council, have made it a practice not to do so except in the company of a majority, or of either the United States or the USSR.[190] In this way, they have contributed to the de facto remission of their veto power.

[187] *Id.*

[188] *Id.* at 201.

[189] For a noteworthy attempt to establish a theoretical basis for such a quest in another area of law, see Wechsler, *Toward Neutral Principles of Constitutional Law*, 73 HARV. L. REV. 1 (1959).

[190] U.S. Mission to the United Nations, List of Vetoes Cast in Public Meetings of the Security Council (Apr. 14, 1988). Only once did the People's Republic of China stand alone in its veto in

This example illustrated that coherence mandates a connectedness between various component parts of a rule or code; between several applications of a rule in various instances; and between the general principles underlying a rule's application and those implicated in other rules. The General Agreement on Tariffs and Trade of 1947[191] further illustrates these aspects of coherence. Its most basic provision is the most-favored-nation clause, which prohibits members from giving benefits to some trading partners not given to all.[192] As long as this rule is applied consistently in practice, it appears to be coherent and, thus, legitimate. In recent years, however, it has become evident that the MFN provision, if applied consistently to all nations, would undermine rather than advance GATT's underlying purpose by diminishing the trade prospects of some 50 less-developed member countries. GATT therefore adopted a Generalized System of Preferences for these special cases.[193] It allows developed states temporarily to permit preferential access to products of only some states, particularly the "least developed."[194] While GSP is inconsistent with MFN, it coheres with the underlying purpose of GATT, which is to increase trade for all nations. It thus advances the real objectives of GATT. Also, it establishes a standard for distinction between the members to whom MFN is applicable and those temporarily benefited by GSP. That standard connects coherently with boundaries commonly used in other sets of regulations to demarcate coverage. Redistributive principles such as those which underlie GSP are commonplace in the international rule system and justify distinctions that, although creating superficial inconsistencies within rules and the application of rule systems, nonetheless leave the rules coherent and legitimate. The checkerboarding, in other words, is redeemed by being seen as based on a principle that both is consistent with the real intent of the specific rule and connects with that skein of principles integrating various other rules of the international system.

To summarize: coherence, and thus legitimacy, must be understood in part as defined by factors derived from a notion of community. Rules become coherent when they are applied so as to preclude capricious checkerboarding. They preclude caprice when they are applied consistently or, if inconsistently applied, when they make distinctions based on underlying general principles that connect with an ascertainable purpose of the rules and with similar distinctions made throughout the rule system. The result-

---

the Security Council. *Id.* at 9. France has vetoed alone only twice since 1946. *Id.* at 10–11. All United Kingdom vetoes during the last 15 years have been cast with the United States. *Id.* at 12–13.

[191] General Agreement on Tariffs and Trade [hereinafter GATT], Oct. 30, 1947, 61 Stat. (5), (6), TIAS No. 1700, 55–61 UNTS.

[192] *Id.*, Art. 1(1).

[193] GATT Contracting Parties, Decision of Nov. 28, 1979, Differential and More Favorable Treatment Reciprocity and Fuller Participation of Developing Countries, GATT, BASIC INSTRUMENTS AND SELECTED DOCUMENTS, 26th Supp. 203 (1980). *See also* J. JACKSON & W. DAVEY, LEGAL PROBLEMS OF INTERNATIONAL ECONOMIC RELATIONS 1149 (2d ed. 1986).

[194] Decision of Nov. 28, 1979, *supra* note 193, paras. 1 and 6.

ant skein of underlying principles is an aspect of community, which, in turn, confirms the status of the states that constitute the community. Validated membership in the community accords equal capacity for rights and obligations derived from its legitimate rule system.

By focusing on the connections between specific rules and general underlying principles, we have emphasized the horizontal aspect of our central notion of a community of legitimate rules. However, there are vertical aspects of this community that have even more significant impact on the legitimacy of rules.

V. Adherence (to a Normative Hierarchy) and Community

Professor Hart's observation, noted above, that the international arena lacks a "legislature, courts with compulsory jurisdiction, and centrally organized sanctions" leads him to deduce "that the rules for states resemble that simple form of social structure, consisting only of primary rules of obligation, which, when we find it among societies of individuals, we are accustomed to contrast with a developed legal system."[195] Although he acknowledges that international law does have many substantive "primary" rules, such as those specific rights and duties typically enumerated in treaties or developed through customary usage, he nevertheless concludes that the system is primitive, if not illusory, because it lacks those crucial procedural "secondary" rules which permit a rule to change and adapt through legislation and the decision of courts. An even more serious disqualification of the international system, Hart alleges, is its lack of "a unifying rule of recognition specifying 'sources' of law and providing general criteria for the identification of its rules."[196] By a "unifying rule of recognition," Hart means an international equivalent of the U.S. Constitution, or the British rule of parliamentary supremacy, both of which are "ultimate" in that they test the validity of all other rules by standards that are not themselves subject to being tested by reference to any superior rule.

Hart identifies the essential elements of a developed system of rules and then concludes that they are missing at the international level. He thus finds the international community to be the approximate equivalent of a small primitive tribe that has primary rules of obligation about such matters as land and kinship, but no system of governance that allocates and regulates social roles or facilitates, by an established process, the making, changing, application and reinterpreting of these random substantive primary rules.

In effect, Hart considers the international system to be primitive because individual rules lack *adherence* to a rule hierarchy. This is a much more sophisticated critique of the international rule system than the simple Austinian one, which focuses on the absence of a system of coercion. Hart does note the lack of institutionalized coercion but puts greater critical emphasis on the failure of international rules to adhere to a hierarchic rule structure.

[195] H. L. A. Hart, *supra* note 3, at 209. [196] *Id.*

Adherence—a term Hart does not use—is used here to mean the vertical nexus between a single *primary rule of obligation* ("cross on the green; stop on the red") and a pyramid of secondary rules about how rules are made, interpreted and applied: rules, in other words, about rules. These may be labeled *secondary rules of process*. Primary rules of obligation that lack adherence to a system of secondary rules of process are mere ad hoc reciprocal arrangements. They are not necessarily incapable of obligating parties that have agreed to them. They may even connect coherently with the underlying principles of distinction found in other rules to create a horizontal skein that is an aspect of community. But the degree of legitimacy of primary rules that only cohere is less than if the same rule were also connected to a pyramid of secondary rules of process, culminating in an ultimate rule of recognition. A rule, in summary, is more likely to obligate if it is made within the procedural and institutional framework of an organized community than if it is strictly an ad hoc agreement between parties in the state of nature. The same rule is still more likely to obligate if it is made within the hierarchically structured procedural and constitutional framework of a sophisticated community rather than in a primitive community lacking such secondary rules about rules.

Hart's critique of the community of states as small and primitive is still widely accepted. Even those who think that the system is at a more sophisticated stage of development might well concede that Hart's misgivings are not wholly unjustified. The recurrence of wars, other conflicts and unremedied injustices invites the appellation "primitive."

The misgivings, however, need to be kept in perspective. Of course, there *are* lawmaking institutions in the system. One has but to visit a highly structured multinational negotiation such as the decade-long Law of the Sea Conference of the 1970s to see a kind of incipient legislature at work. The Security Council, the decision-making bodies of the World Bank and, perhaps, the UN General Assembly also somewhat resemble the cabinets and legislatures of national governments, even if they are not so highly disciplined and empowered as the British Parliament, the French National Assembly or even the U.S. Congress. Moreover, there *are* courts in the international system: not only the International Court of Justice, the European Community Court and the regional human rights tribunals, but also a very active network of quasi-judicial committees and commissions, as well as arbitral tribunals established under such auspices as the Algiers agreement ending the Iran hostage crisis.[197] Arbitrators regularly settle investment disputes under the auspices and procedures of the World Bank and the International Chamber of Commerce. Treaties and contracts create jurisdiction for these tribunals and establish rules of evidence and procedure.[198]

[197] *See* Declaration of the Government of the Democratic and Popular Republic of Algeria Concerning the Settlement of Claims by the Government of the United States of America and the Government of the Islamic Republic of Iran, DEP'T ST. BULL., No. 2047, February 1981, at 3, *reprinted in* 75 AJIL 422 (1981), 20 ILM 230 (1981).

[198] The World Bank approved the Convention on the Settlement of Investment Disputes Between States and Nationals of Other States, Mar. 18, 1965, 17 UST 1270, TIAS No. 6090,

The international system thus appears on close examination to be a more developed community than critics sometimes allege. It has an extensive network of horizontally coherent rules, rule-making institutions, and judicial and quasi-judicial bodies to apply the rules impartially. Many of the rules are sufficiently determinate for states to know what is required for compliance and most states obey them most of the time. Those that do not, tend to feel guilty and to lie about their conduct rather than defy the rules openly. The system also has means for changing, adapting and repealing rules.

Most nations, most of the time, are both rule conscious and rule abiding. Why this is so, rather than that it is so, is also relevant to an understanding of the degree to which an international community has developed in practice. This silent majority's sense of obligation derives primarily not from explicit consent to specific treaties or custom, but from *status*. Obligation is perceived to be owed *to a community of states as a necessary reciprocal incident of membership in the community*. Moreover, that community is defined by secondary rules of process as well as by primary rules of obligation: states perceive themselves to be participants in a structured process of continual interaction that is governed by secondary rules of process (sometimes called rules of recognition), of which the UN Charter is but the most obvious example. The Charter is a set of rules, but it is also about how rules are to be made by the various institutions established by the Charter and by the subsidiaries those institutions have created, such as the International Law and Human Rights Commissions.

In addition, obligation is owed not only to the rules of the game, but also *to the game itself*. This is symptomatic of a community organized by a pyramid of secondary rules at whose apex is an ultimate rule or set of rules of recognition. The ultimate rule defines the community. If the game were football, the ultimate rule of recognition would be the one justifying the statement that what is being played is not baseball or tennis, but football. Thus, when the umpire calls a "foul," the legitimacy of that judgment derives ultimately from those rules which define the activity as football rather than some other sport. In the international system, the game of nations does have its own ultimate, defining set of rules by which the validity of all subsidiary rules—secondary procedural as well as primary substantive—may be tested.

A community is sophisticated when it has such an *ultimate rule of recognition*. In the United States, France, Germany and many other countries this is in the form of a written constitution. In the United Kingdom, however, the existence of an ultimate rule of recognition must be established deductively, since there is no written law defining the community. Nevertheless, it is

575 UNTS 159, which established the International Centre for Settlement of Investment Disputes. *See* Broches, *The Convention on the Settlement of Investment Disputes: Some Observations on Jurisdiction*, 5 COLUM. J. TRANSNAT'L L. 263 (1966). For U.S. implementing legislation, see Convention on the Settlement of Investment Disputes Act of 1966, Pub. L. No. 89-532, §2, 80 Stat. 344 (codified at 22 U.S.C. §§1650, 1650a (1982)). Under certain circumstances, parties to a dispute may arbitrate in the International Chamber of Commerce Court of Arbitration.

demonstrable that parliamentary supremacy qualifies as an ultimate rule of recognition because it owes its legitimacy only to public acquiescence, or to the corporate act of social commitment sometimes metaphorically described as a social contract. Its validity, unlike all the community's other secondary and primary rules, cannot be tested by reference to any other law. No statute makes Parliament supreme, nor can any law curb that supremacy. Indeed, if an act stipulated that it could only be repealed by a two-thirds majority, Parliament could delete that two-thirds requirement by a simple majority vote.[199] The rule of parliamentary supremacy defines the legitimacy of all other laws, but its own legitimacy is undefined, and thus *ultimate.* The rule is autochthonous: one "sprung from the earth itself."

Both the British Parliament and the U.S. Constitution are repositories of ultimate power unfettered by superior authority. Both the rule of parliamentary supremacy in Britain and the rules embodied in the Constitution of the United States are ultimate secondary rules of process by which the legitimacy of all primary rules of obligation may be tested and established. A rule of ultimate recognition operates with such extraordinary power to validate a subsidiary pyramid of rules—both other secondary rules of a procedural nature and primary rules of obligation—because the ultimate rule is accepted by a community that is defined by that rule. The ultimate set of rules also defines the status of each member of the community; that is to say, each member's status derives from the recognition of membership. Rejection of the ultimate rule by the members constitutes revolution and is the only option for discarding the ultimate rule (which, in some states but not in others, may be changed—as distinct from being overthrown—but only in strict accordance with its own terms). Acquiescence, on the other hand, is demonstrated tautologically, by compliance. Ultimate rules of recognition cannot be validated by reference to any other rule. All other secondary rules of the community are inferior to, and validated by, the ultimate rule or set of rules.

It is the nature of community, therefore, both to empower authority and to circumscribe it by an ultimate rule or set of rules of recognition that exists above, and itself is not circumscribed by, the system of normative authority. Does such a notion of community exist internationally, among states? Do nations recognize an ultimate rule or set of rules of recognition or process by which the legitimacy of all other international rules and procedures can be tested, a rule not itself subject to a higher normative test of its legitimacy, a rule that simply *is*, because it is accepted as font of the community's collective self-definition?

If the international community were merely a playing field on which states engaged in various random, or opportunistic, exchanges or interac-

[199] In perhaps the most eloquent statement of Parliament's unlimited legislative authority, Sir Edward Coke has declared that its "power and jurisdiction . . . is so transcendent and absolute, that it . . . hath sovereign and uncontrollable authority in the making, confirming, enlarging, restraining, abrogating, repealing, reviving, and expounding of laws." E. COKE, FOURTH INSTITUTE 36, *quoted in* A. DICEY, INTRODUCTION TO THE STUDY OF THE CONSTITUTION 41 (9th ed. 1939).

tions, it would be easy to conclude that this was a truly primitive aggregation, a rabble, lacking the organizing structure of secondary rules of process and, of course, an ultimate secondary rule. This, rather than any absence of coercive force, would indeed justify the appellation "primitive." The international community, however, demonstrably is not like that. States—whatever their occasional rhetorical excesses—recognize that they are not sovereign. They accept that they are members of a sophisticated community with secondary rules and with what amounts to a constitution or ultimate rules of recognition. States also recognize that they derive validation from membership in this community.

The nonsovereignty of states and the existence of a set of ultimate community rules can be demonstrated by examining the way treaties operate from the perspective of those that become parties to them. It is quite wrong to think that treaties bind states *because* they have consented to them. If states were sovereign, the mere act of entering into a treaty could not "bind" them in any accurate sense. States are not bound only because they agree to be bound, in the sense in which neighbors in an apartment building might informally agree, for their mutual convenience, to turn off their television sets by 10 o'clock every evening. Those neighbors are at liberty to disregard their obligation whenever it does not suit their purpose. Nor are states obligated by treaties the way individuals are bound by a contract. In municipal law, contracts are binding because their sanctity is prescribed and enforced by the state.[200] True, most contracts operate without recourse to state sanctions, but the sanctions remain in reserve.

Treaties thus do not exactly fit either model. They are not like the free-will agreement among neighbors, which is valid only as long as it continues to suit everyone's purpose; and they are not contracts made under the authority of a sovereign and enforceable by the full authority of the state, through either compelled specific performance or an award of damages. Treaties obviously cannot be binding in the sense of being sanctioned by an Austinian sovereign; but a treaty also cannot be said to be binding only because two or more sovereign states voluntarily agree to carry it out. "Sovereign" means *unbindable.* A treaty ratified by a truly sovereign state could only *declare*, never *bind*, that state's free will. If the state were indeed sovereign, then, no matter what it had signed, it would nevertheless remain free to terminate its consent at any time, just as the sovereign British Parliament cannot legislate a law that can only be amended by a two-thirds major-

[200] While the term "contract" is susceptible of many definitions, whatever else a contract may entail, it is agreed that it is "a promise, or set of promises, for breach of which the law gives a remedy, or the performance of which the law in some way recognizes as a duty." 1 WILLISTON ON CONTRACTS §1 (3d ed. 1957); RESTATEMENT (SECOND) OF CONTRACTS §1 (1981). *See also* 1 A. CORBIN, CONTRACTS §3 (1963) (which defines a contract to include "a promise enforceable at law directly or indirectly"). In some jurisdictions, courts will routinely mandate specific performance of the promise. *See, e.g.*, Dawson, *Specific Performance in France and Germany*, 57 MICH. L. REV. 495 (1959). The Anglo-American legal system, however, prefers to impose damages at least equal to the value of the breached promise. *See, e.g.*, J. CALAMARI & J. PERILLO, THE LAW OF CONTRACTS 580–604 (1977).

ity. If states were sovereign, entering into a treaty would be nothing more than evidence of their state of mind for the time being.

Notably, states never claim this. They act, instead, as if they were bound. They believe themselves to be bound—which can only be understood as evidence of their acquiescence in something demonstrable only circumstantially: an ultimate rule of recognition. In the international community "sovereignty"—however fragile—resides in the rule, and not in the individual states of the community. States seem to be aware of this rule's autochthony. They act in professed compliance with, and reliance on, the notion that when a state signs and ratifies an accord with one or more other states, then it has an obligation, superior to its sovereign will. The obligation derives not from consent to the treaty, or its text, but from membership in a community that endows the parties to the agreement with status, including the capacity to enter into treaties.

The most recent instance of this perception of an international rule superior to the specific acquiescence of any particular state is to be found in the advisory opinion rendered by the International Court of Justice on April 26, 1988, at the request of the United Nations General Assembly.[201] At issue was a conflict between provisions of a U.S. law that required the closing of the Observer Mission of the Palestine Liberation Organization,[202] and the obligation assumed under the UN Headquarters Agreement.[203] The Court stated unequivocally that it was "the fundamental principle of international law that it prevails over domestic law,"[204] that "the provisions of municipal law cannot prevail over those of a treaty."[205] The U.S. judge (Stephen M. Schwebel) added that "a State cannot avoid its international responsibility by the enactment of domestic legislation which conflicts with its international obligations" under a treaty.[206] Unanimously, the Court accepted that clear limitation on the sovereignty of states imposed by membership in the international community.

In Hart's words, the "view that a state may impose obligations on itself by promise, agreement, or treaty is not . . . consistent with the theory that states are subject only to rules which they have thus imposed on them-

[201] GA Res. 42/229B (Mar. 2, 1988).

[202] The Observer Mission status was created by GA Res. 3237, 29 UN GAOR Supp. (No. 31) at 4, UN Doc. A/9631 (1974). The closure of the mission is required by the Anti-Terrorism Act of 1987, title X of the Foreign Relations Authorization Act, 1988 and 1989, Pub. L. No. 100-204, tit. X, §1001, 101 Stat. 1331, 1406 (codified at 22 U.S.C.A. §§5201–5203 (West Supp. 1988)).

[203] *See* Agreement Regarding the Headquarters of the United Nations, June 26, 1947, *supra* note 115.

[204] Applicability of the Obligation to Arbitrate under Section 21 of the United Nations Headquarters Agreement of 26 June 1947, 1988 ICJ REP. 12, 34, para. 57 (Advisory Opinion of Apr. 26).

[205] Greco-Bulgarian "Communities," 1930 PCIJ (ser. B) No. 17, at 32 (Advisory Opinion of July 31).

[206] 1988 ICJ REP. at 42 (Schwebel, J., sep. op.).

selves."[207] Rather, "*rules* must already exist providing that a state is bound to do whatever it undertakes by appropriate words to do."[208] This hypothetical notion itself is actually set out in the text of a global treaty defining the law of treaties,[209] a document establishing a body of secondary rules of process. Even so, the binding force of the treaty codifying the law of treaties cannot emanate from the agreement of the large majority of states that have ratified it. It must come from some ultimate, generally accepted unwritten rule of recognition that is fundamental to any real understanding of the nature of international obligation.

If there is an ultimate set of secondary rules of process that embodies an abstract sovereignty and confers legitimacy in the international community, what are its other provisions? As with the foregoing rule, *pacta sunt servanda*, the other components of an ultimate rule of recognition can only be hypothesized and demonstrated circumstantially by habitual state deference. Thus, the rule that treaties are binding is itself modified by the rule that treaties are *void ab initio* if they are against the community's basic public policy, that is, if they violate the community's ultimate (peremptory) norms.[210] A treaty to commit genocide, for example, would be invalid for this reason. A related notion that appears to qualify as part of the ultimate rule of recognition pertains to the binding obligation imposed on state conduct by global custom. There is widespread acknowledgment by states that they are obligated by international customary rules, whether or not they agree in any specific instance with the import of a rule. This was recently reiterated by the International Court of Justice in the case brought by Nicaragua against the United States, where the latter was held to be obligated by an extensive array of customary norms despite an evident desire to pursue its self-interest in a manner incongruent with those rules.[211]

There are other parts of the ultimate rule that can be deduced from the practice of states in adhering to it *as an incident of statehood* rather than as a consequence of their specific consent. For example, new states are deemed to acquire the universal rights and duties of statehood not because they have agreed but because they have joined the community.[212] Similarly, new states may "inherit" rights and duties from a "parent" state[213] not by virtue of

[207] H. L. A. HART, *supra* note 3, at 219. [208] *Id.*

[209] Vienna Convention on the Law of Treaties, *supra* note 33, Art. 26.

[210] *Id.*, Art. 53.

[211] Military and Paramilitary Activities in and against Nicaragua (Nicar. v. U.S.), Merits, 1986 ICJ REP. 14 (Judgment of June 27).

[212] It is a well-established principle that a new state to the international community is automatically bound by the rules of international conduct existing at the time of admittance. *See* 1 L. OPPENHEIM, *supra* note 77, at 17–18. Even Tunkin concedes that if it enters "without reservations into official relations with other states," a new state is bound by "principles and norms of existing international law." *See* Tunkin, *Remarks on the Juridical Nature of Customary Norms of International Law*, 49 CAL. L. REV. 419, 428 (1961).

[213] There has been wide debate over the rights and obligations a successor state can inherit from its parent. The 19th-century doctrine of universal succession maintains that all the rights and duties of the parent pass to the successor. *See* O. UDOKANG, SUCCESSION OF NEW STATES

their consent but as a concomitant of status. Successor governments, too, automatically inherit rights and obligations.[214]

One more example of a part of the ultimate rule of recognition is the previously noted notion of state equality. UN Charter Article 2(1) specifically restates this rule, and no state since Hitler's Germany has claimed anything to the contrary. All states are bound by a rule of state equality as a concomitant of their membership in the community of nations. In the words of U.S. Chief Justice John Marshall in an 1825 decision, *The Antelope*, "No principle of general law is more universally acknowledged than the perfect equality of nations."[215]

It is therefore circumstantially demonstrable that there are obligations that states acknowledge to be necessary incidents of community membership. These are not perceived to obligate because they have been accepted by the individual state but, rather, are rules in which states acquiesce as part of their own validation; that is, as an inseparable aspect of "joining" a community of states that is defined by its ultimate secondary rules of process. It is even possible to conclude that the members of the global community acknowledge—for example, each time they sign a treaty or recognize a new government—*that statehood is incompatible with sovereignty*. They acknowledge this because they must, so as to obtain and retain the advantages of belonging to an organized, sophisticated community, advantages only available if ultimate sovereignty resides in a set of rules of universal application. That is why states behave as if such rules existed and obligated.

To put the matter another way, a "community" of states exists. It has at least some important secondary rules of recognition. These rules are "associative obligations," to use Dworkin's term,[216] which fasten onto all states because of their status as validated members of the international community. Only by stretching the notion of "consent" beyond its natural limits can these specific associative obligations be said to have been assumed consensually, even though they may sometimes be restated in a treaty. Dworkin rightly points out that "associative" rules of obligation are interpretive,[217] defining what a member owes others in the community in general. Thus, the obligation to honor treaties is acquired associatively, rather than by specific consent; and it is owed generally towards all members of the community. This is universally acknowledged. It is inconceivable, for example,

---

TO INTERNATIONAL TREATIES 122–24 (1972). At the other extreme is negativist theory, which holds that a successor inherits no rights and obligations, but begins with a tabula rasa. *See* D. O'CONNELL, STATE SUCCESSION IN MUNICIPAL LAW AND INTERNATIONAL LAW 14–17 (1967). The truth lies somewhere in between, with certain rights and duties of the parent devolving upon the successor. *See* 1 L. OPPENHEIM, *supra* note 77, at 120. Hart further points to evidence that changes in a state's circumstance may automatically accord it new rights and duties, for example, when it acquires new territory giving it a coastline. H. L. A. HART, *supra* note 3, at 221.

[214] Tinoco Case (Gr. Brit. v. Costa Rica), 1 R. Int'l Arb. Awards 369 (1923), *reprinted in* 18 AJIL 147 (1924).

[215] The Antelope, 23 U.S. (10 Wheat.) 66, 122 (1825).

[216] R. DWORKIN, *supra* note 7, at 196.

[217] *Id.* at 197.

that a state would announce that it would no longer be bound by treaties or custom. The obligation, moreover, cannot be extinguished by renouncing a consent that was never given, but only by extinguishing the status that is the real basis of the obligation.

According to Dworkin, a true community, as distinguished from a mere rabble, or even a system of random primary rules of obligation, is one in which the members

> accept that they are governed by common principles, not just by rules hammered out in political compromise. . . . Members of a society of principle accept that their political rights and duties are not exhausted by the particular decisions their political institutions have reached, but depend, more generally, on the scheme of principles those decisions presuppose and endorse. So each member accepts that others have rights and that he has duties flowing from that scheme . . . .

Nor are these rights and duties "conditional on his wholehearted approval of that scheme; these obligations arise from the historical fact that his community has adopted that scheme, . . . not the assumption that he would have chosen it were the choice entirely his."[218]

Moreover, the community "commands that no one be left out, that we are all in politics together for better or worse."[219] And its legitimizing requirement of rule integrity "assumes that each person is as worthy as any other, that each must be treated with equal concern according to some coherent conception of what that means."[220]

Does that accurately describe the social condition of the nations of the world in their interactive mode? The description does not assume harmony or an absence of strife. According to Dworkin, an "association of principle is not automatically a just community; its conception of equal concern may be defective."[221] What a rule community, a community of principle, does is to validate behavior in accordance with rules and applications of rules that confirm principled coherence and adherence, rather than acknowledging only the power of power. A rule community operates in conformity not only with primary rules but also with secondary ones—rules about rules—which are generated by valid legislative and adjudicative institutions. Finally, a community accepts its ultimate secondary rules of recognition not consensually, but as an inherent concomitant of membership status.

In the world of nations, each of these described conditions of a sophisticated community is observable today, even though imperfectly. This does not mean that its rules will never be disobeyed. It does mean, however, that it is usually possible to distinguish rule compliance from rule violation, and a valid rule or ruling from an invalid one. It also means that it is not necessary to await the millennium of Austinian-type world government to proceed with constructing—perfecting—a system of rules and institutions that will exhibit a powerful pull to compliance and a self-enforcing degree of legitimacy.

[218] *Id.* at 211.

[219] *Id.* at 213.

[220] *Id.* at 214.

[221] *Id.*

[7]

THE NORMATIVE FORCE OF HABIT: INTERNATIONAL CUSTOM AND SOCIAL THEORY

by

Martti Koskenniemi*

International lawyers - like any observers of human behaviour - are also amateur social theorists. In seeking to understand what goes on in the international society they necessarily do this from the vantage point of a theory. For the meaning human behaviour - social actions and events - does not come before the observer's eyes "an sich". It appears through multilayered, even chaotic complexes of facts, ideas and texts. Reaching an understanding involves establishing meaningful relationships between these disparate facts, ideas and texts. This again requires that we are in the possession of a code for making distinctions - separating the essential from the non-essential, the cause from the effect, the rule from the regularity, and so on.[1] This code is our more or less explicit social theory. Only by possessing such a code we can understand human behaviour and, by extension, events or actions concerning groups or nations.

My intention in this article is to show how the modern international lawyer's argument about customary law is controlled by a set of assumptions about the interpretation of human behaviour and how the inconclusive discussion among social theorists about interpretation is reproduced as the

---

* Dr., Councellor, Permanent Mission of Finland to the United Nations

1 "One cannot simply study the practice of States as evidence of law because it is logically inconceivable to examine any evidence without a priori criteria of relevance and significance..." A. Carty, The Decay of International Law? A Reappraisal of the Limits of Legal Imagination in International Affairs (Manchester 1986) p. 95.

indeterminacy of lawyers' argument about custom.[2] I shall argue that modern lawyers have adopted a "social conception of law" which blinds them from seeing that when seeking to understand social behaviour, they do this from the perspective of a code - a material theory of justice.

Modern lawyers have assumed that justice cannot be discussed in a rationally controllable fashion. They have also accepted the democratic premise that social constraint can only be based on rules and principles whose application is rationally conrollable. This has forced them to assume that there exists a method whereby they can understand the meaning of social behaviour - whether it encapsulates unwritten law, for example, - as if it were a fact of nature: as if meaning resided immediately on the surface of that behaviour, capable of being grasped by any external observer in an "objective" fashion - without regard to political evaluation.

But this assumption conflicts with their professional experience. For international lawyers constantly disagree about valid custom and about the methods for finding it. That their argument about customary law remains unpersuasive and leads into familiar dilemmas or dead-ends can be explained by their dogmatic reliance on the social conception of law. In order to develop more persuasive and imaginative arguments about custom, international lawyers should start taking justice seriously - though this might mean that they should rethink their modernism, or at least their exclusion of political considerations from statements about valid law.

---

2 This Article develops and partly reproduces the argument in Chapter 6 of my From Apology to Utopia; the Structure of International Legal Argument (Helsinki 1989).

1. THE TWO POSITIONS

For modern lawyers - and no less modern international lawyers - law is a social phenomenon. It does not reside in abstract and unverifiable notions of natural law or principles of justice. The very identity of modern legal doctrines lies in their denial that in order to know the law's content one should know something about what is good or right in human behaviour. "Good" and "right" are subjective notions which cannot be rationally discussed. For the modern lawyer, law is enmeshed in the actual social life in which social agents - States - participate. To find out law, lawyers should look at society.[3]

But of course, not everything in society is law. Some behaviour - perhaps even most of it - and many institutions, bear no relationship to legal standards. A behaviour may reflect private desire, liens of family or friendship, hostility, or calculations of political strategy, for example. While some forms of behaviour undoubtedly signify the creation or observance of legal standards, other forms of behaviour are simply irrelevant from a legal point of view.

To tell us what law there exists in society, the lawyer must distinguish between legally irrelevant and legally relevant behaviour and tell us just in what the legal relevance of a behaviour resides. While the pre-modern lawyer tried to penetrate into notion of the good and the just in order to determine the character (legal/illegal) of a behaviour, the modern lawyer looks at that behaviour itself to find out its legal status. The meaning of

3 This is best evidenced by the standard modern style of preceding textbook analyses with a description of the "International society" or the "political framework" of legal rules. The assumption is that law is determined by society and that, consequently, the legal method should elucidate the content of law by reference to phenomena in the social field. For standard examples fo this argument, see Koskenniemi, op. cit., Ch. 1 n. 1; Ch. 3 n. 217 and the criticism in ibid. pp. 466-471.

behaviour resides in that behaviour itself, not in some external code of purposes or values.

Modern lawyers reject speculation about the good and the just because there seems to reign complete confusion about these matters. They want to have a scientific - objective, controllable - way to decide the controversies about what is applicable law.[4] But their enterprise, as their he look upon State behaviour and come up with an argument that something is, or is not, customary law, is wrought with philosophical problems. Though international lawyers may sometimes have claimed to know the normative Kraft der Faktischen, it seems hardly likely that they should have smashed Hume's Guillotine without anyone working in political philosophy having heard about it - just as unlikely, in fact, as that they could have broken away from the hermeneutic circle to establish the meaning of human action without having to assume an essentially political position.

By what justification, indeed, may the international lawyer claim that he knows the meaning of State behaviour? What is it, precisely, that he means when he claims to have found such meaning? There are, to put it crudely, two types of answer to these questions.

1.1 Materialism: modernism, phase I

It seems natural to assume that understanding an aspect of human behaviour really requires looking closely enough, and long enough, at that behaviour, compare it with

---

4 The standard argument is that naturalism is indemonstrable, subjective and thus "confuses" law with politics. Through its manipulability it merely serves to legitimize tyranny. See, e.g., J.H.W Verzijl, <u>International Law in Historical Perspective</u> (Leiden 1968) pp. 391-393; S. Sur, <u>L'intérprétation en droit international public</u> (Paris 1974) pp. 25-32; H. Kelsen, <u>Principles of International Law</u>, ed. & rev., Robert M. Tucker, (New York-Chicago-San Francisco-Toronto-London 1966) p. 443. See also J.L Brierly, <u>The Law of Nations</u>, 6th ed. (Oxford 1967) p. 22.

other forms of behaviour and thus slowly arrive at an understanding of its meaning. When lawyers first started assuming that law is a social, instead of a theologico-moral or natural fact they also started focusing more closely on the actual behaviour of social agents.[5] Let me call this "materialism".

Being social, law became also a historical matter. It was no accident that 19th century international lawyers used so much of their energy to writing about how nations, or their representatives had conducted themselves in the past. Having rejected arguments about man's nature or God's will as subjective speculation, and wishing to establish a truly scientific discipline of international law which could proceed by merely arranging facts under suitable headings, there was little else what they could write about: diplomatic law became a law about what diplomats had done.[6]

This view and style is no exclusivity of the 19th century. The contemporary international lawyer, too, declares that:

> "The significant question to ask about international law is whether the use of that term is in accordance with an accurate observation and study of the conduct of States."[7]

One needs not be an observant of "realism" nor an adherent to any policy-science approach to feel that international law has more to do with the study of the facts of

---

5 Among the programmatic works of the 19th Century, concentrating on method, in this respect, see e.g., K. Kaltenborn von Stachau, Kritik des Völkerrechts (Leipzig 1847); A. von Bulmerincq, Systematik des Völkerrechts von Hugo Grotius bis auf die Gegenwart (Karow, Dorpat 1858); T.A. Walker, Science of International Law (London 1893).

6 The typical - and influential - example being perhaps H. Wheaton, Elements of International Law, the text of 1866 reprinted with notes in Carnegie Endowment for International Peace, Classics of International Law (No. 19) (Oxford-London 1936). See also generally Koskenniemi, op. cit., pp. 106-127.

7 P. Jessup, A Modern Law of Nations (New York 1952) p. 6.

State behaviour than contemplation of the goodness of sovereign action. As two hundred years ago, calls for methodological reform are still usually calls for a more accurate, sociological, behaviour-looking scholarly practice. Indeed, questioning the dictum that to know the law one should know the behaviour may even seem a somewhat eccentric leap into academic marginalization.

This type of materialism - looking strictly at society, conceptualized as "behaviour" - may seem eminently reasonable for at least the following three reasons:

First, it avoids naturalism - the view that certain acts by their inherent nature are such as to have a certain normative meaning. Did not the Enlightenment arise precisely out of the realization that views on these matters were hopelessly divided and that there was no rational way to solve disagreement. The fiction of there being natural norms only seemed to give formal legitimacy to tyrannical practices. At least Rousseau thought that Grotian naturalism was so flexible as to accommodate any monarch's petty perversion.[8]

Second, it avoids formalism - the assumption that certain propositions have the status of law merely because their logical properties. In this way it avoids making law out of fiction. Materialism's implicit reliance on effectiveness also makes it possible to believe in law as a function of policy.

Thirdly, it makes it easier to fit the study of law within the modern conception of science, so heavily influenced by the methods of natural sciences. Though the methods of human science may be controversial, this may only reflect its "undeveloped" character. It does not have to make us abandon the assumption of some profound similarity between it and natural science. Most importantly, it

---

8 J.J. Rousseau, The Social Contract, Transl. & Intr. by M. Cranston, (Harmondsworth 1986) pp. 51-53.

seems that only by preserving this isomorphy - and its centralmost tenet, the separation of the subject and object of scientific enquiry - may it be assumed that statements about the law's normative content may be attached with the label "true".

1.2 Psychologism: modernism, phase II

But a purely materialistic conception creates problems. If law were simply a matter of externally observable behaviour, and nothing else, then any conquest, any reign of terror - any status quo - may claim to be legally sanctioned. Not only is there the logical problem that materialism cannot distinguish between behaviour which is legally relevant and which is not, in its complete equation of law with power it loses the law's social function: under it, law becomes a non-normative apology, a post hoc justification for any actually effective policy.[9]

This concern in modern legal theory is well illustrated in the well-known criticism by H.L.A. Hart of Austinian positivism. Now John Austin had, during the 1830's, argued that to be scientific, the statements of legal science had to be verifiable. To be verifiable, those statements were to address questions of fact. In social life, facts were what citizens actually did - whom they actually obeyed. So he extrapolated that law ("properly so-called") was expressed in the commands of a superior which induced the conforming behaviour of the citizen - the inferior. Of course, on that test, international law would fail. There was no superior-inferior relationship and consequently no habitual obedience by sovereigns of each other - hence no law either.[10]

---

9 See, e.g., H. Lauterpacht, International Law, vol. I, pp. 341-344.

10 J. Austin, The Province of Jurisprudence Determined, Introduction by H.L.A. Hart (London 1954) pp. 9-18, 126.

For naturalist lawyers, of course, such a conception remained unconvincing. But not so to many others who felt that to deny Austin's point was to relapse the study of law into the kind of superstition from which the Enlightenment had attempted to emerge it. Its refutation without assuming an openly naturalistic - that is, political - position was only possible by a move to psychologism, as undertaken in Hart's criticism.

Hart observed - as many others had done - that Austinian positivism was unable to make a difference between law and the gunman's order. Both may receive habitual obedience. Yet, to call the latter "law" would give a fundamentally distorted picture of the social relationships involved when looked at from an "internal", psychological point of view. Gunman's orders are obeyed because of fear or use of physical violence. Obeying a law involves a much more complex psychological relationship with the legislator. In most cases, laws are obeyed because citizens have internalized the legal structure, they have recognized that obeying laws is a matter of duty and not one of mere constraint.[11]

By the explication of the psychological motives in social behaviour it becomes possible for Hart, and others, to make a distinction between law and power. Famously, Winchian sociology generalizes this lesson: it is simply this "internal aspect" of behaviour which allows us to understand it correctly. To understand behaviour, one must not only look at its external form. One must grasp its sense to the behaving person himself.[12]

This move into psychology provides the recourse to distinguish between law and physical force without having to assume a naturalistic (political) criterion to do this.

---

11 H.L.A. Hart, The Concept of Law (Oxford 1961) p. 91 et seq.

12 P. Winch, The Idea of a Social Science and Its Relation to Philosophy (London-Henley 1977).

If the assumption is rejected that acts are not good or bad (right or wrong) in themselves, we may distinguish between legitimizing silence (in the form of acquiescence, or estoppel) and silence induced by fear of constraint only by referring to the motives which induced such silence.

1.3 From materialism to psychologism and back

1.3.1 Circularity

The problem with this move to psychology lies in the difficulty of grasping any social agent's motives in their authenticity. True, modern hermeneutics, in particular, but also more pragmatic methodologies of anthropology or history have stressed the need for a "fusion of horizons" between the researcher and the agents on whose behaviour his enquiry is directed. It may be assumed that we can reach subjective motives by emphatical imagination - usually assumed to be within our reach only after prolonged stay with the people whose understandings we hope to understand.[13]

Whether or not such methods work succesfully in sociology is one thing. But it seems pointless to tell the lawyer, or the judge, to aim at a fusion of understandings in this way in order to find out the law. He has neither the time nor the capacity to enter into an imaginative assimilation of other people's thoughts. Nor would his clients be satisfied if he explained his opinion or judgement as a result of such an enquiry. How, then, can the lawyer find out the motives of social actors (of parties to a contract, for example). The usual answer is this: one need not reach an actual, psychological motive. It suffices that one grasps what a "reasonable man" would have thought,

---

13 See, e.g., H-G. Gadamer, Philosophical Hermeneutics (Berkeley - Los Angeles - London 1977); R.G. Collingwood, The Idea of History (Oxford 1946).

or what motive the act itself - "externally" - seems to single out.

The construction of tacit consent is a typical example. Frustrated at attempts to find real consent of the parties behind some transaction, contract lawyers - just as international lawyers, in fact - have usually assumed that consent can be "inferred" from the character of the behaviour. Reference may be made to what a reasonable man might have thought, or what the legitimate expectations might have been. But, and here is the dilemma: this assumption - the assumption of tacit consent - assumes what was to be proved: namely that we can know what the behaviour meant ("externally") in order to make an "inference" about psychological motives. But we needed to know psychological motives precisely because we did not know the act's meaning merely by looking at its external appearence.[14]

So, psychologism must show us a reliable practical way of knowing what other people think without referring to how they act. For assuming that we can know the thoughts of other people merely by looking at what they do contradicts psychologism's principal justification: we needed to look into motives precisely because acts in themselves - in their external form - were incapable of showing their real meaning. There is a vicious circle. Modern social theories say that in order to know the meaning of behaviour, you must look at the intent behind it. But when asked to explain how they can know this intent, they refer back to the character of the behaviour itself.

1.3.2 Indeterminacy

A second dilemma is even more fundamental, though perhaps not quite so evident. For it is not at all certain that mere reference to subjective understandings salvages

---

14 See generally Koskenniemi, op.cit., pp. 284-291.

lawyers from the kind of apologism which Hart detected in Austinian positivism. Since the discovery of the unconscious, and the theory of ideology, one has had to reckon with the existence of the possibility that one's subjective motives are only an illusion, a distorted reflection of externally (or internally) induced forces. In such case, the meaning of the act is not clarified, but rather obscured, by the actor's real, psychological understanding. Any sociological study of the act must then transcend the (merely) subjective psychology of the actor, to explicate the real sense of his action.[15]

The demand for critical distance brings us back to the need to have a theory which allows us to understand and evaluate social behaviour without having to rely on subjective understandings. The problem now concerns the justification of those meanings - and norms - which we thus achieve. How can we justifiably invoke meanings which we have received as external observers against the deviating meanings held by the social agents themselves? Creating distance between "real" and "subjective" meaning seems to lead us just in the kind of camouflaged authoritarianism which the Enlightenment project taught us to be wary about. It looks like coercion under the argument that one knows better than people themselves what lies in their interests.

I do not think that there is any magic way to make the problem disappear. People who want to infer norms from behaviour will always have to struggle between simple psychologism and a materialism which says that some acts may be right or wrong regardless of how the acting persons view

15 Though hermeneutics is needed to overcome the limitations of positivism, Critical Theory is needed to avoid the former's intrinsic relativism. See further A. Giddens, General Problems in Social Theory; Action, Structure and Contradiction in Social Analysis (London 1983) pp. 244-5; A. MacIntyre, Against the Self-Images of the Age (London 1983) pp. 213-229 and generally R.J. Bernstein, Beyond Objectivism and Relativism; Science, Hermeneutics and Practice (Oxford 1983) pp. 165-169, 171 et seq.

them. What these people - including international lawyers - can do is to downgrade the expectations regarding the degree of authority their inferences possess and to aim at individualized solutions in particular normative disputes which seem the most just in the particular context. This, I shall argue, is what international lawyers have, even if secret, been doing - despite their theories.

2. INTERNATIONAL CUSTOM IN THE GRIP OF SOCIAL THEORY

The function of a doctrine of customary law is to create space for norms which are neither fully materialistic - that is, assume that the sense of a behaviour can be known without looking at what somebody intends - nor fully psychological - assume that the sense of a behaviour coalesces with its sense to somebody. In other words, custom is needed to have a law between natural law and agreement. This is hoped to achieve by combining materialism and psychologism. Custom is argued in a materialistic way to separate it from agreement (treaty) by stressing the external nature of the acts in which it is expressed. It is argued in a consensual way to distinguish it from natural law:

> "The classic theory of custom depends on a delicate, indeed precarious equilibrium between two opposing concerns: on the one hand, to permit customary rules to change without demanding the inidividual consent of every State; on the other hand, to permit individual States to escape being bound by any rule they do not recognize as such..."[16]

Conventional arguments about custom manifest constantly the tension between these two delimitations. Custom

---

16 P. Weil, "Towards Relative Normativity in International Law", 77 AJIL (1983) pp. 433-4.

cannot be fully materialistic without it needing the backing of a non-consensual theory about the objective justness of certain forms of behaviour. A fully materialistic custom is a form of natural law. But it cannot be fully psychological, either, without the implication that it is no more than a formless consensus - and binding only on States sharing the common view and to the extent that they so do.

In what follows I shall expose the structure of conventional arguments about customary law. I shall proceed by first showing the necessity for a "two-element theory" of custom. I shall then show why this theory is unsatisfactory as neither element can be ascertained in any reliable, non-political way. Finally, I shall show that lawyers secretly rely on unexplicated theories of justice and equity when arguing about the presence or absence of custom in behaviour. My conclusion will consist of an appreciation of the role of justice and equity - that is, politics - in our characterization of habitual forms of State behaviour.

2.1 Conventional Argument about Custom

Conventional theory attempts to construct a theory of custom between natural law and treaty. Therefore, by a near-unanimous orthodoxy, it includes two elements in its definition of custom:

1) a psychological element - the _opinio juris_;
2) a material element - State practice.[17]

---

17 For the acceptance of this "two-element theory" in case-law, see ICJ: Asylum Case, ICJ Reports 1950 pp. 276-7; North Sea Continental Shelf Cases, Reports 1969 p. 44 (§ 76-77); Libya-Malta Continental Shelf Case, ICJ Reports 1985 p. 29 (§ 27); U.S. Military and Parlamilitary Activities Case, ICJ Reports 1986 pp. 97, 108-109, (§ 183, 207). For doctrine, see M. Sørensen, _Les sources de droit international_ (Copenhagen 1946) pp. 84-111; K. Wolfke, _Custom in Present International Law_ (Wroclaw 1964) pp. 20-58; K. Marek, "Le

The function of the psychological element is to account for the law's "internal aspect" which distinguishes it from simple coercion. The material element aims to ensure that law-ascertainment can be understaken without having to rely on what States say they accept at any moment. Neither element can be dismissed or preferred to the other without this engendering immediately the objection that custom is either apologist (because it makes no distinction between might and right) or utopian (because it cannot demonstrate its norms in a tangible fashion).

Because both elements seek to delimit each other's distorting impact, the theory of custom needs to hold them independent from each other. But this it cannot do. Attempting to identify the presence of the psychological element, it draws inferences (presumptions) on the basis of material practice. To ascertain which acts of material practice are relevant for custom-formation, it looks at the psychological element (i.e., "those acts count which express the _opinio juris_"). The psychological element is defined by the material and _vice-versa_.[18] This circularity

---

problème des sources du droit international dans l'arret sur le plateau continental de la Mer du Nord", VI RBDI (1970) pp. 55-6; H.W.A. Thirlway, _International Customary Law and Codification_ (Leiden 1972) p. 46 et seq; E. Suy, _Les actes juridiques unilateraux en droit international public_ (Paris 1962) p. 217 et seq.; A. Vamvoukos, _The Termination of Treaties in International Law: The Doctrines of Rebus Sic Stantibus and Desuetude_ (Oxford 1985) pp. 248-260. See also the very useful P. Haggenmacher, "La doctrine des deux éléments du droit coutumier dans la pratique de la cour internationale", 90 RGDIP (1986) pp. 5-125.

18 Interestingly this is reflected in the often noticed ambiguity in the wording of Article 38(1)b of the ICJ Statute. This speaks of "custom as evidence of general practice, accepted as law". The wording hesitates between associating "custom" with material practice or the acceptance of that practice by States at large. Finally, it ends up in associating it with neither. "Custom" becomes third undefined category which is capable of being "evidence" of the presence or absence of the remaining two. But this seems nonsense: either something is relevant because it encapsulates a practice or an acceptance thereof. A third category (such as natural law) seems excluded. Therefore, modern lawyers read the formulation as simply "unfortunate" rest content with the two-element theory and start going about in a circle by identifying relevant practice through its assumed "acceptance" and

prevents doctrine from developing a determinate method of custom-ascertainment. It is led to determining custom in terms of an equity which it can itself only regard as arbitrary.

2.1.1 The Rejection of Pure Materialism

In order to see why both elements seem necessary, it is useful to consider, as a first move, three deviant theories which, by expressly denying the relevance of the psychological element, manifest an inadmissible materialism.

First, there is the view which holds custom as simply a repetition of similar acts over a period of time. In Kelsen's early work the need for a psychological element was rejected as logically impossible: something could not become a norm for the reason that States already thought it was one. Moreover, it was virtually impossible to prove the psychological element. It was, for Kelsen, simply an offshoot of the autolimitation view which tried to explain custom in terms of consent.[19]

The well-known difficulty with this view is that it includes either too much or too little within custom. If all practice is law-creating, then everything is regulated and no State can act in a manner different from they way in which it has acted. Conversely, if everything States do is law-creative, then no State can act illegally. This view is incapable, not only of making the distinction between legal custom and conventions of courtesy and of explaining discretion in matters of foreign policy, but it also fails to distinguish between custom and behaviour induced by threat

---

inferring that acceptance from material practice. For standard analysis, see, e.g., Wolfke, op.cit., pp. 22-23.

19 H. Kelsen, "Théorie du droit international coutumier", 1 RITD (1939) pp. 263-265.

or use of force. A meaningful custom must be something else than an unexceptionable command for States to behave as they have behaved.[20]

A second strategy of doing away with the psychological element tries to identify as relevant practice such behaviour which corresponds to material criteria of justice. It is suggested, for example, that a practice amounts to custom if it is in "conformity with the social needs of a legal order" or if it corresponds to "reasonableness" or "moral utility".[21] To this view it can be objected that even if it is able to distinguish between binding and non-binding usages, it still cannot distinguish custom from norms of courtesy which correspond to some social needs. Not all sense of moral or social obligation, even if in conformity with behaviour, creates law and not all law need to correspond to such criteria. But the even more important objection concerns the naturalistic - political - chamantsi of this suggestion. Because "justice", "social need", "reasonableness" and "moraly utility" are *subjective* political notions, they cannot be used in order to achieve a determinate delimitation between practice which is and which is not law. Such conceptions can be justifiably opposed to States only if they are linked with what States

---

20 For this standard criticism, see e.g. L. Le Fur, "Règles générales du droit de la paix", 54 (RCADI 1935/4) pp. 198; Sørensen, op.cit., p. 105; J. Kunz, "The Nature of Customary International Law", 47 AJIL (1953) p. 667; G. Fitzmaurice, "The General Principles of International Law; Considered from the Standpoint of the Rule of Law", 92 RCADI (1957/2) pp. 103-104; M. Akehurst, "Custom as a Source of International Law" XLVII BYIL (1974-75) pp. 33. The view was later abandoned by Kelsen. See Kelsen, op.cit., (*supra* n. 4) p. 440. The argument is explicit in: ICJ: North Sea Continental Shelf Cases, ICJ Reports 1969 p. 44.

21 L. Kopelmanas, "Custom as a means of the Creation of International Law", XVIII BYIL (1937) p. 148. See also Scelle (oral argument) in: ICJ: Asylum Case, ICJ Pleadings, vol. I, pp. 119-120; J.P. Müller, *Vertrauensschutz im Völkerrecht* (Köln-Berlin 1971) pp. 88-89; M. McDougal, "The Hydrogen Bomb Tests in Perspective and the International Law of the Sea", 49 AJIL (1955) p. 361; G.C. Venturini, "La portée et les éffets juridiques des attitudes et des actes unilateraux des états", 112 RCADI (1964) t. II, p. 389 et seq.

have thought of as "justice", "social needs" etc. But this will require a study of what States will or believe, in other words, it will have to make reference to the *psychological element* and give up full materialism.[22]

According to a third, and a more apparently plausible strategy, a conduct becomes binding, not because it expresses any *opinion juris* or a principle of material justice but because *other* States have the right to rely on the continuation of the conduct a State has once chosen. In this view, it would be the legitimate expectations of other States - a *Vertrauensprinzip*, or a "principle of fairness" - which combine with material behaviour to make it binding.[23]

This construction does away with general custom altogether. Under it, custom becomes a set of bilateral relations, dependent of cognizance and reliance on one State's behaviour by another. The problem, however, is that this approach must either rely on naturalist theory about the kinds of expectations created by a form of conduct or base itself on the scrutiny of the subjective attitudes of the *other* state (in which case it would combine a psychological element with itself). The former approach is adopted by lawyers arguing that legitimate expectations or good faith sometimes demand that a State not change its conduct. But this seems similar to the view which based custom on justice and engenders the familiar objections against naturalism. How do we know which expectations are "legitimate" or the content of the good faith or the justice principle? Can we impose a conception of legitimacy or good faith on a State which does not accept it? To avoid

---

22 B. Stern, "La coutume au coeur du droit international, quelques réflexions", in *Le Droit international; Unité et Diversité, Mélanges offerts à Paul Reuter* (Paris 1981) pp. 493-494. See also Kelsen, loc.cit., (*supra,* n. 19) pp. 265-266.

23 Müller, op.cit., pp. 7-103; H. Günther, *Zur Entstehung von Völkergewohnheitsrecht* (Berlin 1970) pp. 155-159; P. Reuter, *Droit international public,* 5e éd. (Paris 1976) pp. 94-95.

naturalism, we might focus on actual reliance. But this leads us into a study of the psychology of those States and leaves open the question how it is possible to oppose one State's expectations on another State which perhaps never intended to continue its once-adopted conduct.

Doing away with the psychological element will either result in an inability to distinguish fact and law or pure naturalism. The psychological element is needed in order to avoid these consequences.

2.1.2 The Rejection of Pure Psychologism

A second deviationist strand has taken seriously the criticisms discussed above but has been unable to understand why the material element is needed at all. To explain why a theory of custom cannot rely on the psychological element ("internal aspect") alone is difficult because this element emerges in so many disguises. For a proper understanding of the problems involved, it is necessary to consider the different varieties of the claim according to which custom is essentially a matter of State psychology (even if a full discussion would require going into some deeply philosophical problems). The psychological element is associated variably with:

1) a collective (national, popular) unconscious;
2) tacit agreement;
3) the belief by a State that something is law;
4) the will by a State that something be law.

In addition, there is fifth and a much stronger version of this view which grounds the primacy of psychology on the following claim:

5) "law cannot be dissociated from what States will or believe".

In the following sub-sections I shall argue that these views either betray a hidden materialism, enter into contradiction with themselves or, ultimately, fall into crude apologies for existing power.

2.1.2.1 The Psychological Element as the Material One: collective unconscious

The opinio juris was introduced into the theory of custom by the German historical school of law in the 19th century. Customary law was now portrayed not merely as a repetition, or imitation, of similar acts but as a manifestation of the nation's collective unconscious, emerging from the nation's spirit and history. Similarly, international custom - if distinguished from national customs - was to reflect the spirit and history of the group of nations which it regulated.[24]

From the introduction of such a view it is a short leap into questioning the need for a material element in the first place. If the law is based on a collective, unconscious "spirit", it seems pointless to regard previous behaviour as an additional requirement (that is, to make reference to such behaviour in any other way than as evidence of this spirit). Bluntschli, for example, writing in 1872, refrained from speaking of "custom" at all. His nonwritten international law coalesced with the "Rechtsbewusstsein der Menschheit". Past usages may or may not have significance but only as evidence of the consensus gentium, not because of their independently normative force.[25]

---

24 For reviews, see P. Guggenheim, "Les principes de droit international public", 80 RCADI (1958/1) pp. 36-59; Wolfke, op.cit., p. 52; C. Rousseau, Droit international public, tome I (Paris 1970) pp. 323-324; A. D'Amato, The Concept of Custom in International Law (Cornell, Ithaca 1971) pp. 44-50; Carty, op.cit., pp. 30-35.

25 J.C. Bluntschli, Das moderne Völkerrecht des civilisierten Staaten als Rechtsbuch dargestellt (Nordlingen 1872) pp. 3-7, 63-64; A.W. Heffter, Das Europaische Völkerrecht der Gegenwart, Siebente Ausgabe (Berlin 1882) pp. 5-6, 21-22.

Such an argument, however, is not really a psychological one at all. The argument from a collective unconscious ("spirit", purpose, history, essency, etc.) does not coalesce with an argument about the real - "arbitrary" - psychological will of the nation or its people. The latter are seen as only more or less adequate external manifestations of the normative spirit, residing outside anybody's psychology. Savigny, for example, took pains to demonstrate the internal contradictions of the view which associated the opinio juris with conscious will. Such a view could not explain why this arbitrary will should be binding. Will's binding force could rest only on a non-psychological principle of the national spirit.[26]

Such an argument is based on the naturalistic assumption that a nation has an intelligible essence. And this is the reason why later lawyers have been unable to accept it.[27] For who could tell what the nation's "spirit" or "essence" was? For modernism, national spirit was a mere myth, a fictitious and utopian construction. To achieve concreteness, modern lawyers have been driven to identify the national spirit in a psychological way, by means of conscious will, a vote.

2.1.2.2 Tacit Agreement

Many lawyers have associated the psychological element simply with a general will among States to be bound. This makes custom lose its specificity in respect of agreement, or consensus. The traditional requirements of generality, consistency and duration become superfluous or, at best,

---

26 F.K. von Savigny, System des heutigen Römischen Rechts, Erster Band (Berlin 1840) Buch I, Kap. I pp. 13-16, 34-44.

27 For a criticism, see H. Triepel, Völkerrecht und Landesrecht (Leipzig 1899) pp. 31-32; Kelsen, loc.cit., (supra, n. 19) pp. 360-361.

evidence of any possible consent behind them. If agreement exists, custom exists. The attraction of this view is well put by Chaumont:

> "A notre avis, sauf si l'on considère la coutume comme ayant une mystérieuse autorité venue soit des hauteurs de la métaphysique, soit des profondeurs du subconscient des groupes humains, c'est-à-dire, pour reprendre l'expression du professeur Reuter, comme un 'phénomène irrationnel', on ne peut échapper à la logique de l'accord".[28]

In other words, to associate custom with something beyond what States will is to adopt an indefensibly naturalist position.

But such a view is vulnerable to the objections against any full psychologism: It creates a non-normative law which differs from State to State and changes as the State's opinion does. It fails to explain how custom can bind "generally" or can continue to bind States which have changed their minds.

To become acceptable, doctrines escape into the tacit agreement construction and manipulate the ambiguity inherent in it.[29] For tacit agreement may be explained from two perspectives. To avoid naturalism, lawyers may say that their tacit agreement norm is binding because it reflects what States will.[30] To avoid psychologism, they can now say

---

28 C. Chaumont, "Cours général en droit international public", 129 RCADI (1970-/1) p. 440. The modern "classical" proponents of this view are D. Anzilotti, Cours de droit international, premier volume (Paris 1929) pp. 73-74; K. Strupp, Les règles générales de droit de la paix, 47 RCAD (1934/1) p. 301 et seq. See also G. Tunkin, Theory of International Law (London 1974) p. 124. For the doctrine of instant custom (i.e. purely psychological custom), see also B. Cheng, "United Nations' Resolutions on Outer Space: Instant International Customary Law", 5 IJIL (1965) pp. 23-48. See also B.L. Ferrari-Bravo, "La coutume internationale dans la pratique des Etats", 192 RCADI (1985/3) pp. 314-316.

29 See Koskenniemi, op.cit., pp. 284-291.

30 See e.g. E. Zoller, La bonne foi en droit international public (Paris 1977) pp. 274, 280-1.

that their norm can be ascertained independently of psychological enquires, by merely looking at behaviour.[31] Tacit agreement is a stategy to reconcile materialism and psychologism. But the reconciliation fails. Pressed by argument, tacit agreement theorists are vulnerable to the objections directed at both.

Initially - to avoid naturalism - tacit agreement lawyers argue that their custom is binding because it expresses consent. But this is vulnerable to the objection that real consent cannot be known to an external observer. To assume that it <u>can</u> be known is indistinguishable from full naturalism if thereby is meant that an observer's account of what a State wills can <u>override</u> what the State itself reports it wills or has willed. It is a strategy to introduce authoritarian opinions in a democratic disguise. If it cannot override conflicting State report, then it cannot avoid the problems inherent in full psychologism.

For these reasons, tacit agreement lawyers emphasize, as a second move, that they do not speak of real consent but only consent inferred from the way States have behaved. But what is it that allows such inference?[32] It cannot be "real will" because the argument started from the premise that real will cannot be known by an observer - at least not better than by the State itself. It was such as to create expectations, or reliance, in others.[33] But reliance - actual or possible - cannot be a <u>condition</u> for the emergence of custom. For it fails to explain why somebody should be entitled to rely on the continuation of a conduct <u>before</u> it became normative. To continue, one should have a theory

---

31 See e.g. T. Gihl, "The Legal Character of Sources of Law", 1 <u>Scandinavian Studies in Law</u> (1957) p. 69.

32 M. Virally, "Panorama du droit international contemporain; cours général du droit international public", 183 RCADI (1983/5) p. 179.

33 See e.g. Müller, op. cit., <u>passim</u>.

about when is legitimate to rely and when not. But this would have to be a fully non-psychological theory vulnerable to standard criticisms against full naturalism: it seems incapable of justifying in a credible way its preferred conception of legitimacy.

Thus, tacit agreement lawyers must either fall back on full psychologism or full materialism: they must assume that they can, in some way, know the agent's real will - and know it so as to justifiably override the agent's own report of what it willed. Or they must assume that they know the real, non-psychological essence of a form of behaviour and that such normative essence is capable of overriding justifiably anyone's view of it. Both seem unacceptable as equally totalitarian.

2.1.2.3 The Psychological Element as Will and Belief

A first thing to notice about the orthodox use of the opinio juris is its ambiguous character. Different views on this may be grouped into two. The psychological element might either be:

1) the belief or conviction of the State that something is law;

2) the will of the State that something be law.

The opinio might be understood either as pertaining to what the State knows or believes or it might be thought of as a voluntas, a conscious, law-creating will. These could be called, respectively, the declaratory and the constitutive approaches to the psychological element.[34] They are not merely different but mutually exclusive and defined by this exclusion. The declaratory view holds that custom arises independently of will and that the intervention of the

---

34 Fitzmaurice, loc.cit., (supra, n. 20) p. 102; Stern, loc.cit., pp. 482, 485-488. See also Suy, op.cit., pp. 223-229.

psychological element is necessary only to make the law known, not to create it. The opinio juris is, on this view, an effect and not the cause of obligation. The constitutive view, again, grounds custom on State will and denies it any existence independently of such will. The opinio is the direct reason for custom's binding character.

The declaratory view is merely a restatement of the materialist approach to custom while the constitutive view seems to make custom indistinguishable from agreement. In order to escape the objections considered above, standard doctrinal argument makes use of both senses of the opinio in a happy mixture, resorting to one when argument seems too psychological, the other when too materialistic.

Much judicial practice seems to occupy initially the declaratory position. In the Lotus Case (1927), the PCIJ associated the psychological element with "being conscious of having a duty".[35] In the North Sea Continental Shelf Cases (1969) the ICJ required that material practice be associated with:

> "... a belief that the practice is rendered obligatory by the existence of a rule of law requiring it."

It observed that:

> "... need for such belief, i.e. the existence of a subjective element, is implied in the very notion of the opinio juris sive necessitatis."[36]

---

35 PCIJ: Lotus Case, PCIJ Ser. A 10 p. 28.

36 ICJ: North Sea Continental Shelf Cases, ICJ Reports 1969 p. 44 (§ 77). See also ibid. p. 28, 46 (§ 37, 89). This formulation is sometimes criticized as it seems inapplicable to customary rules creating rights or competences. See generally I.L. MacGibbon "Customary International Law and Acquiescence," XXXIII BYIL (1957) pp. 117, 127-128, 144; Akehurst, loc.cit., (supra, n. 20) pp. 37-38. But see Thirlway, op.cit., p. 49.

In both cases, the Court rejected the claim concerning the existence of binding custom. States were not bound because it was not established that their actions had been motivated by a belief in the existence of custom.

Other formulations have been more equivocal. The Court has sometimes required that the practice be "accepted as law" or that it manifests the "view" of States that it is binding.[37] In the U.S. Military and Paramilitary Activities Case (1986) the Court based the normative status of certain General Assembly resolutions on the "attitude" taken by States in this matter.[38] It is unclear whether such expressions connote something that the States "willed" or that they "believed" was law. In the latter case, however, the Court's discussion of the relevant UN resolutions tends towards a declaratory view. The customary norms (of non-use of force and self-defense) seemed to exist ex ante the resolutions (in particular the 1970 Friendly Relations Declaration) or other documents in which the opinio juris - variably treated as a "recognition" by States that something is law or that they "regard" it to be so - was expressed. Their adoption - and hence the opinio - was treated by the Court as confirmation, not creation of custom.[39]

Under the declatory view, the opinio juris is an opinion, or a conviction, of States that something already is law, not a will that something become law. Haggenmacher summarizes:

> "... tous ces termes ont en commun de relever du domaine de la connaissance; inversement, aucune

---

37 ICJ: Asylum Case, ICJ Reports 1950 p. 277; Nottebohm Case, ICJ Reports 1955 p. 22; Right of Passage Case, ICJ Reports 1960 p. 40. See also ICJ: US Nationals in Morocco Case, ICJ Reports 1952 pp. 199-200.

38 ICJ: US Military and Paramilitary Activities Case, ICJ Reports 1986 pp. 99-100 (§ 188).

39 Ibid. pp. 99-101 (§ 188-189).

> d'entre eux ne se rattache au domaine de la volonté ... l'opinio juris n'est pas une acte de volonté visant à promouvoir une norme autant que lex ferenda; elle apprehende au contraire la norme comme déjà existante et pleinement valable.[40]

Only by thus associating the opinio with knowledge instead of will it seems possible to preserve custom's more normative character vis-à-vis treaty. By implying that custom is valid regardless of State will doctrine seems able to oppose it on States which do not, at the moment of application, accept it.

But a purely declaratory view remains incapable of explaining how a customary rule may arise in the first place. Surely, as Kelsen observed, something cannot become law by the belief that it already is law.[41] This is not merely an academic's pet dilemma. It shows that the declaratory view is premised on the acceptance of pure materialism. It assumes that the emergence of custom is independent from its recognition by States. As such, it will remain vulnerable to criticisms against other materialist theories. It will either fail to make the distinction between binding and non-binding usages or use unverifiable criteria to make it. To escape these objections, "will" must have constitutive role as well.

Some lawyers have attempted a compromise between the constitutive and declaratory views by explaining custom-emergence as a gradual process during which the psychological element undergoes gradual transformation. There is first a politically motivated will - an opinio necessitatis - which gradually strengthens into opinio juris, a belief that the behaviour has become a matter of law. The

---

40 Haggenmacher, loc.cit., p. 11.

41 For discussion, see e.g. Kelsen, op.cit., (supra, n. 4) p. 253 et seq.; Kunz (supra, n. 17) p. 667; Wolfke, op.cit., p. 70; Akehurst, loc.cit., p. 32; Thirlway, op.cit., pp. 47-55; Stern, loc.cit., pp. 482-484, 487.

starting-point is an act of political convenience by a State. It is followed by similar acts by other States - a gradual acceptance of this practice so that it finally "turns into" law.[42] Van Hoof and Meijers believe custom-formation to be a three-stage process during which a practice first delienates the content of the future rule. This is followed by a process whereby State authorities come to regard the practice as binding and, subsequently, the appearence of external manifestations which show that the rule has become generally accepted.[43]

Such explanations may describe better or worse how beliefs about or practices relating to a rule develop. But this brings in nothing to solve the problem. We are still unable to reveal how the transformation from a political opinio necessitatis into a legally motivated opinio juris was possible. Now, we may believe that the former stage only delienates the content of a rule which is, as it were, proposed for acceptance or rejection. But this merely defines the opinio necessitatis as a de lege ferenda view - a belief that something is not law although it should be - and leaves unexplained how it may transform itself into a belief that the proposed rule already is law. Thus, we must assume that the rule is already definitely established at the opinio necessitatis stage, the stage of political will:

> "The opinio necessitatis in the early stages is sufficient to create a rule of law, but its continued existence is dependent on the subsequent practice accompanied by opinio juris."[44]

---

42 Suy, op.cit., pp. 233-235, 238, 260-262.

43 G.J.H. van Hoof, Rethinking the Sources of International Law (Deventer 1983) pp. 93-97; H. Meijers, "How is International Law Made? - The Stages of Growth of International Law and the Use of Its Customary Rules", IX NethYBIL (1978) p. 3 et seq. See also M. Villiger, Customary International Law and Treaties (Dordrecht-Boston-Lancaster 1985) pp. 29-30.

44 Thirlway, op.cit., p. 56.

The only way to solve the dilemmas involved in a declaratory theory about the *opinio juris* is to reject that theory altogether: the *opinio* becomes a matter of will, not of knowledge.

The constitutive view about the *opinio juris* can also be supported by reference to judicial practice affirming the obligation-creative character of consent. The ICJ's refusal to hold the Federal Republic of Germany bound by the equidistance rule as it had not consented to it in the *North Sea Continental Shelf* Case (1969) encapsulates this assumption.[45] It explains better the case of "instant custom". Here the emergence of a will is a necessary and sufficient condition for custom to emerge. The psychological element is one directed to the future, not the past. Stein observes:

> "... *opinio juris* is no longer seen as a consciousness that matures slowly over time ... but instead a conviction that instantaneously attaches to a rule believed to be socially necessary or desirable".[46]

We cannot compromise and hold the psychological element as partly an object of knowledge, partly an object of will. Modernism is premised on a dualistic psychology. The categories of will and knowledge are, in it, fundamentally separate. Their separation reflects opposition of what is subjective and what objective. An object of will exists merely by virtue of having been willed. And, of course, anybody can will anything. An object of knowledge, however, has an existence independent from the process of knowing itself. If we think that rules of law emerge from being

---

45 ICJ: North Sea Continental Shelf Cases, ICJ Reports 1969 pp. 25-27 (§ 27-32).

46 T.L. Stein, "The Approach of the Different Drummer. The Principle of the Persistent Objector in International Law", 26 Harv. ILJ (1985) p. 465.

willed, then any knowledge about some extra-voluntary reality is merely superfluous. If we believe that their existence is grounded in something else than will, then it becomes singularly irrelevant to refer to whatever anyone might will.

At least two objections could be made against the above argument. In the first place, it seems overburdened with antropomorphism. How can we speak of "will" or "belief" or make a meaningful distinction between the two in respect of such corporate entities as States? And secondly, does not the association of the psychological element with "will" rather than "belief" make it impossible to separate between lex lata and lex ferenda?

The argument does rest on an antropomorphism. But if this is objectionable it is resorted to only because this is the manner we discourse about international law. The different forms of consensualism, imputability as well as doctrines about the vitiating effect of duress or error, for example, are premised on assuming the reality of State psychology. The domestic analogy makes it necessary to thinkof custom in terms of mental acts by States.[47]

It may be true that it is difficult - even impossible - to distinguish between what States will and what they believe. But the point is that the very structure of liberal modernism (the common distinctions between legislation/adjudication and law/politics, for example) leads into making the difference between will and belief and holds it as crucial. The assumption that law is different from politics by being more "objective" than this carries with it the distinction between (subjective) will and (objective)

---

47 Thus it is sometimes suggested that what is needed is to identify the pertinent decision-makers to study their psychology. See e.g. Sørensen, op.cit., p. 108-109. But see the critical remarks by Bourquin (oral argument) in ICJ: Right of Passage Case, ICJ Pleadings, vol. IV, p. 507; D'Amato, op.cit., pp. 35-41.

knowledge. If we believe that international law is law, then we must assume that the processes whereby States will something and know something are different. States must be assumed capable of leading a schitzophrenic existence - being legislators in a "private", subjective capacity and judges in a "public" objective one.

The association of the psychological element with "will" does affect the possibility to distinguish between emerging and valid law.[48] If anything can be law by the mere fact that States will it then there is no basis for the distinction. Lex ferenda is merely a description of a State's subjective hope that what it wills (and what thus is law to it) will became generally willed (that is, general law).

2.1.2.4 The Phenomenological Claim and the Consequences of Psychologism

There is a final, strong version of psychologism, expressed in D'Amato's argument according to which international law:

> "... is entirely phenomenological; it does not exist apart from the way representatives of States see it.[49]

It is the apparently unobjectionable character of this claim which leads modern doctrine to privilege the psychological element in its theory of custom. What basis would there be to hold something as law which States would not so

---

48 In particular, it undermines statements such as those by the ICJ in the Fisheries Jurisdiction Cases, ICJ Reports 1974 p. 23 (§ 53) and Tunisia-Libya Continental Shelf Case, ICJ Reports 1982 p. 37 (§ 23) according to which a clear distinction was to be made with what States had willed at the III UNCLOS and what was present law on the matter.

49 D'Amato, op.cit., p. 34.

hold? This is a variant of the "realist" criticisms of an autonomous natural or positive law. Law is what States think is law.[50]

According to this view you may discuss as much as you wish about the duration, generality, consistency or moral appropriateness of a practice but the fact remains that if States recognize something as custom then, for all practical purposes, it is custom. And conversely, however much converging practice you might be able to come up with as evidence for a rule, it still would not amount to custom if States do not accept it as such.

Lawyers have had little difficulty to interpret case-law in this sense. In the Wimbledon Case (1925) the PCIJ seemed to ascribe to a pure psychologism by concluding that the rule according to which artificial waterways connected to open seas and permanently used could be assimilated to natural straits in respect of warship passage was valid as custom because of a "general opinion" among States to that effect.[51] In the Lotus Case (1927) it rejected the French view that the practice of abstaining from the exercise of jurisdiction over foreign vessels in the High Seas had become a customary rule as the abstentions had not been based on States' "being conscious of having a duty to abstain".[52]

The Asylum Case (1950) supports psychologism in two ways. First, the Court refrained from accepting as custom a practice which had not been motivated with a subjective sense of obligation.[53] Second, it held that even if such

---

50 See e.g. J. Brierly, The Law of Nations, 6th ed. (Oxford 1967) p. 61; I. Brownlie, Principles of Public International Law, 3rd ed. (Oxford 1979) p. 2. See also Villiger, op.cit., p. 21.

51 PCIJ: Wimbledon Case, PCIJ Ser. A 1 p. 28.

52 PCIJ: Lotus Case, PCIJ Ser. A 10 p. 28.

53 ICJ: Asylum Case, ICJ Reports 1950 p. 286.

practice had been established it still would not have been applicable to Peru which had not accepted it.[54] In several other cases, too, what has seemed important has not been the presence of a material practice but whether the States have accepted the rule.[55]

If these cases are read together with the Court's view that a practice need not be universal nor followed for a long period - indeed, in the Fisheries Jurisdiction Cases (1974) it was sufficient that a "general consensus" had emerged[56] - then the consequence is clear: custom emerges with the sole emergence of the psychological element. Whatever States agree in regarding binding is binding - and only in respect of the State which so regards. If material criteria of generality, consistency or duration are relevant, they are only so as evidence of the presence or absence of psychological acceptance.

But if the psychological condition (be it "will" or "belief") is necessary and sufficient for something to be custom, then we lose the basis for holding a custom binding on a State which has not accepted it and will not accept it at the moment of application. This is so because under the liberal ideal of the Rule of Law nobody can justifiably claim to know better than the State itself what it is that a State has willed or believed. Were this otherwise, liberal-democratic politics would lack foundation. To base custom on the argument of "knowing better" makes it indistinguishable from naturalism and vulnerable to the objections against it. To base it on what other States have ac-

---

54 Ibid., ICJ Reports 1950 pp. 227-278.

55 See ICJ: Nottebohm Case, ICJ Reports 1955 p. 22; Right of Passage Case, ICJ Reports 1960 p. 40; North Sea Continental Shelf Cases, ICJ Reports 1969 p. 44-45 (§ 78); US Military and Paramilitary Activities Case, ICJ Reports 1986 pp. 97-8 (§ 184, 185).

56 ICJ: Fisheries Jurisdiction Cases, ICJ Reports 1974 p. 24 (§ 53).

cepted violates sovereign equality.[57]

By making custom co-existent with what States will or believe - psychological consensus - the phenomenological claim will destroy its normative character. It engenders the Austinian conclusion that international law is simply an aggregate of State opinions. If these opinions differ, we lack a standpoint from which justifiable preference can be made. It is not only that we are unable to apply a custom against objecting States. Such custom, even if we could identify it, would be completely non-normative as it would change with changing attitudes among States - attitudes, moreover, which we can know only post facto and by asking the States themselves.[58]

To avoid this conclusion, we should leave the phenomenological view and hold that some non-psychological criteria are needed in order for custom to emerge and be identified. We must go back to materialism.

2.1.3 The Re-Emergence of Materialism

Because of the unacceptable conclusions of pure psychologism, doctrine tends towards reconciliation by a tacit consent argument - materializing the psychological element. Intent is inferred from material behaviour. Behaviour is understood to manifest or "articulate" acceptance.[59] Atten-

---

57 Haggenmacher, loc.cit., is, I think, correct in arguing that the "psychological element" works as a strategy to make decisions seem acceptable because consensually based pp. 109-110, 115-116. It cannot be controlling because we have no "privileged access" to others' psychological reality and because we are unable to infer it from a theory of justice. Similarly Stein, loc.cit., holds the subjective element simply a fictional juristic construction, p. 476.

58 "an obligation whose scope is left to the free appreciation of the obliged, so that his will constitutes a legally recognized condition of the existence of the duty, does not constitute a legal bond. H. Lauterpacht, The Function of Law in the International Community (Hamden 1966) p. 189.

59 See generally D'Amato, op.cit., pp. 74-88.

tion is directed away from a search of the "real" <u>opinio juris</u> to the material practice, assumed to be relevant as "proof" thereof. Law is still <u>justified consensually</u> but, it seems, now capable of <u>non-consensual ascertainment</u>.

It is easy to interpret jurisprudence in this way. In the <u>Lotus</u> Case, one would have expected that the Court's rejection of the rule invoked by France due to the assumed lack of the <u>opinio juris</u> would have been accompanied by an examination of what States had willed or believed when refraining from exercizing High Seas jurisdiction. But no such examination was carried out. All that the Court looked at was the material practice of abstention.[60] Likewise, in the <u>Asylum</u> and <u>North Sea Continental Shelf</u> Cases, the Court rejected the existence of custom by merely examining what States had done, not their motivations.[61] Other cases manifest this lack of a specific method for ascertaining the <u>opinio juris</u>, too.

The Court's apparent reliance on the "general consensus" at the 1960 Conference on the Law of the Sea regarding the 12-mile fishery zone in the <u>Fisheries Jurisdiction</u> Cases did not imply an unequivocal view in favour of the custom-forming effect of "pure" consensus. For, as the Court itself noted, this matter was not in dispute. In respect of the coastal State's preferential rights within the 50-miles zone - the real object of the dispute - the Court made a survey of post-1960 practice in the North West and North East Atlantic Fisheries commissions in which all three of the disputants were members. The rule on preferential rights was based on this practice.[62]

---

60 See comments by Günther, op.cit., p. 66; Haggenmacher, loc.cit., pp. 69-71.

61 ICJ: Asylum Case, ICJ Reports 1950 pp. 277, 286. See also Haggenmacher, loc. cit., pp. 50-51 and further pp. 57-61.

62 ICJ: Fisheries Jurisdiction Cases, ICJ Reports 1974 pp. 24-27 (§ 55-60). See also joint sep. op. ibid. pp. 47-52.

111

There exist no means for the ascertainment of the presence of the psychological element which would be independent of an ascertainment of the generality, consistency and duration of practice.[63] In this sense, the material element is primary and the opinio merely a hypothesis based on it. Sørensen summarizes his study of the practice of the PCIJ in following words:

> "... ni la Cour ni les juges dissidents ne se sont jamais interessés à l'élement psychologique pour affirmer l'existence ou non-existence d'une coutume. La pratique générale et constante leur a suffi pour conclure qu'une coutume avait été née ... On a recouru à l'élement psychologique seulement dans le sens négatif que son absence empêche l'affirmation d'une règle coutumière.[64]

But even this seems to exaggerate the role of the psychological element. Also in cases where the Court's finding has been in the negative, there seems to have existed no specific method for ascertaining its absence. Lack of material practice has been sufficient. Virally observes:

> "... the Court, though it pays lip-service to the concept of opinio juris and though it has had occasions to speak of the 'consciousness of a legal duty', is concerned less with analysis of mental sates than with the examination and assessment of the facts proved."[65]

Among students of ICJ jurisprudence this conclusion is near-unanimous.[66] The Court examines material practice and

---

63 Thus, in the US Military and Paramilitary Activities Case, ICJ Reports 1986, the Court concluded that: "... existence in the opinio juris of States of the principle of non-intervention is backed by established and substantial practice", pp. 106-107 § 202).

64 Sørensen, op.cit., pp. 101, 108-111.

65 M. Virally, "The Sources of International Law", in Sørensen, ed., Manual of Public International Law (Glasgow 1968) pp. 134-5.

66 See e.g. Günther, op.cit., p. 70; Wolfke, op.cit., pp. 54, 121-129; M. Bos, "The Identification of Custom in International Law", 25 GYIL (1982) pp. 32-

makes a presumption about State will or belief on the basis of it. In order to avoid the non-democratic implication that States are bound irrespective of consent, the justification for this is received from the assumption that material practice reflects what States will or believe. Even a tacit agreement theorist such as Strupp is forced into this position. Having first declared that the only element in custom is the psychological one, he goes on to argue that the content of the custom-agreement is to be ascertained from material practice. And he proposes no other way to determine it.[67]

But to say that material practice creates a presumption about consent does not, by itself, go far enough to make that practice normative. The point is whether such presumption can be rebutted or not. If it can be rebutted, then we are back in full psychologism.[68] For the only kind of evidence which can rebut a presumption created on perception of material acts is the State's own knowledge about its will or belief. As we cannot claim to "know better" we have nothing to argue against a State which says that a behaviour is not binding on it because it did not manifest its subjective consent.

Therefore, if we wish to achieve the original aim of having a custom which binds non-accepting States, too, we must regard the presumption as non-rebuttable. But this is just another way of taking a fully materialistic position. A practice now binds regardless of whether it manifests real, psychological consent. And this position is vulner-

---

37; K. Skubiszewski, "Elements of Custom and the Hague Court" 31 ZaöRV (1971) pp. 843, 353-854; Meijers, loc.cit., p. 18-20; Akehurst, loc.cit., p. 38; Stein, loc.cit., p. 476.

67 Strupp, loc.cit., pp. 302, 304, 309 et seq.

68 C.H.M. Waldock, "General Course on Public International Law", 106 RCADI (1962/2) p. 51.

able to the now familiar criticism; it will either 1) fail to distinguish between binding and non-binding usages, or 2) assume the existence of a naturalistic criterion for making the distinction. We have seen that the psychological element was included precisely in order to achieve the former distinction without having to rely on naturalism. If the psychological element loses its reality, its independently normative force, then we fall back into pure naturalism and the criticisms directed at it.

2.1.4 The Re-Emergence of Psychologism: the circle closes

To achieve binding force the theory of custom privileged the material element over the psychological one. But this led into the difficulty of distinguishing between custom-forming and other practice. Standard argument makes this distinction by assuming that the criterion is whether or not the practice "reflects" State will or belief to be bound. But this is circular. For it assumes that the "wills and beliefs" can be known <u>independently</u> of the practice whose normativity we study - a position which was excluded by our argument about the need to look at material practice in the first place. Circularity could be avoided if there existed a general rule (whatever its status) as to which practices are custom-forming and which not. But no such rule exists. Indeed, inasmuch as we take seriously the view that law is matter of wills and beliefs, then we must realize that anything can reflect State will or belief about the law - any act may be creative of custom.

Consequently, a flexible concept of custom-forming practice has developed. As it was suggested in 1950 by the ILC, in addition to positive acts by States, at least the following may be cited as "evidence of customary international law": "treaties, decisions of national and international courts, national legislation, diplomatic correspondence, opinions of national legal advisers, practice of international organizations...".[69] The list is not exhaustive. Statements by public officials, a State's representatives at international conferences, municipal laws and acts by national courts, bi- and multilateral treaties, among other "practice" have also been held relevant.[70] Indeed, there is no reason to exclude any category of acts of statements because anything, including silence and abstention, may manifest what a State wills or believes to be customary law. Schwarzenberger observes:

> "For a rule of customary international law to emerge, no particular form is required ... All that matters is that the generality of subjects of international law accept the rule as law."[71]

The matter is put even more clearly by Akehurst:

> "... any act or statement by a State from which views can be inferred from international law...[72]

is custom-formative. The same conclusion is arrived at in the recent studies by Villiger, Ferrari Bravo and others. Anything can count as custom-formative practice provided that it only reflects State views about what is law in the matter.[73]

Lawyers have observed difficulties in such abundance of evidentiary materials.[74] If the sole criterion for some-

---

69 Report of the ILC to the General Assembly, YILC (1950), vol. II, pp. 368-372.

70 See Koskenniemi, op.cit., pp. 382-384 for references.

71 G. Schwarzenberger, The Dynamics of International Law (Milton 1976) p. 6.

72 Akehurst, loc.cit., pp. 43-44.

73 Villiger, op.cit., p. 7; Ferrari Bravo, loc.cit., p. 261. Similarly Bos, loc.cit., pp. 22-23; I. Detter-Delupis, The Concept of International Law (Uppsala 1987) p. 112.

74 R. Jennings, "What is International Law and How Do We Tell it When We See it?" XXXVII Schw. JB (1981) p. 69.

thing to count as custom-forming practice is whether it "reflects" the *opinio juris*, then we in fact lack the criterion altogether. For in order to be able to make use of such criterion, we should already know the *opinio juris*. In such case, however, the reference to any material practice would be superfluous - for it was relevant only as a "presumption" about the *opinio* which, it was assumed, can be really known only to the State itself. The construction is hopelessly circular.

It might be objected that all this is simply theoretical *finesse*. In practice it is usually evident from the act itself whether it manifests the *opinio* or not. To say that we should know the State's view in order to appreciate the relevance of such action would, in this view, be - although correct in principle - inapplicable in practice.

But State actions do not immediately reveal the meaning which they carry to the acting State. They need to be interpreted. Take, for example, the view which holds UN General Assembly resolutions as custom-forming "practice". Do we have the right to assume that a positive vote reflects the State's views about the law? This is quite uncertain. The vote may have been given as a political gesture, a confirmation of an alliance, for example, and be wholly unrelated to what the State regards as law. It may also have been given due to pressure exerted by a powerful State or in order to embarrass one's adversary. In neither case does it "reflect" any *opinio juris* in the State concerned. Moreover, it is possible to interpret the constant voting at the UN in the light of a widespread conviction within States that the resolutions will only exceptionally survive in the minds of other States. States vote freely because they have virtual certainty that no-one will cite the resolutions against them as binding law. In other words, it is possible (and frequent) to interpret UN decision-making in the light of the assumption - evidenced by the lack of full powers of State representatives - that it is non-binding. If this is so, then we cannot infer anything "automatically" from their voting-practice. On the contrary, we can interpret or evaluate the significance of a resolution only _after_ we know what the States in fact willed or believed when voting.

Take another example. State A lets State B's warships enter its ports without permit or notification. Is this relevant evidence of a customary rule allowing such entry? State A's motives may be interpreted at least in the following three ways: 1) it wishes to allow _all_ military ships into its ports without permit or notification but holds this merely a matter of political convenience, not one of duty; 2) it allows only B's ships to do this because of a special relationship between them; 3) it does not think that any warships should enter any State's ports without previous notification or permit but lets B's ships to do this because of fear or pressure by it. We do not know whether A's action can be interpreted as custom-forming practice nor, if it can, which rule it supports.

The problem of intepreting State action in respect of treaties is well-known. Is the fact that States conclude bilateral investment treaties evidence of custom which is in conformity or in conflict with the effective compensation clauses in such treaties? What about the evidentiary value of lump sum agreements whereby less than full compensation has been awarded? How should one interpret delimitation agreements which use the equidistance principle? Do these support the customary nature of the equidistance rule or have such treaties been concluded precisely because custom has not seemed to include an unequivocal rule in favor of equidistance? All such agreements may be understood both ways:[75] as confirmations of a pre-existing custom (in which

---

75 In the Dispute between Libyan American Oil Co. (LIAMCO) and the Government of the Libyan Arab Republic XX ILM (1981), the Arbitrator regarded lump sum agreements as evidence of a custom which did not provide for full compen-

case we remain puzzled about the point in concluding them) or as conscious departures from custom (in which case custom's generally binding nature is lost). Neither interpretation is automatic or natural. It would be tempting to say that their value is what the States intended their customary value to be. But this is petitio principii: we have referred to treaties as evidence of custom in order to escape making assumptions about the actual, subjective views of States. As a result, we are left with nothing apart from a general reference to contextual evaluation. Or as De Visscher points out, the matter cannot be decided by any rule at all. It must be left:

> "... à la discrétion du juge qui se décide en fonction des particularités d'espèce.[76]

Just as friendship and hostility may be expressed in the same acts (e.g. intervention), so too any act may be cited to express the most varied kinds of wills or beliefs. A State may pay damages caused by its industrial or military activities but not because it would accept a rule of law conferring liability on it but in order to remove the political tension between it and the injured State. A State may extend its fishery jurisdiction zone hoping or believing that this will not trigger off similar claims by other States and thinking its claim justified only by virtue of

---

sation, pp. 72-73. However, lump sum agreements were regarded as deviations from customary standard by the Iran-US Claims Tribunal: Sedco Inc. v. National Iranian Oil Company and Iran XXV ILM (1986) p. 633. On the relevance of equidistance agreements, see the conflicting positions by Libya and Malta in ICJ: Libya-Malta Continental Shelf Case, ICJ Reports 1985 p. 38 (§ 44). See also the Equalization of Burdens Taxation Case (Federal Constitutional Court, FRG, 4 May 1968) 61 ILR (1981) (the question of the custom-creative character of bilateral tax exemption agreement: such character was recognized in the Report by M. Seidl-Hohenveldern but rejected by the Court which treated them as exceptions) pp. 173-178.

76 C. De Visscher, Problèmes d'intérprétation judicaire en droit international public (Paris 1963) p. 233.

its special circumstance. A State may resort to violence for peaceful motives and refrain from war only because it has not yet developed the capacity for victory. Even open statements frequently rather hide than express State wills and beliefs. And so on.

The absurdity of believing that State practice would somehow be capable of an automatic interpretation is well-reflected in doctrines about the custom-forming significance of abstention from positive acts.[77] Consider, for example, absence of positive acts in the fields of disarmament, commercial space travel or deep seabed mining. Surely it cannot plausibly be held that because States have not engaged in such activities, a customary rule now prohibits them from so doing. Besides consent in a binding rule, silence or non-action may denote indifference, conscious non-participation in something considered illegal, lack of technical capacity, political maneuvre or whatever. It is impossible to make any presumptions about the opinio juris on the basis of such silence as a matter of general rule. It may be seen as relevant or irrelevant only after we know the will or belief which prompted the silence in the first place.

The same applies more generally: we cannot automatically infer anything about State wills or beliefs - the presence or absence of custom - by looking at the State's external behaviour. The normative sense of behaviour can be determined only once we first know the "internal aspect" - that is, how the State itself understands its conduct. But if, to know custom, we have to know first the internal aspect, then we face the problem of how we can "know" a State's opinions in any reliable way and, in case the State

---

77 It is commonly assumed that abstention may be just as custom-formative as positive acts. See e.g. Sørensen, op.cit., pp. 98-101; MacGibbon, loc.cit., p. 120-123; Akehurst, loc.cit., pp. 8-10; Rousseau (supra, n. 24) p. 317. See also Y. Blum, Historic Titles in International Law (The Hague 1965) pp. 44-46.

puts torward a different view about its opinion, claim that "we know better".

To sum up: doctrine about customary law is indeterminate because circular. It assumes behaviour to be evidence of the opinio juris and the latter to be evidence of which behaviour is relevant as custom. To achieve binding force, doctrine looks at the psychological element from the perspective of the material; to avoid naturalism, it looks at the material element from the perspective of the psychological. But it can permanently occupy neither perspective without becoming vulnerable to criticisms from the other. The movement between perspectives continues interminably.

This proves fatal to the practice of problem-solution. Any proposed solution - that is, any attempt to cease the shifting of perspectives at some point - will have to appear as either non-normative (because it prefers psychology to behaviour) or naturalist (as it privileges behaviour over psychology). Though we can justify anything that States will or believe as custom we must also constantly remain vulnerable to the objection that our justification is inadmissible as a legal solution.

2.2 Resulting Dilemmas: general/particular, stability/change

To illustrate how the doctrine of custom fails to provide material resolution to normative problems, I shall take a look at how it lends equal support to contradicting arguments about the generality and particularity of custom and about the significance of its early and late origin. Being unable to establish priority between such arguments, doctrine defers substantive resolution into contextual evaluation under a principle of equitableness - evaluation which is, by the doctrine's own assumptions, undetermined by law.

2.2.1 General vs. Particular

Alongside the idea of custom as general law there exists an interpretation of custom as an aggregate of reciprocal inter-State relationships.[78] The former view stresses custom's normativity, its capacity to override individual State will, the latter emphasizes custom's consensual character, its dependence on State will. Both are illustrated in standard arguments about the generality of custom vs. the principle of persistent objector, general vs. particular custom and the relations between custom and treaty. The problems encountered result from doctrine's inability to prefer either of its two interpretations.

Initially, it may be noted that in cases where it has found no written law, the ICJ has consistently looked at both "general law" and whatever obligations the States involved in a dispute before it may have accepted inter se - by means of estoppel, acquiescence or recognition, for example ("special law"). In such cases, the Court has assumed neither of these approaches as superior to the other. Sometimes it has first looked at the Parties' consent and behaviour, sometimes at general custom. It has turned to the one only once it has found the other inconclusive. Never has it found incompatibility between the two nor discussed possible priority in case of conflict.[79] It has avoided establishing a normative hierarchy between general

---

78 See, e.g. McDougal, loc.cit., pp. 356-8; K. Venkata Raman "Toward A General Theory of International Customary Law", in Reisman-Weston, eds. Toward World Order and Human Dignity. Essays in Honor of Myres S. McDougal (New York-London 1976) p. 368 et seq.

79 Instructive in this respect is the way in which the Court argued about customary obligations relating to the continental shelf in the North Sea Continental Shelf (1969), Tunisia-Libya (1982) and Gulf of Maine (1984) cases. In each, the Court looked - in varying order - to general as well as special law and in each found that they did not contradict each other. See further Koskenniemi, op.cit., pp. 389-392.

law (the will and behaviour of the community) and special law (the will and behaviour of the individual State) - thus avoiding violating sovereign equality.

This lack of hierarchy renders discourse indeterminate. The special and general law cannot be equally valid as they are based on conflicting premises. The sense of the former is that State assent as expressed in its behaviour is creative of obligations. To be effective, such assent must be capable of overriding any general law. The argument about the binding nature of general custom is premised on the materialistic assumption that such custom binds even against conflicting will and conduct. The indeterminacy of the Court's approach is hidden by its conclusion that both point in the same direction. General practice is in harmony with special will and behaviour. This allows it to by-pass the question of hierarchy. But it is quite uncertain whether such an assumption of harmony between consent and general law can be consistently maintained. This is easiest to see by a discussion of the hidden materialism in discourse about the "requirement of generality" and how this is betrayed by an unleashed psychologism behind the persistent objector doctrine.

The ambiguous relationship between the two approaches is manifested in the curiously inconclusive discussion about the generality of a practice to have eligibility for custom. The question "how many States are needed" cannot even be meaningfully discussed unless we have first decided to prefer either psychologism or materialism.

For a purely psychological theory of custom, a "requirement of generality" has no normative status at all. Custom binds only States which have consented to it. "Generality" becomes a description of the custom's scope of application, not a condition for its validity.[80] Even as a

---

80 This is admitted by such tacit agreement lawyers as van Hoof, op.cit., pp. 111-112; Skubiszewski, loc.cit., p. 830; Suy, op.cit., pp. 220-221.

presumption of consent, "generality" cannot have normative force. For if the presumption is rebuttable (as it must be, under the psychological theory), the only way to rebut it is that the State denies its consent. In which case it is that consent (or lack of it) which settles the question of normativity and no need for a presumption arises.

A normative requirement of generality can exist only in a materialistic theory of custom which assumes that a practice may be binding even on non-consenting States. For clearly, to argue that the requirement of generality means that all States must have participated in it is merely a restatement of the psychological position. But as the ICJ noted in the North Sea cases, equidistance could be binding on the Federal Republic without its assent if other States had accepted it in a manner "both extensive and virtually uniform".[81] The whole discussion about how extensive must a practice be to be valid as custom is meaningful only on the assumption that once that degree has been attained, the rule binds all States. But this conclusion can be objected with the standard argument against majority legislation. The persistent objector doctrine is needed to safeguard non-consenting States' sovereign equality.

Although case-law on the persistent objector is thin, doctrine has overwhelmingly assumed it.[82] This is understandable. It is not merely an annex in the general theory of custom. It makes the views of other States something

---

81 ICJ: North Sea Continental Shelf Cases, ICJ Reports 1969 p. 43 (§ 74); Asylum Case, ICJ Reports 1950 ("constant and uniform usage") p. 276. Similarly, US Military and Paramilitary Activities Case, ICJ Reports 1986 p. 98 (§ 186). For the view that full uniformity is not needed, see further Claim against the Empire of Iran Case (Supreme Federal Court, FRG, 30 April 1963) 45 ILR (1972) pp. 61-62; National Iranian Oil Co. Pipeline Contracts Case (Oberlandsgericht, 4 May 1982) 65 ILR (1984) p. 214.

82 For standard cases, see ICJ: Asylum Case, ICJ Reports 1950 pp. 277-278; Anglo-Norwegian Fisheries Case, ICJ Reports 1951 p. 131. For doctrine, see e.g. Brownlie, op.cit., supra, n. 50, pp. 10-11; Akehurst loc.cit., p. 24-25; J. Charney, "The Persistent Objection Rule and the Development of Customary International Law", LVI BYIL (1985) pp. 1-24; Stein, loc.cit., pp. 457-482.

less than jus cogens vis-à-vis the non-consenting State. Sovereign equality requires a State to have the right to protest against a norm or refrain from recognizing a situation which it finds non-acceptable.[83]

But this doctrine has an uneasy relationship with the requirement of generality. If all States which have not accepted a custom may classify themselves as persistent objectors, then the normativity of general custom is lost. Can we establish the category of persistent objectors in a way which is opposable to non-accepting States and allows regarding at least some of them bound?

The persistent objector doctrine has not been regarded as a threat to custom's normativity because it is assumed that the objector cannot prevent the emergence of a customary norm but only its application to itself.[84] But in many cases this does not correspond to what is objected against. The objection may concern the norm's erga omnes validity, not merely its application. Arguably, this is the case with United States opposition to the customary nature of prohibition of unilateral seabed mining and Soviet Union's opposition towards the rule of restricted immunity. These States deny that any such custom has emerged.[85] It is because the objection can always be formulated in such a manner that we remain incapable of delimiting the category of persistent objectors.

In principle, as persistent objectors qualify only States which have voiced their objection before the rule's emergence. If this temporal criterion were absent, then no rules would be applicable to non-accepting States. But it may be circumvented by directing objection to the rule's emergence instead of its application. Let us take a hypo-

83 See e.g. Suy, loc.cit., pp. 47-80.

84 Akehurst, loc.cit., p. 24; Charney, loc.cit., pp. 2-3.

85 Stein, loc.cit., pp. 460-463.

thetical argument. State A objects to the application of rule X against it. It argues that X is not valid as custom. To this, B might answer that in order to invoke the persistent objector rule A should have protested already when X emerged. But this is not at all what A is disputing. It accepts the orthodox interpretation of the persistent objector doctrine but points out that "how could I have protested before because I never realized that there was a rule-creation process going on?". This is crucial. If B wishes to remain consistent with the assumption about sovereign equality behind the persistent objector doctrine, then it is not open for it to say "but you should have known" and press upon that point. To insist that A "should have known" by reference to what other States know, for example, or some standard of reasonableness, is to imply that A might be bound even if *it really* did not know - and thus impose other States' will and knowledge or a naturalistic standard on A. Both implications seem unacceptable.

By first challenging the very existence of a custom or at least one's knowledge thereof it remains possible for a State to oppose the application of the custom in respect of it. Even if the State is hard pressed so as not to be able to deny the *inter alios* existence of the norm, it will still have the possibility of qualifying itself as a persistent objector as it may argue that it learned about the norm (or that the norm was intended to apply in respect of it, too) only now and thus voice its "objection" at the moment of application.

Similar considerations apply to the question whether treaties prevail over custom or *vice-versa*. Though some lawyers have suggested a general priority of the treaty, most writers recognize that no *prima facie* hierarchy exists.[86] This is a natural consequence of the view which

---

86 See, e.g., G. Schwarzenberger, *International Law*, vol. I (London 1949) p. 16; H. Lauterpacht, *International Law*, vol. I (Cambridge 1970) pp. 86-89;

sees custom only as a kind of unwritten treaty. But it follows also from the inability to consistently prefer jus cogens over consent. Accent is put on eliminating conflicts by interpretation, i.e., by manipulating the sense of the treaty process or the custom so as to make prima facie conflicts disappear.[87]

In the North Sea Continental Shelf Cases (1969), the Court seemed to adhere to a lex specialis rule in its consideration of the relations between the 1958 Convention and custom. It observed.

> "... the provisions of the Convention will prevail in the relations between the parties, and would take precedence of any rule having a more general character, or deriving from another source."[88]

But this is contradicted by the Court's distinction, considered above, concerning the consensual character of treaty and the non-consensually binding nature of general custom. Clearly, if this distinction was correct, or if at least some customs have jus cogens character - as commonly assumed - then such generalized preference is simply illegitimate. Moreover, it is generally accepted that subsequent custom may abrogate earlier treaties by desuetude or modify them.[89] This is obviously true also vice-versa - indeed the point of many treaties has been to avoid applying an earlier custom inter partes, that is, to create an

---

Kelsen supra, n. 4 p. 438; Virally, op.cit., pp. 170-171; Akehurst, loc. cit., pp. 275-278; Sørensen, op.cit., supra, no. 17, p. 237-251; Sur, op. cit., p. 163-166.

87 Common methods being either reading the treaty "against the background" of custom or, in a reverse way, holding treaty as "evidence" of custom. For the former, see e.g. ICJ: Gulf of Maine Case, ICJ Reports 1984 p. 291 (§ 83). For the latter, see ICJ: North Sea Continental Shelf Cases, ICJ Report 1965 p. 41 (§ 71).

88 ICJ: North Sea Continental Shelf Cases, ICJ Reports 1969 p. 24 (§ 25).

89 Obviously, this may be explained either subjectively, as a result of further agreement, or objectively, as a result of change of circumstances, see,

exception to old custom while some multilateral treaties have intended to replace old custom altogether.

Whatever character a treaty or a custom might have seems determinable only through a contextual evaluation, not by any general rule.[90] The same conclusion can be reached also by considering the equally problematic matter of priority between general and particular customs.[91] The problems inherent in each of the standard suggestions (lex specialis, lex posteriori) are well-known and thoughtful discussion of the tension between the two regularly points to an ad hoc evaluation of the circumstances and the normative significance of the conflicting norms. The problem is, how can such evaluation be imposed on a state which fails to share the evaluer's view of contextual significance? If it can be imposed nevertheless, then we seem to be arguing on the basis of the assumption that matters of political value - different conceptions of contextual equity - are capable of legal (objective decision). If it cannot, then we have nothing to legal solve the conflict with.

2.2.2 Time and Customary Law: The antinomy of stability and change

The problem of time in relation to customary law has two aspects. First, the duration of a practice for a determined period may be suggested as a criterion for dis-

---

e.g., Air Services Agreement Arbitration, 69 RGDIP (1965) pp. 249-255; Vamvoukos, op.cit., pp. 220, 225-227, 266-303. See also Thirlway, op.cit., pp. 130-132; Villiger, op.cit., p. 215 et seq.

90 Relevant factors being then, for example, the possible jus cogens character of the custom or the treaty, the treaty's character as "codifying" or its purpose of creating a special regime among the parties, the objective of the treaty and the social importance of the custom and so on. It is in fact difficult to think of any principled limits to the criteria involved in such assesment. On treaties creating "special regimes" or "special law", see e.g. ICJ: US Nationals in Morocco Case, ICJ Reports 1952 p. 199-201; Gulf of Maine case, Reports ICJ 1984 p. 300 (§ 114).

91 See Koskenniemi, op.cit., pp. 395-398.

tinguishing custom-formative practice from mere usage. Second, the duration of practice may also be a criterion for distinguishing conduct which is in conformity with the law from behaviour which is not. Although these are aspects of the same concern, namely the concern to relate law closely to how States behave while still maintaining critical distance towards how they have behaved, they are here discussed separately in order to show the doubly unsuccesful result of doctrine's attempt to achieve a reconciliation. Once more, doctrine is led from general statements about the need to "balance" stability and change into contextual studies about the equitableness of alternative solutions.

The requirement of repetition of a behaviour, including both the duration of a practice and its consistency,[92] seems an intuitively natural element in custom. But it is unclear whether that requirement has any real normative force. To uphold it against conflicting State consent seems difficult. If States agree in holding something as "custom", what basis is there to deny it as such, even if it were not accompanied by long-standing and consistent practice?

Lately, the discussion about required duration has been devoured by the doctrine of instant custom. If one act may create custom, then to speak of any requirement of duration is superfluous. The element of time - like that of generality - loses its normative nature and becomes a description of one class of customary norms.[93] It is true, of

---

92 ICJ: Asylum Case, ICJ Reports 1950 p. 276; US Nationals in Morocco Case, ICJ Reports 1952 p. 200; Right of Passage Case, ICJ Reports 1960 p. 40; North Sea Continental Shelf Cases, ICJ Reports 1969 ("virtual uniformity") p. 43 (§ 74). See also Interpretation of the Treaty between USA and Italy Arbitration, 72 RGDIP 1968 p. 484. Common to these cases, however, is that the requirement of time rather more acted as evidence of one State's tacit consent or acquiescence in a bilateral context than any independently normative requirement. See also Mac Gibbon, op. cit., XXXIII BYIL (1957) pp. 119-121.

93 Hence, many argue that duration is not at all a necessary ingredient in custom. See, e.g. Wolfke, op.cit., pp. 67-68; Blum, op.cit., pp. 52-

course, that the doctrine of instant custom has not secured full acceptance. But the objections relate more to its classification as "custom" than to its character as law. It seems difficult to deny the status of law from a consensus, even if not accompanied by positive acts, which States agree to hold binding.

Time as a criterion distinguishing between custom and usage has direct connexion with the materialistic and psychological arguments about custom. The former perspective emphasizes law's autonomy and normative character. It may be associated with a claim for stability. Law cannot be infinitely flexible and custom's social role is precisely to resist unwarranted, hasty change. Under this view, the requirement of duration possesses independent normative value as against (arbitrary) will. The more ancient the custom, the more normative it is. The psychological perspective emphasizes law's concreteness, its role as an instrument of politics, of will. In order to fulfil its social function, custom must be responsive to social change. But it cannot only accomodate change, it must speed it up, help in the creation of a better society. From this perspective, custom's point is precisely in its flexibility, its non-formal nature and its capacity to create law through instant consensus. The more ancient the custom, the more obsolete it is.

Both approaches alone lead into absurd results. A purely materialistic position freezes custom into a general command for States to do what they have always done. A purely psychological position cannot provide the security and stability for which law is enacted in the first place. It accepts any new will or act as a potential change in

---

53; G. Fitzmaurice, "The Law and Procedure of the International Court of Justice 1951-1954: General Principles and Sources of Law", XXX BYIL (1953) pp. 31; 15-16; Ferrari Bravo, loc.cit., pp. 247-250.

law. Neither position can be preferred as a matter of general rule. Somehow, the demands of stability and change need to be "balanced".[94] To do this, we should argue from an external criterion of justice which can be used to delimit these *prima facie* plausible arguments *vis-à-vis* each other.

One consequence of this dilemma is doctrine's inability to explain change in customary law while preserving its normative force. From a purely psychological perspective, explaining change in custom is no problem. Some States have merely started behaving in another manner and that, for them, settles all there is to settle. But this is simple apologism. To preserve (old) custom's normative character, we must assume that the only manner in which customary rules can change is by States first breaking the law until this law-breaking becomes so general that it becomes the rule. But this runs counter to the *ex injuria non jus oritur* and the *pacta sunt servanda* principles as well as assumes the non-existence of *jus cogens*. Efforts to deal with this problem counter similar dilemmas as effort to explain custom-formation in terms of different stages. At some point, they must accept the psychological assumption that (old) law becomes obsolete because States no longer will it.

The only way to avoid denying the normative character of "old" custom and the *ex injuria* or *pacta sunt sevanda* principles - without taking a fully psychological view - is to assume that a fundamental change of circumstances has taken place outside the law which has made old custom obsolete and justified the new one. This resembles the *rebus sic stantibus* doctrine, held generally valid in respect of treaties. If we think of custom as tacit agreement, then there exists no difficulty to apply the *rebus* doctrine in respect of custom, too. However, care should be taken not

94 Lauterpacht, op.cit., pp. 248-250; van Hoof, op.cit., pp. 103-104.

to include into "fundamental change" a change in State practice or the opinio juris. This is, of course, a change in customary law, pure and simple. If the "fundamental change" doctrine is to have meaning in respect of custom, it must denote a change, not in the law but in the conditions, for a particular State, of its carrying out its customary duties.

Stated in such manner, the rebus doctrine becomes indistinguishable from aplying equity in order to release a State from obligations which have become too burdensome. This brings out the fact that at issue in the "balancing" of stability and change are not so much views about the significance of time as different conceptions of what is equitable in certain circumstances and what is not.[95] We cannot reach "justice" through the use of some legally formulated temporal metaphor. We must know justice before we can give conflicting formal-temporal criteria definite priority.

Let me illustrate these difficulties by reference to the intertemporal law doctrine. The question is whether the legal effects of a fact or a situation in the past should be evaluated on the basis of the law contemporary with it or on the basis of law valid at the time of application. The classical formulation of the doctrine by Max Huber contains two elements. First:

---

95 See also E. MCWhinney, UN Lawmaking: Cultural and Ideological Relativism and International Lawmaking in an Era of Transition (Paris-New York 1984) pp. 2937; P. Tavernier, Recherches sur l'application dans le temps des actes et des règles en droit international public (Paris 1970) pp. 43-44. It is precisely this "political" aspect of the rebus doctrine which has been focus of criticism. See, e.g., Lauterpacht, op.cit., (supra n. 58) pp. 270-272; Carty, op.cit., pp. 65-66. In the Fisheries Jurisdiction Cases, ICJ Reports 1973, Iceland disputed the validity of the compromissory clause in a 1961 Exchange of Notes between it and, respectively, the United Kingdom and the Federal Republic of Germany, as well as the applicability of the customary 12-mile fishing zone on the basis of changed circumstances, p. 18 (§ 35). That the Court held that argument as relevant - though not decisive - and saw the matter as one of "balancing" is manifested in the way it constructed the applicable law on the basis of an equitable appraisal of the applicants' historic and Iceland's preferential interests, ibid., ICJ Reports 1974 pp. 30, 33 (§ 69, 78).

> "... a juridical fact must be appreciated in the light of the law contemporary with it, and not the law in force at the time when a dispute in regard to it arises."[96]

But there is more:

> "The same principle which subjects the act creative of a right to the law in force at the time the right arises, demands that the existence of the right, in other words its continued manifestations, shall follow the conditions required by the evolution of law".[97]

The first statement expresses the principle of the law's non-retroactivity. Support for it may be sought from two directions. It can be argued psychologically by reference to the need to honour original State will and in a non-psychological fashion, referring to the need for legal security. But the second statement points in the opposite direction. It provides that the validity of a right at each period of time should be evaluated by reference to the law in force at that time. It may also be argued from two perspectives, by reference to present State will and the need to make law responsive to social change.

Both legs of the intertemporal law doctrine have been criticized in a predictable fashion. The principle of non-retroactivity has seemed excessively conservative and non-responsive to changing conceptions of justice.[98] The principle of retroactivity has seemed to create insecurity and destability and violate original intent.[99] Neither position can fully overrule the other. Making a hierarchy between

---

96 Island of Palmas Case, II UNRIAA p. 845.

97 Ibid. p. 839.

98 E. McWhinney, "Time Dimension in International Law", in Makarczyk, ed., Essays in international law in honour of Judge Manfred Lachs (The Hague 1984) pp. 180-181.

99 P.C. Jessup. "The Palmas Island Arbitration", 22 AJIL (1928) pp. 739-740; Tavernier, op.cit., pp. 271-276.

them is possible only through an anterior view about the justice of such hierarchy in a particular case.

This problem may be illustrated by reference to the South West Africa (1966) and Namibia (1971) cases. Though the cases concern treaty interpretation, they provide a good illustration of how the law can be used so as to generate opposite but equally valid outcomes in the stability/change conflict.

In the former case, the Court asked itself whether the claimants had a legal interest in the subject-matter of their claim and answered this in the negative after an extensive analysis of the mandates system as it existed under the League of Nations' period.[100] To determine the claimants' rights:

> "... the Court must place itself at the point in time when the mandate system was being instituted ... the Court must have regard to the situation as it was that time ...".[101]

In other words, the Court held that rights flowing from an international convention had to be interpreted by reference to the law in force at the time of its conclusion. By contrast, in the Namibia opinion it construed the South African mandate in view of ideas which had gained international acceptance only after the League's dismissal. The Court observed that the relevant parts of the Covenant were "evolutionary". Therefore:

> "The Court must take into consideration the changes which have occurred in the supervening half-century, and its interpretation cannot remain unaffected by the subsequent development of law."[102]

---

100 ICJ: South West Africa Case, ICJ Reports 1966 p. 18 (§ 6) et seq.

101 Ibid. p. 23 (§ 16). This is, of course, simply a restatement of the non-retroactivity principle.

102 ICJ: Namibia Case, ICJ Reports 1971 p. 31 (§ 53). This principle is particularly often applied in respect of human rights instruments. See, e.g.,

The Court now held that the mandate was to be interpreted in light of present law.

This contrast is further highlighted by the manner in which the Court dealt with the "sacred trust of civilization" concept. In the South West Africa case this was considered a "moral ideal" which was, divested of such "specifically legal character" that it could have been creative of rights and obligations in the League.[103] In the Namibia opinion, the sacred trust was used as an "evolutionary" concept which was associated with the present law's objectives of "self-determination and independence".[104]

These conflicting outcomes are usually understood so that in the former case the Court preferred stability (that is, past over present) in the latter, change (that is, present over past). Depending on the critic's perspective, the Namibia Case is either seen as a healthy move away from a mistaken precedent or a political decision ignoring established law. Either one or the other contains an incorrect application of law. But these interpretations fail to understand that it is possible to argue both cases on the basis of established law because it is that law itself which is contradictory; neither outcome can be challenged within the system.

Many have argued that while the South West Africa case was decided on the basis of original intent (of the drafters of the Covenant) the Namibia opinion used teleo-

---

ECHR: Tyrer Case, Ser A 26 pp. 15-16 (§ 31); Marckx Case, Ser A 31 p. 19 (§ 41). See also joint diss. op. ECHR: Deumeland Case, Ser A 100 (arguing that the principle is enshrined in the Vienna Convention of the Law of Treaties) p. 35-36 (§ 12).

103 ICJ: South West Africa Case, ICJ Reports 1966 pp. 34-35 (§ 49-59).

104 ICJ: Namibia Case, ICJ Reports 1971 p. 31 (§ 52-53).

logical and equitable considerations.[105] In other words, the contrast is explained by the former case manifesting a psychological, the latter a justice-based approach. The question of the possible non-conformity of the cases with the law would then seem to depend on whether the law in fact prefers consent or justice.

But if the law really preferred consent or justice, it would seem vulnerable to the objections of being too dependent on or too independent from what States actually will. The same applies to the two cases. To be acceptable, neither can make such preference. And in fact, both avoid making it. It is thus possible to produce a contrary explanation of the contrast between them. For while the South West Africa case did make express reference to original intent, such intent was construed by reference to the text of Article 22 of the Covenant. There is no study whatsoever of State intentions which would have been independent of a study of this text. Quite the contrary, the Mandates system was interpreted "having regard to the structure of the League" in what seemed like a thoroughly systematic - materialistic - and not a will-based argument at all.[106]

On the other hand, the Namibia opinion may be understood in thoroughly consensual light. First, the Court was careful to read its "teleological" interpretations in light of the intent of League members. The parties to the Convenant "must... be deemed to have accepted" the "evolutionary" character of the "sacred trust" concept.[107] Second,

---

105 G. Schwarzenberger, International Law, vol. III (London 1976) p. 149 et seq; B. Bollecker-Stern, "L'avis consultatif du 21 juin 1971 dans l'affaire de la Namibie (Sud-Ouest Africian)", XVII AFDI (1971) pp. 287-298.

106 ICJ: South West Africa Case, ICJ Reports 1966 pp. 28-29 (§ 33).

107 ICJ: Namibia Case, ICJ Reports 1971 p. 31 (§ 53). Particular attention was given to the rejection of the idea of annexation in the negotiations which preceded the adoption of Article 22 of the Covenant, p. 28 (§ 45), 30 (§

the Namibia opinion seems consensualist also in its effort to accomodate the views ("philosophy", writes judge Fitzmaurice) of the present UN majority.[108]

In other words, both cases assume the correctness of a consensualist and a materialistic (teleological, "systemic") way of looking at the opposition past law/present law. The consensualist strand manifests itself in the way both cases seem to base themselves on the consent of original drafters and the present UN community. The materialistic stand manifests itself in the way both cases argue about previous behaviour, texts, teleology and system.

This argumentative structure - the way both cases assume that the law makes no priority between consent and material justice - renders both cases coherent and simultaneously makes them vulnerable to contrasting criticisms about which (or whose) consent is relevant and what justice says. These are the points at which the cases - and their critics - diverge. Scholars have criticized the 1966 case as it failed to give effect to the consent of present UN community and worked with a conservative theory of justice. And judge Fitzmaurice's criticism of the 1970 case is based on the overruling of original consent in favour of an anarchic theory of justice.

But neither outcome - and neither criticism - can be preferred within the system. For this would imply that we can know consent or justice in an objective way - a position inadmissible under the Rule of Law. It is not the law's or the Court's preference for past or present which explains the contrast between the two cases. No such gen-

---

5). Thus Bollecker, loc.cit., argues that the "teleological" interpetation was linked with an analysis of the subjective wills and interests of South Africa and other League members at the time, pp. 291, 296.

108 Thus judge Fitzmaurice, diss. op. ICJ: Namibia Case, ICJ Reports 1971 criticized the opinion for interpreting the mandate in a subjective, political way by, giving effect to the "philosophy" or intentions of "different organs fifty years later", p. 223.

eral preference exists. Which is to be preferred depends on what can be proved consensually or by recourse to justice. The contrast between the two cases is a contrast in the interpretations of the Court of what is required by consent or justice.

In order to make a definite preference between these interpretations ("What did the drafters relly intend?", "what was the system of the League really like?", What does present UN Community really wish?", "what does 'evolution' require?" etc.) we should be able to know real consent or justice in an objective way. But such knowledge is not open to us. Ultimately, it is for this reason that the Court could prefer past as well as present and still remain within a formally coherent argument. But because both cases turn on contestable interpretations about consent and justice, both are open to challenge by somebody whose interpretations differ. The contrast between the two cases is a contrast between different interpretations of what kind of and whose consent it is that counts and which kind of teleology it is that is working. But these are questions to which no legal answers can be given.

The making of a decision between claims of stability and change is always both contextual and indeterminate. It is contextual because we are able to make a preference only by looking at contextual will and justice. It is indeterminate because there exist no specifically legal criterion whereby differing views about will and justice could be resolved.

3. BEYOND THE SOCIAL CONCEPTION OF LAW: CUSTOM AS CONTEXTUAL JUSTICE

For the modern lawyer, it is very difficult to envisage, let alone to justify, a non-written law which would not be based on will or behaviour. Though standard account of sources of international law includes "general principles of law recognized by civilized nations" as a distinct category of normative materials, it is not principles of (political) justice which are meant thereby.[109] Modern lawyers usually assume that such principles, too, are based on acceptance or translate themselves to actual behaviour against which statement about them can be tested. Were we to assume that law may exist in, or be verifiable as against, principles which bear no necessary relationship with how (at least some) States behave or what they will, we would have moved away from the social conception of law. Our new conception would then simply appreciate conduct from the point of view of its conformity with some criterion of goodness (or justice, equity). This, in the orthodox view, would be to give up the modern project altogether and start assuming, either, that principles of justice indeed may be dicussed in a rationally controllable fashion, or that legal argument is no more than assertion of subjective desires.

In this final section I shall argue that even modern doctrines of international law have constant recourse to notions of justice when seeing norms in the way States behave. Neither materialism nor psychologism can be carried through without the intervention of notions of justice. These notions, however, are very difficult to justify. We cannot justify them by reference to how States have behaved or what they will because we can see meaning in behaviour or will only _through them_. Hence the dilemma of modern doctrine: how to deal with justice without falling back into naturalism or pure subjectivism. There is no easy way out from this dilemma. Disagreements about notions of

---

109 See, e.g., M. Koskenniemi, "General Principles; Reflexions on Constructivist Thinking in International Law", XVIII Oikeustiede-Jurisprudentia (1985) pp. 117-163; op.cit., (_supra_, n. 2) pp. 353-357.

justice are, and will remain, disagreements about the political good.

3.1. Contextualization

It does not seem at all possible to establish a general custom, opposable to a State, by means at looking at general State practice and the opinio juris. This is so because the argument is circular: we have recourse to material practice only because there seems to exist no way to find out what the general opinio juris is without asking each state itself. But we cannot simply hold all material practice as binding, either. In order to distinguish between normative and non-normative behaviour we need either to posses a theory of the intrinsically normative character of some forms of behaviour - a theory of material justice - or focus on the meaning of the behaviour by the States themselves - a possibility excluded by our previous denial of it being possible to know the opinio independently of its manifestations in behaviour.

Hence, the doctrine of custom looks beyond its general theory. This takes place in two moves. Fist, there is the move to think about custom as a set of bilateral "opposabilities".[110] Second, the normative sense of bilateral opposability is construed with the help of an undefined equity.

There is a view which regards custom as a process in which States constantly present claims vis-à-vis each other

---

110 The term "opposability" is derived from ICJ: Anglo-Norwegian Fisheries Case, ICJ Reports, 1951 in which the Court (in the French text) observed that the Norwegian system of straight base-lines had, on the basis of consolidation, become "opposable à tous les Etats", p. 138. Later, in the Fisheries Jurisdiction Cases, ICJ Reports 1974, the Court discussed the Icelandic extension of its fishery zone on the basis of whether it was "opposable" to the claimant States, p. 29 (§ 68).

and acquiesce in them.[111] The merit of this view lies in its concreteness. The law need not be ascertained in an abstract, erga omnes manner. Obligation is based on a particular legal relationship which is understood to reflect an individual norm. Merrills writes:

> "... opposability of particular claims is a far more significant issue than their conformity with an uncertain customary rule".[112]

Analytical mind is immediately tempted by such reduction of abstract categories into particular relationships. Even a rapid glance at the jurisprudence of the ICJ shows that it has tended to base obligation rather on the specific relationship between the disputing States than general rules. In the Anglo-Norwegian Fisheries Case (1951), it established British obligation on its "prolonged abstention" from protesting against Norway's system of drawing the baselines of its territorial sea.[113] In the Right of Passage Case (1960) the applicable norm was inferred, instead of some general law concerning transit thorugh foreign territory, from the parties past behaviour vis-à-vis each other.[114] In the South West Africa Case

---

111 See e.g. D'Amato, op.cit., p. 18; McDougal, op.cit., (supra, n. 21) pp. 356-358; MacGibbon, loc.cit., pp. 115-117; Wolfke, op.cit., pp. 63-54, 121-129; Skubiszewski, loc.cit., p. 824; Miller, op.cit., p. 100-103; Venkata Raman, loc.cit., pp. 368-371 et seq.

112 J.G. Merrills, J.G: Anatomy of International Law (London 1976) p. 5.

113 ICJ: Anglo-Norwegian Fisheries Case, ICJ Reports 1951 pp. 118, 138-139. The character of the Norwegian system as a historic right, as pointed out by some of the judges, did not signify any general rule to that effect, merely the opposability of the Norwegian system on the United Kingdom. See Hackworth, declaration, ibid, p. 144; Hsu Mo, sep. op. ibid, p. 154. Even judge Read, dissenting, did not dispute the Court's approach, merely the fact that the system had become opposable, ibid. p. 191.

114 ICJ: Right of Passage Case: ICJ Reports 1960 p. 39.

(1966) the very rationale behind dismissing the claims of Ethiopia and Liberia was based on interpreting the issue in terms of bilateral relations instead of rules or principles valid *erga omens*.[115]

Likewise, the Court's strategy in the *Fisheries Jurisdiction* and the *Nuclear Tests* (1974) cases to re-interpret the Applicant's claims so as not to concern general custom but the opposability of the respondent's practice towards the Applicants - though much criticized - was a strategy to bilateralize the dispute. In both cases, ruling one way or the other in respect of the existence of the alleged customary rules (concerning 50-mile fishery zones and the legality of nuclear testing) would have involved the Court in the midst of a political conflict.[116]

---

115 ICJ: South West Africa Case, ICJ Reports 1966 p. 54 (§ 100). A further strategy of bilateralization has occurred in connexion with the way the Court has turned down applications to intervene in the proceedings to protect one's legal interest in the case in pursuance of Article 62 of the ICJ Statute. The Court has held that Article 59 of the Statute which restricts the effects of a judgement to the parties in the case already provides sufficient protection. See, e.g., ICJ: Tunisia-Libya Continental Shelf (Application of Malta for Permission to Intervene) Case, ICJ Reports 1981 p. 16 (§ 28) et seq; 20 (§ 35). Libya-Malta Continental Shelf (Application of Italy for Permission to Intervene) Case, ICJ Reports 1984 p. 18 (§ 28) et seq; 26 (§ 42). The effect of this view is, of course, that the Court defines itself unable to pronounce anything on matters of general law. For a criticism of this strategy, see, e.g., *Jennings*, diss.op., ibid. p. 148 et seq, pp. 157-160.

116 ICJ: Fisheries Jurisdiction Cases, ICJ Reports 1974 p. 6 (§ 11). See further ibid. p. 34 (*dispositif*). The Court felt capable of discussing the issue on a bilateral basis after it had rejected the "narrow interpretation" of the applications according to which its jurisdiction would have been restricted to determining the general law on the issue. As the Court saw it, the task entrusted to it related to the "respective rights in the fishery resources" of the parties and that deciding this would require to "take into consideration all relevant elements in administering justice between the parties", ibid. pp. 20-22 (§ 42-48). See also ICJ: Nuclear Tests Cases, ICJ Reports 1974 pp. 260-263 (§ 25-30). The Court observed: "The original and ultimate objective of the applicant [Australia, MK] was and has remained to obtain the termination of these tests; thus its claim cannot be regarded as being a claim for a declaratory judgement", p. 263 (§ 30).

Contextualization serves as a strategy to avoid the difficulties in arguing about general custom. General rules are both hard to find and applying them may seem like an abstract, inflexible way of dealing with controversies which are invariably invested with particularized aspects. As the law must anyway bear a relationship to consent, it seems only natural to focuse on what the disputants have said or done *inter se*.

3.2 Custom as Justice

It seemed difficult to appreciate the significance of custom's two elements - practice and the *opinio juris* - without a contextual evaluation. Bilateralization helped to delimit the relevant context into relations between two States. It is through looking at the past behaviour of those two States that the non-written (customary) law between them can be discerned.

But a first thing to notice is, of course, that not *all* past behaviour in a bilateral relationship creates norms. How to distinguish, then, between past acts which may, for example, constitute acquiescence, or estoppel, and those which may not? The standard answer is the psychologist one. Past behaviour binds if it encapsulates consent, psychological will to be bound. This is the course taken by the ICJ in the *Nuclear Tests* Case (1974) in order to explain why a past declaration could be interpreted so as to amount to a unilaterally assumed obligation. Such declaration creates obligation:

> "When it is the intention of the State making the declaration that it should become bound..."[117]

The same is frequently argued about other statements as well as actions or non-action by a State. They might be

---

117 ICJ: Nuclear Tests Cases, ICJ Reports 1974 p. 267 (§ 43). See also e.g. ICJ: Gulf of Maine Case, ICJ Reports 1984 p. 307 (§ 138-139).

interpreted so as to amount to unilateral assumptions of an obligation in a bilateral relationship if intended to have that effect.

But such a purely psychological explanation cannot, of course, be accepted. It is not only virtually impossible to find out what a State's real, psychological intention at some point in time might have been. Even assuming that such intention could be known by an external observer it would be difficult to justify how it could be authoritative against the report of a "change of mind" by the State itself. A move away from pure psychologism is needed. And, as one might expect, this move is also taken by the ICJ in the Nuclear Tests Case (1974). Having affirmed that declarations bind if they have been intended as binding, the Court immediately throws another consideration into the picture. A purely intent-based justification would have to accept that a State might change its mind and thereby avoid obligation. But this is unacceptable. Therefore, declarations bind also because:

> "One of the principles governing the creation and performance of legal obligations ... is the principle of good faith..."[118]

The same point is continuously made by reference to the need to protect other States' reliance or "acting upon" a statement, act or silence of a State.[119] It is clearly necessary that, sometimes, such reliance is protected even when the behaving State never intended to create an obligation. This seems to be the very sense of the much-belaboured estoppel doctrine, for instance. But this construction faces the difficulty of having to justify its concep-

---

118 ICJ: Nuclear Tests Cases, ICJ Reports 1974 p. 268 (§ 46); See also ICJ: Gulf of Maine Case, ICJ Reports 1984 p. 305 (§ 130).

119 For a discussion and further references and case-analyses on these points, see Koskenniemi, op.cit., pp. 264-341.

tion of good faith, or of legitimate expectations, or of the reasonable man standard as against the possible deviating view on the same matter of the behaving State.

By what principles is a dispute between two deviating conceptions of good faith (or reasonableness, for example) decided? These cannot be principles written in a legal code - for the reference to good faith is intended precisely to avoid laying down, in a detailed manner, legal conditions of trustworthiness. Neither can they be principles which the States themselves might have intended (psychologically) because other actors' psychologies are not open to external observers. The point is that to decide between deviating conceptions cannot be done by other means than through a code of value, of significance. And this would be a code which cannot be justified in reference to the legal system whose very meaning it attempts to clarify.

The social conception of law is in a dilemma: it cannot construe the normative sense of past behaviour in a bilateral relationship on the parties' real, psychological intent because such intent can neither be known nor authoritatively opposed to the State's own deviating view thereof. But it cannot base it on a non-psychological principle, either, because such principle will immediately look like a natural (poltitical) principle, based on non-verifiable and contested value-preferences. The social conception of law will simply destruct itself in its search for a binding law. This self-destruction may be summarized in the following steps:

1) Doctrine starts with materialism; past behaviour binds simply because it is there - a verifiable fact. But all past behaviour cannot reflect or constitute a rule which makes such behaviour mandatory. A principle is needed to distinguish between normative and non-normative behaviour. Two types of principles might be envisaged: either they are principles existing within the psychologies of the acting

States or they exist independently of such psychologies.

2) Doctrine opts for psychologism; behaviour binds if it reflects intent to be bound. But real intent cannot be ascertained without asking the State itself - and thereby losing the law's constraining force;

3) Doctrine moves back into materialism; intent is "in-ferred" from material behaviour. But not all behaviour allows making this inference. We cannot check the inference against real, psychological will - as usually suggested - as we had already ruled out the possibility to know intent "better" than the State itself;

3a) Doctrine takes up a new form of materialism; it as-sumes that the (non-psychological) criteria for dis-tinguishing between normative/non-normative behariour could refer to good faith, reasonableness or legitimate expec-tations. But if these criteria refer to other States' acting upon, or their actual reliance, then we face the problem to explain why such reliance was justified in the first place. To do this, we should have a theory of legit-imate expectations. But such (a fully non-psychological) theory is a theory of natural justice and as such inadmis-sible under the social conception;

3b) A third materialist variant simply assumes that some kinds of behaviour automatically allow inferences about be-haviour. Different criteria have been suggested to recog-nize such forms of behaviour. These may have included the governmental status of the acting entities, the publicity of the acts, the duration and intensity of the behaviour, and so on. But no such criteria seem decisive and none of them is fully supported by international practice. The point is, of course, that the interpretation depends on the context. Often the same form of behaviour might, in differ-ent contexts, carry different meaning. A State may resort to war for peaceful motives and refrain from the use of force only because it has not yet developed the capacity for victory.

Intervention may follow from friendship as well as hostility. And so on. Besides, what is needed is that we _justify_ our construction against a deviating construction. In such case we can hardly persist in assuming that behaviour has meaning in some "natural" way (which our opponent has somehow curiously failed to grasp);

3c) A final form of materialism might justify itself by reference to the intrinsic value of the behaviour or the context in which it was made. But this, of course, is a naturalist criterion. How does one defend a view about _intrinsic_ value (i.e., a value independent of anyone's views about it)? Theories about intrinsic value must, under the social conception, seem only like superstition. Value, we have been taught, is something historically conditioned - it is not historically embedded in the cement of the universe but projected on things and actions by men. Would we not feel this way, we would have difficulty to justify the Rule of Law.

It is, I feel, precisely the well-foundedness of the liberal Rule of Law ideal which is threatened by the turn into equity - a roundabout way of speaking about justice - in modern customary law argument. Let me now explain, if only somewhat briefly, the force and character of this threat.

In the _North Sea Continental Shelf_ Cases (1969) - the _locus classicus_ of modern customary law argument - the ICJ, having first found that both State practice and the _opinio juris_ were inconclusive, explained that customary law on delimitation required that delimitatiation follow "equitable principles".[120] In the _Tunisia-Libya Continental Shelf_ Case (1982), equity became the very goal of delimitation:

---

120 ICJ: North Sea Continental Shelf Cases, ICJ Reports 1969 pp. 46-47 (§ 85).

121 ICJ: Tunisia-Libya Continental Shelf Case, ICJ Reports 1982 p. 59 (§ 70).

146

> "The result of the application of equitable principles must be equitable...The equitableness of a principle must be assessed in the light of its usefulness of arriving at an equitable result".[121]

The same point is captured by the manner the Court treated the interests of Norwegian fishermen in the Anglo-Norwegian Fisheries Case (1951)[122] and its attempt to balance them between the Applicants' historic and Iceland's "preferential" rights in the Fisheries Jurisdiction Cases (1974).[123] In both, the applicable rule was constructed through an identification of the relevant interests and then striking a balance between them. In the Burkina Faso - Mali Frontier Case (1986), the Chamber of the Court expressly extended this approach to terrestial sovereignty disputes as well.[124]

In fact the whole range of customary law relating to delimiting the freedoms of two sovereigns in the absence of written rules is similarly built. Disputes are conceptualized in terms of the juxtaposition of sovereign powers. In the absence of justification to prefer one sovereign to another, the law turns towards equitable compromise. Nationalisation cases provide another example. On the one side, there is the host State's sovereign freedom to nationalize - on the other, the home State's acquired rights: legal practice strikes the needed balance by looking for appropriate or "just" compensation.[125]

---

122 ICJ: Anglo-Norwegian Fisheries Case, ICJ Reports 1951 p. 133.

123 ICJ: Fisheries Jurisdiction Cases, ICJ Reports 1974 pp. 22-30.

124 ICJ: Burkina Faso - Mail Frontier Case, ICJ Reports 1986 pp. 567-568 (§ 28).

125 See, e.g., Dispute between the Government of Kuwait and the American Independent Oil Co. (Aminoil) 66 ILR (1984) p. 602-603, 607-609; Libyan-American Oil Co. (Liamco) v. the Government of Libyan Arab Republic XX ILM (1980) pp. 74, 76-77 (§ 145, 150-151). See also comment in O. Schachter, "International Law in Theory and Practice: General Course in Public International Law", 178 RCADI (1982/5) pp. 323-326.

The legal regime of transboundary damage is a further example: the work of the International law Commission on the topic of liability for injurious consequences of acts not prohibited by international law reads like an extended gloss on the rule that conflicts among sovereigns must be settled by the contextual balance - taking all interests into account.[126] Transfrontier pollution typically involves a juxtaposition of the economic interests in State A with the environmental interests in State B. A law which would simply prefer one type of interests vis-à-vis another would seem unacceptable. In a world of sovereign equality it would fail to reflect adequately sovereign preference. Therefore, a virtually uniform legal opinion thinks that the law in such cases directs one to the search of contextual compromise.[127]

Dealing with disputes involving claims for the foreign sovereign's immunity or extraterritorial jurisdiction (mirror-image situations), legal practice has little other to offer than a reference to good faith and balancing interests.[128]

---

126 See, in particular the "Schematic Outline" in Quentin-Baxter: Third Report. YILC (1982), vol. II/1 pp. 62-64. See also idem: First Report. YILC (1980), vol. II/1 p. 161 and generally pp. 156-162. See also comments in D. Magraw, "Transboundary Harm; the ILC's Study of 'International Liability'", 80 AJIL (1986) pp. 311-313, 327.

127 See M. Koskenniemi, "International Pollution in the System of International Law", XVII Oikeustiede-Jurisprudentia (1984) pp. 128-164 and the notes therein. See, in addition, J.G. Lammers, "'Balancing the Equitites in International Environmental Law", RCADI Coll. 1984 pp. 153-164; L.F.E. Goldie, "Concepts of Strict and Absolute Liability and the Ranking of Liability in Terms of Relative Exposure to Risk", XVI NethYBIL (1985) pp. 175, 204-238.

128 On the turn to seeking for 'balance of interests' in the practice of settling claims concerning extraterritorial jurisdiction, see W. Meng, "Völkerrechtliche Zulässigkeit und Grenzen Wirtschaftsverwaltungsrechtlicher Hoheitsakte mit Auslandswirkung", 44 ZaöRV (1984) pp. 675-783; A.V. Lowe, "The Problem of Extraterritorial Jurisdiction; Economic Sovereignty and the Search for a Solution", 34 ICLQ (1985) pp. 730-731 et seq. See also the criticism in H. Maier, "Extraterritorial Jurisdiction at a Crossroads:

In each of such enteral fields of customary law - teritory, jurisdiction, damage and compensation, beside a host of others - customary law looks beyond formal rules and strict tests of the practice and opinio and calls for equitable balancing. The duration, consistency or generality of a practice are not decisive - these factors receive significance only through an anterior view of whether they sould, in the circumstances of the case be regarded as significant. If there are two sovereigns, and two histories of sovereign behaviour, with two sovereign interpretations about the sense of cush behaviour, there remains little more for an external observer than to try to balance these interpretations against each other with a view to achieving an accptable ad hoc compromise. Notice the irony: originally the Rule of Law seemed needed because notions of justice had seemed so subjective. Social justice should be what the law said. But rigid rules of law fail to reflect the infinite variability of conflict-situations. To avoid formalism, and the associated risk of non-compliance, the law refers back to justice. The circle is full. The law is what social justice determines it should be.

But if this is so and if the customary law constantly refers us to look for a contextual equity (either by an express rule or an interpretative principle), then we must assume that equity is the core of custom, that it is equity which delimits what States may claim as their customary rights and possess as their customary duties. Custom becomes an extension of a general principle of good faith or reasonableness - of just conduct - which obliges States to take reasonable regard of others and guides lawyers to look for reasonable compromise instead of hard- and fast rules.

An Intersection between Public and Private International Law" 76 AJIL (1982) pp. 295, 318 et seq.

It is indeed sometimes claimed that whether or not a putative norm needs confirmation from State practice or opinio juris depends on the value of that norm. A norm considered essential to peace and security or expressing a "basic universally held moral principle" would retain its validity also against inconsistent State practice - while a jurisdictionary rule, for example, should not be upheld without significant support from State practice.[129] Indeed, it seems difficult to deny that in many cases, international courts or tribunals have been content with very little evidence from such practice when affirming the validity of a rule supported by strong considerations of justice. The brevity with which the ICJ justified its rule of self-defence as "custom" in the U.S. Military and Paramilitary Activities Case (1986) points in the same direction. This was considered being custom less because there was evidence of concurring practice or opinio juris than for its intrinsically just character.[130] And in the Gulf of Maine Case (1984) the Court expressly noted that in addition to regular customary rules "whose presence in the opinio juris of States can be tested by induction based on the analysis of sufficiently extensive and convincing practice" there were also customary rules which did not need such evidence because of their character as "ensuring the co-existence and vital co-operation of the members of the international community".[131]

The move into what are primarily principles of political justice is well evidenced in the present practice of international tribunals and documented by scholars. In the

---

129 Schachter, loc.cit., p. 118; C.W. Jenks, The Prospects of International Adjudication (London-New York 1964) p. 264.

130 See ICJ: US Military and Paramilitary Activities Case, ICJ Reports 1986 p. 94 (§ 176).

131 ICJ: Gulf of Maine Case, ICJ Reports 1984 p. 293 (§ 111).

best recent analysis of the matter, Peter Haggenmacher concludes that custom-ascertainment of necessity involves an analysis and appreciation of the interests at stake to the parties. It is not a matter of simply observing what acts have taken place or what States may have intended. The judge is never confronted with past events in their purity. They appear to him as a set of unconnected, disparateactions and objectives between which he must make a (political) choice.[132] De Visscher observes:

> "Il s'agit donc ici non pas seulement de considérer les régularités observées mais de les évaluer en fonction des impératifs moraux et sociaux qui quident l'effort humain dans sa poursuite d'une organisation meilleure de droit".[133]

But this is a move which is immediately vulnerable to important criticism. For, as Reuter writes:

> "Il y a toujours plusieurs équités possibles et chacune d'entre elles est soustendue par une concéption politico-philosophique différente".[134]

Lawyers have objected against the turn to notions of justice under the guise of equity or equitable principles because this seems to be a turn towards the political, the subjective.[135] Reference to equity has seemed to restate the problem of the subjectivity of notions of justice which it was the task of formal rules to dispose of. It has

---

132 Haggenmacher, loc.cit., pp. 115, 118-124.

133 De Visscher, op.cit., pp. 221, 237-242.

134 P. Reuter, "Quelques réflexions sur l'équité en droit international", XV RBDI (1980-1) p. 179.

135 See especially Gros, diss. op. ICJ: Tunisia-Libya Continental Shelf Case, ICJ Reports 1982 p. 153; McNair, diss. op. ICJ: Anglo-Norwegian Fisheries Case, ICJ Reports 1951 p. 169.

seemed, as judge Oda writes, to "suggest the principle of non-principle".[136]

The starting-point and principal justification of the social conception of law lies in its criticism of arguing from abstract, subjective and unverifiable notions of justice. Because naturalist arguments about the good and the just seemed to bend to suit any sovereign policy Enlightenment lawyers started to argue about the usefulness of basing Government on (concrete, objective and verifiable) rules. The move into arguing about equity constitutes, therefore, a challenge to the very foundations of modern legal thought. Is it, after all, possible to discuss what is equitable (read: what is _just_) in some controllable way, so as to avoid political tyranny? If the answer is negative, what should we think of the apparent necessity of that move? If the reply is positive, what consequence does that have to our ideal of the rule of (formally neutral) law?

4. APPRAISAL

The United Nations General Assembly recently declared the last decade of this millennium the "Decade of International Law".[137] At the initiative of the erstwhile global opposition - the non-aligned States - they have pledged adherence to a global Rule of Law. And they have done this precisely for the same belief as that which animated Vattel's "Droit des Gens". This is the belief in a uniquely rational, non-political mechanism - the legal

---

136 _Oda_, diss. op. ICJ: Tunisia-Libya continental Shelf Case, ICJ Reports 1982 p. 157. Likewise, _Tanaka_, diss. op. ICJ: North Sea Continental Shelf Cases, ICJ Reports 1969 pp. 195-196, _Oda_, diss. op. ICJ: Libya-Malta Continental Shelf Case, ICJ Reports 1985 p. 159 (§ 65).

137 UNGA Res. 44/23, 15 November 1989.

mechanism - capable of curtailing political subjectivism and irrationality, or at least providing a neutral framework within which politics could function.

But we have seen that at least customary international law is not such a "fact of nature" that it could be grasped without the mediation of essentially political theories. Whether explained as a matter of behaviour or a matter of will, we could give sense to custom only through interpretation. And interpretation took place through a conceptual matrix - a code of separating what is just and what is unjust in sovereign behaviour. Few people would say that because there have been over 500 wars or armed conflicts during the past forty years, using armed force has become a customary privilege. To argue something into or out of the category of "customary law" is possible only through a notion of justice. Without such notions of justice, it is impossible to understand social life, let alone to participate in it.

That standard academic customary law theory is so unpersuasive relates to lawyers' attempt to purge it from considerations of political principle and economic causality. Yet, the move to equity is only another name for discussing conflict in terms of what is just and how we get there. That legal practice uses standard customary law theory in justifying its conclusions has become an ever more strenuous ritual.

The Rule of Law is part and parcel of the politics which it hopes to constrain and arguments about the law are arguments of political preference. Lawyers will continue to disagree about custom, and even on the methods for finding it. Depending on the perspective we occupy, we shall persist in seeing different meanings in our actions. There is no such "view from nowhere" which we could occupy, an invisible code which we could reach and which would allow us to combine all existing interpretations, assumptions and projections under some great principle - a consistent, rational whole of normative purpose.[138]

This is hardly a cry of despair. To the contrary, that there is no uniquely rational code embedded outside human passion and desire is the best possible reason for using passion and desire so as to create more acceptable conditions of social life. The less certain we can justifiably be with final results, the more reason we have to work against imperialism.

The Decade of international Law is no shortcut to Utopia. If it teaches us to take political conflict seriously - instead of trying to get rid of it - and leads us to grapple with politics in a truly normative way it will have created something far more valuable.

---

138 See further Koskenniemi, op.cit., (supra, n. 2), pp. 476-501.

Part IV
Rethinking the Substance of International Law

[8]

ARTICLES

THE SOURCES OF INTERNATIONAL LAW

David Kennedy*

I. DOCTRINES ABOUT THE SOURCES OF INTERNATIONAL LAW

International law devotes a great deal of attention to its sources. Scholars have produced a large body of work about both the conditions under which treaties, custom, or general principles of law bind actors and the hierarchy among the various doctrinal forms which might apply in a given instance.[1] Indeed, doctrine and commentary about what

---

* Assistant Professor of Law, Harvard Law School. I would like to thank Clare Dalton, Josh Floum, Kim Goslant, Reinhard Hermes, Duncan Kennedy, and Dan Tarullo for their research assistance, readings, and comments. This article is one part of a larger study of public international legal doctrine being published in 1987 by Nomos Verlag under the title *International Legal Structures*.

1. Most standard treatises and casebooks devote a section to the sources of international law. *See, e.g.*, J. BRIERLY, THE LAW OF NATIONS (5th ed. 1955); I. BROWNLIE, PRINCIPLES OF PUBLIC INTERNATIONAL LAW (3d ed. 1979); L. OPPENHEIM, INTERNATIONAL LAW (8th ed. H. Lauterpacht 1955); 1 M. WHITEMAN, DIGEST OF INTERNATIONAL LAW (1963).

For information devoted to sources in general, see Waldock, *General Course on Public International Law*, 106 RECUEIL DES COURS, 1, 39-103 (1962) (classic British approach focusing on practice and the I.C.J. jurisprudence); McDougal & Reismann, *The Prescribing Function in World Constitutive Process: How International Law is Made*, 6 YALE STUD. IN WORLD PUB. ORDER 249 (1980) (a sociological approach); A. VERDROSS, DIE QUELLEN DES UNIVERSELLEN VÖLKERRECHTS (1973) (a natural law approach); G. Tunkin, *Soviet Theory of Sources of International Law*, in VÖLKERRECHT UND RECHTSPHILOSOPHIE: INTERNATIONALE FESTSCHRIFT FÜR STEFAN VEROSTA 67 (1980) (summarizing the extremely positivist Soviet approach); Virally, *The Sources of International Law*, in MANUAL OF PUBLIC INTERNATIONAL LAW 116 (M. Sørenson ed. 1968) (a classic treatise summary); Baxter, *Treaties and Custom*, 129 RECUEIL DES COURS 44 (1970) (discussing mutual reciprocal influence of treaty and custom upon each other's formation); de Visscher, *Cours général du droit international public*, 136 RECUEIL DES COURS 9 (1972). For information concerning treaties, see T. ELIAS, THE MODERN LAW OF TREATIES (1974) (based on the Vienna Convention on The Law of Treaties); A. MCNAIR, THE LAW OF TREATIES (1961) (a practice-oriented handbook drawing upon British practice; concerned primarily with clarifying rules about specific doctrines such as treaty conclusion rather than with general considerations of validity); P. REUTER, INTRODUCTION AU DROIT DES TRAITÉS (1972); B. SIMMA, DAS REZIPROZITÄTSELEMENT IM ZUSTANDEKOMMEN VÖLKERRECHTLICHER VERTRÄGE (1972); I. SINCLAIR, THE VIENNA CONVENTION ON THE LAW OF TREATIES (1973).

are and what are not the sources of international law are so well developed that further commentary seems unnecessary. The discussion usually revolves around the four classic sources contained in Article 38 of the Statute of the International Court of Justice.[2] Article 38 is addressed to I.C.J. justices and enumerates the various sources they are to examine in finding the law necessary to resolve a case.[3] It has been taken as a convenient catalog of international legal sources generally, and as such, has been the starting point for most discussion in this area. Article 38 reads:

> 1. The Court, whose function it is to decide in accordance with international law such disputes as are submitted to it, shall apply:
>
> a. international *conventions*, whether general or particular, establishing rules expressly recognized by the contesting states;
> b. international *custom*, as evidence of a general practice accepted as law;
> c. the general *principles* of law recognized by civilized nations;
> d. subject to the provisions of Article 59, *judicial decisions* and the

---

For information on customary law, see Akehurst, *Custom as a Source of International Law*, 47 BRIT. Y.B. INT'L L. 1 (1974-1975) (a good survey of contemporary doctrine); A. D'AMATO, THE CONCEPT OF CUSTOM IN INTERNATIONAL LAW (1971) (a balanced and comprehensive treatment); Guggenheim, *Les deux éléments de la coutume en droit international*, in 1 LA TECHNIQUE ET LES PRINCIPES DU DROIT PUBLIC, ÉTUDES EN L'HONNEUR DE GEORGES SCELLE 275 (1950); H. GÜNTHER, ZUR ENTSTEHUNG VON VÖLKERGEWOHNHEITSRECHT (1970) (emphasizes estoppel, or "Vertrauensgrundsatz" as a basis for customary law).

For information on general principles, see Tunkin, *"General Principles of Law" in International Law*, in INTERNATIONALE FESTSCHRIFT FÜR ALFRED VERDROSS 523 (1971); Verdross, *Les principes généraux de droit dans le système du droit international public*, in RECUEIL D'ÉTUDES DE DROIT INTERNATIONAL EN HOMMAGE À PAUL GUGGENHEIM 521 (1968).

For additional sources, see C. DE VISSCHER, DE L'ÉQUITÉ DANS LE RÉGLEMENT ARBITRAL OU JUDICIAIRE DES LITIGES DE DROIT INTERNATIONAL PUBLIC (1972); Falk, *On the Quasi-Legislative Competence of the General Assembly*, 60 AM. J. INT'L L. 782 (1966); R. HIGGINS, THE DEVELOPMENT OF INTERNATIONAL LAW THROUGH THE POLITICAL ORGANS OF THE UNITED NATIONS (1963); Skubiszewski, *A New Source of the Law of Nations: Resolutions of International Organizations*, in RECUEIL D'ÉTUDES DE DROIT INTERNATIONAL EN HOMMAGE Á PAUL GUGGENHEIM 508 (1968); E. SUY, LES ACTES JURIDIQUES UNILATÉRAUX EN DROIT INTERNATIONAL PUBLIC (1962).

2. Most textbooks make this reliance explicit. *See* I. BROWNLIE, *supra* note 1, at 3 *passim*; NGUYEN QUOC-DINH, P. DAILLER & A. PELLET, DROIT INTERNATIONAL PUBLIC 105, 108 (2d ed. 1980); E. MENZEL & K. IPSEN, VÖLKERRECHT 75 (2d ed. 1979); A. VERDROSS, *supra* note 1, at 38 *passim*. For a critical analysis of this reliance, see McDougal & Reisman, *supra* note 1, at 259-60 ("It has become almost a ritual presentation among commentators to make Article 38 . . . the central focus of exposition.").

3. I.C.J. CHARTER art. 38. Article 38 replicates a similar provision in the statute of its predecessor, the Permanent Court of International Justice. The I.C.J. provision suggests a stronger intention that the enumerated sources are *general* sources of international law by adding after "the Court" the words "whose function it is to decide." *See* NGUYEN QUOC-DINH, P. DAILLER & A. PELLET, *supra* note 2, at 108-09; A. VERDROSS, *supra* note 1, at 98.

teachings of the most highly qualified publicists of the various nations, as subsidiary means for the determination of rules of law.

2. This provision shall not prejudice the power of the Court to decide a case *ex aequo et bono*, if the parties agree thereto.

Contemporary analyses of source doctrine generally begin with an abstract definition of each of the sources enumerated in Article 38, developing the boundaries of these categories.[4]

Treaty law, for example, considers the theoretical prerequisites for in-

---

4. Treatments of treaty law differ only in the level of abstraction at which treaties are defined. The most abstract definition is perhaps Kelsen's: "A treaty is an agreement normally entered into by two or more states under general international law." H. KELSEN, PRINCIPLES OF INTERNATIONAL LAW 454 (2d rev. ed. R. Tucker 1966); *see* J. STARKE, AN INTRODUCTION TO INTERNATIONAL LAW 457 (8th ed. 1977).

> A treaty may be defined, in accordance with the definition adopted in Article 2 of the [Vienna] Convention, as an agreement whereby two or more States establish or seek to establish a relationship between themselves governed by international law. So long as an agreement between States is attested, any kind of instrument or document or any oral exchange between States involving undertakings may constitute a treaty, irrespective of the form or circumstances of its conclusion.

Id. at 454 (coupled with a system for categorizing treaties by the form of their creation, *id.* at 458); *see also* NGUYEN QUOC-DINH, P. DAILLER & A. PELLET, *supra* note 2, at 111.

> Le traité désigne tout accord couclu entre deux ou plusieurs sujets du droit international, destiné à produire des effets de droit et régi par le droit international.

A still more concrete definition is:

> Unter einem [völkerrechtlichen] Vertrag verstehen wir eine ausdrückliche oder durch konkludente Handlungen zustandegekommene, vom VR [Völkerrecht] bestimmte Willenseinigung zwischen zwei oder mehreren Staaten oder anderen Völkerrechtssubjekten, in denen sich diese zu bestimmten einseitigen oder korrespondierenden, gleichen oder verschiedenen, einmaligen oder wiederholten Leistungen, Unterlassungen oder Duldungen verpflichten.

A. VERDROSS & B. SIMMA, UNIVERSELLES VÖLKERRECHT 270 (1976). For an interesting "programization" of this abstract approach, see I. V. MÜNCH, VÖLKERRECHT IN PROGRAMMIERTER FORM 53-82 (1982). These abstract definitions are usually coupled with abstract limitations in the form of categorizations of permissible treaties defined by the form of their conclusion. *See, e.g.*, J. STARKE, *supra*, at 400-05. Treaties are limited, for example, by contrast to private agreements or declarations of political intention. Münch, *Non-Binding Agreements*, 29 ZEITSCHRIFT FÜR AUSLÄNDISCHES ÖFFENTLICHES RECHT UND VÖLKERRECHT [ZAÖRV] 1 (1969); *see* Dehaussy, *Le problème de la classification des traités et le projet de convention établi par la Commission du Droit international des Nations Unies*, in RECUEIL D'ÉTUDES DE DROIT INTERNATIONAL EN HOMMAGE À PAUL GUGGENHEIM 305 (1968) (describing the classification of treaties). Custom is similarly defined and limited at an abstract level. *See, e.g.*, Hudson, *Article 24 of the Statute of the International Law Commission*, U.N. Doc. A/CN.4/16, *reprinted in* [1950] 2 Y.B. INT'L L. COMM'N 24, 26, U.N. Doc. A/CN.4/SER.A/1950/Add.1:

> Seeking with Brierly [The Law of Nations (4th ed. 1949)] (p. 62) "a general recognition among States of a certain practice as obligatory," the emergence of a principle or rule of customary international law would seem to require presence of the following elements:

cluding some form of words under the heading "treaty." Thus, people who discuss treaties feel that such issues as "capacity,"[5] executive

---

(a) concordant practice by a number of States with reference to a type of situation falling within the domain of international relations;

(b) continuation or repetition of the practice over a considerable period of time;

(c) conception that the practice is required by, or consistent with, prevailing international law; and

(d) general acquiescence in the practice by other States. Of course the presence of each of these elements is to be established (droit être constaté) as a fact by a competent international authority.

Id.

"International jurists speak of a *custom* when a clear and continuous habit of doing certain actions has grown up under the aegis of the conviction that these actions are, according to International Law, obligatory or right." L. OPPENHEIM, *supra* note 1, at 26. Most modern treatises refer to Article 38 of the Statute of the International Court of Justice in lieu of developing their own definition: "international custom, as evidence of a general practice accepted as law." Custom is then limited by abstract consideration of issues such as the degree of "evidence" required. *See, e.g.*, I. BROWNLIE, *supra* note 1, at 4-6. For discussions of related topics such as the meaning of "practice" as acts or verbal statements, see *infra* note 72; the duration of the practice required, see *infra*, note 12; the number of states who must participate, see *infra* note 12; the requirement of "*opinio juris*," see *infra* note 41. For a discussion of the *opinio juris* requirement, compare A. VERDROSS, *supra* note 1, at 104-09 (favoring) with Virally, *supra* note 1, at 134-35 (against) and H. GÜNTHER, *supra* note 1, at 149 (against).

5. Although capacity seems unproblematic for sovereign states (Vienna Convention on the Law of Treaties, *opened for signature* May 23, 1969, U.N. Doc. A/CONF.39/27, art. 6, *reprinted in* 8 I.L.M. 679 (1969), 63 AM. J. INT'L L. 875 (1969) [hereinafter Vienna Convention]; J. STARKE, *supra* note 4, at 466; A. VERDROSS & B. SIMMA, *supra* note 4, at 348), the discussion of the capacity of international organizations and federal states reveals the abstract structure of assumptions underlying capacity doctrine. There is a basic tension between the aim of registering pre-existing capacity and creating reliable or reasonable limits to capacity. The notions of "pre-existing" or "reasonable" capacity which are in turn relied upon reflect either the intention of some pre-existing sovereign capacity or reasonable external values or definitions of sovereignty. Thus, the treaty-making capacity of institutions is deduced either "by implication from their constituent instruments" (Virally, *supra* note 1, at 183) in the so-called "implied powers" approach (A. VERDROSS & B. SIMMA, *supra* note 4, at 350) or "is to be deduced, if at all . . . , from the evidence pointing to its having that sort of personality which involves capacity to make treaties" (Parry, *The Treaty Making Power of the United Nations*, 26 BRIT. Y.B. INT'L L. 110 (1949)). For the view that treaty-making power must be expressly conferred by constituents, see H. KELSEN, *supra* note 4, at 330; J. SCHNEIDER, TREATY MAKING POWER OF INTERNATIONAL ORGANIZATIONS (1959); *see also* L. WILDHABER, TREATY-MAKING POWER AND CONSTITUTION (1971) (describing the capacity of federal states). International law capacity of federal states depends upon the constitution of the federation. *See, e.g.*, Grundgesetz für die Bundesrepublik Deutschland (Basic Law of the Federal Republic of Germany), art. 32 III; Bundesverfassung der Schweizerischen Eidgenossenschaft, art. 8, 9 (Federal Constitution of Switzerland) (establishing a limited treaty-making capacity, although such provisions cannot be relied upon to deceive other sovereigns). For a comprehensive survey of the treaty-making capacity of and performance of treaties by constituent member states in Federal systems, see L. WILDHABER, *supra*, at 278-343. In particular, compare the situation where member states have no power to conclude international agreements: Australia, *id.* at 297-302; USSR, *id.* at 283-84, with the situation where member states may have a limited treaty-making power; Canada, *id.* at 286-89, and the situation where member states have a constitutional power to make treaties: West

"competence,"[6] the "full powers" of plenipotentiaries,[7] the require-

---

Germany, *id.* at 306-7; Switzerland, *id.* at 315-19.

6. This doctrine considers which organs of the state may legitimately conclude treaties. Although the domestic legal order is normally considered controlling, 1 C. ROUSSEAU, DROIT INTERNATIONAL PUBLIC (1970); A. VERDROSS & B. SIMMA, *supra* note 4, at 352, the discourse attempts abstractly and vainly to resolve the international law consequences of derogation from these domestic provisions. The effect of an internal limitation of authority upon other states is seen to depend either upon a vision of the true, pre-existing power of the state concluding the treaty or upon the systematic necessity of establishing reasonable limits of state authority. Each of these views depends in some way upon the other. For example, if the doctrine is to register the true power of the concluding state, it must be based upon either an external vision of state power or recognition of acceptable international rules. Most commentators alternatively distinguish and then blend these approaches. *See, e.g.*, Geck, *The Conclusion of Treaties in Violation of the Internal Law of a Party, Comments on Arts. 6 and 43 of the ILC's 1966 Draft Articles on the Law of Treaties*, 27 ZAÖRV 429 (1967). Geck maintains that the dependence of treaties on internal law is particularly dangerous from the viewpoint of the security of international treaty relations. He concludes that:

> On the basis of almost universally uniform constitutional law, and indeed perhaps even on the basis of a rule of international law, a Head of State is empowered to express binding consent to a treaty . . .
>
> It is, however, at present both necessary and sensible to refer to constitutional law for the answer as to whether other representatives of State are authorised to express consent independently of any authorization by the Head of State.

Id. at 442. For the view that derogation from municipal provisions of authority is not relevant at international law, see H. BLIX, TREATY MAKING POWER 392 (1960). "[T]he evidence of a practice treating constitutional provisions as not directly relevant in international law is both quantitatively and qualitatively more significant than that pointing to the direct relevance of municipal provisions." *Id.* Blix suggests that what practice does support is a "criterion of apparent ability." *Id.* For the view that derogation from municipal authority is internationally relevant, because the pre-existing power had simply not been exercised, see TRIEPEL, VÖLKERRECHT UND LANDESRECHT 236 (1899). For the mixed view that such derogation is sometimes relevant, see Vienna Convention on the Law of Treaties, *supra* note 5, at art. 46 (holding a violation of internal law relevant if the violation is manifest, the provision is of fundamental importance and concerns competence to conclude treaties). The International Law Commission, which drafted the Convention, was "extremely cautious" in formulating Article 46. Nahlik, *The Ground of Invalidity and Termination of Treaties*, 65 AM. J. INT'L L. 736, 740 (1971); *see also* Cahier, *La violation du droit interne relatif à la competênce pour conclure des traités comme cause de nullité des traités*, 54 RIVISTA DI DIRITTO INTERNAZIONALE 226 (1974); Kearney, *Internal Limitations on External Commitments: Article 46 of the Treaties Convention*, 4 INT'L LAW. 1 (1969). Kearney analyzes Article 46 (originally I.L.C. draft Article 43) as a:

> middle ground between opposing schools of thought classically grouped under the convenient umbrellas of monism and dualism. The monists, holding the view that internal law and international commitments are one, deduced from this concept of unity that international commitments which did not meet internal limitations on making treaties are unlawful because of a failure of consent. The dualists, holding the distinctness of internal and international law, concluded that while a treaty obligation may be invalid internally because of failure to comply with constitutional requirements, the international obligation is unimpaired if it measures up to international law requirements, because these requirements do not comprehend any reference to the internal law. There is an essential bootstraps element in each position because the conclusion depends upon acceptance of a semantic assumption.

ments and effects of signature or ratification,[8] or the requirements of

---

Id. at 3. Nevertheless, Kearney appears to rely on a dualist interpretation of Article 46 in his attempt to elaborate its coherent meaning.

> Is the solution that has been finally worked out the best available solution? It is certainly not the rule that would have the greatest appeal to either the fervid nationalist or the perfervid internationalist. But the all-or-nothing approach of true believers rarely supplies a workable formula for a work-a-day world. When the desirable aim of upholding the stability of the international treaty structure collides with the laudable end of placing some domestic checks and balances upon the making of international commitments, the reasonable solution should be a compromise that protects both sets of interests to the maximum extent.
>
> The essential decision in reaching such a compromise is allocation of the burden of proceeding. . . .
>
> The decision underlying [article 46] . . . is to accord *prima facie* validity to the appearance of authority subject to the limitation of an objectively evident violation of a fundamentally important internal law. The review of the problem has demonstrated above that this solution is amply supported, not only by legal theory, but by consideration of practical consequences.

Id. at 21.

7. "Full powers" is defined:

> a document emanating from the competent authority of a state designating a person or persons to represent the state for negotiating, adopting or authenticating the text of a treaty, for expressing consent of the state to be bound by a treaty, or for accomplishing any other act with respect to a treaty. . . .

The Vienna Convention on the Law of Treaties, *supra* note 5, at art. 2(1)(c): The extremely formal nature of this doctrine exists in some tension with its reliance upon a substantive view of "competent" municipal authority and of the impact of international law of failure to negotiate on the basis of full powers. Article 7(1) provides that:

> A person is considered as representing a State for the purpose of . . . expressing the consent of the State . . . if:
>
> (a) he produces full powers; *or*
>
> (b) it appears from the practice of the States concerned or from other circumstances that their intention was to consider that person as representing the State . . . .

Moreover, under Article 47,

> if the authority of a representative to express the consent of a State to be bound by a particular treaty has been made subject to a specific restriction, his omission to observe that restriction may not be invoked as invalidating the consent expressed by him unless the restriction was notified to the other negotiating States prior to his expressing such consent.

See J. STARKE, *supra* note 4, at 401; J. JONES, FULL POWERS AND RATIFICATION (1946). For examples of the doctrine's invocation, see 1 C. ROUSSEAU, *supra* note 6, at 80.

8. Signature and ratification doctrine defines in a formal way the abstract end steps in treaty creation. These formal acts separate binding and non-binding instruments. *See* Bolintineanu, *Expression of Consent to be Bound by a Treaty in the Light of the 1969 Vienna Convention*, 68 AM. J. INT'L L. 672 (1974); I. BROWNLIE, *supra* note 1, at 603-04 (a good doctrinal summary); SMETS, LA CONCLUSION DES ACCORDS EN FORME SIMPLIFÉE (1969). Ratification, like full powers, is discussed as a municipal and international law event. Article 2(1)(b) of the Vienna Convention, *supra* note 5 defines ratification as "the international act . . . whereby a state establishes on the international plane its consent to be bound by a treaty." *Cf.* "capacity" doctrine, *supra* note 5; *see also infra* notes 59 & 65 and accompanying text. On the hierarchical relation between signature and ratification, see I. BROWNLIE, *supra* note 1, at 603-04; J. STARKE,

registry and deposit[9] need abstract explanation. Mitigating circumstances such as duress, or *force majeure*[10] complete the affirmative pre-

---

supra note 4, at 479-81.

9. Designed to prevent secret agreements or make a determinative text available, these doctrines provide for the registry and deposit of reservations, ratifications, and treaty texts with one or more states or international organizations. I. BROWNLIE, *supra* note 1, at 590-91. The discourse about these doctrines contrasts a view of registry as a nonsubstantive recognition of the underlying instrument and as in some way the act which gives the instrument international force. These strands structure discussion of the role of the repository and of the requirement that "[e]very treaty . . . entered into by any member of the United Nations . . . shall . . . be registered with the Secretariat." U.N. CHARTER art. 102. In one view, for example, the repository is an impartial communicator of reservations, in another, the decisive acceptor of reservations. *See* Rosenne, *More on the Depository of International Treaties*, 64 AM. J. INT'L L. 838 (1970) (updating Rosenne, *The Depository of International Treaties*, 61 AM. J. INT'L L. 923 (1967)). After a general discussion of the function of deposit, the author concludes "that a depository notified of reservations incompatible with the object and purpose of a treaty must communicate the text of the reservation to the other states concerned and leave it to them to decide the question of compatibility." *Id.* at 852. Similarly, under one view of U.N. Charter article 102, the provision that "[n]o party to any such treaty or international engagement which has not been registered in accordance with the provisions of paragraph 1 of this Article may invoke that treaty or engagement before any organ of the United Nations" imposes a condition on the validity of the underlying instrument. In another, this merely adds an international law sanction to failure to register. *See* I. BROWNLIE, *supra* note 1, at 609-10; Geck, *Die Registrierung und Veröffentlichung völkerrechtlicher Verträge*, 22 ZAÖRV 173 (1962).

10. Instances of invalidity on the grounds of error, fraud, or the threat or use of force against the person of a representative are little known in international practice. *See* Nahlik, *supra* note 6, at 741; Waldock, *Second Report on the Law of Treaties*, [1963] 2 INT'L L. COMM'N Y.B. 36 (1963). Nevertheless there is hardly a treatise which does not deal abstractly and often at length with these mitigating factors. *See, e.g.*, E. MENZEL & K. IPSEN, *supra* note 2, at 327; 1 C. ROUSSEAU, *supra* note 6, at 143; Virally, *supra* note 1, at 201-04. Coercion of a state by use of force is uniformly viewed to mitigate consent. *See* Vienna Convention on the Law of Treaties, art. 52, *supra* note 5, at 891, providing: "a treaty is void if its conclusion has been procured by the threat or use of force in violation of the principles of international law embodied in the Charter of the United Nations." *Id.* The discourse concerns the extent to which all treaties can be understood to be coerced by the underlying positions of power. This arises in abstract discussions of the binding force of peace treaties and the mitigation of economic coercion. *See* Parry, *The Law of Treaties*, in MANUAL OF PUBLIC INTERNATIONAL LAW 175, 202 (M. Sørenson ed. 1968) (on peace treaties); Stone, *De Victoribus Victis: The International Law Commission and Imposed Treaties of Peace*, 8 VA. J. INT'L L. 356 (1967). Some claim to have resolved this by requiring that duress be legitimized by international law.

> Durch Art. 2 Abs. 4 SVN wurde (jedoch) jede zwischenstaatliche gewaltsame Selbsthilfe mit Ausnahme von Notwehr und Nothilfe gemäss Art. 51 SVN . . . verboten. Somit ist seither jeder Vertrag nichtig, der durch einen unter Verletzung der Grundsätze der USVNO gegen einen Staat ausgeübten Zwang herbeigeführt wurde.

A. VERDROSS, *supra* note 1, at 62-63. For a discussion on economic duress, see *id.* at 62 (economic and political duress not mitigating factors); *cf.* INSTITUT FÜR INTERNATIONALE BEZEIHUNGEN DER AKADEMIE FÜR STAATS UND RECHTSWISSENSCHAFT DER D.D.R., 1 VÖLKERRECHT 251 (H. Kröger ed. 1973) [hereinafter DDR LEHRBUCH]. "Unter 'Gewalt' [muss] auch jede Art politischer und insbesondere ökonomischer

conditions for treaty making.[11] Those who consider custom elaborate the psychological and physical prerequisites to treating mere habit as "custom." They talk about how frequently a norm must be respected, and by whom, before it becomes a customary norm.[12]

Those who consider both major sources likewise elaborate the condi-

Zwangsanwendung . . . [verstanden werden]." *Id.*

11. One of the most important doctrines abstractly limiting the ambit of treaty law concerns the possibility of reservations. As enshrined by the Vienna Convention, *supra* note 5, (Articles 19-23), reservation doctrine blends a "contractual conception of the absolute integrity of the treaty as adopted" (I. BROWNLIE, *supra* note 1, at 605-06) with a deference to the "purpose and *raison d'être* of the convention" (Reservations to the Convention on Genocide, 1951 I.C.J. 21 (Advisory Opinion of May 28)). For an analysis of three modes of discourse about reservations to multilateral treaties, see Koh, *Reservations to Multilateral Treaties: How International Legal Doctrine Reflects World Vision*, 23 HARV. INT'L L.J. 71 (1982); *see also* Mendelson, *Reservations to the Constitution of International Organizations*, 45 BRIT. Y.B. INT'L L. 137 (1971); Sinclair, *Vienna Conference on the Law of Treaties*, 19 INT'L & COMP. L.Q. 47, 53-60 (1970); Reports of the Commission to the General Assembly, U.N. Doc. A/6309/Rev.1, *reprinted in* [1966] 2 Y.B. INT'L LAW COMM'N 169, 205, U.N. Doc. A/CN.4/SER.A/1966/Add.1 [hereinafter Reports of the Commission].

12. Formerly, for example, it was maintained that only an "immemorial" practice could give rise to a customary rule. Virally, *supra* note 1, at 131. This was slowly eroded. A classic statement of the prerequisite practice required only "practice over a considerable period of time." Hudson, *supra* note 4, at 26. Modern discourse prefers other factors, as indicated in the now famous statement of the I.C.J. in the *North Sea Continental Shelf Cases*; "[a]n indispensable requirement would be that within the period in question, short though it might be, State practice, including that of States whose interests are specially affected, should have been both extensive and virtually uniform." North Sea Continental Shelf Cases (Ger. v. Den., Ger. v. Neth.) 1969 I.C.J. 2, 43 (Judgment of Feb. 20). Some authors suggest that the time element has become fully irrelevant. *See, e.g.*, Cheng, *United Nations Resolutions on Outer Space: "Instant" International Customary Law?*, 5 INDIAN J. INT'L. L. 23, 35 (1965) (coining term "instant customary law"); *see also* Baxter, *Treaties and Custom*, 129 RECUEIL DES COURS 25, 44 (1970). "If all States were today to declare that the State of law is that foreign States are not entitled to immunity in national courts, that would be the law, even though it had theretofore been acknowledged that the law is just the opposite." *Id.* The progressive abandonment of the time element has led to a focus on how many states, or, more accurately, *which* states must participate to create custom. *See infra* note 72; E. MENZEL & K. IPSEN, *supra* note 2, at 81 ("derjenigen Staaten . . . die ein besonderes Interesse . . . [an der betreffenden Norm] haben.") Each of these attempts at abstract delimitation contained an element of deference to the consent of underlying sovereigns or registry of already binding norms and one of norm creation. This is most clearly seen in the discourse about the states which must participate. It relies upon a vision either of the relative importance of various states or of the nature of the norm being created. That each strand depended upon the other has been recognized by those who suggest that this discourse has failed in its attempt to delimit custom independently of the content of the norms themselves on the basis either of practice or sovereign intention. *See, e.g.*, A. D'AMATO, *supra* note 1, at 92.

> A more difficult question, insisted upon by many writers, relates to the number of acts (or restraints) necessary to satisfy the material element of custom formation. However, such an inquiry is misleading. There is no metaphysically precise (such as "seventeen repetitions") or vague (such as "in the Court's discretion") answer possible. States simply do not organize their behavior along absolute

tions under which treaties and customs cease to be sources of international law, due to abrogation,[13] denunciation,[14] changed circumstances (*rebus sic stantibus*),[15] or subsequent custom.[16] When discussing

> lines. There is no international "constitution" specifying when acts become law. Rather, states resort to international law in claim-conflict situations. In such instances, counsel for either side will attempt to cite *as many acts as possible.*

Id. (emphasis in original).

13. The abstract discourse about the replacement of the old custom with new perenially oscillates between an approach which would imagine practice and sovereign authority to create and merely to recognize norms. A. D'AMATO, *supra* note 1, at 97.

> Unquestionably customary law has changed over the years, and thus any theory must incorporate the possibility of change into its concept of custom. In particular, an "illegal" act by a state contains the seeds of a new legality. When a state violates an existing rule of customary international law, it undoubtedly is "guilty" of an illegal act, but the illegal act itself becomes a disconfirmatory instance of the underlying rule. The next state will find it somewhat easier to disobey the rule, until eventually a new line of conduct will replace the original rule by a new rule.

Id. Although one writer has suggested that "[t]he Vienna Convention prescribes a certain presumption as to the validity and continuance in force of a treaty," I. BROWNLIE, *supra* note 1, at 496, abrogation (termination by all parties) is possible if the treaty so provides (Vienna Convention, art. 54, *supra* note 5) in an abstract provision about validity of its own, by consent of all parties (article 54) or by the conclusion of a later treaty (article 59). Discourse about these doctrines, while independent of the substance of the treaty itself, blends a consensual theory, which relies upon a vision of underlying sovereign authority, with a justice-based "nature of the obligation" theory, which relies upon a vision of the limits of consent. *See* 1 C. ROUSSEAU, *supra* note 6, at 206-07; Simma, *Reflections on Article 62 of the Vienna Convention on the Law of Treaties and its Background in General International Law*, 2 ÖSTERREICHISCHE ZEITSCHRIFT FÜR ÖFFENTLICHES RECHT [ÖZÖR] 5 (1970).

14. The denunciation doctrine limits and justifies unilateral abrogation. *See supra* note 13. Denunciation is permitted if the treaty expressly or impliedly so provides (Vienna Convention, *supra* note 5, at arts. 54, 56) or if another party materially breaches. The discourse again blends a consensual strand, relying upon a vision of sovereignty, with a "material" breach of a provision "essential to the accomplishment of the object or purpose of the treaty" (article 60), relying upon a vision of implied consent. *See* A. DAVID, THE STRATEGY OF TREATY TERMINATION (1975); B. SINHU, UNILATERAL DENUNCIATION OF TREATY BECAUSE OF PRIOR VIOLATIONS BY OTHER PARTY (1966); Briggs, *Unilateral Denunciation of Treaties*, 68 AM. J. INT'L L. 51 (1974); *see also* Nahlik, *supra* note 6, at 736-56 (examining the development of the relevant provisions of the Vienna Convention).

15. The doctrine of "fundamental change of circumstances" has become embodied in Article 62 of the Vienna Convention. Few issues were as strongly debated as the inclusion of this cause in the Convention. Fervent supporters of the doctrine suggested that it constituted an implied restriction to the binding force of any treaty which could contribute to the stability of agreements. Lyssitzyn, *Stability and Change: Unilateral Denunciation or Suspension of Treaties by Reason of Changed Circumstances*, 61 AM. SOC'Y INT'L L. PROC. 186 (1967). Opponents of the doctrine argued that it would undermine the stability of consensual agreements. Nahlik, *supra* note 6, at 748; *see also* Poch de Caviedes, *De la clause "rebus sic stantibus" à la clause de revision dans les conventions internationales*, 118 RECUEIL DES COURS 109, 138-39 (1966) (in the absence of an automatic decision by an impartial organ on all the issues involved, the *clausula* is open to abuse as a handy means of avoiding compliance with burdensome treaty obligations).

sources of law not included in the Article 38 list, such as the acts of international institutions, what seems to need explaining is whether they fit within the classic forms.[17]

---

16. *See supra* note 12. Commentators agree that custom can overrule itself. The question is when. Discourse considers the relative thresholds which abstract components of custom creation (duration, frequency, etc.) must overcome to change previous custom. *See* E. MENZEL & K. IPSEN, *supra* note 2, at 83 (statement of the classic position); *see also* Akehurst, *supra* note 1, at 19 (developing "a very strong presumption against *change* in the law" and a weaker presumption against formulation of new custom). "In particular, a great quantity of practice is needed to overturn existing rules of customary law. The better established a rule is, the greater the quantity of practice to overturn it." *Id.* [footnotes omitted].

17. Some commentators suggest that the acts of certain international institutions, particularly resolutions of the U.N. General Assembly, are binding. Their justifications generally assimilate these acts to more traditional sources either by suggesting that similar thresholds of consent or intention are met or by indicating that while such resolutions may not themselves be authoritative, they are constitutive of more traditional sources; particularly of custom. For support of the first sort, see J. CASTAÑEDA, LEGAL EFFECTS OF UN RESOLUTIONS 2-21 (1964) (categorizing diverse resolutions to systematize the "extraordinarily complex" law-creating function of the UN; concluding that "internal" resolutions, "determinations" concerning facts, and resolutions relying upon "external" legal foundations such as treaties or "declarations" are binding because sufficient intention is present); *see also* G. TUNKIN, THEORY OF INTERNATIONAL LAW 162-76 (W. Butler trans. 1974). In general, the Soviet international law literature views resolutions of international organizations as a source of international law. Tunkin adds, however:

> [t]o say . . . that the resolutions of international organizations are sources of international law if they have been recognized by a state in no way defines the place of these resolutions in the process of forming norms of international law. . . . [A] norm of international law results . . . only when there is a concordance of the wills of states relating to recognition of a particular rule as a norm of international law.

Id. at 163-64; *see also* Falk, *supra* note 1, at 784 (suggesting that there is a "rather indefinite line that separates *binding* from *non-binding* norms governing international behavior"). "Thus the formal limitations of status, often stressed by international lawyers, may not prevent resolutions of the General Assembly, or certain of them, from acquiring a normative status in international life." *Id.* Falk, *supra*, justifies this binding force by asserting:

> The degree of authoritativeness that a *particular* resolution will acquire depends upon a number of contextual factors, including the expectations governing the extent of permissible behavior, the extent and quality of the consensus, and the degree to which effective power is mobilized to implement the claims posited in a resolution."

Id. at 786 (emphasis added). For support of the second sort, maintaining that UN resolutions function as contributors to the formation of conventional sources, see Virally, *supra* note l, at 162; A. VERDROSS & B. SIMMA, *supra* note 4, at 329-32; R. HIGGINS, *supra* note 1, at 5 ("Resolutions of the Assembly are not *per se* binding: though those rules of general international law which they may embody are binding on member states, with or without the help of the resolution. But the body of resolutions as a whole, taken as indications of a general customary law, undoubtedly provide a rich source of evidence." (footnote omitted)); Panel Discussion, *The Effect of U.N. Resolutions on Emerging Legal Norms*, 1979 AM. SOC. INT'L L. PROC. 300 (an informative discussion concluding that the legal power of UN resolutions is not due to their being binding *per se*, but rather to their substantial influence upon the development of inter-

Such an inquiry might consider the sense in which U.N. resolutions are constitutive of custom or interpretively derivative of the Charter treaty.[18] There seems to be some hesitation about simply adding another source to the list.

The important thing about these inquiries into the scope and meaning of the sources considered is the pervasive attempt to delimit boundary conditions for the category in an abstract way, independent of the particular content of the norms whose source is being considered. The sense that it is important to elaborate a theoretical boundary which has an on-off quality reflects the shared understanding among those doing this work that the abstract categories will control the content of the norms, rather than merely register them. Some of the most modern treatises acknowledge this explicitly by pairing their abstract discus-

---

national law via more traditional and acknowledged sources such as customary law). Those who oppose the treatment of resolutions as *sui generis* sources of law do so on similar grounds. *See, e.g.*, Virally, *supra* note 1, at 160-62; A. VERDROSS & B. SIMMA, *supra* note 4, at 329-33; *see also* J. MÜLLER, VERTRAUENSSCHUTZ IM VÖLKERRECHT 250 (1971); Sloan, *The Binding Force of a "Recommendation" of the General Assembly of the United Nations*, 25 BRIT. Y.B. INT'L L. 1 (1948):

> There are circumstances under which a resolution of the General Assembly produces important juridical consequences and possesses binding legal force. As a general rule, however, resolutions, for lack of intention or of mandatory power in the Assembly, do not create binding obligations in positive law . . . .
>
> Although a large majority supports the view that mere recommendations have no *legal force*, the opinion also prevails that [they] possess *moral force* and should, as such, assert great influence. . . .
>
> The exact nature of this moral force is not easy to define . . . . [However], the view that the expression "moral force" has no positive content and is merely a diplomatic way of indicating that there is no legal, i.e., binding, force cannot be accepted.

Id. at 31-32; *see also* Gross, *The International Court of Justice and the United Nations*, 120 RECUEIL DES COURS 313 (1967).

> In regard to some resolutions members may record their view that they recognize the principles contained in them as constituting or reflecting international law . . . . Some resolutions like General Assembly resolution 1514(XV) may be stepping stones towards a principle of international law. . . .
>
> A resolution or declaration of the General Assembly, putting it at its highest, could be regarded as *opinio juris*, but . . . unless it results in uniform conduct could not be regarded as a rule of law.

Id. at 375-76. There is widespread consensus that such resolutions as these admitting states to membership, promulgating rules of procedure, or establishing subsidiary bodies are legally binding on all members because of the degree of consent which they represent. *See, e.g.*, W. FRIEDMANN, THE CHANGING STRUCTURE OF INTERNATIONAL LAW 139 (1964); Fitzmaurice, *The Law and Procedure of the International Court of Justice, 1951-1954: Questions of Jurisdiction, Competence and Procedure*, 34 BRIT. Y.B. INT'L L. 1, 3-7 (1958); Johnson, *The Effect of Resolutions of the General Assembly of the United Nations*, 32 BRIT. Y.B. INT'L L. 97, 121-22 (1955-56); Tammes, *Decisions of International Organs as a Source of Law*, 94 RECUEIL DES COURS 265, 316 (1958).

18. *See supra* note 17 and accompanying text.

sions of sources with a distinct discussion of the "reality" or "force and effect" of the sources which they have abstractly elaborated.[19]

In addition to defining abstractly the boundaries of the sources under consideration, the scholarly literature considers limits of various sorts to the force of each source. For example, scholars consider the municipal effects of international norms,[20] the force of treaties upon non-signatories[21]

---

19. *See, e.g.*, B. WESTON, R. FALK & A. D'AMATO, INTERNATIONAL LAW AND WORLD ORDER 80-101, 116, *passim* (1980) (the discussion devoted to "sources" is followed by a subchapter entitled "The Reality of International Law" which considers how and why states obey each type of international legal norm). The term "reality of international law" was popularized by Jessup, *The Reality of International Law*, 18 FOREIGN AFF. 244 (1940); *see also* Friedmann, *General Course in Public International Law*, 127 RECUEIL DES COURS 39, 76 (1969).

20. One of the most abstract of sources discourse concerns the general relationship between international and municipal law. This is done both generally, as an inquiry into their relative authority and separation, and specifically, as an inquiry into the process by which an international norm can be imported into municipal law by, for example, transformation, adoption, or execution. Both types of inquiry proceed independently of the norms themselves. Both blend reliance upon a vision of pre-existing national sovereignties which must be internationally registered or recognized with reliance upon a region of pre-existing international sovereignties which must be municipally registered or constituted. *See* B. WESTON, R. FALK & A. D'AMATO, *supra* note 19, at 163-89 (1980) (providing examples of this discourse). On the approach of the Vienna Convention, see Hostert, *Droit International et Droit Interne dans la Convention de Vienne sur le Droit des Traités du 23 Mai 1969*, 1 ANNUAIRE FRANÇAIS DU DROIT INTERNATIONAL 92 (1969). For a discussion on monism and dualism, see 1 C. ROUSSEAU, *supra* note 6, at 37-48 (criticizing each doctrine by relying upon the other); *see also* E. MENZEL & K. IPSEN, *supra* note 2 (concluding that a modified endorsement of both theories is possible); Virally, *supra* note 1, at 165-71 (surveying both positions). For a discussion on municipal incorporation of international law, see I. BROWNLIE, *supra* note 1, at 45-50.

21. Conventional doctrine provided that "[a] treaty does not create either obligations or rights for a third state without its consent." (Vienna Convention on the Law of Treaties, *supra* note 5, at art. 34). While assent to benefits may be implied if "the contrary is not indicated," burdens must be expressly accepted in writing. *Id.* at art. 35. The strands of reliance upon a consensual vision of pre-existing sovereign authority and upon a justice based vision of the authority of the community are displayed in discourse about the treatment of multilateral treaties as constituting or expressing customary international law. Argument approving and disapproving the entry into custom of such treaties relies alternatively upon notions of internationalized consent and decentralized justice. All these discussions proceed independently of the content of either the treaty or customary regime. *See* A. D'AMATO, *supra* note 1, at Ch. 5 (unqualifiedly supporting the possibility that such treaties are binding as custom either because they create custom or because they reflect it). Baxter, *infra* note 70, illustrates several trends, including both treaties as evidence of custom: "My thesis is that . . . 'general practice' or international custom may be found in treaties and that treaties may therefore exercise their effects, *qua* evidence of customary international law, upon non-parties." *Id.* at 51. Or later: "If certain treaties both bind the parties and form evidence of customary international law, they will be the instruments of harmonization of the law on a widespread basis. . . . The simplicity of the use of a treaty rule and its widespread acceptance by others makes it a convenient short-cut for non-parties," *id.* at 102, and treaties as constitutive of custom: "The rule of a treaty becomes general inter-

and successor states[22] or of custom upon new states[23] or those beyond

national law in the same way that a practice accompanied by the necessary *opinio juris* may come to dominate customary international law." *Id.* at 103. Baxter concludes that there is an interplay between codification and progressive development. *Id.* at 41; *cf.* Akehurst, *supra* note 51, at 42-49, 53 (requiring intent to transform treaty into custom). "The better view would appear to be that treaties, like other forms of State practice must be accompanied by *opinio juris* in order to create customary law." *Id.* at 44. Or later: "Sometimes a treaty which is not accompanied by *opinio juris* may nevertheless be imitated in subsequent practice; but in such cases it is the subsequent practice (accompanied by *opinio juris*), and not the treaty, which creates customary law." *Id.* at 53. Denmark and the Netherlands sought to combine these elements in a progressive approach requiring all of them in the *North Sea Continental Shelf Cases*:

> "[T]he process of the definition and consolidation of the emerging customary law took place through the work of the International Law Commission, the reaction of governments to that work and the proceedings of the Geneva Conference;" and this emerging customary law became "crystallized in the adoption of the Continental Shelf Convention by the Conference."

North Sea Continental Shelf Cases (W. Ger. v. Den.; W. Ger. v. Neth.) 1969 I.C.J. 3, 38 (Judgment of Feb. 20). For the Soviet viewpoint emphasizing consent, see North Sea Continental Shelf Cases, *supra*, at 154 (diss. op. Koretsky, J.). In Soviet views of international law, treaties take paramount precedence over customary international law as they rest upon the express agreement of states. The dissenting opinion of Judge Koretsky is particularly important for the weight he attaches to the development of "the general principles of the law of the continental shelf," which he found to have taken shape even before the Geneva Conference of 1958. *Id.* at 158 (diss. op. Koretsky, J.). However, this position stands in contrast to Tunkin's view that conventional and customary rules of international law are created on a basis of agreement and that "to become a norm of international law of universal application [a customary norm of limited application] should be recognized by all the states." *See* Tunkin, *Coexistence and International Law*, 95 RECUEIL DES COURS 1, 18 (1958); *cf.* Rozakis, *Treaties and Third States: A Study in the Reinforcement of the Consensual Standards in International Law*, 35 ZAÖRV 1, 1-80 (1975).

> [D]ue to the increasing emphasis upon individual consent, custom is becoming more and more identified with treaties. In fact it is almost becoming as voluntarist a process as a treaty is; and thus, easy inferences of customary law-creation are replaced by rigid requirements of proof. It is therefore evident that custom and treaties are approaching each other and that the former is losing its relative advantage over the latter which lay in its being a less voluntarist process of law-creation.
>
> At the same time, however, consensualism may rejuvenate custom and make it viable in the long run. In an international system where treaties will unquestionably play the role of the most usual tool of international legislation, custom may prove very valuable by playing the equally important role of assisting, as a universally recognized process, changes of law in all cases where the inelasticity of written law does not allow rapid modifications to cope with new needs.

Id. at 39-40; *see also* Cahier, *Le Problème des effets des traités à l'égard des états tiers*, 143 RECEUIL DES COURS 589, 589, 604 (1974) (discussing that, in principle, treaties affect only the contracting parties and doubting that in the absence of conventional mechanisms, silence of a state could be considered as consent).

22. The Vienna Convention on the Law of Treaties leaves the question of the effect of state succession on treaty obligations expressly open. Vienna Convention, *supra* note 5, at art. 73. There are two opinions. Some believe that successor states are not bound. *See, e.g.*, Castren, *Obligations of States Arising from the Dismemberment of Another State*, 73 ZAÖRV 753, 754 (1951) ("To the succeeding states the treaties concluded by the former state are *res inter alios acta*"); MCNAIR, *supra* note 1, at 601 ("Newly

established states which cannot fairly be said to involve political continuity with any predecessor, start with a clean slate in the matter of treaty obligations"); E. MENZEL & K. IPSEN, *supra* note 2, at 189. These writers generally emphasize the consensual nature of treaty obligations but make an exception for treaties which must remain reliable as a matter of international stability, such as those establishing boundaries, or riparian rights. *See* 2 D. O'CONNELL, STATE SUCCESSION IN MUNICIPAL LAW AND INTERNATIONAL LAW 12-23, 273-291 (1967); O. UDOKANG, SUCCESSION OF NEW STATES TO INTERNATIONAL TREATIES (1972); Virally, *supra* note 1, at 277. Others hold that while a new state may have a qualified right to repudiate "unequal" provisions, the treaty remains binding to take into account the legitimate interests of the other state. These authors, while emphasizing the systemic importance of the reliability of treaties, indicate the importance of an exception for provisions to which the new state could not consent consistent with its identity or its purpose in the succession struggle. These two aspects of the discourse blend reliance upon consent and external notions of international justice differently. *See, e.g.*, L. CHEN, STATE SUCCESSION RELATING TO UNEQUAL TREATIES (1974). Chen agrees with the general position of the commentators that "there is no single answer to the general questions of state succession to treaties," *id.* at 232, but advocates a substantive investigation of the "unequalness" of each treaty. "In an unequal treaty the disparity of the power bases of the contracting parties is translated into unequal rights or obligations for the contracting parties." *Id.* After this determination, "[a]ccording to contemporary international law an unequal treaty is voidable, and thus it should be a legitimate reason for nonsuccession." *Id.* at 235. This approach, in Chen's view, ensures that "[p]roper treaty relations can thus be established among the predecessor, successor, and other concerned states to redress past grievances and achieve international equity and justice." *Id.* at 241. For a contrasting emphasis on the consent element in the unequal treaty exception, see O. UDOKANG, *supra* at 487-508. "While a new state may be reluctant to assume those treaty obligations which are not in conformity with its basic interests, or with the essential object of its independence, subrogation to certain other rights and obligations under treaties concluded on its behalf by the predecessor may well prove indispensable not only to the progressive development of its domestic economy, but to its very participation in international life." *Id.* at 492-93. Udokang thus supports Chen's position regarding unequal treaties, on the ground that they are regarded by new states as "void *ab initio*, on the ground that they are calculated to enshrine and protect the 'predatory interests' of the colonial powers." *Id.* at 220-21. The extreme form of the neo-universalist position holds that all treaties would devolve *ipso jure* upon a new state, to protect systemic stability while any new state might denounce the treaty if it was contrary to its basic interests, to protect its consensual authority. *See* C. JENKS, THE COMMON LAW OF MANKIND 94 (1958); 2 D. O'CONNELL, *supra* at 23-25. The Soviet position, as expressed by Korovin, advocates devolution of all treaties to protect the consensual nature of the obligations with an exception for unequal treaties on grounds of equity:

> Every international agreement is the expression of an established social order, with a certain balance of collective interests. So long as this social order endures, such treaties as remain in force, following the principle of *pacta sunt servanda*, must be scrupulously observed. But if in the storm of a social cataclysm, one class replaces the other at the helm of the state, for the purpose of reorganization not only of the economic ties, but the governing principles of internal and of external politics, the old agreements in so far as they reflect the preexisting order of things, destroyed by the revolution became null and void. To demand of a people at last freed of the yoke of centuries the payment of debts contracted by their oppressors for the purpose of holding them in slavery would be contrary to those elementary principles of equity which are due to all nations in their relations with each other.

U.S. Dept. of State, in 2 M. WHITEMAN, *supra* note 1, at 777. Many modern authors have abandoned the discourse of abstract solution to this controversy in favor of a

the region who may not have participated in its formulation.[24] Along

---

description of the varied state practice. *See, e.g.*, Meron, *International Practice as to Succession of New States to Treaties of Their Predecessors*, 10 INDIAN J. INT'L L. 459 (1970):

> International practice as to succession to treaties is not sufficiently abundant and uniform to permit an attempt at generalization . . . . The practice is more dictated by public policy of the respective states than by any legally accepted principle . . . . That does not mean that a state may be safely and freely allowed to avail itself of the advantages of the treaty when it suits it to do so and repudiate it when its performance is onerous.

Id. at 476. Meron proposes that "we have to follow a pragmatic, problem-oriented, step-by-step approach. Each case has to be scrutinized carefully taking into account a number of factors." *Id.* at 477. Although Meron suggests reference to the "nature of the treaty" among other factors, he retains the distanced and abstract discourse which would determine a hierarchy of "natures" before it would allow the treaty to determine its own scope. The apparent distance from substance of this aspect of sources doctrine has almost been overcome as its reliance either upon a vision of interests or of justice has been exposed. For further development of this tendency, see Keith, *Succession to Bilateral Treaties by Seceding States*, 61 AM. J. INT'L L. 521, 546 (1967) (holding that the solution depends upon "(a) the nature and function of the treaty in question; (b) the method of secession; and (c) the circumstances of the conclusion of the treaty . . . . The first factor is obviously of great importance. . . ."); *see also* U.S. State Dept., in 2 M. WHITEMAN, *supra* note 1, at 993.

23. *See infra* notes 85-88 and accompanying text. The unanimous opinion of Western commentators is that new states are bound by custom upon their coming into being as states. A. D'AMATO, *supra* note 1, at 191-93; E. MENZEL & K. IPSEN, *supra* note 2, at 82. This position is usually based on a vision of the communal nature of statehood. It is usually paired with an exception should new states not consent. *See, e.g.*, Akehurst, *supra* note 1, at 28 ("[T]he opposition of new states to old customs is bound to cast doubt on the customs"). The Soviet bloc theorists, by contrast, argue that because custom is consensual, new states are not bound without their consent. *See, e.g.*, G. TUNKIN, THEORY OF INTERNATIONAL LAW 127-33 (W. Butler trans. 1974). This consent-based theory is usually combined with a willingness to imply consent when the new state begins to act like a state on the grounds of reciprocal fairness. *See* H. BOKORNÉ-SZEGŐ, NEW STATES AND INTERNATIONAL LAW (1970).

24. The idea of regional or bilateral custom is generally justified on the basis of consent, or at least is seen as more directly connected to state consent than general custom. *See* D'Amato, *The Concept of Special Custom in International Law*, 63 AM. J. INT'L L. 211 (1969). D'Amato argues that:

> the requirement of a showing of consent is a mistaken view . . . because of a widespread failure to draw a basic distinction between special (or "local" or "particular") customary international law and general customary international law. . . . The stringent requirements of proof of consent in [the three cases decided by the World Court] thus do not apply to the large body of general norms of international law binding upon all states, but rather apply only in similar cases of "special" custom.

Id. at 211-12. Consequently, unlike general customary norms, special custom seems binding only upon those who have participated in its creation. This seems to be the practice of the I.C.J.

> The Party which relies on a custom of this kind must prove that this custom is established in such a manner that it has become binding on the other Party. The . . . Government must prove that the rule invoked by it is in accordance with a constant and uniform usage practised by the states in question. . . .

Asylum Case (Colom. v. Peru) 1950 I.C.J. 266, 276 (Judgment of Nov. 20). *See* Falk, *supra* note 1, at 782 (discussing the idea that "some tangible evidence of consent on

this vein, the literature has considered the hierarchical relationship among the various Article 38 sources.[25]

---

the part of the state that is bound" is required). Other commentators, however, emphasizing the non-consensual nature of custom as opposed to treaty, argue that a custom which has grown up among some of the states belonging to a well-defined group is binding upon all members of that group. Just as the consensual position was willing to imply consent in some cases, so commentators of this persuasion are willing to except members of the group who opposed the custom. *See* H. THIRLWAY, INTERNATIONAL CUSTOMARY LAW AND CODIFICATION 136-37 (1972) (admitting that it is difficult for the non-consensual approach "to ascertain exactly what are the boundaries of the 'community' to which the custom in question is to be treated as applying," but charging that "[t]he view that local custom is binding only on states which have expressly agreed to it is fundamentally an assertion of the view that custom is based upon acceptance."); *see also* Akehurst, *supra* note 1, at 29-30 (discussing this view).

25. The relative authority of various sources is most often discussed in contrasting treaties and custom. Advocates of all logically available positions exist. For the proposition that there is no hierarchy, see NGUYEN QUOC DINH, P. DAILLER & A. PELLET, *supra* note 2, at 104 (source equality reflects social equality): "En effet, à l'absence de hiérarchie organique dans la société internationale correspond l'absence de toute hiérarchie entre les sources"; E. MENZEL & K. IPSEN, *supra* note 2, at 43 (source equality flows from textual equality); *see also* Barile, *La structure de l'ordre juridique international*, 161 RECUEIL DES COURS 9 (1978). "[L]e rapport entre droit international spontané (ou de la conscience) et droit international écrit (nous nous référions justement aux accords dont nous discutons dans ce chapitre) ne devait pas être celui d'une subordination du second au premier mais celui d'une interdépendance réciproque."
Id. at 92. For the proposition that treaty is superior to custom, see Right of Passage over Indian Territory (Port. v. India) 1960 I.C.J. 6, 90 (Judgment of Apr. 12) (Quintana, J. dissenting); Akehurst, *The Hierarchy of the Sources of International Law*, 47 BRIT. Y.B. INT'L L. 273 (1974-1975) (summarizing the positions of other authorities and the differing results which occur when a treaty is more or less specific than a rule of custom, earlier or later in time, intended to overrule, or be overruled, and other similar conflicts). For the proposition that treaty is inferior to custom, see C. PARRY, THE SOURCES AND EVIDENCES OF INTERNATIONAL LAW 53 (1968). "Treaties, then, are binding because there is a rule of customary international law to that effect." *Id.*; *see also* Fitzmaurice, *Some Problems Regarding the Formal Sources of International Law*, in SYMBOLAE VERZIJL: PRESENTÉES AU PROFESSEUR J.H.W. VERZIJL 153, 157 (1958) (treaties are not a source of law, but rather a source of obligation under the law); *see also* L. OPPENHEIM, *supra* note 1, at 28:

> But it must be emphasized that, whereas custom is the original source of International Law, treaties are a source the power of which derives from custom. For the fact that treaties can stipulate rules of international conduct at all is based on the customary rule of the Law of Nations that treaties are binding upon the contracting parties.

Id.; *see also* 1 P. GUGGENHEIM, TRAITÉ DE DROIT INTERNATIONAL PUBLIC 57 (1953); G. SCELLE, MANUEL ÉLEMENTAIRE DE DROIT INTERNATIONAL PUBLIC 577 (1948). Because Article 38 lists "treaty" before "custom" in enumerating the sources of law, some commentators have suggested that if this does not create a hierarchy it suggests at least a procedural order in which sources are to be examined to see whether they can dispose of a case at hand. In a given case, the judge should begin by seeking applicable rules of treaty law, turning to custom or ultimately to general principles when treaty does not "dispose" of the case. This approach is said to combine the rules of *lex specialis* (since treaties are usually more specific) and *lex posterior* (since treaties are often more recent). There are also commentators who conclude exactly the opposite. *See* E. MENZEL & K. IPSEN, *supra* note 2, at 94:

> Die Rechte und Pflichten der Staaten sind in erster Linie durch verträgliche Ver-

In addition to considering the abstract hierarchy of treaty and custom at great length,[26] the sources literature devotes a great deal of energy to the idea that the power of states to make treaties runs out when it confronts a supercustomary norm of *jus cogens*.[27] Likewise, and far

> einbarungen festgelegt. . . . Es steht den Staaten frei, untereinander Regeln zu vereinbaren, die von Normen des Gewohnheitsrechts abweichen. Verträge schränken insoweit den Geltungsbereich des Völkergewohnheitsrechts und der allgemeinen Rechtsgrundsätze ein. Man kann folglich *in dem dargestellten sinne* von einem Vorrang der Verträge vor anderen Quellen des Völkerrechts sprechen. Dadurch ist allerdings nicht ausgeschlossen, dass umgekehrt verträgliche Regelungen durch Gewohnheitsrecht beseitigt werden.

Id.; *see also* 1 H. LAUTERPACHT, INTERNATIONAL LAW 87 (1970). "When a controversy arises between two or more States with regard to a matter regulated by a treaty, it is natural that the parties should invoke and that the adjudicating agency should apply, in the first instance, the provisions of the treaty in question." *Id.*; *cf.* Jenks, *The Conflict of Law Making Treaties*, BRIT. Y.B. INT'L L. 401, 451-53 (1953) (even in the situation of a conflict between law-making treaties, the first approach to resolution should be based on an analysis of the provisions of the treaties, aided by the presumptions and rules of construction that have developed about treaty interpretation). Jenks considers that these presumptions are similar to those that "exist in respect of statutes and contracts, and the applicability of the same principles to treaties was recognized at an early stage in the development of international law." *Id.* at 451. In the final analysis, Jenks adopts a legalistic stance, seeing the avoidance of controversy lying in the domain of "considerable improvement in the technical legal equipment. . . ." *Id.* at 452. The perspective which is taken to the hierarchy of treaty and custom depends in part upon the understanding which a writer has of the power of consent and of the extent to which each source enshrines consent. McDougal and Reisman describe this phenomenon:

> The initial itemization of "international conventions" prompts some commentators to champion agreements as an important "direct, conscious, and purposive" modality for law creation, offering the closest approach to the deliberate and explicit formulations of legislative processes in national societies. From this perspective, agreements may be both "formal" for the parties and others, and "material" or "evidentiary" sources of the expectations about authority and control which comprise customary law. Other commentators, however, find it difficult to understand how agreements, which in some versions of inherited international myth are supposed to "bind" only the immediate parties, can create "obligation" for third parties. Posing the problem as a quest for "consent" rather than for empirical expectations about the probable course of future decision, such commentators distinguish between the creation of "law" and the creation of "obligations," and insist that even agreements can derive their "binding" quality only from "a rule of customary law to that effect." This would appear greatly to subordinate agreements to custom as an exclusive law creating modality.

McDougal & Reisman, *supra* note 1, at 261 [footnotes omitted]. For a general treatment of the relative authority of other sources, see Akehurst, *supra* note 1, *passim*.

26. *See supra* notes 6-8.

27. The doctrine of *jus cogens* or *peremptory norm* is defined by the Vienna Convention on the Law of Treaties quite concretely as "a norm accepted and recognized by the international community of states as a whole as a norm from which no derogation is permitted and which can be modified only by a subsequent norm of general international law having the same character." Vienna Convention, *supra* note 5, at art. 53. A more general definition is provided by A. VERDROSS & B. SIMMA, *supra* note 4, at 264; "Normen, die im gemeinsamen Interesse aller Staaten gelten und tief im allgemeinen Rechtsbewusstsein verankert sind." *Id.*; *see also* Verdross, *Ius Dispositivum and Jus*

more often, custom or treaty norms run out when they contravene certain other, superior norms of *jus dispositivum*.[28] These doctrines are disconnected from the content of the particular norms of custom which overrule treaty and *vice versa*. Although commentators often remark that no one has ever "found" a norm of *jus cogens*,[29] some hierarchy seems to need to be established in order to develop an internally coher-

---

Cogens in International Law, 60 AM. J. INT'L L. 55 (1966); Lachs, *The Law of Treaties. Some General Reflections on the Report of the I.L.C.*, in RECUEIL D'ÉTUDES DE DROIT INTERNATIONAL EN HOMMAGE À PAUL GUGGENHEIM 391, 398 (1968).

28. *See supra* note 25 for general discourse about the hierarchical relations among sources. *Jus dispositivum* is discussed far less often than *jus cogens* in contemporary scholarship. Because it is thought to include all norms which are not *jus cogens*, and can therefore be changed by subsequent, more authoritative norms, its abstract dimensions are negatively implied by the myriad discussions of *jus cogens*. Most norms of treaty law are considered replaceable by subsequent agreement. Most customary norms can be replaced by subsequent custom. These possibilities are justified by more basic norms, such as "freedom to conclude treaties," which cannot be so changed. Paradoxically, the concentration of the literature upon *jus cogens* would be replaced by a concentration upon *jus dispositivum*, if the number of norms recognized as *jus cogens* increased. Then one would need to ask, in considering changing a treaty, if the specific norms were, in fact, *jus dispositivum*. The theoretical concentration upon the exceptional category thus reflects the concern of scholarship to delimit the sources of law abstractly. *See, e.g.*, Verdross, *supra* note 27, at 55 (discussing *jus dispositivum* and *jus cogens* in international law).

29. Some writers have tried to catalog norms of *jus cogens*. *See, e.g.*, Ago, *Droit des traités à la lumière de la Convention de Vienne*, 132 RECUEIL DES COURS 297, 324 (1971) (a somewhat less comprehensive survey than Whiteman); A. VERDROSS & B. SIMMA, *supra* note 4, at 265-66; Whiteman, *Jus Cogens in International Law with a Projected List*, 7 GA. J. INT'L & COMP. L. 609 (1977) (the most ambitious list to date). Most authors are far more sceptical that an example of *jus cogens* might be found. *See, e.g.*, Mann, *The Doctrine of Jus Cogens*, FESTSCHRIFT ULRICH SCHEUNER 399 (1973); Schwarzenberger, *The Problem of International Public Policy*, 18 CURRENT LEGAL PROBS. 191 (1965); 1 C. ROUSSEAU, *supra* note 6, at 150; J. SZTUCKI, JUS COGENS AND THE VIENNA CONVENTION ON THE LAW OF TREATIES 93 (1974) (concluding that his survey of modern practice "seems to justify the conclusion that there is not a single application of the concept of peremptory norms"). Sztucki dramatically separates the doctrinal discussion from practice, noting:

> the references to *jus cogens*, or to other similiar constructions, in . . . opinions . . . belong to the doctrine of international law rather than to practice, since the inter-state obligations remain unaffected by such opinions.
>
> All the known cases of recognition of certain norms as binding independent of the respective conventional obligations, as well as all the known cases of avoidance or nullification of treaties, touch, in fact, upon other matters than the category of *jus cogens*, and can be explained without any need of resorting to the concept of peremptory norms, unless one departs from a preconceived idea that peremptory norms should be looked for and arrived at at any price.
>
> . . . .
>
> Therefore, in the light of international practice, the question whether the concept of *jus cogens* has been "codified" or "progressively developed" in the [Vienna] Convention, may be answered only in the sense that there has been nothing to codify.

Id. at 94.

ent and sufficiently independent scheme of authority.[30] Otherwise, the scheme might produce equally authoritative norms among which one would then be obliged to choose on the basis of their content. These hierarchical discussions elaborate the relative authority of treaties or custom which are general or specific,[31] multilateral or bilateral,[32] universal or regional,[33] and earlier or later.[34]

The sense that hierarchy needs explaining, like the sense that the abstract boundaries of enumerated sources need elaboration, reveals

30. *See generally supra* note 25. In general, regardless of their content, conflicts among the three major sources (treaty, custom, and general principles) are discussed in terms of such abstractions as *lex posterior derogat legi priori*, *lex specialis derogat legi generali*, *lex superior derogat legi inferiori*, etc. *Jus cogens* comes top of the heap as the ultimate *lex superior*. *See supra* notes 44-45. Other sources (judicial decisions or the writings of publicists) are regarded as "subsidiary" to the big three. *See* Akehurst, *supra* note 25, at 280-81.

31. A specific norm is generally regarded as superior to a general rule, of either custom or treaty. It is unclear whether "specific" refers to the content of the norm, or to the size of the group whose consensus gave it force. Some basic principles overrule specific rules. Sometimes world custom could overrule regional custom, and multilateral obligations override bilateral. But sometimes the reverse is true. These issues are discussed in terms of the relative strength of the intention of those responsible and in terms of general systemic notions of justice. *See* Akehurst, *supra* note 1, at 31 (regional custom beats universal custom); Barile, *Structure de l'ordre juridique international*, 161 RECUEIL DES COURS 9 (1978); E. MENZEL & K. IPSEN, *supra* note 2, at 95 (discussing cases in which the *lex specialis* rule creates no clear hierarchy). *But cf.* 1 A. SERENI, DIRITTO INTERNAZIONALE 174 (1956) (arguing that a later general custom overrides a special earlier custom).

But in view of the strong presumption against changes in the law, see A. D'AMATO, *supra* note 1, at 60-61; Akehurst, *supra* note 1, at 19; Lauterpacht, *Sovereignty over Submarine Areas*, 27 BRIT. Y.B. INT'L L. 376, 393 (1950), this result would follow only if there was clear evidence that the parties to the special custom were applying the new general custom *inter se* and no longer applying the old special custom. *But cf.* G. TUNKIN, TEORIIA MEZHDUNARODNOGO PRAVA 504-05 (1970) (applying the principle of *lex specialis derogat generalis* to the relationship between the norms of socialist and general international law).

See also Osakwe, *Socialist International Law Revisited*, 66 AM. J. INT'L L. 596, 599 (1972): "Nothing in [the] general international law . . . precludes the existence of a local international legal order that would regulate relations between states belonging to the same regional (ideological) bloc." *Id.* at 597. Specifically on the conflict of special and general treaty obligations, see A. MCNAIR, *supra* note 1, at 218-24 (regarding this as a rule of interpretation, not authority, he emphasizes the parties' intent which he recognizes is complicated when a hierarchy among treaties with different parties must be constructed).

32. Bilateral treaties are often viewed as more specific than multilateral treaties. The general obligations of multilateral treaties, partly because they relate to third parties, and partly because the intention in ratifying them was to create fundamental obligations, can overrule or aid in the interpretation of bilateral treaties. *See supra* notes 25 & 31.

33. Usually universal custom is considered to be opposable by regional custom. *See supra* notes 25 & 31.

34. Unless the earlier norm was more specific (or more fundamental) the later norm controls. *See supra* notes 25 & 31.

the shared sense that sources discourse is meant to delimit abstractly and authoritatively the norms which bind states in such a way that they might remain free to establish and disagree about the content of those norms as their interests or a natural order might dictate. Discussions of both the extent and hierarchy of sources produce doctrines which do not rely on the content of the norms whose source they identify. Each of these types of discussion suggests that the problem which sources doctrine addresses is the abstract definition of the authoritative set of norms binding states.

II. ARGUMENT ABOUT THE SOURCES OF INTERNATIONAL LAW

International law about sources is more than a set of doctrinal boundaries and hierarchies. Sources doctrine is also a quite well worked out argumentative practice about the authority or "binding nature" of various legal instruments. The arguments which people make about the sources of international law—in treatises, articles, opinions, and so forth—are like the various doctrines which comprise the law of sources in that they define and limit what various sources mean and how they relate to one another in an abstract fashion. This abstract detachment from the content of the norms whose authority they delimit is also characteristic of arguments about the application of particular sources doctrines to particular fact situations.

In sources argument, one characteristically seeks to convince someone that a state which does not currently believe it to be in its interests to follow a given norm should do so anyway. Sources rhetoric provides two rhetorical or persuasive styles which we might call "hard" and "soft." A "hard" argument will seek to ground compliance in the "consent" of the state to be bound. A "soft" argument relies upon some extraconsensual notion of the good or the just. Of course there is no *a priori* reason to divide the "sources" of law, or the persuasive reasons for compliance into these two categories. Indeed, it is difficult to classify the various classic sources as either "hard" or "soft," and it seems intuitively obvious that fulfilling promises is an important dimension of justice and *vice versa*. Nevertheless, it turns out that arguments about sources doctrine often rhetorically contrast these two sets of ideas. It will be easier to analyze exemplary sources argument after considering the ways in which one might argue about sources doctrine in a somewhat stylized fashion. As I have defined them, hard and soft sources are mutually exclusive categories which together account for all possible sources that might be imagined. Hard sources are grounded in consent. Soft sources are grounded not in consent. Moreover, to be coherently grounded, a source may not be both. The point of a consent-based source is that it *binds*: that it is authoritative even when other considerations—including notions of the good—push an actor in another direction. The point of soft sources is that they are *authoritative*: that they bind even the state which does not imagine compliance to be in its interest—which does not consent. In a schematic and preliminary way, we can imagine the arguments which might be made on behalf of hard and soft sources in a world of autonomous states. Suppose that one sovereign (State 1) when invoking a norm against another (State 2) argues that the norm invoked is authoritative and binding because it is "hard." A hard source is binding because the state to be bound has agreed that it is binding, so that compliance will not threaten its autonomy. State 2 might make several responses. It might make a factual argument, claiming, for example, that it had not in fact agreed, or had agreed only subject to a condition which had not been fulfilled. Leaving these arguments aside for the moment (or imagining that they are resolved in favor of State 1), State 2 might attack the hard source directly. It might argue that if its consent is the basis for its being bound, it has changed its mind, or did not intend to consent in the first place.

These classic responses force State 1 to argue that such change is not permissible. The reasons offered may be many: because if everyone did, it would be a mess; because State 1 would not want its treaty partners to do so; because you just have to keep your word, etc. One might invoke a doctrinal expression of these conclusions such as *pacta sunt servanda*.

State 2, against whom the norm is being invoked, might respond that these norms or considerations have nothing to do with its consent. If they do, State 2 might simply reinvoke its initial objection that it does not *now* consent to this application or interpretation. Perhaps State 2 is willing in similar circumstances to let its treaty partners off as well, or finds the state of the system less important than its own release from this particular norm. In responding, State 2 has forced State 1 to shift gears and argue from some non-consensual perspective. To State 2, all hard sources have become soft sources in disguise.

Imagine, however, that State 1 originally argues from a soft perspective; claiming, for example, that the norm is binding on State 2 because it is in some sense just. State 1 might admit that it is arguing from a soft perspective, suggesting that without this norm the international system would not be "equitable" or "workable" or whatever soft codeword seems appropriate. State 2 might make a number of responses. It might argue about the meaning or application of this soft norm in this case, arguing, for example, that the system would be "just" or whatever, even if it were not bound. Leaving this response aside for the moment, or assuming that it is resolved in favor of the norm invoking state, State 2 might directly attack the soft source. It might assert that it has a different idea of softness, a different image of the system or of justice. Although the visions of softness which might proliferate in the ensuing argument might be patterned in some fashion, if we ignore for the moment the *content* of State 2's response, it seems predicated on the notion that the norm-invoker cannot convincingly invoke its *own* idea of softness. If State 2 is to be bound because of the "justness" of the norm, State 1 must have some way of defending the norm on that plane, without merely asserting power against State 2's sovereignty. Among equal sovereigns, "justice" must be negotiated, or voted to agreement. To State 2, all the soft arguments seem to have been hard arguments in disguise.

These hypothetical arguments reflect the relationship between hard and soft sources as well as their incompatibility and exclusivity. Although one cannot make both sets of arguments together, the proponent of a given norm must continually switch from one rhetoric to the other. When pressed, the hard defender of a norm can be forced to concede that the norm can only be binding if it is soft. Likewise, the defender of a soft norm can be forced to defend his norm in hard terms. Because neither set of arguments can be convincing by itself and neither can trump the other, argument within this structure could go on endlessly without resolution.

This hypothetical set of arguments is similar to the way people actually argue about doctrines concerning the sources of international law. They argue in ways which contrast norms based on sovereign consent but which must be externally validated outside consent (perhaps by implication from "objective" facts) with externally supplied norms which must be subjectively justified and defined by sovereigns. These two strands of argument are present in the discourse about all such traditional sources as treaties, custom, general principles, or the writings of judges and publicists.

Moreover, arguments about sources are related to each other as the hypothetical structure of hard and soft suggests. Arguments about the authority for an international norm appeal either to some form of sovereign consent, or to some ideal outside of consent. In the rhetoric of sources argument, these are exclusive possibilities, and no coherent single appeal can be simultaneously to both. In the world of equal and autonomous sovereigns imagined by those who engage in sources argument, a norm is authoritative either because states say so, or for some other reason which overrides consent. By definition, to be authoritative, consent must overrule other sources of authority. Likewise, to be authoritative, a nonconsensual source must be able to overrule consent. Yet neither of these sources alone can justify a doctrinal choice. On the one hand, we are unable to explain why consent should be binding against a dissenter (and in every contentious case someone will by definition object) without reference to a higher norm. On the other, we cannot explain the content of extraconsensual norms except by reference back to consensual standards.

This argumentative pattern reflects the image of inter-sovereign life characteristic of sources discourse generally. Sources discourse establishes an abstract basis for authoritatively binding states within a normative order without derogating from their separate and autonomous sovereign authority. The autonomy of sovereigns ensures the attractiveness of hard sources while their separation requires that they be permitted to limit their own consent in a fashion which reveals all hard sources to be soft. The possibility of an external normative order grounding its equality and mutual respect suggests the appeal of soft sources, while the independence of a normative structure from any single content for that order requires that all soft sources rely upon hard sources for their content. The attempt to delimit an abstract system of sources, free of the content of either state interest or of external value, is reflected in the hypothetical rhetorical patterns which I have outlined.

To the extent sources argument pursues these twin rhetorics, moreover, it continues the problematic which motivates it. In order to fulfill the desire for an autonomous system of normative sources, argument about the sources of international law, like sources doctrine itself, includes strands associated both with normative autonomy and normative authority. Sources argument is interesting both because it pursues a rhetorical strategy of inclusion and because it manages the relations between these two rhetorical strands so as to "solve" the problem of sources discourse as a whole. It seems that if the "hard" can lie down with the "soft" in sources argument, sovereigns will be able to remain autonomous within a binding normative order.

The solution furnished by sources doctrine and argument is not so much a matter of logic as it is a practice of continued movement between these two rhetorics which creates an image or a feeling of resolution. Doctrines are not defined by choosing between the hard and the soft. In fact, doctrines can only be produced if the extremes of hard and soft argumentation can be avoided. Neither alone could sustain doctrines of normative authority. Because these arguments may always be elaborated into conflicting and exclusive global visions, doctrines must include them both by limiting each so as to render them compatible. Without this careful limitation of extreme visions of hard and soft visions, doctrines are in constant danger of dissolution.

Various rhetorical devices for including these two rhetorical strands in sources discourse can be identified both in arguments which define, limit, and order various sources and in concrete arguments about the application of various source doctrines. In this section, I consider arguments of a most general sort about the meaning of various sources, the relations among sources, and the assimilation of new sources to those which are traditionally accepted. In the next sections, I take up argument about the application of various sources doctrines in particular exemplary cases.

The initial embrace of these two rhetorical approaches by sources discourse as well as one technique for managing any tension between them—placing them in a rather simple hierarchical relationship—can be seen in discussion about the boundaries between and within doctrines about the basic sources. It is difficult to categorize the sources of Article 38 as either soft or hard. Treaties seem quintessentially hard: the ultimate expression of sovereign consent. Custom, by contrast, and certainly "general principles," seem soft: binding because it is just to do things as they have been done, to preserve expectations or reinforce a natural selection of wise norms.[35] In general, positivists, who eschewed soft sources, preferred treaties to custom.[36] Naturalists, by con-

35. *See, e.g.*, Kunz, *The Nature of Customary International Law*, 47 AM. J. INT'L L. 662, 664 (1953) (criticizing the idea that custom is the discovery of pre-existing natural law).

36. *See supra* notes 6-8 (concerning hierarchy of custom and treaty). Nineteenth century positivists often embraced extreme versions of this position, holding, for example, that no norm could be binding except on the parties who agreed to it, and for as long as they agreed to it. This led to an observational style of scholarship. *See, e.g.*, J. MOSER, GRUNDSÄTZE DES JETZT ÜBLICHEN EUROPÄISCHEN VÖLKERRECHTS IN FRIEDENSZEITEN (1750). Usually, conventions are viewed as most persuasive because, in the words of Article 38(1)(a) of the Statute of the International Court of Justice, they "establish rules especially recognized by the contesting states." The preference for treaties is thus usually associated with a preference for consensual rules. *See* Bishop, *General Course of Public International Law*, 115 RECUEIL DES COURS 147 (1965).

> First among the sources of international law . . . [are] "international conventions" . . . . As between the parties to them, treaties . . . lay down clearly expressed, deliberately chosen rules. . . .
>
> [W]hen one compares the position of treaties in international law with various instruments in domestic law, we find treaties having to take the place, internationally, occupied domestically by contracts, legislation, conveyances, constitutional documents, and other instruments. . . . Treaties may, as between the parties, override previously existing rules of customary international law, modifying the law as parties wish.

trast, often emphasized custom and general principles of justice.[37] But the discourse of naturalism and positivism corrupted these pure forms.

Positivists, defending the authoritativeness of treaties, raised the soft norm *pacta sunt servanda* to a new status, extending the validity of treaty-based norms to those who had not explicitly consented on the grounds that treaty following was just.[38] They also reinterpreted custom and general principles to be binding because they too expressed consent, even if by implication.[39] They developed doctrines of custom-

Id.; *see also* Baxter, *supra* note 1, at 36-74:

> In the first place, the treaty is clear evidence of the will of States, free of the ambiguities and inconsistencies characteristic . . . of evidence of State practice.
>
> . . .
>
> Secondly, the convention . . . constitutes one common statement of the law by virtually all States, which does not require the process of harmonization and reconciliation that normally goes into the extraction of a rule of law from the hodge-podge of evidence presented to a tribunal or other form of decision-maker.

Id. at 36-37. When the commentator is less concerned with consent or, more probably, sees the consensual and nonconsensual element of both treaty *and* custom, the text will tend to treat them equally, resolving conflicts in terms of technical and procedural abstractions. *See, e.g.*, Akehurst, *supra* note 25, at 275:

> It is sometimes said that treaties prevail over custom by virtue of the maxim of *lex specialis derogat generali*. It often happens that the subject matter of a treaty is more specific than a customary rule, or that the States bound by a treaty are fewer than the States bound by a customary rule. But it is equally possible that a customary rule may be more specific than a treaty, or that a special custom binding a small number of States may conflict with a multilateral treaty binding a large number of States; in such cases the maxim *lex specialis derogat generali* causes the customary rule to prevail over the treaty.
>
> Where the maxim *lex specialis derogat generali* provides no clear guidance, or where it is shown not to reflect the intentions of the States concerned, it seems that treaties and custom are of equal authority. The later in time prevails.

Id.

37. *See supra* notes 6-8.

38. Successor and third states are usually considered bound by at least those treaties which have become customary law. Opinion differs as to the additional categories of treaties which bind successor states. *See supra* note 22; *see also* 2 D. O'CONNELL, *supra* note 22, at 352 *passim*; O. UDOKANG, *supra* note 22, at 327-402.

39. *See, e.g.*, Baxter, *supra* note 1, at 31 (customary international law finds its origins in the will of states); DDR LEHRBUCH, *supra* note 10, at 259 ("Der Nachweis *der Existenz einer gewohnheitsrechtlichen Norm erfordert . . . den Nachweis des Willens der Staaten, . . . zu der von ihnen praktisch geübten Verhaltensweise rechtlich verpflichtet zu sein.*") (emphasis in original). So pervasive has this positivizing tendency been that no contemporary author imagines custom to be binding solely as an expression of justice or of historical wisdom. Only norms of *jus cogens* are now understood in this way. *See supra* note 29. Even modern naturalists concede that custom is a matter of "will." *See, e.g.*, A. VERDROSS & B. SIMMA, *supra* note 4, at 282 n.17.

> Wir ersehen daraus [aus der Tatsache, dass ein persistent opposer nicht an eine neuentstandene customary norm gebunden wird], dass auch eine gewohnheitsrechtliche Bindung durch Konsens, wenn gleich nicht durch einen "stillschweigenden Vertrag" entsteht. Zwar beruht jeder Vertrag auf einem Konsens, aber nicht umgekehrt, da ein Vertrag immer eine durch Erklärungen oder konkludente Handlungen erzielte Willenseinigung (consent) voraussetzt,

ary law which reflected this sense of its reliance upon consent: custom was to be binding only upon those who participated in its formulation,[40] and in general only existed when the repeated practice of states was coupled with a psychological intent to be bound.[41]

Naturalists likewise corrupted the softness of custom and the hardness of treaty. They sought to extend custom and general principles by

---

> während ein Konsens auch aus einem passiven Verhalten, aus einer widerspruchslosen Duldung geschlossen werden kann. Richtig sagt daher Tammes, *The Status of Consent in International Law*, [2 NETHERLANDS Y.B. INT'L L. 11 (1971)] ein "tacit consent" sei eine "contradictio in terminis."

Id.

40. *See supra* notes 21-23 (elaborating on consent to be bound).

41. The "*opinio juris*" requirement was classically formulated by Judge Negulesco to be "the mutual conviction that the recurrence is the result of a compulsory rule." Jurisdiction of the European Commission of the Danube, 1927 P.C.I.J. (ser. B) No. 14, at 105 (Advisory Opinion of Dec. 8) (Negulesco, J., dissenting). The importance of this requirement to the formation of custom has been generally recognized as positivism has come to dominate international legal scholarship. Guggenheim relates that the *opinio juris* requirement had appeared in the positivist writings at the end of the 18th century. Guggenheim, *Contribution à l'histoire des sources du droit des gens*, 94 RECUEIL DES COURS 1, 52-53, 53 n.1 (1958). Some contemporary authors who rejected it early in their careers have since changed their minds. *Compare* 1 P. GUGGENHEIM, TRAITÉ DE DROIT INTERNATIONAL PUBLIC 46-48 (1953) (disapproving of *opinio juris*) *with* P. GUGGENHEIM, TRAITÉ DE DROIT INTERNATIONAL PUBLIC 102-05 (2d ed. 1967) (approving of *opinio juris*); *see also* Kelsen, *Théorie du droit international coutumier*, 1 REVUE INTERNATIONALE DE LA THÉORIE DU DROIT, 253 *passim* (1939) (strict *opinio juris* not required); H. KELSEN, *supra* note 4, at 307 *passim* (claiming that "the second element is . . . that they must be convinced that they fulfill, by their actions or abstentions, a duty, or that they exercise a right"). For a discussion of this change in the views of Guggenheim and Kelsen, see G. TUNKIN, *supra* note 23, at 120-21. The recent discourse about the *opinio juris* requirement blends a subjective attempt to assess the true motives of compliers and an objective strand, willing to infer intent from certain behavior patterns. *See* Akehurst, *supra* note 1, at 31-42 (contrasting modern attempts to define *opinio juris*); Virally, *supra* note 1, at 133; I. BROWNLIE, *supra* note 1, at 8 (*opinio juris* "in fact a necessary ingredient"); Barberis, *L'Opinio juris comme élément constitutif de la coutume d'après la Cour de la Haye*, 50 R.D.I. 563 (1967). *Compare* 1 H. LAUTERPACHT, *supra* note 25, at 63 (advocating a "flexible" approach requiring some subjective sense of "obligation" in order "to emphasize the distinction between international custom and international courtesy") *with* Skubiszewski, *Elements of Custom and the Hague Court*, 31 ZAÖRV 810, 839-45, 853-54 (1971). Skubiszewski interprets the Hague approach to be that "the Court reduces the *opinio juris* to a certain aspect of the practice and implicitly denies the subjective nature of the second element of custom. Further, the Court has never explained the nature of this subjectiveness." *Id.* at 854. He concludes that *opinio juris*:

> is not psychological in nature, and this is so for the obvious reason that there is no "State Psychology" as only a human being possesses mind and soul. The Court describes the element of *opinio juris* as "subjective," probably to contrast it with the "objective" nature of material facts that compose the practice. But the belief as to the legal nature of the rule of behavior that follows from the practice is not the result of any psychological process. This belief—and it is again an inexact term in the circumstances—follows from the acceptance of the legal nature of the rule by the States.

Id. at 840 (footnotes omitted).

arguing that these most accurately represented the way in which sovereigns wanted to be treated.[42] They also reinterpreted treaty law to be binding as an expression of community judgment about the justice of the norms included.[43] This led them to give a special status to some general treaties like the original Hague protocols, the Kellogg-Briand Pact, or the United Nations Charter and subsequent human rights related treaties.[44] Consequently, general principles are valid when "recognized" and custom when "accepted" as law.[45] Moreover, the International Court of Justice may decide a case *ex aequo et bono* "if the parties agree thereto."[46]

---

42. *See, e.g.*, A. D'AMATO, *supra* note 1, at 75.

> The articulation of a rule of international law—whether it be a new rule or a departure from and modification of an existing rule—in advance of or currently with a positive act (or omission) of a state gives a state notice that its action or decision will have legal implications. In other words, given such notice, statesmen will be able freely to decide whether or not to pursue various policies, knowing that their acts may create or modify international law. *This voluntaristic aspect of international law is precisely what makes it acceptable to nation-state decision-makers.*

Id. (emphasis added).

43. *See supra* note 25 (describing the transformation of multilateral treaties into norms of customary law); *see also* Baxter, *supra* note 1, at 57 (concluding that "[t]reaties that do not purport to be declaratory of customary international law at the time that they enter into force may nevertheless with the passage of time pass into customary international law").

44. Some provisions of these treaties (such as Article 2(4) of the United Nations Charter precluding international interference with matters of domestic jurisdiction) are considered by some to have become *jus cogens. See* Reports of the Commission, *supra* note 11, at 247-49; *see also* A. MCNAIR, *supra* note 1, at 215-16 (considering the General Treaty for the Renunciation of War and the United Nations Charter to be binding upon non-signatories). The Hague Protocols and the Kellogg-Briand Pact, due partly to the sweep of their object, have often been given special status as constitutive of custom. *See* 1 THE TRIAL OF GERMAN MAJOR WAR CRIMINALS: PROCEEDINGS OF THE INTERNATIONAL MILITARY TRIBUNAL SITTING AT NUREMBERG, GERMANY 41-42, 44 (1946); JUDGEMENT OF THE INTERNATIONAL MILITARY TRIBUNAL FOR THE FAR EAST 413-30 (1948).

45. I.C.J. CHARTER art. 38(1)(c)-(1)(d).

46. Article 38(2) of the Statute of the International Court of Justice provides for "the power of the Court to decide a case *ex aequo et bono*, if the parties agree thereto." This provision, in the otherwise heavily positivist Statute has never been the basis for the Court's jurisdiction, and is hardly mentioned in most treatments of the Court's jurisdiction. *See, e.g.*, I. BROWNLIE, *supra* note 1, at 27; A. VERDROSS & B. SIMMA, *supra* note 4, at 337-38. *Ex aequo et bono* refers to a decision on the basis of equity, involving elements of compromise, conciliation, and friendly settlement in cases where no norm of international law seems able to provide a solution. Several naturalist authors have noted the role which equity plays in the usual jurisprudence of the Court. *See, e.g.*, A. VERDROSS & B. SIMMA, *supra* note 4, at 337-38 (speaking of "ausserrechtliche Billigkeit"); de Visscher, *supra* note 1, at 13; I. BROWNLIE, *supra* note 1, at 27 (equity in international law may be understood in a different sense, as "an important factor in the process of decision"); Pirotte, *La notion d'équité, dans la jurisprudence récente de la Cour internationale de justice*, 77 REVUE GÉNÉRALE DE DROIT INTERNATIONAL PUBLIC 92 (1973). The I.C.J. has expressed this role:

Sources discourse as a whole embraces the tension between hard and soft by allocating it as the difference between custom and treaty. Discourse about each source avoids the difficulties of singleminded reliance upon either hard or soft by repeating the maneuver. Because each of the classic sources had this double nature, each seemed protected from the inadequacy of either hard and soft tendency. The discourse of sources as a whole is able to appeal both to sovereign authority and sovereign equality. These two aspirations can be embraced by sources discourse precisely because they can be allocated to different doctrinal boxes.

Despite this allocation, commentators have sought to characterize Article 38 as either dominantly hard or soft, and continue to differentiate sources from one another by their relative hardness or softness. These argumentative practices of differentiation and characterization are as important to the overall project of sources discourse as are the embracing practices of inclusion and allocation. Without a sense of *both* the distinctiveness of consent and justice *and* of their inseparability, sources discourse could not reflect both sovereign autonomy and equality. At this preliminary point we might think of argument about the sources of international law as an endless project of differentiation and recombination. The difficulty is to relate these two practices to one another. One technique of accomodation, which is quite apparent even at this preliminary point, is the rhetorical development of hierarchical relations among dimensions of sources doctrines that have been differentiated as relatively hard or soft. This practice characterizes argument both about the relationship among sources and about doctrines defining each source which might be thought of as either hard or soft. Traditional commentators, for example, have seen Article 38 as the expression of a positivist vision of international law.[47] By this they mean that

---

> Whatever the legal reasoning of a court of justice, its decisions must by definition be just, and therefore in that sense equitable. Nevertheless, when mention is made of a court dispensing justice or declaring the law, what is meant is that the decision finds its objective justification in considerations lying not *outside but within the rules*, and in this field it is *precisely a rule of law that calls for the application of equitable principles*.

North Sea Continental Shelf Cases (W. Ger. v. Den.; W. Ger. v. Neth.), 1969 I.C.J. 3, 48 (Judgment of Feb. 20) (emphasis added).

47. *See, e.g.*, 1 H. LAUTERPACHT, *supra* note 25, at 86-87:

> The order in which the sources of international law are enumerated in the Statute of the International Court of Justice is, essentially, in accordance both with correct legal principles and with the character of international law as a body of rules *based on consent* to a degree higher than is the law within the State. The rights and duties of States are determined, in the first instance, by their agreement as expressed in treaties.

Id.; *see also* E. MENZEL & K. IPSEN, *supra* note 25, at 94; 1 C. ROUSSEAU, *supra* note

Article 38 seems to weight sources based in consent more than those based elsewhere. Of course, if each source were actually equally groundable in both consent and justice, such a characterization would not be possible. Commentators who characterize Article 38 positivistically rely both on the order in which the sources are listed, and upon the way they are described. They treat the order as a hierarchy, from the most to the least consensual source: treaties before custom before general principles before judicial decisions before publicists.[48] Moreover, judicial decisions and the writings of publicists are included only as "subsidiary" means for the determination of rules of law. They are least convincing because they are least consensual. Both custom and general principles, moreover, are described in such a way as to be grounded in consent rather than in a vision of the justice of tradition.[49] Those who would loosen the positivism of international legal theory accept this characterization, avoiding the "extreme positivism" of Article 38 in part by concentrating on custom and general principles, which they regard as midway between hard treaties and soft theories of justice.[50]

Creating a hierarchy among sources based on a frozen characterization of each source as more or less "consensual" advances the project of

6, at 395-97. The traditional socialist view is that consent is the primary source of international legal principles which leads Tunkin to conclude that "these principles and norms are created primarily by . . . treaties . . . ." G. TUNKIN, *supra* note 17, at 441. The East Germans conclude likewise that, "Sie [die socialistische Völkerrechtsliterature] betrachtet den völkerrechtlichen Vertrag einhellig als *die Hauptquelle des gegenwärtigen Völkerrechts*." DDR LEHRBUCH, *supra* note 10, at 215 (footnote omitted).

48. *See supra* note 47.

49. *See* VIRALLY, *supra* note 1, at 135 (stating that "[the] obligatory character [of customary law] follows from the general consent on the part of states, and this is what Article 38 seeks to convey when it speaks of 'a general practice accepted as law' "); *see also* DDR LEHRBUCH, *supra* note 10, at 210: " 'allgemeine Rechtsgrundsätze' . . . *sind völkerrechtliche* Grundsätze, die entweder über völkerrechtliche Verträge oder im Wege des Völkergewohnheitsrechts Bestandteil des Völkerrechts geworden sind und deren allgemeine Anerkennung die Folge allgemein . . . eingegangener (ausdrücklicher oder stillschweigender) Vereinbarungen ist."

This approach is particularly evident in those texts which emphasize the importance of multilateral treaties (traditionally hard sources) as evidence of customary norms. *See supra* note 25; *see also* Baxter, *supra* note 1, at 38 (maintaining that multilateral treaties are declaratory or even constitutive for new customary law because of "the accuracy with which it reflects the will of States, clarity, near universality, contemporaneity, and sense of legal obligation").

50. *See* B. SIMMA, *supra* note 1; *see also* D'Amato, *The Concept of Special Custom in International Law*, 63 AM. J. INT'L L. 211 (1969) (maintaining that consent is the basis for special, but not general custom); D'Amato, *Manifest Intent and the Generation by Treaty of Customary Rules of International Law*, 64 AM. J. INT'L L. 892 (1970) (remarking that custom requires proof of "manifest intent," an objective standard, which can be especially well met by certain multilateral treaties).

domesticating the tension between authority and normative criticism within sources doctrine as a whole. Although both tendencies are present they do not seem to conflict with each other because they have been confined to doctrinal categories which are not equivalent. In one vision, treaty is the master of custom because it is more consensual, in another the reverse. Which of the various permutations one adopts is less important than the overall project of establishing distinctions and hierarchies. It protects the image of a doctrinal resolution to the social problem of conflicting authority centers.

Sometimes, however, the instability of the characterizations upon which this argumentative pattern relies becomes apparent. When this happens, other rhetorical techniques of resolution are available. Of these, the most significant is probably doctrinal proliferation. This instability and the proliferative response can be seen in discourse about new sources of international law and in discussion of the specific doctrines which define and limit each source.

Commentators often discuss new sources of international law in ways which characterize them as either hard or soft.[51] When these two rhetorical strands are used in this way, it is difficult to terminate the discussion in any definitive way—not so much because new sources each entertain both hard and soft rhetorics as because each can be characterized as either hard or soft and neither characterization alone seems a persuasive basis for the new source's authority. Resolutions of the United Nations General Assembly have been treated in precisely this fashion. Since the General Assembly formally has no general legislative function in public international law, Article 38 makes no mention of its various textual outputs. Commentators have nevertheless struggled to think about United Nations resolutions within the rhetoric of sources.

General Assembly resolutions are thought to be binding to the extent that they express state consensus or systemic justice.[52] Those who ar-

---

51. *See supra* notes 17-18.

52. *See supra* notes 17-18. Some commentators supporting the binding nature of United Nations Resolutions do so on the basis of the form of their adoption and emphasize their consensual nature. Others rely upon their content and emphasize their justness. Others rely on both. For the first type, see G. TUNKIN, *supra* note 17, at 176: "[T]he binding force of the provisions contained in the resolution is based not on the resolution itself . . . but on the agreement of the States who voted for the resolution . . ."; *see also* Falk, *supra* note 1, at 782-83 ("[T]he jurisprudential basis for attributing a limited legislative status to those resolutions of the Assembly is that they are supported by a consensus of the membership"); Higgins, *The United Nations and Lawmaking: The Political Organs*, PROC. AM. SOC'Y INT'L L. 37, 37-38 (1970) (explaining that the political organs of the United Nations engage in the development of customary international law); E. MCWHINNEY, INTERNATIONAL LAW AND WORLD REVOLUTIONS 80 (1967); C. JENKS, LAW, FREEDOM AND WELFARE 83-100 (1963).

gue that they express consent are opposed by the argument that General Assembly delegates lack the requisite capacity or intent.[53] Those who argue that resolutions embody principles of systemic justice are opposed by argument that resolutions express a mere passing consensus—rule or tyranny of the majority.[54]

Commentators of the second type are harder to find, since few defend the innovative position that Resolutions are binding with the non-positive and hence innovative argument that they express justice. *See* J. CASTAÑEDA, *supra* note 17, at 5 ("the legal value of these pronouncements is not uniform: it depends not only on the organ that approves them and on their form, but also, and especially on their content"). A strong advocate of this position is M. BEDJAOUI, TOWARDS A NEW INTERNATIONAL ECONOMIC ORDER (1979). Bedjaoui calls for a law whose principles are derived from its purpose, and "the primary concern of the law today is the establishment of a new international economic order." *Id.* at 132. Focusing on the "normative actions" of organizations, he calls for "ending referral to the traditional sources of international law" because they do not serve this purpose, whereas "the development of resolutions as a means of formulating international law is linked with the very evolution of that law, which has become a law of transformation for a purpose." *Id.* at 140. For advocacy of both positions, see J. BRIERLY, THE BASIS OF OBLIGATION IN INTERNATIONAL LAW 1-67 (H. Lauterpacht & C. Waldock eds. 1958) (all obligations in international law can be traced directly or indirectly to the consensus of states or to some universal system of natural rights or duties).

53. Those who rely on the formal consensual nature of resolutions are opposed by arguments cast in the rhetoric of the inadequacy of form or of the absence of underlying substantive authority which would legitimize the form. Thus, commentators argue either that the requisite intent was missing or the requisite power to forge consensus did not rest with the United Nations organ in question. *See, e.g.*, Sloan, *supra* note 17, at 31 ("As a general rule, however, resolutions, for lack of intention or mandating power in the Assembly, do not create binding obligations in positive law."); Virally, *supra* note 1, at 160 ("The Charter contains no general provision regarding the legal effects of General Assembly resolutions. Consequently, as a manifestation of the principle of sovereignty they generally have no binding force on members."); A. VERDROSS & B. SIMMA, *supra* note 4, at 330-31 ("Deklarationen können nur dann für die Mitgliedstaaten verbindliche Völkerrechtsnormen erzeugen, wenn dieses Organ dazu zuständig wäre . . . . Eine Erweiterung der Zustandigkeit ist jedoch bisher weder auf förmlichem Weg noch durch eine Verfassungswandlung . . . erfolgt"). Regarding the lack of intent, see Arangio-Ruiz, *The Normative Role of the General Assembly of the United Nations*, 137 RECUEIL DES COURS 419 (1972):

> As everybody in the United Nations is convinced that recommendations are *per se* not mandatory, States tend to embellish their image by putting forth draft resolutions. Other states tend naturally to support such drafts. And potential or natural opponents are often reluctant to face the risk of tarnishing or spoiling their own image by opposing the proposal openly or by casting a negative vote.

Id. at 457.

54. Those who justify the binding nature of resolutions by reliance upon their material expression of right values are opposed by a rhetoric which challenges the legitimacy of resolutions as substantive expressions of justice, seeing them instead as expressions of formal voting arrangements or power. Even those supporting the binding force of resolutions in these terms consequently rely simultaneously upon a consensual element, limiting their advocacy to generally or nearly unanimously adopted resolutions. The problem of the dissenter remains. *See* Sohn, *The Development of the Character of the United Nations*, in THE PRESENT STATE OF INTERNATIONAL LAW AND OTHER ESSAYS 39, 50 (M. Bos. ed. 1973) (noting that when an interpretation of the Charter is

It would not be possible to argue both that General Assembly resolutions are binding as reflections of a passing consensus and that the delegates lacked capacity to consent. Likewise, it would not be possible to argue both that the apparent lack of consent did not matter (because the resolutions were just) and that the undesirable redistributive consequences had to be accepted because the resolutions were expressions of consent. The incompatibility of these rhetorical strategies can most clearly be seen in attempts to argue United Nations resolutions into the box of international custom. If custom is a matter of consent, resolutions do not fit because the practice of the very states who voted for them indicates that consent was not given. If custom is valid because it embodies the value and justice of tradition, then the United Nations resolutions are too instant. They cannot, however, be *both* too instant to be traditional and too implied to be consensual.[55]

The difficulty posed by this tension within argument about a single potential source of law might be handled in a number of ways. We might imagine, for example, that although United Nations resolutions "reflect" tradition, their textuality keeps them somewhat displaced from custom and that although United Nations resolutions are "indicative" of international consensus, their institutional form distinguishes them from treaties. Approached in this way, United Nations resolutions occupy a sort of free space between consent and justice—grounded in both, if in a somewhat ambiguous fashion. A mediating rhetorical strategy of this sort has obvious advantages, but it is quite unstable, for those sceptical about the binding authority of United Nations resolutions can attack it from either direction.

A much more common response to the unstable incompatibility of

---

not generally accepted it is without binding force); Conforti, *Le rôle de l'accord dans le système nations unies*, 142 RECUEIL DES COURS 203, 253 (1974) (objecter not bound despite justice of resolution); D'Amato, *On Consensus*, 8 CAN. Y.B. INT'L L. 104, 121-22 (1970) (remarking that a resolution does not bind a dissenting state merely because there is a declaration of consensus).

55. Most treatise writers feel obliged to take a stand on the binding nature of United Nations resolutions. Efforts at organizing this burgeoning literature have attempted to develop sophisticated methods of differentiating the positions and developing some theory which could unite a fairly wide range of them. No one has focused on the deeper structure of these various argumentative positions. *See* Gross, *The United Nations and The Role of Law*, 19 INT'L ORG. 537 (1965). After distinguishing two extreme positions, that resolutions are not binding and that the General Assembly has a "legislative or quasi-legislative function," Gross deploys the rhetoric of consent to demonstrate that resolutions are not binding. *Id.* at 555-58; *cf.* Arangio-Ruiz, *supra* note 53 (surveying the various idiosyncratic positions which have been developed between the two extremes distinguished by Gross and commenting sceptically upon the elaborate distinctions necessary to maintain "one foot in one spot and the other foot or a hand in another").

the two strands of sources rhetoric is to embrace and submerge them by creating further doctrinal distinctions and hierarchies. This technique is easiest to see by returning to doctrines limiting and defining various traditional sources. At first, doctrines governing entry into and departure from treaty and custom follow the rhetorical lines established by argument differentiating one source from another. Thus, for example, treaty and custom having been initially distinguished as respectively hard and soft, doctrines about entry into treaty seem more preoccupied with consent than doctrines about entry into custom.

Doctrines about the creation of custom and treaty reflect a sense that what needs explaining about a treaty is its hard basis in consent, while what needs explaining about custom is its soft basis in the natural order of the system, or, in recent discourse, the conditions under which consent can be implied. Thus, discussion of the creation of treaties is preoccupied with the conditions under which a state which will be bound by a treaty has indeed consented to its terms. A treaty is binding when properly signed and when ratified by the appropriate internal state organs.[56] From this perspective, executive competence to conclude treaties depends upon the extent to which, under constitutional law, the executive can speak for the state.[57] Ratification is viewed as a substantive process for registering consent.[58] In this view reservations are thought to be freely possible until ratification, although they must be accepted by other signatories.[59] Duress or *force majeure* mitigate the consent of states.[60]

---

56. *See supra* notes 5-9.

57. *See supra* notes 5 & 7.

58. *See supra* note 8; *see also* Virally, *supra* note 1, at 192-93 (justifying treating ratification as final act of consent to provide "breathing space" for subjective national reflection after signature). The formal approach to the subjective consent represented by requiring ratification is often replaced by a direct requirement that the subjective intent be present, however it is shown. *See* Bolintineanu, *supra* note 8, at 673. "The underlying principle of the provisions concerning the expression of consent to be bound by a treaty is the autonomy of the will of the negotiating states." *Id.* Bolintineanu further adds: "[w]e share, therefore the opinion that the Vienna Convention has eliminated the distinction between formal and informal treaties, both being placed on the same level and thus reflecting the 'decline of form' in international law and the procedural autonomy of the negotiating states." *Id.* at 678.

59. *See* I. Brownlie, *supra* note 1, at 605-06 (observing that this hard approach to reservations rests on a "contractual conception of the absolute integrity of the treaty as adopted"). Since the Vienna Convention this view has been softened, at least for multilateral treaties. *See infra* note 65 and accompanying text; Koh, *supra* note 11, at 95-105, 115-16.

60. *See supra* note 10. The Western approach to duress is typically hard, focusing only on the elements of formal consent. Socialist and third world authors significantly soften this approach, focusing upon the "unequal" substance of the treaty as a consequence of political or economic pressures. *See infra* note 66.

The initial discussion of the creation of custom, by contrast, concerns doctrines for measuring the pulse of the international system as a whole.[61] Doctrines about the number and importance of states who must follow a practice for it to be binding upon all states suggest limits on the ability of each state to have consented to its being bound.[62] Gone are doctrines about ratification, or subjective internal agreement by the states to be bound.

Argument about these doctrines of treaty and custom law displays a more complex weave of hard and soft rhetoric. Each doctrine about the creation of a treaty norm balances hard and soft considerations. Often this balance takes the form of an "objective approach" to measuring the consent of the state. Executive competence is discussed in terms of what is reasonable or just for other states to expect the executive to have the power to commit.[63] Signature and ratification act as limits on consent; binding the state even when not intended to bind, and limiting the state's ability to change its mind.[64] The acceptability of reservations is thought to depend upon their compatibility with the "object and purpose" of the treaty rather than upon their acceptance, and the power to reserve is understood to be limited.[65] Duress either does not

61. *See supra* notes 12-13.

62. *See supra* note 12.

63. This is easiest to see in modern doctrine as enshrined in Article 46 of the Vienna Convention on the Law of Treaties. *See* Vienna Convention, *supra* note 5, at art. 46. In fact, the expectations of foreign states seem more strongly protected in modern doctrine than municipal constitutional provisions, since a violation of internal competence provisions is only relevant if the provision concerned is one expressly regarding competence to conclude treaties, is of "fundamental importance" and is "manifestly" violated. The effect of this softening has been to make the subjective internal lack of executive capacity irrelevant at international law.

64. Ratification, the last act of consent, is also the act which gives the treaty a presumptive life of its own, independent of consent. *See* I. BROWNLIE, *supra* note 1, at 604; E. MENZEL & K. IPSEN, *supra* note 25, at 304; *see also supra* note 8.

65. *See supra* note 59. This modern softer approach to reservations was first stressed by the International Court of Justice in the Reservations to Convention on Genocide:

> [A] State which has made and maintained a reservation which has been objected to by one or more of the parties to the Convention, but not by others, can be regarded as being a party to the Convention if the reservation is compatible with the object and purpose of the Convention . . . .

1951 I.C.J. 15, 21 (Advisory Opinion of May 28). The Vienna Convention incorporates this approach to the extent that the old free reservation-acceptance approach has become an exception. Vienna Convention, *supra* note 5, at art. 20(4), (5). *See* I. BROWNLIE, *supra* note 1, at 605-06 (the best short survey of reservation doctrine describing this switch). The meaning of "compatible" or of the "object and purpose" of the treaty are often given a hard interpretation even in this soft approach, although this is by no means necessary. *See id.* at 590 (maintaining that "compatibility" might be determined "by a majority rule," on the basis of the "fundamental" nature of some provisions, or that "each state decides for itself whether reservations are incompatible"); *see*

mitigate when the state to be bound could not have known the relevant consent was forced or mitigates consent out of a sense of unfairness in the result rather than through implying a lack of subjective consent in "unequal" treaties.[66]

Sometimes, this rhetorical balancing proceeds by reinterpreting hard doctrines of treaty creation as expressions of justice rather than consent. Thus, for example, doctrines about consent such as signature and ratification are justified as the embodiment of justice, protecting the ability of the consenting state to bind itself in the interests of the community.[67] Likewise, the softer doctrines of treaty creation, like the ob-

---

also Waldock, *supra* note 1, at 65-66 (viewing the "compatibility" doctrine as unsuitable for adoption as the "general criterion for determining the status of a reserving state as a party" because it cannot be objectively defined without violating sovereign autonomy and viewing it instead as a "valuable concept for consideration by both the States formulating reservations and other signatories"). Some "pragmatic" authors promote avoiding these contradictions by adopting a "sensible" approach to achieving "the rule calculated to promote the widest possible acceptance of whatever measure of common agreement can be achieved and expressed." Reports of the Commission, *supra* note 11, at 206.

66. *See supra* note 60. In the third world and socialist view, treaties are invalid if unequal, regardless of the subjective consent of the relevant government, which may, after all, have been suffering from false consciousness. This approach has been rejected by the West, in most cases. *See, e.g.*, A. VERDROSS, *supra* note 1, at 62. For socialist advocacy of this view, see DDR LEHRBUCH, *supra* note 10, at 251; Lukashuk, *The Soviet Union and International Treaties*, [1959] SOVIET Y.B. INT'L L. 44, 45-50; Detter, *The Problem of Unequal Treaties*, 15 INT'L & COMP. L.Q. 1069, 1082-83, 1086 (1966) (citing examples such as agreements "forced" on a state as the price of freedom, perhaps allowing an ex-colonial power to maintain economic control over new states, and concluding: "We submit here that the very contents of a treaty ought to be examined when the question of validity is discussed: the material contents of the instrument ought to be accepted as a separate ground of voidance, irrespective of whether the treaty has been concluded under force or ought to be revised/rescinded according to the principle *rebus sic stantibus*."). For the third world expression of this approach, see M. BEDJAOUI, *supra* note 52; Abi-Saab, *The Newly Independent State and the Rules of International Law, An Outline*, 8 HOWARD L.J. 95, 108 (1962); Sinha, *Perspective of the Newly Independent States on the Binding Quality of International Law*, 14 INT'L & COMP. L.Q. 121 (1965).

> The newly independent States believe that political and economic privileges have been extorted by the colonial powers in the past from the peoples of Asia and Africa. On becoming independent, these States increasingly rely on the argument that "unequal" or "inequitable" treaties thus extracted, and treaties imposed by duress, are invalid *ab initio*. Accordingly, they declare that it is the right of the State which was obliged to enter such treaties to terminate them by denunciation.
>
> *Rebus sic stantibus* is frequently resorted to by the newly independent states in order to terminate their inherited burdens. The doctrine is invoked by them not only on the basis of justice but also because a treaty fails to accord with the present position of power in the world.

Id. at 123-24.

67. *See* Kearney & Dalton, *The Treaty on Treaties*, 64 AM. J. INT'L L. 495 (1970) (the treaty as "the mechanism without which international intercourse could not exist, much less function . . . the cement that holds the world community together"); M.

jective view of consent, are seen as ways of protecting the subjective ability of the other state to know the terms upon which it binds itself.[68]

Similarly, doctrines about the creation of custom combine hard and soft approaches. Often this blending is visible in the subjective, consensual element in each doctrine. Custom is created not merely by habitual repetition, for example, but requires also *opinio juris*: an intent to be bound, or a recognition that compliance with the habitual norm resulted from a sense that it was binding.[69] In this approach, doctrines

---

MCDOUGAL & W. REISMAN, INTERNATIONAL LAW IN CONTEMPORARY PERSPECTIVE 1119 (1979) (emphasizing the community-serving functions of treaties).

> The special importance of agreements among the strategies of states resides in the fact that, in the absence of centralized legislative institutions in the world arena, agreements offer one of the closest approaches to the considered and deliberate prescription of future policies which is the characteristic function of constitutive legislative institutions in municipal arenas.

Id; *see also* 1 H. LAUTERPACHT, *supra* note 25, at 59.

68. *See* A. VERDROSS & B. SIMMA, *supra* note 4, at 391-92:

> Der (subjektiven) Konsenstheorie wird die [objektive] Vertrauenstheorie gegenübergestellt, die nicht danach fragt, welcher Regelung die Vertragsparteien *zugestimmt* haben, sondern was sie vernünftigerweise voneinander *erwarten* können, wenn sie bestimmte Erklärungen abgeben oder ein bestimmtes Verhalten beobachtet haben. An die Stelle des Konsenses tritt somit die rationale Auslegung des Textes durch den Schiedsrichter oder Richter.

Id. This approach is often visible in discussions of interpretation. *See* Favre, *L'interprétation objectiviste des traités internationaux*, 17 SCHWEIZER JAHRBUCH FÜR INTERNATIONALES RECHT 75 (1960):

> Donner une interprétation raisonnable d'un texte, c'est, de la part du juge, introduire un élément nouveau, objectif, dans l'accord des parties. C'est opérer la balance des intérêts en présence . . . c'est arrêter, à la place des parties, ce qu'un homme juste et "raisonnable" aurait fait s'il avait eu à rédiger l'accord.

Id. at 82; *see also* Falk, *On Treaty Interpretation and the New Haven Approach: Achievements and Prospects*, 8 VA. J. INT'L L. 323 (1968); Gottlieb, *The Conceptual World of the Yale School of International Law*, 21 WORLD POL. 108 (1968).

69. On *opinio juris* generally, see *supra* note 41. Although most commentators now agree that a subjective element is necessary for the consensual creation of custom, it is unclear how proof of that element should be provided. This discourse reposes the opposition of hard and soft tendencies. *Opinio juris* was conceived as the subjective, motivational, or intentional element of custom which, along with objective practice could create custom. It seemed required to distinguish "mere habit" or "courtesy" from law. *See* I. BROWNLIE, *supra* note 1, at 4-8 (explaining that states differentiate between obligation and use). But *opinio juris* must be inferred from practice as well. This objective approach to *opinio juris* (itself the subjective element in the hard, consensual approach to custom, a soft source) was expressed by the International Court of Justice in the North Sea Continental Shelf Case: "State practice should have been both extensive and virtually uniform in the sense of the provision invoked—and should moreover have occurred in such a way as to show a general recognition that a rule of law or legal obligation is involved." North Sea Continental Shelf Cases (Ger. v. Den.; Ger. v. Neth.), 1969 I.C.J. 3, 43 (Judgment of Feb. 20). This approach is made more explicit by Judge Lachs in dissent: "In sum, the general practice of States should be recognized as prima facie evidence that it is accepted as law. Such evidence may, of course, be controverted—even on the test of practice itself, it shows much uncertainty and contradiction." *Id.* at 231-32; *see also* Sørensen, *Principes de droit international public*, 101

about frequency and the importance of those who must participate in custom building emphasize the ability to register consent. Thus, relatively more states will need to participate, or those who will be bound will need to participate more directly.[70] In this view, doctrine should downplay the importance of the states who must consent in favor of a more universal approach, or should treat "important" as meaning those affected by the norm most adversely rather than those whose impor-

---

RECUEIL DES COURS 1 (1960). Various attempts have been made to determine what practice is an objective measure of this intent. The most successful views blend hard and soft tendencies most elegantly. Consider, for example, the view that *opinio juris* is an objective warning protecting the power freely to consent, which can therefore only be satisfied by practice following an articulated norm:

> The articulation of a rule of international law . . . in advance of or concurrently with a positive act (or omission) of a State gives a State notice that its action or decision will have legal implications. In other words, given such notice, statesmen will be able freely to decide whether or not to pursue various policies, knowing that their acts may create or modify international law. . . . [T]he absence of prior notification that acts or abstentions have legal consequences is an effective barrier to the extrapolation of legal norms from patterns of conduct that are noticed *ex post facto*.

A. D'AMATO, *supra* note 1, at 75. Akehurst expresses the subjective view of *opinio juris* clearly: "Practice creates a rule of customary law that particular conduct is obligatory, if it is accompanied by statements on the part of States that such conduct is obligatory," and distinguishes his approaches subjectively: "The traditional view implies, even if it does not state expressly, that *opinio juris* consists of the *genuine* beliefs of States. It is submitted, however, that a statement by a State about the content of customary law should be taken as *opinio juris* even if the State does not believe in the truth of its statement." Akehurst, *supra* note 1, at 36-37 (footnote omitted). In practice, however, these elements can hardly be distinguished or combined. Either there is a continuous conduct which is evidence of a legal duty which will finally be regarded as sufficient, or the conduct will *consist* of expressions of *opinio juris* unaccompanied by "real actions." Kelsen suggested that the *opinio juris* requirement served no other purpose than to conceal the role played by the judge in the creation of customary law. *See* Kelsen, *Theorie du droit international coutumier*, *supra* note 41, at 266.

70. This heightened sensitivity to the consensual nature of customary law in doctrines about creation of custom is expressed in Baxter, *supra* note 12, at 44; Akehurst, *supra* note 1, at 16.

> A rule of customary law is established if it is accepted by the international community, and . . . the number of States taking part in a practice is a more important criterion of acceptance than the number of acts of which the practice is composed, and a much more important criterion than the duration of the practice.

Id.; *see also* Virally, *supra* note 1, at 135: "The obligatory character (of custom) follows from the general consent on the part of states . . . . The qualities of continuity and generality, requisite in order that an international practice may give rise to a custom, reflect the presence of this consent." *Id.* The number of states necessary to create custom is less when there is no conflicting practice because general consent is more likely in such circumstances and greater when a previous rule of custom is to be overruled. *See* Akehurst, *supra* note 1, at 18-19; *cf.* Fisheries Jurisdiction Case (U.K. v. Nor.), 1951 I.C.J. 116, 151-52 (Judgment of Dec. 18) (sep. op. Alvarez, J.); S.S. "Lotus" Case (Fr. v. Turk.), 1927 P.C.I.J. (ser. A) No. 10, at 34 (Judgment of Sept. 7) (diss. op. Loder, J.).

tance can be measured in terms of some external standard.[71]

Sometimes, hard rhetoric in doctrines about the creation of custom recharacterizes soft doctrinal positions as ways of emphasizing consent rather than justice. Thus, for example, the physical requirement of habitual compliance will be seen as a way of ensuring subjective consent, on the grounds that actions speak louder than words.[72] The soft doctrine that universal consent is not necessary will be seen as a way of permitting states to develop their subjective intentions without being hindered by recalcitrant or uninterested states.[73] The soft sense that "important" states who understand the system should surely consent to ensure wise rules is understood to reflect not the wisdom of those who

---

71. Most writers follow the I.C.J. on this point: "State practice, including that of States whose interests are specially affected should have been both extensive and virtually uniform." North Sea Continental Shelf Cases (W Ger. v. Den., W. Ger. v. Neth.), 1969 I.C.J. 3, 43 (Judgement of Feb. 20). *See, e.g.*, A. VERDROSS & B. SIMMA, *supra* note 4, at 281; Baxter, *supra* note 1, at 66 ("The practice of those States particularly affected by the treaty must count heavily"), *cf.* Akehurst, *supra* note 1, at 22 ("Suggestions are often made that the practice of some states is more important than the practice of other states . . . the author has already attacked such suggestions. . . .").

72. *See supra* note 69; *see also* A. D'AMATO, *supra* note 1, at 88 ("A claim is not an act . . . [C]laims . . . , although they may *articulate* a legal norm [i.e., they may be evidence of *opinio juris*] cannot constitute the material component of custom"); Anglo-Norwegian Fisheries Case (U.K. v. Nor.), 1951 I.C.J. 116, 191 (Judgment of Dec. 18):

> Customary international law is the generalization of the practice of States. This cannot be established by citing cases where coastal States have made extensive claims, but have not maintained their claims by the actual assertion of sovereignty over trespassing foreign ships. . . .
>
> The only convincing evidence of State practice is to be found in seizures, where the coastal State asserts its sovereignty over the waters in question by arresting a foreign ship and by maintaining its position in the course of diplomatic negotiation and international arbitration.

Id. at 191 (diss. op. Read, J.).

73. *See* 1 H. LAUTERPACHT, *supra* note 25, at 62 ("It is clear that if absolute and universal uniformity were to be required, only a very few rules could rank as general customary rules of international law."). The persistent objector doctrine makes the creation of a new customary rule possible even against outspoken and consistent opposition of a state. This doctrine, developed by the Anglo-Norwegian Fisheries Case (U.K. v. Nor.), 1951 I.C.J. 116 (Judgment of Dec. 18), is adopted by most writers. *See, e.g.*, 1 H. LAUTERPACHT, *supra* note 25, at 66; H. THIRLWAY, *supra* note 24, at 110; Virally, *supra* note 1, at 137. *cf.* A. D'AMATO, *supra* note 1, at 261 (applying the doctrine to "special," but not "general" custom). Although one could say that the consensual nature of custom is jeopardized by this doctrine, most defenders of "persistent objector doctrine" argue that it protects the ability of a large number of states to establish norms consensually and not be frustrated by a single state. *See* 1 H. LAUTERPACHT, *supra* note 25, at 66.

> The fact that universal consent is not required for the creation of custom and that general consent is sufficient, is not a factor pointing to the irrelevance of consent in the creation of custom; it is merely a factor pointing to the irrelevance of the consent of every single state.

Id.

have struggled to dominance, but the greater burden not to counter the subjective consent of the important states.[74] Likewise, the hard positions emphasizing consent of the specially affected can be reimagined so as to enshrine the just notion that the specially affected are also most likely to produce good norms.[75]

A similar rhetorical pattern structures doctrines about the extent of the force of treaty and customary international law. In the first instance, doctrines about the ability of treaties to bind municipally or to bind third and successor states seem preoccupied with measuring the extent of consent. Treaties are binding internally if enacted as municipal legislation,[76] if so provided by internal constitutional law,[77] or if "self-executing," a characterization that depends primarily upon the intent of the parties to create a self-executing document.[78] Treaties bind third parties and successor states if they accept the obligation,[79] and give third parties rights if such was the intent of the signatories.[80]

---

74. *See* Akehurst, *supra* note 1, at 23 (it is harder to overlook the state whose practice is more frequent or famous than that of other states); A. D'Amato, *supra* note 1, at 96-97 (states with highly sophisticated international legal practice are more likely to be given more weight in developing customary consensus).

75. *See, e.g.*, North Sea Continental Shelf Cases (W. Ger. v. Den., W. Ger. v. Neth.), 1969 I.C.J. 3, 126 (Judgment of Feb. 20) (diss. op. Lachs, J.) (emphasizing the participation in the Continental Shelf Convention of interested states "who are actively engaged in the exploration of continental shelves").

76. This is the approach of the United Kingdom and the Scandanavian countries. *See* I. Brownlie, *supra* note 1, at 50 (describing techniques of statutory enactment); Waldock, *supra* note 1, at 131 (describing practice of British courts which "refuse to apply treaties modifying legal rights or obligations within domestic law unless Parliament has first enacted a law expressly incorporating the treaty into domestic law").

77. A number of states adhere to the principle that treaties made in accordance with their respective constitutions bind the courts without any specific act of incorporation. This practice is described by I. Brownlie, *supra* note 1, at 52; Mosler, *Application du droit international public par les tribuneaux nationaux*, 91 Recueil des Cours 625 (1957); Waldock, *supra* note 1, at 130.

78. This is the United States approach. *See* Fujii v. California, 38 Cal. 2d 718, 721, 242 P.2d 617, 620 (1952) ("In determining whether a treaty is self-executing courts look to the intent of the signatory parties as manifested by the language of the instrument"). For a survey of United States practice, see J. Russotto, L'application des traités self-executing en droit américan (1969). For a comprehensive and revealing analysis of the hard and soft strands of argument in the discourse about self-executing treaties, see N. Grabar, Limit on the Self-Execution of Treaties in United States Doctrine (1982) (unpublished manuscript, on file Harvard Law School Library).

79. *See supra* notes 21-22. This is codified in Article 35 of the Vienna Convention on the Law of Treaties which allows third parties to be bound if they "expressly accept that obligation in writing." Vienna Convention, *supra* note 5, at art. 35. In practice, separate "devolution" agreements generally govern the transfer of obligations to successor or third parties.

80. *See supra* notes 21-22. This doctrine was formulated by the Permanent Court of International Justice in the Free Zones of Upper Savoy and the District of Gex Cases (Fr. v. Switz.), 1932 P.C.I.J. (ser. A/B), No. 46, at 147 (Judgment of June 7) ("It cannot be lightly presumed that stipulations favorable to a third State have been

Each of these doctrines, however, is also associable with softer notions of justice. Sometimes this takes the form of an objective approach to consent. Intent to be self-executing can be implied from the treaty itself—perhaps from its objective clarity.[81] Successors are bound if it is reasonable to expect them to have intended to be bound—if they have not abrogated or denounced the treaty.[82] Moreover, these characteristically hard positions are simply reinterpreted as expressions of justice rather than consent. For example, treaties are thought to be self-executing when that appears required by the nature of the provision regardless of any implication about consent.[83] Successors are not bound by unequal treaties while successors are bound and third parties receive rights when it would be unjust to allow otherwise.[84] These soft positions can also be reinterpreted as methods of protecting the subjective intentions of the other contracting parties to know to what it is they have agreed.

In the first instance, by contrast, doctrines about the extent of the force of custom seem governed by custom's ability to register justice or the nature and requirements of the international system. Nonparticipants in the process of custom formation such as new states and those outside the region in which the custom is developed are bound if the rule seems justly to suit their situation as well, or if it is a wise norm or one associated with other basic norms defining the nature of the system like "reciprocity" or "sovereignty" or "equity." Successor states and governments are bound because they partake in the international system whose nature customary norms express.[85]

---

adopted with the object of creating an actual right in its favour. There is, however, nothing to prevent the will of sovereign States from having this object and this effect."). *See* Jiménez de Aréchaga, *Treaty Stipulations in Favor of Third States*, 50 AM. J. INT'L L. 338 (1956). The classic examples of such treaties are the United Nations Charter (particularly Article 35(2) permitting non-members to call upon the Security Council in some cases), and treaties regulating canals or international straits. *See* 1 C. ROUSSEAU, *supra* note 6, at 187-88.

81. *See supra* note 78.

82. *See supra* notes 12 and 14. This is the approach of the classic neo-universal succession theory which implies consent by successor states and devolves all treaty obligations upon them *ipso jure* unless the new state opts out by denunciation should the treaty seem incompatible with its basic interests. *See* C. JENKS, *supra* note 22, at 94; 2 D. O'CONNELL, *supra* note 22, at 23-24.

83. *See supra* note 78; I. BROWNLIE, *supra* note 1, at 53 ("the term [self-executing] is also used to describe the *character* of the rules themselves"); *see also* Foster v. Neilson, 27 U.S. (2 Pet.) 253, 314 (1829) (developing objective approach to self-execution).

84. *See* sources quoted *supra* note 23.

85. Although most classic commentators argue against the "unequal treaty" exception on the basis of hard arguments (*see supra* note 22), they base their opposition to the *tabula rasa* theory of state succession in soft arguments. *See* Waldock, *supra* note

Nevertheless, discourse about these doctrines is also animated by a harder emphasis on consent. Sometimes this rhetorical change in emphasis is expressed by countervailing doctrines. Successor states, new states and extra-regional states should only be bound, in this version, to customs which they accept or helped (perhaps as colonies) to develop.[86] The soft doctrines, however, are also interpreted to express consent rather than justice. New states should be bound by custom because they consent to it by participating in the international system to whose nature they consent and from which, in exchange for their consent to consensual norms, they have received the "advantages" of statehood.[87] Doctrines which have been rhetorically characterized as consensual are also often reinterpreted as expressions of a concern for objectivity and justice. For example, successor states and ex-colonies should only be

---

1, at 52 (emphasizing reciprocity):

> [T]he fundamental objection to it [the *tabula rasa* approach] is that it really denies the existence of a general international legal order and the new States have at least as much to lose as anyone else from a denial of the validity of existing international law. If consent is so far the basis of customary law that a new State may reject any customary rule it chooses, how can it be said that an older State is not free, vis-à-vis the new State, to reject any customary rule that it may choose. Either there is an international legal order or there is not.

Id.; *see also* Virally, *supra* note 1, at 138 (emphasizing equity):

> This is beyond dispute: nothing else would be acceptable either to the new state concerned or to the other states. As a result, the new state becomes bound by all those rules of international customary law which are applicable indifferently to all independent states. By its entry into the international community the new State acquires the status of an independent state, with all the rights and obligations which are attached to that Status by general international law.

Id.; *cf.* Sørensen, *Principes de droit international public*, 101 RECUEIL DES COURS 1, 45-46 (emphasizing basic norms of international system):

> A l'encontre de cette opinion on pourrait opposer l'argument suivant. D'après la doctrine classique, les règles coutumières ne se limitent pas à imposer des obligations aux états nouveaux. Elles créent également des droits en leur faveur et à la charge des états anciens, par exemple le respect de leur souveraineté territoriale.

Id.

86. *See supra* note 23. This is the position of voluntarist socialist doctrine. *See* G. TUNKIN, *supra* note 23, at 129.

87. *See supra* note 23; *see also* G. TUNKIN, *supra* note 23, at 179. "If however, a new State enters without reservations into official relations with other countries, this signifies that it accepts the specific complex of principles and norms of prevailing international law as being the basic principles of relations among states." *Id.*; *see also* DDR LEHRBUCH, *supra* note 10, at 264 (emphasizing both hard and soft bases for implication):

> Da [die neuen Staaten] diese Beziehungen zu den schon bestehenden Staaten aufnehmen und entwickeln wollen, ergibt sich daraus, dass es ihren *Interessen* und ihrem *Willen* entsprechen wird, solche Normen des Völkergewohnheitsrechts, die für die Entwicklung derartiger Beziehungen wesentlich und international weitgehend anerkannt sind, als auch für sich bindend anzusehen . . . sie stimmen damit diesen Normen zu.

Id. (emphasis added).

bound by those customs which they helped to create because this is the only way to ensure that the system of norms reflects the interests of states which it binds, itself a condition of justice.[88]

Taken as a group, doctrines about treaties and custom also blend hard and soft in a repetitive fashion. Just as treaty and custom seem differentially hard and soft, doctrines limiting the extent of the force of treaty or customary law have a similar but inverse structure. If doctrines of treaty creation seem consensual (ratification, for example), they are tempered by exceptions which are based in justice (like *rebus sic stantibus*). If doctrines of custom creation seem based on a conception of the good, they are tempered by doctrines providing for consensual opting out (persistent opposer, etc.). These subordinate doctrines, moreover, are inferior "exceptions" to doctrines about the creation of treaty or custom.

The presence of these two streams in treaty law is easy to uncover. Throughout the Vienna Convention on the Law of Treaties consent vies with justice and subjective consent vies with objective consent for supremacy as the source of obligation to abide by treaty law.[89] Some-

88. *See supra* notes 22-24. These considerations are blended by M. BEDJAOUI, *supra* note 52. *Cf.* Anand, *Riole of the "New" Asian-African Countries in the Present International Legal Order*, 56 AM. J. INT'L. L. 383, 388 (1962):

> International law has in fact come to be accepted by these countries except where it is still found to support past colonial rights. . . . There is never any plea for its over-all rejection. The "new" countries have come to accept international law as such and they always plead their cases according to its rules. They in fact claim to be "scrupulous" adherents to it. They believe it acts as a protection for them because they are the weaker members of international society.

Id.

89. The Vienna Convention, *supra* note 5, contains four major substantive sections, which consider treaty formation (conclusion and entry into force), treaty compliance (application, observation, and interpretation), treaty modification or amendment, and treaty lapse (invalidity, termination, and suspension). In the first instance, it seems that the first two parts are in some tension with the latter pair. The first deal with the binding force of treaties, the latter with derogations from that force. Moreover, the first two are primarily cast in terms of consent, the latter in terms of justice. Thus, the first contain primarily doctrines about registering and understanding consent, while doctrines of duress or changed circumstances form the main body of the latter two sections. This potential tension is avoided throughout the document by adoption of what might be thought of as a principle-exception framework. Consent operates as the *primary* source of obligation until it is trumped by an exception in situations of injustice. The treatment of consent as *primary* is reinforced by the characterization of the justice component as an *exception*. Yet the very nature of an exception, of course, is that it overrules the principle, and is in that sense *primary*. This framework is repeated within each of the sections, a repetition which reduces sensitivity to the polarity of principle and exception. Thus, for example, the fundamental rule of consent is coupled with a "good faith" requirement and the section about treaty formation is littered with the unresolved invocations of an objective approach to consent. *See* Vienna Convention, *supra* note 5, at art. 26. This objective approach, coupled with the good faith requirement, allows justification of the consensual aspects of the first two major sections in

times these two strands are kept apart. Modern hornbooks consider separately the formal *pacta sunt servanda* rule and the obligation of good faith governing treaty obligations.[90] Sometimes they are blended together. Article 26 of the Vienna Convention incorporates both: "every treaty in force is binding upon the parties to it and must be performed by them in good faith."[91] Throughout the Convention, absolute duty is coupled with a good faith lubricant, and the formal triggers for duty or release from duty to perform are paired with an exception for unjust results, or implied contravention of intended results.

Emphasis on the *pacta sunt servanda* rule is often supported by arguments about consent, while good faith obligations and exceptions for duress or *rebus sic stantibus* are usually associated with the view that treaties are binding as expressions of justice.[92] These associations are also familiar when reversed. The *pacta sunt servanda* rule seems a con-

---

terms of social justice. In part III, justice concerns are fundamental, yet are introduced as exceptions, or limits on consent. Thus, for example, Article 31 reads: "a treaty shall be interpreted in good faith in accordance with the ordinary meaning to be given to the terms . . . in the light of [the treaty's] object and purpose," thus introducing nonconsensual elements as *additions* to the basic intentional basis which are understood to supplement or explicate the subjective intent. *Id.* at art. 31. Thus, those soft elements which are introduced in this section of the treaty are cast in terms of consent, just as the consensual elements of the earlier sections were cast in terms of social justice. Likewise, the basic provision for *jus cogens* (Article 53) which sets limits on the scope of the freedom to make treaties is stated as an *exception* to general freedom and cast in terms of consent, defining *jus cogens* thus: "for the purposes of the present Convention, a preemptory norm of general international law is a norm *accepted* and *recognized* by the international community of States as a whole. . . . " *Id.* at art. 53 (emphasis added).

90. *See, e.g.*, 1 C. ROUSSEAU, *supra* note 6, at 53; W. HOLDER & G. BRENNAN, THE INTERNATIONAL LEGAL SYSTEM (1972); M. MCDOUGAL & W. REISMAN, *supra* note 67.

91. Vienna Convention, *supra* note 5, at art. 26.

92. *See supra* note 89; *infra* note 94; *see also* I. BROWNLIE, *supra* note 1, at 595, 599; E. MENZEL & K. IPSEN, *supra* note 25, at 329-30. The principle of good faith is connected to the idea of justice in the jurisprudence of the Permanent Court of International Justice and International Court of Justice. Waldock observes that the "good faith" idea has been regarded as a "general principle of law" in the sense of Article 38 of the Statute of the Court. Waldock, *supra* note 1, at 58-59; *see* Certain German Interests in Polish Upper Silesia (Ger. v. Pol.), 1926 P.C.I.J. (ser. A) No. 7, at 30, 37-39 (Judgment of May 25); Free Zones of Upper Savoy and the District of Gex (Second Phase) (Fr. v. Switz.), 1930 P.C.I.J. (ser. A) No. 24, at 12 (Order of Dec. 6); Conditions of Admission of a State to Membership in the United Nations, 1948 I.C.J. 57, 79-80 (Advisory Opinion of May 28). When expressed in this way, the two principles seem at odds with one another, a contradiction which most commentators seem to acknowledge with such observations as "[t]reaties are inviolable, but not forever" (International Law Commission, Summary Records of the Fifteenth Session, 694th meeting, remarks by Anado, [1963] 1 Y.B. INT'L L. COMM'N 135, 142) or "[t]he principle of a respect for treaty obligations is one of the pillars of international law. . . . At the same time, the *pacta sunt servanda* rule cannot be fetishized" (Haraszti, *Treaties and Fundamental Change of Circumstances*, 146 RECUEIL DES COURS 1, 59 (1975)).

dition of justice,[93] while the good faith or *rebus sic stantibus* rules seem restatements of the consensual force of norms.[94]

The interesting point, however, is not this duality, apparent throughout the doctrines of both treaty and custom, but the various ways in which this polarity can be rhetorically managed. Sometimes this is achieved by reference to an interpretive method which "complements" the rhetorical emphasis of the doctrine in question. Arguments for an intent-based interpretation of soft norms and a justice-based interpretation of hard doctrines have been analyzed elsewhere.[95] Despite the appearance of resolution which such an approach gives these doctrines, however, once an intent-based approach is chosen, it remains difficult

93. *See supra* note 29; *see also* A. VERDROSS & B. SIMMA, *supra* note 4, at 295-96.

94. The treatment of good faith or *rebus sic stantibus* as "implied" terms in the treaty is standard in most texts, just as it is standard to justify *pacta sunt servanda* as a matter of social justice. *See* J. MÜLLER, *supra* note 17 (*rebus sic stantibus* is an implied term in all treaties); *see also* C. FENWICK, INTERNATIONAL LAW 454 (4th ed. 1965). Fenwick posits that all international contracts are entered into under certain implied conditions, which accompany the express conditions of the treaty and are equally part of the "valuable consideration" which forms the essence of the contract. This view is criticized strongly by the International Law Commission as "a fiction by which it was attempted to reconcile the dissolution of treaties in the consequence of a fundamental change of circumstance with the rule *pacta sunt servanda*." Reports of the Commission, *supra* note 11, at 258. Many commentators are now forthright about this contradiction. *See* C. FENWICK, *supra* at 458.

> [I]nternational law must continue to witness the struggle of two conflicting principles: on the one hand the necessity of stability in international relations and on the other hand the demand for such changes in the legal situation created by past treaties as will meet the requirements of present justice. . . [I]n international relations a way must be found to make obligation and justice coincide, with perhaps a margin on the side of obligation in the interest of that law and order which is the primary condition of justice.

Id. Many continue to blend the two strands by treating them as matters of "interpretation" which must be carried out so as to reflect both. *See, e.g.*, Lissitzyn, *Treaties and Changed Circumstances*, 61 AM. J. INT'L. L. 895, 896 (1967).

> Thus viewed, the problem of the effect of a change of circumstances on treaty relationships becomes in principle one of interpretation—of establishing the shared intentions and expectations of the parties. This approach is consistent with . . . the principle of *pacta sunt servanda* . . . A treaty is not breached if it is not applied in circumstances in which the parties did not intend or expect it to be applied. Indeed, to expect performance contrary to shared expectations not only could be regarded as inconsistent with good faith, but could also produce resentment which would undermine rather than promote stability.

Id. For a discussion on the history of the clause, see Haraszti, *supra* note 92, at 46 *passim*.

95. *See supra* note 94; *see also* Gross, *Treaty Interpretation: The Proper Role of an Impartial Tribunal*, AM. SOC'Y INT'L. L. PROC. 108 (1969); Larson, *Between Scylla and Charybdis in Treaty Interpretation*, 63 AM. J. INT'L. L. 108 (1969) (contrasting the extreme positions of Falk, *On Treaty Interpretation and the New Haven Approach: Achievements and Prospects*, 8 VA. J. INT'L L. 323 (1968) and Metzger, *Treaty Interpretation and the United States-Italy Air Transport Arbitration*, 61 AM. J. INT'L. L. 1007 (1967)).

to stabilize whether one should concentrate upon formal expressions of intent or supply what must have been the parties' intention, or what would have been a reasonable state's intention under the circumstances had the problem been foreseen.

I am more interested in rhetorical strategies of closure which rely upon the relationships among doctrinal strands and characterizations. For these strategies, the important thing to understand about these various doctrinal discussions is not only the recurring applicability of hard arguments in soft contexts and *vice versa.* Far more crucial is the potential these sub-doctrines offer, because they are differentiated and defined by the same tendencies which differentiated custom and treaty, to support the sense that the overall doctrinal structure has this tension under control. For example, each doctrine about the creation of treaty or custom can be set off against an exception which expresses the opposite tendency. By setting the rule against the exception, tempering it by its rhetorical opposite, sources argument can appear to have taken both hard and soft considerations "into account" and thereby reach closure in particular cases. This combination of differentiation and hierarchically organized recharacterization through proliferation suits doctrines about treaty and custom to rhetorical strategies which will sustain the hard and soft images of international law as a whole.

To develop argumentative strategies for embracing and containing these tensions, I explore discourse about four doctrines: one creating binding obligations and one ending obligation for both treaty and custom. Treaty obligations seem consensually created. Dropping a treaty obligation before its fulfillment seems appropriate only when some extraconsensual standard provides an alternative to the harsh fulfillment of the original intent. Of course, it would also be possible to examine *pacta sunt servanda* from the perspective of its "good faith" softener and think of *rebus sic stantibus* as an implied term of the original treaty. To investigate the rhetorical possibilities opened up by these associations, I consider a series of doctrinal arguments about "unilateral declarations" and *rebus sic stantibus.* I then consider arguments about custom creation and termination which utilize similar, if often opposing, rhetorical strategies.

A. The Case of Unilateral Declarations

Argument about the binding force of unilateral declarations at international law takes place in what might be thought of as the most consensual corner of sources discourse. As such it seems exemplary of treaty doctrine as a whole, and the techniques for managing the relationship between hard and soft strands of sources rhetoric seem particularly vivid. The relationship between unilateral declarations and treaties is difficult to grasp. From one perspective, all legally binding acts are unilateral, to the extent that bilateral and multilateral acts are composed of separately binding unilateral promises.[96] From another perspective, however, even acts which seem unilaterally binding are bilateral in the sense that they can only be binding if another party can call upon the obligation.[97] These two visions of the distinctiveness of unilateral acts seem differentially hard and soft. Those who imagine unilateral acts to have a separate legal significance might seem to rely upon a consent-based approach to legal obligations. In this view, even multilateral treaties are composed of individual obligations, binding because of the consent of the state agreeing to be bound. Analysts characterize multilateral treaties as unilateral obligations by relying upon this consensual element. In this extreme hard view, other systemic or relational considerations distinguishing multilateral arrangements would not affect to the authoritative nature of the obligation. Similarly, those who emphasize the systemic or bilateral nature of unilateral acts might rely upon a soft vision of obligation. States might seem bound, even by a unilateral act, because of the expectations which it has raised in others.

These associations might be reversed. We might focus on the unilateral nature of all acts in an objective way, seeing their binding character in communal acceptance. Alternatively, we might suppose that it is the unilateral components of multilateral acts which bind because these reflect the systemic conditions applicable to each sovereign. An approach emphasizing the multilateral nature of unilateral acts, more-

96. *See* Rubin, *The International Effects of Unilateral Declarations*, 71 AM. J. INT'L L. 1, 8 (1977).

97. *See, e.g.*, Franck, *World Made Law: The Decision of the ICJ in the Nuclear Test Cases*, 69 AM. J. INT'L L. 612, 617 (1975):

> "[C]ommon lawyers, reared in the culture of "consideration," have difficulty accepting as truly binding a unilateral commitment wholly devoid of anything like a grain of mutuality. . . .
>
> At common law, reliance is a necessary ingredient: acts or abstentions based on the assumptions that the unilateral promisor will keep his word."

Id.; *see also* E. SUY, *supra* note 1, at 111: "La détection de ces promesses purement unilatérales exige un effort de recherche minutieux afin de déterminer si, derrière la façade de l'unilatéralité formelle d'une déclaration de volunté, ne se cache pas une bilatéralité de fond." *Id.* American scholars in particular have little enthusiasm for the idea, advanced by Suy, Reuter, Rousseau, and other French and Italian writers that some unilateral acts alone are binding. In modern texts, the term "unilateral acts" does not appear in the index. *See, e.g.*, B. WESTON, R. FALK & A. D'AMATO, INTERNATIONAL LAW AND WORLD ORDER; L. HENKIN, R. PUGH, O. SCHACHTER & H. SMIT, INTERNATIONAL LAW: CASES AND MATERIALS (1980).

over, might rely on hard arguments. An objective approach to unilateral declarations might seem appropriate because it protects the subjective will of the other states. Consequently, even in what might seem the hardest corner of sources doctrine we find both hard and soft arguments available.

Although it has often been recognized that unilateral acts and declarations sometimes create international legal obligations, it is clear that not all such declarations do so.[98] A number of criteria have been suggested for distinguishing the binding from the nonbinding unilateral declaration. Some rely strictly upon the declarant's intention to be bound, and some supplement their reliance upon intention with some more systemic factor, such as reliance, raised expectations, or the existence of another state which could reasonably have had its expectations raised and thus has standing to hold the declarant to its word.[99] The

98. Pfluger was one of the first to dedicate a treatise to the subject of unilateral acts and declarations. *See* E. PFLUGER, DIE EINSEITIGEN RECHTSGESCHÄFTE IN VÖLKERRECHT (1936). An important monograph is E. SUY, *supra* note 1. *See also* sources cited *supra* note 97. Rubin, *supra* note 96, at 28 questions: "Whence came the Court's conviction that such unilateral declarations are binding?" and concludes that the pronouncement of the Court appears to have been *ultra vires* because it comes:

> Not from any treaty . . ., thus not from Article 38(1)(a) of the Statute of the Court; not from any known international custom as evidence of a practice accepted as law, thus not from Article 38(1)(b) of the Statute; not from any principle accepted by Anglo-American courts or commentators or from "any general principles of law," thus not from Article 38(1)(c) of the Statute; and indeed, not from the unequivocal writings of any publicists or judicial decisions that have focused squarely on the question, thus not from Article 38(1)(d) of the Statute.

Id. (footnote omitted).

99. Several theories have been advanced to justify the binding force of unilateral declarations. Some rely upon "good faith" or principles of community justice; others upon the "intention" of the declarant or the reasonable intention of the listener; and still others on some formulaic blend of the two like "*pacta sunt servanda.*" For the first type, see Schwarzenberger, *The Fundamental Principles of International Law*, 87 RECUEIL DES COURS 195, 312 (1955):

> If a subject of international law chooses to take up a position in relation to a matter which is legally relevant and communicates this intent to others it is bound within such limits to accept the legal implications of such a unilateral act. . . . No doubt, in the formative stage of this rule, the obnoxiousness of self-contradictory behavior and *venire contra factum proprium* assisted in creating the *opinio iuris sive necessitatis* which marks the border-line between international comity and international customary law.

Id.; *see also* Jacqué, *A Propos de la Promesse Unilatérale*, in MÉLANGES À PAUL REUTER 326 (1981). For texts of the second sort, see Fitzmaurice, *supra* note 17, at 230:

> Such a [unilateral] Declaration may or may not create binding legal obligations . . . it seems fairly well settled that it can and will do so only if clearly intended to have that effect, and held out, so to speak, as an instrument on which others may rely and under which the declarant purports to assume such obligations.

Id. For texts which combine these two approaches, see P. REUTER, DROIT INTERNATIONAL PUBLIC 142 (5th ed. 1976):

> Une promesse, faite unilaterale en faveur d'un, de plusieurs ou de tous les Etats

apparently harder of these two positions, in which an intentional declarant is bound, may rely on the actual subjective intent of the declarant, or may imply that intent from the circumstances. In the extreme, the subjective intention of the declarant may only be known from what the declarant claims to have been his subjective intent. This very extreme approach removes softer considerations to rhetoric about evidence and the nature of proof. Argument about unilateral declarations, like the doctrines of treaty law generally, thus seems continually to complement its primarily hard rhetoric with a softer alternative.

The classic unilateral declarations case exemplifies various strategies for managing the relationship between these two strands of sources rhetoric. The 1974 Nuclear Tests case between Australia and France arose out of objections by Australia to French nuclear testing in the South Pacific.[100] During 1974, the President of the French Republic made a series of public statements to the effect that since advancing technology would permit future testing to be conducted underground, France would cease atmospheric nuclear testing.[101] The International Court of Justice sought to determine whether these statements legally bound France to refrain from further atmospheric tests.[102]

A number of rhetorical strategies were available to Australia and France. One way of structuring the possibilities in accordance with their relative reliance upon consent might be the following:

> (ou d'une organisation) peut-elle engager son auteur à l'égard de cet Etat (ou organisation) de ces Etats? Il n'y a aucune raison de ne pas l'admettre lorsque la promesse est manifestement faite avec cette intention. Cette affirmation est basée sur le principe de la bonne foi et plus spécialement sur l'obligation de respecter les convictions que l'on fait naître par son comportement.

Id.; *see also* A. VERDROSS & B. SIMMA, *supra* note 4, at 344:

> Die überwiegende Lehre anerkennt die Verbindlichkeit eines Versprechens, wenn der versprechende Staat eine solche begründen wollte *und* die anderen Staaten ihr Verhalten nach diese Erklärung orientiert haben. Die Verbindlichkeit des Versprechens besteht also, um das Vertrauen, das andere Staaten einer solchen Erklärung entgegenbringen, zu schützen.

Id. (emphasis added). For a text of the third type, see E. SUY, *supra* note 1, at 45.

100. Nuclear Tests Case (Austr. v. Fr.), 1974 I.C.J. 253 (Judgment of Dec. 20).

101. Parts of these statements are quoted by the Court itself. *Id.* at 265, 266.

102. The issue was not originally presented to the Court in this way. Rather, Australia complained that the tests violated substantive international law and sought a judgment to that effect. During the proceedings, various French government officials made public statements to the effect that the testing program was to be terminated. The Court, taking cognizance of these statements, declined to reach the merits of Australia's claim, holding instead that France was bound by its unilateral statements to discontinue testing. Ironically, Australia had actually stressed in urging the Court to reach the merits their sense that France was *not* bound by these statements. France did not appear. The judgment considered the claim that France was bound as though France would oppose and Australia support that ruling.

Australia: (Hard) Intent to be bound alone binds. The unilateral declaration is binding.

France: (Hard) Intent binds, but we did not intend to be bound. These were merely "policy statements." Moreover, if intent binds only we can know our intent.

Australia: (Softening) Intent binds, but must be judged by the evidence.

France: (Hard) If intent binds, we now change our intent: all statements of intent must reserve the possibility of changing our mind.

Australia: (Soft) This is not possible because it would upset systemic values like the fairness of fulfilling reasonable expectations or reliance or of keeping one's promises.

France: (Soft) We accept those systemic values, but no one should have relied since we were not bound and it was not a promise.

Australia: (Hard) I have ten states here who did rely, including ourselves and only I can interpret my reliance. You must keep your word regardless of whether you thought it was a promise so that I might rely and be able to consent informedly.

France: (Soft) Our approach to the systemic values which are implicated here is different. It seems equitable or fair to let us remain unbound.

Australia: (Hard) Accepted and recognized norms are otherwise.

In this hypothetical oral argument, France is able repeatedly to invoke Australia's principle against her, forcing her to switch from hard to soft arguments. Were the argument to continue, each party would be driven through incompatible positions. Of course, it would be surprising if any or even most of these arguments were to be found in the International Court of Justice opinion, or, for that matter, in the pleadings. The aim of the argument is to terminate this potentially endless dialogue in a persuasive fashion. In the International Court of Justice opinion, this was accomplished by switching repeatedly between two incompatible perspectives. The Court's opinion considers whether a unilateral declaration can be binding, under what conditions this may be true, and who may decide these questions. At each stage the judgment embraces the contradictory tendencies illustrated by the hypothetical debate.

The substantive portion of the Court's judgment begins with a statement of what it takes to be the rule of applicable law: "It is well recognized that declarations made by way of unilateral acts, concerning legal or factual situations, may have the effect of creating legal obligations."[103] This conclusion is supported by two different principles. First, the Court argues that unilateral declarations are binding because and to the extent that they express the intention of the declarant to be bound. This classic hard argument is expressed as follows:

> When it is the intention of the State making the declaration that it should become bound according to its terms, that intention confers on the declaration the character of a legal undertaking, the State being thenceforth legally required to follow a course of conduct consistent with the declaration.[104]

This approach is picked up in the dissenting opinion of Judge de Castro, who uses it to support the conclusion that France cannot be bound by these "policy statements."

> For a promise to be legally binding on a State, it is necessary that the authorities from which it emanates should be competent so to bind the State (a question of internal constitutional law and international law) and that they should manifest the intention and will to bind the State (a question of interpretation).[105]

On the other hand, the Court justifies the conclusion that unilateral declarations are binding with soft arguments about the systemic requirements of good faith:

> One of the basic principles governing the creation and performance of legal obligations, whatever their source, is the principle of good faith. Trust and confidence are inherent in international co-operation, in particular in an age when this co-operation in many fields is becoming increasingly essential. Just as the very rule of *pacta sunt servanda* in the law of treaties is based on good faith, so also is the binding character of an international obligation assumed by unilateral declaration. *Thus interested States may take cognizance of unilateral declarations and place confidence in them*, and are entitled to require that the obligation thus created be respected.[106]

Commentators reflect this dual basis for the binding nature of unilateral declarations. Macdonald and Hough, for example, summarize the holding of the Nuclear Test case as follows: "In order to find that a statement imposes a binding obligation, it is essential to find that the person making the statement intended it to do so. The issue is not whether in the circumstances the person should be bound but rather whether he intended to be bound."[107] Eric Suy restates the view that binding acts are "une manifestation de volonté . . . à laquelle une norme de cet ordre juridique rattache des conséquences cor-

103. *Id.* at 267.
104. *Id.*
105. *Id.* at 374.
106. *Id.* at 268 (emphasis added).
107. Macdonald & Hough, *The Nuclear Tests Case Revisited*, 20 GER. Y.B. INT'L. L. 338, 352 (1977).

respondantes à la volonté."[108] On the other hand, Macdonald and Hough conclude: "The binding character of unilateral declarations is based on the need for good faith (trust and confidence) in international relations."[109]

Invoking both theories presents the Court with a rhetorical problem, for these two approaches could as easily appear incompatible as complementary and might each as easily support the conclusion that unilateral declarations should not be binding. This potential for rhetorical contradiction and indeterminacy needs to be appreciated in order to understand the delicacy of the Court's resolution.

Although the Court argues that the binding nature of unilateral declarations can be grounded in the intent of the declarant, reliance upon the subjective intentions of the declarant opens up the possibility that France should be allowed to change its mind. Commentators seem to recognize this point when they suggest that if the declaration were *binding*, it must not have been truly unilateral. Intent alone cannot support the idea of obligation.

Also, it seems questionable that, if the French declaration was binding, it was unilateral. As Suy points out, "La détection de ces promesses purement unilatérales exige un effort de recherche minutieux afin de déterminer si, derrière la façade de l'unilatéralité, formelle d'une déclaration de volunté, ne se cache pas une bilatéralité de fond." If a declaration is made in response to a request for such a declaration, it is bilateral. And if France's statements constituted an undertaking, it is plausible to view them as a response to Australia's request for such an undertaking.[110]

The hard intent-based approach seems to preclude the binding nature of purely unilateral obligations, requiring what at first seemed the softer rule; that purely unilateral obligations are not binding:

> The ICJ's logic seems odd in positing a system in which states are *not* conceived as constantly negotiating with each other, but in which unilateral acts have legal results identical to the results they would have if states were constantly negotiating with each other. Those problems cannot wholly be avoided, but they can be minimized by confining the discussion to a more superficial level by avoiding the discussion of the theory that underlies the conception of the legal effects of "unilateral" acts that the Court seems to have had in mind.[111]

---

108. E. Suy, *supra* note 1, at 22. On unilateral acts, see *supra* notes 96-97; Schwarzenberger, *supra* note 99, at 548-61; M. Hudson, The Permanent Court of International Justice, 1920-42, 631-36 (1943).

109. Macdonald & Hough, *supra* note 107, at 341.

110. *Id.* at 354; E. Suy, *supra* note 1, at 111.

111. Rubin, *supra* note 96, at 9.

To this commentator, the hard consent-based approach which the Court seemed to adopt appeared to require a community which the Court precluded.

> Thus, analyses that reflect a view of the international order as emphasizing sovereign equality and independence, as regarding all acts by states as essentially "unilateral" but part of a system of constant adjustment of rights and obligations in which legal significance is given to each of those acts, are simply inconsistent with the ICJ's basic approach.[112]

Although the Court argues that the systemic interests in predictability and good faith require that unilateral obligations be binding, one might as easily imagine a world in which the expectation of obligation arose only when registered by the community by acceptance, consideration, or exchange. The principle of good faith could be thought to require only that bilateral, or systemicly implicated obligations are binding. Good faith would then seem incompatible with the *unilateral* nature of a unilateral declaration. Perhaps this is what commentators mean when they argue that "if France's statements constituted an undertaking," it might better be seen to be bilateral. One commentator pointed to the incompatibility of the soft "good faith" approach and the *unilateral* aspects of the norm which the Court invoked:

> But since no concept of "good faith" can make binding a policy declaration or other pronouncement that is *not* binding because not conceived as binding by any party concerned, to argue that "good faith" alone creates the obligation is to argue in support of an obvious absurdity.[113]

This same commentator noted that from a hard approach, all binding acts are unilateral.

> Every legally significant act in a legal system that posits individual legal personality is, in a sense, unilateral. Thus, in most if not all legal systems that have a concept of contract, the contractual tie is created by the law giving legal value to various acts of the several parties to the transaction.[114]

Despite the ambiguity of each principle's meaning for the binding nature of unilateral declarations, moreover, each of these two principles, seems to require the abandonment of the other. If states are to remain free and if the independence of intent means anything, the state ought to be able to decide when it is bound—free of external requirements of good faith. If any system of good faith is to endure, on the other hand, states cannot remain free to change their minds once having given their word. This problem might be thought of as the tension

112. *Id.*
113. *Id.*
114. *Id.* at 8 (footnote omitted).

between the extreme forms of positions which when limited might coexist. To test that vision, we must examine how the Court was able to make these two justifications seem compatible.

The opinion rendered these two principles compatible in part by expressing each in a way which affirmed its opposite and denied itself. We have seen that each principle has two elements, one which supports and one which opposes unilateral declarations. The Court exploited this rhetorical diversity to blend both approaches in a way which seemed to support the binding nature of unilateral declarations. The soft argument of good faith was made to seem compatible with the intent-based hard argument by emphasizing the manifestation of each which supported the bindingness of unilateral declarations. For example, the systemic conditions of justice were understood to mean protecting the freedom of each sovereign.

In the Court's opinion, the soft principle of good faith was made compatible with the seemingly intent-based rule in two ways. First, the Court emphasized that good faith protects the ability of other states to "place confidence in" and "rely upon" unilateral statements in making their own subjective calculations. The good faith argument, then, is able to remain consistent with a hard intent-based approach because it associates itself with Australia's interests, not those of France. Second, the soft argument simply embraces the content of intent. The ability of France to bind itself depends upon the systemic value of good faith. Thus, the hard intent-based norm, like the rule of *pacta sunt servanda*, is seen to be based on good faith because those intending to bind themselves must "assume" they can do so. The Court was able to make the two strands of its justification seem consistent in part because the soft alternative is presented in a hard manifestation.

As we have seen, however, a purely hard position could as easily devour the bindingness of undertakings. The Court, in arguing that bindingness is in fact an intent-favoring norm, must elaborate this hard, intent-based argument so as to prevent its association with France's ability to redefine the terms of its own obligations. This the Court accomplishes in two ways. First, the Court emphasizes the subjective freedom of *other* states who must be able to rely on French good faith. Second, and more importantly, the Court elaborates the meaning of an intent-based system of unilateral declarations in such a way as to deny France the freedom to define its own intent.

This the Court accomplishes in two steps. First, it suggests that intent is to be objectively measured by the way in which another state could be expected to view French statements. This objective approach, in turn, is justified by both hard and soft arguments. Second, the Court switches discussion from the choice between French and Australian consent to an issue of the Court's appropriate role. The arguments for the Court's role in assessing evidence operate like arguments about objective measurement of consent to prevent the intent argument from precluding a finding of obligation.

These arguments occur in the context of the Court's discussions of the conditions under which a state is bound by its unilateral statement. Although dissenting Judge de Castro argues that only unilateral acts which are accepted can bind; "[h]ence—and this should not be forgotten—any promise (with the exception of *pollicitatio*) can be withdrawn at any time before its regular acceptance by the person to whom it is made (*ante acceptationem, quippe iure nondum translatum, revocari posse sine injustitia*)."[115] By contrast, the Court holds "that the unilateral undertaking resulting from these statements cannot be interpreted as having been made in implicit reliance on an arbitrary power of reconsideration."[116] The Court also holds:

> An undertaking of this kind, if given publicly, and with an intent to be bound, even though not made within the context of international negotiations, is binding. In these circumstances, nothing in the nature of a *quid pro quo* nor any subsequent acceptance of the declaration, nor even any reply or reaction from other States, is required for the declaration to take effect, since such a requirement would be inconsistent with the strictly unilateral nature of the juridical act by which the pronouncement by the State was made.[117]

This softening of the emphasis on France's intent is justified because France so intended. The question before the Court is how to distinguish instances of such binding intention from other statements. In one view, the only consistent method is to let France decide. De Castro writes:

> [I]n my view the attitude of the French Government warrants . . . the inference that it considers its statements on nuclear tests to belong to the political domain and to concern a question which, inasmuch as it relates to national defence, lies within the domain reserved to a State's domestic jurisdiction.[118]

The Court picks up this approach in holding that the obligation is coterminous with French intent: "The Court finds further that the French Government has undertaken an obligation the precise nature and limits of which must be understood in accordance with the actual terms in which they have been publicly expressed."[119]

115. Nuclear Tests Case (Austr. v. Fr.), 1974 I.C.J. 253, 374 (Judgment of Dec. 20).
116. *Id.* at 270.
117. *Id.* at 267.
118. *Id.* at 375.
119. *Id.* at 270.

Indeed, they go so far as to indicate that no requirements about the form which an intentional statement can or should take could be compatible with the notion of the obligation being based in consent.

> With regard to the question of form, it should be observed that this is not a domain in which international law imposes any special or strict requirements. . . . Thus the question of form is not decisive. As the Court said in its Judgment on the preliminary objections in the case concerning the *Temple of Preah Vihear*:
>
> > "Where . . . as is generally the case in international law, which places the principle emphasis on the intentions of the parties, the law prescribes no particular form, parties are free to choose what form they please provided their intention clearly results from it." (*I.C.J. Reports* 1961, p. 21)

The Court further stated in the same case: " . . . the sole relevant question is whether the language employed in any given declaration does reveal a clear intention. . . ."[120]

Nevertheless, the Court recognizes that a purely subjective approach is not compatible with the notion of obligation: "Of course, not all unilateral acts imply obligation; but a State may choose to take up a certain position in relation to a particular matter with the intention of being bound—the intention is to be ascertained by interpretation of the act."[121] This is immediately limited to reflect the hard nature of this basic argument by the sentence which follows: "When States make statements by which their freedom of action is to be limited, a restrictive interpretation is called for."[122]

The Court squares this objective approach with the consent based argumentation in two ways. First, it interprets the objective approach to reflect the *true* subjective intention of the declarant.

> In announcing that the 1974 series of atmospheric tests would be the last, the French Government conveyed to the world at large, including the Applicant, its intention effectively to terminate these tests. It was bound to assume that other States might take note of these statements and rely on their being effective.[123]

---

120. *Id.* at 267-68.
121. *Id.* at 267.
122. *Id.*
123. *Id.* at 269. Thomas Franck describes this approach to intentionality:
Intentionality, as the Court said, must be the test. But the intention cannot be determined solely by reference to the speakers' state of mind but must also take into account that of the listeners. A spokesman for state policy—like the President of France, who speaks with the solemn voice of "acts of the French state,"—must be taken to intend the natural consequences of his words just as actors are assumed, in law, to intend the natural consequences of their acts. If a state speaks, though an ostensible agent, and the statement contains an express commitment to a course of future conduct by that state, it should not be neces-

Second, the Court squares the objective test with a consent-based approach by suggesting that objective interpretation is the Court's function, as a way of protecting France from the willfulness of Australia's interpretation.

> It will be observed that Australia has recognized the possibility of the dispute being resolved by a unilateral declaration, of the kind specified above, on the part of France, and its conclusion that in fact no "commitment" or "firm, explicit and binding undertaking" had been given is based on the view that the assurance is not absolute in its terms, that there is a "distinction between an assertion that tests will go underground and an assurance that no further atmospheric tests will take place," that "the possibility of further atmospheric testing taking place after the commencement of underground tests cannot be excluded" and that thus "the Government of France is still reserving to itself the right to carry out atmospheric nuclear tests." The Court must however form its own view of the meaning and scope intended by the author of a unilateral declaration which may create a legal obligation, and cannot in this respect be bound by the view expressed by another State which is in no way a party to the text.[124]

Having thus blended these two strands, the Court describes its interpretive process so as to juxtapose the hard and soft elements of its argument in adjoining sentences:

> The validity of these statements and their legal consequences must be considered within the general framework of the security of international intercourse, and the confidence and trust which are so essential in the relations among States. It is from the actual substance of these statements, and from the circumstances attending their making, that the legal implications of the unilateral act must be deduced. The objects of these statements are clear and they were addressed to the international community as a whole, and the Court holds that they constitute an undertaking possessing legal effect.[125]

Judge Barwick, in his dissent, after reference to a similar confluence of hard and soft factors concludes:

> There seems to be nothing, either in the language used or in the circumstances of its employment, which in my opinion would warrant, and certainly nothing to complete, the conclusion that those making the statements were intending to enter into a solemn and far-reaching international obligation. . . . I would have

---

> sary to inquire whether the state intends to be bound, but merely whether the states with an interest at stake could reasonably assume that the statement constituted a commitment.

Franck, *supra* note 97, at 616-17 (footnote omitted). Macdonald & Hough take the opposite view: "To 'assume' that a state 'intends' to be bound if other states 'could reasonably assume that the statement constituted a commitment' is to express this view in terms of a convenient, but misleading fiction." Macdonald & Hough, *supra* note 107, at 354.

124. Nuclear Tests Case (Austr. v. Fr.), 1974 I.C.J. 253, 268-69 (Judgment of Dec. 20).

125. *Id.* at 269.

> thought myself that the more natural conclusion to draw from the various statements was that they were statements of policy. . . .[126]

To summarize, the Court made the hard argument for the binding nature of unilateral declarations seem compatible with the good faith strand of its argument and with the idea of obligation by reinterpreting intentionality in soft terms. In the course of elaborating the meaning of an intent-based approach to unilateral declaration, the Court was again faced with a choice between two alternatives: an objective and a subjective one. The Court chose the objective one, thereby downplaying the subjective nature of its initial intent based approach. This was revealed in the arguments which the court made to defend this choice. First, the Court reinterpreted the subjective approach which it rejected to be incompatible with true intent-based subjectivism: if France could interpret its own consent it could not bind itself. Second, it reinterpreted the objective alternative to be truly reflective of the subjective approach, in terms, paradoxically, first of Australia's interests, then of those which France must have had. Any tension between these two positions is finessed by focusing on the court's role.

Argument about the application of doctrine about unilateral declarations illustrates one way in which the hard and soft strands of sources argumentation can be blended and stabilized. The elegance of the Court's opinion resides in its management of the relationship between two approaches to unilateral declarations which have the potential to contradict each other and themselves in important ways.

B. The Case of *Rebus sic Stantibus*

Doctrines governing release from consensual obligations (e.g., denunciation, termination, impossibility, or the emergence of a new peremptory norm of *jus cogens*),[127] like those governing entry into consensual obligations are discussed in the rhetorics of both consent and justice. Although some of these doctrines (particularly denunciation and termination) seem primarily consensual, most seem to temper a consensual obligation with more systemic considerations. The doctrine of "changed circumstances" or "*rebus sic stantibus*" is exemplary in its rhetoric and structure.[128]

The doctrine of *rebus sic stantibus* has been discussed in both hard and soft terms. Some commentators emphasize that a state may be released from its consensual obligations when the parties would have in-

126. *Id.* at 448-49.
127. *See supra* notes 14-16, 89-92 and accompanying text.
128. *See supra* notes 15, 89-92 and accompanying text.

tended release had they considered the potential for circumstances to so evolve.[129] Indeed, the doctrine is often referred to as the "*clausula rebus sic stantibus*" to emphasize the implication of a release clause into the treaty obligations which it modifies. The Permanent Court of International Justice, in the *Free Zones of Upper Savoy and the District of Gex* expressed this consensual approach to *rebus sic stantibus*:[130]

> The argument in favor of the view that the stipulations establishing the zones have lapsed is that these zones were created in view of and because of the existence of a particular state of facts, [and] this state of facts has now disappeared. . . .
>
> To establish this position it is necessary, first of all, to prove that it was in consideration of the absence of customs duties at Geneva that the Powers decided, in 1815, in favour of the creation of the zones. There is nothing in the text of the treaties to support this, and the only occasion on which the Swiss representative at the Allied gathering in 1815 is shown to have relied on the absence of customs at Geneva was when he endeavored to secure the withdrawal of the French customs along the whole frontier from Basle to Geneva—an effort in which he was not successful . . . .
>
> As the French argument fails on the facts, it becomes unnecessary for the Court to consider any of the questions of principle which arise in connection with the theory of the lapse of treaties by reason of change of circumstances. . . . [131]

Others, however, have understood the doctrine of *rebus sic stantibus* to be primarily designed to rectify extraordinary, if also unanticipated, harshness.[132] Both of these strands find expression in most analyses of

---

129. *See* C. FENWICK, *supra* note 94; C. HILL, THE DOCTRINE OF "REBUS SIC STANTIBUS" IN INTERNATIONAL LAW (1934):

> The definition of the doctrine of *rebus sic stantibus* generally given by the older writers on international law and accepted by many writers today states that the obligations of a treaty terminate when a change occurs in those circumstances which existed at the time of conclusion of the treaty and whose continuance formed, according to the intention or wills of the parties, a condition of the continuing validity of the treaty. . . .
>
> This definition of the doctrine is merely a principle for carrying out the intention of the parties to the treaty and is not at all an objective rule of international law which operates to terminate the obligations of the treaty irrespective of the original will of the parties.

Id. at 8-9 (footnote omitted); *see also* Lissitzyn, *supra* note 94, at 889-92 (giving examples of similar statements by other commentators).

130. Free Zones of Upper Savoy and the District of Gex (Fr. v. Switz.), 1932 P.C.I.J. (ser. A/B) No. 46 (Judgment of June 7).

131. *Id.* at 156, 158.

132. *See supra* note 94 (discussing views on implied terms of treaties). *See, e.g.*, A. VERDROSS & B. SIMMA, *supra* note 4, at 420:

> Nach der richtig verstandenen *objektiven* theorie handelt es sich bei der *clausula rebus sic stantibus* weder um eine tatsächliche noch um eine subintellegierte Vertragsklausel, sondern um einen objektiven vr [völkerrechtlichen] Grundsatz . . . . Die entscheidende Frage geht also dahin, ob sich die Umstände nach Vertragsschluss so wesentlich geändert haben, dass den Parteien die Erfüllung des

the doctrine. In the following passage, for example, Wharton begins with a hard description of the consensual basis of the doctrine, softens this by suggesting that the changed elements need not have been specifically intended to lead to lapse of duties (this would collapse the doctrine of *rebus sic stantibus* into that of material conditions) but need have been merely a "strong inducement" to the adversely affected party, and concludes with a soft standard limiting *rebus sic stantibus* to situations of "unreasonable sacrifice."

> A treaty may be modified or abrogated under the following circumstances:
> (7) When a state of things which was the basis of the treaty, and one of its tacit conditions, no longer exists.
> In most of the old treaties were inserted the "*clausula rebus sic stantibus*", by which the treaty might be construed as abrogated when material circumstances on which it rested changed. To work this effect it is not essential that the facts alleged to have changed should be material conditions. It is enough if they were strong inducements to the party asking abrogation.
> The maxim "*Conventio omnis intelligitur rebus sic stantibus*" is held to apply to all cases in which the reason for a treaty has failed, or there has been such a change of circumstances as to make its performance impracticable except at an unreasonable sacrifice.[133]

Article 62 of the Vienna Convention of the Law of Treaties restates this dual approach.

> 1. A fundamental change of circumstances which has occurred with regard to those existing at the time of the conclusion of the treaty and which was not foreseen by the parties, may not be invoked as a ground for terminating or withdrawing from the treaty unless:
>
> > (a) the existence of those circumstances constituted an essential basis of the consent of the parties to be bound by the treaty and
> > (b) the effect of the change is radically to transform the extent of obligations still to be performed under the treaty.[134]

Vertrages *bona fide* nicht mehr zugemutet werden kann.

Id.; *see also* Haraszti, *supra* note 92, at 47:

> [T]here is in international law a rule of general validity and operating independently of the agreement of the parties at treaty-making, which in the event of a fundamental change of the circumstances existing at the conclusion of the treaty authorizes either party to terminate the treaty . . . . This, in our opinion, [the] solely acceptable doctrine, rejecting all fictions, best suits conditions.

Id.

133. 2 F. WHARTON, A DIGEST OF INTERNATIONAL LAW OF THE UNITED STATES, § 137a, at 161 (1886).

134. Vienna Convention, *supra* note 5, at art. 62. Lissitzyn, summarizing state practice with regard to *rebus sic stantibus*, emphasized these two elements. Lissitzyn, *supra* note 94, at 911. The hard consent based approach is cast here as a "general community policy."

> In the several instances of state action just reviewed, which are illustrative rather than exhaustive of recent practice, the governments invoking the changes of cir-

Presenting these two dimensions of the *rebus sic stantibus* doctrine side by side is shrewd, for either alone seems incapable of supporting an escape from consensual obligations. If the true intent of the parties is thought the exclusive basis for extinguishing a consensual duty, the doctrine of *rebus sic stantibus* seems indistinguishable from the norm *pacta sunt servanda* and can mean no more than that express conditions must be met and termination clauses honored. If, on the other hand, the doctrine is to look beyond what the parties specifically intended, it seems that the doctrine becomes a substantive set of notions about justice or equity unconnected to the treaty itself—disconnecting

---

> cumstance can all be regarded as maintaining in effect that their actions were not inconsistent with the general community policy of protecting and effectuating ascertained or reasonably imputable shared expectations of parties to international agreements. In short, these instances support the view that the problem of the legal effect of changes of circumstances on treaty relationships is one of determining the parties' shared intentions, expectations and objectives, that is, a problem of interpretation.

Id. at 911 (footnote omitted). The Harvard Research in International Law restates this hard vision of *rebus sic stantibus*, but describes the two alternate, soft approaches. It identifies, moreover, both a subjective and an objective stand to the hard approach.

> The idea common to most concepts of the doctrine is that a treaty becomes legally void in case there occurs a change in the state of facts which existed at the time the parties entered into the treaty. It is generally admitted, however, that not every change in those facts terminates the binding force of a treaty . . . . Many writers affirm that a change in the state of facts terminates the binding force of a treaty only when the parties entered into the treaty with reference to this state of facts and envisaged its continuance unchanged as a determining factor which moved them to undertake the obligations stipulated.
>
> . . . .
>
> Although the doctrine of *rebus sic stantibus* as conceived . . . above is based upon the idea of a relation between the binding force of the treaty and a continuance of a state of facts essentially unchanged, because the parties intended that the continuance of the state of facts should be a condition of the binding force of the treaty, two variations of this concept may be distinguished. In the one case, a tacit clause *rebus sic stantibus* is presumed to be contained in every treaty. In the second case, no such tacit clause is presumed for all treaties; but if, upon examination, it is clear that a particular treaty was entered into with reference to the existence of a particular state of facts, the continued existence of which was envisaged by the parties as a determining factor moving them to undertake the obligations stipulated, then the rule of *rebus sic stantibus* applies . . . .
>
> There is a second concept of the doctrine which adopts as a test for determining whether a given change in the state of facts shall render the treaty no longer binding, not the intention of the parties, but a test of quite a different nature. It is that the changes shall be "essential," fundamental or "vital" . . . .
>
> A third concept of the doctrine of *rebus sic stantibus* makes the test of whether or not a change in the state of facts causes termination of a treaty, the fact that fulfillment of the treaty after occurrence of a change in the state of facts would be so injurious to one of the parties that such party has a right under the law or right of necessity to terminate the treaty.

Harvard Research in International Law, *The Law of Treaties*, 29 AM. J. INT'L L. SUPP. 657, 1097-98, 1100-01 (1935).

consensual sources from their mooring in consent.

Despite the strong motive these difficulties provide for a combined rhetorical presentation of the *rebus sic stantibus* doctrine, however, getting the hard to lie down with the soft is no easier here than elsewhere. Hard justifications for *rebus sic stantibus* seem to deny the doctrine's aspiration to temper or depart from treaty law—from the consensual source of the obligation which the doctrine will extinguish. Soft arguments for *rebus sic stantibus*, however, seem to take the doctrine out of sources law altogether, transforming it into a doctrine of substantive international law.

One rather simple strategy used to manage this tension articulates each approach to *rebus sic stantibus* in a way which transforms it into its opposite. For example, intent remains the basis upon which equitable standards can be applied if the parties can be assumed to have intended this derogation from their intent. In this image, the doctrine is not displaced by its hard justification because the intent upon which it is thought to rely is given soft content. Similarly, the soft rhetoric does not displace the doctrine from the field of treaty law because those conditions of justice which interrupt the consensual obligation such as "fundamental," "vital," "necessary," and so forth, are themselves situated, perhaps by implication, in the intent of the states parties. Equity is treated to mean enforcement of the *fundamental* nature of the treaty.

This rather elementary rhetorical strategy takes a characteristic form in argument about the application of the doctrine of *rebus sic stantibus*. A legal dispute over the doctrine normally arises only when there is disagreement about whether *rebus sic stantibus* indeed excuses failure to perform some particular treaty obligation. Typically, one state claims to be excused from its obligations over the objection of a state, a court or a commentator. Each position advanced in such an argument is typically associated with one or the other strands of the *rebus sic stantibus* doctrine. For example, the state claiming to be excused might argue that *rebus sic stantibus* leaves it able to determine when circumstances have changed sufficiently to have been outside the contemplation of its consent. This subjectivist position seems associated with the hard strand of the *rebus sic stantibus* doctrine: that its justification lies in its fulfillment of consent. Those opposing release from duty might respond by interpreting *rebus sic stantibus* so as to impose an external standard on the subjective consent of the state seeking release. This response would rely upon the soft strand of *rebus sic stantibus*: that its justification lies outside consent. As the debate develops, each side might seek to augment its position by reference to the alternative rhetorical strand. The trick, for advocates as for tribunals or commentators who seek to sort out these claims, is to blend these elements into an argument which supports either release from or fulfillment of the initial obligation.

Various approaches to this problem are illustrated by the arguments made in regard to the 1941 United States suspension of its participation in the International Load Line Convention regulating certain aspects of maritime shipping.[135] Claiming that the Convention had presumed a situation of peaceful commerce, President Roosevelt, relying on an opinion by Acting Attorney General Francis Biddle, declared the Convention "suspended and inoperative." The President's proclamation suggests that the *rebus sic stantibus* doctrine gives the United States the "right" unilaterally to suspend the Convention.

> WHEREAS the conditions envisaged by the Convention have been, for the time being, almost wholly destroyed, and the partial and imperfect enforcement of the Convention can operate only to prejudice the victims of aggression, whom it is the avowed purpose of the United States of America to aid; and
>
> WHEREAS it is an implicit condition to the binding effect of the Convention that those conditions envisaged by it should continue without such material change as has in fact occurred; and
>
> WHEREAS under approved principles of international law it has become, by reason of such changed conditions, the right of the United States of America to declare the Convention suspended and inoperative:
>
> NOW, THEREFORE, I, Franklin D. Roosevelt, President of the United States of America, exercising on behalf of the United States of America an unquestioned right and privilege under approved principles of international law, do proclaim and declare the aforesaid International Load Line Convention suspended and inoperative in the ports and waters of the United States of America, and in so far as the United States of America is concerned, for the duration of the present emergency.[136]

The position that *rebus sic stantibus* gives states a unilateral right of revocation is supported by some international law commentators. Lissitzyn's commentary on the draft articles of the Vienna Convention is exemplary:

> Strictly speaking, there is no requirement in all cases that nonperformance be preceded or accompanied by a formal notice to the other parties, although concern for orderliness, prudence and courtesy make the giving of such notice generally desirable. If the treaty operates as municipal law, a formal enactment or proclamation may be necessary.
>
> The exercise of the right to cease or limit performance does not depend on the

135. The text of the Convention appears at 47 Stat. 2228 (1933).

136. Proclamation No. 2500, Aug. 9, 1941, 6 Fed. Reg. 3,999 (1941); revoked as of Jan. 1, 1946 by Proclamation No. 2675, Dec. 21, 1945, 10 Fed. Reg. 15,365 (1945).

specific consent of the other party or upon a third-party decision.[137]

The opposing view, that unilateral suspension is not compatible with *rebus sic stantibus*, is advocated by other commentators—generally by those who emphasize that a purely consensual approach to *rebus sic stantibus* would either collapse the doctrine into treaty law or lead to an unqualified ability to avoid treaty obligations. Hyde's 1945 treatise is exemplary: "It requires . . . something more than the sheer power of a contracting State to disregard with impunity the terms of a valid treaty, in order to establish a legal right to do so."[138]

Of course, neither of these two positions can be fully supported using only a hard or a soft rhetoric. Although unilateral suspension seems associated with a hard consensual rhetoric, if the United States were allowed unilaterally to suspend its treaty obligations, the subjective intent of the other signatories would seem threatened. Moreover, if a unilateral capacity to suspend were within *their* contemplation, it would seem to limit America's ability to bind itself in such a way that performance could not be suspended in this way. The unilateral suspension position seems to demand a soft as well as a hard defense.

Similarly, although the position that the United States should not be permitted unilaterally to suspend the Convention seems associated with some extra-consensual or systemic justification, it also seems that if America is unable to determine the limits of its own obligations when circumstances change, an important systemic interest in sovereign autonomy would be threatened. Moreover, such an extra-consensual approach threatens the norm of *pacta sunt servanda* to which *rebus sic stantibus* is merely an exception. Consequently, opposition to the unilateral suspension position seems to demand a hard as well as a soft rhetoric.

In light of these rhetorical demands, it is not surprising that the President's declaration cited the likelihood of "prejudice" to the "victims of aggression, whom it is the avowed purpose of the United States of America to aid."[139] Since both rhetorical styles seem compatible with and indeed demanded by both positions, the rhetorical challenge is

137. Lissitzyn, *supra* note 94, at 911-12.

138. 2 C. HYDE, INTERNATIONAL LAW 1523 (2d rev. ed. 1945). The Swiss Federal Court followed this approach in its 1923 decision, In re Lepeschkin, 49(1) Entscheidungen des Schweizerischen Bundesgerichtes 188, 194-97 (1923), 1951 JOURNAL DU DROIT INTERNATIONAL (Clunet) 1135, 1137-38 (1924), 2 ANN. DIG. 323, 334-35 (1923-24).

139. Similarly, the systemic interest invoked by the Swiss Federal Court as it limited the unilateral right to suspend is one of *notice* "through the usual international law channels." *See* In re Lepeschkin, 2 ANN. DIG. 323, 325 (1923-24).

to express them in such a way as to seem compatible with one another and with the position being advocated. Both those opposing and those supporting Roosevelt's proclamation did this quite elegantly by elaborating a form of each strand which embraced the other.

The President's assertion of a unilateral right to suspend the Convention was defended by Acting Attorney General Francis Biddle.[140] Biddle manages the rhetorical difficulties generated by his position in two moves. First, he treats the unilateral suspension right as a mere matter of "procedure" which reflects a preexisting lapse in the obligation. As a procedural matter, unilateral suspension does not seem to threaten the idea of international obligation. Instead it is a mere expression of the (absent) obligation.

> As to the procedure to be adopted by the Government that relies on the principle of *rebus sic stantibus*, it may well be that ordinarily the procedure would call for the government to inform the other parties to the treaty with respect to the matter and request agreement for termination or suspension of the treaty. The matter of procedure, however, does not affect the right of termination or suspension . . . . The fundamental character of the change in conditions underlying the treaty . . . leaves the Government of the United States entirely free to declare the treaty inoperative or to suspend it for the duration of the present emergency.[141]

Biddle then turns to the obligation itself. As indicated in this short passage from his argument, that obligation depends upon the characterization of the changes which have occurred as "fundamental" in some sense. Biddle's second move is to a soft rhetoric of "emergencies" and "fundamentality." This move allows Biddle to sidestep the suggestion that a unilateral suspension would contravene the obligation's basis in the consent of other states by grounding both the obligation and the suspension in a set of general systemic considerations. The problem is that a soft rhetoric threatens either America's unilateral right or the treaty context of the claim for *rebus sic stantibus*. Biddle avoids this by elaborating the extra-consensual conditions which govern the procedural right to suspend in terms of the intention of the parties. Fundamental, to Biddle, means fundamental *to the treaty. Rebus sic stantibus* is triggered when there has been "essential" change in the "basic conditions" upon which the treaty "was founded."

> It is a well-established principle of international law, *rebus sic stantibus*, that a treaty ceases to be binding when the basic conditions upon which it was founded have essentially changed. Suspension of the convention in such circumstances is the unquestioned right of a state adversely affected by such essential change.

---

140. 40 Op. Att'y Gen'l 119 (1941).
141. *Id.* at 123.

> It is sometimes said that the change which brings the principle into operation must be essential or fundamental. But whether or not this is an integral part of the principle itself, there can be no doubt that the changed conditions affecting the Load Line Convention are most essential and most fundamental.[142]

Biddle argues that obligations lapse with change in the "assumptions" upon which the treaty was based. He does not suggest that these assumptions are within the unilateral authority of one party to interpret. He treats their lapse as a matter of *fact* which remains only to be procedurally registered.

> It is clear from its general nature that the convention was a peacetime agreement. As stated in its preamble the contracting governments entered into it "to promote safety of life and property at sea by establishing in common agreement uniform principles and rules with regard to the limits to which ships on international voyages may be loaded . . . ." This general purpose, as the terms of the convention demonstrate, was to be achieved by limiting international competition in the loading of cargo vessels. That peacetime commerce and voyages were assumed as the basis of the convention is also demonstrated by the nature of its detailed provisions and regulations. A perusal of them leaves no doubt that peacetime commerce was a basic assumption of the treaty. The present situation with respect to shipping is a wholly different one. Conditions essential to the operation of the convention, and assumed as a basis for it, are in almost complete abeyance . . . . International shipping is not being carried on under normal conditions subject to agreements arrived at for the purpose of regulating international voyages freely undertaken and completed. On the contrary, the actual destruction of vessels engaged in such commerce, however loaded, is one of the principal means by which the war is now being conducted among various of the contracting parties . . . . It is well known that the international sea lanes are the rendezvous for varied instrumentalities of war set loose for the destruction of shipping. It is equally well known that a serious shortage exists in shipping in the case of numerous, if not all, signatories to the convention, including those whose defense the Congress has declared essential to the defense of the United States . . . . In short the implicit assumption of normal peacetime international trade, which is at the foundation of the Load Line Convention, no longer exists.
>
> Under these circumstances there is no doubt in my mind that the convention has ceased to be binding upon the United States.[143]

Biddle thus develops his argument for the American suspension of the Convention in two steps. He begins with a hard assertion of the American right, but casts it as a matter of procedure, dependent upon the lapse of an acknowledged international obligation. He then grounds this lapse in general notions about what is "fundamental" to a treaty, understood to have been in the contemplation of the Convention signatories. His unilateral interpretation of these systemic notions, even of

142. *Id.* at 121-23.
143. *Id.* at 120-21.

the consent of other signatories, is treated as a matter of fact rather than of unilateral assertion. Biddle's argument is interesting because he blends hard and soft rhetorics by allowing each to deny itself. The unilateral right to terminate is a procedural dependent of the obligation and the general obligation is an expression of collective intent which can be unilaterally noticed.

Interestingly, commentators attacking the American position deployed similar rhetorical strategies. Professor Briggs developed a strong opposition to Roosevelt and Biddle in a commentary which appeared in the American Journal of International Law in 1942.[144] Briggs identifies a contradiction within Biddle's argument between his reliance upon consent and obligation. To the extent Biddle relies upon arguments about the general nature of the treaty, the *rebus sic stantibus* doctrine which Biddle invokes should be unnecessary. To the extent Biddle relies upon the consent of treaty signatories, the unilateral aspect of his argument seems undercut.

> The necessity for suspending a convention which has assertedly already ceased to be binding through the operation of an alleged principle of international law is not clear to the writer. Nor is it clear why circumstances of admittedly general application should lead to the suspension of the treaty only by the United States.[145]

Briggs argues that the doctrine of *rebus sic stantibus* does not contemplate unilateral suspension of treaty obligations, citing Professor Chesney Hill and the Harvard Research Draft on the Law of Treaties, itself also cited for the opposite proposition by Biddle.

> Indeed, Mr. Biddle, if interested in one of the most able and comprehensive analyses of state practice on the subject, might well have consulted Chesney Hill's *The Doctrine of "Rebus Sic Stantibus" in International Law*, which states:
>
>> Despite any theoretical objections to the contrary, it remains true that customary international law lays down the rule that a party who seeks release from a treaty on the ground of a change of circumstances has no right to terminate the treaty unilaterally, and that recognition that the doctrine is applicable must be obtained either from the parties to the treaty or from some competent international authority.[146]

Briggs criticizes Biddle's suggestion that the United States has an absolute right to control the ambit of its own obligations, a position which seems to Briggs to be incompatible with the possibility of systemic obligation.

144. Briggs, *The Attorney General Invokes Rebus Sic Stantibus*, 36 AM. J. INT'L L. 89 (1942).
145. *Id.* at 93.
146. *Id.* at 94.

> This surprising, and, indeed, reckless and unnecessary, espousal by the United States of a much questioned doctrine by which Germany, Italy, Japan, and Soviet Russia might equally well justify the suspension, termination, or even violation, of inconvenient treaties renders desirable an examination of the conditions and legal principles set forth by the Attorney General in his opinion.[147]

Briggs returns to this theme later in his commentary, criticizing the unilateral approach for reading any systemic element out of the *rebus sic stantibus* doctrine. His opposition to the unilateral position blends hard and soft considerations. To a certain extent, he fears that reliance upon unilateral action by the United States will devour the systemic elements of justice encapsuled in the idea of "extraordinary circumstances." He also recognizes that the unilateral approach, by allowing a single state to impose its conception of "necessity" upon its treaty partners, might derogate from the ability of other states freely to enter into treaties. His critique of unilateralism, then, is not merely a critique of the hard institutionalization of consent which it seems to represent. It is simultaneously a suggestion that subjective notions of necessity are incompatible with the consensual rights of the community. Unilateralism threatens consent as well as justice.

> The Attorney General concedes that "ordinarily" a state which relies on the principle of *rebus sic stantibus* should "request agreement" of the other parties for termination or suspension of a treaty, but believes this a mere matter of procedure which does not affect the right of termination. This arbitrary rejection of one of the essential elements of the concept of *rebus sic stantibus* suggests that the suspension of the International Load Lines Convention is not so much based on the principle of *rebus sic stantibus* as upon some vague and slippery doctrine of state necessity. One is reminded of Secretary of State Cordell Hull's assertion that certain rules of Hague Convention XIII, which he admitted are declaratory of international law in "ordinary" circumstances, cease to be binding in situations "extraordinary in character." One recalls also the statement of Professor Josef L. Kunz that there are "the politicians—often, consciously or unconsciously, also among men who want to be considered as scholars—who have always so conveniently two international laws . . . one for one's own nation and those we like, the other against the nations we do not like."[148]

This double strategy is a difficult one to sustain. In arguing that unilateral suspension renders the obligation system hostage to the whim of a single state, Briggs threatens his image of the *rebus sic stantibus* doctrine, for it is precisely to protect the system of obligations that Biddle interprets *rebus sic stantibus* in terms of the "necessary" and "fundamental." To the extent Briggs relies upon soft rhetoric, he threatens to reduce his image of *rebus sic stantibus* doctrine into either Biddle's

147. *Id.* at 90.
148. *Id.* at 94-95 (footnotes omitted).

necessity approach or to expand it into a rule of substantive public international law. Briggs thus faces exactly the inverse of the contradiction which he identifies in Biddle's argument.

To reduce this threat, Briggs introduces consensual elements into his argument. Indeed, his soft approach seems to imply nothing beyond the consent of the parties themselves. His text investigates at great length the extent to which the parties intended that the United States would be free of its obligations should war arise.

> Moreover, the evidence presented by the Attorney General fails to establish that the parties to the convention—the purpose of which was to establish minimum safety regulations—intended that the occurrence of war should release the parties from the obligations assumed. The fact that safety of life and property at sea is noticeably less evident in time of war than in time of peace proves neither the desirability of relaxing those safety regulations which continue to be possible nor that the parties to the convention in question so intended.[149]

His soft rhetoric about the *rebus sic stantibus* doctrine is not grounded in what seems to have been fundamental to the treaty, but rather in what the parties seem actually to have contemplated.

> Nevertheless, the few states which have invoked [the *rebus sic stantibus* doctrine] have been in agreement on one point: the doctrine has been "clearly based juridically upon the intention of the parties at the time of the conclusion of the treaty."
>
> To what extent was a unilateral right to terminate the International Load Lines Convention because of "changed conditions" envisaged by the parties to that treaty?[150]

Two difficulties arise from Briggs's development of soft rhetoric. First, he is confronted with the same choice between subjective and objective notions of intent which he criticizes Biddle for failing to resolve.[151] Second, this consensual interpretation of systemic obligation

---

149. *Id.* at 93.

150. *Id.* at 90 (footnote omitted). This is the approach used by Brierly in his short treatise on international law.

> Neither a treaty in international law nor a contract in English law is dissolved merely by a change in circumstances; they are only dissolved if a term can fairly be read into them providing that in the event which has happened they *are* to be dissolved. Both doctrines attempt not to defeat but to fulfil the intention . . . of the parties.

J. BRIERLY, *supra* note 1, at 262.

151. Both views are expressed by commentators who follow Briggs's interpretation of justice in terms of intent. Hyde expresses these two prongs as follows:

> If changed conditions ever serve in principle to confer upon a contracting State the right to free itself from obligations laid down in a treaty, it is because those conditions mark the existence of a new order of things which in a broad sense were not contemplated by the parties at the time of the conclusion of their agreement and which render highly unreasonable a demand for performance . . . .

could reduce the doctrine of *rebus sic stantibus* to that of *pacta sunt servanda*, negating the soft perspective it was designed to rescue.

Briggs does not resolve this difficulty. Perhaps because his argument, unlike that of Biddle, is less a defense of some action than a critique, he never reintegrates his reliance upon the treaty language into a soft rhetoric of justice. Like Biddle, Briggs could have utilized a distinction between procedure and substance, or fact and law to do so, perhaps arguing that the treaty language was merely one procedural manifestation of the systemic requirements of obligation. Instead, he edges quite close to the abyss of an absolute hard rhetoric—ironically exactly the abyss he felt the right to unilateral suspension would open up. As Briggs sees it, there seem no circumstances except those enumerated by the parties and hence covered by other release doctrines which could safely trigger the *rebus sic stantibus* doctrine under this approach.

> ' In 1930 maritime experts representing thirty states drafted and signed at London the International Load Lines Convention in order, as the preamble states, "to promote safety of life and property at sea by establishing in common agreement uniform principles and rules with regard to the limits to which ships on international voyages may be loaded." The treaty came into force between fifteen of the signatories, including the United States, on January 1, 1933, and by September 1, 1935, had been ratified or acceded to by 36 "governments." The convention contains no provision permitting its suspension in time of war by either belligerents or neutrals, but Article 25 stipulates that the convention may be denounced at any time after it has been in force for five years, such denunciation not to take effect until twelve months after it has been received. Article 20 states, in part, that "modifications of this Convention which may be deemed useful or necessary improvements may at any time be proposed by any Contracting Government . . . and if any such modifications are accepted by all the Contracting Governments . . . this Convention shall be modified accordingly." It is clear that no provision of the treaty authorizes the action taken by the United States Government, which was neither a denunciation subject to one year's notice, nor a proposed modification in the line of improvement, subject to unanimous acceptance,

---

> That which causes a demand for performance to be unreasonable, and which, conversely, clothes a party with freedom to rid itself of the obligation to perform is the coming into being of a new condition of affairs which was not only not brought to the attention of the parties when they concluded their agreement, but also one which, if it had then been brought to their attention, would have necessarily produced common acknowledgement that the agreement would be inapplicable, and hence permit a party to regard it as no longer binding in case that condition or situation should subsequently arise.

2 C. Hyde, *supra* note 138, at 1524-27. Chesney Hill comments similarly:

> A change of circumstances becomes relevant to the obligatory force of a treaty only in so far as it is related to the wills of the parties to the treaty at the time of the conclusion of the treaty. It is not an objective rule of international law which is imposed upon the parties, but is a rule for carrying the intention of the parties into effect.

C. Hill, *supra* note 129, at 77.

but was a unilateral declaration that the treaty was immediately "suspended and inoperative" in so far as the United States is concerned.[152]

Although quite different in their conclusions, Briggs and Biddle have quite similar rhetorical styles. Each blends consensual and extra-consensual considerations by interpreting each to embrace its opposite. In this, their arguments about *rebus sic stantibus* are similar to arguments about unilateral declarations. Although these two doctrines of treaty law (one about beginning and the other about terminating a consensual obligation) present these rhetorics in different ways, they share a set of rhetorical strategies for mixing the hard with the soft. Taken together, these two doctrines introduce a similar blend of hard and soft to treaty doctrine as a whole. Although both are doctrines about treaty law a seemingly consensual source of international law, treaties, unilateral declaration doctrine, because it concerns the creation of consensual obligations, seems to concern the binding nature of consent most directly. *Rebus sic stantibus*, on the other hand, seems to be about the soft conditions under which consent-based obligations fall. Taken together the rule (unilateral declaration) and the exception (*rebus sic stantibus*) allow treaty law itself to embrace the tension between hard and soft rhetoric. Although these two doctrines were thus defined by this initial differentiation, each in turn embraced and managed the tension within itself. As a whole we see within treaty law a rhetorical pattern of proliferating differentiation and recombination managing what might otherwise seem a tense relationship between an absolute sovereign autonomy to consent and a systemic pattern of legal obligation.

C. THE CASE OF CUSTOM

Although both the form and the authoritative basis for international customary law are generally considered to be less consensual than the form and basis for treaty law, the law of custom, like treaty law, blends consensual and non-consensual rhetorics. The strategies used to blend these elements in argument about custom are similar to those which animated argument about doctrines of treaty law. Interestingly, however, arguments about custom arrange their reliance upon hard and soft rhetorics differently than treaty law argument. Indeed, custom seems in many ways the rhetorical mirror image of treaty law.

That the law of custom, like treaty law, should contain both consensual and non-consensual doctrines and rhetorical tendencies is unsurprising. As a general matter, international custom is seen both as an

152. Briggs, *supra* note 144, at 91 (footnotes omitted).

ersatz treaty, raising the same issues about consent which were raised by treaty law, and as an expression of the requirements and equity of the interstate system.[153] Just as sovereign consent was predominant in the theory and doctrine of treaty law, in custom the non-consensual element is generally thought to predominate.[154] Although custom is generally thought to be found in repeated state behavior, as a formal matter custom might be written and indeed is often thought to have been expressed in the form of a multilateral treaty. As we saw in the case of unilateral declarations, moreover, consensual rhetoric can ground oral statements and behavioral practices as well as written expressions of sovereign will.

As was true of treaty law, some doctrines about custom seem hard and others soft. In particular, it seems that doctrines about the creation of custom seem to be about the conditions of justice or the nature of the system of international law, while doctrines about the limits of custom seem to be about the failure of consent by the state to be bound. This doctrinal arrangement—exactly the inverse of doctrines about creating and terminating an obligation of treaty law—seems to follow from custom's predominantly non-consensual nature. For example, Waldock begins his elaboration of the doctrines of custom formation in a way which reflects his soft view of custom, finding it:

> clear that, if a custom becomes established as a general rule of international law, it binds all States which have not opposed it, whether or not they themselves played an active part in its formation. This means that in order to invoke a custom against a State it is not necessary to show specifically the acceptance of the custom as law by that State; its acceptance of the custom will be presumed so that it will be bound unless it can adduce evidence of its actual opposition to the practice in question. The Court in applying a general custom may well refer to the practice, if any, of the parties to the litigation in regard to the custom; but it has never yet treated evidence of their acceptance of the practice as a sine qua non of applying the custom to them.[155]

Initially it seems that custom is formed in a way which might render state consent irrelevant—just as treaty law initially seemed oblivious to the systemic implications of its consensually generated rules. But the softness of this doctrine is tempered in several ways. It seems that a

153. *See supra* notes 40-45 and accompanying text.

154. Waldock's summary of these two dimensions of custom is exemplary:

> The view of most international lawyers is that customary law is not a form of tacit treaty but an independent form of law; and that, when a custom satisfying the definition in Article 38 is established, it constitutes a general rule of international law which, subject to one reservation, applies to every State.

Waldock, *supra* note 1, at 49.

155. *Id.* at 50 (footnote omitted).

customary rule cannot form against the opposition of a sovereign and will lapse when confronted with a later consensually adopted doctrine—just as a treaty could not form against the opposition of some systemic norm of *jus cogens* and would lapse when confronted with either a later "peremptory norm" or a "fundamental" change of circumstances. Waldock's formulation suggests that sovereign consent to systemic rules is presumed, not irrelevant. He extends this approach in developing a reservation to his general statement about custom formation:

> The reservation concerns the case of a State which, while the custom is in process of formation, unambiguously and persistently registers its objection to the recognition of the practice as law . . . . [t]he rule so created will not bind the objectors; in other words, . . . in international law there is no majority rule even with respect to the formation of customary law."[156]

Moreover, it seems that although custom is discovered in practice, that practice must be accompanied—even motivated—by a sovereign acknowledgement that the practice is norm-generating or compliant. This requirement of *opinio juris* is reminiscent of the requirement that treaty law, although the expression of sovereign will, be expressed in an appropriate, communally recognized form.

At the level of doctrinal structure, custom and treaty law differentiate themselves from one another by reversing the arrangement of their internal components. Custom seems softer than treaty because doctrines about getting into custom are softer — tempered by consent — while doctrines about initiating treaty obligations are harder — tempered by systemic considerations. Treaty seems harder than custom because it confines systemic considerations to the exceptional doctrines about lapse — tempered by consensual implication — while custom confines consensual considerations to exceptional doctrines about lapse — tempered by *jus cogens.*

Since custom doctrine mixes consensual and extra-consensual considerations, argument about the application of these doctrines is rhetorically quite similar to argument about treaty law doctrine, if often somewhat inverted. In the *Anglo-Norwegian Fisheries Case*, the United Kingdom objected to the method by which Norway delimited its territorial waters, claiming that Norway thereby violated a customary norm of international law.[157] Norway responded that such a norm did not exist, or, that if it did, it did not apply to the Norwegian coast.

156. *Id.* at 49-50.

157. Anglo-Norwegian Fisheries Case, (U.K. v. Nor.) 1951 I.C.J. 116 (Judgment of Dec. 18).

Norway defended this position in part by opposing the claim that a general norm had been created, relying on a somewhat more consensual vision of customary creation than had the United Kingdom. Norway claimed, moreover, never to have consented to the general rule and to have consistently and successfully opposed its application to the rocky and deeply indented Norwegian coastline. Norway also claimed that the combination of Norwegian practice and the acquiescence of other sovereigns, including the United Kingdom, created an opposing and permissive customary norm which could be invoked against the United Kingdom. Sometimes they cast this opposing norm as an exception for such peculiar coastlines and sometimes they styled it a "historic title." The United Kingdom opposed this norm of custom much as Norway had opposed theirs.

Thus, like many custom cases, the *Fisheries* opinion contains arguments about the creation and limitation of two different and opposing customary norms. Each party argued for and against a norm of custom—and did so by weaving hard and soft rhetorics together in ways familiar from argument about unilateral declarations or *rebus sic stantibus*. As a result, what looks like a limit to one customary norm is also the creation of another and the opinion must decide between two customary norms, each both justified and opposed in hard and soft rhetorics.

The Court ruled that the Norwegian delimitation method did not contravene international law.[158] In reaching this conclusion, the Court found both that the proposed United Kingdom norm was not binding on Norway and that the proposed Norwegian scheme was binding on the United Kingdom. Initially, the Court supported the first proposition with consensual and the second with non-consensual rhetoric. The Court rejected the United Kingdom's claim that a general customary norm bound Norway in the following terms:

> The claim of the United Kingdom Government is founded on what it regards as the general international law applicable to the delimitation of the Norwegian fisheries zone
>
> . . . .
>
> In these circumstances the Court deems it necessary to point out that although the ten-mile rule has been adopted by certain States both in their national law and in their treaties and conventions, and although certain arbitral decisions have applied it as between these States, other States have adopted a different limit. Consequently, the ten-mile rule has not acquired the authority of a general rule of international law.
>
> In any event the ten-mile rule would appear to be inapplicable as against Nor-

158. *Id.* at 143.

way inasmuch as she has always opposed any attempt to apply it to the Norwegian coast.

. . . .

The Court, having thus established the existence and the constituent elements of the Norwegian system of delimitation, further finds that this system was consistently applied by Norwegian authorities and that it encountered no opposition on the part of other States.

. . . .

The Court considers that too much importance need not be attached to the few uncertainties or contradictions, real or apparent, which the United Kingdom Government claims to have discovered in Norwegian practice. They may be easily understood in the light of the variety of the facts and conditions prevailing in the long period which has elapsed since 1812, and are not such as to modify the conclusions reached by the Court.

In the light of these considerations, and in the absence of convincing evidence to the contrary, the Court is bound to hold that the Norwegian authorities applied their system of delimitation consistently and uninterruptedly from 1869 until the time when the dispute arose.[159]

On first reading, it seems that the Court rejects application of the United Kingdom norm to Norway primarily because Norway has not consented. A second reading complicates the image. We know that Norway has not consented—has opposed the United Kingdom norm—because Norway has succeeded in creating a "system of delimitation" which has been "consistently" applied without "opposition"—has, in other words, generated what might be thought of as an opposing norm of customary law binding upon the United Kingdom despite its apparent unwillingness to comply. So long as both norms (or both the United Kingdom's norm and its exception) are expressed consensually, they coexist uneasily. It seems difficult to explain why the Court should conclude that "too much importance need not be attached" to "uncertainties or contradictions" in the Norwegian practice while finding the fact that "other States have adopted a different limit" dispositive in concluding that the ten-mile rule "has not acquired the authority of a general rule of international law."

The Court avoids a direct clash between two consensually supported norms by moving to a softer defense of the Norwegian system—emphasizing practice rather than *opinio juris* and stressing the interests of local fishermen who have traditionally been economically dependent upon fish caught in the disputed regions. The Court defends the Norwegian system in the following terms:

These ancient concessions tend to confirm the Norwegian Government's contention that the fisheries zone reserved before 1812 was in fact much more exten-

---

159. *Id.* at 126, 131, 136-37, 138.

> sive than the one delimited in 1935. It is suggested that it included all fishing banks from which land was visible, the range of vision being, as is recognized by the United Kingdom Government, the principle of delimitation in force at that time. The Court considers that, although it is not always clear to what specific areas they apply, the historical data produced in support of this contention by the Norwegian Government lend some weight to the idea of the survival of traditional rights reserved to the inhabitants of the Kingdom over fishing grounds included in the 1935 delimitation, particularly in the case of Lopphavet. Such rights, founded on the vital needs of the population and attested by very ancient and peaceful usage, may legitimately be taken into account in drawing a line which, moreover, appears to the Court to have been kept within the bounds of what is moderate and reasonable.[160]

After reciting the geographic peculiarities of the northern Norwegian coast, the Court emphasizes the soft realism of accepting the Norwegian position.

> In these barren regions the inhabitants of the coastal zone derive their livelihood essentially from fishing.
>
> Such are the realities which must be borne in mind in appraising the validity of the United Kingdom contention that the limits of the Norwegian fisheries zone laid down in the 1935 Decree are contrary to international law.[161]

As a rhetorical matter, of course, an extra-consensual defense stressing consistency and competitive access could as easily have been used to support the ten-mile rule. Moreover, such a defense of the Norwegian rule invites a consensual response which focuses on gaps in the Norwegian practice and in the acquiescence of foreign states. Indeed, the United Kingdom argued that its previous attitude had at most been one of benign neglect rather than *opinio juris*, in any case displaced by its current opposition.

The key rhetorical moment, however, was achieved when the deadlock between two consensual norms was broken. Once the Court had characterised one rule in consensual terms and the other in extra-consensual terms, its argument took on a certain momentum. The Norwegian rule became "the" rule which needed to be displaced. The rest of the opinion was a rhetorical mopping up operation, deploying the strategies we encountered in the cases of unilateral declarations and changed circumstances to make the soft lie down with the hard.

This mopping up operation proceeded by exploiting the fact that both a hard and a soft rhetoric were available both to support and oppose each norm. The Court turned from a soft defense of the Norwegian system to a hard offense against the United Kingdom's opposition

160. *Id.* at 142.
161. *Id.* at 128.

to it, arguing that the absence of opposition indicated that the United Kingdom had consented to the Norwegian system, whatever its actual intent.

> From the standpoint of international law, it is now necessary to consider whether the application of the Norwegian system encountered any opposition from foreign States.
>
> . . . .
>
> The general toleration of foreign States with regard to the Norwegian practice is an unchallenged fact. For a period of more than sixty years the United Kingdom Government itself in no way contested it . . . . It would appear that it was only in its Memorandum of July 27, 1933, that the United Kingdom made a formal and definite protest on this point.
>
> The Court is thus led to conclude that the method of straight lines, established in the Norwegian system, was imposed by the peculiar geography of the Norwegian coast; that even before the dispute arose, this method had been consolidated by a constant and sufficiently long practice, in the face of which the attitude of governments bears witness to the fact that they did not consider it to be contrary to international law . . . .[162]

This offensive use of hard rhetoric against the United Kingdom is tempered in two ways so as not to clash directly with the United Kingdom's consensual claims. First, the Court tempers its hard opposition to the United Kingdom's proposed norm by suggesting that the ten-mile rule—as applied to Norway—is incompatible with certain systemic considerations "inherent the nature of the territorial sea:"

> In this connection, certain basic considerations inherent in the nature of the territorial sea, bring to light certain criteria which, though not entirely precise, can provide courts with an adequate basis for their decision, which can be adapted to the diverse facts in question.
>
> Among these considerations, some reference must be made to the close dependence of the territorial sea upon the land domain. It is the land which confers upon the coastal State a right to the waters off its coasts. It follows that while such a State must be allowed the latitude necessary in order to be able to adapt its delimitation to practical needs and local requirements, the drawing of base-lines must not depart to any appreciable extent from the general direction of the coast.
>
> Another fundamental consideration, of particular importance in this case, is the more or less close relationship existing between certain sea areas and the land formations which divide or surround them. The real question raised in the choice of base-lines is in effect whether certain sea areas lying within these lines are sufficiently closely linked to the land domain to be subject to the regime of internal waters. This idea, which is at the basis of the determination of the rules relating to bays, should be liberally applied in the case of a coast, the geographical configuration of which is as unusual as that of Norway.
>
> Finally, there is one consideration not to be overlooked, the scope of which

162. *Id.* at 138, 139.

> extends beyond purely geographical factors: that of certain economic interests peculiar to a region, the reality and importance of which are clearly evidenced by a long usage.[163]

Second, the United Kingdom's acquiescence is implied objectively from its practice, rather than found subjectively in *opinio juris*, in contrast to the Court's approach in evaluating the French unilateral declarations in the *Nuclear Tests* cases.

> The United Kingdom Government has argued that the Norwegian system of delimitation was not known to it and that the system therefore lacked the notoriety essential to provide the basis of an historic title enforceable against it. The Court is unable to accept this view. As a coastal State on the North Sea, greatly interested in the fisheries in this area, as a maritime power traditionally concerned with the law of the sea and concerned particularly to defend the freedom of the seas, the United Kingdom could not have been ignorant of the Decree of 1869 which had at once provoked a request for explanations by the French Government . . . .
>
> . . . .
>
> The notoriety of the facts, the general toleration of the international community, Great Britain's position in the North Sea, her own interest in the question, and her prolonged abstention would in any case warrant Norway's enforcement of her system against the United Kingdom.[164]

This softer assessment of the United Kingdom's rule might need to confront the Court's soft argument favoring the Norwegian practice, forcing the Court to choose between the systemic value of open seas and the systemic value of "natural prolongation" as expressions of sovereignty just as it might have seemed necessary to choose between Norwegian and United Kingdom fishermen when the Court justified the Norwegian rule in soft terms. The Court deploys a number of rhetorical strategies to avoid such a direct choice.

One strategy is to return to a hard justification for the Norwegian exception to the United Kingdom rule—precisely the position which was downplayed when the Court was expressing the United Kingdom's rule in hard terms. This time, however, the Norwegian opposition is tempered by soft considerations of systemic principle to which the Norwegian delimitation must, of course, comply.

> The Norwegian Government does not deny that there exist rules of international law to which this delimitation must conform. It contends that the propositions formulated by the United Kingdom Government in its "conclusions" do not possess the character attributed to them by that government. It further relies on its own system of delimitation which it asserts to be in every respect in conformity with the requirements of international law.

163. *Id.* at 133.
164. *Id.* at 138-39.

. . . .

> It does not at all follow that, in the absence of rules having the technically precise character alleged by the United Kingdom Government, the delimitation undertaken by the Norwegian Government in 1935 is not subject to certain principles which make it possible to judge as to its validity under international law. The delimitation of sea areas has always an international aspect; it cannot be dependent merely upon the will of the coastal State as expressed in its municipal law. Although it is true that the act of delimitation is necessarily a unilateral act, because only the coastal State is competent to undertake it, the validity of the delimitation with regard to other States depends upon international law.[165]

Another strategy is to express the systemic, softer basis for the Norwegian rule in terms of a customarily accepted scheme of "historic title" in the establishment of which the United Kingdom, like other states, has participated.

> By "historic waters" are usually meant waters which are treated as internal waters but which would not have that character were it not for the existence of an historic title. The United Kingdom Government refers to the notion of historic titles both in respect of territorial waters and internal waters, considering such titles, in both cases, as derogations from general international law. In its opinion Norway can justify the claim that these waters are territorial or internal on the ground that she has exercised the necessary jurisdiction over them for a long period without opposition from other states, a kind of *possessio longi temporis*, with the result that her jurisdiction over these waters must now be recognized although it constitutes a derogation from the rules in force. Norwegian sovereignty over these waters would constitute an exception, historic titles justifying situations which would otherwise be in conflict with international law.
>
> As has been said, the United Kingdom Government concedes that Norway is entitled to claim as internal waters all the waters of fjords and sunds which fall within the conception of a bay as defined in international law whether the closing line of the indentation is more or less than ten sea miles long.[166]

Although the Court's opinion has not directly confronted either the choice between Norwegian and British consent or between systemic interests in Norwegian and British fisheries or in open seas and historic titles, it has produced an elegant and persuasive account of its decision for Norway. One might say that the decision expresses a preference for historic title, or Norwegian fisheries or British consent, but the decision does not rhetorically present these choices. Similarly, one might say that the opinion, although primarily "about" customary law, is important primarily for its doctrinal expression of consensual doctrines of estoppel and persistent opposition which here trump the customary norm. But the opinion itself weaves an elegant blend of consensual and non-

165. *Id.* at 126, 132.

166. *Id.* at 130-31. Judge Hackworth concurs on the basis of this connection. *Id.* at 144.

consensual rhetoric on behalf of one customary norm and against another. This blend is created much as it was created in the International Load Line Convention materials and in the *Nuclear Tests* opinions—by interpreting soft doctrines in consensual terms and supporting consensual norms with systemic considerations.

The major difference is that the opening moment, in which the Court chooses to consider treating Norway's system as the norm which will lapse only in the face of persistent opposition by the United Kingdom, is cast in soft rhetoric, whereas in the earlier cases we considered, the norm was established in hard rhetoric and then lapsed in the face of systemic considerations, however consensually expressed. This moment reveals something about rhetorical strategies of decision. These shifting rhetorical possibilities can be mobilized in a way which seems tilted in favor of Norway by exploiting the contrast between consensual and nonconsensual norms rather than by expressing a direct choice for the Norwegian system. In this, the opinion reaches persuasive closure in much the way the doctrinal system achieves doctrinal distinctiveness—by expressing doctrines in differentially hard and soft rhetoric.

In both situations, moreover, *extreme* versions of the two rhetorical strands are avoided by interpreting each in terms of the other, thus allowing them to coexist easily. Thus, the Court saves the apparent effectiveness of hard arguments by treating them as capable of objective systemic definition. In the first instance, the Court uses an objective practice-based approach to British consent, finding in a benign practice a willingness to live with the Norwegian system. On the other hand, the Norwegian will is understood to be bound by systematic considerations of justice. Both consensual strands of the Court's argument are thus given soft interpretations. Similarly, although the Norwegian rule is supported and the United Kingdom norm is opposed by soft arguments, these soft arguments are defined by historically acknowledged practices.

The opinion of the International Court of Justice in the *North Sea Continental Shelf Cases* develops, but never quite resolves, similar arguments about the creation and limitation of a special norm of customary law.[167] Germany, Denmark, and the Netherlands, having agreed that the boundaries of their adjoining continental shelves should be determined by agreement, requested the Court to state the rules of international law, if any, which should be taken into account. The judgment, confined to an analysis of the relative authority of alternative legal norms, was almost exclusively concerned with sources doctrine.

167. (W. Ger. v. Den., W. Ger. v. Neth.) 1969 I.C.J. 3 (Judgment of Feb. 20).

As it turned out, moreover, the Court did not feel it necessary definitively to choose among norms or to specify in any detail how any norm should be applied to the continental shelf in the North Sea: "The Court is requested . . . to decide what are the applicable 'principles' and rules of international law. The Court is not asked actually to delimit the further boundaries which will be involved. . . ."[168]

Denmark and the Netherlands proposed that the shelf be delimited in accordance with the principle of "equidistance" which they argued was binding upon the Federal Republic. Because the German North Sea coast is deeply indented, this rule would have allocated much of the oil rich outer shelf to Denmark and the Netherlands. The Federal Republic proposed that the "just and equitable share" rule bound Denmark and the Netherlands to allocate Germany a portion of the shelf proportional to the relative length of Germany's coastline, despite its indented shape.

The Court presented the arguments for both rules in a similar order. First, the Court treated the contentions of both sides that their proposed norm could be deduced from the first principle of continental shelf doctrine: that the right to continental shelf dominion is based upon the "natural prolongation" of the sovereign's coastal territory. The Court reaffirmed the principle of "natural prolongation" but rejected both of the interpretations offered by the parties.

Although the Court rejected the two interpretive claims in slightly differing ways, both were treated as insufficiently consensual expressions of a systemic norm. As a result, the second half of the Court's opinion compared hard justifications for the two rules. This approach is thus quite different from that of the *Fisheries* case which created a sense of rhetorical progression by contrasting hard and soft justifications. Here the Court considers both proposed rules from a soft perspective and then from a hard perspective. This approach makes it far more difficult for the Court to weave a persuasive and continuous rhetorical fabric—and it is perhaps well that the opinion confronted no narrative demand for decisiveness.

Let us follow these two argumentative presentations in turn. Although the first stage of the opinion treats the two proposed norms from a soft perspective, this uniformity is hardly necessary, for the parties appear to have presented slightly divergent arguments for their proposed interpretation of the "natural prolongation" principle. Indeed, the Court seems to have struggled to transform each into a springboard for a similar parallel investigation of consent.

---

168. *Id.* at 13.

As presented by the Court, the Germans sought to interpret the soft standard so that it might depend upon their participation in delimitation according to its terms, rendering the automatic and nonconsensual "natural prolongation" principle dependent upon actual usage and a consensual settlement of claims. They thus seemed to be grafting a consensual requirement onto a systemic argument of principle. The Court rejected this argument by stressing the systemic and principled nature of "natural prolongation" as an extension of sovereignty—excluding any necessity of sovereign participation in its interpretation.

> It will be convenient to consider first the contentions put forward on behalf of the Federal Republic. The Court does not feel able to accept them. . . . The doctrine of the just and equitable share appears to be wholly at variance with what the Court entertains no doubt is the most fundamental of all the rules of law relating to the continental shelf, enshrined in Article 2 of the 1958 Geneva Convention, though quite independent of it,—namely that the rights of the coastal State in respect of the area of continental shelf that constitutes a natural prolongation of its land territory into and under the sea exist *ipso facto* and *ab initio*, by virtue of its sovereignty over the land, and as an extension of it in an exercise of sovereign rights for the purpose of exploring the seabed and exploiting its natural resources. In short, there is here an inherent right . . . . Furthermore, the right does not depend on its being exercised. . . .[169]

By emphasizing the inherency of "natural prolongation" rather than "participation" in sovereignty, the Court drove a wedge between the two halves of the German argument, forcing a consensual defense of the proportionality approach.

The Court approaches the soft arguments for the Danish-Dutch norm quite differently. It presents arguments for the equidistance principle in exclusively soft terms—precisely the terms in which it rejected the proportionality norm—and rejects them as insufficiently grounded in German consent. The opinion considers and rejects the view that the equidistance principle is implied by the idea of natural prolongation and is hence "a rule that is part of the corpus of general international law;—and, like other rules of general or customary international law, is binding on the Federal Republic automatically and independently of any specific assent, direct or indirect, given by the latter."[170]

The Court could have structured its rejection of the Danish-Dutch norm parallel to its rejection of the German norm, as incompatible with the inherency of "natural prolongation" in sovereignty. Equidistance, by tying the principle of "natural prolongation" to the formal equality

169. *Id.* at 21-22.
170. *Id.* at 28.

of sovereigns, would have introduced a hard element into a principle which expresses the systemic respect for territorial configurations. Instead, the Court rejects the Dutch-Danish norm for being *insufficiently* grounded in sovereign consensual autonomy.

> The *a priori* argument starts from the position . . . according to which the right of the coastal State to its continental shelf areas is based on its sovereignty over the land domain, of which the shelf area is the natural prolongation into and under the sea. From this notion of appurtenance is derived the view which, as has already been indicated, the Court accepts, that the coastal State's rights exist *ipso facto* and *ab initio* without there being any question of having to make good a claim to the areas concerned, or of any apportionment of the continental shelf between different states. . . . Denmark and the Netherlands, for their part, claim that the test of appurtenance must be "proximity," or more accurately "closer proximity:" all those parts of the shelf being considered as appurtenant to a particular coastal state which are (but only if they are) closer to it than they are to any point on the coast of another state . . . .
>
> The conclusion drawn by the Court from the foregoing analysis is that the notion of equidistance as being logically necessary, in the sense of being an inescapable *a priori* accompaniment of basic continental shelf doctrine, is incorrect . . . . A review of the genesis and development of the equidistance method of delimitation can only serve to confirm the foregoing conclusion . . . .
>
> [A]t no time was the notion of equidistance as an inherent necessity of continental shelf doctrine entertained. Quite a different outlook was indeed manifested from the start in current legal thinking.[171]

On the one hand, the Court seems to have deployed a rhetorical strategy familiar from the *Fisheries* case. By rejecting the two proposed interpretations of the natural prolongation principle with arguments which differentially emphasize the hard and the soft, the Court has generated a sense of movement forward, placing a burden upon the Dutch to prove consent, and eliminating the German norm from further consensual consideration. On the other hand, however, the Court has created a difficulty for itself. By rejecting the German norm for attempting to introduce consensual elements into natural prolongation and rejecting the Dutch argument for insufficiently demonstrating the consensual basis for their interpretation of the natural prolongation principle, the Court has preserved the soft integrity of the principle—without creating a preference for either interpretation. The Court seems confronted with an awkward choice. Either they can maintain the high ground and interpret "natural prolongation" themselves—an alternative which stands uneasily with the justification for their rejection of the Danish-Dutch interpretation—or they can shift to a more purely consensual rhetoric—which will need to leave their purified sys-

171. *Id.* at 29, 32, 35.

temic principle somewhat behind. They choose the latter.

The remainder of the opinion is devoted to the Danish and Dutch claim that Germany is bound to the equidistance rule because it is part of the body of consensual custom or treaty law which binds Germany. The trouble is that unmoored from the discussion of systemic considerations, an argument cast purely in terms of sovereign autonomy and consent seems unable to generate any particular rule. Although Denmark and the Netherlands presented consensual arguments of both treaty and custom for equidistance, Germany asserted that it had not or did not consent.

Limited to the idea that subjective consent is to be the basis for customary norms, the Court is confronted with two classically polar claims. On the one hand, it seems to require that Germany be bound by whatever norm Denmark and the Netherlands subjectively claim to have consented to on the basis of their objective and reasonable belief that Germany had bound itself thereto. The idea that objective or implied consent is to be the basis of obligation seems in Danish hands to devour any subjectively based German protest to imposition of the proposed customary norm. On the other hand, the idea of implied consent seems incompatible with the notion that Germany is bound by its consent.

Having rejected the soft arguments attributed to the Netherlands and Denmark, the Court examines what it treats as fallback positions which justify binding the Federal Republic by its consent. The equidistance principle was alternatively to be considered binding because Germany had signed a treaty (Geneva Convention) containing it, or had assented to the treaty's contents, or because the treaty declared preexisting positive customary law, or crystallized new law, or because the treaty rule had since become a customary norm through the assent of the international community.

As presented by the Court, Germany responds to each of these hard arguments in consensual terms, terms which would ordinarily compel the Danish and Dutch to abandon their consensual justification for the rule and return to the soft argumentation which the Court had already rejected. Germany was not bound by the treaty because it never intended to be bound, and had not ratified, despite its signature and unilateral declarations assuming the treaty's obligations. Germany argued further that it did not accept either a prior customary law declared or an emergent law crystallized. Moreover, Germany rejected the view that new custom had been created because the requisite subjective intent was missing.

The Dutch and Danish responded to each of these objections by moving to implication: German consent could be implied even absent ratification, or, supported by Judge Lachs in dissent, *opinio juris* must be implied from conduct.[172] Germany countered that it had been a consistent dissenter to precisely this rule, whatever the norm's customary status elsewhere.

The Court adopts the German point of view at each stage in this exchange. Germany is not bound by the Convention which contains the equidistance rule. Germany is not bound by its unilateral acceptance of the Convention because it did not intend to be bound.[173] The Convention did not "crystallize" the equidistance principle as a customary norm because it was proposed "by the [International Law] Commission with considerable hesitation, somewhat on an experimental basis,"[174] with insufficient consensus to produce custom. Even when the Court considers somewhat softer, more systemic responses to Germany's arguments, it rejects them. Thus, the equidistance rule is not binding as custom because not sufficiently consciously accepted by states over a long enough period of time to have registered sufficient consent.

> With respect to the other elements usually regarded as necessary before a conventional rule can be considered to have become a general rule of international law, it might be that, even without the passage of any considerable period of time, a very widespread and representative participation in the Convention might suffice of itself, provided it included that of States whose interests were specially affected. In the present case, however, the Court notes that, even if allowance is made for the existence of a number of States to whom participation in the Geneva Convention is not open, or which, by reason for instance of being land-locked States, would have no interest in becoming parties to it, the number of ratifications and accessions so far secured is, though respectable, hardly sufficient . . . .
>
> As regards the time element, the Court notes that it is over ten years since the convention was signed, but that it is even now less than five since it came into force . . . . Although the passage of only a short period of time is not necessarily, or of itself, a bar to the formation of a new rule of customary international law on the basis of what was originally a purely conventional rule, an indispensable requirement would be that within the period in question, short though it might be, State practice, including that of States whose interests are specially affected, should have been both extensive and virtually uniform in the sense of the provision invoked;—and should moreover have occurred in such a way as to show a general recognition that a rule of law or legal obligation is involved.
>
> . . . .

172. *Id.* at 231. Judge Lachs stated: "it is surely over-exacting to require proof that every state having applied a given rule did so because it was conscious of an *obligation* to do so." *Id.*

173. "The Federal Republic was one of the signatories of the convention, but has never ratified it, and is consequently not a party. . . ." *Id.* at 25.

174. *Id.* at 38.

> The essential point in this connection—and it seems necessary to stress it—is that even if these instances of action by non-parties to the Convention were much more numerous than they in fact are, they would not, even in the aggregate, suffice in themselves to constitute the *opinio juris*;—for, in order to achieve this result, two conditions must be fulfilled. Not only must the acts concerned amount to a settled practice, but they must also be such, or be carried out in such a way, as to be evidence of a belief that this practice is rendered obligatory by the existence of a rule of law requiring it.[175]

The dissenting opinions differed with the majority on one or another of these points, preferring a somewhat softer approach. Judge Lachs was willing to imply *opinio juris*, which he regarded as merely a matter of "evidence," and to do so on the basis of fewer instances over a shorter period so that the law could remain "commensurate with the rate of movement of events which require legal regulation."[176] In the end, Judge Lachs takes a softer approach:

> For to become binding, a rule or principle of international law need not pass the test of universal acceptance. This is reflected in several statements of the Court, e.g.: "generally . . . adopted in the practice of States" (*Fisheries, Judgment, I.C.J. Reports* 1951, p. 128). Not all States have . . . an opportunity or possibility of applying a given rule. The evidence should be sought in the behaviour of a great number of States, possibly the majority of States, in any case the great majority of the interested States . . . .[177]

Judge Tanaka, in his dissent, is willing to eliminate reliance upon the subjective consent altogether.

> Next, so far as . . . *opinio juris sive necessitatis* is concerned, it is extremely difficult to get evidence of its existence in concrete cases. This factor, relating to internal motivation and being of a psychological nature, cannot be ascertained very easily, particularly when diverse legislative and executive organs of a government participate in an internal process of decision-making in respect of ratification or other State acts. There is no other way than to ascertain the existence of *opinio juris* from the fact of the external existence of a certain custom and its necessity felt in the international community, rather than to seek evidence as to the subjective motives for each example of State practice, which is something which is impossible of achievement.[178]

Judge Sørensen is willing to take an objective approach to *opinio juris*, citing Sir Hersch Lauterpacht.

> Unless judicial activity is to result in reducing the legal significance of the most potent source of rules of international law, namely, the conduct of States, it would appear that the accurate principle on the subject consists in regarding all

175. *Id.* at 42-43, 44.
176. *Id.* at 230.
177. *Id.* at 229.
178. *Id.* at 176.

> uniform conduct of Governments (or, in appropriate cases, abstention therefrom) as evidencing the *opinio necessitatis juris* except when it is shown that the conduct in question was not accompanied by any such intention (Sir Hersch Lauterpacht: *The Development of International Law by the International Court*, London 1958, p. 380).
>
> Applying these considerations to the circumstances of the present cases, I think that the practice of States referred to above may be taken as sufficient evidence of the existence of any necessary *opinio juris*.[179]

Rather than blending the hard with the soft, the Court simply stresses the hard, leaving the soft to the dissenting opinions. In this, the majority and the dissent have differentiated themselves from one another by monopolizing the rhetorical tendencies which also differentiate doctrines from one another. This rhetorical strategy, while it effectively banishes the proposed Danish-Netherlands rule, has a difficult time coming up with an alternative. In rejecting the soft Danish-Netherlands argument, the Court indicated the dependence of soft argument on hard consensus for which it had criticized the German position. Having completed its rejection of the Danish position, the Court never considers the hard arguments which Germany may have advanced for the proportionality rule.

The Court was perhaps fortunate, given its rhetorical approach, that the parties had agreed not to save it from the task of knitting, from opposed protestations about lack of consent, a coherent norm to apply to the delimitation. Having considered both sets of soft arguments and rejecting them with a rather hard analysis, not much was left out of which to fashion a decision. The parties were content to have the equidistance rule eliminated and the Court did not actively defend an alternative rule, or even the absence of that rule. The result was the anticlimactic conclusion that the parties must "agree" to an apportionment which must be in accord with "equitable principles" including equidistance and "a reasonable degree of proportionality." At the last moment, the Court returns to a more persuasive combination strategy:

> It was, and it really remained to the end, governed by two beliefs;—namely, first, that no one single method of delimitation was likely to prove satisfactory in all circumstances, and that delimitation should, therefore, be carried out by agreement (or by reference to arbitration); and secondly, that it should be effected on equitable principles.[180]

The Court suggests that this combination is what most people mean [hard] by the idea of natural prolongation [soft]. This consensus leads to the conclusion that:

179. *Id*. at 247.
180. *Id*. at 43.

> On a foundation of very general precepts of justice and good faith, actual rules of law are here involved which govern the delimitation of adjacent continental shelves . . ., namely:
>
> (a) the parties are under an obligation to enter into negotiations with a view to arriving at an agreement . . .;
>
> (b) the parties are under an obligation to act in such a way that, in the particular case, and taking all the circumstances into account, equitable principles are applied,—for this purpose the equidistance method can be used, but other methods exist and may be employed, alone or in combination, according to the areas involved;
>
> (c) for the reasons given . . . the continental shelf of any state must be the natural prolongation of its land territory and must not encroach upon what is the natural prolongation of the territory of another State.
>
> . . . .
>
> [I]n the course of the negotiations, the factors to be taken into account are to include:
>
> (1) the general configuration of the coasts of the Parties, as well as the presence of any special or unusual features;
>
> (2) so far as known or readily ascertainable, the physical and geological structure, and natural resources, of the continental shelf areas involved;
>
> (3) the element of a reasonable degree of proportionality, which a delimitation carried out in accordance with equitable principles ought to bring about between the extent of the continental shelf areas appertaining to the coastal state and the length of its coast measured in the general direction of the coastline, account being taken for this purpose of the effects, actual or prospective, of any other continental shelf delimitations between adjacent states in the same region.[181]

III. CONCLUSIONS ABOUT SOURCES DISCOURSE

The elaborately articulated modern doctrine and argument about the sources of international law are strikingly abstract and independent of the specific norms of process or substance whose authority it establishes.[182] The authority of various sources, their limitations, and the hierarchical relationship among sources do not depend upon the content of norms. Argument about the authority of various norms, when conducted in the rhetoric of sources doctrine, proceeds independently of the norm's particular content or application. At the same time, however, modern sources discourse is a distinctly doctrinal affair. Argu-

---

181. *Id.* at 46-47, 53-54.

182. Not only are "sources of law" perceived to be a topic sufficiently unified to be the subject of separate monographs and books, *see supra* note 1, they are generally treated separately in casebooks and treatises. *See, e.g.*, W. Bishop, International Law (3d ed. 1971); J. Brierly, *supra* note 1; I. Brownlie, *supra* note 1; L. Henkin, R. Pugh, O. Schachter & H. Smit, *supra* note 97; A. Verdross, *supra* note 1; Waldock, *supra* note 1.

ment about the binding nature of particular international legal norms may be abstract, but it is neither theoretical nor political. Norms are legally binding which fit within one of a series of doctrinally elaborated categories, not when a persuasive argument about political interest or theoretical coherence can be made for their observance.

In establishing, delimiting, and hierarchically arranging the categories of authoritative norms in a way which is both doctrinal and yet independent of particular legal doctrines, sources discourse has developed a variety of puzzling rhetorical patterns. Throughout sources discourse, doctrines and arguments repeatedly invoke a distinction between consensually and non-consensually based norms. Most of the rhetorical strategies developed by sources discourse can be understood to recapitulate in one form or another this basic distinction. It is used to distinguish treaties from custom, to contrast various schools of thought about the nature of custom, to divide arguments for and against the application of specific norms in various situations, and in dozens of other ways throughout the materials on sources.

For all this repetition, however, the distinction between consensual and non-consensual sources or doctrines or positions remains frustratingly fluid. These two opposed themes present rhetorical possibilities and strategies more than decisive identifications and differentiations. The important point is that using these rhetorical themes to articulate and distinguish the sources of law gives sources discourse a doctrinal feel without presenting the choice between two norms as a substantive clash between two substantive doctrinal schemes or two sovereigns.

Although a sources discourse which operated completely within the rhetoric of either consent or systemic considerations would also seem doctrinal, it would not be able to avoid presenting a more substantive face. A consensual rhetoric could certainly differentiate and prioritize norms in an abstract way, but in choosing among two norms one would need to choose between the claims of two sovereigns about their autonomous consent. A purely extra-consensual rhetoric, while it would obviously avoid this problem, would have a difficult time avoiding a more substantive seeming choice among various systemically grounded norms. By combining these two rhetorics, sources discourse can defend its independence from sovereign autonomy and substantive legal regulation.

In this survey of sources discourse I have presented a few of the more obvious strategies for combining these incompatible rhetorics. The most apparent rhetorical strategy of combination is simply repetition—differentiating various doctrines from one another as hard and soft and then repeating the distinction in distinguishing each doctrine from its exception or interpreting doctrinal strands which have once been characterized and perhaps adopted as hard in soft terms. Arguments about the fluid and proliferating doctrinal field which results from this repeating practice of distinction and recombination are often able to combine both rhetorics by careful management of an argument's order—establishing a disjuncture between hard and soft arguments in order to create a sense of decisive forward movement, much as the doctrinal corpus used notions of hierarchy to accommodate sources which were characterized as both hard and soft.

If we think of these various strategies together, the rhetorical patterns seem less fluid. Taken as a whole, sources doctrine seems to favor consensual rhetoric. Consensual doctrines seem to dominate, and consensual interpretations of softer doctrines seem most compelling. The doctrinal hierarchy seems tilted in favor of a rhetoric of consent. Sources argument as a whole, however, seems tilted towards the systemic authority of legal norms. Indeed, sources rhetoric as a whole seems to move toward law and away from sovereign autonomy. A certain systemic authority seems to be taken for granted in rhetoric which is most emphatic about its consensual foundation. In this way, sources discourse seems to combine both rhetorics. That sources discourse can be doctrinal indicates its systemic basis. That it speaks incessantly about consent insulates it from a substantive legal regime. The argument and doctrine taken together seem to move from sovereign autonomy toward systemic authority.

So long as consensual rhetoric seems associable with sovereign autonomy and extra-consensual rhetoric with sovereign cooperation or international solidarity, these patterns suggest something about the goal or project of sources discourse. Sources discourse, so long as it seems hard, guarantees that the legal order will not derogate from—indeed will express—sovereign authority and autonomy. So long as it seems soft, sources rhetoric guarantees that the international legal order will not be hostage to sovereign whim. So long as hard sources rhetoric remains different from soft rhetoric, can seem superior to soft rhetoric and is able to coexist with soft rhetoric, the international legal order can seem to express and transcend sovereign power.

The important point, however, is not simply the coexistence of these two rhetorics. Each must also *temper* the other in important ways and the discourse as a whole must seem to move forward from autonomy to community. Let me take up these two additional dimensions in turn. Although it is difficult to see exactly why, it seems that contemporary sources discourse is uncomfortable with both hard and soft rhetoric in their extreme forms. One could imagine a sources discourse which was dependent either upon sovereign will or upon the content of the individual norms which made up the international legal order. Imagining such systems suggests something about the motivation for the elaborately hybrid contemporary doctrine and argument about international legal sources.

Were sources discourse completely derivative of other doctrines, it might simply describe the places where one might look to find descriptions of state behavior or elaborations of norms whose authority was derived from someplace else. Interestingly, international law scholars writing before 1648 characteristically spoke of sources in this way.[183] Their derivative approach to sources was indicated in part by the dispersal of sources doctrine throughout other doctrinal discourse.

A scholar who imagined that the authority of norms was well established elsewhere and who wanted only to describe the ways in which these rules were manifested, could have had a much smaller abstract discussion. He would not be concerned about abstractly identifying the relative hierarchy of his sources. The norms themselves would do that for him. More powerful norms would simply be more powerful, or would say they were more powerful, and there would be no particular reason to suspect that this hierarchy depended upon the way in which a norm was made known. Moreover, such a scholar would not need to delimit the boundaries of his sources very clearly in an abstract fashion. The boundaries of the body of norms would be logically independent of the form of their manifestation. The norms would be limited by their content, not the particular catalog in which they were found. Pre-1648 discussions of the sources of international law did not consistently establish a hierarchy among sources, but suggested that norms from each catalog might, depending upon their content, overrule those of another. Likewise, they did not abstractly delimit their various catalogs. Instead, they suggested that each was limited by the norms which filled it. For example, natural law was defined by the norms which were natural and necessary. These were then elaborated. The category or "source" ended when norms of this sort ran out.

We might also imagine a sources discourse which simply catalogued norms which comported with sovereign will. Such an approach would threaten other doctrinal fields. As the articulation of the content as well as the form of power, sources discourse would no longer simply ground doctrines of process and substance. A scholar who imagined discourse

183. For a discussion of the concepts of the sources of legal authority in the work of primitive scholars Vitoria, Suarez, Gentili, and Grotius, see Kennedy, *Primitive Legal Scholarship*, 27 HARV. INT'L L.J. 1 (1986).

about the "sources" of international law to be descriptive of catalogs of state interests would have a different sense of what needed explaining in doctrines about the sources of international law. He would not need to establish a hierarchy among the sources he considered. When norms conflicted, the norm expressing the more important sovereign interest or the more forceful sovereign will would predominate. There would be no reason to assume that the form of their manifestation could be an accurate guide to their relative strength. Likewise, such a scholar would not be particularly interested in abstractly defining and limiting the various catalogs he felt one could refer to for the content of state interest. The state interests or patterns of authority which were sources would limit the body of norms, and the catalogs would be defined by the norms which filled them, rather than *vice versa*.[184]

Contemporary people who talk about sources are not content to say that states obey rules because it is in their interest to do so and that we look to custom, treaty, etc. to discover what is in their interest. Rather, these people accept that the state is best situated to understand and follow its own interests. They want to know the source of norms which bind sovereigns who do not perceive the obligation to be in their own immediate interests. They are looking for the source of norms which can bind the dissident, the nonconformist, the state which wants to do something else. There would be no legal dispute in need of normative resolution unless there was a conflict of interest, unless two states thought their interests could best be served by acting in different fashions. To resolve that dispute by looking for the source of norms only in state interest would lead us only to the conflict.

Likewise, people who talk about sources are not content to say that they are discussing only the ways in which a higher order which animates and therefore binds the state system is made known. They want to acknowledge the authority of states to differ about the content of such a higher order and seek in their discourse about sources to deter-

---

184. During the extreme period of positivism in the mid-nineteenth century, when a view of international law quite similar to this dominated, the writing of abstract casebooks fell out of fashion in the Anglo-Saxon world, to be replaced by catalogs of state behavior and exercises of sovereign will. *See, e.g.*, H. WHEATON, HISTORY OF THE LAW OF NATIONS IN EUROPE AND AMERICA (1845); H. WHEATON, ELEMENTS OF INTERNATIONAL LAW (1866) (containing a short non-abstract list of sources of the practices guiding international life as indicated by prior publicists). Although this was not true in continental Europe during this period, the treatises produced there often lacked an abstract discussion of the validity of various sources. *See, e.g.*, F. HOLTZENDORF, HANDBUCH DES VÖLKERRECHTS (1887); F. VON LISZT, DAS VÖLKERRECHT (1898) (stating "nur die Rechtsüberzeugung der Staaten vermag Recht zu schaffen"); H. HALLECK, INTERNATIONAL LAW, OR RULES REGULATING THE INTERCOURSE OF STATES IN PEACE AND WAR (1861).

mine which of several possible manifestations of such a higher order is authoritative. Indeed, the contemporary scholar discussing the sources of international law does so distinctly from his elaborations of the content of the norms of international law. He tries to develop an abstract set of doctrines about the sources of international law which are independent of the content of the norms which result and of the authorities which produce them. This would only seem worth doing if it seemed that something about the content of international law hinged on this abstract discussion; if the ensuing catalogs of norms were defined by the abstract discussions and not *vice versa*. This would seem true if the authority of the various norms depended upon their inclusion in the abstractly defined categories; if sources discourse was about the justification and limitation of normative authority.

Paradoxically, then, the hesitancy to adopt either extreme position about the basis for international normative authority preserves the authority of sources discourse. People who discourse about the sources of international law are trying to do two things. They seek the norms which can bind states against their own perception of their interests. They seek to elaborate the normative order in a way which does not presume away the diversity of state interests. Sources discourse argues about the normative forms which can bind states without overthrowing their authority. The discourse is not about the form of the catalog of norms. It is about the sources of normative authority in a system of autonomous sovereigns.[185]

Thus it seems that the rhetorical tendency to temper hard with soft in sources discourse is more than a persuasive technique. It expresses a hesitancy to embrace either of the extremes with which it flirts. We might think of sources discourse as a whole as sustaining its distinctive position of independence and authority by *invoking* in a hyperbolic way

185. *See* 1 G. DAHM, VÖLKERRECHT (1958) (presenting extensive doctrinal discussions): "Das Problem ist damit in aller Schärfe gestellt: Wie kann es in einer nicht auf über-und Unterordnung, sondern auf Gleichberechtigung *souveräner* Staaten beruhenden Gemeinschaft Völkerrecht geben?" *Id.* at 8; *see also* Barile, *La Structure de l'ordre juridique international*, 161 RECUEIL DES COURS 9 (1978):

> La règle en question répond, en premier lieu, aux principes de souveraineté et d'indépendance des états, membres fondamentaux de la communauté internationale. Le principe de parité entre les états, étroitement lié à celui de leur souveraineté et de leur indépendance, qui, du reste, est à la base également de toutes les autres normes du droit des traités (que l'on pense aux règles qui garantissent d'une certaine façon, plutôt limitée à vrai dire—voir le paragraphe 13 de ce chapitre, la liberté du consentement et aux autres qui déterminent les vices et la nullîté des accords) s'exprime, dans la règle *pacta sunt servanda*, dans la valeur *inter partes* des traités . . . .

Id. at 80.

images of sovereign autonomy and systemic authority which it is unwilling to embrace. Rather than combining hard and soft rhetorics, we should think of sources discourse as *excluding* the referents of both hard and soft rhetoric. In one way, this exclusion preserves the autonomy and authority of sources doctrine. But in another way, this exclusion refers us away from sources discourse and establishes a substantive legal fabric which remains comfortable with sovereign autonomy. Thought of this way, a sources discourse which deploys the rhetorical strategies which I have outlined seems self-effacing rather than assertive.

The rhetorical proliferation and continual displacement characteristic of sources discourse typifies this self-effacing authority. The rhetorical style and direction of sources discourse, is thus related to its supplemental position within doctrinal discourse as a whole. Neither itself authoritative nor descriptive of an authority located elsewhere, sources doctrine maintains an uneasy independence from other doctrine while leading us towards the substantive legal order. Paradoxically, discourse about the authoritative source of international legal norms occupies a space in modern doctrinal work at once fundamental and trivial. Its importance has a logical flavor. In an era assuming the centrality of origins, doctrines about the authority of authoritative norms seem logically prior to doctrines of substance or process. They are usually presented first in international legal treatises. Moreover, in an era distinguishing theory and doctrine by their relative levels of abstraction from a particular notion of reality, doctrines about the sources of law seem more intimately connected to the structure of the systemic power apparatus than do the individual and specific doctrines whose authority they validate. Sources discourse seems theoretically superior to doctrines of substance or process. As we might expect from this viewpoint, this discourse is very closely related to much theoretical work. Sources discourse is the doctrinal counterpart to the obsession of theory with questions of the legitimacy, strength, and authority of international law.[186]

On the other hand, despite this apparent doctrinal priority, sources discourse functions as the last resort of all doctrinal argument. Only when the persuasive power of other doctrines is diminished are advocates forced to say: "this doctrine or outcome may not be persuasive or coherent, but it is authoritative." Consequently, one might only uncover the structure of arguments about the sources of international law after

186. *See* Kennedy, *Theses About International Law Discourse*, 23 GER. Y.B. INT'L L. 353 (1980).

theoretical and other doctrinal argument had run out. Moreover, despite the theoretical superiority of sources discourse, doctrines about sources seem derivative of a systemic vision articulated first in doctrines of process or substance—where, for example, the "sovereign" whose consent will ground a source will be defined. In argument, sources discourse plays a supplemental role, validating and supplanting a constellation of sovereign authorities produced by doctrines of substance and process.

The key to understanding the structure of sources doctrine is this paradoxical position anterior and inferior to other doctrine. Sources discourse is distinct from other doctrines, allowing space for theoretical elaborations of authority within doctrine. It formally precedes other doctrines as theory formally encompasses doctrine, yet it supplements other doctrinal discourse. One way of thinking about the significance of the rhetorical strategies characteristic of sources doctrine is to see them as managers of this supplemental separation or dependent autonomy from other doctrines. Another way of approaching the same issue, however, is to think of these rhetorical maneuvers as translations into doctrine of difficulties encountered by international legal theory.

At first, the hard and soft rhetorics characteristic of sources doctrine seem reminiscent of positivism and naturalism. We might associate positivism with the view that sources discourse could supplant other doctrines by mapping the interests of state authority. Maintaining the supplemental position of sources discourse (its dependence upon an authority apparatus articulated elsewhere) seems similar to avoiding the pitfalls of an extreme positivism which postulates an authority which it cannot ground. We might associate naturalism with the view that sources discourse could be consumed by doctrines of substance and process. Maintaining the independent position of sources discourse (its ability to validate other norms) seems similar to the dilemma of an extreme naturalism which posits an order to which it cannot give content. In this view, we would equate the struggle to blend hard and soft rhetorics with the dilemma confronting a theory of international law which is to be neither naturalist nor positivist.

Like our preliminary associations of hard and soft rhetorics with images of an independent and a dependent discourse of sources, these preliminary associations simplify naturalism and positivism. Each of these theoretical positions, which developed after the collapse of primitive scholarship, like contemporary sources discourse, were aimed at resolving the division of authority and order. Although they tended towards these two extremes, each school offered a mediation of the relation between order and autonomy. Sources discourse likewise situates itself between two extremes which it expresses only hyperbolically—only as it excludes them. The problem of sources discourse, like the problem of international legal theory, is to achieve a mediation—to carve out an independent and yet supplemented position within doctrine. But the problem within doctrinal discourse of this type is somewhat different.

Perhaps it is easiest to think of sources discourse as a translation of these theoretical concerns into doctrine—as the transposition of theoretical scepticism into doctrinal proliferation. In theoretical literature, the problem of realism and idealism is presented directly. International legal theory argues directly on behalf of the international legal order against the scepticism of either the political realist or the moralist. Whether positivist or naturalist, the theoretician must respond to the posited or hypothetical absence of an international legal order. As a result, the theoretician must posit and justify the authority of legal norms—indeed by arguing their consensual origin or justice.

In sources discourse, by contrast, the legal order is always already presumed and one is always arguing for some norms against others. Sources discourse seems to argue against the normative order—expressing its authority against the substantive regime on behalf of its origin—even as it establishes that regime by removing us from theoretical scepticism and opposition. As a result, the management of hard and soft rhetorics, while similar to the management of natural and positive justifications for an international legal order, seems to reverse their tone. Here, for example, consensual rhetoric seems to reassure the sovereign while critiquing substantive order even as it establishes the authority of the source. In theoretical literature, by contrast, positivism seems to respond to the realist with evidence of practice. The net result of these two discoursive enterprises is to sustain a sense of movement towards and into doctrine.

Discourse about sources searches abstractly to delimit the norms which bind sovereigns in a way which relies neither on the interests of sovereigns nor on some vision of the good which is independent of state interests. The search is for a decisive discourse—not for a persuasive justification—which can continually distinguish binding from nonbinding norms while remaining open to expressions of sovereign will. The argumentative moves made by those engaged in sources discourse reflects this central goal.

The result is a discourse of evasion which constantly combines that which it cannot differentiate and emphasizes that which it can express only by hyperbolic exclusion. Pursued in this fashion, sources doctrine moves us forward from theory towards other doctrines which it supplements, remaining both authoritatively independent and parasitic. This paradoxical position between theoretical discourse and the doctrines of substance and process is maintained by endlessly embracing and managing a set of ephemeral rhetorical differences. The turn to sources doctrine thus seems to provide an escape from fruitless theoretical argument, moving us towards legal order, precisely by opening up an endlessly proliferating field of legal argumentation.

[9]

SOVEREIGNTY IN ABEYANCE: Self-Determination and International Law

NATHANIEL BERMAN*

TABLE OF CONTENTS

*Mellon Lecturer in Law and Social Order at Amherst College. J.D. Harvard Law School, 1985. I would like to thank Gerald Frug and David Kennedy for their comments on earlier drafts of this article.

> All peoples have the right to self-determination; by virtue of that right they freely determine their political status and freely pursue their economic, social and cultural development.
>
> — General Assembly Resolution 1514 (1960)

I. Self-Determination as a Form of Argument

A. Introduction

"Self-determination" refers to the right claimed by a "people" to control its own destiny — despite the fact that such a people has not yet achieved the status of "statehood" under international law. Traditionally, only statehood could confer international legal personality and its attendant rights and duties upon a group. A group seeking self-determination is, by definition, one which feels that it has been excluded, albeit unjustifiably, from the community of legal individuals recognized by international law. Hence the paradox involved in the notion of a legal right to self-determination: how can international law recognize a right accruing to an entity which, by its own admission, lacks international legal existence?

As generally conceived by international law, the international community is composed of already-constituted and commonly recognized states.[1] To be sure, there may be no universally accepted definition of statehood.[2] Nonetheless, there is general agreement with the criteria for statehood given by the Convention on Rights and Duties of States: a) a permanent population; b) a defined territory; c) government; and d) capacity to enter into relations with other States.[3] In the traditional view, claims of legal right by non-state groups and their members, "being internationally unrecognised . . . must be clothed in the garb of state rights before they can be put forward internationally."[4]

---

[1] *See, e.g.*, U.N. Charter art. 4, para. 1: "Membership in the United Nations is open to all other peace-loving states which accept the obligations contained in the present charter and, in the judgment of the Organization, are able and willing to carry out these obligations."

[2] *See, e.g.*, *Western Sahara*, 1975 I.C.J. 12, 43-44.

[3] Convention on Rights and Duties of States, Dec. 26, 1933, art. 1, 49 Stat. 3097, T.S. No. 881, 165 L.N.T.S. 19.

[4] W.E. Hall, A Treatise on International Law 53 (A.P. Higgens ed. 8th ed. 1924). Hall condemns the "dangerous vagueness" of the principle of self-determination. *Id.* at 54 n.2.

The "traditional view," as I have sketched it above, has, of course, been criticized from various perspectives in recent decades. To cite a notable example, Kelsen has declared that the traditional theory that only states are the subjects of international law is no longer tenable. H. Kelsen, Principles of International Law 180 (1972). Instead, Kelsen analyzes the specific differences between the ways that states, individuals and others may be considered to be subjects of international law. *See*

Such a vision of international society conforms to the rationalist liberal vision of formally equal individuals united in states, each governed by domestic law; these formally equal states, in turn, constitute the legal community governed by international law. An applicant for membership in the United Nations "must *be* a state";[5] those who present their credentials to sit in such international fora claim to *represent states*; states, in turn, purport to represent a particular population and territory. Groups seeking self-determination assert that they have been excluded from this system.

Such claims pose a twofold challenge to the purportedly seamless system of representation. On the one hand, the claim may be garbed in the language of cultural particularism, asserting that a given state is *incapable* of representing a group of people because of their cultural difference. Such a particularist claim must appear as irrational to a formal conception in which homogeneous individuals are represented by states.

On the other hand, the claim may be articulated as simply a corrective to the failures of representation, asserting only that a given state does not, *as a matter of fact*, represent a particular group. Rather than objecting to the concept of formal representation, the group would assert that the state has failed to live up to its neutral representative function. In either case, such claims of invidious exclusion pose a profound challenge to the integrity of the international legal community.[6]

---

generally C.A. Norgaard, The Position of the Individual in International Law (1962) (summarizing opposing theoretical positions).

In this essay, however, I focus solely on the challenge to the traditional view posed by the idea of self-determination. The complex conceptual and historical relationship between the development of the idea of self-determination and other revisions in the traditional concept of international law lies beyond the confines of this analysis.

[5]Conditions of Admission of a State to Membership in the United Nations, 1948 I.C.J. 57, 62 (emphasis added).

[6]For a discussion of the relationship between the formal and particularistic elements in self-determination, sometimes associated, respectively, with democracy and nationalism, or with "subjective" and "objective" approaches, see *infra* text accompanying note 129. *See also* B. Neuberger, National Self-Determination in Postcolonial Africa (1986), ch. 2: "Democratic Determination or National Determinism?"

The inextricability of these two elements in modern self-determination claims renders problematic attempts at inclusion through reforms of a "due process" variety. Thus, France attempted to evade the demands of self-determination by incorporating its colonies on the basis of formal equality. *See* the Preamble to the 1946 French Constitution:

> France forms with the peoples of its overseas territories a union based upon equality of rights and duties, without distinction of race or religion. . . . [R]ejecting any system of colonization based upon arbitrary power,

The existence of a legal right of self-determination continues to be hotly disputed, from logical, jurisprudential and practical perspectives. Nevertheless, the contention that such a right has come into being in the period following World War II rests on strong grounds. Such a contention may be defended by reference to decisions of the International Court of Justice (I.C.J.), resolutions of the U.N. General Assembly, state practice and the writings of commentators. These same sources allow for a description of the content of such a right — although no such description could be free from controversy even if couched in highly flexible terms. A description of the subjects, methods and content of the right of self-determination might run as follows: a) self-determination is a right of peoples that do not govern themselves, particularly peoples dominated by geographically distant colonial powers;[7] b) the identity and desires of such

> she guarantees to all equal access to public office and the individual or collective exercise of rights and liberties.

This attempt was rejected by the U.N. General Assembly in its call for "self-determination and independence" for the Algerian people "on the basis of respect for the unity and territorial integrity of Algeria. . . ." G.A. Res. 1573, 15 U.N. GAOR Supp. (No. 16) at 3, U.N. Doc. A/4684 (1960). The states who requested the inclusion of Algeria on the agenda of the General Assembly had stated that "[t]he position in Algeria is the direct result of colonial conquest, and the people of Algeria cannot be said to have exercised their right to self-determination. . . ." 10 U.N. GAOR Annex 1 (Agenda Item 64) at 2, U.N. Doc. A/2924 and Add. 1 (1955).

[7]The United Nations Charter declared that the establishment of international relations on the "principle" of self-determination was one of its central purposes. U.N. CHARTER art. 1 para. 2. The General Assembly subsequently recognized self-determination as a "right" in countless resolutions, perhaps the most important of which were G.A. Res. 1514, 15 U.N. GAOR Supp. (No. 16) at 66, U.N. Doc. A/4684 (1960) and G.A. Res 2625, 25 U.N. GAOR Supp. (No. 28) at 121, U.N. Doc. A/8028 (1970). Both the *International Covenant on Economic Social, and Cultural Rights and the International Covenant on Civil and Political Rights and Optional Protocol to the International Covenant on Civil and Political Rights*, G.A. Res. 2200, 21 U.N. GAOR Supp. (No. 16) at 49, U.N. Doc. A/6316 (1966), recognize the right to self-determination in their first articles. The International Court of Justice (I.C.J.) has recognized the right to self-determination in, for example, *Namibia*, 1971 I.C.J. 16, 31 and in *Western Sahara*, 1975 I.C.J. 12, 31. *See generally* A. CRISTESCU, THE RIGHT TO SELF-DETERMINATION: HISTORICAL AND CURRENT DEVELOPMENT ON THE BASIS OF UNITED NATIONS INSTRUMENTS 17-24 (1981).

Although many of these sources state that the right applies to "all peoples," it has generally been interpreted as limited to those subjected to certain forms of domination, especially colonialism. I discuss the rationale for this limitation below. The legal source for such a limitation may be found in the recurrent linkage of the right to self-determination with a condemnation of colonialism. General Assembly Resolution 1514, generally recognized as the turning point in the inter-peoples may be ascertained through several means, including plebiscites, international commissions of inquiry and reference to the relevant historical and political facts, such as the actual struggles of a people to assert its identity;[8] and c) while self-determination may take various forms, including continued association with an existing state, a strong preference is placed on the bestowal of statehood on the people in question.[9]

In this essay, I attempt neither to prove the existence of a legal right to self-determination nor to advocate a particular position with regard to the many ambiguities in my preceding description of the meaning of such a right. Rather, I seek to understand the terms and the structure of con-

---

national acceptance of self-determination as a right, was entitled, "Declaration on the Granting of Independence to Colonial Peoples." G.A. Res. 1514, 15 U.N. GAOR Supp. (No. 16) at 66, U.N. Doc. A/4684 (1960). As I discuss below, this resolution condemned secession, implicitly limiting self-determination to decolonization. In the *Western Sahara* case, the I.C.J. referred to the "*principle* of self-determination as a right of peoples, and its *application* for the purpose of bringing all colonial situations to a speedy end. . . ." 1975 I.C.J. 12, 31 (emphasis added).

[8]The method used to determine the application of self-determination to a particular case depends, in part, on the underlying conception of self-determination. *See infra* text accompanying note 21. For a review of the various methods used in the post-World War II period, see A. RIGO SUREDA, THE EVOLUTION OF THE RIGHT OF SELF-DETERMINATION 294-324 (1973). The I.C.J. has recognized the validity of a flexible approach in determining the "freely expressed wishes of the territory's peoples," holding that an actual consultation with the population may not always be necessary. *Western Sahara*, 1975 I.C.J. 12, 33.

[9]General Assembly Resolution 1541 provided for three legitimate methods of decolonization consistent with the principle of self-determination: independence, free association or integration with an existing state. G.A. Res. 1541, 15 U.N. GAOR Supp. (No. 16) at 29, U.N. Doc. A/4684 (1960). *See also Western Sahara*, 1975 I.C.J. 12, 32; G.A. Res. 2625, 25 U.N. GAOR Supp. (No. 28) at 121, U.N. Doc. A/8028 (1970). Most sources, however, manifest a strong presumption for independence - for example, in the constant coupling of the terms "self-determination and independence" as though they were synonymous. General Assembly Resolution 1514 specifically condemns any "pretext" for the delaying of independence for colonial peoples. G.A. Res. 1514, 15 U.N. GAOR Supp. (No. 16) at 66, U.N. Doc. A/4684 (1960). The I.C.J. has stated that the "ultimate objective of the sacred trust [of League of Nations Mandates] was the self-determination and independence of the peoples concerned." *Namibia*, 1971 I.C.J. at 31. As a matter of international practice, many commentators would agree with the substance of Roger Fisher's view that the U.N. Special Committee of Twenty-Four on decolonization "appeared to act as an international lobby for absolute independence regardless of the consequences." Fisher, *The Participation of Microstates in International Affairs* 1968 PROC. AM. SOC'Y INT'L L. 164, 168. *See also* Rapoport, *The Participation of Ministates in International Affairs, Id.* at 155, 157 (U.N. views independence as the "preeminent," though not exclusive, form of decolonization). *But see* Esfandiary, *Comments, Id.* at 170. *See also infra* notes 104–117 and accompanying text.

temporary discussions of the issue. Specifically, I will examine the two central elements of the paradox of self-determination: 1) the nature of the competence of law to bypass the state system in order to reach questions of self-determination; and 2) the nature of the entities, the "selves," which may be entitled to this extraordinary legal right to become a full-fledged right-holder.

In analyzing these two major themes, I will seek to understand: first, the broad conceptual and historical paradoxes which form the background of contemporary discussions of these issues; second, the ways in which the genesis of the principle has facilitated the development of certain characteristic forms of argument about self-determination; and third, the manner in which those arguments may be marshaled to justify a particular form of self-determination. In short, I attempt to show how, far from remaining an abstraction to be denounced or canonized, the idea of self-determination has evolved into a richly textured form of argument, providing a fruitful framework for discussion of some of our most basic jurisprudential dilemmas.

B. Between Law and Sovereignty

Self-determination appears, at first, to be a contemporary example of ideas that challenge legal thought by posing the problem of law's relationship to sources of normative authority lying beyond the normal rules of a functioning legal system. Such challenges may confront positive law with its presumed source in natural law or may urge legal discourse to look to the realms of morality or politics when fundamental issues arise. The difficult issues raised by self-determination, moreover, call to mind the impasses into which these traditional debates have led. It is my thesis, however, that, in its contemporary form, the discourse of self-determination provides a novel framework in which these quandaries may be discussed and a useful perspective on those impasses. In self-determination, legal discourse has developed a doctrine with an extraordinary status: a legal doctrine which, within certain exceptional situations or domains, discusses the limitations of the conceptual basis of law and outlines the conditions for the temporary suspension of the ordinary legal framework.

The extraordinary quality of self-determination lies in its position between the concepts of international law and state sovereignty. In its normal functioning, international law may be seen as complementing state sovereignty: law restrains sovereigns from abusing their prerogatives and thereby protects an international society based on the state system. Critical reflection, however, reveals the conceptual instability latent in this functional balance. Very different conceptions of international society result depending on whether, and to what extent, law or sovereignty is granted ultimate primacy. We are familiar with the vicissitudes of such reflections from the historical debates between various versions of positivism and naturalism.[10]

These debates may be recalled quickly, if somewhat schematically. Thus, on the one hand, one may privilege sovereignty, relegating law to the role of servant of state prerogatives. In such a conception, law's limits would be determined by reference to sovereign consent; depending on the historical form of such a conception, law would be excluded from such domains as would interfere with the basic elements of sovereign will. From this perspective, international law would derive the justification for its powers from its subordinate position in relation to sovereigns and its legitimacy would derive from its ability to serve their goals.

Alternatively, international law may be viewed as resting on a source of legitimacy independent from sovereign will. Some holding this view have even claimed that a system based in sovereign consent is logically incompatible with a stable legal system. International law would be required to look elsewhere for its normative basis — a transcendental source of a religious, ethical or philosophical nature.

In recent decades various schools of thought have arisen seeking a way out of the law/sovereignty conundrum. Functionalism, integration theory, transnational law, regime theory and global policy studies have all sought a framework which would bypass the traditional dichotomy.[11] It is my thesis that, from within international legal doctrine itself, a discourse has developed which provides a nuanced manner of thinking about the dichotomy in surprising ways. This discourse — that of self-determination — does not pretend to do away with the traditional dichotomy, but rather, offers a new and fruitful manner of setting its polar terms in relationship to each other.

Groups claiming a right of self-determination ask international law to assert that the adjudication of legal rights to population and territory cannot always be based on sovereignty. On the contrary, they seek legal confirmation of the idea that sovereignty over people and territory must itself be derived from another source, that of the "people" it claims to

---

[10]The vast literature on the debate between positivism and naturalism need not be reviewed here. For a well-documented, if partisan, summary of the conceptual debate, see T.C. CHEN, THE INTERNATIONAL LAW OF RECOGNITION 17-29 (1951).

[11]The work of Myres McDougal and his associates, of course, represents the most sustained legal effort to transcend an abstract opposition between law and sovereign power by expanding the frame of analysis to include a multiplicity of decision-makers, institutional commitments and procedures. For a concise statement of this position, see McDougal, *Law and Power*, 46 AM. J. INT'L L. 102 (1952). *See generally* M.S. MCDOUGAL AND F.P. FELICIANO, LAW AND MINIMUM WORLD PUBLIC ORDER (1961). For a description of alternatives to "political realism" in the study of international relations, see M.S. SORROS, BEYOND SOVEREIGNTY: THE CHALLENGE OF GLOBAL POLICY 10-19 (1986).

represent. This claim presents a dual jurisprudential challenge corresponding to the two articulations of self-determination I outlined above. On the one hand, claims of self-determination confront a positivistic acceptance of sovereignty's claims of representation with a transcendental criterion of legitimacy — the "people" — which would play the role traditionally occupied by ethics or reason in naturalistic jurisprudence. On the other hand, they challenge the rationalistic conception of representation with a claim for power based on group identity. The former challenge confronts mere sovereign power with its failure to meet the criteria of impartial reason; the latter challenges neutral legal reason with a claim for group power.

In the modern discourse of self-determination, these seemingly incompatible challenges function together as a unified form of argument. Rather than taking one side in the age-old debate between positivism and naturalism, sovereignty and law, the discourse of self-determination provides an arena in which they may contend. As we shall see, self-determination is viewed in the literature as an "exceptional" doctrine and it is this quality which enables it to serve this function.

Issues of self-determination arise in unusual temporal or spatial gaps in the legal system. These gaps arise when, as a result of a set of circumstances — be they political, historical, ideological — sovereignty has been called into question and, with it, the functioning of normal law. The "exceptional" quality of self-determination signifies that the ensuing confrontation between normative bases of law constitutes a *limited suspension* of the usual legal norms. The situation is ultimately directed back towards the quotidian complementarity of law and sovereignty. In discussions of self-determination, consequently, arguments that privilege either legal or sovereign authority are constantly met by those that privilege the other.

The discourse of self-determination flourishes in the conceptual and real hiatuses in international society. Rather than being positioned on one side or another in the law/sovereignty dilemma, it weaves a textured discourse between them. In this way, its very marginality to normal international law enables it to occupy a privileged conceptual role in international law, illuminating law's basic conceptual dilemmas.

This privileged conceptual role may not be minimized through reduction to specific historical circumstances or to a particular political stance. One might be tempted today to view the significance of self-determination as lying in a specific historical experience — the massive wave of decolonization that swept the globe after World War II.[12] This historical period, the argument might go, was shaped by a particular conjuncture of circum-

[12]Thus, in 1973, with the elimination of most forms of classic colonialism, S.P. Sinha posed the question: *Is Self-Determination Passé?*, 12 COLUM. J. TRANSNAT'L L. 260 (1973).

stances in which the idea of self-determination played an important role. Now that this period is past, law should resume its ordinary framework without reflecting on the conceptual implications of self-determination. Self-determination, from this perspective, would seem like a noble idea that was put into practice but is now essentially irrelevant.

Nevertheless, many of the key conflicts in the world continue to be framed in terms of claims of self-determination. From the Middle East to New Caledonia, such claims, and the passions they evoke, are at the center of the urgent concerns of more than one great power. Many contemporary disputes involving assertions of self-determination pose exceptionally "hard cases": unusual competing claims of two arguably non-European peoples (Palestine), areas where the indigenous people constitutes an electoral minority (New Caledonia), etc. Yet is it not true that close examination reveals that most particular cases, in the area of self-determination as in other legal fields, are "hard cases" in their own unique way? The stubborn persistence of certain struggles for self-determination and the recurrent cropping-up of new claims and new struggles testify to the seeming inevitability of confronting the conceptual and practical riddles posed by the idea. The story of self-determination appears destined to be played out anew in ever-changing contexts.

Nor can our ambivalent relationship to the idea be resolved through political contextualization. Self-determination has been the rallying cry of various sides of the political spectrum during the course of its history. The idea that would come to be called the right of self-determination during World War I may be traced to the French Revolution and the European response to the Napoleonic Wars.[13] Over the course of two centuries, however, it has been adopted by the forces of the political left and right, by liberals and reactionaries, by Bolsheviks and Nazis, by centrists and Third World revolutionaries.[14] A history of the vicissitudes of the idea of self-determination could, in fact, provide a useful perspective from which to write a general history of Europe in the nineteenth century and of the world in the twentieth.

The conceptual challenge posed by self-determination, then, transcends any particular political or historical context. Rather, whatever its occasion, the idea of self-determination poses a general challenge to international law's normative foundation, questioning the unreflective ac-

---

[13]*See* A. COBBAN, NATIONAL SELF-DETERMINATION 4-7 (1945).

[14]*See* W. OFUATEY-KODJOE, THE PRINCIPLE OF SELF-DETERMINATION IN INTERNATIONAL LAW 39-66 (1977); Sinha, *supra* note 12; R. Emerson, *Self-Determination Revisited in the Era of Decolonization*, 9 HARVARD UNIVERSITY CENTER FOR INTERNATIONAL AFFAIRS: OCCASSIONAL PAPERS (1964); A. COBBAN, *supra* note 13, at 4-15, 35-43; E. HULA, NATIONAL SELF-DETERMINATION RECONSIDERED (1945); E.H. CARR, THE FUTURE OF NATIONS: INDEPENDENCE OR INTERDEPENDENCE? (1971).

ceptance of the complementarity of law and sovereignty. Self-determination confronts international law with the latent conflict between these principles — and between the jurisprudential conceptions that would accord primacy to one or the other. If modern international law may be viewed as oscillating between these competing conceptions of the relationship between legal and political authority, the doctrine of self-determination may be understood as a hinge upon which this oscillation turns. It belongs neither to one conception nor the other; rather it discusses the conditions and limits of the oscillation between the two. The debates over whether self-determination may be considered as a legal doctrine or as a mere moral principle stem from this intermediate position of this idea between competing conceptions of the foundation of legal legitimacy. Self-determination is, indeed, marginal to both systems; its discourse flourishes in their hostile encounter and its strategy consists of playing each off against the other.

II. International Legal Competence Over Claims of Self-Determination

A. *Introduction*

Given the troublesome nature of the idea of self-determination, it is not surprising that its role in contemporary international law has received radically different appraisals from those deeply involved in thinking about the international legal system. An authority such as Sir Gerald Fitzmaurice, a former member of the International Court of Justice, finds the concept of self-determination incompatible with international law. To be sure, he acknowledges some "sympathy" with the "principle . . . politically considered."[15] "[J]uridically," however, Fitzmaurice finds that "the notion of a 'legal right' of self-determination is nonsense."[16]

On the other hand, some view self-determination as the cornerstone of the international legal system, rather than as a moral or political curiosity. A study prepared by a U.N. Special Rapporteur declared that the principle of self-determination underlies the other fundamental principles of international law, including that of the equality of states.[17] From this perspective, self-determination is "the most important of the principles of international law concerning friendly relations and cooperation among states."[18] Moreover, this principle "entails international legal rights and

---

[15]Fitzmaurice, *The Future of Public International Law and the International Legal System in the Circumstances of Today* in Institut de Droit International, Evolution et Perspectives du Droit International 196, 233 (1973).

[16]*Id.* at 233.

[17]A. Cristescu, *supra* note 7, at 25.

[18]*Id.* at 117, 119.

obligations";[19] self-determination, for this U.N. study, is a "universally recognized right under contemporary international law"; a right of a "general and permanent" character.[20]

Nor does the vigorousness of this debate find resolution in the writings of those who seek to ground such conceptual disputes in the realities of modern international practice. Some commentators feel that the idea of self-determination, though somewhat empty as an abstract idea, has slowly acquired content through years of adaptation to particular situations by states and international organizations.[21] In contrast to repeated statements by the U.N., however, another commentator who examined state practice concluded: "All peoples do *not* have the right to self-determination: they never have had it, and they never will have it."[22]

Such widely varying views suggest that general assertions about self-determination generate more controversy than insight on the matter. Rather than simply rejecting such general statements, however, I will attempt to discover the specific ways in which the articulation of such views can lead us into a more textured understanding of self-determination. I will do so by examining two extreme examples of such views, a rigorously legal-formalist rejection of self-determination and a valorization of it as the legal arm of a political struggle.

1. A Formalist Rejection

As though insisting stylistically as well as conceptually on the marginality of the concept, Sir Gerald Fitzmaurice relegates the bulk of his arguments against self-determination to a footnote in a long essay devoted to the contemporary state of international law.[23] Nevertheless, his reflections afford much insight into the paradoxical nature of the idea of a legal right of self-determination. Before proceeding to a detailed analysis, I would like to quote the core of Fitzmaurice's argument:

> The initial difficulty is that it is scarcely possible to refer to an entity as an entity unless it already is one, so that it makes little juridical sense to speak of a claim to *become* one, for in whom or what would the claim reside? By definition, "entities" seeking self-determination are not yet determined internationally, or the case

[19] *Id.* at 18.

[20] *Id.* at 22.

[21] *See, e.g.*, W. OFUATEY-KODJOE, *supra* note 14, at 11, 19. Ofuatey-Kodjoe rejects the views of writers who present "definitions of self-determination derived from political theories or ideological principles." He advocates, instead, focusing attention on the "wealth of diplomatic practice" that has "provided a consensual nexus among states as to the scope of the principle."

[22] R. EMERSON, *supra* note 14, at 64.

[23] Fitzmaurice, *supra* note 15, at 233 n. 85.

> would not arise. Can they therefore possess "rights" under international law, and in what way, juridically, could the corresponding obligations be postulated? Alternatively, if they do possess such rights, they are entities which are already determined internationally, and the case has passed beyond, and is no longer on, the self-determination plane. The logical impasse involved can really only be avoided by assuming the existence of something to which international law is still a stranger, namely rights residing not in particular entities, but in the international community at large. . . .[24]

Fitzmaurice's discussion of self-determination comes in a section of his essay devoted to outlining rigorously the formal notion of "equality before the law." His terse analysis of the "logical impasse involved" is impressive and seemingly irrefutable on its own terms. Fitzmaurice assumes an international system composed of already-constituted states. Such a system must be viewed as always already functioning. All references to the origin of the system can only be viewed as irrelevant, indeed logically impossible: "[i]t is scarcely possible to refer to an entity unless it already is one, so that it makes little juridical sense to speak of a claim to *become* one, for in whom or what would the claim reside?"[25]

All entities that have a *right* to membership in such a system *are already* members. Membership in the international community is grounded, at one and the same time, in the sheer fact of an entity's existence as a state *and* in the legal sanction given by international legal recognition. By contrast, this same logic tells us that " 'entities' seeking self-determination are not yet determined internationally." Thus, the very condition of not being "determined internationally" which gives rise to claims for self-determination puts such claims outside the pale of international law. Conversely, if those putting forth such claims were able to obtain international jurisdiction, their claims to self-determination would no longer be pertinent; they would be "entities which are already determined internationally and the case [would have] passed beyond, and [would] no longer [be] on, the self-determination plane." Nor, as we shall see, would the admirable logic governing such a view of the international legal system be incapable of accommodating such established doctrines as those governing recognition and state succession.[26]

---

[24] *Id.*

[25] *Id.*

[26] *See, e.g., id.* at 224-26 and my discussion, *infra* notes 81-103 and accompanying text. The complementarity between fact and law found in the passage on self-determination may be viewed as consistent with Fitzmaurice's general desire for a synthesis between positivism and naturalism. He views international law as based on both "a positive quality and a root in the nature of man," a view he finds embodied in the formula, "general principles of law recognized by civilized nations." *Id.* at 310-11.

In Fitzmaurice's conception of the membership of the international community, then, factual and legal existence cannot be separated. There is no legal instance that has the power to confer a legal right to self-determination — a right which is tantamount to a legal right of an extralegal entity to acquire legal status. A legal instance asserting such a power would, by definition, be overreaching the limits of legal discourse. An instance asserting such a power would, in effect, be claiming that it is the repository of that "something to which international law is still a stranger, namely rights residing not in particular entities but in the international community at large." Nor could an extra-legal entity such as a people, prior to the conferral of legal status, lay claim to any right to such status: the "logical impasse involved" is a Catch-22 for would-be self-determiners.

In this way, both international law, as an abstract conceptual power, and concrete peoples, as merely factually existing entities, lie beyond each other's reach prior to the acquisition of the legal and factual indicia of statehood by the people. The accession to such indicia must lie outside the sphere of legal rights. Only states, grounded both in fact and law, can lay claim to "rights" under international law.

For Fitzmaurice, the story of how such states came into being must be bracketed when one comes to analyze a functioning legal system. By contrast, a story about the genesis of states would inevitably focus on the ways in which factual realities and claims of moral or legal right interacted in the turmoil of the state's political and cultural birth. We need look no farther than the history of the American Revolution to verify this insight.

Fitzmaurice, however, in his demonstration of the logical impossibility of the idea of self-determination from the standpoint of juridical logic makes implicit reference to the seeming irrepressibility of the idea in legal discourse. I refer to his distinctive use of the phrase "determined internationally," as in his discussion of entities that are or are not "already determined internationally." In Fitzmaurice's view, only states are "determined internationally"; peoples, the potential "subjects" of self-determination, are not. The puzzle inherent in the phrase, "determined internationally," is that the past participle, "determined," necessarily refers back to a *process* of determination: a moment when an entity, that had not yet been "determined internationally," had had that "determination" conferred upon it by a "determiner." Yet, both the existence and validity of such a process is explicitly excluded from legal discourse by Fitzmaurice's argument: Fitzmaurice excludes the possibility that international law allows of an instance, a "something," which could dispense rights that do not already adhere to a legally recognized entity. For legal discourse, the process of determination, the attainment of the indicia of statehood, has always already occurred; if it has not, the entity in question does not exist in the eyes of the law.

Nevertheless, Fitzmaurice's use of the past participle implies the inescapability of talking about that past, whether real or mythic. It is as though a description of the "logical impasse involved" in a jurisprudential contradiction inevitably leads to a discussion of that which lies outside the system of concepts creating that "impasse": as though a clear articulation of such logical impasses inevitably leads to opening the system of concepts to an alternative history or logic. The articulation of Fitzmaurice's seemingly unassailable logical opposition to the idea of self-determination points to the ever-present possibility of challenging a functioning legal system to justify its legitimacy by telling the story of its founding moments. In responding to such a challenge, law's limits expand beyond the bounds of its formal logic.

2. A Substantive Endorsement

I now turn to a perspective which lies, at least from a jurisprudential point of view, at the opposite end of the spectrum from that of Fitzmaurice. Such a perspective would reject the idea that the validity and limits of the concept of self-determination could be discovered through formal criteria of legal logic. On the contrary, this second approach would seek to understand self-determination by rooting it in a particular political and historical context. The right of self-determination, in this view, would be neither embodied in an abstract, universal legal norm nor left to the discretion of the international community. Rather, the right accrues to those groups who have been subject to domination, indeed, to a particular historical form of domination, that of colonialism.

Such a conception is a variant of what has been called the "equality theory" of self-determination.[27] One may give the name of "equality theories" to those theories which view the right of self-determination as the right of dominated peoples to achieve equality in relation to those who dominate them.[28] Such theories would look at the relationship of force

[27] *See* W. OFUATEY-KODJOE, *supra* note 14, at 29.

[28] *See id.* at 156. *Cf.* Bassiouni, *"Self-Determination" and the Palestinians*, 1971 PROC. AM. SOC'Y INT'L L. 31, 33. " 'Self-determination' becomes a right whenever: a given collectivity is prevented or seriously impeded from freely adhering to or exercising its values, beliefs and practices on the indigenous territory which they inhabit (or from which have been removed) by another collectivity by coercive means." The Kenyan delegate to the 1963 OAU Summit offered another formulation of this theory, in the context of the debate over secession: "The principle of self-determination has relevance where FOREIGN DOMINATION is the issue. It has no relevance where the issue is territorial disintegration by dissident citizens." L.T. FARLEY, PLEBISCITES AND SOVEREIGNTY: THE CRISIS OF POLITICAL ILLEGITIMACY 17 (1986).

The equality theory thus responds to the argument, advanced by the critics of

existing between two entities, be they "peoples" or "states," to determine which of the entities may claim a right of self-determination. Thus, the right is never a universal legal abstraction but, rather, may only be discovered on the basis of a substantive analysis of a particular situation.

This theory was originally identified with the Bolsheviks' claim of self-determination for the subject peoples of Eastern Europe and the overseas colonies of Western European countries.[29] In the post-World War II era, the equality theory was applied to what we now know as the Third World. Despite the equality theory's origins, it now governs the common understanding of self-determination. The massive postwar decolonization is usually understood in terms of an equality theory of self-determination as applied to the relationship between Europe, on the one hand, and Africa and Asia, on the other.

The ways in which such an approach to self-determination differ from a formalist approach, such as that of Fitzmaurice, are evident. It is important, however, to note the features which the two approaches have in common. Like the formalists, the equality theorists would deny to an international legal instance a discretionary role in the granting of full status to entities seeking self-determination. To be sure, each theory would reject such a role for its own reasons.

The equality theory would reject such a role because of the kinds of *limits* an international instance might set on the right of self-determination. For example, Article 22 of the Covenant of the League of Nations provided for mandates, rather than for self-determination, for those territories whose populations were not prepared for the "strenuous conditions of the modern world."[30] The attitude underlying that Article would be thoroughly repudiated by the equality theory. Such a repudiation was expressed in the U.N. General Assembly Resolution which rejected all alleged grounds to avoid the granting of independence: "Inadequacy of political, economic, social or educational preparedness should never serve as a pretext for delaying independence."[31]

Thus, like Fitzmaurice, the equality theory cannot accept the international community as the repository of rights which it might dispense

---

self-determination, that a logical extension of this right would "seem to give to each individual human being a right to be an independent country" if he so desires. Eagleton, *The Excesses of Self-Determination*, 31 FOREIGN AFF. 592, 596 (1953). At the same time, it rejects the idea that an ethnic group may secede even if it has not been the victim of oppression. *See* W. OFUATEY-KODJOE, *supra* note 14, at 162-63 (discussing lack of international support for the independence of Katanga and Biafra).

[29] *See* W. OFUATEY-KODJOE, *supra* note 14, at 30.

[30] LEAGUE OF NATIONS COVENANT art. 22.

[31] G.A. Res. 1514, para. 3, 15 U.N. GAOR Supp. (No. 16) at 66, U.N. Doc. A/4684 (1960).

without being strictly governed by the presence of an actual or potential sovereign. No balancing tests, no weighing of conditions, no evaluations on a case-by-case basis — for the equality theory, the right of self-determination is grounded in the political context, not in cautious adjudicatory decisions.[32] Once again, the right would adhere in entities, not in the international community. To be sure, *contra* Fitzmaurice, such entities would be precisely those which had not yet been fully "determined internationally." "Peoples" would be able to claim that they were the full and sufficient measure of legitimate authority over populations and territory.

Even the proponents of various forms of the equality theory, however, seek to gain acceptance for self-determination as a *legal* concept, a concept with reasonable limits, rather than merely a prescription for unlimited and irresponsible claims.[33] Thus, W. Ofuatey-Kodjoe, a Third World writer sympathetic to a variant of the equality theory,[34] condemns a view of self-determination which would identify it with a "right" of revolution. Such a "right," he explains, would be "illogical."[35] In his view, recognizing an unlimited "right to revolt" would "represent a negation" of a legal right of self-determination.[36]

---

[32] I have described an ideal-type of the "equality theory," rather than the full views of a particular theorist. Nothing would prevent a particular variant of this theory from according a discretionary element as a supplement to the general right of subjugated peoples. For example, Bassiouni, whose general definition of self-determination reflects an equality theory, incorporates such a discretionary auxiliary as an equitable limitation on the broad legal right. Bassiouni states that "as a remedy, the equitable application" of the right "is limited by the rights of others and the potential injuries it may inflict as weighed against the potential benefits it may generate." Bassiouni, *supra* note 28, at 33.

[33] The effort to limit self-determination to a legally manageable form is, in part, a response to those who would view its uncontrolled expansion as a recipe for anarchy. The empirical question about the effects of a broad interpretation of the principle, however, is still subject to debate. *Compare* e.g., R. Higgins, The Development of International Law Through the Organs of the United Nations 104 (1963) *with* Bowett, *Self-Determination and Political Rights in the Developing Countries*, 1966 Proc. Am. Soc'y Int'l L. 129, 130.

It has also been argued, from other quarters, that the unlimited expansion of the concept would be a method of justifying colonialism. This argument was made during the debates on the "Belgian Thesis" during the early 1950's. *See, e.g.*, 9 U.N. GAOR C. 4 (419th mtg.), U.N. Doc. A/C.4/SR.419 (1954); 7 U.N. GAOR C.4 (275th mtg.) U.N. Doc. A/C/Sr. 275 (1952); 7 U.N. GAOR C.4 (255th mtg.), U.N. Doc. A/C.4/SR.255 (1952). *See also infra* note 117.

[34] "The beneficiary of the right of self-determination is a self-conscious politically coherent community that is under the political subjugation of another community." W. Ofuatey-Kodjoe, *supra* note 14, at 156.

[35] *Id.* at 53.

[36] *Id.*

Rather, Ofuatey-Kodjoe insists that the existence and content of a legal right of self-determination must be gleaned from a careful study of international practice. This inquiry, he finds, shows the importance of "subjugation" as an element of the definition of groups entitled to the right. In the contemporary period, this subjugation has come to be identified largely with colonization.

Ofuatey-Kodjoe recognizes that such a limitation cannot be defended on "logical" grounds once the right of self-determination has been conceptualized and universalized as a legal norm. He contends, however, that such logic is simply "irrelevant" until groups other than colonized peoples have obtained "access to the international political arena" in order to assert their claims.[37]

With this formulation, Ofuatey-Kodjoe's attention to substantive practice rejoins Fitzmaurice's privileging of formal logic. Both assert that the only groups who may assert the right are those which have somehow already gained a status within the international community. For Ofuatey-Kodjoe, as for Fitzmaurice, that status would be indistinguishably one of fact and of right: those who may *legally* assert rights are those who are *actually* present on the international stage pressing their claims. The process of reaching that stage lies beyond law, in the realm of politics or morality.

Nonetheless, Ofuatey-Kodjoe's conception, like that of Fitzmaurice, contains a tantalizingly ambiguous formulation. In the case of Ofuatey-Kodjoe, the ambiguity lies in the idea of "access" to the international arena. For Ofuatey-Kodjoe that arena is the international political arena, rather than that of the international legal system in the formal sense. Nonetheless, "access," like "determination" implies a *process*, a founding moment, of gaining entry into the international community. Such a process, again, is not one in which fact and law are already united, but one in which claims achieve recognition through the interaction of empirical realities and the moral or legal evaluation and organization of those realities.

The idea of obtaining "access" to the international forum resembles nothing so much as familiar doctrines concerning court jurisdiction: the ways in which parties seek jurisdiction and the factors that enter into judicial assertions of jurisdiction. As has often been observed, courts who rule on their own jurisdiction are involved in a paradoxical exercise. For, whatever their decision, the mere arrogation of the right to decide the jurisdictional question already involves a jurisdictional assertion of some kind: a claim of the right to decide. Law is always present and always exerts its influence in some way — even when it only does so by ruling that the matter at hand "is not properly before the court."

---

[37] *Id.* at 128.

Self-determination involves law in a similar paradox. The idea of a right to attain the status of a right-holder lies at the very limit of legal discourse. Any attempt to exclude such a matter from law's competence must necessarily discuss that which it excludes. The attempt to avoid such discussion of the process whereby a group reaches law's threshold tends to culminate in an ambiguous formulation straddling the boundary between that which lies within the competence of law and that which lies beyond.

The best legal texts that grant law competence over self-determination do not evade the paradox of law discussing its own limits. Rather, they place it at the center of their portrayal of the exceptional character of self-determination as a legal doctrine. These writings narrate those moments in which "access" is gained and "determination" is achieved. Such moments occur in extraordinary times when sovereignty is disrupted and normally marginal legal forms and doctrines move to the center of international law. Such moments of "access" and "determination" belong neither wholly to the world of impartial law nor to that of brute fact: rather, they belong to the paradoxical province of self-determination.

B. An Exceptional Competence

The quandaries left unresolved by the two commentators discussed above become central for those texts that have focused on the critical procedural issue inherent in the idea of self-determination: the question of the source and nature of international competence over self-determination. In the preceding discussion, I highlighted the difficulty of articulating a manageable, legal right of self-determination. In the formalist view, self-determination appeared logically empty and therefore absurd; in the substantive view, the idea threatened to become a mere plaything of politics and therefore dangerously uncontrollable. Those who have focused on the question of international competence seek a way out of these dilemmas.

In his comprehensive study of the subject, A. Rigo-Sureda cites a common objection about the emptiness of the idea of self-determination, *viz.*, that self-determination is "in fact ridiculous because the people cannot decide until somebody decides who are the people."[38] In response, Rigo-Sureda explains that the openness of the concept shows its inextricable link with the issue of international competence, specifically, with an institutional framework competent to deal with such questions. Rigo-Sureda asserts that "when Pres. Wilson launched his programme of self-

[38] A. RIGO SUREDA, *supra* note 8, at 28 (citing I.W. JENNINGS, THE APPROACH TO SELF-GOVERNMENT 55-56 (1956)).

determination he had in mind an organisation capable of deciding when and to whom self-determination would apply."[39]

Placing the question of international competence at the head of a consideration of self-determination promises to illuminate the obscurities of a purely formalist or substantive approach. From this new perspective, the establishment of a competent international legal instance is at the core of any working doctrine of self-determination. The process of "determination," of the means by which groups gain "access" to the international arena, becomes an essential consideration.

Yet, the shift in emphasis to such a legal instance and its capacity as a decision maker threatens to carry with it the dilemmas that resulted when the focus was on the "people" and its capacity as a right-holder. What are the limits of international legal discretion over claims of self-determination? How much independence is to be accorded to international law's ability to inquire into the legitimacy of sovereign control of people and territory? What sanctity and stability remains for the state system as the core of international law once an international legal instance acquires the ability to extend legal rights to entities without full legal existence?

1. The Limits of Discretion

An inquiry into the source of international competence over self-determination may be usefully prefaced by a brief discussion of the uses to which this competence may be put: specifically, whether a finding that a people has a legitimate claim to self-determination necessarily entails a right to statehood. Such a discussion of what one might call the "remedies" portion of the doctrine of self-determination[40] appears to lie at the opposite end of the spectrum from a discussion of the source of legal competence; nonetheless, it is important to know what sort of power such a legal source must be able to justify.

Many of the founding documents of the right of self-determination declare that statehood does not constitute the only manner of realizing the right. For example, the U.N. General Assembly has declared that "free association or integration with an independent state or the emergence into any other political status freely determined by a people" can also constitute "modes of implementing" the right.[41] Nonetheless, U.N. practice and the language of other documents indicate a strong presumption that independence is the preferred result once a legitimate claim has been established.[42]

---

[39] *Id.* at 28. *See also id.* at 101.

[40] *See* Bassiouni, *supra* note 28, at 33.

[41] G.A. Res. 2625, 25 U.N. GAOR Supp. (No. 28) Annex 1 at 124, U.N. Doc. A/8028 (1970).

[42] *See supra* note 9.

Some commentators, arguing vigorously against such a presumption, have urged a more flexible interpretation. Such arguments have arisen in the context of "mini" or "micro" states, as well as in cases where states other than the original colonial power have made claims over the territory in question.[43] Roger Fisher, for example, has contended that statehood should be viewed as only one of a "wide array of fluid arrangements to meet the varying needs of small peoples and territories."[44] Those who argue for such a range of options do not do so, as did the League Covenant, on the paternalistic grounds of the lack of preparedness of the indigenous populations. Rather, they argue on the grounds of practical considerations, such as the political difficulties that "micro-states" would face and the devalorization of international bodies some of whose members would represent such states.[45]

Thus, one commentator contends that the mere "desire, unity and territorial basis" of a group are insufficient grounds to justify the granting of statehood. Rather, various "other matters" must be considered. For example:

> Independence for an ambitious group may be dangerous for the community of nations. The new state may be weak or quarrelsome, and bring upon itself the attack of a covetous or injured or aggressive neighbor. . . The group seeking independence may be located at a strategic point which the community cannot afford to have weakly held; it may control a strategic waterway of wide importance; it may have within its area natural resources which it is incapable of developing but which the community needs. Does the mere fact that resources vital to the whole community happen to be located within an area to which a group wants exclusive title require the community to surrender control over it?[46]

Such a perspective clearly places us within an entirely different framework than that of Fitzmaurice or Ofuatey-Kudjoe. In this new framework, the international community not only possesses the authority to rule on claims to self-determination but may consider its own interests, including its own economic and political interests, in doing so.

---

[43] *Id.*

[44] Emerson, *Self-Determination*, 65 Am. J. Int'l L. 459, 472 (1971) (citing Fisher, *The Participation of Microstates in International Affairs*, 1968 Proc. Am. Soc'y Int'l L. 166).

[45] The fear that an overbroad practice of self-determination would devalorize the very concept of the state, as well as the international community formed by states, dates back to the earliest legal discussions of self-determination. *See, e.g., Report of the International Committee of Jurists on the Aaland Islands Question*, League of Nations O. J. Spec. Supp. 3, at 5 (1920).

[46] Eagleton, *supra* note 28, at 601.

This perspective, however, entails certain risky conceptual implications. The desire to grant the international community such substantive power over decisions about self-determination arises, in most cases, from a desire to protect the state system. Both the political and the conceptual prestige of statehood is viewed as in danger of erosion by an indiscriminate granting of independence. Yet once the international instance is granted the considerable authority to evaluate considerations both of law and interest in evaluating claims to independence, the limits of that authority become problematic. For example, there is no logical reason for the limitation of such geopolitical considerations to the cases of "ministates" rather than to classic cases of decolonization. Nor can such an approach explain the general limitation of self-determination to the Third World — one can surely imagine definitions of global interest which would look favorably on claims to self-determination by minorities inhabiting large industrialized countries.

One may understand this issue of limits as the familiar problem of maintaining a defined sphere of law in the face of a Realist-style insertion of policy considerations. Yet in the international context, this problem has a distinctive quality because of the necessity of understanding law in relation to sovereignty. Although perhaps motivated by a desire to protect the integrity of state sovereignty through a regulatory legal regime, the "fluid arrangements" school cannot logically limit the implications for sovereignty of according such broad legal discretion in matters of self-determination. A consistent, if extreme, extension of the proliferation of "fluid arrangements" governed by an international regulatory regime would be a conception of the authority of international law over people and territory as a *substitute* for sovereignty.

The "fluid arrangements" school shows the stakes involved in the challenge posed to international law by the idea of self-determination: the questioning of source of the limits of international law. Such a questioning may come from a radical attack on the state system or from a regulatory attempt to protect it. Once law is allowed to retell and evaluate the founding narratives of states, it threatens to speak too much, raising questions that some would rather leave dormant — and that others may find echoing back to them from their supposed geopolitical and jurisprudential opponents. With its discretion thus extended, law threatens to overwhelm an unquestioning acceptance of sovereignty as well as the automatic application of self-determination even in cases of decolonization.[47]

[47]Thus, enlarging the discretionary power of the international law to its full extent would threaten *both* the traditional authority of states *and* the rights of "all peoples" to self-determination. Such an extension of law could perhaps be seen as correlative to an extension of the concept of the "self" of self-determination beyond particular "peoples" to the world's people as a unified whole. An unlimited concept of in-

The essential distinctiveness of international competence over self-determination lies in its novel response to this issue of law's limits. It is not a matter of a simple substitution of one ground, law, for another, sovereignty, but of providing an arena constituted by their interplay. An understanding of this arena requires a return to the direction to which my analyses of Fitzmaruice and Ofuatey-Kodjoe pointed: the need to analyze the nature and source of the competence of an international legal tribunal to treat questions of self-determination. I turn to the *Aaland Islands* case, perhaps the first legal opinion in which an international tribunal discussed the nature of its competence over self-determination, a discussion that may still be viewed as the classic source for our ideas about the subject.

2. International Law in Transition: The *Aaland Islands* Case

A dispute between Finland and Sweden over the Aaland Islands in the aftermath of World War I provided the occasion for one of the first extended legal discussions of self-determination.[48] The core of this path-breaking opinion, issued in 1920 by a distinguished Commission of Jurists appointed by the League of Nations, concerns the competence of international law to treat of such matters. Finland had objected to international legal jurisdiction, arguing that disposition over the territory was a matter of internal Finnish jurisdiction.[49] Sweden, on the other hand, sought international legal recognition of its own sovereignty over the islands.[50] Sweden argued that the Aalanders had shown their desire to be united with Sweden through their political and military struggles.[51]

---

ternational law could thus be viewed as embodying the sovereignty of an unlimited, i.e., universal, "people." *Cf.* Lansing, *Notes on World Sovereignty*, 15 AM. J. INT'L L. 13 (1921). As I shall show below, the modern discourse of self-determination depends precisely on a limitation of both legal and sovereign authority, a limitation that emerges from the critical tension between them.

[48] On the Aaland Islands affair generally, see, e.g., J. BARROS, THE AALAND ISLANDS QUESTION: ITS SETTLEMENT BY THE LEAGUE OF NATIONS (1968); F.H.A. COLIJN, LA DÉCISION DE LA SOCIÉTÉ DES NATIONS CONCERNANT LES ILES D'ALAND (1923).

[49] *Report of the International Committee of Jurists on the Aaland Islands Question*, LEAGUE OF NATIONS O.J. SPEC. SUPP. 3 (1920) [hereinafter Aaland Islands Report]. It should be noted that the League appointed a second commission whose findings differed considerably from those of the Jurists. *See* A. RIGO-SUREDA, *supra* note 8, at 111-17; J. BARROS, *supra* note 48, at 300-33. The League's decision was heavily influenced by the second commission's views. *Id.* My discussion, however, is limited to the opinion of the Jurists, which has been more significant for the future development of self-determination doctrine.

[50] Aaland Islands Report *supra* note 49, at 5.

[51] *Id.* at 3.

The Jurists rejected Finland's jurisdictional objections. They began their opinion by acknowledging that, generally, "the right of disposing of territory is essentially an attribute of the sovereignty of every state."[52] Similarly, a dispute over whether a particular group is to be granted the right to "determin[e] its own political fate" is one which, "under normal conditions . . . International Law leaves entirely to the domestic jurisdiction of the state" exercising sovereignty over the territory in question.[53] Moreover, they declared that the principle of the right of peoples to self-determination could not be considered as an established part of positive international law.

War, revolution and occupation, however, had disrupted the Aaland Islands' normal legal status. The Jurists applied an emphatic version of the distinction between fact and law to describe the way in which these events affected the islands' legal status. Such political upheavals as those endured by the islands occur "as facts and outside the domain of law";[54] they are among those "situations of fact which, to a large extent, cannot be met by the application of normal rules of positive law."[55] Extraordinary events, like those transpiring on the Aalands, overwhelm "normal" law's ability to provide guidance for political life.

The Jurists trace this suspension of ordinary legality to the disruption by political turmoil of a clearly defined sovereign authority. Sovereignty, explain the Jurists, is fundamental to international law:

> [I]f the essential basis of these rules, that is to say, territorial sovereignty, is lacking, either because the State is not yet fully formed [*n'a pas encore pris complètement naissance*] or because it is undergoing transformation or dissolution, the situation is obscure and uncertain from a legal point of view and will not become clear until the period of development is completed and a definite new situation, which is normal in respect to territorial sovereignty, has been established.[56]

For the Jurists, then, the "essential basis" of law is sovereignty, at least in normal times. However, in the absence of a stable sovereign, an absence that may be occasioned by the pangs of the sovereign's birth or the crisis of its death, the legal situation becomes "obscure and uncertain." This equivocal situation is one of a "transition" from fact to law, from a "*de facto* situation to a normal situation *de jure*."[57]

---

[52] *Id.* at 5.
[53] *Id.*
[54] *Id.* at 9.
[55] *Id.* at 6.
[56] *Id.*
[57] *Id.*

During the period of this "transition," where the "normal" rules of law are suspended, a new set of rules finds its appropriate context. Specifically, "[u]nder such circumstances, the principle of the self-determination of peoples may be called into play."[58] Sovereignty and the normal rules of international law, including law's limited jurisdiction, are temporarily suspended; a different kind of international legal jurisdiction, a jurisdiction empowered to apply the doctrine of self-determination, takes their place. The Jurists add that transformations in the political and cultural as well as legal spheres mark the "obscure and uncertain" period of transition: "New aspirations of certain sections of a nation, which are sometimes based on old traditions or on a common language and civilization, may come to the surface and produce effects"[59] in such periods. In this turbulent period the "essential basis" of international law must be sought elsewhere than in sovereignty.

The opinion thus draws an essential connection between the questions of self-determination and that of a new kind of international legal competence. In normal times, international law finds its justification, its "essential basis," in the safeguarding of sovereignty; in extraordinary times, it grounds itself in the transformations that occur during the suspension of sovereignty. The appropriateness of the invocation of this new legal complex can only be determined on the basis of a detailed empirical analysis — specifically, a detailed investigation as to whether the situation is one of those "transitions" from a factual to a legal situation. In the case of the Aaland Islands, a determination of the appropriate basis of international law depends on the question of whether the situation prevailing on the islands "is of a definite and normal character, or whether it is a transitory or not fully developed situation."[60]

This question can only be decided on the basis of "the principal historical facts" in the birth of new nations after World War I.[61] Accordingly, the Jurists recount, at great length, the political and military events surrounding the shifting situation with regard to sovereignty over both Finland and the Aaland Islands. They conclude that stable political authority was substantially disrupted during the period of upheaval; at times, this disruption led Finland to default completely on its sovereign responsibilities and powers ["de veritables carences de souveraineté"[62]].

The travails of Finland's birth as a nation and of the Aaland Islanders as a people make appropriate the invocation of a novel international law which may competently discuss conflicting claims to population and ter-

---

[58] *Id.*

[59] *Id.*

[60] *Id.* at 6-7.

[61] *Id.* at 7.

[62] *Id.* at 13.

ritory without reference to sovereignty. International law may, under such conditions, reach beyond the state system to investigate the claims of extralegal groups to legal status and to determine the future of the population and territory. The goal, however, is to restore a "normal" situation, to restore the complementarity of law and sovereignty.

What is at stake here are alternative forms and bases of international law, not merely opposing jurisdictional positions. The Finnish Minister Enckell, who had argued the case for Finland before the Commission, declared that the Jurist's conclusions could not be justified "[u]nless a new international law is to be called into existence" by the decision.[63] Rather than mere lawyerly hyperbole, this statement grows out of a developed conception of international law that cannot admit the jurisprudential validity of self-determination.

In support of his argument, Enckell quotes Rivier's treatise on international law for the proposition that sovereignty "originates law." Enckell comments:

> The two ideas of right and of fact are so closely bound up with that of sovereignty that one can no more understand the expression *de jure* sovereignty than the expression *de facto* sovereignty, for in sovereignty, which is the supreme power, *de facto* and *de jure* coincide.[64]

In this jurisprudential vision, international law originates upon a basis of states, sovereign in both fact and law, into whose origins in real and ideological turmoil one may not inquire. Disrupting the indissolubly legal and factual legitimacy of this basis would, in this view, result in the disruption of law itself. In the alternative view propounded by the Jurists, the disjunction of fact and law, the period of transition from one to the other during the crisis of sovereignty, is the very basis upon which a new international law can flourish.

Thus, rather than merely deciding a jurisdictional question, the *Aaland Islands* opinion recounts the birth of an alternative international law, an international law that is, in turn, competent to discuss the birth of states. With the rupture of the complementarity of law and fact, the foundations of international law become a matter for discussion. Law may now inquire into the processes by which groups come to assert their collective will, by which they begin to acquire the indicia of international "determination," by which they obtain "access" to the international stage.

---

[63] *Preliminary Observations by the Finnish Minister on the Report of the Committee of Jurists*, 2 LEAGUE OF NATIONS O.J. 66, 67 (1921).

[64] *Supplementary Statements Made to the Council of the League by the Finnish Minister*, 2 LEAGUE OF NATIONS O.J. 75, 76 (1921), *citing* 1 RIVIER, PRINCIPLES OF INTERNATIONAL LAW 55 (1896).

The arrogation of power by this extraordinary international law appears to represent a victory, however temporary, over the principle of sovereignty. Indeed, it would be tempting to borrow an image from corporate law to describe this victory: international law, in deciding questions of self-determination, "pierces the veil" of the state system to reach the underlying facts. Such an assertion of law's power would be appropriate in those stormy times when the state system goes into disarray, no longer able to provide the real and conceptual guidance demanded of it.

Such a description, however, would miss the distinctiveness of the Jurists' conception. In deciding questions of self-determination, law does not confront "facts," but rather, "transitions" between facts and law. In moving beyond sovereignty to the underlying equities, law is confronted with the striving of those concerned for sovereign power over their destinies. Those seeking self-determination wish to delegitimize the authority of existing sovereigns and to augment the authority of law *in order to* achieve sovereign status.

The complementarity of fact and law, in which one may justifiably forget the conflict between the positive and the transcendental, sovereign and legal authority, is replaced by a complex articulation of that conflict. The text of self-determination is woven through this articulation of contradictory jurisprudential urges. One discusses self-determination as long as the appeals from sovereignty to law and back again can shape a productive rhetorical form. The final shape of a particular form of the doctrine, the "holding" of a given text or period, is determined by the particular manner in which the articulation is performed.

3. "Sovereignty in Abeyance": McNair's *South West Africa* Opinion

"It may seem a far cry from the Aaland Islands to South West Africa."[65] Nevertheless, legal writings on self-determination are marked by a certain set of problems which reappear in widely varying contexts. Such writings tend to describe the extraordinary quality of self-determination and its ramifications for international law in a series of homologous, though not identical, images.

In his separate opinion in the 1950 *South West Africa* Case, Judge McNair discussed at length the system of mandates established by the League of Nations, a system that seems to differ considerably from the crisis situation that evoked the purportedly "transitory" jurisdiction in the *Aaland Islands* opinion.[66] McNair's opinion focuses on the question of the status of South Africa's League Mandate over Namibia after the dissolution of the League. McNair concludes that the Mandatory system created an

---

[65] *South West Africa* Case, 1950 I.C.J. 128, 154 (sep. op. McNair).

[66] *Id.* at 153-55.

"objective" international legal regulation governing the territories concerned. Such regulation creates "real" rights not limited to the contracting states. Such rights "acquire an objective existence which is more resistant than are personal rights to the dislocating effects of international events."[67] The Mandate created a status *in rem* for the territory.[68] The legal obligations of a Mandatory Power, therefore, survive the dissolution of the League.

In McNair's description, then, the Mandatory system seems to be the opposite of the international jurisdiction over self-determination embodied in the section of the *Aaland Islands* opinion discussed above. For McNair, the Mandates create an international jurisdiction designed to be "resistant" to change in the face of international "dislocations"; the *Aaland Islands* Jurists viewed precisely such "dislocations" as calling forth the novel form of jurisdiction that empowers law to act on claims of self-determination.[69]

Nevertheless, when discussing the nature of the relationship between the Mandatory Power and the territory over which it exercises its powers, McNair uses imagery that embodies a conception of the role of international law in the context of self-determination analogous to that of the Jurists. McNair declared that the usual concept of sovereignty was inappropriate to such a situation:

> The Mandates System (and the "corresponding principles" of the [U.N.] Trusteeship System) is a new institution — a new relationship between territory and its inhabitants on the one hand and the government which represents them internationally on the other — a new species of international government, which does not fit into the old conception of sovereignty and is alien to it. The doctrine of sovereignty has no application to this new system. *Sovereignty over a Mandated Territory is in abeyance*; if and when the inhabitants of the Territory obtain recognition as an independent State, as has already happened in the case of some of the Mandates, *sovereignty will revive and vest in the new State.*[70]

McNair views this "abeyance" of sovereignty as analogous, though not identical, to the common law institution of the trust, "whereby the property

---

[67] *Id.* at 157.

[68] *Id.* at 156-57.

[69] It should be noted that the contrast I describe between McNair's opinion and that of the *Aaland Islands* Jurists applies only to the first part of the *Aaland Islands* decision, the section concerned with self-determination. McNair's concept of "objective" international law actually derives from the second part of the *Aaland Islands* opinion, *viz.*, that portion concerned with the 1856 Convention on the demilitarization of the islands. *See* Aaland Islands Report, *supra* note 49, at 14-19.

[70] 1950 I.C.J. at 150 (sep. op. McNair) (emphasis added).

(and sometimes the persons) of those who are not *sui juris* . . . can be entrusted to some responsible person as a trustee or *tuteur* or *curateur*."[71] Among the principles central to such an institution that McNair found pertinent to the Mandate system are that the trustee "is not in the position of the normal complete owner"[72] and that he must "carry out . . . the mission confided to him for the benefit of some other person."[73] In the case of the Mandates, the trust was to be managed for the benefit of the "dependent peoples"[74] occupying the territory — specifically, for their "material and moral well-being and the[ir] social progress."[75]

There are thus two images at work in McNair's opinion, images which are not wholly compatible. First, there is the image of the common law trust for those who, "such as a minor or a lunatic,"[76] cannot manage their own affairs. McNair acknowledges that the analogy with private common law cannot wholly satisfy in the international context — presumably, because the character of sovereignty in its relation to international law does not correspond exactly to the character of the individual in relation to domestic law. He thus finds it necessary to do away with sovereignty in relation to the Mandated territory. In the absence of sovereignty, the focus shifts to the "rights and duties of the Mandatory" as defined in the "international agreements creating the system and the rules of law they attract."[77] International law thus becomes directly empowered to administer the territory and dispense "rights and duties" without regard for sovereignty; the Mandate System, as a "new institution," has apparently created a new international law which can do without sovereignty as the basis for the legal representation of people and territory within it.

Such an interpretation receives a correction with the idea of the "abeyance" of sovereignty. International law receives its new status not from the abolition of sovereignty but only from its latency. Between death and birth, sovereignty may "revive and vest" in the near future as has "already happened" in the new postwar period of decolonization. When the "inhabitants of the Territory obtain recognition"[78] — and we are reminded of the mysteries of such "obtaining" — the trust will collapse and with it this "new" international law which dispensed with sovereignty.

As in the *Aaland Islands* opinion, the paradox of self-determination — the assertion of a right to become a right-holder — finds its legal cor-

[71]*Id.* at 149.
[72]*Id.*
[73]*Id.*
[74]*Id.* at 148.
[75]*Id.* at 155.
[76]*Id.* at 149.
[77]*Id.* at 150.
[78]*Id.*

relate in an exceptional "new" international competence. The establishment of such a competence rests on a lapse of sovereignty and a consequent arrogation of legal power to dispense "rights and duties" over people and territory. This extraordinary jurisdiction, however, is shaped and delimited by the "sacred trust"[79] — the goal of the eventual "revival" of sovereignty in the formerly "dependent" peoples.[80] This extraordinary international legal competence, then, is "new" not merely in a one-time historical sense; rather, it is always a freshly occurring, novel competence arising in the hiatus of legal normality.

C. Related Doctrines: State Succession and "Premature Recognition"

The perspective from which I have discussed the role of self-determination in international law raises the question of the relationship between self-determination and other, more traditional international legal doctrines. I have stressed the transitional function of self-determination: both in a conceptual sense, bridging the law/sovereignty dilemma, and in a temporal sense, providing the conditions and limits for international jurisdiction in times of crises of sovereignty. Yet, transitions in international life occur constantly: the birth, death and transformation of states and governments have been features of modern history for a long time. In order to understand the distinctiveness of self-determination, we must understand its relationship to other legal doctrines developed to cope with the transformations of the shape of international society.

For purposes of comparison, the most important of these doctrines concern the succession of states and the recognition of the statehood of insurgents by third countries. "State succession" means the "replacement of one State by another in the responsibility for the international relations of territory."[81] There are two issues involved in state succession. The first, sometimes called "succession in fact," concerns the question of whether the old state has remained in existence or has been replaced by a new state; the second, sometimes called "succession in law," concerns the legal effects of succession, i.e., the determination of which of the legal respon-

---

[79]*Id.* at 147-49 (discussing the meaning of the "scared trust" in Article 22 of the League Covenant).

[80]McNair's concept of the "abeyance of sovereignty" makes the eventual reacquisition of sovereignty a somewhat contingent matter. By 1971, the I.C.J. was certain that "the ultimate objective of the sacred trust was the self-determination and independence of the peoples concerned." *Namibia*, 1971 I.C.J. 16, 31.

[81]Vienna Convention on Succession of States in Respect of Treaties, U.N. Doc. A/Conf. 80/31 (1978), Art. 2 (b). *See generally* I. Brownlie, Principles of International Law 76-79 (1966); K. Marek, Identity and Continuity of States in Public International Law (1954).

sibilities of the old state remain binding on the successor state.[82] These two issues are interrelated, at least in part: the stand one will take on what responsibilities should devolve on a new state cannot be separated from theories about the essence of statehood and the kinds of changes required for a state to be considered as a new entity.[83]

The relevant comparison with self-determination concerns the way in which international law treats questions of "succession in fact," i.e., those concerning the kind of transformations required for international law to decide that a succession of states has occurred. Although there has been much debate on the subject, the requirements are quite strict by all standards. Thus, according to one treatise, a "state remains one and the same International Person in spite of changes in its headship, in its dynasty, in its form, in its rank and title, and in its territory."[84] Another treatise declares that

> [e]ven when internal change takes the form of *temporary dissolution, so that the state, either from social anarchy or local disruption, is momentarily unable to fulfill its international duties*, personal identity remains unaffected; it is only lost when the permanent dissolution of the state is proved by the erection of fresh states, or by the continuance of anarchy so prolonged as to render reconstitution impossible or in a very high degree improbable.[85]

Among the changes that affect the identity of a state and induce succession are a real union between two or more states, a loss of independence, the merger of one state into another, and the annexation and fragmentation of states.[86]

The important point here is not so much the detail of these doctrines as the perspective from which international law considers these questions. In the *Aaland Islands* opinion, temporary anarchy and dislocation provided the space for legal creativity; in the passage just cited, it mandates legal forbearance. In succession doctrine, law is concerned with identifying the sovereign to whom legal responsibility is to be attributed. The determination of whether the old sovereign has survived or whether a new sov-

---

[82]O. UDOKANG, SUCCESSION OF NEW STATES TO INTERNATIONAL TREATIES 107-9 (1972).

[83]D.P. O'Connell associates the view that successor states inherit all of its predecessor's obligations with the Hegelian view of the state and the opposite view with the Austinian view. He calls for a pragmatic approach which would lead to an intermediate case-by-case evaluation of the legal effects of succession. *See* O'Connell, *Independence and Problems of State Succession*, in THE NEW NATIONS IN INTERNATIONAL LAW AND DIPLOMACY (W.V. O'Brien ed. 1965).

[84]L. OPPENHEIM, INTERNATIONAL LAW: A TREATISE 153 (H. Lauterpacht ed. 8th ed. 1955) (emphasis added).

[85]W.E. HALL, *supra* note 4, at 21 (emphasis added).

[86]L. OPPENHEIM, *supra* note 84, at 154-6.

ereign has been born is oriented toward a determination of this attribution of legal obligations and the scope of these obligations.

By contrast, the concept of self-determination does not seek to situate itself on one side or the other of the crisis of sovereignty, but, rather, in the midst of that crisis. The question is whether other legal principles than those which seek to attribute obligations to responsible sovereigns have come into play. The discourse of self-determination thrives in the duration of the crisis rather than with a *post hoc* evaluation of whether, and with what result, the crisis has come to a decisive conclusion.

We can bring out this feature of self-determination more clearly through reference to certain aspects of debates concerning the recognition of new states by third countries. In the traditional view, the decision to grant or withhold such recognition lies outside the sphere of law. States, retaining complete discretion, could base their decision solely on policy considerations — regardless of the objective characteristics of the entity in question. In this traditional view, prior to recognition, such a community "possesses neither the rights nor the obligations which international law associates with full statehood."[87]

Legal discussions of recognition for those adhering to this traditional view concern not the decision to recognize, which lies outside the "orbit of law," but, rather, the legal consequences entailed by such decisions. Such discussions focus primarily on the debate between the "declaratory" and "constitutive" theories: whether recognition should be considered merely "declaratory" of a state which already has a legal existence on the basis of its factual nature or whether recognition by other states is actually "constitutive" of the new state's existence.[88]

The view that no duty of recognition exists appears to be consistent with the views of Fitzmaurice and others in relation to self-determination. For such views, states owe no more duty to entities that seek full legal personality prior to their attaining such status under law than they do to "peoples" who have not yet been "determined internationally." With the absence of a duty of recognition, the achievement of the indicia of statehood lies beyond the competence of legal discourse; law must remain ignorant of processes whose legal consequences it is nonetheless required to assess.

These theoretical consequences hold with greater consistency for those adhering to a strict constitutive view of recognition than for those supporting the declaratory view. Nonetheless, as Lauterpacht cogently argues, the true conceptual crux rests not on the question of whether recognition

---

[87]H. Lauterpacht, Recognition in International Law 2 (1947). In the discussion that follows, I discuss only the recognition of States and not the separate issues of the recognition of governments and belligerents.

[88]*Id.* at 1-2. *See also* I. Brownlie, *supra* note 81, at 82-4.

is declaratory or constitutive but on that concerning the obligatory character of recognition.[89] As long as recognition remains discretionary, it continues, for both the declaratory and the constitutive positions, to lie outside the orbit of law, and remains vested with a political, rather than a legal, character.[90]

Lauterpacht argues for a duty to recognize once an entity has reached the objective characteristics of statehood. In support of this view, Lauterpacht finds it necessary to confront the following question, which should be familiar from my discussion of Fitzmaurice: "[I]s it permissible to assert the existence of a duty in relation to an entity which is incapable of possessing and asserting rights?"[91] Fitzmaurice found the analogous dilemma jurisprudentially fatal in the context of self-determination; in the context of recognition, Lauterpacht offers two answers which he views as conclusive.

First, Lauterpacht argues, states could be said to owe such a duty not to the entity seeking recognition but to the international community as a whole.[92] A duty to recognize means that states must evaluate the situation in accordance with law rather than mere state interest; in carrying out this duty, states are thus acting in "their capacity as organs of international law."[93] Secondly, Lauterpacht suggests that an entity not yet recognized in law can nevertheless possess a right, although that right is "unenforceable and, therefore, imperfect."[94]

Lauterpacht's discussion of "premature recognition" illuminates his conception of states acting as "organs of international law." The rule against premature recognition poses issues quite close to those associated with self-determination and often arises in situations involving claims of self-determination.[95] The doctrine concerns the permissibility of the recognition by third countries of the statehood of entities or groups struggling for independence from a parent state. During such a conflict states are said to have a "duty not to recognize" the statehood of the insurgents as long as the outcome is in doubt.[96] The duty not to recognize continues unless and until a "new state has in fact come into being" as a result of

---

[89]H. Lauterpacht, *supra* note 87, at 76.

[90]*Id.*

[91]*Id.* at 74.

[92]*Id.*

[93]*Id.* at 6.

[94]*Id.* at 74.

[95]*See generally* J.A. Salmon, La Reconnaissance D'Etat 36-45 (1971); R.H. Sharp, Nonrecognition As a Legal Obligation: 1775-1934 (1934); W.E. Hall, *supra* note 4, at 105.

[96]*See, e.g.*, P.C. Jessup, A Modern Law of Nations 52 (1948); W.E. Hall, *supra* note 4, at 105.

the insurgency.[97] This situation does not arise unless the "conflict with the parent State has been substantially won."[98] Premature recognition by another state constitutes not a neutral legal act as in other acts of recognition but as a bellicose "participation in the conflict."[99] The parent state will rightly consider such recognition to be a hostile act in relation to itself.

Lauterpacht strongly supports the rule against premature recognition and, indeed, appears to view it as a necessary complement to his theory. For Lauterpacht, premature recognition is an "act of intervention and an international delinquency"[100] because it "constitutes an abuse of the power of recognition."[101] The rule governing premature recognition gives "expression to the objective requirements which make the grant of recognition legally permissible," conditions which are identical, in his view, to those which make such a grant obligatory.[102]

The above discussion shows that the issues implicated in self-determination as a matter for legal discourse carry us well beyond doctrines about recognition. In the traditional view, the decision to recognize and thus grant legal status to a previously "undetermined" entity simply lies outside law. Yet, even when the line between law and politics is extended in the manner of Lauterpacht to the decision to recognize, recognition doctrine stops well before the domain claimed by self-determination.

For Lauterpacht, just as for the traditional view, states, acting as "organs of international law," must attend the resolution of struggles for power before they may grant any full recognition to the new entity. Premature recognition intervenes in an unclear situation, a situation whose outcome cannot be predicted. One cannot, from the perspective of recognition doctrine, assert the intervention of law in such a situation without such an intervention being considered an act of violence. A properly legal recognition of an insurgency, rather than a political assertion of power, depends on an objective evaluation of the chances for the permanent success of the insurrection.[103]

---

[97]C.C. Hyde, International Law 152-53 (2d ed. 1945).

[98]*Id.* at 152-53.

[99]*Id.*

[100]H. Lauterpacht, *supra* note 87 at 8.

[101]*Id.* at 9.

[102]*Id.* at 11.

[103]W.E. Hall, *supra* note 4, at 105-7. In a related context, the *Aaland Islands* Jurists expressed the distinction between recognition as a full legal act and recognition as intervention in an unclear situation in terms of their characteristic contrast between "normal" and extraordinary times: "The experience of the last war shows that the same value cannot be attached to the recognition of new States in war time. . . as in normal times; further, neither were such recognitions given with the same object as in normal times." Aaland Islands Report, *supra* note 49, at 8.

Yet it is precisely such an intervention into an unsettled situation that is performed by self-determination. Unlike both succession and recognition doctrine, self-determination is not motivated by a desire to locate and delimit the holder of sovereign responsibility. Rather, it derives its existence from the gap in sovereignty and the opportunities that can exist only in that gap. With the doctrine of self-determination, law detaches itself from its role as an impartial arbiter between competing sovereigns.

This difference between the nature of self-determination and recognition means that the positions of Lauterpacht and Fitzmaurice are not mutually exclusive even though they give opposite answers to strikingly similar dilemmas in their respective contexts. One may agree with Lauterpacht that states are under an obligation to recognize entities that have attained the indicia of statehood *and* with Fitzmaurice that a right to self-determination is juridical nonsense. Those seeking self-determination lack some of the indicia of statehood — often, for example, that of an effective government. They seek recognition of a right to attain those indicia. This right involves a qualitative leap from Lauterpacht's right to recognition.

In the language of recognition doctrine, law in the form of self-determination would have become a "party to the conflict." From a passive role as judge, it would become an interventionist actor. It would exercise not law, but power. In the terms in which I have described it, however, this alternative, between impartial judge and interventionist participant, is inadequate to capture the role of the law in self-determination. Self-determination serves as a transition — neither crowning sovereignty as king nor replacing it with an omnipotent international law on the model of domestic law. Rather, it serves as a suspension of normal law, devoting itself to a dynamic conflict between positive and transcendental conceptions of legitimacy.

III. Law And The "Self" of Self-Determination

The problem which I posed at the beginning of this essay concerned the possibility of international law's ability to recognize the rights of those admittedly beyond its ordinary purview. In the section on international competence, I tried to show how commentators and jurists justify the right of international law to decide questions of self-determination by reference to a suspension of the normal foundations of international law. The opinions of the Jurists in the *Aaland Islands* case and of McNair in *South West Africa* provided eloquent images for the way in which certain extraordinary situations suspend the established complementarity of law and sovereignty while remaining teleologically directed towards its reconstitution. These images suggest a novel conception of the stance of international law in its adjudication of questions of self-determination. In the section on the relatively more conventional doctrines that deal with issues similar to those implicated in self-determination, I attempted to highlight the distinctiveness of the stance found in those opinions.

If "normal" international law treats mainly of sovereigns, the extraordinary international law of *self*-determination is concerned with nonstate "selves." I turn, therefore, to examine the nature of such "selves." As in my discussion of legal competence, I will begin with a set of relatively abstract debates concerning the"self" and then proceed to an analysis of the way the opposing elements structuring these debates are woven together to produce textured forms of legal argument.

A. Historical and Conceptual Controversies

The "self" that merits the right to determine its own future has received many different definitions. I will divide these controversies into two groups, those concerned with historical changes in the definition of the "self" and those concerned with problems in the underlying conceptual framework. The terms of the historical debate do not directly correspond to those on the conceptual level; the terms of each discussion, however, are often used to explain or justify particular positions in the other. I will first discuss the way in which commentators have understood the historical changes in the bearer of the right to self-determination, changes which are often seen in conjunction with views about the evolution of international law. I will then turn to the conceptual debate, structured by a dichotomy between subjective and objective views of national selfhood. Finally, I will show the way in which two significant I.C.J. opinions employ historical and conceptual arguments in a complex justification of a particular interpretation of the "self" of self-determination.

1. Secession, Decolonization and History

Writers employ various narrative images to describe the history of self-determination, some portraying a smooth development, others describing various forms of rupture. These historical accounts focus on changing definitions of the "self" in terms of the relationship between the group seeking self-determination and the state in actual sovereign control. Specifically, these accounts discuss the issue of decolonization versus secession: does a valid assertion of "selfhood" arise exclusively from domination by geographically distant powers or may groups occupying territory contiguous to the sovereign state also assert the right on the basis of other identifying features? Commentators have drawn conflicting lessons from international legal history on this issue.

Those emphasizing continuity in the history of self-determination often link this history to a vision of international law as progressively unfolding from early modern times through the critical moment in which self-determination became its cornerstone. The U.N. study[104] discussed earlier exemplifies this approach. The study traces the gradual unfolding of the principle of self-determination from its origins in the French Revolution through its consolidation in a legal right in the post-World War II period.[105]

For the study, this progressive development of international law into a system based on self-determination culminates in international law's ability to distinguish between authentic and specious claims of self-determination. The great divide between authentic and specious claims lies between self-determination, identified primarily with decolonization, and "secession." The same 1960 U.N. resolution which declared unequivocally that "all peoples have the right to self-determination," also states: "Any attempt aimed at the partial or total disruption of the national unity and territorial integrity of a country is incompatible with the purposes and principles of the United Nations."[106]

The resolution, thus, unequivocally commands adherence to the two apparently incompatible goals of self-determination and national unity. The U.N. study resolves this tension through an appeal to the historical progress of international legal consciousness: "the international community is mature enough now to be able to distinguish between genuine self-determination and self-determination used to disguise an act of secession."[107] The U.N. study thus combines a description of the current state of the accepted limits of self-determination — as applying primarily to decolonization — with a teleological justification of this situation — a normative conception of the history of international law.

Shorn of this teleology, the study's account is generally accepted as a history of self-determination in the twentieth century. Thus, it is possible, with one commentator, to divide the history of self-determination into two periods according to the differential acceptance of the twin ideas of secession and decolonization. In the first period, immediately following World War I, self-determination applied to "ethnic communities, nations or nationalities primarily defined by language or culture," who "were authorized to disrupt the existing states."[108] Self-determination was brought into play as a guiding principle for administering the breakup of the Ottoman and Austro-Hungarian empires, leaving the overseas possessions of Europe generally untouched. In the second period, the decades following World War II, self-determination was applied so as to allow "the inhabitants of former European colonies, however haphazardly assembled by the colonial

---

[104]*See supra* notes 17-20 and accompanying text.

[105]A. Cristescu, *supra* note 7, at 17-18.

[106]G.A. Res. 1514, 15 U.N. GAOR Supp. (No. 16), U.N. Doc. A/4684 (1960).

[107]A. Cristescu, *supra* note 7, at 26.

[108]Emerson, *supra* note 44, at 463.

Power, [to] take over pre-existing political units as independent states."[109] The first period was concerned with the rights of minorities to "secession"; by contrast, the second period rigorously denied the legitimacy of "secession."[110]

One manner of putting into question the teleological view would be to expand the historical span under consideration — both by moving back in time and by anticipating possible future developments of the doctrine. In this way, one commentator distinguishes four waves of accession to independence, in which secession and decolonization alternate:

1) the decolonization of Latin America during the early nineteenth century, a phenomenon inspired by the French and American revolutions;

2) the gaining of independence "par détachment ou par démembrement" of various European nations, primarily during the mid-nineteenth century and post-World War I eras — a phenomenon governed by the principle of nationality;

3) the decolonization of Africa and Asia between 1930 and the early 1960's;

4) the struggles for independence "par détachement ou par sécession" in various parts of the world, primarily from the 1960's to the present (Katanga, Biafra, Singapore, Bangledesh, etc.).[111]

According to this commentator, the current period would be primarily one of secession, a phenomenon as yet unacknowledged in legal doctrine. From this perspective, the U.N. study's historical justification of the exclusion of secession from its definition of self-determination cannot be sustained.

Above, I related the U.N. study's teleological justification of its views on secession to its conception of the history of international law; similarly, a view of the discontinuity in the history of self-determination may be associated with an analogous conception of international legal history. The idea of a discontinuous history of international law has been sharply stressed by those who have been concerned with self-determination as a disruption of the European nature of international law. There are at least two versions of this disruption. The first relates the incorporation of self-determination into international law to the story of the wresting of international law away

---

[109] *Id.*

[110] The distinction between secession and self-determination has been criticized from various perspectives. *See, e.g.*, Mojekwu, *Self-Determination: The African Perspective* in SELF-DETERMINATION: NATIONAL, REGIONAL AND GLOBAL DIMENSIONS 221, 226-36 (Y. Alexander & R.A. Friedlander, ed. 1980); L.C. BUCHHEIT, SECCESSION: THE LEGITIMACY OF SELF-DETERMINATION (1978); J.F. GUILHAUDIS, LE DROIT DES PEUPLES À DISPOSER D'EUX-MÊMES 33-35 (1976).

[111] J. BROSSARD, L'ACCESSION À LA SOUVERAINETÉ ET LE CAS DU QUÉBEC 39-42, 74-77 (1976).

from domination by the West. Thus, in justifying the invasion of Portuguese Goa by India, the Indian delegate to the United Nations characterized it as the mere return of territory to its rightful owner.[112] The Portuguese occupation, he argued, had been illegal and, therefore, the territory had never legally passed out of Indian sovereignty. The Indian delegate grounded his arguments in a certain conception of international law, a conception that gave wide latitude to the exercise of self-determination. He rejected all contrary legal arguments on the grounds that they were based on an illegitimate, because European, international law:

> If any narrow minded legalistic considerations — considerations arising from international law as written by European law writers — should arise, these writers were, after all, brought up in the atmosphere of colonialism. I pay all respect to Grotius, who is supposed to be the father of international law and we accept many tenets of international law. But the tenet . . . which is quoted in support of colonial powers having sovereign rights over territories which they won by conquest in Asia and Africa is no longer acceptable. It is the European concept and it must die.[113]

In his opinion in the 1971 *Namibia* case, the Vice President of the I.C.J., Fouad Ammoun, offered a somewhat different version of historical discontinuity. Judge Ammoun views legal history not as the story of a succession between an older, European system and a newer, Third World system, but as part of an ongoing struggle between European and Non-European concepts, a struggle with ancient roots and diverse historical phases. Judge Ammoun extensively recounts the historical origin of the concept of human equality, the concept he views as underlying the doctrine of self-determination.[114] This concept, he writes, originated with the philosopher Zeno who was not European because he came from Sidon. Ammoun further argues that the Greeks, including Plato and Aristotle, were opposed to human equality. The idea of equality was transmitted to the Age of Reason through the influence of Stoicism on Papinius and Ulpian, "the greatest of the Roman juriconsults, who were of Phoenician origin."[115] In this way, the institution of the legal doctrine of self-determination becomes the symbol of a modern triumph of the non-European position in this perennial conceptual and political contest.

Nevertheless, despite Ammoun's conception of competing European and Third World principles, he constructs his argument that self-determination has become part of international law in a traditional manner:

---

[112]For this debate, see generally 16 U.N. SCOR (987th mtg.), U.N. Doc. S/PV 987 (1961).

[113]*Id.* at 11.

[114]*Namibia* , 1971 I.C.J. 16, 77-78.

[115]*Id.* at 78.

cataloging its increasing recognition in U.N. documents, interstate treaties and state practice.[116] One may question the consistency of these two methods of analysis: if history is marked by struggle between incompatible principles, and if law must be seen in the context of those struggles, how can we retain the idea of the gradual evolution of a principle into a legal right? The idea of the incremental evolution of a legal right would seem to require a view of a continuous legal history. Ammoun's historical vision thus appears to be hopelessly contradictory.

This differential treatment of history, however, in which certain periods or phenomena are treated as continuous and others as discontinuous, is characteristic of the discourse of self-determination. As I argue throughout this essay, rather than forming a mere logical inconsistency, this feature must be seen as the effect of an historical vision in which periods of disruption alternate with those of restoration; the discourse of self-determination can only be understood in the context of a form of argument in which both elements are deployed to yield particular positions in specific cases. It is the peculiar quality of the legal discourse of self-determination to combine unconventional jurisprudential ideas, such as a radically discontinuous legal history, with more traditional conceptions in order to give prudent legal form to normally extralegal notions. I explore this characteristic of the discourse further in my discussions of Judge Ammoun's opinions in Part III.

The theme of self determination as a disruption of the European framework of international law has moved us somewhat away from the question of the particular forms of self-determination (secession, decolonization, etc.). Nevertheless, these diverse readings of history — continuity and rupture, succession and struggle — have become important for the construction of arguments about self-determination. Competing positions on the continuous or discontinuous nature of that history may be viewed as structuring the arguments over the "Belgian Thesis" in the early 1950's — arguments which opposed a view of self-determination as decolonization against a view that would extend it to indigenous peoples within metropolitan states.[117] Moreover, these diverse historical images

[116] *Id.* at 63-67.

[117] The debates over the "Belgian Thesis" concerned the interpretation of Chapter XI of the U.N. Charter, which provided for certain reporting requirements for states administering "non-self-governing territories." U.N. CHARTER, art. 73(e). Belgium argued that the term "non-self-governing territory" should apply to those regions of certain states, particularly those in Latin America, inhabited by indigenous peoples culturally, ethnically, and economically distinct from the ruling majorities in those countries. Latin American and other Third World states responded that the term "non-self-governing territory" applied only to traditional colonies governed by geographically distant powers. *See generally* Kunz, *Chapter XI of the*

have become an important method for structuring arguments about the "self" in which both terms of a seemingly irreconcilable conceptual dichotomy are productively deployed in particular cases. I now turn to that dichotomy.

2. Conceptions of the "Self"

The manner in which legal writers justify a particular form of self-determination, such as decolonization, depends on their manner of deploying the underlying dichotomy about the "self" of self-determination. Two main conceptions of "peoplehood" structure the debate about the "self": one focusing on relatively "subjective" factors in determining the identity of the "self", the other on relatively "objective" factors.[118] The first conception views the "self" as constituted primarily by the aspirations and efforts of a people to achieve self-determination, what one writer calls "a common subjective attachment."[119] This view is sometimes called the "political" concept of nationality: "The definition of the nation, as the

---

U.N. Charter in Action, 48 AM. J. INT'L L. 103 (1954).

Conceptually, this debate could be seen as rooted in the question of whether self-determination and related doctrines, such as those contained in Chapter XI, are universal norms of international law like all others, emerging from the traditional bases of consent and custom and neutral in application — or if, on the contrary, self-determination must be seen essentially in terms of the rupture introduced by particular historical events. Thus, the Belgian delegate argued that the obligations laid down in Article 73 were of a general nature and apply to all member states which are responsible for the progress of backward indigenous peoples living within their territories. 7 U.N. GAOR, C.4 (253rd mtg.) para. 17, U.N. Doc. A/C.4/SR.253 (1952). 7 U.N. GAOR C.4 (402nd mtg.) para. 46, U.N. Doc. A/C.4/SR.402 (1952). The Ecuadorean delegate attacked this position by asserting that "it would convert the whole world into a vast colonial system." 7 U.N. GAOR C.4 (257th mtg.) para. 5, U.N. Doc. A/C.4/SR.257 (1952). These positions could be seen not so much as contradictory as incommensurable — opposing a universal, continuous conception of self-determination applicable in all times and places to a conception stressing the emergence of the right in the context of a particular historical disruption.

To be sure, the holders of each position also attacked the other on its own terms. Thus, the Belgian delegate defended his thesis as the true anti-colonialist position — asserting that rule by Latin American governments over indigenous peoples was a direct continuation of European colonialism. 9 U.N. GAOR C.4 (419th mtg.) para. 25, U.N. Doc. A/C/SR.419 (1954). Similarly, the Guatemalan delegate challenged the Belgians' universalist pretentions; the Belgians' supposed attempt to extend the rights of non-self-governing peoples, he claimed, were simply "intended to justify colonialism and not to hasten its disappearance." 7 U.N. GAOR C.4 (255th mtg.) para. 32, U.N. Doc. A/C.4/SR.255 (1952).

[118] *See, e.g.*, W. OFUATEY-KODJOE, *supra* note 14, at 36.

[119] *Id.* at 78.

term is used in the theory of self-determination, is essentially political. The nation is a community that is, or wishes to be, a state."[120]

The opposite conception focuses on certain objective characteristics of a group of people. These characteristics may include a common territory, ethnicity, language or culture. One commentator has traced the origin of a focus on this last objective factor, that of culture, to Central Europe, where the "idea of the cultural nation . . . acquired priority over the political conception of the nation," leading to a view of nationality as an "objective rather than subjective fact."[121] The "political" conception, in this view, belongs to Western Europe.

Some writers relate the origin of the two conceptions to complexities of nineteenth century European intellectual and political history. In this way, the "subjective" conception may be traced to the democratic ideals of 1789 and the influence of Rousseau; the "objective" conception would stem from Romantcism and be more associated with the events of 1848.[122] According to Cobban, the heterogeneity of the two conceptions remained largely ignored during the nineteenth century; what we now might call struggles for self-determination were formed by their historically fortuitous synthesis in the ideology of democratic nationalism. The twentieth century, for Cobban, has seen the rupture of this synthesis: "[W]e are bound to conclude that the association between nationalism and democracy, and, therefore, the theory of self-determination itself, may have been the result, not of their innate interdependence, but of historical accident."[123]

Indeed, an exclusive focus on either the subjective or objective conception may be associated with opposite forms of self-determination and the corresponding roles for international law. An exclusively objective focus, for example, could do away with any form of consultation with the actual population that forms the "people" in question. All members of a "people" — defined by some given criterion, such as language or ethnicity — would deserve to inhabit a state governed by fellow members of their

---

[120] A. Cobban, The Nation State and National Self-Determination 108 (1969).

[121] *Id.* at 115.

[122] *See generally* P. Vergnaud, L'Idée de la Nationalité et de la Libre Disposition des Peuples dans ses Rapports avec L'Idée de L'Etat (1955); 1 E.H. Carr, The Bolshevik Revolution 1917-1923, 410-415 (1951).

[123] Cobban, *supra* note 13, at 7. The various ways of linking the subjective and objective components in the theory of self-determination with the democratic and nationalistic trends in nineteenth century Europe must be understood in the context of general theories of modern nationalism. *See generally*, T.V. Sathyamurthy, Nationalism in the Contemporary World (1983); A.D. Smith, Theories of Nationalism (1983); L.L. Snyder, Global Mininationalisms: Autonomy or Independence (1982); A.D. Smith, Nationalism in the Twentieth Century (1979); R. Redslob, Le Principe des Nationalités (1931).

group. The consequences of such a conception as applied by the Nazis to neighboring territories occupied by ethnic Germans need not be reviewed here.

Nevertheless, such reliance on an objective criterion would render international law's adjudicatory task much simpler. Legal inquiry could maintain the appearance of neutrality and objectivity through a mechanical focus on a specific index of "peoplehood." However, the term "self-*determination*," with its democratic overtones, would be harder to justify.

A purely subjective conception, on the other hand, seems to be associated with an extremely passive role for international law. Law would merely be required to assist in the struggles of any group of people for an altered political status. Such a perspective raises the specter of uncontrollable secession, confirming the worst fears of chaos invoked by the critics of self-determination. To be sure, international law would still be obligated to determine what counted as the expression of a people's desire for self-determination.

It should be noted that the "equality theory" I discussed above may be cast either in subjective or objective terms. If all subjugated peoples merit self-determination, then a legal inquiry could proceed in relatively objective fashion — assuming, of course, one arrived at a definition of subjugation. Alternatively, one could look at a people's struggle for self-determination as evidence of subjugation, thus making the inquiry a relatively subjective matter.

Some have suggested that the two tests for "peoplehood" should be combined: a "people" would have the right to self-determination if it is characterized by certain objective indicia *and* expresses its desire, by political or military means, to change its political status.[124] This solution appeals to the desire for a moderate, nonpartisan approach and appears to offer a reasonable way for limiting self-determination to a manageable group of cases.[125]

[124] J. F. GUILHAUDIS, *supra* note 110 at 36-42. Guilhaudis traces the origin of this synthesis of the two conceptions to the definition of a nation given by the nineteenth century Italian jurist and statesman Mancini: "une société naturelle d'hommes amenés par l'unite de territoire, d'origine, de coutume et de langues a une communauté de vie et de conscience sociale." *Id.* at 40-41. This definition would permit an impartial adjudication of the authenticity of separatist claims. *Id.* at 42. The case, however, would only be ripe for adjudication if the people had manifested its desire for independence through political struggle. *Id.*

Guilhaudis's views thus resemble those of Ofuatey-Kodjoe whose definition of the "beneficiary" of self-determination I cited at *supra* note 34. It should be noted that, like Ofuatey-Kodjoe, Guilhaudis requires a prior political struggle to enable a group to activate international legal competence over such claims.

[125] "La conception de Mancini permet done de faire le partage entre les vrais et les faux mouvement séparatistes. C'est ce qui explique, qu'a des nuances pres, les auteurs nonengagé's s'y soient ralliés." J.F. GUILHAUDIS, *supra* note 110, at 42.

Nevertheless, one may question the possibility of simply combining the two contradictory ideas. It would be difficult for an inquiry in a particular case to avoid giving dispositive power to one of the two conceptions — often, indeed, to the conception opposed to that obstensibly being implemented. For example, one may seek to poll the population in order to fulfill the subjective component of the test; in order to do so, however, one would have had previously to define the appropriate electoral unit. Presumably, such a delimitation would rely on an objective analysis of the situation. This objective analysis could thus potentially predetermine the outcome of the subsequent expression of the people's will.[126]

Similarly, the objective component of the inquiry would depend on a prior conception of which of many possible national characteristics should be viewed as critical. Presumably, if the legal inquiry wished to avoid imposing ethnocentric prejudice in this inquiry, it would choose the dispositive characteristic on the basis of a phenomenological study of the culture concerned. The objective inquiry would ultimately depend on an investigation into the cultural elements privileged by the population in question. Thus, the objective analysis would be dependent upon the prior subjective consideration.[127]

For these and similar considerations, I would conclude that, either alone or in combination, the abstract conceptual positions are inadequate to provide a determinative answer to the meaning of the "self." Rather

---

[126]In the case of the British Cameroons, for example, the U.N. Trusteeship Council asked the Visiting Mission to determine the appropriate method of consultation with the wishes of the people. The Mission declared that the population in the northern and southern sections should be consulted separately. A. Rigo Sureda, *supra* note 8, at 163-66. The Mission declared that the "distinction to be drawn between the northern and southern sections is a question of fact." *Id.* at 164. The decision to hold separate plebiscites in the two sections decisively influenced the outcomes. *Id.* at 166-67. *See also id.* at 151-63 (the case of British Togoland).

[127]*See, e.g.*, Mojekwu, *supra* note 110. Mojekwu argues against the uncritical retention of colonial frontiers for independent African states. Those frontiers, he claims, "cut across traditional boundaries and ethnic societies," thus violating the self-determination of peoples. *Id.* at 230. Mojekwu defines a people in objective terms as "a cultural nation." His definition, however, is not universal. Rather, the manner in which self-determination is to be applied in a particular context must defer to prevailing cultural views about the definition of nationhood. In Africa, he contends, the notion of "communal rights" dictates a conception of self-determination opposed to that stemming from Western conceptions of the individual and state sovereignty. *Id.* at 231-34. *Cf. Western Sahara*, 1975 I.C.J. 12, 125-26 (sep. op. Dillard) (relationship of people to government authority in religious societies must not be evaluated according to standards appropriate to secular western-oriented societies).

than looking to these positions for dispositive guidance, we must look to their productive combination in complex legal texts. Rather than seeking to combine them in a coherent test that may be mechanically applied, we must turn to the manner in which they structure the discourse of self-determination as a form of argument.

B. Self-Determination as Decolonization: Two Exemplary Cases

1. Introduction

In my discussion of the nature of legal competence over claims of self-determination, I explored the way in which the terms of an abstract dichotomy became the basis for a textured argument for an exceptional form of legal competence. Analysis of the discussions of the "self" has also led us to an apparently irresolvable set of contradictory conceptions. The best legal texts on the "self" do not seek a way out of this impasse on the level of logical abstraction. Rather, they draw on the opposed conceptions to articulate complex arguments in particular cases. The opposed conceptions are not simply added together but are set in a critical relationship to each other in the formation of the argument. I turn, therefore, to the most important recent I.C.J. cases on the principle of self-determination, the 1971 *Namibia* case and the 1975 *Western Sahara* case; I will particularly focus on the separate opinions of Judge Ammoun in those cases, opinions which most fully marshal the range of argumentative resources in modern discussions of the issue.

The dynamics of this critical form of argument are informed by the dual stance of international law in matters of self-determination that we discovered in the analysis of the nature of legal competence. On the one hand, law must be able to assert its own power of analysis, seeking equities that transcend sovereignty. On the other hand, law is accorded this extraordinary power to dispense with the principle of sovereignty so that it may assist in the emergence of a new sovereign, thereby restoring law to a more modest role.

This dual task may produce certain ambivalent expressions analogous to those — such as "determination" and "access" — found in the procedural context. For example, in Judge Ammoun's opinion in the 1971 *Namibia* case, self-determination is viewed as rooted in

> . . . man's inevitable, irreversible drive towards equality and freedom. . . . The texts, whether they be laws, constitutions, declarations, covenants or charters do but define it and mark its successive phases. They are a mere record of it.[128]

It would be hard to know whether such a formulation should be viewed as expressing a subjective or an objective approach. The difficulty is fo-

[128] 1971 I.C.J. at 73.

cused in the use of the idea of "drive," an idea as ambiguous in this legal context — where it appears to carry both political and cultural, or even quasi-natural, implications — as it has been in psychoanalytic discourse — where the term carries meanings related both to the human psyche and to animal instinct.[129]

On the one hand, the passage may be interpreted as focusing on a people's aspirations towards equality, and would thus represent a "subjective," political, conception of self-determination. It is difficult to understand the role the passage gives to "texts" in such a process. The part played by "texts" in the political development of a nation can hardly be viewed as secondary. If a nation is defined by the strength and quality of its aspiration toward autonomy, surely the role of education, study and polemical writing would be central.

On the other hand, one could focus on the "inevitability" and "irreversibility" of the "drive" as representing a relatively objective conception. In this view, self-determination is merely the legal acknowledgement of a natural force, embedded in the objective characteristics of a particular people. "Texts" would, indeed, play a secondary role in such a naturalistic conception. Yet, deference to such a mere force of nature would be hard to justify.

The ambivalence focused in Ammoun's "drive" and similar formulations resembles that found in other ambiguous expressions in the discourse of self-determination, some of which I have discussed above. The recurrence of such expressions stems from the peculiar position of self-determination as a concept bridging traditional legal contradictions and providing an arena for their deployment. Each such expression plays a specific role in its own domain. In the substantive area, such an expression directs us to rethink the classical opposition between an activist and a deferential judicial attitude toward the "facts" in a case.

In contrast with the justification of legal competence over the matter, discussions of the *application* of the right of self-determination in a particular case often seem to adopt a deferential attitude to the political forces at work. Such an attitude would appear to call for law, its competence justified, to become a simple instrument for enabling legitimate claims of self-determination to acquire the stamp of international legal approval, claims whose legitimacy and limits derive from non-legal sources.

A consistent adoption of such a deferential attitude, however, is impossible in practice for reasons essential to the idea of a right to self-determination. In discussing such a claim, law is engaged in the task of

---

[129]For similar quasi-naturalistic formulations, compare the views of Redslob that a nation has a "tendance naturelle à se constituer en état" and of Grotius, who believed that secession was justified when founded on a "nécessité vitale." BROSSARD, *supra* note 111, at 74-75.

according rights to those who lack the indicia of right-holders. Law thus always acts in a creative capacity, aiding in the birth of a new sovereign power. A situation raising an issue of self-determination is inherently uncertain, containing elements pointing towards different possible conclusions.

2. The *Namibia* and *Western Sahara* Cases

In the 1971 *Namibia* case and the 1975 *Western Sahara* case, the I.C.J. explicitly recognized the principle of self-determination as part of international law. These cases raised, among other things, issues concerning the "self" similar to those I have discussed above. In his separate opinions filed in those cases, Judge Ammoun treated these issues at great length, a treatment highlighting the creative quality of international legal argument.

In the *Namibia* case, the Court was asked by the Security Council for an advisory opinion concerning South Africa's occupation of Namibia in the face of resolutions by the U.N. revoking its League of Nations Mandate and declaring illegal its continued occupation of the territory.[130] This question depended on a prior inquiry into the propriety of those U.N. actions, specifically on whether the U.N. had the power to revoke South Africa's League of Nations Mandate and whether it had grounds for revocation. The Court's discussion of self-determination came in its interpretation of the nature of the Mandate, particularly of the concept of the "sacred trust" bestowed upon the Mandatory Power.[131] The Court's interpretation of the "sacred trust" in light of the principle of self-determination contributed to its holding that the Mandate over Namibia was revocable in the face of a material breach.

The Court agreed with the U.N. that such a material breach had occurred, *inter alia*, because of South Africa's policy of *apartheid*.[132] The Court rejected South Africa's contention that it should consider South Africa's motives for applying that policy. The Court held that, regardless of motivation, *apartheid* constituted a violation of South Africa's duties

---

[130]S.C. Res. 284, 25 U.N. SCOR (1550th mtg.) at 16, U.N. Doc. S/9892 (1970). The General Assembly had declared, in G.A. Res. 2145, 21 U.N. GAOR Supp. (No. 16) at 2, U.N. Doc. A/6316 (1966), that South Africa had conducted its administration of Namibia in violation of its obligations under the Mandate, the U.N. Charter and the Universal Declaration of Human Rights; the General Assembly, accordingly, terminated the Mandate. The Security Council reaffirmed this position in a series of its own resolutions, culminating in S.C. Res. 276, 25 U.N. SCOR (1529th mtg.) at 17, U.N. Doc. S/9620 (1970), to which S.C. Res. 284 specifically refers.

[131]*Namibia*, (sep. op. Ammoun). 1971 I.C.J. at 31-32.

[132]*Id.* at 56-57

under the Mandate, as well as its obligations under the U.N. Charter to "observe and respect, in a territory having an international status, human rights and fundamental freedoms for all without distinction of race."[133]

Judge Ammoun chided the Court for not going far enough in drawing the implications for international law of the principle of self-determination.[134] In his treatment of the substantive issues in the case, Ammoun's opinion asserts that the denial of the Namibian people's right to self-determination was among the key breaches of the Mandate by South Africa, whereas the Court had only discussed the general principle of racial equality.[135] For Ammoun, therefore, this case provided the opportunity for applying the principle of self-determination to a concrete case involving a dispute about "selfhood," a matter untouched by the Court.

South Africa had, in effect, presented the rather perverse argument that *apartheid* was a means to self-determination for the various subgroups inhabiting Namibia. South Africa contended that

> . . . natives in the south-west of Africa had never formed a people, and that, because of the ethnic and sociological differences which divide them and set them against each other, only the policy of separate development based upon their tribal institutions could ensure their social well-being and progress.[136]

South Africa's argument was a selective valorization of possible objective indicia of peoplehood. It rejected the idea that the mere presence in a territorially unified area can serve to form groups into a unified "people," claiming that such co-presence is merely an historical accident and has no legal significance. Rather, South Africa claimed that objective "ethnic and sociological differences" are essential attributes of the groups concerned and should govern the determination of the pertinent "selves."[137] One might summarize South Africa's position as a view of history as accidental and of sociology as essential.

In response, Judge Ammoun made several historical observations. He rejected the idea that a plurality of ethnic groups precluded the existence of a unified people by pointing to the many nations who have been composed of heterogeneous groups.[138] He extensively reviewed the history of the ancient African state system.[139] This review showed that Africa was historically structured by political organization, rather than by the merely contingent co-presence of diverse ethnic groups on neighboring lands.

---

[133] *Id.* at 57.

[134] *Id.* at 67.

[135] *Id.* at 81.

[136] *Id.* at 85.

[137] *Id.*

[138] *Id.*

[139] *Id.* at 86-87.

Perhaps most intriguingly, he noted that the Namibian people "had, before the days of the colonial regime, taken part in the making of great empires."[140]

These arguments express a complex blend of subjective and objective conceptions. Ammoun's description of the political activity characterizing African history appears at first to represent a subjective conception, rooted in the aspirations and struggles of the people. This "subjective" political activity gives unity to nations composed of objectively diverse ethnic or cultural groups. Yet, Ammoun's narrative also meets the South African argument on its own, objective terms. Ammoun is attempting to show that an analysis based on the objective historical background suffices to refute any claim based on putative "sociological differences."

This combination of subjective and objective factors is made possible by a differential treatment of distinct historical periods. The political activity valorized by Ammoun occurred in the ancient past. Thus, although references to such activity are a hallmark of a subjective approach, the place of the political events in a semi-sacred past enables them to be considered as part of the objective characteristics of the Namibian people.

This special use of history is highlighted by Ammoun's positive reference to the "making of great empires" as a political act showing the dignity of the Namibian people's objective, historical existence.[141] This reference is somewhat paradoxical because of the strong *anti*-imperialist tenor of Ammoun's text — a text rooted in the denunciation of the "plague" of European colonialism.[142] Ammoun's historical perspective, thus, is a textured one. History, including historical conquest, is alternatively revered as sacred myth and denounced as profane violence.

For Ammoun, there is an ancient political history which may become enshrined in the objective qualities of a people; there is also a relatively modern history whose effects on the unity of nations are to be viewed as contingent disruptions of the essence of those nations. In the first period of history, empire-building has the dignity of the unified activity of an ancient people; in the second period, empire-building is a "plague" rather than a human activity. Apparently objective "sociological differences" are to be attributed to the deleterious effects of that "plague."

The "plague" of colonial conquest serves as the occasion for the appropriate intervention of the international law of self-determination. This "plague" marks the dividing line between the history to which law must defer and the history which it must critically evaluate for the distorting effects of illegitimate domination. The "plague" of colonialism gives rise to the need for an international law of self-determination, a law

[140] *Id.* at 85.
[141] *Id.* at 86.
[142] *Id.*

whose goal would be to restore the world to its true history, free from the distorting effects of colonialism.

The 1975 *Western Sahara* case also confronted the I.C.J. with many of the central issues of the law of self-determination. Spain, which had ruled the Western Sahara since the late nineteenth century, had agreed to hold a referendum to determine the wishes of the people for the future of the territory.[143] Morocco and Mauritania each claimed sovereignty over part of the Western Sahara, claims that together encompassed the entire territory.[144] These two states based their claims on legal ties that existed at the time of colonization between the Western Sahara and Morocco and the "Mauritanian entity," a nonstate predecessor to Mauritania.[145] The U.N. General Assembly asked the I.C.J. for an advisory opinion on the legal status of the Western Sahara at the time of colonization and urged Spain to postpone the referendum until the Court's decision.[146]

The legal arguments between Spain and the two African states turned on the relationship between the two cardinal principles of G.A. Res. 1514: self-determination and territorial integrity. One can see the argument of Morocco and Mauritania as a claim for the indissociability of the two principles in the idea of decolonization. Self-determination, in this context, would mean restoring the territorial integrity of a state rent by colonial conquest.[147] Spain, on the other hand, maintained that the imminent holding of a referendum, in accordance with the self-determination principle of Resolution 1514, rendered the U.N.'s historical questions irrelevant.[148] In addition to this disagreement about the historical meaning of self-determination, the dispute also raised the underlying conceptual issue concerning the "self." For Morocco and Mauritania, a decision about the

---

[143]*See* G.A. Res. 3292, 29 U.N. GAOR Supp. (No. 31) at 353, para. 3 U.N. Doc. A/9631 (1974); *Western Sahara*, 1975 I.C.J. 12, 29; *see also* Judge Ammoun's comments on Spain's motives, 1975 I.C.J. at 100-01 (sep. op. Ammoun).

[144]1975 I.C.J. at 66.

[145]*Id.* at 26-27.

[146]*See* G.A. Res. 3292 *supra* note 143. The General Assembly asked the Court for an advisory opinion on two questions: "I. Was Western Sahara . . . at the time of colonization by Spain a [*terra nullius*]?" and, if not, "II. What were the legal ties between this territory and the Kingdom of Morocco and the Mauritanian entity?" *Id.* As the Court decided the former question unanimously in the negative, *see* 1975 I.C.J. at 68-9, I focus on the answers to the latter issue.

[147]1975 I.C.J. at 29-30. In his separate opinion, Judge Petrén elaborated the concept of a "law of decolonization" which would balance the principles of self-determination and territorial integrity. *See id.* at 110 (sep. op. Petren). This conception should be viewed as analytically distinct from a view of the two principles as embodying a unitary idea of self-determination.

[148]*Id.* at 29.

pertinence and form of the subjective method of holding a referendum must be informed by a prior objective analysis of the historical facts.[149]

The Court agreed with Morocco and Mauritania that the historical issues were not moot because of the "measure of discretion" afforded the General Assembly in the decolonization process.[150] The Court reasoned that the historical analysis could have an effect on the eventual procedures adopted for decolonization, though it declined to specify its view of the nature of such an effect.[151] In its general discussion of self-determination, though, the Court had noted that "special circumstances" could render unnecessary an actual consultation with the population in question.[152]

On the substantive issue, the Court held that no ties of sovereignty existed between the Western Sahara and either Morocco or the Mauritanian entity at the time of colonization, although both had other "legal ties" to the territory or its population.[153] The Court stressed that the "legal ties" of Morocco and the Mauritanian entity "overlapped", indicating the "difficulty of disentangling the various relationships existing in the Western Sahara region at the time of colonization by Spain."[154] The Court concluded, therefore, that the ties between the Western Sahara and the other states should not affect the implementation of the principle of self-determination "through the genuine and free expression of the will of the peoples of the Western Sahara."[155]

The Court's opinion is thus based on principles similar to those I discussed in relation to the *Aaland Islands* opinion and McNair's *South West Africa* opinion. The Court views the principle of self-determination as fully applicable because the situation in the Western Sahara at the time of colonization was entangled from a legal point of view, beset by overlapping claims falling below the factual or legal criteria of sovereignty. This ambiguous historical situation, frozen by colonization, calls for the implementation of self-determination principles, discretion over which is left to the General Assembly.

---

[149] *Id.*

[150] *Id.* at 36.

[151] *Id.* at 37.

[152] *Id.* at 33. Two judges who filed separate opinions were less reticent. Judge Ammoun declared that consultation was unnecessary in the context of a "legitimate struggle for liberation from domination." *Id.* at 99 (sep. op. Ammoun). Judge Singh stated that the holding of a referendum, which he appeared virtually to identify with the principle of self-determination, could be dispensed with only if the result would be a foregone conclusion or in the presence of some other "special feature" of the case. *Id.* at 81 (decl. Singh).

[153] *Id.* at 48-49, 63-64.

[154] *Id.* at 67.

[155] *Id.* at 68.

Judge Ammoun filed a separate opinion to object to the minimization by the Court of the legal ties between Morocco and the Western Sahara. In writing this opinion, Ammoun further elaborated upon the method of analysis for identifying the "self" in the context of decolonization that he employed in the *Namibia* case. This method consists of structuring conflicting arguments through reference to a disrupted history.

In supporting Morocco's claims over the disputed territory of Western Sahara, Ammoun cites both subjective and objective arguments. On the one hand, he refers "above all to the common aspirations which have ultimately constituted the ties which as a matter of law link the elements of one and the same nation."[156] On the other hand, he taxes the majority opinion with "disregard[ing] the notion of territory."[157]

Ammoun, however, is confronted with certain disturbing manifestations of cultural independence and separatist struggle among the inhabitants of the Western Sahara. These phenomena directly cast doubt on Ammoun's subjective argument; they also call into question the territorial argument — is the contiguity of the Western Sahara and Morocco a sign of national unity or of mere accidental location? Ammoun responds with an argument quite similar to his refutation of the South African position in the *Namibia* case:

> [T]he colonizers sought to win over the colonized peoples to their own civilization, in order to bind them more closely to themselves. . . . If this is indeed the explanation for the origin of a certain autonomous way of life on the part of the tribal populations in Western Sahara, one can similarly suppose that the present separatist tendencies . . . are also the result of a foreign presence.[158]

In contrast with his description of the distortions created by *this* "foreign presence," Ammoun declares authentic and legally binding the ties between Morocco and Western Sahara, ties created through pre-colonial, intra-African military conquests.[159] Once again, certain phases of history are valorized as authentic parts of the national heritage, others as mutations caused by a foreign, specifically a European, invader.

Ammoun restates in this opinion that legal documents — the writings of "jurists, statesmen, constitutions and declarations, and the United Nations Charter — have merely recognized and solemnly proclaimed" the right to self-determination whose sources lie in the struggles of the peoples concerned.[160] Yet, this pronouncement must be viewed in light of Ammoun's actual work in the opinion, his marshalling of an array of theo-

---

[156] 1975 I.C.J. at 85.
[157] *Id.* at 101.
[158] *Id.* at 84.
[159] *Id.* at 96.
[160] *Id.* at 100.

retical and historical arguments to support the ties between Morocco and the Western Sahara. Ammoun devotes much of the opinion to describing the historical legal ties between Morocco and Western Sahara, legal ties taking the form both of domestic legal control of Western Sahara *and* of international legal recognition of those ties. Thus, law, far from "merely recognizing and proclaiming" that which was established in extra-legal political struggles, is viewed as implicated in the history underlying those struggles.

Judge Ammoun's opinions exemplify the creative quality of the legal analysis of self-determination, while appearing merely to defer to the peoples at stake. This dual quality is no mere logical inconsistency; rather, it expresses the dual character of legal authority over claims of self-determination, bypassing sovereignty in the name of sovereignty. Ammoun's critical factual investigations can only be undertaken through marshalling the entire array of argumentative stratagems developed in the discourse of self-determination. Like the Jurists' discussion of legal competence in the *Aaland Islands* opinion, these investigations are justified and guided by the idea of a disruption of the normal legal order, an order in which abstract conceptual pairs are viewed as complementary rather than as standing in seemingly irreconcilable opposition.

In the two cases discussed above, Judge Ammoun deploys the various seemingly contradictory argumentative moves to produce a cogent argument for a well-defined and limited legal doctrine of the "self." One may surely disagree with the *content* of any or all of Ammoun's historical or ideological presuppositions. Nonetheless, the method and structure of his argument are informed by the legacy of over a half-century of self-determination jurisprudence.

Ammoun elaborates a particular concept of a disrupted history as the fulcrum of his argument. This concept of a disrupted history functions, on the level of the substantive issue of the "self," in an analogous fashion to the "transitions" between law and fact, those turbulent moments of the dissolution of sovereignty, found on the level of the issue of competence. In both domains, self-determination is linked essentially with an extraordinary role for law in the face of temporary anomalies — although those anomalous periods may consist of entire historical eras.

For Ammoun, colonial conquest destroys the possibility of relying, for a true account of the identity of the population, on either the legal sovereign or the positive facts — including, at times, the empirical consciousness of the people. Accordingly, international law can intervene critically, rejecting, when necessary, the ostensible claims of the people and the sovereign. Colonization inaugurates a hiatus, a disruption of national history; the law of self-determination intervenes to restore the situation to a point at which an authentic history can again be possible.

On the level of competence, the *Aaland Islands* Jurists carved out a role for an extraordinary international law justified and shaped by the disruption of law and sovereignty. On the level of substance, Ammoun's legal analysis intervenes to critically evaluate national identity, an evaluation legitimized and formed by the disruption of the normal unity of the subjective and objective elements of that identity. The cause of that disruption — for Ammoun, colonialism — creates the need for legal analysis and guides its course. Ammoun evaluates the seeming opposition of the subjective and objective elements of national identity by linking that opposition to the colonial disruption of history. The right to self-determination is the right to overcome that disruption.

Thus, the particular form of self-determination — for Ammoun, decolonization — does not simply derive from a political decision, external to law, to limit an abstract right to certain groups and not others. Nor is the gaining of "access" to this extraordinary legal analysis merely a process by which political life furnishes law with cases for adjudication, an adjudication which would remain unaffected by that process. Rather, the very form and rationale of the legal argument emerges from the recognition of a particular, extraordinary historical dislocation. The gaining of "access" depends on the construction of an argument interpreting a particular historical situation as an extraordinary dislocation of national identity; this historically specific interpretation of the situation *as* such a dislocation will then guide the nature of the remedy proposed. Situated between the opposed subjective and objective elements of national identity, law weaves its argument by reconstituting their unity with reference to that dislocation.

Viewing self-determination as a form of argument, we see that the substance, as well as the occasion, of this legal intervention is guided by the particular nature of the historical disruption. Thus the "people" does not simply exist in brute positivity, waiting to be discovered by law. Rather, the way in which the disrupted elements will be united depends on the dynamics of the particular legal discourse. The recognition of a particular "people" is an effect of a particular form of discursive reconstruction. The "self" of self-determination emerges through the particular textual dynamics of subjective and objective conceptions, dynamics guided by the particular type of disruption giving rise to their conflict. No less than the legal competence over self-determination, the "self" is a form of argument.

IV. Conclusion

The discourse of self-determination, both in its discussion of the nature of its distinctive legal competence and of the "selves" of which it treaties, serves an essentially exceptional conceptual role in international law. In adjudicating the legal rights of extralegal entities to attain legal status, this discourse asserts that a dislocation has arisen in the legal order.

This dislocation consists of a dual rupture in the functional complementarity of law and sovereignty, posing a challenge of both a normative and factual character. On the one hand, those who should have attained legal status have remained outside law's purview: the positive legal community fails to correspond to the community as it ought to be. On the other hand factual events have rendered it impossible to look to sovereign control for dispositive guidance. This dual challenge is evoked in a series of paradoxical formulations in discussions of the origin of legal competence over claims to self-determination.

With the idea of a legal right to self-determination, law asserts that it is competent to remedy this dislocation by temporarily reaching beyond its ordinary limits. This extension of law's boundaries is justified by the disruption of the complementarity of sovereign and legal authority. For both the Jurists of *Aaland Islands* and for Judge Ammoun, this disruption occurs through the impossibility for law to rely on the existing sovereign control for dispositive guidance.

In the *Aaland Islands* opinion, this dual impossibility resulted from the factual overwhelming of sovereign control and, hence, of normal law, by extraordinary political events. These events render the situation "obscure and uncertain" from a legal as well as a factual perspective, a situation in which factual and legal components are confused, are in a state of "transition" from one to the other. In Ammoun's opinions, law can no longer trust in positive sovereign control because colonialism has caused a great divide in history, ushering in a period in which the factual situation has lost its normative authority for legal analysis. The "obscurity and uncertainty" of this period derives from the "plague" of colonialism, a factual event with a peculiar normative power to disrupt history.

For both conceptions, law must confront an anomalous situation involving inchoate claims over population and territory. On a conceptual level, this situation results from the rupture between ideas that are normally complementary: the positive and the normative elements of legal authority, the subjective and objective components of national identity. This rupture cannot be mended simply by siding with one element or the other: the goal is a restoration of their harmony.

The legal discourse of self-determination, therefore, can never consist in a mechanical application of the pertinent categories. Rather, it is essentially a form of argument: the weaving together of opposed conceptions through textual composition. Each conception is set in a critical relationship to the other, the whole ordered by the particular manner in which the idea of disruption is deployed.

The characterization of self-determination as an anomalous doctrine varies with the particular writer: Ammoun's modern opinions accord self-determination a role in positive international law inconceivable to the Jurists. Nonetheless, for Ammoun, no less than for the Jurists, the idea of a right of groups to attain the status of right-holders must always embody the notion of an aberrant dislocation in the legal order. This dislocation provides a broad field for legal analysis, although the goal remains to achieve the constriction of that field. The work of remedying an episodic dislocation such as that of the status of the Aaland Islands may require a less stable right than when the dislocation is viewed as that accomplished by hundreds of years of colonialism. The juridic method, however, is the same: allowing the extraordinary competition of opposed conceptions, a competition occasioned and structured by a particular concept of historical disruption and aimed at the reconstitution of an unreflective harmony in a restored legal order.

I have elaborated some of the ways in which the discourse of self-determination has acquired a conceptual and historical legacy of particular resources of argumentation. The advocacy of a particular form of self-determination requires the production of complex legal texts which appropriate and rework that legacy. The terms of the debates become woven into a fabric of argument whose dynamics depend on the writer's particular conception of historical disruption. From these textual dynamics emerge both the "law" and the "self" of self-determination. Neither juridical absurdity nor sacred cornerstone, the right to self-determination has evolved into a textured form of argument, a particular logical and rhetorical practice. The moment in which sovereignty reposes in abeyance is the moment of opportunity for forms of legal creativity, forms whose full potential we perhaps cannot yet fully anticipate.

[10]

COMMENT/BOOK REVIEW

An Understanding of the Relationship Between International Legal Discourse and Third World Countries

Surakiart Sathirathai*

The perceptions of Third World analysts and actors about international law center on the role of law in resolving international economic and political disputes. Since specific issues in such disputes arise in a variety of legal materials—e.g., resolutions of the United Nations and its specialized agencies—it is difficult to analyze Third World perceptions through any one particular document. However, because Judge T.O. Elias is recognized as a leading scholar on international legal thought in the Third World, his most recent book *The International Court of Justice and Some Contemporary Problems*[1] is an appropriate starting point. The book focuses on the practices of the International Court of Justice (ICJ) and the role of law as they affect developing states. In addition, the book describes present Third World legal thought and its possible future trends. Finally, Elias' arguments are fine examples of typical liberal legal discourse. To bring about a just and acceptable scheme of international participation it is important to critically analyze such liberal legal discourse.

I. THIRD WORLD LEGAL THINKING AND DISCOURSE.

The International Court of Justice and Some Contemporary Problems discusses a variety of issues facing Third World states from a liberal

---

* S.J.D. candidate, Harvard Law School; LL.M., Harvard Law School; M.A.L.D., Fletcher School of Law and Diplomacy; LL.B., Chulalongkorn Law School, Thailand. Part of the analysis in this Comment was inspired by the work of Professor David Kennedy of Harvard Law School. Comments from Professor Oscar Schachter of Columbia Law School, who provided particularly insightful criticisms from a liberal viewpoint, also proved of great benefit. Finally, the author wishes to express his gratitude to Professor David Kennedy and Professor Daniel K. Tarullo of Harvard Law School for their extensive critical comments on earlier drafts of this essay. Of course, any errors are to be attributed to the author.

1. T.O. ELIAS, THE INTERNATIONAL COURT OF JUSTICE AND SOME CONTEMPORARY PROBLEMS (1983). T.O. Elias is Judge and President of the International Court of Justice (ICJ). He has been a Justice on the ICJ since 1976. He served as Vice-President of the ICJ from 1979 to 1982 and as Acting President in 1982.

legal[2] point of view.[3] Judge Elias' liberal thought permeates that discussion in three distinct areas. The first area is the importance of international law for Third World countries. The second area centers on the connection between state sovereignty and state participation as they affect both the development of international law and discourse about it. And, in the third area, Judge Elias suggests that the ICJ is the proper medium for the just and acceptable participation of the Third World in the international order.

In discussing the importance of international law for Third World countries, Judge Elias focuses both on those practices of the ICJ which insure the just participation of states in the international system and on the impact of current legal thinking on economic and development issues. As to the former, of particular concern for the role of the ICJ (parts I and V of the book) are the issues of jurisdiction, the non-appearing respondent, provisional measures, the right of intervention in a case before the ICJ, the doctrine of intertemporal law, and the ICJ's particular role *vis-à-vis* the African states. With regard to economic and development issues (parts II, III, and IV), Elias portrays the shift from political to economic concerns in international relations. To demonstrate this shift, he considers recent changes in the concepts of sovereign immunity and commercial transactions, and the work of international institutions in legal, social and economic fields. Further, Elias emphasizes the "right to development" as the important link between the New International Economic Order (NIEO) and human rights.

The concepts of state sovereignty and state participation in international activities underlie Elias' choice of topics and his discussion of

2. For a definition of liberalism as a conception which offers a total world view that delimits our ideas about society and about the possible ways to revise our thinking, *see generally* R. UNGER, KNOWLEDGE AND POLITICS (1975). *See also* Robert Gordon's statement in *New Developments in Legal Theory*: ". . . [L]iberal legalism . . . [is a belief structure] that abstracts particular relationships between real people . . . into relations between entirely abstract categories of "individuals" playing the abstract social roles of "owner", "employee", etc." in THE POLITICS OF LAW: A PROGRESSIVE CRITIQUE 288 (D. Kairys ed. 1982).

3. Article 38(1)(d) of the Statute of the International Court of Justice includes opinions of distinguished legal scholars as one of the sources of international law upon which the Court should base its decision. It reads:

> 1. The Court, whose function is to decide in accordance with international law such disputes as are submitted to it shall apply:
>
> d) subject to the provisions of Article 59, judicial decisions and teachings of the most highly qualified publicists of the various nations, as subsidiary means for the determination of rules of law.

Statute of the International Court of Justice, 1970 YEARBOOK OF THE UNITED NATIONS 1013. The Statute entered into force on October 24, 1945.

Therefore, Judge Elias' discussion will significantly contribute to the study of the future of international legal system.

legal principles.[4] Elias explicitly recognizes the relationship between legal principles and the concepts of sovereignty and participation when he states that:

> The realisation of the new international economic order is an essential element for the effective promotion of human rights and fundamental freedoms . . . . The resolution emphasized that it is of paramount importance for the promotion of human rights and fundamental freedoms that *member States undertake specific obligations through accession to, or ratification of international instruments in this field*. [i.e. sovereign cooperation and participation concepts] . . . . Finally, the resolution insists that the experience and *contribution of the developed and developing countries* should be taken into account by all organs of the United Nations System, in their work related to human rights and fundamental freedoms.[5] (emphasis added)

The formulation of legal frameworks and mechanisms to compliment the concepts of state participation and state sovreignty greatly concerns the Third World. For example, issues such as the Court's jurisdiction in the case, the non-appearance of parties, and the right of intervention all focus on the question of whether states should be permitted to defend their rights on the international plane. The right of access to international fora is in turn a question of state participation, yet the right of access is also grounded in the concept of state sovereignty. But any decision involving such issues as jurisdiction, non-appearance, etc., is based on the choice between the sovereign authority of an institution (such as the ICJ) and the equality of states (sovereign cooperation) coming before that institution. Similarly, state involvement in economic and social activities (part II), the NIEO's role (part III), and human rights (part IV) also present the tension between authority and cooperation.

Third, Elias' discussion reflects his opinion that recent developments in international law will serve the interests of the Third World (and

4. For example, in discussing the right to intervention in a case before the ICJ, Judge Elias argues that requiring the Court to determine jurisdiction initially might hamper the development of international law, because states would be likely to abstain from coming to the ICJ. T. ELIAS, *supra* note 1, at 92. He also notes that requiring compulsory jurisdiction might ". . . encourage wider participation in international judicial activities generally." *Id.* Further, in part V (the ICJ and Africa) Judge Elias indicates that deciding which states have standing to press claims before the ICJ affects participation on the international plane. *Id.* at 341–350. Another example appears when Judge Elias suggests that the United Nations and its specialized agencies help to shape the economic order, by having states participate more equally. *Id.* at chs. 11,12. Finally, he also points out the importance of regional cooperation and institutions for human rights and economic development. *Id.* at ch. 13.

5. *Id.* at 250.

the interests of the international community generally).[6] For example, he states: "In the author's view, experience has shown that *the application of methods of general legal theory, of legal history and of comparative law* permits us to be optimistic that the *lawyer will play an important role* in the evolution of the new international economic order."[7] (Emphasis added.) With regard to the evolving role of the ICJ, Elias states:

> . . . [t]he Court has shown a growing awareness of the General Assembly resolutions 171(II) of 14 November 1947 and 3232 (XXIX) of 12 November 1974, the one calling upon the Court to apply the resolutions and other relevant determinations of the Assembly in their Judgments and the other to attempt as far as possible in their Judgments principles of progressive development of international law.[8]

However, such liberal legal discourse lacks a significant analysis of the structural conflicts between legal doctrines and concepts, and of the relationship of these doctrines and concepts to the current development of international law. In ignoring such structural analysis, one can too easily draw connections between state participation and international harmony and community,[9] and the role and the desired development of law. The liberal legal approach misunderstands the relationship between law and what happens in reality, and thereby undermines the effort to achieve acceptable and just state participation in a more cohesive international community. Structural analysis, though, offers a way of achieving such a state of affairs by reimagining the relationship between law and what happens in reality.

Accordingly, this Comment will analyze the sets of doctrinal and

6. Judge Elias explicitly states his concern about the ICJ's role. For example, he comments that the decision in Aegean Sea Continental Shelf (Greece v. Turk.), 1976 I.C.J. 3 (Interim Protection Order of Sept. 11) may make both applicant and non-appearing respondents hesitatant to come to the ICJ to resolve disputes. *Id.* at 60. Such hesitation might hamper the ICJ's ability to solve international problems. Also, Elias argues that states should not view the exercise of the right to intervention as an unfriendly gesture: "So intermingled have the economic, technological and geographical interests of States become today that they must expect the possibility that their bilateral disputes might impinge upon the interests of a third State . . . ." *Id.* at 92. He views the ICJ as an impartial entity. *See also Id.* at 50–51, 60–61, 66, 70, 76, 105, 110, 113–15, and 117–18.

7. *Id.* at 236.

8. *Id.* at 10. Elias also quotes Justice Jessup: "The attempt is made here to stress the importance of the International Court of Justice as a developer or clarifier of rules of international law whether the rules be found in intenational conventions or in the more elusive customary law[.]" *Id.*

9. The notion of international community and harmony relies on an image of fraternity in international relations. Such a notion connotes a state of affairs that is charectarized by toleration and mutual acceptance and understanding, and not by antagonism or bitter strife. That notion, however, is distinctly not neo-realist.

conceptual conflicts[10] that the legal liberal overlooks.[11] The first step is to develop the two sets of doctrinal conflicts, and to reveal the unsuccessful liberal attempt to mediate those conflicts in order to justify other legal and political objectives. Examples will aim at the structural connection between ICJ practice and the international law of development. The next step is to bring out the indeterminacy of the meanings of the two *concepts of sovereignty*, i.e. sovereign authority and cooperation. That indeterminacy shows that the way liberals mediate the doctrinal conflicts consists of simply choosing one meaning of sovereignty or the other to arrive at a workable discourse about the just participation of states. After bringing out the relationships between the two sets of doctrinal conflicts and the concepts of sovereignty and participation, this Comment will point out the emptiness of the *concept of participation* and its domination by politics, human interests, and human desires—a domination which legal discussion tries very hard to conceal.

Only a structural analysis allows a real understanding of states' legal and economic relations. Such an understanding is the foundation for a reconstructed vision of the role of law and the relationships among states. A reconstructed vision would accomodate diverse political perspectives and human interests and would help to develop a way of thinking about international relations that is more congenial to all states.

II. STRUCTURAL ANALYSIS OF THIRD WORLD LEGAL THINKING AND DISCOURSE.

A. *Doctrinal Conflict and Mediating Techniques.*

1. Politics and Law in Conflict, and the Failure of Legal Measures to Mediate that Conflict: Substance and Procedure.

The two areas of law discussed in Elias' book—practices of the ICJ and the international law of development—have an underlying struc-

10. The term "doctrinal conflicts" refers to conflicts of law and politics and conflicts of rights and duties. The term "conceptual conflicts" refers to conflicts involving the meaning of sovereignty.

11. The following literature is the basis of the analysis in this Comment: Unger, *The Critical Legal Studies Movement*, 96 HARV. L. REV. 563 (1983); Kennedy, *Theses About International Law Discourse*, 23 GERMAN Y.B. INT'L L. 353 (1980); Kennedy, Book Review, 21 HARV. INT'L L.J. 301 (1980); Kennedy, International Legal Structures (unpublished manuscript, available at the Harvard Law School library); Kennedy, *The Structure of Blackstone's Commentaries*, 38 BUFFALO L. REV. 209 (1980); THE POLITICS OF LAW: A PROGRESSIVE CRITIQUE 11–64, 281–293 (D. Kairys ed. 1982); R. GEUSS, THE IDEA OF A CRITICAL THEORY (1980); R.M. UNGER, KNOWLEDGE AND POLITICS (1975).

tural connection. In both areas of law, Elias distinguishes law from politics.[12] The ICJ itself employs that distinction. For example, the ICJ often uses procedure and discretionary powers to label certain issues or cases either as 'law' or as 'politics'. The ICJ feels obligated to deal only with legal disputes. However, the distinction between political and legal questions is unclear.

The *Nuclear Tests* cases[13] demonstrate the inseparable nature of law and politics. After the ICJ accepted a French unilateral declaration as legally binding to limit future French nuclear testing, the ICJ found no need to provide further remedies that would insure France's compliance with its own declaration. It reasoned that: "Whilst it had found that a State had entered into a commitment concerning its future conduct, it is not the ICJ's function to contemplate that it will not comply with it."[14] Implicitly, the ICJ regarded France's future conduct as a political issue, and the legally binding nature of the French declaration as a legal issue. The ICJ separated out the legal issue and argued that it would not make the political determination that France would break its promises (i.e. it would not make a subjective prediction about France's future conduct). The ICJ decided to label that determination political because it wished to protect France's sovereign authority. Consequently, it managed to police the boundary of France's sovereign authority, while giving to Australia—the state for whose benefit the declaration was made—a duty to respect France's promises (sovereign cooperation). The ICJ essentially avoided a difficult substantive issue by proceduralizing it. Since the ICJ was unsure of the exact criteria for distinguishing law from politics, it employed the procedural side of the law (discretionary power) to avoid discussing substantive issues.

---

12. *See* T. ELIAS, *supra* note 1, at 26–28, 55–57. Politics in this context refers to subjective choice, not decision by rules and/or the area of free reign left to states by virtue of their sovereignty.

13. Nuclear Tests (Austl. v. Fr.), 1974 I.C.J. 253 (Judgment of Dec. 20); Nuclear Tests (N.Z. v. Fr.) 1974 I.C.J. 457 (Judgment of Dec. 20). *See* T. ELIAS, *supra* note 1, at 52–57, 100–18.

Australia and New Zealand each brought an application before the Court instituting proceedings against France for holding atmospheric nuclear tests over the Pacific Ocean. The French government stated that the Court was not competent to hear the case, and that it would not accept the jurisdiction of the Court. Australia and New Zealand requested the Court to grant the interim protection measures (article 41 of the Statute of the Court). The Court subsequently granted such interim measures, which directed France to stop carrying out any further tests in the Pacific pending a final decision. Yet France still carried out nuclear tests in the interim. Subsequently, the ICJ examined the unilateral statement made by France that it would stop the tests. Over the strong protests of many jurists, the ICJ went on to hold that the statement was legally binding. However, since the only issue before the Court was the termination of such atmospheric tests, and since France undertook to stop the tests by that declaration, there was no longer any dispute for the ICJ to adjudicate.

14. T. ELIAS, *supra* note 1, at 55–56.

Although Elias also strongly criticizes the ICJ's handling of the French declaration, his criticisms replicate the fundamental contradictions between law and politics[15] and between substance and procedure:

> On what must be regarded as a questionable extension of *the principle of customary international law*, the Court made the bold assertion that the maxim *pacta sunt servanda* applied to treaties just as it applies to unilateral declarations. *This looks like judicial law-making* in its *most naked form, as there is no warrant for this proposition* either in jurisprudence, in doctrine, or in judicial or arbitral decisions.[16] (emphasis added)

Elias believes that the French declaration should not be regarded as legally binding according to "the principle of law." He admonishes the ICJ for engaging in politics, but himself relies on political criteria in arguing that such unilateral declarations should not be binding. He states:

> Now, these unilateral declarations could hardly be regarded as binding upon their makers because
>
> (i) France had all along refused to give any undertaking to both complainants, and
>
> (ii) France had not taken any part in the proceedings before the Court nor had it made the statements as part of any undertaking to the Court.[17]

That is a shift from politics to law. Elias mediates (i.e. makes conflicts seem to disappear) the conflict between politics and law by appealing to a strictly legalistic argument. Nonetheless, that legalistic argument relies on France's behaviour as a basis for legal decision—which is a political criterion.[18] Elias constructs a different discourse which shares the same problems as that of the ICJ: his arguments separate law from politics to serve pre-set policy objectives. Judge Elias does not help us to understand the proper role of the ICJ in creating and protecting a scheme of just state participation in an international community. Nor does he enable us to reconstruct a proper vision about the devel-

15. *See* the critique of legal objectivism in Unger, *supra* note 11, at 566–570.

16. T. ELIAS, *supra* note 1, at 105.

17. *Id.* at 105–106.

18. Elias sets out a "principle of law" that serves the goal of protecting France's sovereign authority. To justify this "principle of law" Elias does not formalistically defer to other legal rules, but instead argues that what France does or does not do determines its legal obligation. In other words, Elias does not succeed in arguing strictly from other legal rules. His formulation imports political ideas about the nature of sovereign authority.

opment of law and states' economic and legal relations. Instead, he leads us to a vicious circle where people of different political ideologies mediate conflict and manipulate thinking for their own ends.

Elias' treatment of the ICJ and Africa (chapter 17) further illustrates the foregoing analysis.[19] In the South West Africa (first phase) case,[20] the ICJ granted Ethiopia and Liberia *locus standi* to present their claims, a procedural move. However, in the second phase of the case (1966),[21] the ICJ denied these two African states *locus standi* when it was unsure how to deal effectively with the substantive issues of their case against South Africa. Only in 1970, after criticism from the international community, did the ICJ decide against South Africa substantively. While procedure was used to permit Liberia and Ethiopia to participate in the case, the same procedure later barred them from participation. Similarly the ICJ decided to reach the substantive issues in 1970 where it had previously decided not to do so.[22] The ICJ used the procedural and substantive sides of the law to justify each of two incompatible results.

These cases illustrate that law and politics cannot be separated, and that conflicts between the two can neither be resolved nor mediated through mere application of the procedural side of the law.[23] Further, the fact that procedure and substance can yield contradictory results affecting states' participation[24] demonstrates that any attempt to move from substance to procedure reveals and mirrors the inseparability of law and politics. It also reflects the failure of mediating techniques to yield particular solutions. If this policy of the ICJ is still pursued, it

---

19. *Id.* at ch. 17, pt. V.

20. *South West Africa* (Eth. v. S. Afr.; Lib. v. S. Afr.), 1962 I.C.J. 319 (Judgment of Dec. 20; First Phase). See *infra* note 17.

21. *South West Africa* (Eth. v. S. Afr.; Lib. v. S. Afr.), 1966 I.C.J. 6 (Judgment of July 18; Second Phase). Ethiopia and Liberia, acting in the capacity of states which were members of the former League of Nations, brought this action alleging South African contraventions of the League of Nations Mandate for South West Africa (that mandate required the Mandatory to promote the material and moral well-being and social progress of the inhabitants of the territory). In the first phase of the case, South Africa had objected to the jurisdiction of the ICJ and to the standing of Ethiopia and Liberia to sue. *See supra* note 20. The ICJ held that it had jurisdiction under article 7, which provides that any dispute arising between the Mandatory and another member of the League shall be submitted to the ICJ. Therefore, both states had *locus standi* in presenting the case. In the second phase, however, the ICJ considered similar issues, but it concluded that the states had not established any legal right regarding the subject matter of the present claim (i.e. no standing). The case was dismissed.

22. Legal Consequences for States of the Continued Presence of South Africa in Namibia (South West Africa)—Notwithstanding Security Council Resolution 276, 1971 I.C.J. 16 (Advisory Opinion of June 21).

23. T. ELIAS, *supra* note 1, at 6–8.

24. For example, the use of procedure in the first phase of the *South West Africa* case (1962) could have led to a result desired by the international community. *See supra* note 20. However, the ICJ used substantive norms in 1970 to declare the illegality of the continued presence of South Africa in Namibia.

will create a large loophole in judicial practice, obstructing the ICJ's function of ensuring an acceptable and just participation.[25]

The ICJ has also used law to conceal injustice in political and developmental issues. Judge Elias emphasizes the shift from political to economic concerns in the new international economic order.[26] The NIEO approach presents a body of new legal concepts created to regulate economic activities. Procedural law is the cornerstone of the NIEO framework. The framework contains ideals of cooperation, consultation, nondiscrimination, proclamation of legitimate rights, and so forth,[27] and leaves most of the important substantive issues to be resolved by negotiation or by some kind of bilateral agreement. Similarly, part IV of the General Agreement on Tariffs and Trade (GATT)[28] is a declaration of intention and leaves the resolution of substantive issues outside its framework. The only clear substantive law approach is found in article 2(2)(c) of the Charter of Economic Rights and Duties of States (CERDS). Several questions arise here. First, does this new trend towards procedural law add anything new to economic order? Second, how does this new legal order affect the concept of participation? Finally, is it true that international actors have shifted their focus and concern from politics to purely economic issues? A closer analysis of the Multilateral Trade Negotiations (MTN) agreement on the Generalized System of Preferences (GSP) provides some answers to the above questions.[29]

---

25. *See* U.N. CHARTER, ch. I, art. 1. *See also* ch. IV, art. 9, para. 1; art. 18, para. 1.

26. T. ELIAS, *supra* note 1, at 234–35.

27. See, for example, the Preamble, chapter I and chapter II, articles 3–14, 17–20, etc. of the Charter of the Economic Rights and Duties of States G.A. Res. 3281 (XXIX), 29 U.N. GAOR Supp. (No. 31), U.N. Doc. A/9631 (1974); Declaration on the Establishment of a New International Economic Order, G.A. Res. 3201 (5-VI), U.N. GAOR (6th Special Session), Supp. (No. 1), U.N. Doc. A/9559 (1974); Program of Action on the Establishment of a New International Ecomomic Order, G.A. Res. 3202 (5-VI), U.N. GAOR (6th Special Session), Supp. (No. 1), U.N. Doc. A/9559 (1979); paragraphs 1–3 of the Multinational Trade Negotiation: Differential and More Favourable Treatment, Reciprocity and Fuller Participation of Developing Countries, decision of Nov. 28, 1979, GENERAL AGREEMENT ON TARIFFS AND TRADE, BASIC INSTRUMENTS AND SELECTED DOCUMENTS, 35th Sess., Supp. (No. 26) at 203; The preamble and article 3 of the UNCTAD: Agreement Establishing the Common Fund for Commodities, U.N. Doc. TD/IPC/CONF/L.15 (1980), and Corr. (1980); Resolution on the Permanent Sovereignty Over Natural Resources, G.A. Res. 1803 (XVII), 17 U.N. GAOR Supp. (No. 17), U.N. Doc. A/5217 (1962). The resolution was restated many times under the conference relating to the NIEO. Of the above, perhaps only the Common Fund Agreement spelled out substantial issues. However, the operation of the Fund has been sluggish.

28. Part IV of the GATT concerning trade and development was included in the GATT in 1965. *See* GENERAL AGREEMENT ON TARIFFS AND TRADE, BASIC DOCUMENTS AND SELECTED DOCUMENTS vol. I (1952). Of course, pressure from the LDCs forced special concern and treatment for the Third World with regard to tariffs and trade practices.

29. MTN, *supra* note 27. Paragraph 3 of the MTN states:

> Any differential and more favourable treatment [i.e. preferential tariff treatment] provided under this clause
>
> (a) shall be designed to facilitate and promote the trade of developing countries and not to raise barriers.

Paragraph 7 of the MTN agreement reads:

> The concessions and contributions made and the obligations assumed by developed and less-developed contracting parties under the provisions of the General Agreement [the GATT] *should promote the basic objectives of the Agreement* . . . .
>
> "Less Developed Contracting parties expect that *their capacity to make contributions* to negotiated concessions or take other *mutually agreed action* under the provisions and procedures of the General Agreement *would improve* . . . and they would accordingly expect to *participate more fully* in the *framework of rights and obligations* under the General Agreement.[30] (emphasis added)

The provision was carefully phrased to avoid touching upon any sensitive substantive issues regarding international economic activity. Since the less developed countries (LDCs) favor sovereign cooperation, paragraph 7 stresses cooperation by the developed countries (DCs) to make it acceptable to the LDCs. But paragraph 7, however cloaked in procedural rhetoric, conceals the concept of graduation, which determines when and at what stage a country is an LDC eligible to receive special treatment.[31] Therefore, graduation preserves the sovereign authority of the DCs to determine a country's eligibilty. The political power of the DCs lies somewhere within the procedural language of the provision. The graduation concept disadvantages LDCs because it uses ambiguous criteria to determine when LDCs assume obligations under the principles of the GATT. The fundamental question is whether paragraph 7 protects the Third World from subjective criteria of preferential treatment imposed by the DCs, or whether it protects the DCs' interests by giving them a right to determine which LDCs should be treated specially. Yet the decision to protect the LDCs' rights to preferential treatment is subject to the DCs' discretion. Such discretion is subjective and highly politicized. It consists of a choice between the application of the principle of discrimination or nondiscrimination—a choice which internal and/or external political pressure will influence. Liberal legal discourse surrounding paragraph 7 will therefore fail to mediate the conflict between law and politics.

This corresponds to article 18 of the CERDS which states: "Developed countries should extend, improve and enlarge the system of generalized non-reciprocal and nondiscriminatory tariff preferences to the developing countries . . . ." CERDS, *supra* note 27.

30. *See* MTN, *supra* note 27, para. 7.

31. Lecture by Professor Daniel K. Tarullo of Harvard Law School in his class "International Economic Regulations" (Fall, 1982). The concept is employed by the DCs to determine which LDC has already "graduated" from developing status and has acquired developed status. This decision determines when a particular LDC is no longer eligible to receive preferential treatment. This concept also is applied to the very least-developed countries in the same manner as above. *See also* Frank, *The 'Graduation' Issue for LDCs*, 13 J. WORLD TRADE L. 289–302 (1979).

Further, attempting to shift from political to purely economic concerns does not work. Instead, politics and economics are intertwined, and both sets of concerns influence the law's role in helping to design mechanisms which hide conflicting views and interests. Law only conceals old dilemmas. Therefore, law contributes very little to the new international economic order. Legal discourse is only a tool to mediate the conflict between law and politics. At best, legal discourse provides a framework for arguments about sovereign authority and/or cooperation concepts. Which arguments ultimately succeed depends upon which group of states one intends to influence.

Instead, one might argue that concepts of sovereignty influence lawyers to employ liberal legal discourse to mediate conflicts between law and politics. Such mediation of conflicts in turn enables lawyers to discuss and implement one concept of sovereignty or the other. Thus, concepts of sovereignty themselves would mediate the dilemma presented by the choice between conflicting alternatives. For example, paragraph 7 uses the sovereign cooperation concept to separate law from mere politics, ostensibly by establishing a procedural standard. However, since paragraph 7 fails to separate law from politics, concepts of sovereignty are simply manipulable legal discourse. And, by their nature, concepts of sovereignty do not necessarily benefit any particular group of states.

2. Rights and Duties in Conflict, and the Failure of Measures to Mediate that Conflict: Substance and Procedure.

The procedural nature and aspects of law often justify the separation of rights from correlative duties. But similar structural problems permeate both areas of law covered in Elias' book. For example, the ICJ often faces the conflict between its duty to adjudicate legal issues (in order to solve disputes and promote international harmony) and its right to decide whether it will adjudicate a given case. The following cases exemplify that conflict.

In the *Fisheries Jurisdiction Case*,[32] the *Nuclear Tests Cases*,[33] and the *Aegean Sea Continental Shelf Case*,[34] the ICJ overruled strong objections to its jurisdiction when it considered issues of provisional measures and jurisdiction.[35] In the *Aegean Sea Continental Shelf Case*, it explicitly

32. Fisheries Jurisdiction (U.K. v. Ice.), 1972 I.C.J. 12 (Interim Protection Order of Aug. 17); Fisheries Jurisdiction (U.K. v. Ice.), 1973 I.C.J. 302 (Order of July 12); Fisheries Jurisdiction (Fr. v. Ice.), 1973 I.C.J. 99 (Interim Protection Order of June 22).

33. Nuclear Tests (Austl. v. Fr.), 1973 I.C.J. 99 (Interim Protection Order of June 22); Nuclear Tests (N.Z. v. Fr.), 1973 I.C.J. 313 (Continuance of Interim Protection Order of July 12).

34. *See Aegean Sea Continental Shelf*, *supra* note 6, at 3.

35. "Provisional measures" refers to the ICJ's power to safeguard the rights of parties pending final decision. Article 41(1) of the Statute of the International Court of Justice reads: "1) The

decided that it could and should deal with the requests for interim measures, leaving final determination of jurisdiction until later phases in the cases. In all the cases, the ICJ felt that its duty was to protect the respective rights of the parties, as well as to promote international harmony.[36] Elias fully agrees with this jurisprudential posture of the ICJ:

> To follow the course advocated by those who wanted the issue of jurisdiction settled *in limine litis* would be to go against the grain of the exercise of the Court's normal judicial functions, thus making it possible for a party objecting to the jurisdiction in such a case in effect to veto all proceedings in any dispute brought before the Court, irrespective of the merits or the demerits of the case for either side; *such a course might result in endangering international peace and security, contrary to the United Nations Charter.*[37] (emphasis added)

As a result, in deciding these cases the ICJ ignored the rights of the other parties, which the exercise of the ICJ's procedural power impairs.[38] That procedural power (discretion) enabled the ICJ to rely on a duty (to promote international harmony) argument as the basis for its decision. It is unclear whether the ICJ will use the same reasoning in the future if it decides that, under certain circumstances, granting of the provisional measures will impair peace and security. Significantly, in the *Nuclear Tests* cases,[39] the ICJ exercised its procedural power when it used only a rights argument as a basis for decision. The ICJ avoided discussing the substance of the case (i.e., the validity of French nuclear tests, the legality of the French unilateral declaration, and the consequences of the tests and the declaration). Instead, it focused on the procedural elements of the case deciding that once the declaration was accepted as binding, it could not question the

---

Court shall have the power to indicate, if it considers that circumstances so require, any provisional measures which ought to be taken to preserve the respective rights of either party . . . ." *See supra* note 3.

36. T. ELIAS, *supra* note 1, at 67–83.

37. *Id.* at 76.

38. Elizabeth Mensch in *The History of Mainstream Legal Thought* points out the problem that the ICJ ignores:

> *Moreover, in every dispute, both sides' interests and goals can be asserted and formulated in terms of rights.* In a nuisance case, for example, one party's 'right' to complete security from the other's invasion can be countered by an equally coherent 'right to complete freedom to use property as one chooses.' *Thus, instead of a preexisting right that compels a particular* result, *there are, in fact, conflicting (and contradictory) rights between which the Court must always choose.* It is the legal *choice* which then determines the result and forms the so-called right. (emphasis added)

D. Kairys, *supra* note 2, at 27.

39. *Nuclear Tests*, 1974 I.C.J. 253, *supra* note 13.

future conduct of the state. The ICJ exercised its right to determine that future litigation would affect international relations adversely:

> *The Court therefore sees* no reason to allow the continuance of proceedings which *it knows* are bound to be fruitless. While judicial settlement may *provide a path to international harmony*, in circumstances of conflict, it is nonetheless true that the needless continuance of litigation is an obstacle to such harmony.[40] (emphasis added)

In this case, the ICJ disregarded its duty to protect the interests and safety of the affected parties (Australia and New Zealand). Thus it also disregarded its duty to protect just participation, i.e. international harmony and community.[41] Yet the ICJ often relies on such duties to reach the substantive issues in similar cases.

Whenever right and duty clash, the ICJ separates the two, basing its decision on one without reference to the other. The ICJ's procedural power enables it to make such a choice without the embarrassment of addressing unsolved substantive issues. The ICJ can use either right or duty arguments as bases of decisions to reach the same result. Therefore, right and duty cannot be separated.[42] The use of procedure to hide the subjective choice, once revealed, is no longer convincing. The failure of the legal measures to mediate the conflict between rights and duties partly reveals why the ICJ has not yet effectively promoted just and acceptable participation among states.

Elias makes a very important connection between human rights and the new international economic order when he talks of the "right to development."[43] He cites several General Assembly resolutions, including the Secretary General's Report: ". . . [t]he Concept of development . . . encompasses the realization of the potentialities of the human person in harmony with his community, seeing the human power as the subject and not a mere object of the development process."[44] He agrees and points out some principal concerns regarding

40. *Id.* at 271; T. ELIAS, *supra* note 1, at 55.

41. *See supra* note 25.

42. The relationship between legal rights and duties was first treated analytically by Wesley Hohfeld in his famous article, *Some Fundamental Legal Conceptions as Applied in Judicial Reasoning*, 23 YALE L.J. 16 (1913). Under the Hohfeldian scheme eight basic legal rights are divisible along two lines. First, four distinct legal entitlements (rights, privileges, immunities, powers) are contrasted with four opposites (duties, no-rights, disabilities, liabilities). *Id.* at 30. The opposites merely denote the absence of entitlement. Second, the four entitlements imply correlative concepts involving action or inaction on the part of another party—either the state or a person. Thus, a right implies a correlative duty (a privilege, a no-right, an immunity, a disability; a power, a liability;). *Id.* at 31.

43. T. ELIAS, *supra* note 1, at 238–41.

44. Secretary General's Report, U.N. Doc. E/CN4/1334, *cited in id.* at 240.

the right to development. These concerns include reviewing progress in development, the need for improved coordination of United Nations human rights efforts, and the need to integrate human rights standards into development plans.[45] He concludes that ". . . the right course to pursue in the establishment of the new international economic order, especially as concerns the developing countries, *is to promote economic and social rights pari passu civil and political rights in the fostering of the right to development*."[46] (Emphasis added.)

The notion of a right to development is problematic since it focuses on the existence and enforcement of rights (procedure), but not correlative duties (substance). Mediation of the conflicts between rights and duties through proceduralizing avoids substantive issues which disturb both DCs and LDCs. Yet inevitably both the LDCs and the DCs will raise those disturbing issues. For example, if the DCs guarantee the right to development they will want to know what their rights and the LDCs' corresponding duties are. Likewise, the LDCs will want to know what duties the DCs have assumed, if any at all. The LDCs and DCs will raise questions of duty even if they do not specifically use the language of duty, because rights naturally implicate correlative duties and vice versa.[47] For example, the LDCs' right to development requires a foundation for such a right, i.e., the DCs must have duties to do some things for the LDCs. Conversely, the DCs' rights also require a foundation: the LDCs must acknowledge certain responsibilities. LDCs and DCs have always avoided an open discussion of duties. The fact that rights have correlative duties has not been a main concern under the new idea of international order. DCs and LDCs avoid the language of duty to increase the short-run participation of both groups of states in international activities. Such avoidance works against the LDCs' own self-interest.

The MTN agreement under the GSP shows how procedural language mediates the conflict between those rights and duties which affect the LDCs' interests. Under paragraph 7 of the GSP, the right of the LDCs to preferential treatment does not exist because of the DCs' duty to extend such a right. Instead, the DCs retain the right to determine through the concept of graduation whether or not they will extend preferential treatment. Thus, the DCs' duty to give or the LDCs' right to receive preferential treatment depends on the DCs' right to determine subjectively whether such rights and duties exist. The DCs threaten to control the LDCs' rights through the concept of graduation.

45. *Id.* at 242–43.

46. *Id.* at 245.

47. *See supra* note 41. *See also* Holmes, J. *in* The Western Maid, 257 U.S. 419, 433 (1922): "Legal obligations that exist but cannot be enforced are ghosts that are seen in the law but that are elusive to grasp."

Elias notably recognizes the indivisibility of rights, and the danger which may arise in dividing them: "It is almost impossible to separate the two sets of rights since they are indivisible. Any attempt to separate civil and political rights from economic and social rights *would inevitably lead to difficulties in practice.*[48] (Emphasis added.) He states that rights cannot or should not be separated because of difficulties in practice. How then, can one separate rights from their inevitably corresponding duties, and still expect that an acceptable international order will result?

3. The Relationship Between Liberal Strategy and the Doctrinal and Conceptual Conflicts.

In discussing international law, one must bear in mind two sets of relationships—the relationship between the doctrinal conflicts of law and politics and rights and duties, and the relationship between the conceptual conflicts of state participation and state sovereignty. With regard to the doctrinal conflicts, the mediation of the rights/duties conflict is in itself a mediation of the conflict between law and politics. For example, an LDC's right to preferential treatment arises independently from the DCs' correlative duties. Such separation of right and duty mediates the rights/duties conflict and also conceals the DCs' political decision behind the procedural language of paragraph 7.[49]

With regard to the conceptual conflicts, the mediation of the rights/duties conflict in turn implicates the principles of sovereign cooperation and authority. A good example is the GSP. The DCs' duties to grant preferential treatment under the MTN do not arise from the correlative rights of the LDCs (the MTN agreement deferred to the sovereign authority of the DCs). Rather, the DCs have the power, or right, to decide whether an LDC has a right to such treatment. The mediation of the rights/duties conflict and its relationship to sovereign cooperation find reflection in Judge Elias' own remarks: "Clearly, *negotiations and multilateral meetings* [i.e. cooperation] are necessary in this regard and these negotiations must be sensitive to the *historical realities of both the developing and the developed countries.*"[50] (Emphasis added.)

The phrase "historical realities" enables one to discuss current development of law without touching the sensitive issue. Elias might mean that the DCs have to compensate for the disadvantageous position of the LDCs by extending to them favorable treatment in economic relations (i.e. cooperation). However, such a compensatory maneuver may mean that the DCs, while extending help, should

48. *See* T. ELIAS, *supra* note 1, at 246.
49. Paragraph 7, *supra* page 13.
50. T. ELIAS, *supra* note 1, at 164.

design a mechanism to retain some control of world economic development (i.e. cooperation but with authority). While supporting the LDCs' position, Elias seems to confirm the second interpretation: "The challenge to international law and to international lawyers is to devise legal instruments in such a way that the *aspirations and rights of no state or people are promoted at the expense of other states or peoples*."[51] (Emphasis added.) Beyond this, the DCs must mediate and conceal the rights/duties conflict, for example, in making the language of paragraph 7 seem compatible both with the idea of sovereign cooperation and with the idea of sovereign authority. Indeed, the DCs cannot promote the rights and aspirations of the LDCs without taking corresponding measures to protect the DCs' own interests.

B. *Concepts of Sovereignty—Their Conflicting Meanings and Relationships to Doctrinal Conflicts and Participation.*

Two concepts of sovereignty play a crucial role in international relations—that of sovereign cooperation and that of sovereign authority.[52] As Elias observes:

> . . . [I]n legal terms, it will be necessary to rethink a whole series of the *relations between legal principles of freedom of States* [sovereign authority] and of non-governmental economic actors like the transnational corporations of formal *and substantive equality between States* [sovereign cooperation] and of international solidarity. This rethinking must have regard for economic, political and legal facts of the infrastructure of the international economic order as well as the nature of the problems to be solved.[53] (emphasis added)

51. *Id.*

52. In addition to Judge Elias' recognition of the two meanings of the concepts of sovereignty below, other legal scholars have, in various instances, discussed both concepts of sovereignty. For example, Judge Alvarez stated in his Individual Opinion in the *Corfu Channel Case* that:

> By sovereignty, we understand the whole body of rights and attributes which a State possesses in its territory, to the exclusion of all other States, and also in its relation with other States.
>
> Sovereignty confers rights upon States [i.e. sovereign authority] and imposes obligations on them [i.e. sovereign cooperation] . . . .
>
> [A]nd we must now adopt a conception of it which will be in harmony with the new conditions of social life. *We can no longer regard sovereignty as an absolute and individual right of every State*, as used to be done under the old law founded on the individualist regime [i.e. sovereign authority] . . . . Today, owing to social interdependence and to the predominance of the general interests, the States are bound by many rules which have not been ordered by their will [i.e. sovereign cooperation]. (emphasis added)

Corfu Channel Case (U.K. v. Alb.), 1949 I.C.J. 4, 43 (Judgment of Apr. 9). *See also* L. Henkin, R. Pugh, O. Schachter, and H. Smit, International Law: Cases and Materials 256–96 (1980); I. Brownlie, Principles of Public International Law, part III, chapters VI and VII (3rd. ed. 1979); J. Brierly, The Law of Nations: An Introduction to the International Law of Peace, part V ("States") (5th ed. 1955).

53. T. Elias, *supra* note 1, at 235.

Legal liberals mediate the doctrinal conflicts to support and legitimate a particular vision of sovereignty and also use various concepts of sovereignty to mediate doctrinal conflicts. Further, the twin concepts of sovereignty have contradictory meanings and interpretations, which have been embodied simultaneously in international law.

While the authorizing statute of the Court, for example, recognizes the sovereign authority of each state by making ICJ jurisdiction compulsory *only* when states declare acceptance of its jurisdiction (the optional clause),[54] the same article recognizes the ICJ's authority (as a neutral institution) to decide whether it has jurisdiction.[55] When the ICJ exercises its discretionary power,[56]it relies on a hidden concept of sovereign cooperation. Theoretically, states vest their sovereignty in the ICJ, authorizing it to act on their behalf in deciding the issue of a given state's status in international affairs. Similarly, under the NIEO, CERDS accepts sovereign cooperation as a cornerstone of the Third World economic and legal movement,[57] while at the same time explicitly recognizing the sovereign authority of developing states to assess the appropriate compensation for nationalization according to their own domestic law.[58] The conflict between competing concepts of sovereignty is reproduced in many current legal documents and

54. Article 36(2) of the Statute of the International Court of Justice reads: "The States parties to the present Statute may at any time declare that they recognize as compulsory *ipso facto* and without special agreement, in relation to any other State accepting the same obligation, the jurisdiction of the Court in all legal disputes . . . ." 2 A DIGEST OF THE DECISIONS OF THE INTERNATIONAL COURT 1264 (K. Marek ed. 1978). Of course, that article does not preclude states from accepting jurisdiction in other ways. For example, states can accept jurisdiction through optional protocols attached to treaties or through subsequent consent (*forum prorogatum*).

55. Article 36(6) of the Statute of the International Court of Justice reads: "In the event of a dispute as to whether the Court has jurisdiction, the matter shall be settled by the decision of the Court." *Id.*

56. For example, the Court exercised its discretion to decide whether or not it had jurisdiction in United States Diplomatic and Consular Staff in Teheran (U.S. v. Iran), 1980 I.C.J. 3 (Judgment of May 24); Case Concerning Factory at Chorzow (Ger. v. Pol.), 1927 P.C.I.J., Ser. A, No. 8 (Judgment of July 26).

57. The Preamble of the Charter of Economic Rights and Duties of States (CERDS) enunciates that idea clearly:

> *Reaffirming* the fundamental purpose of the United Nations, . . . and the achievement of international co-operation in solving international problems in the economic and social fields,
>
> *Affirming* the need for strengthening international cooperation in these fields,
>
> *Reaffirming* further the need for strengthening international cooperation for development . . .

G.A. Res. 3281, 29 U.N. GAOR Supp. (No. 31) at 51, U.N. Doc. A/9631 (1975).

58. Article 2 of the CERDS states:

> 2. Each State has the right:
>
> (c) To *nationalize*, expropriate or transfer ownership of foreign property, in which case *appropriate compensation* should be paid by the State adopting such measures . . . . In any case where the question of compensation gives rise to a controversy, *it shall be settled under the domestic law of the nationalizing State* and by its tribunals . . . ." (emphasis added)

Id. at 52.

problems. The emphasis on one concept of sovereignty to the exclusion of the other results from several invalid assumptions.

The first such assumption is that the twin concepts of sovereignty have clearly distinguishable meanings. However, in many instances, sovereign cooperation means the same thing as sovereign authority. For instance, the concept of sovereign cooperation contains elements of the concept of sovereign authority. When states grant sovereignty to an institution (such as the ICJ) to perform functions relinquished by them, such an institution takes on sovereign authority of its own in performing those functions. Thus, for the ICJ to promote sovereign cooperation it needs such an endowment of sovereign authority (either through the United Nations or individual consent) from all states. Similarly, under the NIEO, states must vest sovereignty (sovereign cooperation) in that institution to make it acceptable and to allow it to perform its functions convincingly. In all cases, when states grant power to institutions to create international cooperation, those institutions necessarily take on aspects of sovereign authority. Yet, the threat remains that the DCs will control such institutions to promote *their* sovereign authority and their subjective interests.[59]

Conversely, sovereign authority contains an element of sovereign cooperation. If a state wants to have sovereign authority, it must show respect for other states and for international institutions. The international community (states, international institutions), gives sovereign authority to a state. Therefore, a state will only have sovereign authority when it demonstrates that it is willing to participate in a scheme of international cooperation. Accordingly, if a state were to assert sovereign authority without respecting similar rights for others, the United Nations, the ICJ, or the whole international system would collapse.[60] In the area of development, for example, an LDCs' power to regulate foreign investment according to its own law entails the duty to adhere to international norms which afford foreign investors some protection. Because such protection does not exist in article 2(2)(c) of the CERDS[61] (i.e. sovereign cooperation is totally separated from sovereign authority) the Charter was not accepted by most industrialized countries.[62]

59. *See, e.g.*, UNCTAD: Agreement Establishing the Common Fund for Commodities, U.N. Doc. TD/IPC/CONF/L.15 (1980), and Corr. 1 (1980). The Common Fund Agreement, article 21, establishes a system of weighted voting that is based on the amount of capital that a state contributes. The DCs are, of course, those countries which are able to contribute a more substantial amount of capital to the Fund. They therefore have more votes allocated to them, even though they account for a fewer number of states. The institution is inevitably in the control of the DCs.

60. Of course, there have been cases where the Court's decisions have not been complied with by parties concerned. *See* United States Diplomatic and Consular Staff in Teheran, *supra* note 56.

61. *See supra* note 58.

62. The Charter was not ratified by many of the industrialized countries. The countries

Since the meanings of the two concepts of sovereignty interconnect, legal discourse that separates them is politically motivated.[63] The application of one or the other concept in a certain case really depends upon the political policies of the most powerful group of states in a particular period of time. At root, this dependence stems from the failure to separate law from politics. The interconnected and inseparable meanings of the sovereign concepts may answer some questions asked by Elias:

> Is it likely that there will never be a new international economic order if states *do not accept restrictions of the exercise of their sovereign rights in external* and even internal economic policies, as far as those policies have substantial external effects for other States? *In other words: is the concept of States' sovereignty compatible with the concept of a new international order?*[64] (emphasis added)

Liberals typically separate the concepts of sovereign cooperation and sovereign authority and attempt to employ one without the other in legal documents. But, since the two concepts are indivisible, neither liberal maneuver can succeed.

Discourse relying on a particular concept of sovereignty merely mediates the conceptual conflicts within the concept of sovereignty itself. By recognizing that, we can understand another relationship between the two sets of doctrinal conflicts and the conceptual conflict within the idea of sovereignty. Sovereignty concepts are goals *for* mediating doctrinal conflicts, as well as means *to* mediate such conflicts. Importantly, however, the reverse relationship also exists. To mediate the two sets of doctrinal conflicts is to mediate the conflicting yet inseparable meanings of the concept of sovereignty.[65] Bringing out the underlying structure of legal discourse will encourage equal participation and international harmony and community. For example, defining the LDCs' right to development without corresponding duties

---

opposed on both the vote in the Second Committee and in the General Assembly were: the U.S., Belgium, Denmark, Federal Republic of Germany, Luxembourg and the United Kingdom. Abstaining were: Austria, Canada, France, Ireland, Israel, Italy, Japan, the Netherlands, Norway and Spain.

63. Just as the attempt to distinguish *stare decisis* from mere judicial policymaking is politically motivated. *See* Kairys, *supra* note 2, at 11–17, esp. 17.

64. T. Elias, *supra* note 1, at 236.

65. Settling on a characterization of some international event as either law or politics or separating rights from duties automatically implicates one concept of sovereignty or the other. Thus, for example, when the ICJ labels an issue as "political" it is *ipso facto* promoting the notion of sovereign authority. By refusing to interfere in the realm of subjective decision-making or in the sphere of state sovereignty, the ICJ delegates or affirms the rights of such states to abide by their own decisions—i.e., sovereign authority. Conversely, if the ICJ labels an issue as "law," it *ipso facto* promotes notions of sovereign cooperation. By asserting its sovereign authority, the ICJ forces states to participate and agree on common "objective" goals. The same reasoning applies to rights and duties.

mediates the rights/duties conflict in a way which only strengthens the sovereign cooperation concept. Focusing on either the DCs' or the LDCs' duties would raise issues of the DCs' sovereign authority to grant the power to determine both their own and the LDCs' duties. Once again politics and law intertwine.

C. *The Concept of Participation: Meaning and Domination.*

An analysis of liberal legal discourse concerning Third World states, the role of law, and the ICJ should focus on the concept of participation. Liberals mediate doctrinal and conceptual conflicts to foster participation, yet they also use the concept as a means for mediating such conflicts. Participation, though, does not have a rigid intrinsic meaning. Instead, different political ideologies and complex human desires and interests alter the meaning of participation. For example, when the DCs are strong politically, they view the concept of sovereign authority—the concept which delegates power to the DCs—as fostering the goal of participation. Yet when the LDCs are strong politically, they view the concept of sovereign cooperation (which promotes the influence of the LDCs) as fostering the goal of participation. Both DCs and LDCs structure legal discourse to fit their political interests. Since the LDCs' political influence has increased recently, discourse about participation has focused on the sovereign cooperation concept. However, because the DCs still want a certain degree of control, a hidden framework of DC authority still coexists with the cooperation concept. Again, paragraph 7 of the MTN Agreement on the GSP and the Common Fund Agreement are good examples of such a hidden framework.[66]

States motivated by different political interests thus use the device of mediation to reach and justify their various goals. The existence of these powerful political goals explains the numerous attempts and failures to mediate the conflict between law and politics in international relations. Such attempts and failures have characterized state relations. We cannot change this phenomenon. However, we can and must do the following. First, we must analyze states' relations in order to understand them. A lack of thorough analysis, although allowing advocacy of certain doctrines, concepts and developments, will result in a false vision of state relations and of what should be done. Second, we should restructure the play of human desires and interests. The aim is to create a new vision of international relations that will reduce discord and promote international harmony and community.

---

66. Because of the weighted voting system, the DCs still have powers to control the operation of the Common Fund. *See also supra* note 26 with regard to the MTN agreement on the GSP.

III. A RESTRUCTURED VISION OF INTERNATIONAL RELATIONS.[67]

Liberal legal thought may help us to move closer to a more acceptable international order, since the liberal concept of state participation promotes pluralism rather than totalitarianism.[68] Yet to improve upon the liberal approach we need to understand all of the relationships among doctrines and concepts which justify and encourage participation. We must expose the underlying structural dilemmas of pluralism to serve better the interests of all parties. Eventually the underlying political aims of liberal mediating techniques will be uncovered and states will become skeptical about the structure of pluralism. However, structural analysis and the approach of this Comment will modify liberal mediating techniques and will reimagine the role of law in international relations. Since a variety of human interests and desires motivate and animate liberal mediating techniques, any new approach must deal with those interests and desires. Such a new approach will protect equal and just participation for states and will promote international harmony and community. The new approach must recast the role of law and create an alternative vision of state participation.[69]

Law will still have an important role in bringing about a just system of international relations. However, current visions of the legal system must be restructured before the critical power of law can affect state behaviour positively. Of course, law is crucial for any organized society. Yet any new vision must reveal the hidden manipulation and domination in law, so that actors will not be able to use law as a tool to take advantage of others, and so that others will not blindly accept such domination. Further, lawyers must not abuse the structure of law to appear to solve certain doctrinal problems while in reality serving some pre-set policy objectives. Even if unintentional, such subterfuges will not create workable or just agreements among states. For example, using the procedural side of the legal structure to make conflicts of law and politics seemingly disappear will not convince any states once they understand the inseparability of law and politics. In the long run, liberal legal rhetoric cannot really solve international problems, nor can it protect the real interests of the international community.

---

67. *See* D. KAIRYS, *supra* note 2, at 286–91. The argument there explains the ultimate aims of a structural analysis and the power of a reconstructed vision.

68. Liberal ideas of pluralism advocate broad-based state involvement in international affairs. If this ideal were carried out in practice, it would make absolute domination by one state impossible.

69. These are goals of critical theory. Instead of conceiving of international relations problems as problems of control over objective events in the world, i.e. conceiving of them as scientific problems, this Comment focuses on problems that arise when states fail to realize their true interests. The goals of critical theory may seem foreign to those who usuallly think of international problems in scientific terms. But as Guess states:

Law should be the first step to dispute settlement or to reaching acceptable agreements, not a tool for manipulation. In other words, law should be used as one of the means towards ends, and not as an end itself. Law must help to create more appropriate negotiation processes and more ways of making people from different political cultures realize that they share problems of the same nature.[70] Law must also make people aware of common goals and potential compromises. Restructuring our vision of the role of law in those ways will bring law closer to reality, and will thereby foster long run international cooperation which is at once just and acceptable yet not riddled with hidden domination. Proceduralizing legal conflict—the method currently utilized to mask doctrinal conflicts and underlying interests—should be avoided. Such a method widens the gap between law and reality, brings in dominating factors, and disrupts the route to international harmony and community. Therefore, a participation approach coupled with a restructured vision will help eliminate the gap between law and reality.

A participation approach begins with an alternative vision of the relationship among states. That approach in turn will restructure our vision of law and its application. Currently, states resort to building and using legal structures and concepts which favor their interests. For example, the belief that sovereign cooperation notions should be strengthened to increase the number of participating states, the separation of right from duty to satisfy LDCs, and the separation of law from politics to make institutions look impartial are all manipulable. Yet the illusion of objectivity persists. The vision of "one world"[71] offers an alternative approach to participation. This vision will push at social, national, and cultural boundaries, and lead to the acceptance and sharing of different beliefs and concepts. Such a vision will end the antagonistic use of law and politics. In other words, the "one world" vision does not rely on political, legal, or economic coercion in international relations. That vision portrays law as merely a first step toward international cooperation with mutual understanding, but

---

> Scientific theories have as their aim or goal successful manipulation of the external world; they have 'instrumental use'. If correct they enable the agents who have mastered them to cope and thus pursue their chosen ends successfully. Critical theories aim at emancipation and enlightenment, at making agents aware of hidden coercion, thereby freeing them from that coercion and putting them in a position to determine where their true interests lie.

R. Guess, The Idea of a Critical Theory 90 (1982).

70. Yet law must also stress and promote the awareness and appreciation of cultural variety.

71. *See* the statement of John Comenius, 1666:

> We are all citizens of one world, we are all of one blood. To hate a man because he was born in another country, because he speaks a different language, or because he takes a different view on this subject or that, is a great folly. Desist, I implore you, for we are all equally human—Let us have but one end in view, the welfare of humanity; and let us put aside all selfishness in consideration of language, nationality, or religion.

not as the solution. A vision of "one world" will help lead to more acceptable international activities and to lasting and just agreements among states.

Of course, translating a "one world" vision into practice will be difficult. There is a significant difference between having an image of "one world" and consciously realizing the full import of that vision. Yet the abstract discovery that international activities are manipulated through the mediation of doctrinal and conceptual conflicts, and by different political beliefs which result from complex human interests and desires, may trigger enlightened thinking about international legal and economic relations (or participation). Such enlightenment will in turn lead to a deeper picture of what the "one world" vision involves. Clarifying the image, by casting it as a specific program designed to elucidate and overcome the hidden liberal structures, the vision of "one world" could become part of international practice.

Restructuring the vision of international legal and economic relations is not enough, though. Ultimately we must reshape the nature of human interest and desire,[72] to get to the root of the problems of domination inherent in the concepts of participation and mediation technique. Training one's mind and thinking[73] is necessary if the alternative vision is to be implemented effectively. Saying that we all are in one world differs from truly realizing and feeling that we all really are. A deep commitment and awareness[74] will lead to substantive

---

72. The venerable Ajahn Maha·Bua, one of the most respected Buddhist monks, stated:

> Human Desire always interferes with the untrained mind. It fills the mind with a sense of antagonism, destruction, irrationality in obtaining what a human being wants. This Human Desire is naturally with a human being. It works for the self. It raises one's ego to be self-centered. For example, if a ruler (whose untrained mind is controlled by Human Desire) says that he will do x for the benefit of the people, this often results in his own benefit. It results in this way because, naturally, Human Desire controls mind to work for the self. (author's trans.)

AJAHN MAHA BUA, WHERE IS THE RELIGION? 251 (Bangkok, 1979).

73. *See supra* note 72. The venerable Ajahn Chah states:

> To practice Buddhism is the training of one's mind. This is the most important point. Buddhism is the philosophy of mind.
>
> The untrained mind races around following its own untrained habits (e.g. a person does things as he desires regardless of others' suffering.) Therefore, whatever it may be of worldly habits, lessen them, go against their power. Don't just do as you like, don't indulge in your thoughts. Stop this slavish following. You must constantly go against the stream of ignorance. This is called 'Discipline'. (author's trans.)

AJAHN CHAH, PHODHIYAN 76–84 (Bangkok, 1982).

74. Ajahn Chah states:

> The duties of the practicing Buddhist are mindfulness (conciousness), collectedness, and contentment. These things stop the habits of the mind. And why should we bother to do this? If you don't bother to train your mind, it remains wild, following the ways of nature. It is possible to train that nature so that it can be used to advantage. (author's trans.)

Id.

Thus, consciousness is a very important factor in training the mind. Consciousness will control the interference of "Human Desire" with the mind and provides unbiased rationale, thoughtfulness and forgiveness. The venerable Ajahn Tede explains:

action towards realizing the vision, and will avoid superficial action which masks subjective choices. A deep commitment requires individual training of mind and thinking to stabilize one's self-awareness. Such training will result in a greater willingness to share ideas and to accept differences in the international community. The training suggested is an inward look at oneself to correct oneself, and an outward look at others to help them—conscious forgiveness and the reduction or elimination of egoism.[75] Egoism is the most important cause of different visions of the world. Unbridled egoism leads to hostile international relations and to the use of law, economics, and ideology to achieve what suits personal or narrow group interests. It is impossible to eliminate egoism entirely, but such training will produce a sense of the universal aims and aspirations of all states, and will thereby lay the foundation for the implementation of the "one world" vision.

CONCLUSION

This Comment began by discussing the relationship between two major areas of law analyzed by Judge Elias: the role of the ICJ in insuring just participation and the international law of development. Those two relatively dissimilar areas of law share the same aim—participation. Liberal legal discourse has mediated doctrinal and conceptual conflicts to create an image of impartiality and to justify the goal of participation. The same dilemma occurs among the sets of conflicts; the mediation of those conflicts always serves a pre-set political goal. This pre-set goal makes the meaning of participation indeterminate and reveals that different political ideologies and human interests dominate that concept.

A new vision of law portrays it as a means and not as an end. Law, by its nature, cannot conceal domination. Law can only give a form and shape to states' relations, but it can never reshape the *structure* of such domination. The goal of participation, accompanied by the vision of one world and by a new understanding of law, would promote just and acceptable international relations.

> Consciousness is a self awareness. Mind is a thinking. Consciousness can control mind. If it is under our power, we will not be misled or trapped by our mind (i.e. a constant self-awareness guides one's thinking to a true rationale). Thus, we can order it. For example, it must not be angry. Mind is always clear and calm.

AJAHN TEDE, EXPLANATION OF DHARMA (DHARMA TESANA) 234 (1983).

Practicing Buddhism, to conclude, focuses on the natural awareness (a result of a constant consciousness). Natural awareness is different from knowledge. There can be a diversity of knowledge between different individuals. However, such diversity no longer matters once the natural awareness is achieved. Natural awareness makes one's mind self-controlled at all times even without one's knowing it. The constant self-controlling mind will help one to be enlightened and see the true rationale.

Id. at 27.

75. *See supra* note 72.

Achieving international harmony and community is not the specific responsibility of lawyers or politicians. Relying solely on law and lawyers will not help us to achieve that end. Rather, it is *everyone*'s responsibility to restructure and to implement his or her vision about legal roles, and about participation. Putting a vision of one world into practice is particularly difficult, but not impossible nor too idealistic. The process of creating a vision of one world is particularly difficult, but it is neither impossible nor too idealistic.

[11]

Two Models for a Rawlsian Theory of International Law and Justice

DANIEL W. SKUBIK*

I. INTRODUCTION

John Rawls' *A Theory of Justice*[1] is a massive, impressive volume. As Barry notes in his critique, "[i]t weighs in at over a quarter of a million words—about equivalent to three books of the average length of modern books devoted purely to analysis and argument. . . . [F]rom the first page to the last it is simply crammed with arguments."[2] Yet, for all the topics thoroughly investigated which inform the arguments for his theory of justice as fairness, the book is just as crammed with assumptions,[3] caveats,[4] and questions which cannot be either (further) pursued or considered except in passing.[5]

This need not be a severe drawback on its face. Too many authors implicitly incorporate these limiting devices without notice to the reader, making analysis cumbersome and difficult. By being explicit, Rawls has done his readers and critics valuable service. On the other hand, it is difficult to gauge the success of the over-all argument for justice as fairness when the reader begins to accumulate a number of reservations. Just how important are certain caveats or unanswered queries to Rawls' theory?

The purpose of this paper is to explore but one of these troublesome areas of reservations and queries which arise with Rawls' full account of his theory of justice and to chart the consequences of troubling these waters. The area of focus here selected is the intimated extension of justice as fairness between societies to develop a theory of global reciprocity. Our focus then, will be limited to the problems arising from Rawls' account of international justice and the principles which can be derived from an original position for a law of nations. It is in exploring this account that we hope to analyze and to expand upon a number of the assumptions and workings of the domestic theory of justice as fairness provided in the text.

---

* B.A., B.S., California Baptist College; M.A. (hons.) University of Melbourne; J.D., UCLA College of Law. Currently in private practice as a Legal and Political Risk Consultant in Canberra, Australia.

1. J. RAWLS, A THEORY OF JUSTICE (1971)[hereinafter cited as TJ].

2. B. BARRY, THE LIBERAL THEORY OF JUSTICE 1 (1973).

3. Phrases such as "I assume," "it seems reasonable," "seems widely agreed that," and "we may suppose," occur frequently throughout the work.

4. *See* TJ, *supra* note 1, sec. 42 at 265, opening remarks of sec. 42 on economic theory. *See also id.* sec. 69 at 452.

5. *E.g.*, closing remarks of sec. 59 on non-ideal theory. *Id.* sec. 59 at 391. *See also* opening remarks of sec. 18 on principles for individuals. *Id.* sec. 18 at 108.

Although Rawls expresses the belief that his account of international justice naturally leads to principles for a law of nations with which we are familiar,[6] it is not at all obvious that this should be so. In fact, we might wonder at such an innocuous outcome being the ready result of extrapolations from domestic principles of justice which were themselves derived from such controversial devices as maxims with no less controversial results like lexical ordering in the special conception. And we shall quickly discover that analyzing these ready extrapolations will be extremely troublesome. This is so for two reasons: (1) the treatment accorded the derivation and application of principles for international law is so minimal as to be near lacking;[7] and (2) the assumptions underlying this treatment and their consequences for international justice are never dealt with systematically.[8]

Indeed, we shall find little guidance even in the mass of secondary literature generated since the publication of Rawls' treatise. The few articles which do direct themselves to the account of international justice tend to focus only upon preliminary questions of the theory's structure,[9] usually relating to issue-specific applications like the assumption of self-sufficiency and the politics of the difference principle,[10] or the principle of non-intervention and the politics of human rights.[11] The questions are then always pursued within a general framework of contemporary non-ideal international relations.

While these articles raise significant questions, a theoretical frame-

---

6. *Id.* at 387

7. In fact, fewer than two full pages are dedicated to the discussion of principles of international law. *Id.* at 377-79. These pages are within the general discussion of conscientious refusal in time of war. *Id.* sec. 58, at 377-82. Other references are mere notes that the principles for the law of nations will not be taken up except in passing. *Id.* at 8, 108, 115.

8. In addition to the references cited in the previous note, an important paragraph for our purposes occurs in *id.* at 457. There an assumption is bared but altogether this seems precious little in 587 pages of dense text. Nonetheless, this lack of systematic discussion, however curious, should not be taken to indicate that Rawls dismisses the issue. Two of Rawls' subsequent articles in defense of his domestic theory also collaterally address the issue of international scope, particularly as regards the nature of the basic structure he is attempting to construct. *See* Rawls, *The Basic Structure as Subject*, in VALUES AND MORALS, 47, 57, 70 (A. Goldman & J. Kim eds. 1978). [hereinafter cited as BSS]. *See also* Rawls, *Kantian Constructivism in Moral Theory*, 77 J. PHIL. 515, 524 (1980) [hereinafter cited as KCMT], where he defends his notion of "self-contained national community". The fact that he broaches the topic of international justice from the detailed framework of societal justice which he does provide indicates an expectation that his theory can be naturally extended. TJ, *supra* note 1, at 377. Framing this extension and tracing its consequences are the tasks of this essay.

9. *E.g.*, D'Amato, *International Law and Rawls' Theory of Justice*, 5 DEN. J. INT'L L. & POL'Y 525 (1975).

10. Representative of this is the work by Beitz, *Justice and International Relations*, 4 PHIL & PUB. AFF. 360 (1975). This article appears in revised and expanded for in C. Beitz, POLITICAL THEORY AND INTERNATIONAL RELATIONS pt.3 (1979).

11. Wicclair, *Rawls and the Principle of Nonintervention*, in JOHN RAWLS' THEORY OF SOCIAL JUSTICE 289 (H. Blocker and E. Smith eds. 1980)

work for an ideal strict compliance theory for international justice remains unexplicated, both by Rawls and his critics. It is this missing framework and its applications which we shall attempt to supply in the remainder of this essay. In fact, after uncovering some ambiguities and questionable assumptions, it will become possible to develop clearly two disparate models of well-ordered societies existing as subjects of international justice. It is argued that both models are consistent with Rawls' overall treatment of justice and both receive the "Rawlsian" label. Model 1 is based upon the primary presentation found in *A Theory of Justice*; Model 2 is that theory which develops from questioning some of the conceptual ambiguities of society and international law grounding Model 1.

As might be expected, the consequences of these models' developments and operations are quite dissimiliar. The subsequent part of this essay will explore the development of these two models, detailing the special features of their original positions. Based upon their respective positions, an exposition is formulated detailing principles to be chosen from behind their respective veils of ignorance. Here, Model 1 will closely follow the limited account presented by Rawls. Model 2, on the other hand, will begin to diverge in the description of its original position, yielding strikingly different principles than those acknowledged under Model 1.

Part III completes the substance of the essay with a close examination of some of the practical consequences of the operations of both models in three hypothetical situations of international import. Based on the theoretical and practical analyses generated, the paper concludes with a summary evaluation of the models coherence and stability under the Rawlsian device of reflective equilibrium. The question proposed is: "Which model more closely matches considerations of justice as fairness in an international arena"? Let us proceed to develop an answer.

II. THEORY

Rawls' aim is to present a sophisticated social contract conception of justice. Being so framed, it is not surprising that his theory incorporates familiar elements found in the social compact theories of Locke, Rousseau and Kant. But, justice as fairness is an attempt to transcend these traditional conceptions by generalizing at a higher level of abstraction.[12] Thus, while one of the central features of Rawls' theory of justice is a description of an initial status quo in which participants meet to formulate and agree (contract)[13] upon principles for establishing a well-ordered society (a common central feature of social contract theories), no particular society or form of government is envisioned (as is usually the case). Rather, general principles for ordering the basic structure of society (and,

---

12. TJ, *supra* note 1, at viii, 3 and 11.

13. *See* Hampton, *Contracts and Choices*, 77 J. OF PHIL. 315 (1980), where it is argued that this initial status quo, Rawls' "original position," effectively eliminates altogether a contractarian interpretation of the resulting theory of justice.

thereby, any society) are in view.

Derivation of such general principles is made possible through the careful structuring of a hypothetical initial situation which is fair towards all. That is, based upon a philosophical anthropology familiar to Kant, the hypothetical ought to be so structured as to respect the freedom and equality of human beings as moral agents. Conversely, the hypothetical ought to nullify the accidents of natural endowments and the contingencies of social circumstance. Man *qua* man is hereby represented in the initial situation and general principles for (generic) society can be meaningfully sought.

That the description of this initial situation plays a prominent role in the development of a conception of justice for Rawls is evident not only in that his theory is contractarian, but is presaged in the very name of his theory. It is the description, itself, of an "appropriate initial status quo which insures that the fundamental agreements reached in it are fair. This fact yields the name 'justice as fairness'."[14] Now, he admits that there exist numerous characterizations of such an initial situation. Proffered interpretations will vary

> depending upon how the contracting parties are conceived, upon what their beliefs and interests are said to be, upon which alternatives are available to them, and so on. In this sense, there are many different contract theories. Justice as fairness is but one of these. But the question of justification is settled, as far as it can be, by showing that there is one interpretation of the initial situation which best expresses the conditions that are widely thought reasonable to impose on the choice of principles yet which, at the same time, leads to a conception that characterizes our considered judgments in reflective equilibrium.[15]

Justice as fairness, it is argued, best satisfies these criteria. Considerations of fairness then will help shape the favored philosophical interpretation of the conditions which characterize this initial situation. Such conditions and their ramifications for principles of domestic justice are discussed by Rawls under four headings: the circumstances of justice, the formal constraints of the concept of right, the veil of ignorance, and the rationality of the parties.[16] The initial situation so characterized is what Rawls designates the original position. What will constitute the focus of our discussion in this part is the interpretation of the conditions noted above, as given by Rawls, when extended to encompass the sphere of international justice as defined by our models.

A. *Model 1.*

In beginning to develop an original position for our first model, it should be noted that the conditions discussed by Rawls under two of the

---

14. *Id.* at 17.
15. *Id.* at 121.
16. *Id.* secs. 20-25, at 118-50.

headings previously mentioned—the formal constraints of the concept of right and the rationality of the parties—do not require extensive reanalysis and need not detain us. We can readily subsume the discussion on generality, universality, publicity, ordering and finality within the international scope of Model 1. Since these constraints "hold for the choice of all ethical principles,"[17] they easily extend to our forum and are, in fact, desirable conditions as given.

Likewise, his discussion of mutual disinterestedness (limited altruism), lack of envy, use of effective means and strict compliance, however individually debatable,[18] can be incorporated without greatly influencing development of our model. Indeed, desiring to develop a Rawlsian model, Rawls' presentation should be adopted or incorporated wherever feasible. As he has signalled no necessity to reevaluate these conditions when discussing international principles, the rationality of the parties shall also be taken as given.

On the other hand, the remaining two headings—the circumstances of justice and the veil of ignorance—and their conditions present some difficulties. Within the framework provided by Rawls, the reader is signalled that modifications of these conditions are required when extending the original position to encompass an international setting. Passing hints are given concerning the substance of some changes.[19] The extent of any other modifications is less clear. Our interpretative task involves an analysis of all necessary modifications, their effects upon the participants and any (new) constraints for international principles resulting from a modified original position. In an effort to chart these necessary modifications and their effects, let us begin by reviewing Rawls' passing sketch of an international original position, the changes he envisions, and the assumptions he invokes.

For Rawls, derivation of principles of justice for a law of nations is the final choice problem in a three-item agenda for the participants in the original position.[20] The first choice problem focuses upon those principles

---

17. *Id.* at 130.

18. *See, e.g.*, Simson, *Another View of Rawls' Theory of Justice*, 23 EMORY L.J. 473 (1974). *See also* R.P. WOLFF, UNDERSTANDING RAWLS (1977), for a critical commentary on these points.

19. It is assumed that those in the orginal position should act as representatives of their nations to develop fundamental principles as between states; and that although still deprived of most specific information—such as the nation to which they do/will belong, its particular circumstances and their own place in it—these representatives are to benefit from a partial "lifting of the veil" and do know that (1) nation-states are the historical reality of the day, and (2) these, like individuals-in-society, will have conflicts of interests. This thinner veil assumption is placed in relative time for us in TJ, *supra* note 1, at 109f; it lies between the initial original position stage (no specific societal data injected into deliberations) of the four-stage sequence. Note that the former assumption appears to eliminate any notion of an individual having a claim against a state. Neither apparently does a nation which is not also a state have any such claims.

20. *See* the schematic diagram provided, *id.* at 109. Principles are to be chosen for (I) social systems and institutions, (II) individuals, (IIa) natural duties, (IIb) obligations, (IIc)

of justice which order the basic structure of individual societies. The solution to this problem is his two principles of justice as lexically ordered in the special conception. Arriving at and defending this solution consumes the greatest portion of his energies, as he argues for justice as fairness and against competing conceptions like average utility.

The second choice problem concerns the various principles of obligation and natural duties as these apply to individuals. Although no complete or systematic account pertaining to this choice problem is offered, that this problem is encountered as the second item on the original position agenda means

> the choice of principles for individuals is greatly simplified by the fact that the principles for institutions have already been adopted. The feasible alternatives are straight-way narrowed down to those that constitute a coherent conception of duty and obligation when taken together with the two principles of justice.[21]

Certain examples and arguments disclosing the substantive nature of this coherent conception briefly appear, in four widely separated sections,[22] involving a principle of fairness coupled to various positive and negative natural duties, including those of justice, mutual aid, mutual respect and refraining from doing harm or injury.

Assuming this order of choice problems, when the participants reach the end of this second agenda item of business, they will have agreed upon a set of

> principles of right as these apply to their own society and to themselves as members of it. Now at this point one may extend the interpretation of the original position and think of the parties as representatives of different nations who must choose together the fundamental principles to adjudicate conflicting claims among states.[23]

But before moving directly to a choice of principles, it will be necessary to reexamine our initial situation. As previously noted, although no changes in the understanding or interpretation of the original position were required as the argument moved from the first item of institutional principles to the second item of individual natural duty, differences in construction and interpretation of the original position are required as the participants move to choice item three, the law of nations. These changes occur in three categories: (1) our conception of the parties, (2) the circumstances of justice, and (3) the veil of ignorance.

The most straightforward change confronts us in the first category, our conception of the parties. No longer do the participants represent

---

permissions, and (III) the law of nations. "The Roman numerals express the order in which the various sorts of principles are to be acknowledged in the original position." *Id.* at 110.

21. *Id.* at 334 (footnote omitted).

22. Secs. 18 and 19 describe the principles for individuals. *Id.* secs. 18, 19 at 108-17. Secs. 51 and 52 argue their acceptance as essential part of a conception of right.

23. *Id.* at 377-78

continuing persons as mutually disinterested individuals. In addition, no longer do the participants have in view the ordering of only the basic structure of a single, undefined society. Rather, given that a society is now assumed to be defined by the modern conceptual and actual boundaries of a nation-state, the participants find themselves representing different nations in an initial situation where they are to choose principles for structuring the relations between these new, higher-order parties.[24] Thus, it can reasonably be assumed (though it is not absolutely clear) that the parties—the nation-states so represented, are all well-ordered societies and that these well-ordered societies need (desire?) to choose principles to order their interaction and to adjudicate any conflicting claims.

The second category of the circumstances of justice also incorporates a number of changes.[25] In part, these changes in interpretation are due to the change of forum, since we are now dealing with global cooperative schemes or boundaries. However, not the least of the changes are in response to the shift in understanding of the conception of the parties inhabiting the original position. The circumstances require sufficient reinterpretation so that it makes sense to ask if, and how, they might apply to well-ordered nation-states as parties. For example, the second circumstance of justice indicates that parties are expected (though certainly not required) to have divergent fundamental basic beliefs. How are we to understand this expectation in relation to a number of well-ordered socie-

24. A number of interesting queries arise here, for example in fullfilling their representative functions, do the participants actually come from different nations or merely reason as if they are from different nations (rather like reasoning as if they were risk averse)? *Id.* at 172. This is unclear because the subsequent contractual arena, a constitutional convention in the four-stage sequence, appears to involve the identical participants; yet clearly, only a single society is there in view and the participants are once again only continuing persons. *Id.* at 196. Is representation divided o allow one participant per nation, or more than one? Might nation A have one representative while nation B has three? These questions may seem trivial, but they are tied to the much more important issue of legitimacy of representation. By what authority or conception of right can the participants move from their status as continuing persons to wholesale representatives of nations? As Rawls notes in reference to his domestic principles of justice, "the hypothetical nature of the original position invites the question: why should we take any interest in it, moral or otherwise"? *Id.* at 587, 21. An attenuated representation in a hypothetical original position to encompass the international forum would appear to enhance the difficulties in formulating an adequate response.

25. Rawls describes the circumstances of justice as the normal conditions which characterize the objective and subjective factors of human cooperation which confront individuals in (or in formation of) a well-ordered society. He deals with these factors in some detail. *Id.* sec. 22 at 126-30. These factors may be summarized in the following manner: (1) conditions of moderate scarcity exist; (2) there is a divergence of fundamental interests and ends, and a variety of opposing and incompatible beliefs; and (3) the scheme of basic institutions is a more or less self-sufficient and productive scheme of social cooperation for mutual good. "Society" is here viewed as a "cooperative venture for mutual advantage" *Id.* at 520. The summary is culled from the enumeration of the twelve features involved in the concept of a well-ordered society in Rawls, *Reply to Alexander and Musgrave*, 88 Q. J. ECON. 633, 635 (1974), where they appear as conditions (8)-(10). For a critical discussion and comparison of Hume's and Rawls' use of such factors when characterized as circumstances of justice, see Hubin, *The Scope of Justice*, 9 PHIL. & PUB. AFF. 3 (1980).

ties, all of which are ordered by the same coherent set of institutional and individual principles?

Perhaps the best way to understand this circumstance in the immediate context is to distinguish two levels of meaning. At the higher level of abstraction, it is certainly true that justice is the fundamental interest of all well-ordered societies. In this there will be no divergence. But we should not therefore conclude from this convergence that we are approaching an international society whose fundamental agreements belie a need for principles of international justice. Rawls does, for example, present constitutional democracy as a type or structure which can conform to his principles and, thereby, be just. But he never argues that only constitutional democracies are just. Similarly, ownership of the means of production could conceivably be private of public, capitalistic or socialistic, in nature and still conform to the demands of justice.[26]

At a somewhat lower level of abstraction, then, it should not be surprising to see a variety of societal structures as each nation-state attempts to fulfill this interest of justice in differing forms. Based on these type or structural differences, it should also not be surprising to discover that two of more well-ordered societies, striving towards justice, develop divergent goals and opposing beliefs. Thus, the focus of the question posed by this circumstance is not whether disputes or conflicts will arise, but on what basis they are to be resolved if and when they do. Interpreted in this light, the second circumstance of justice is readily incorporated into the new original position.

Unfortunately, the remaining two circumstances of justice pose more difficult problems of reinterpretation and incorporation. They will not be so easily maneuvered into place. Turning to the first circumstance, we find the statement that conditions of moderate scarcity exist. While this condition makes reasonable sense when individuals within a single society are in view, it does not have any apparent application to and between well-ordered societies of nation-states. Recall the numerous phrases employed to designate these boundaries of cooperation: "a closed system isolated from other societies"[27] . . . "self-sufficient scheme of social cooperation"[28] . . . " a closed and self-sufficient system of cooperation."[29] To the extent that a well-ordered society is truly self-sufficient, a condition of any overall level of scarcity has little meaning or application. If self-sufficiency and closedness holds, any principles of interaction or adjudication that might be chosen would merely lie unused; no conflicts would ever arise, for no reciprocal interaction would ever be necessary. Any contacts which might occur would be handled simply on an ad hoc basis.

---

26. *Id.* at 195 and 280. This discussion assumes, of course, that it makes sense to speak of nations as having distinctive goals and beliefs. Whether this assumption is legitimate is examined in the discussion concerning the veil of ignornance, *infra.*

27. *Id.* at 8.

28. BSS, *supra* note 8, at 70.

29. KCMT, *supra* note 8, at 524.

Presumably, Rawls is prepared to relax the supposition of self-containment when treating the law of nations.[30] This is again not wholly clear, but given such a relaxation a plausible reading of this circumstance is that "moderate scarcity" might refer to the wide and uneven distribution of natural and other resources throughout the world. Being a matter of general knowledge for the parties, this fact of uneven distribution would be known and considered. Thus, every country might be expected to be able to supply some, or perhaps even most, of its needs for a time. Yet, no country could reasonably expect to perpetually supply all of its needs from internal resources alone. Too may natural resources are non-renewable and chances are that some natural and technological resources will be lacking entirely. Sooner or later, the society will be required to seek to supplement its own resources by reaching outside its territorial borders. In such instances, principles of interaction and adjudication are mandatory. This same line of reasoning applies as well to the internal development of technological and other resources for use and export. Principles of reciprocity as between states will then be needed to order necessarily expanding contacts of state parties. If this interpretation holds, the circumstance can be reworded or understood to state that conditions of unevenly distributed and limited resources exist as between societies of nation-states, giving rise to conflicting claims. Still, this interpretation remains only plausible.

The third circumstance of justice relates directly to the first and requires elucidation before the latter can be made firm. The third circumstance states that a scheme of basic institutions exists which is (more or less) self-sufficient and productive for mutual good. Again, while this condition reads reasonably well when individuals in society are in view, that such a scheme exists in the international forum is patently not the case. (Emphasis here is on the lack of a pre-defined scheme of authoritative institutions in the model; a debatable contemporary historical void is here only of contingent and secondary interest or concern.) Even were the wording modified to indicate that such a scheme "can" or "might" exist, we would still run headlong into statements like those above which noted self-sufficiency, or this capstone: "a well-ordered society is a closed system; there are no significant relations to other societies, and no one enters from without, for all are born into it to lead a complete life."[31] Understood definitively, no degree of relaxation short of repudiation will get around such firm statements concerning the nature of the parties.

Nevertheless, the enterprise need not be abandoned just yet. One option remains. It could be maintained that a statement like "there are no significant relations" simply recognizes the factual situation at the time the parties enter this stage in the original position to organize institutional structures to administer principles of adjudication. If such a read-

30. TJ, *supra* note 1, at 457.
31. KCMT, *supra* note 8, at 536.

ing were permissible, we could reinterpret this third circumstance to indicate that a scheme of basic institutions "needs" or "ought" to be established which "can" order interaction and adjudicate conflicting claims between parties, based upon fundamental principles yet to be contracted, due to the conflicts conceivably arising under the first two circumstances of justice as reinterpreted in the discussion above.

Of course, this is no longer, strictly speaking, a mere factual claim of circumstance. It contains a normative element, as well. But such a reading should not come as a complete surprise or generate too great an apprehension, since the parties already have a significant set of institutional and individual principles to hand. Breakdown in the original position leading to statal egoism in the international forum would not likely be deemed desirable by parties who are otherwise commited to and are striving for justice. If this "ought" is conceded, the understandings reached should allow incorporation of these reinterpretations in an international original position. This analysis should also complete our discussion of the changes required in category two.

Only one category remains, the third category of the veil of ignorance. Like the change in the first category pertaining to the parties, this presentation is relatively straightforward. But it also raises similar problems of justification. Recall that during the first two agenda items in the original position, no specific information is available to the participants.

> No one knows his place in society, his class position or social status; nor does he know his fortune in the distribution of natural assets and abilities, his intelligence and strength, and the like. Nor, again, does anyone know his conception of the good. . . . More than this, I assume that the parties do not know the particular circumstances of their own society. That is, they do not know its economic or political situation, or the level of civilization and culture it has been able to achieve. The persons in the original position have no information as to which generation they belong.[32]

This passage focuses upon the negative aspects of their position, what they do not know. The only particular facts available are that the circumstances of justice (and whatever these imply) apply to their society. Positively, other passages indicate that there are to be no limitations on general information, such as political and economic theory, laws of human psychology and the basis of social organization.[33] While Rawls has been severely critized for the thickness of the veil,[34] his response is firm.

> The parties are not to be influenced by any particular information that is not part of their representation as free and equal moral per-

32. TJ, *supra* note 1, at 137.

33. *Id.* at 137-138.

34. One of the strongest critiques is provided by Hare, *Rawls' Theory of Justice*, 23 PHIL. Q. 144 (1973).

> sons . . . unless this information is necessary for a rational agreement to be reached. . . . Even if these [thinner veil] restrictions led to the same principles, the thicker veil would still be preferable, since these principles are then connected more clearly to the conception of free and equal persons.[35]

Turning to the ever so slight lifting of this veil for the third agenda item, we find the introduction of an assumption and its corresponding particular information. The assumption is that societies of the participants are to be characterized as nation-states and this new bit of information is revealed to them in their representative capacities. Other restrictions being equal, "the original position is fair between nations; it nullifies the contingencies and biases of historical fate."[36]

Time will not be spent working out reinterpretations of all the restrictions noted in the preceding passages as they relate to nation-states. Most are easily converted and understood in their new context. However, it should be noted that the veil-lifting prescribed severely diminishes the universal application of this original position. Since the formative rising of the nation-state is a relatively recent political phenomenon, dating back little more than 350 years,[37] it can no longer be said that the parties "have no information as to which generation they belong." Perhaps this assumption is simply a calculated concession to the present era of world history in which we live. But, when only 350-odd years of nation-state contingencies are nullified . . . when the parties can reasonably assume a recent time frame in world history, it is difficult not to conceive this concession as morally arbitrary in a model otherwise devoted to ideal theory. This criticism does no damage to the actual operation of the model; yet, it does appear to limit its effective moral range.

A more serious problem arises in the context of nation-state parties which does affect the operation of the model. Unless some organic assumptions of society previously rejected are brought into play,[38] it seems extremely difficult to understand what it means to transfer the free and equal moral status of persons to national societies. If, indeed, this transfer cannot be made, it is not clear that the argument for requiring a thicker veil should prevail. On a thinner account, all particulars could be known (e.g. the actual distribution of all resources and the stages of development—political, cultural and economic—of the nations represented). Only the personal characteristics, including nation-state citizenship, of the representatives would remain behind the veil to insure the requisite

---

35. KCMT, *supra* note 8, at 549-50.

36. TJ, *supra* note 1, at 378.

37. While scholars differ as to datings, there is little disagreement that the origin of the modern state is tied to the neologism of "sovereignty," which concept began to flourish in the early 17th century. For representative discussion see H. KRABBE, THE MODERN IDEA OF THE STATE (Sabine & Shepard trans. 1922); *see also* A. D'ENTREVES, THE NOTION OF THE STATE 89-103 (1967).

38. TJ, *supra* note 1, at 264.

level of fairness.

On the other hand, it can be argued that free and equal moral status does pertain to society as a collective. Rawls' early rejection of an organic conception of society is arguably a rejection of "organ-ism" and not the concept of collective responsibility and accountability. His discussion of community and use of phrases such as "legitimate interest" in possessive relation to society bear out this interpretation. Although a full-account of a philosophical sociology is lacking in his treatise, the following gloss is consistent with Rawls' presentation.

> The notion of moral or collective personality—in which "personality" has a proper analogical value—applies to the people as a whole in a genuine manner: because the people as a whole (a natural whole) are an ensemble of real individual persons and because their unity as a social whole derives from a common will to live together which originates in these real individual persons.[39]

Based upon such an interpretation of collectivity, the transfer of free and equal moral status can be made in the new original position with the result that the thicker veil would still be preferable.

Discussion of the veil of ignorance closes the account of original position modifications. To conclude this rather lengthy discussion, a summary chart follows. The column on the left (headed I and II) notes the first and second choice problems relating to domestic institutional and individual principles. The column on the right (headed III) provides a summary of those conditions reinterpreted in light of the third choice problem relating to principles for a law of nations. Having now developed the structure for an international original position, we can begin to examine the solution to this third choice problem by indicating those principles which would be chosen under the model. But before actually turning to these principles of international justice, one analytic chore remains. It is first necessary to briefly examine the constraints of choice, or derivation and acknowledgement, as these apply to the reasonings of the parties in the original position.

39. J. MARITAIN, MAN AND THE STATE 16 n.11 (1951).

	I and II	III
Formal constraints of the concept of right	Universality, generality, publicity, ordering finality	Universality, generality, publicity, ordering, finality
Rationality of the parties	Mutual disinterestedness (limited altruism) lack of envy, use of effective means, strict compliance	Mutual disinterestedness (limited altruism), lack of envy, use of effective means, strict compliance
Conception of the parties	Free and equal continuing persons	"Free and equal" well-ordered nation-state societies
Circumstances of justice	1) Moderate scarcity exists	1) Unevenly distributed and limited natural, technological and other resources exist as between nations
	2) Divergent fundamental interests, opposing and incompatible beliefs	2) Convergent fundamental interest, but (probable) divergent goals and opposing beliefs
	3) A scheme of basic institutions exists for mutual good	3) Need to establish basic institutions for reciprocal relations
Veil of ignorance	no specific information available to parties as moral agents—thick veil obtains	parties are known to be modern-type nation-states which are responsible collectives; veil is thick, but thinner than for items I and II

SUMMARY CHART OF MODEL 1
ORIGINAL POSITIONS

The first constraint resting upon the parties is that any feasible set of alternatives embracing international principles must be narrowed such that acknowledgment is consistent with the institutional and individual principles already chosen. Just as the individual principles of the second choice problem had to form a coherent conception when taken with the constitutional principles of the first choice problem, international principles are to conform to the outlines of this previously established coherent conception. Taken together, all three sets of choice-solutions should form a coherent table of principles for a theory of justice as fairness.

The second constraint to be considered is based upon one of the conditions of the rationality of the parties. According to the condition of strict compliance, the principles finally acknowledged will constitute the basis for an ideal theory of international justice. That is, "the parties can rely on each other to understand and act in accordance with whatever principles are finally agreed to. Once principles are acknowledged the parties can depend on one another to conform to them."[40] Because of this constraint, the parties can be expected to concentrate on selecting those principles of reciprocal advantage for well-ordered nation-states which will become the foundation for the basic institutions of a well-ordered society of nations. The stress on well-orderedness means that the parties need not be overly concerned with developing rules for just wars or general sanctioning powers, save as these relate to the problem of assurance: given human nature, a "stabilizing device" might be required to allay suspicion or lack of confidence between the parties due to the possibility of the "free rider" problem when an otherwise ideal scheme is implemented.[41] This possibility ties the ideal theory envisioned to partial compliance theories and real-life conflict (thereby indicating the place and value of ideal theory in a non-ideal world), but partial compliance is not the theme of Rawls' work or our Rawlsian models. Since the parties are to assume good faith, the problem of assurance need only be mentioned or sketched in passing.[42]

With these two constraints in mind, the parties can now consider the principles required to solve the third choice problem of international relations. Indeed, assaying the very conception of the parties as free and equal entities, the first principle of international justice to be acknowledged would be immediately apparent. This is the basic principle of equality: "Independent peoples organized as states have certain fundamental equal rights."[43] This principle corresponds to the free and equal status of individuals and is the consequence of the transfer of moral status of individuals to nation-states based upon the notion of collectivity in

40. TJ, *supra* note 1, at 145.

41. *See* Rawls' discussion of penal sanctions in a well-ordered society, *id.* at 240f, 267f and 315.

42. *Id.* at 8f, 245 and 351. Some of the problems of application will be appraised in the next part of this article.

43. *Id.* at 378.

the original position.

Equality is a basic or fundamental principle in that contingent factors are not to affect recognition of this essential quality. This feature of the principle of equality is also a familiar part of contemporary international legal thinking. An early international contract theorist, commenting on the moral equality of nations, notes that

> just as the tallest man is no more a man than a dwarf, so also a nation, however small, is no less a nation than the greatest nation. Therefore, since the moral quality of men has no relation to the size of their bodies, the moral equality of nations also has no relation to the number of men of which they are composed.

This same author also goes on to argue that the fundamental rights and obligations of all nations are the same, even as between powerful and weak nations, and that right is never to be measured by might.[44] A more recent 19th century international legal theorist puts the case succinctly when he writes,

> equality cannot be affected by the casual qualities or attributes of a State, such as antiquity, population, extent of territory, military power, form of the constitution, title of its sovereign, state of civilization, respect which it enjoys, etc. No one of these considerations can justify the least difference or the slightest distinction between nations considered as moral persons. . . .[45]

Lest there be any doubt, we might interpolate that "[n]o one or any combination of these considerations" affects the principle of equality as between states.

This principle of equality seems required by the very structure of the original position and the constraints outlined above. What is not clear is how this principle, once acknowledged, should influence further deliberation. Interpretation and extension of an egalitarian principle should proceed cautiously and in concert with prior principles.

Equality of the parties easily led in the first choice problem to a principle of greatest equal liberty in treating individuals-in-society,

> [b]ut in the society of states the need is not for greater liberty for the individual states, but for a strengthening of the social bond between them, not for the clamant assertion of their rights, but for a more insistent reminder of their obligations towards one another. . . . [I]t is not improbable, and it is certainly desirable, that there should be a

44. C. WOLFF, JUS GENTIUM METHODO SCIENTIFICA PERTRACTATUM secs. 16-18 (1764); original reproduced and translated in 2 volumes in THE CLASSICS OF INTERNATIONAL LAW 15-16 (J. Scott ed., J. Drake trans. 1934). Though Wolff relies on, and Rawls denies, a self-evident natural law, both present contractual theories for international relations and justice.

45. 1 C. CALVO, DICTIONNAIRE DE DROIT INTERNATIONAL PUBLIC ET PRIVE 286 (1885). Cited in full by E. DICKINSON, THE EQUALITY OF STATES IN INTERNATIONAL LAW 100-101 (1920); cited in part by Johnston, *The Foundations of Justice in International Law*, in THE INTERNATIONAL LAW AND POLICY OF HUMAN WELFARE 122 (MacDonald ed. 1978).

movement towards the closer interdependence of states.[46]

Granted the author is not here speaking to parties in a Rawlsian original position, the caution is nonetheless legitimate. Although the parties would be loath to acknowledge a principle requiring interdependence, they would also be wary, given the model conditions outlined, of choosing a principle or interpretation of equality which might hinder establishing reciprocal relationships for mutual advantage. Rather, based upon these model conditions, a principle of equality should be so interpreted to help form the very basis of cooperation, not merely differentiation or hostility.

If interdependence in some from is probable, even desirable, then a basic institutional structure is required to develop a framework for responsible interaction. A reciprocating equality in relations cannot reasonably be expected to evolve in an atmosphere of statal egoism. The principle of equality could not be preserved under such a scheme. To found a reciprocal structure, two more basic or fundamental principles will need to be acknowledged. The first of these is the basic principle of obligation, know traditionally as the principle of *pacta sunt servanda*—treaties or agreements are to be observed. This principle is interpreted so as to encompass the individual analog of fairness, combined with the duty of mutual respect.[47] So rendered, the principle establishes the contours of reciprocity in statal relations.

The second of these additional principles which should be acknowledged or chosen is based, like that of equality, on the conception of the parties behind the veil of ignorance. This conception requires the acknowledgment of continuing collective responsibility. That is, once collective responsibility is recognized and the transfer of free and equal status is made from individuals to nations in the original position, accountability cannot later be shed.[48] Nations must acknowledge and take responsibility for their international claims and actions.

These three principles form the basic triad for the international structure of Model 1. They would be readily acknowledged as flowing

46. J. BRIERLY, THE LAW OF NATIONS, 50-51 (6th ed. 1963). Brierly's text is Rawls' one and only cited authority for international affairs. We are even told that Brierly's work "contains all that we need here" for the development of international principles of justice. TJ, *supra* note 1, at 378).

47. Remember that at the time of the transfer of moral status, individual principles had already been acknowledged. Unless the contrary can be cogently argued, such individual duties as these will also have transferred. For purposes of discussion under this model, we shall assume they do, in fact, transfer legitimately to states; counter arguments could not be successful. *Cf.* the statal duties outlined in Schachter, *Towards a Theory of International Obligation*, 8 VA. J. INT'L L. 300 (1968).

48. Not all legal theorists would agree. *E.g.*, Kelsen argues that collective responsibility is a characteristic of primitive peoples and primitive legal systems. As an international law develops, he would hope to see collective responsiblity diminish. Only in this critical light does he admit, that collective responsibility is one of the characteristics elements of international law. *See* H. KELSEN, LAW AND PEACE IN INTERNATIONAL RELATIONS 25-26 (1942). *But cf.* Cheng, *Justice and Equity*, 8 CURRENT LEGAL PROBS. 185 (1955).

from the combinations of principles, constraints and conditions facing the parties. But, these principles also imply a second-order triad of corollaries: self-determination (linked to the principle of equality), self-defense (linked to the principle of collective responsibility) and self-limitation (linked to the principle of *pacta sunt servanda*). These three additional principles are the consequence of holding the first triad as basic to international relations.

In this context, self-determination means that each nation's conception of the good, being based in equality, is deemed legitimate and of equal worth. Given that the particularities of specific conceptions are unknown behind the veil, the parties could not reasonably agree to a principle which might allow ranking of conceptions, thereby possibly putting their nation's conception in jeopardy. Any other principle permitting one nation's predominance over or interference in the internal affairs of another state, due solely to differing conceptions of the good, could not be acknowledged or tolerated.

The corollary of self-defense, in this context, signifies not so much the violence of warfare or military sanctions (remember that the parties are well-ordered states), but addresses in light of collective responsibility the right inhering to press claims based upon a nation's conception of the good. Since all conceptions are deemed to be equal in worth under self-determination, the claims based in these conceptions must be allowed to equally compete for resources.[49]

Finally, the meaning of self-limitation, which in this context is linked to the *pacta* principle is two-fold. It acknowledges that a state has the fundamental right to (a) entirely withhold a claim or claim of value, and (b) restrict the scope of any claims which it can otherwise put forward under self-defense. This corollary recognizes the independence of each party to operate on the basis of its conception of the good and no party can require another to act in accordance with its interpretation of the other's best interest.[50]

Taken together, these six principles form a complete foundation for erecting a basic structure of background justice in the international arena. Such was their derivation that these principles also form a coherent set when aligned with the solutions and constraint of the first two choice problems of the model. This result closes the section and completes our initial task for the first Rawlsian model of international justice.

49. Rawls' indication of the traditional principles and meanings of self-determination and self-defense appear at TJ, *supra* note 1, at 378. *But cf.* French & Gutman, *The Principle of National Self-Determination*, in PHILOSOPHY, MORALITY AND INTERNATIONAL AFFAIRS 138 (Held ed. 1974), where "nation" and "state" self-determinations are differentiated.

50. These corollaries may appear somewhat trivial, but they become important considerations in later rule development and effectiveness. As such, they would be acknowledged as principles in this original position. *See* Wildeman, *The Philosophical Background of Effectiveness*, ESSAYS ON INTERNATIONAL LAW AND RELATIONS 355 (Meijers & Vierdag eds. 1977).

We have developed its original position for an international forum and have acknowledged the principles to be chosen under this model. We turn in our next section to the complementary task of developing an original position for and acknowledging principles to be chosen under Model 2.

B. *Model 2.*

Under Model 1, the original position agenda contained three items or choice problems: principles were to be acknowledged for the basic institutional structure, the natural duty of individuals and finally, the law of nations. These problems were to be solved in the order given, so that international principles could be selected only after a coherent set of institutional and individual principles had first been established. This coherent set of principles would, in turn, narrow the range of feasible alternatives for international principles, so that, at the conclusion of all choice problems, the three solutions could form a complete and coherent table of principles for a theory of justice as fairness. That the choice problems were so framed was largely due to an assumption incorporated in Rawls' theory of society. This assumption operated so as to circumscribe the denotations of community and society, making both terms synonymous with the modern notion of the nation state.[51]

Model 2 is the outcome of an attempt to break free of these restrictions in accord with the Kantian emphasis so often acknowledged in justice as fairness. This model is based upon distinctive understandings of the concepts of community and society. "Community" here designates a

---

51. TJ, *supra* note 1, at 457. We discover the assumption which has been implicitly operating throughout his argument when in section 69, "*The Concept of a Well-Ordered Society*," the reader is informed that he is to "*assume that the boundaries of these schemes [i.e., the complex of major social institutions] are given by the notion of a self-contained national community*." That this notion implies the importation into theory of the modern concept of the nation-state is made clear in later writings where the concept of the basic structure is refined:

> Now by assumption the basic structure is the all-inclusive social system that determines background justice. (Observe that I leave aside here the problem of justice between nation.)
>
> . . . .
>
> The reason for doing this is that, as a first approximation, the problem of social justice concerns that basic structure as a closed background system. To start with the society of nations would seem merely to push one step further back the task of finding a theory of background justice. . . . We are better prepared to take up this problem for a society (illustrated by nations) conceived as a more or less self-sufficient scheme of social cooperation and as possessing a more or less complete culture.

BSS, *supra* note 8, at 57, 70 (footnote omitted). This approach is reiterated in *Kantian Constructivism*:

> I am leaving aside two important matters: [one being] questions of justice between societies (the law of nations). . . . I shall simply proceed on the idea that we may reasonably begin with the basic structure of one society as a closed and self-sufficient system of cooperation.

KCMT, *supra* note 8, at 524.

factual description of the nature of man as man-in-the-world; "society" characterizes those voluntary relationships which develop as an expression of this community within a fixed or definite territory. These distinctions are maintained by acknowledging the fact of community as being prior to and therefore separate from the phenomenon of society, and that which is [to be] regulated by major institutions (i.e. a basic structure) of international (understood as global) scale is essentially the former fact, not the latter phenomenon.

Rawls' own description of the sociability of man, coupled with his Kantian emphasis, points to a narrower notion of society and a broader notion of community.[52] Consider the Stoic notion of a world-wide cosmopolis:

> The positive substitute wherewith the Stoics thought to replace the ordinary relations of civil society was by a citizenship of the world. No preceding system had been able to overcome the difficulty of nationalities.
>
> . . . .
>
> If human society . . . has for its basis the identity of reason in individuals, what ground have we for limiting this society to a single nation, of feeling ourselves more nearly related to some men than to others? All men . . . are equally near, since all equally participate in reason.[53]

Similarly, in emphasizing the freedom and equality of moral persons (especially as rationally autonomous agents in the original position), Rawls himself, following Humboldt, speaks of "the notion of the community of mankind."[54] If such a notion of the community of man is more than mere wish-projection, then a corresponding concept of society should be developed which is not tied to specific political structures (whether ancient city-state or modern nation-state), but is rather derived

52. TJ, *supra* note 1. Just as "various conceptions of justice are the outgrowth of different notions of society against the background of opposing views of the natural necessities and opportunities of human life," we can only fully understand any particular conception of justice by making "explicit the conception of social cooperation from which it derives" *Id.* at 9-10. Detailed discussion of Rawls' notion of society is provided in section 79, "The Idea of Social Union." *Id.* at 520. *See also infra* note 58.

53. REICHEL, THE STOICS, EPICUREANS AND SCEPTICS 326, 328 (Zeller trans. 1962). For further discussion, see E. ARNOLD, ROMAN STOICISM at 275 (1911), where it is argued that the "world-state is held together neither by force nor statecraft, but goodwill." For examples of primary materials, see 4 SENECA, DE OTIO 1; 8 SENECA, DE OTIO 2; 1 EPICTETUS, DISCOURSES 9, and 4 MARCUS AURELIUS, MEDITATIONS 4. Phrases such as "citizen of the cosmos" and "fellow citizens of a common [read 'universal'] political community" frequently recur in Stoic discourse on politics. By proceeding in this way, we can quite readily follow Kant when he notes that "the idea of a cosmopolitan right is not fantastical, high-flown notion of right, but a complement of the unwritten code of law—constitutional as well as international law—necessary for the public rights of mankind in general and thus for the realization of perpetual peace. E. KANT, PERPETUAL PEACE: A PHILOSOPHICAL ESSAY 21 (Smith trans. 1948).

54. TJ, *supra* note 1, at 523.

from this notion of human community. This approach permits development of an ideal theory of international justice uninfluenced by historical politics. International law and international justice, in this context, are individual-oriented, working through particular societies. This runs contrary to the modern context and Rawls' own particular derivation of international law and justice principles which are nation-state oriented and which deny individual standing. But just such a derivation seems much closer to his intent and Kantian approach.

Given that in this second model only one basic community structure is in view, we should expect the choice problems to be formulated differently. Indeed, being now unhindered by the assumption of societal nation-states with individuated basic structures, choice problem number one (involving principles for an institutional or basic domestic structure) and choice problem number three (involving principles for an international structure) logically collapse into a single agenda item. Thus, under Model 2, the original position agenda contains but two items or choice problems: principles are to be acknowledged for (1) the basic institutional structure [of global community], and (2) the natural duty of individuals. As to the order of acknowledgment, Rawls' defense for a hierarchy for choosing principles for the basic structure prior to those for natural duty remains valid here: "while it would be possible to choose many of the natural duties before those of the basic structure," some natural duties and obligations "presuppose principles for social forms. . . . That principles for institutions are chosen first shows the social nature of the virtue of justice. . . . "[55] Principles for the basic community structure, then, will still be acknowledged first.

As previously noted, a more definite structuring of an original position for our model is required before moving to the choice of principles. Following our earlier format as a guide to development, analysis begins with the conditions for structuring an original position as discussed by Rawls under the four headings of the circumstances of justice, the formal constraints of the concept of right, the veil of ignorance and the rationality of the parties.

Since we begin in Model 2 with the very first agenda item, there will be no need to investigate multiple hierarchical original positions. But, as we proceed, it will become desirable to juxtapose the two original position descriptions detailed under Model 1 with the single original position of Model 2. In fact, many of the conditions outlined for the first original position for the first two agenda items under Model 1 (designated M1A for discussion) will appear unchanged in the original position under Model 2 (M2). Other conditions under M2 will synthesize some of the additional features found in the original position for the third agenda item under Model 1 (M1B). This should not be too surprising since we are dealing with a choice problem in M2 which partakes of both Model 1

55. *Id.* at 110.

elements. (This triple comparison will culminate in a chart detailing all three original positions under both models.)

Turning now to the conditions which define the structure of the original position M2, it is again apparent that those of universality, generality, publicity, ordering and finality (*viz.* the formal constraints of the concept of right) can be readily subsumed as proper conditions holding for the choice of all ethical principles. Likewise, though disagreement may not have abated, those conditions of mutual disinterestedness (limited altruism), lack of envy, use of effective means and strict compliance (*viz.* the conditions of the rationality of the parties) can be incorporated to develop a Rawlsian model. Also, keeping with our model definition, the conception of the parties poses no difficulty and is similar to the conception found in M1A: since individuals comprise the component actors of international community, the parties are conceived to be individual participants acting as continuous persons; the participants are not acting as societal or national representatives. Thus, the difficulties of representative justifications do not arise under Model 2 as they did under Model 1.

This quick overview allows a setting aside of three sets of conditions. No real problems for incorporation in the structure of M2 confront us. The only conditions requiring broader analysis are those falling under the headings of the circumstances of justice and the veil of ignorance. To briefly review, the circumstances of justice specify that (1) conditions of moderate scarcity exist; (2) there is a divergence of fundamental interests and ends, with a variety of opposing and incompatible beliefs; and (3) the scheme of basic institutions is a self-sufficient and productive scheme of social cooperation. How are these conditions to be understood in M2?

Regarding the first circumstance, synthesis is greatly simplified. Participants in M2, representing continuing persons, will readily understand that conditions of moderate scarcity exist as between the parties: natural and other resources are not abundant enough to meet every claim; additionally, not only are resource levels finite, but uneven global distribution will skew the factor of availability itself. Nor will it be difficult to interpret and apply the condition of moderate scarcity to and between non-self-contained and non-self-sufficient societies established by individuals' circumscribed collective relations in the world community. Given the parties knowledge of general facts, they will recognize that skewed individual and societal access to unevenly distributed resources of limited store creates individual, intra- and inter-societal conflicting claims. Thus, the first circumstance of justice in M2 can be read in the following manner: natural, technological and other resources are unevenly distributed and of limited store, yielding a condition of moderate scarcity as to and between individual and societal claims. In short, conditions of moderate scarcity exist in the world community.

The second circumstance of justice can be approached in similar fashion. Once again, participants in M2 will have little difficulty in interpreting the scope of divergent fundamental interests and incompatible beliefs as between the parties. Acting as "rational agents of construction"[56] with a conception of the good (though they know not what the substance of that conception entails—an element of the veil in all accounts), the parties can reasonably entertain the assumption that not all conceptions are congruent. They would rather expect these various conceptions to clash and to produce many (though surely not all) of the conflicting claims recognized under the first circumstance of moderate scarcity.

Societies would also be expected to have divergent interests, goals and beliefs. Societies, arising from the collective relationships of groups of individuals situated territorially in the world community, are bound to take upon themselves, as collectives, the beliefs and aspirations of its individual members as communicated through societal organizational channels (whatever form these[57] may take). Now this certainly does not mean that any single society so described is necessarily homogeneous and must develop a common belief or interest pattern which only conflicts with another society's incompatible singularly defined belief or goal. Organizational channels of communication being imperfect mechanisms at their operational best, some level of internal conflict seems inevitable, even if stability is never threatened. On the other hand, though societal heterogeneity might be the more common experience, it is just as certainly not required. Two (or more) societies, more or less internally homogeneous, might develop patterns which are incompatible and then come into contact and conflict. The point is that just as with claims to resources, conflicts can be expected under this circumstance at multiple levels. Consider the following actors and the possible basic conflict situations:

56. KCMT, *supra* note 8, at 520.

57. The indefinite referent "these" is purpose fully ambiguous. Not only beliefs and goals, but organizational channels, can be expected to take multifarious forms in M2 societies. Recall that the choice problem of principles for ordering any single society is not an agenda item in M2. Here, only the basic institutional structure of community is of concern.

Society A:	Society B:	Unassociated:
individual member P	individual member R	individual S
individual member Q		individual T

INDIVIDUAL CLAIMS IN CONFLICT	(1) P v. Q (individual members of same society)
	(2) P v. R (individual members of different societies)
	(3) Q v. S (individual societal member/unassociated individual)
	(4) S v. T (unassociated individuals)
INDIVIDUAL/SOCIETAL CLAIMS IN CONFLICT	(5) P v. A (individual societal member/own society)
	(6) Q v. B (individual societal member/different society)
	(7) T v. A (unassociated individual/any society)
SOCIETAL CLAIMS IN CONFLICT	(8) A v. B (any two societies)

BASIC CONFLICT
SITUATIONS

Due reflection permits the incorporation of the second circumstance of justice in M2 with but the addition of a clarifying phrase. The circumstance will now read that there is a divergence of fundamental interests and ends, with a variety of opposing and incompatible beliefs as to and between individuals and societies.

Before turning to the third and final circumstance of justice involving the scheme of basic institutions, a brief review of the role of the basic structure would be helpful. Recall that the basic structure is the closed background system of major institutions which distributes fundamental rights and duties and determines the division of advantages of cooperation. In Model 2, the basic structure is that closed system of major international institutions whose object is justice. This scheme of basic institutions distributes the fundamental rights and duties and determines the division of advantages of communal (i.e. individual and societal) cooperation.[58]

The difficulty arising in M2 with this third circumstance is alike to the problem encountered in M1B—a prescribed scheme of institutions does not appear to exist. Despite this superficial similarity, the problem here is not so acute. Given Model 1 assumptions, a predefined scheme to generate international community was lacking and could not be assumed. It had to be supposed that the need for interaction would be recognized and acted upon to aid resolution of the third choice problem. Under Model 2 assumptions, international community, like the concept of socia-

---

58. This central point concerns the scope of the application of justice as fairness: that is, determination of what size and sort of community or associative activity over which the theory of justice extends—the realm of its operation. In Rawls' discussion of sociability, we were led to the notion of social union. Kelsen, *supra* note 48. This notion might best be understood in the context of coordinated activity of a group of individuals who share final ends and common activities which are declared to be) intrinsically valuable. TJ, *supra* note 1, at 525. Since the group is of indefinite size, we can speak of families and friendships—as well as familiar and larger associations of clubs, churches, universities, and professional or trade unions—as forms of social unions. Accordingly, a well-ordered community "is itself a form of social union. Indeed, it is a social union of social unions" TJ, *supra* note 1, at 527.

Yet, justice as fairness does not provide a general theory for evaluating or directing the course of all social unions:

> In many if not most cases these principles [of justice as fairness] give unreasonable directive. To illustrate: for churches and universities different principles are plainly more suitable. Their members usually affirm certain shared aims and purposes as essential guidelines to the most appropriate form of organization.

BSS, *supra* note 8, at 49. Such social unions are subjects of justice, but they are not the subjects to which the theory addresses itself. Rather, its concern and the domain over which the theory applies is the primary subject of social justice, and "the primary subject of justice is the basic structure" of community. TJ, *supra* note 1 at 7; similar formulations are employed at 54, 84. The principles of social justice apply then to the "social union of social unions" and "the way in which the major social institutions distribute fundamental rights and duties and determine the division of advantages from social cooperation" *Id.* at 7. That is, justice is the object of the basic structure of a well-ordered community. Thus, while the basic structure of Model 1 narrowly encompassed nation-state society, the basic community structure of Model 2 encompasses global community. *See* Cheng, *supra* note 49.

bility, is a factual description of the nature of man and interaction (with interactive conflict) at all levels is reasonably assumed as a natural result of this factual description. Put in slightly different perspective, just as sociability "guarantees" collectives, community "guarantees" collective interaction. This latter form of expression is somewhat misleading because it obscures our vision of individual characters. Nevertheless, it makes clear that patterns of interaction and adjudication will develop and it is the right of the basic structure to order those patterns of cooperation and adjudicate any conflicts which arise between parties. Thus, to acknowledge principles for agenda item number one in M2 does not create *ex nihilo* a scheme of basic institutions; rather, given the facts of community and the first two circumstances of justice already noted above, principles are to be chosen to order the scheme of basic institutions, which structure is bound (as opposed to the "can" or "need" in M1B) to arise, for the sake of justice.

In light of this analysis, it should be noted that the closed background system recognized by this third circumstance of justice leads to an expansion of the chart of basic conflict situations previously outlined. Three additions are necessary to complete the chart for M2:

Individual/Basic Community Structure (BCS) claims in conflict
(9) P v. BCS (individual societal member/BCS)
(10) S v. BCS (unassociated individual/BCS)
Societal/BCS claims in conflict
(11) A v. BCS (any society/BCS)

With this clarification in hand, the third circumstance in M2 should read that for a scheme of basic institutions to exist for mutual advantage, principles must be chosen to order relations according to the dictates of justice.

The final category of conditions requiring examination are those of the veil of ignorance. As previously noted, the thickest veil possible is desired; instead of starting with full information and then excluding just enough to eliminate contingent factors, a Rawlsian veil excludes all information and then adds "just enough" so that rationally autonomous agents can reach agreement. However, the factor of the thickness of the veil in all situations is also directly related to the hierarchical position of the agenda item being considered and its assumptions. Veil thickness in M1B was greatly influenced by the fact that the choice of principles for a law of nations was the third of three agenda items or choice problems. Incorporation of certain contingent factors at that point in the original position affected both the conception and knowledge of the parties, and compromised the ideal value of the theory.

Veil thickness in M2, on the other hand, is nearly identical with that of M1A. Given that both deal with their respective number one agenda items, this is an expected and desirable outcome. Behind these thick veils, the parties in M1A and M2 are not influenced by any particular information which can inappropriately influence their representation as free and equal moral persons. As a result, the ideal value of M2 is maintained. In fact, given the slight twist of interpretation required of some factors due to the delineation between community and society, the veil of M2 is nominally thicker than veil of M1A. Following is a partial demonstrative list of such veil conditions:

> No one knows his place in society *or if he is a member of a society*
> . . .
> The parties do not know the particular circumstances of *any society*
> . . .
> They do not know *any society's* economic or political situation, or the level of civilization and culture
> . . .
> They do not know any particular circumstances of *international community*
> . . .
> They do not know the *international community's* economic or political situation, or the level of civilization and culture. . . .[59]

This analysis of the veil of ignorance concludes discussion of the conditions required to structure the original position under Model 2. All the necessary elements have been considered. (Following is a comparative chart detailing all three original positions formulated under both models.) We can now deal with the M2 agenda item of choosing principles of international justice.

59. TJ, *supra* note 1, at 137. Emphasis supplied to indicate M2 additions.

	M2	M1A	M1B
Formal constraints of the concept of right	Universality, generality, publicity, ordering, finality	Universality, generality, publicity, ordering, finality	Universality, generality, publicity, ordering, finality
Rationality of the parties	Mutual disinterestedness, lack of envy, use of effective means, strict compliance	Mutual disinterestedness lack of envy, use of effective means strict compliance	Mutual disinterestedness, lack of envy use of effective means, strict compliance
Conception of the parties	free and equal continuing persons	Free and equal continuing persons	Free and equal well-ordered nation-state societies
Circumstances of justice	1) Conditions of moderate scarcity exist as to and between individuals and non-self sufficient/non-self-contained societies	1) Moderate scarcity exists	1) Unevenly distributed and limited natural and others resources exist as between nations
	2) Divergent fundamental interests and opposing and incompatible beliefs as to and between individuals and societies	2) Divergent fundamental interests, opposing and incompatible beliefs	2) Convergent fundamental interest, but divergent goals and opposing beliefs
	3) A basic scheme will exist, but principles must be chosen to order relations for reciprocal advantage	3) A basic scheme exists for reciprocal advantage	3) A basic scheme needs to exist for reciprocal good
Veil of ignorance	No specific information available—nominally thicker than M1A	No specific information available—thick veil	Specific information that parties are nation-states existing as collectives known by participants

ORIGINAL POSITIONS FOR RAWLSIAN MODELS

Once again, any constraints on choice solutions flowing from the conditions in the original position should be briefly covered before turning to the derivation of principles, itself. To this initial coverage we turn below.

The discussion of the choice of principles under Model 1 opened with an examination of two constraints which were laid upon the parties. The task of acknowledging international principles to solve the third choice problem was put under the constraints of coherence and strict compliance and thereunder was the task discharged. But are these same constraints to be found here?

Unlike the parties under the first model, participants in Model 2 should face no coherence constraints in their deliberations. Since the first, not the third agenda item is being considered, no prior principles need be taken into account; none exist. Only the basic assumptions or conditions of the model confront the parties here. On the other hand, the condition of strict compliance is a feature of all three original positions outlined in previous discussion. As one of the present model conditions defining an element of the rationality of the parties, the participants can reasonably assume each other's good faith. That is, all can be expected to receive and act in accordance with whatever principles are finally acknowledged. Since the parties rely on this as a condition of the model, they will not be generally concerned with sanctioning powers to induce compliance. Only the psychological (motivational) problem of assurance in implementing an ideal scheme is of any particular concern and this consideration should solely affect the participants' reasonings in the subsequent operation of the model, not while here acknowledging basic principles. Thus, the only comparable operative constraint on reasoning towards international principles of justice under Model 2 is the model restriction that ideal, not partial compliance theory is envisioned.

Turning to the actual choice of principles under the model, it might be helpful to begin by taking a closer look at the conditions of the first original position for Model 1 and the solution to its first agenda item or choice problem, i.e. Rawls' domestic theory of justice as fairness. Given the striking similarities between the structures of the original positions M1A and M2, it would perhaps become possible to adopt some of Rawls' reasonings or conclusions from the former domestic situation where similar conditions are met in our Rawlsian international model. In fact, by taking this slightly discursive route, it becomes possible to argue that Rawls' solution to M1A (*viz.* the general and special conceptions of domestic justice involving his two principles)[60] is also the solution—with a

60. The formulation of Rawls' general conception of justice rests upon the following intuitive argument: Looking at the problem of the choice of principles from the viewpoint of one of the participants, it would not be reasonable to expect agreement on a principle granting a greater than equal share in any division of the primary goods. Neither would it be rational to put oneself at a (possible) disadvantage by agreeing to a principle distributing less than an equal share. If this fairly states the case, the sensible thing to do is to initially

few appropriate modifications—to M2.

How are we to understand Rawls' general and special conceptions as possible solutions to M2? Turning to the conditions fo the structure for M2, what differences exist and how might any difference affect the reasonings of the original position participants? If the solution to M1A is to form a basic solution to M2, the hypothetical should be similarly structured.

In fact, perusal of the original positions' comparative chart indicates that the conditions outlined for M1A and M2 are nearly identical. Where differences do occur, they are usually matters of phraseology, not of substance. The one difference which indicates more than mere turn-of-phrase can be seen in the third circumstance of justice. In M1A, the scheme of societal institutions comprising a basic structure is assumed to presently exist. This scheme is a factor to be considered irrespective of the participants' time of entry. Although not pursued in previous discussions, this assumption is an important one (and, of course, factually arguable in historical perspective), removing Rawls' theory from the mainstream of contract theories. This is evident in that Rawls does not attempt to create or legitimate social union and basic schemes (something past theorists have taken great pains to establish with their social contracts); rather, the Rawlsian contract seeks only to order that which already exists for the sake of justice.

The third circumstance of justice is rendered somewhat differently in M2, with slightly different implications. Here, the scheme of institutions comprising a basic community structure is only assumed to be assured of coming into existence. Behind the veil, the participants cannot know

---

acknowledge principles of equality establishing equal liberty, equality of opportunity and an equal distribution of income and wealth. These principles of equality lead to the formulation of a general conception of justice which can be expressed as follows: All social values—liberty and opportunity, income and wealth, and the bases of self-respect—are to be distributed equally unless an unequal distribution of any, or all, of these values is to everyone's advantage (TJ, at 62). The formulation of Rawls' special conception rests upon an argument for ranking these primary goods which yield certain priority rules. These rules, in turn, work to order the principles of justice. Without rehearsing all the arguments presented, the final statement takes the following form: *First Principle*—each person is to have an equal right to the most extensive total system of equal liberties compatible with a similar system of liberty for all. *Second Principle*—social and economic inequalities are to be arranged so that they are both: (a) to the greatest benefit of the least advantaged, consistent with the just savings principle, and (b) attached to offices and positions open to all under conditions of fair equality of opportunity. First Priority Rule (The Priority of Liberty)—Liberty can be restricted only for the sake of liberty. There are two cases: (a) a less extensive liberty must strengthen the total system of liberty shared by all, and (b) a less than equal liberty must be acceptable to those with the less liberty. Second Priority Rule (The Priority of Justice over Efficiency and Welfare)—The second principle of justice is lexically prior to the principle of efficiency and to that of maximizing the sum of advantages; and fair opportunity [2(b)] is prior to the difference principle [2(a)]. *Id.* at 302-03, statement of two cases in second priority rule omitted. (This is the final compilation of several provisional forms developed during argument for the theory.)

whether such institutions already substantially exist or are only in early developmental or formative stages. The historical question is left open. What they do understand is that principles are required to order these institutions for mutual good under justice. Again, this Rawlsian contract does not create social union, but it does recognize the imported normative element of legitimation also found in M1B. That is, M2 explicitly recognizes the self-legitimating function of justice as a circumstance. M1A does implicitly recognize such a function, but only under the rubric of Kantian autonomy and self-realization.

Is this difference substantive, affecting the reasonings of the parties? Not at all. At least, there should be no substantive difference when reasoning towards basic principles. The conditions of M1A and M2 are effectively the same, though terminology and categories differ in respect of legitimation. Both sets of parties recognize that a basic structure is an inevitable factor in their deliberations and both sets seek mutual good under principles of justice. If this difference is to have any discernible effect, it is only in that a breakdown in deliberations leading to an egoistic stated of nature is not an acceptable option for M2 parties as it might be on some interpretatious of M1A.[61] Where substantive differences can be expected is in the later interpretation of international circumstance. There, conceptual divergence in our models is great (compare M1B with M2). What is required here is only an interpretative discussion of the principles of equality under the Model 2 framework. A few modifications are suggested below. Note that these modifications are due not to any hidden structural difference, but are related to the concepts of community and society under our second model definition.

Modification 1 — As is implicit in Rawls' own discussion, the "persons" entitled to the most extensive total system of basic liberties are not only individual human beings acting as moral agents. Generally speaking, social unions, evidenced for example in families, churches and trade councils, existing as individuated collectives having an organizational "personality" are also to be afforded political liberites.[62] Under Model 2, societies are similarly viewed as second-order social unions ordered by the basic structure of the social union of social unions, the international community. This community scheme distributes rights, advantages and duties to all its members, individuals and social unions (including societies) alike. With this explicit understanding, the first principle of equal liberty is easily adopted in M2.

Modification 2 — Similarly, the principles of equality of opportunity and equal distribution of income and wealth are readily adopted with the understanding that the subjects of these principles remain consistent with the subjects of modification 1. Thus, Model 2 can speak of inter-

61. *Id.* at 136.

62. *See, e.g., id.* sec. 35 at 216-21, "Toleration of the Intolerant," where political parties and religious groups are under consideration.

societal, not just intra-societal, social and economic inequalities in the world community.

Modification 3 — Rawls notes that one of the elements of basic liberty is the principle of free association.[63] What is not clear is whether there exists a freedom to disassociate, although it could be reasonably argued that this latter freedom is implied in the former. So that there is no misunderstanding, this modification makes explicit the freedom to disassociate, notably at the societal level, and to remain unassociated if willing and able. This freedom may be exercised contingent upon one factor: any standing obligations legitimately incurred in association must be discharged. Such a constraint is only reasonable. Rational parties could not otherwise be expected to agree upon a principle which could so consistently work to their detriment. The modification is not intent on providing an escape route, but views social union (e.g. societal membership) as fluid, rather than more-or-less fixed for life. So circumscribed, the freedom is a valuable one in international community.

Modification 4 — One final modification and interpretation is complete. We have spoken of the need to recognize collective personality in relation to specific social unions, but what of collective assets? If they exist (and there is no reason to assume they do not, given acknowledgment of group person-hood), does the general community have any call upon resources individually or collectively possessed? Does mere possession imply a duty to share on a broad scale, or is community sharing simply a good which can be designated the outcome of a supererogatory act? To put the question squarely, should the parties in M2 acknowledge a principle that everyone has duties reciprocal in nature within the community in which he develops? A proper answer would aid understanding the factor of "legitimately incurred obligations" in modification 3 above.[64]

To form a reply, we should note not only that emphasis on community in Model 2 leans in the direction of acknowledging such a principle; Rawls himself suggests acknowledgment of an obligation when he writes, "Now when the maximum criterion is followed, the natural distribution of abilities is viewed in some respects as a collective asset."[65] That is, while the result of the natural lottery is morally arbitrary, development of those distributed assets in not. The community has some degree of right to see those talents used for the benefit of the whole in reciprocal response to community provision of an environment in which the talents can be developed for the benefit of the talents' possessors. Just how this right is to be weighted against a right of personal liberty is ticklish, but that the

---

63. *Id.* at 328-29.

64. Though apparently intruding in some degree onto second choice problem territory of selection of individual duties, the question of institutional obligations appropriately arises here as part of an analysis of the basic structure, especially given the intimate link with the third modification. Obligations linking individuals and institutions should not be expected to necessarily take the same form as those arising between individuals. *Id.* at 335.

65. Rawls, *supra* note 25, at 647.

obligation exists is difficult to deny. That "no man is an island" is no less true because quaint.

Neither is it difficult to understand this obligation in terms of large social unions like societies. In fact, it is much easier to understand an obligation of sharing, for example, excess natural resources than the benefits of personal talents. Such an interpolation seems less a strain on liberty, as well. The participants might well argue in the following fashion:

> Inasmuch as societies are understood to be combined in a supreme community, the individual societies are understood to have bound themselves to the whole, because they wish to promote the common good, but the whole to the individuals, because it wishes to provide for the especial good of the individuals. [Likewise,] if a society is established, individuals bind themselves to the whole, because they wish to promote the common good, and the whole binds itself to the individuals, because it wishes to provide for adequate life, for peace and security, consequently for the especial good of the individuals.[66]

Such obligations, then, are always reciprocal in nature. Being for the common benefit or mutual good, communal obligations would generally be acknowledged by the parties as long as they are founded upon the reciprocity in the community obligation to provide for free and full development of its members.[67]

In light of these four modifications, the parties in M2 would acknowledge the following triad of principles and general conception:

(1) principles of equality
- (a) equal liberty
- (b) equality of opportunity
- (c) equal distribution of income and wealth

(2) principles of free association
- (a) freedom to associate
- (b) freedom to disassociate
- (c) free to be unassociated

(3) principles of obligation
- (a) individuals have duties to community
- (b) individuals may incur duties in social union
- (c) community and union have reciprocal obligations towards members

General conception. All social primary goods—liberties, obligations and opportunities, income and command over resources, and the bases of self-respect—are to be distributed equally unless an unequal distribution of any or all of these goods is to the advantage of the least favored.

---

66. Wolff, *supra* note 44, sec. 12, at 13-14 (the terms "society" and "community" are here inserted, replacing "nation" and "state" respectively.

67. *Cf.* art. 29(1). "Everyone has duties to the community in which alone the free and full development of his personality is possible" and its context as drawn from the Universal Declaration of Human Rights. G.A. Res. 217A, U.N. Doc. A/810 at 71 (1948).

These principles and the general conception naturally flow from the Rawlsian hypothetical, given the great similarities and minor differences between M1A and M2. Although the participants could now proceed to develop parallel arguments for a special conception, it should be noted that the special assumption permitting adoption of a lexical order is not obviously present in Model 2: it cannot be assumed that conditions will admit effective realization of liberties. Priority rules may only come to the fore after much work with a fully developed scheme. Suffice to say that lexical ordering remains the long-run tendency of the general view here as in Model 1. The result would again be nearly identical. But application of a special conception will not be taken for granted.

It should also be noted that the natural duties mentioned above as the solution to the second choice problem in M1A are just as easily assimilated as the solution to the second choice problem in M2. Indeed, natural obligations of fairness, justice and refraining from harm naturally flow from the solution to the first agenda item (specially taking the third principle of obligation into consideration). Taken together, they form a coherent set of Model 2 principles for development of a basic structure for a scheme of just institutions. Acknowledgment of these principles and a general conception for a structural foundation for our model completes this part. We can now turn to the task of outlining in the next part some of the models' practical and theoretical implications in application.

III. PRACTICAL CONSEQUENCES

In turning to analyze and compare the practical consequences of the operations of our Rawlsian models, we shall focus discussion upon three cases or situations which might conceivably arise in the international forum. In this way, the interaction of model principles to specify the parameters of a just resolution can be observed and any differences between the models can be noted. The first two situations presented are types which could occur under either ideal or non-ideal, but its type has been all too common in our 20th century. The resolutions the models propose as being just (especially in the final case) could bear significant weight in relation to any considered judgments of fairness. In all cases, the proposed resolutions provide some insight into the relative strength of the models heretofore developed.

> *Situation 1. The world economy consumes x tons of strategic mineral y during an average annual production schedule. All y at the present time enters the production stream from land mining operations. World reserves are estimated at 25x tons /- 3x tons, which is to say that supplies will be exhausted within 22-28 years at current consumption levels. It is discovered that certain nodules from the deep floor of the Alpha Sea contain significant amounts of y, along with other valuable trace elements. Later research locates a sizeable field of these nodules—estimated yield of 5x tons /- .6 tons—situated at roughly mid-point between bordering coastal societies A and B. Two privately-owned companies (#1 and #2) located in prosperous A are*

> *prepared to attempt deep sea mining operations, either in concert or with societal aid, if an adequate return on their investment can be reasonably assured. The breakeven point is calculated at 3x tons, which includes a 5-year lead time to develop the field and come online plus a 6-year mining schedule of .5x tons/year, leaving a marginal return on yields of 1.4x to 2.6x tons. One publicly-owned company (#3) in developing society B would like to work the field, but requires economic and technical assistance or a partnership venture to do so. The breakeven point is here calculated at nearly 4x tons, which includes a 7-year lead time plus a 12-year mining schedule of .3x tons/year, leaving a marginal return on yields of .4x to 1.6x tons.*

Assuming that technological and cost factors prohibit development of more than one site in this field, who should begin mining, if anyone?

We shall not spend time working out questions of economic efficiency in this or subsequent cases. The data bases are purposefully incomplete for the benefit of generality, but they are also indeterminate for the benefit of justice. As Rawls notes, efficiency is a concern of the background system of institutions to a lesser degree than the concern for justice. That is, justice as fairness provides that the theoretically just parameters must first be established; only then do concerns like efficiency intrude to order the implementation of a solution.[68] Thus, in narrowing analysis of these situations to consideration of fairness, the primary concern of both models becomes the institutional and individual relationships engendered with the case settings.

In this first situation, numerous relationships are in view and the scope of the problem remains rather broad. Even in this simplified case, upwards of ten basic ties and their permutations could be investigated. Lest analysis become too cumbersome, intra-societal and other relationship ties will not be discussed; only the primary relationship between societies A and B are considered below.

Under Model 1, the configuration of basic and corollary principles suggest the following parameters. Assuming A and B are nation-states,[69] B is equal with A (equality) and may of itself determine its need for y and the desirability of mining nodules in the Alpha Sea (self-determination). It can decide its claim is of societal value (collective responsibility) and press that claim in the international forum (self-defense), so long as pressing the claim puts no prior agreement or treaty in jeopardy (pacta principle). B may also later reserve, restrict or withdraw its claim (self-limitation) during any bargaining session. The same analysis pattern applies, *pari passu*, to A. What this analysis does not provide is a neat an-

68. TJ, *supra* note 1, at 9.

69. The model is limited to nation-states and does not appear capable of settling conflicts between non-statal conflicting parties. *E.g.*, what if B were a non-statal nation or society? Neither does the model reach the question of "which company in A?" if the larger issue of "which society?" is resolved in A's singular favor. Some other internal process or model must then be invoked.

swer to the question originally put, "who should begin mining? The model does tell us that, other factors being equal (e.g. there are no applicable bi- or multilateral treaties or international agreements specifically resolving issues of ownership or access to this Alpha Sea floor), A and B should meet as equals at the bargaining table to work out a fair resolution of conflicting claims. But the model cannot, indeed was never meant to, declare a right result before negotiations even begin.

What is perhaps interesting is what arguments cannot be pressed by the parties under Model 1 during a bargaining session. Assuming A and B are both (relatively) well-ordered states, A cannot press B to withdraw its claim or sell its interest at a pittance as a simple function of A's economic superiority. That is not fair dealing for an otherwise just state striving towards an international society based on reciprocal relations. Neither can A press an argument of greater right or privilege founded on technological capabilities. However, A could stress the economic advantage to B of investing in A's venture through company #1 and/or #2, and the diseconomy to both states if B secured the aid it required to go ahead through its company #3.

On the other hand, B need not be persuaded by the force of economic efficiencies, alone. It might highly value technological linkage and the benefit to the society as a whole if #3 could work the field for 12 years, though it might realize only a minimal return above the breakeven point on an accounting ledger. B may insist on its view, but being well-ordered and wanting mutual advantage of all.[70] With the give-and-take of a fair bargaining session, A and B should be able to weigh the relative merits of their claims and strike a mining agreement for the nodules which can be deemed just.

Under Model 2, a more complicated structure makes analysis of this situation relatively more difficult as principle factors and relationships in view necessarily increase. The additional primary relationship considered here is that between the Basic Community Structure (BCS) and societies A and B. This relationship will be discussed along with the other primary relationship between A and B, as in the model above. However, the increase in complexity permits a more tightly drawn set of parameters which looks not only to the process, but to some of the very elements of the result, of what is deemed just. Unlike Model 1, specific resolutions may be forthcoming as information is gathered on the parties and their claims. To that extent, Model 2 works similarly to Rawl's domestic theory

70. We initially ignore here, though it is certainly relevant, the interest other societies have in adding five years' supply of strategic mineral y to world reserves at stable prices. The bargaining process is discussed as if it were between only A and B, but claims would surely be advanced by all user-states; under the model, all have a right to be heard and have the relative merits of their claims weighed in striking any final balance to reach agreement in the forum. The simple addition of states and claims do not, however, result in any change in the model's operation and need not be considered for sake of illustration of model efficacy.

of justice as fairness in that teleological judgments are taken into account while travelling the deontological path of pure (or quasi-pure) procedural justice.

The BCS is responsible to distribute fundamental rights and duties and to determine the division of advantages of cooperation of and for its members, based on the principles and general conception of justice as fairness formulated in Part II. Societies A and B are two such members, whose conflict also involves community advantage. Thus, while we could initially ignore other societal input under Model 1, the BCS must observe community balance from the outset to formulate any final resolution.

To this end, basic questions concerning the status of the societies directly involved must be addressed. For example: what is the relative market share in y of A and B, both as suppliers and users? How would access affect these shares? Is mining y a highly profitable enterprise?[71] If so, how much value would actually flow to society A? Society B? Once these and similar questions receive sufficient statistical input, analysis under the general conception can begin: would access to the field reasonably aid B in attaining community parity (principles of equality)? If B does develop the field, can it meet its community obligations (including price stability and steady delivery over the mining schedule per principles of obligation)? Turning to A, would access too greatly enhance its position in the community? Would this enhancement be offset by A's contribution to the community's least favored? If A were required to aid B, how great a cost is incurred monetarily? How great a price in terms of liberty?

Finally, assuming that the field should be developed (an obvious, though not necessary assumption, questions of conservation and price stability could be addressed as well), what are the possibilities or ramifications of introducing society Z (a developing land-locked society) to the field? In the alternative, what of establishing a central mining enterprise with general community authority for deep-sea-mining operations which would distribute the fruits of its business to societies in need?[72] Without pretending to answer all the issues raised, it can at least be observed that the resulting parameters tend to a much more centrally organized system of cooperation than under Model 1. A and B are not sitting together at a bargaining table alone or with minimal outside input to develop the framework of an agreement. Community factors play a dominant role in a Model 2 analysis. This is not to say that similar issues of organization could not be raised under Model 1. Such questions well might occur with

---

71. This need not refer to monetary input, alone. It can profit a society to grow technologically and to be able to expand inter-societal contacts, as well.

72. *See* the operation of the Enterprise in the text of the Law of the Sea Treaty. The Enterprise (art. 170ff) is the functional production organ of the Authority (art. 156ff), which is an international council in control of the Area (pt. XI) of deep sea resources for the benefit of mankind (art. 140) United Nations Convention on the Law of the Sea, U.N. Doc. A/Conf. 62/122, U.N. Doc. C/N.57(1983). *See also*, R. PLATZODER AND W. VITZTHUM (eds.), SEERECHT—LAW OF THE SEA 69 (1984).

even similar resolutions forthcoming as a result (e.g. Model 1 nation-states could agree on a central enterprise linked to private or statal investments). But the bases for centralized modeling will be quite distinct. This difference is perhaps better illustrated in the next situation.

> *Situation 2. Society C has just harvested a bumper crop of winter wheat far exceeding societal requirements. The goodly yield can be attributed to a number of factors, including careful agricultural management and beneficent weather patterns. At least one-third of the current harvest can be expected to enter the export market, giving good additional return to producers and a boost to C's economy. Nearby, society D is facing another harsh drought and basic foodstuffs are in short supply. With only a small industrial base to draw upon, D's treasury is rather limited and the relatively steep prices of importing grain will keep the society from securing sufficient quantities to avert high levels of severe malnutrition or famine amongst the populace.*

What obligations, if any, does C have with respect to D and its people?

Under Model 1, there exists significant difficulty in defining the conflict involved within this particular case. It is clear that C's abundance could timely aid D through any number of schemes, including lower prices, extension of credits, long-term low-interest loans, grants and gifts, or any combination of these devices. It is conceivably to C's advantage to extend a helping hand now (C might suffer from a future drought and need aid from D's goodly harvest). But there is no clear claim of right that D can advance to secure C's help. Unless reciprocal factors historically exist (perhaps D extended agricultural aid to C in the past and has yet to reap the advantage of that assistance), or some scheme of aid is currently envisioned by treaty or agreement in the international forum (perhaps C and D have a conventional or customary relationship whereby each undertakes to aid the other in such distress), D appears unable to insist on peremptory aid; it can only request supererogatory action from C or others.

Now D can certainly make a general claim of right for itself and its people. As a nation-state, it is equal with all other states and can press its right to survive by requesting aid for its people (self-defense). It can recognize collective responsibility and incur long-term debts to this end and even argue that mutual advantage in international society would be enhanced if a humanitarian assistance scheme were instituted. But what is the relational tie being invoked? In what forum or against whom is this right advanced? Can D perhaps invoke duty "to extend aid if it can do so without excessive risk or loss to itself"?[73]

It appears that until specific agreements or international schemes are established to aid states like D, the right to assistance is an imperfect

---

73. TJ, *supra* note 1, at 114.

right.[74] In the absence of cooperative pacts, each nation will decide to what extent aid can be rendered to others without neglecting internal needs (self-determination), thus, each nation

> must be allowed to abide by its own judgment in determining its action . . . as to whether it can do anything for another without neglect of its duty toward itself; consequently if that which is sought is refused, it must be endured. . . .[75]

In an international society striving towards just or reciprocal interaction, we might well expect a scheme of aid to develop. It is not likely that D would be allowed to collapse or its people die in famine. What is curious, and somewhat troublesome, is D's apparent inability to force resolution of the problem under the model. After presenting its case in all appropriate fora, it must wait for others to decide to act. And if no one does?

Under Model 2, the community's obligation to aid a struggling member is never seriously in doubt. The reciprocal obligation inhering in the relationship between the BCS and D (principle of obligation 3c) and the requirements of the general conception necessitate a positive response to the member's need. Aid will be provided for D and its people.[76] It would thus appear that the models again begin to converge, the difference being that Model 2 aid is certain, while Model 1 aid is only likely, though theoretically problematic. Neither model seems to recognize an enforceable direct obligation that C aid D according to the extent of any excess supply of grain.

---

74. A perfect right carries with it a particularized duty. *E.g.*, Q's perfect right to privacy means that R has a corresponding duty not to invade that private sphere. An imperfect right implies no such correlative determinate duty. *E.g.*, R's imperfect right to sell does not mean that Q has a duty to buy. In situation 2, D has the imperfect right of assistance, but no correlative duty to extend aid from determine states can be implied.

75. Wolff, *supra* note 44, sec. 157, at 85. Wolff develops the distinction between perfect and imperfect rights held by nation-states in ch. II, sec. 156ff. (For analysis of individual relations, it could be useful to contrast Wolff's perfect and imperfect rights with Hohfeld's analysis of jural correlatives and jural opposites, particularly a regards rights/duties and privileges/no-rights, in Hohfeld, *Some Fundamental Legal Conceptions as Applied in Judicial Reasoning*, 23 YALE L. J. 16 (1913), and 26 YALE L. J. 710 (1917).) Wolff goes on to comment in sec. 158, "So, when the price of bread is high, no nation can compel another nation to sell grain to it, even if it has ever so great a supply of grain, and is naturally bound to sell." *Compare* the socially basic human rights defined in Luban, *Just War and Human Rights*, 9 PHIL. & PUB. AFF. 160, 177 (1980), which would permit D to declare a just war against C if the latter refused to supply grain.

76. We ignore here, though it would need to be considered in a more detailed analysis, the distinction between the societal organization (the local system of government and its organizational channels of operations) and the people of the society. Individual members will always have the right to call upon the BCS for help n such circumstances and that call will always be considered in light of available resources. But, systems may be denied the luxury of being propped-up after displaying dangerous ineptitude or (non-ideally) corrupt practices (*e.g.*, could the severity of the draught have been avoided under better administrative processes?). In fairness, questions like these could not be ignored. We do so here only to simplify analysis and to keep the question in comparative focus.

Although this surface result of the models is similar, the bases for any aid rendered are quite distinct. Under both models, the question "what obligations does C have with respect to D?" only carries explicit content if direct links between the societies can be demonstrated (e.g. trading relations, bilateral pacts or social interchange between societal members). If no direct relations or linkages exist, no direct obligations can be inferred. This lack of direct linkage led to the relative uncertainty of an imperfect right under Model 1: D had no one to address with a perfect right of aid, so no one needed to respond with a correlative perfect duty. D was dependent upon another society (like C) to recognize its mutual advantage and/or its natural duty and agree to provide the necessary grain.

What is singularly different about the certain resolution under Model 2 is that the right to aid is a perfect right from the outset. It need not be transformed into a perfect right on the basis of subsequent recognition or agreement. However, this perfect right to aid is not a function of relations, direct or indirect, between C and D. The conflict of this case cannot be construed or framed in simple or even complex inter-societal terms. Rather, the conflict is to be framed as existing between D and the BCS. So framed, an appropriate resolution of this conflict might be worked out in the following stages:

> (1) D has a dire need. D addresses this need to the BCS in terms of a perfect right based upon the reciprocal relation in community membership.
> (2) The BCS acknowledges the need and the right under which it is advanced.
> (3) The BCS calculates the costs involved in meeting D's need and balances available options in light of its duty to the community under the general conception (e.g., how much grain? At what price? From which stores? Through what supply channels? Are other direct obligations involved?)
> (4) The BCS invokes its right in reciprocal relation with C (and/or others) to provide stores from its excess under the fair terms determined in stage (3).
> (5) C responds to the BCS based on its community duty.
> (6) D is supplied through appropriate distributional channels.

In this scheme, direct linkage is not forged (though it may develop) between members. But, interaction for the sake of individuals-in-community is facilitated as the institutions of the basic structure organize and distribute community primary goods.

In turning to discuss the third and final case, we enter the arena of non-ideal or partial compliance theory conditions. Time and space do not permit an analysis of all the variables involved in translating ideal theory into non-ideal settings, but some basic outlines will be drawn to provide a sketch of the issues raised (or avoided) by the models.

> *Situation 3. Society E was once politically homogeneous. Internal disagreements were rare and when they did arise, organizational*

channels easily absorbed this energy and directed it into constructive avenues within the system. Recently, political dissent has increased with a concomitant increase in minority opposition to some of E's internal policies. The system is having difficulty coping with this drive towards heterogeneity and has begun to suppress dissent. When minimal jail terms for infractions of a limited free speech and assembly provision proved ineffective in deterring opposition, prison sentences were lengthened and labor camps were erected. Such internal exile has since become common and opportunities to leave the society are severely restricted. Once relatively open, E is now a closed society. Although the government of E denies it is attempting to quell dissent n this manner, reports of these internal activities continue to come to the attention of other societies.

What obligations, if any do these other societies have in respect of E and its people?

Model 2 provides parameters which can readily be applied to the situation above. Being ultimately responsible for intra-societal, as well as inter-societal, conflict, the BCS must provide a final authoritative forum for this type of individual/societal dispute. If investigation confirms the reports that principles of free association and obligation are being unjustly abridged (specifically, the freedom to disassociate and societal obligations of fairness), the societal system must answer for its unjust actions. (Here, the distinction between the system of government and the people comes to the fore.) As a minimal solution, internal reform acceding to a formal heterogeneity seems required. In the alternative, two (or more) separate social unions might be nurtured as homogeneous replacements. If necessary, the societal form could be disbanded and reorganized along entirely wholly new hierarchical channels. Whatever the solution justice as fairness demands, it would indeed be done.

In such a non-ideal situation, force might be employed to secure the reorganization if resistance were encountered. In this extremity, jus ad bellum principles would need to be invoked and jus in bello principles would need to be developed if not already to hand. A show of force is perhaps problematic for the model, since ideal development ignored just war theory and provided only for problems of assurance. But there is little doubt that principles for just armed conflict would not present an ineffable barrier in developing a partial compliance response.

On the other hand, Model 1 parameters are essentially lacking. Just as the model could not even reach the question of "which company?" in situation 1, the principle of equality and its corollary of self-determination can operate so as to peremptorily preclude interference or even investigation into the internal affairs of another equal, self-determining nation-state. How E treats its own people is its own affair, being between that people and its system of government. Presumably, this shroud is of negligible import when more-or-less just states are in view under an ideal theory of strict compliance. But it is not at all clear that the shroud can be justifiably lifted even under reinterpreted or relaxed principles in a partial compliance international society of Model 1 proportion or design.[77] It seems that Model 1 nation-states have an extremely limited response indeed. Besides lecturing E for its apparent abuse, international society can invoke no particular principle or duty of state relations to chide E. Neither can the distressed people of E invoke any international principles in a call for assistance or internal reform.

If E were simply an example of an errant, over-zealous or cruel administration in an otherwise just international society, a case might be made that the principles informing international society should only apply to those states whose domestic arrangements (continue to) satisfy the two basic principle of domestic justice (per choice problem number one in the model's first original position). Since E is in obvious contravention of the special (and apparently even the general) conception of justice as fairness, international statal equality and non-intervention (self-determination) principles need not apply. The state has placed itself beyond the pale of legitimate invocation of principles of fairness as between states by its own unjust (though internal) actions. Thus, other states desiring to investigate and intervene on (supererogatory) humanitarian grounds might fairly do so.[78]

Unfortunately, this is a weak argument for at least two reasons. First, intervention is still not required by any principles of justice. Those suffering injustice will have to wait (as did society D in situation 2, above) for any aid. More importantly, why should international principles of justice be deemed contingent given the nature of the model? Is a criminal offender in domestic society fairly dealt with if treated inhumanely (i.e., ultra vires principles of justice) when he breaks his tacit "contract" to conform to certain societal laws? Granted the analogy is not perfect, but an argument declaring that primary principles of reciprocal dealing can be set aside if the (third-party) contract is (partially) broken leaves one huge authoritative gap—who decides that a breach exists? and what sanctions apply? Without a recognized authoritative agency to guide the parties in a partial compliance situation, the principle that "principles can be deemed inoperative" is systemically destructive. Such an argument is even more dubious in an international society filled with partial compliance actors ("let he who is without sin cast the first stone"). Once the assurance factors of an ideal theory reveal such insufficiency, the model will begin to breakdown; it must then either evolve of collapse.

---

77. *See, e.g.*, U.N. CHARTER art. 2, para. 4: "All Members shall refrain in their international relations from the threat or use of force against the territorial integrity or political independence of any State, or in any other manner inconsistent with the Purposes of the United Nations."

78. As in situation 2, Luban is prepared to suggest that a war of intervention is justified and even morally "urgent"; views which argue against intervention based upon a principle of self-determination are labelled "obscene" or "perverse," as well as illogical "doublethink." Luban, *supra*, note 75, at 178-81. *Cf.* Wicclair, *supra* note 11, at 298 and 300-01.

Note that under Model 1, the principled inability to act is not directly related to enforcement ability. There is little question that international society could martial sufficient numbers to rout an oppressive regime; its might is sufficient. Neither is the problem directly related to or a function of cost (though cost factors are involved and need to be considered). Rather, the problem lies in the absence of a formal mechanism capable of determining "rightness" in statal dealings under the model. When basic disagreements between the parties result in statal impasse, no authority exists which can cut the Gordian knot.

It might be argued that under Model 1, a more-or-less just international society would agree to precisely such an authoritative agency (like a Security Council or International Court) to meet contingencies where assurance factors are insufficient. Thus, the priorities of nation-state equality and self-determination would be superceded by a principle of community responsibility. But to the extent that states recognize this responsibility and establish a super-statal agency which has recognized, formal declaratory (and, perhaps, enforcement) power, the model has begun evolving into a Model 2 structure with an international BCS.

We are not prepared to argue that Model 2 is the full and natural outcome of modifying Model 1 to meet partial compliance conditions. But with the relative strengths and weaknesses of the models now in view, it is interesting that Model 2 principle seem to lead to practical applications more consistently in accord with considered judgments of fairness formerly encountered. Although the model distinctions in situation 1 were mere adumbrations of variances to come, operational differences began more clearly to appear in situation 2 and are visible in full relief here in situation 3. Having glimpsed some of these more important differences, we turn next to consider the models under Rawls' device of reflective equilibrium. In this concluding part of the essay, we consider what it means to choose one of these models over the other on the basis of justice as fairness.

IV. CONCLUSION

Rawls' device of reflective equilibrium is not novel,[79] but he employs it in a deceptively powerful manner. Striving to establish a deductive connection between his two principles of domestic justice and his original position (proposing that the former's conclusions be logically derivable from the latter's premises), he reaches for a kind of "moral geometry with all the rigor which this name connotes."[80] In working out this geometry, the reader is asked to reflect upon his considered convictions of justice and the conditions of fairness embodied in an original position. If the principles which can be derived (deduced) from an acceptable initial situation of fairness match (yield) firm considered judgments, well and good.

79. TJ, *supra* note 1, at 20 n.7.
80. *Id.* at 121.

If not, modify either the initial situation, or the considered convictions, or both, until a match (equilibrium) is established. If this final coherent view comprehends philosophically favored conditions for an original position, a procedure of justification for the conception of justice exists as well.

This device is useful not only for developing conceptions of justice, but also for examining conceptions offered as just solutions to the problem of social justice in a given context. For example, Rawls first employs a reflective equilibrium to establish his original position and its two special conception principles; he then employs the same device to challenge the value of average utility (finding it a relatively unstable conception) in the societal arena.[81] In similar manner, this part is devoted to applying considerations of reflective equilibrium to the two models of international justice which have been developed in this article.

Focusing attention on three hypothetical cases of international scope, we have examined the questions which the models raised and the parameters or conclusions proposed in respect of coordinating cooperative efforts for resource recovery (situation 1); coordinating relief efforts for the disadvantaged (situation 2); and coordinating response to deviation from just norms (situation 3). In all three cases, Model 2 operated in equilibrium with considered judgments of fairness as it presented a coherent conception of international justice. Coordination was not only just, but other values like efficiency could also appropriately be accounted for in the model's responses. In contradistinction, only in situation 1 did Model 1 similarly operate in equilibrium. As a conception of international justice, this model was found to be relatively unstable in situation 2 and appeared wholly inadequate in meeting the demands of considered convictions of justice in situation 3.[82]

Can Model 1 be salvaged? Can we perform a reflective equilibrium operation and save the patient? If this means modifying considered convictions so that the results noted above can be sustained, probably not. Deeming the results in situation 2 acceptable is less problematic, but the lack of response in situation 3 is difficult, if not impossible, to confirm on reflection. On the other hand, if salvaging the model means toying with the original position, two possibilities come to mind: (1) modify the motivational assumptions of the parties to reach more accommodating princi-

---

81. *Id.* secs. 27 and 28, 161-74.

82. Time and space will not be taken to formulate a full discussion but the inadequacies illuminated are arguably a necessary function of the introduction of a morally arbitrary element defining the scope of Model 1's first choice problem. *See supra* note 25, and accompanying text. Not only model consequences but model principles themselves are subject to reflective equilibrium considerations. Without more, it seems undesirable if not ad hoc to introduce a morally arbitrary delimitation into an otherwise basic, fair position. Thus, consequences aside, we may have strong reason to prefer Model 2's original position and principle over Model 1's. Supporting argument would be analogous to discussion of thick v. thin original position veils of ignorance and their reflection of a basic conception of free and equal persons. *See supra* notes 16-17, 33-34.

ples and results; or (2) modify the structural components of the initial situation. If the first option is taken, it is more likely than not that a Model 2 structuring will be the result. This is what occurred when a modification was attempted in discussion under situation 3, above. If the second option is considered, and pains are taken to avoid imitating Model 2, an equilibrium can conceivably be achieved, but I dare say that the model would no longer be Rawlsian in nature. In the great scheme of things such a result is not devastating, but Rawlsian models are, after all, the theme of this essay.

Should this analysis hold, sufficient data is now available to address the interrogatory originally defining our project, "Which model more closely matches considerations of justice as fairness in the international arena"? On the basis of the findings presented above, we are bound to choose Model 2 over Model 1 as that Rawlsian model of international justice which best expresses a stable and coherent conception of justice as fairness. Having such a model to hand, we, as fully autonomous moral beings, are thereby philosophically justified in selecting that model as our own. *Vade, et tu fac similiter.*

Name Index

www.ingramcontent.com/pod-product-compliance
Lightning Source LLC
LaVergne TN
LVHW102106300926
849161LV00014B/3064
* 9 7 8 0 8 1 4 7 4 6 1 9 6 *